Outlook® 2007 Bible

Outlook® 2007 Bible

Peter G. Aitken

BICENTENNIAL
1807
WILEY
2007
BICENTENNIAL

Wiley Publishing, Inc.

Outlook® 2007 Bible

Published by
Wiley Publishing, Inc.
10475 Crosspoint Boulevard
Indianapolis, IN 46256
www.wiley.com

Copyright © 2007 by Wiley Publishing, Inc., Indianapolis, Indiana

Published simultaneously in Canada

ISBN: 978-0-470-04645-6
Manufactured in the United States of America

10 9 8 7 6 5 4 3 2

For general information on our other products and services or to obtain technical support, please contact our Customer Care Department within the U.S. at (800) 762-2974, outside the U.S. at (317) 572-3993 or fax (317) 572-4002.

Library of Congress Cataloging-in-Publication Data:

Aitken, Peter G.
  Outlook 2007 bible / Peter Aitken.
      p. cm.
  Includes bibliographical references.
  ISBN 978-0-470-04645-6 (paper/website)
  1. Time management—Computer programs. 2. Personal information management—Computer programs. I. Title.
  HF5548.4.M5255A37 2007
  005.5'7—dc22

                                                2007008101

To my dear wife Maxine, whose support and understanding were crucial over the months it took to write this book. Thanks for the neck rubs!

About the Author

Peter G. Aitken has been writing about computers and programming for more than 15 years, with over 45 books to his credit and over 1.5 million copies in print. He has also contributed hundreds of articles and product reviews to magazines and web sites such as *Visual Developer Magazine*, *PC Magazine*, DevX, Microsoft Office Pro, Builder.com, and DevSource. Peter is the proprietor of PGA Consulting, providing custom application development and technical writing services to business, academia, and government since 1994.

Credits

Acquisitions Editor
Katie Mohr

Senior Development Editor
Tom Dinse

Technical Editor
Todd Meister

Production Editors
Felicia Robinson
William A. Barton

Copy Editor
Kim Cofer

Editorial Manager
Mary Beth Wakefield

Production Manager
Tim Tate

Vice President and Executive Group Publisher
Richard Swadley

Vice President and Executive Publisher
Joseph B. Wikert

Project Coordinator
Erin Smith

Graphics and Production Specialists
Beth Brooks
Carrie A. Foster
Denny Hager
Jennifer Mayberry
Heather Pope
Amanda Spagnuolo

Quality Control Technicians
John Greenough
Charles Spencer

Proofreading and Indexing
Linda Seifert and Aptara

Anniversary Logo Design
Richard Pacifico

Contents at a Glance

Contents

Contents

Contents

Contents

Contents

Contents

Contents

Acknowledgments

Though this book may list only one author, it has been a team effort from the initial concept to the dotting of the final "i". My thanks to everyone who helped make this book a reality:

Tom Dinse, Development Editor, who brought his skill and knowledge to essentially every aspect of the book.

Todd Meister, Technical Editor, whose expertise and attention to detail were instrumental in ensuring the book's technical accuracy.

Kim Cofer, Copy Editor, who applied her skills and sharp eye to improving the readability of the text.

Katie Mohr, Acquisitions Editor, whose oversight and guidance kept us on track and on schedule.

Introduction

Welcome to the Microsoft Outlook 2007 Bible. The goal of this book is to provide a complete guide to this popular and useful program and, modesty aside, we think that we have done a terrific job. The Outlook Bible covers Outlook from A to Z, from soup to nuts, so you can be confident that it includes the information you need. Whether you are an Outlook beginner or have experience with earlier versions of the program, this book is designed for you.

Whereas many other programs are devoted to a single task, Outlook is more like a Swiss Army knife. It provides, in a convenient integrated package, all of those tools that most everyone uses on a regular basis—email, a calendar and appointment book, a contacts list, and a to-do list, just to name the most popular components. These tools can be used independently but—and here's where the real power of Outlook comes into play—can also be integrated with each other to provide a sophisticated information and time management system.

There's no getting around it, however—such a powerful program is unavoidably complex. Although Microsoft has made every effort to make Outlook as intuitive and easy to use as possible, any user will benefit from a guide to the program's commands and features. That's where this book comes in.

Is This Book For You?

Like all books in the Bible series, the Outlook Bible is designed to provide a complete guide to the program while remaining accessible to users at all levels of experience. It is neither a simplistic beginner's guide that covers only the basics, nor is it a dense technical tome that can be understood only by nerds and gurus. If you need to learn the fundamentals, you'll find them clearly laid out with plenty of illustrations and step-by-step instructions. When you are ready to dive deeper into Outlook's advanced features, you'll find that information at your fingertips. This book is appropriate for:

- The complete beginner who needs to install Outlook and get her email working as soon as possible.

- The person who has some experience with Outlook and now wants to explore the program's features in depth to use it to its full potential.

- The advanced user who needs to make use of VBA programming, forms, rules, and other of Outlook's more sophisticated abilities.

How This Book Is Organized

This book has been structured to make it easy for you to find the information you want. You can read the book in order from start to finish, or you can jump around and read only those chapters of interest.

Part I starts at the beginning with an overview of Outlook's features. To get the most from any program, you have to know what's available! Then Outlook installation and the elements of the screen are explored.

Part II is devoted to what is probably the most popular part of Outlook—email. You'll learn how to set up your email account, create and send messages, use message attachments, and work with received messages. This part also shows you how to format email messages, how to insert tables and pictures in a message, set email options to work the way you want, and how to protect yourself against junk email.

Part III is all about managing information with Outlook. You'll learn how to use Outlook's sophisticated contacts manager and how to schedule appointments and meetings. This section also covers using notes to keep track of various kinds of information, maintaining a to-do list with the tasks feature, and using the journal to keep track of how you spend your time. Finally, you'll see how to use RSS feeds—a new feature in this version of Outlook—to create a customized view of information from a variety of sources.

Part IV shows you how to get the most out of Outlook. You'll learn how to use categories with all types of Outlook information, a great way to stay organized. You'll see how to use Outlook data files and folders to meet your needs, and how to customize the program and screen to suit the way you work. This section also covers security issues, a topic that no one should ignore. Finally, you'll see how Outlook can be integrated with other Office applications.

Part V delves into using Outlook to develop custom solutions for your messaging and information management needs. You'll learn how to write macros, using the VBA programming language and the Outlook Object Model to automate and customize many Outlook tasks. You'll also see how to design custom forms to provide data management capabilities that are precisely tailored to your needs.

Finally, Part VI explores using Outlook with Microsoft Exchange Server and with SharePoint Services.

Conventions Used in This Book

Many different organizational and typographical features throughout this book are designed to help you get the most of the information.

Whenever the author wants to bring something important to your attention the information will appear in a Caution, Note, Tip, or Warning.

CAUTION This information is important and is set off in a separate paragraph with a special icon. Cautions provide information about things to watch out for, whether simply inconvenient or potentially hazardous to your data or systems.

NOTE Notes provide additional, ancillary information that is helpful, but somewhat outside of the current presentation of information.

TIP Tips generally are used to provide information that can make your work easier—special shortcuts or methods for doing something easier than the norm.

WARNING The information Warnings provide advise you about the serious consequences of performing the procedure or activity described—whether to you, to your data, or to your hardware or software.

Part I

Getting Started

Chapter 1

Getting Started with Outlook

O utlook is one of the most widely used programs in the world. The latest version, called either Outlook 12 or Outlook 2007 (but simply *Outlook* from here on) takes a great program and makes it even better. What is it about Outlook that makes it the one indispensable program on many people's computers?

The way I look at it, Outlook is the digital version of a Swiss Army knife. It doesn't do just one or two things, it does a whole bunch of things — and equally important, it does them well. You may not need all of Outlook's capabilities, but it's a pretty sure bet that you need some of them.

How many people do you know who don't use email? That's one of Outlook's abilities. How about keeping track of contact information for friends, family, and business associates? That's another. Do you need to schedule meetings, appointments, and social engagements? Outlook can help. This is what makes Outlook so popular — it takes a bunch of commonly needed capabilities and rolls them together into a single well-designed and easy-to-use program.

The key concept here is *productivity*. Outlook is carefully designed to integrate information and tasks in a way that will save you time, errors, and headaches.

This chapter gets you started with Outlook by taking you on a quick tour of all the program features. I think this is the first step in learning any program — you need to know *what* it can do before learning *how* to do it! After a look at all the things you can do with Outlook, the chapter ends with some information about what's new in this version of Outlook.

No Instant Messaging?

Strictly speaking, Outlook by itself does not support instant messaging. You can, however, use Outlook in conjunction with any of several compatible IM services.

Even though you may already be addicted to email, here's a look at some of the reasons it is so popular and why Outlook is such a powerful email client:

- Fast — email messages are delivered nearly anywhere in the world almost instantly. Neither the post office nor FedEx can say that!
- Convenient — you can read email messages at your convenience, which is a lot better than being interrupted by the phone every five minutes.
- Free — there's no cost for sending or receiving messages. At most you'll pay a modest fee for your email account, but it's still a lot cheaper than long distance.
- Flexible — in addition to messages you can use email to send photos and other documents to friends, family, and business associates.
- Forms — Outlook lets you design email forms for exchanging specific information.
- Record keeping — Outlook provides powerful tools for organizing and archiving your received and sent messages.

Email is an important aspect of most people's work and personal lives. With Outlook you have a tool that lets you work with email in an efficient and intuitive manner.

Messaging

Who could survive in today's connected world without email? Messaging is at the heart of Outlook's capabilities, and you'll even find some people who use Outlook for email and nothing else — although that's a waste in my opinion. In Outlook, the term *messaging* refers specifically to email — Outlook does not work with instant messaging, chat, or other forms of electronic communication.

Managing Contacts

Information management is Outlook's other main focus, and managing your contacts is an important aspect of that. Outlook's contact management feature is really just a sophisticated address book, but it is designed to be extremely flexible. Figure 1.1 shows an Outlook contact form with an individual's information filled in. This information includes:

- Name, title, and company.
- Phone numbers for business, home, FAX, and mobile.
- Addresses (business, home, and other).
- A photo.

- Email addresses (as many as needed).
- Web page address.
- Instant messaging address.

Of course a contact entry need not include all this information — many will consist of just a name and email address. However, the capability to enter as much or as little information as needed provides you with great flexibility.

An Outlook contact can contain a wide variety of information.

The real beauty of Outlook contacts is that you can easily use and reuse the information in so many ways. This follows the philosophy that you should have to enter any piece of information just once and then be able to use it wherever and whenever it is needed. Among the things you can do with contact information are

- Address email messages.
- Print envelopes for postal mail.
- Automatically dial a contact's phone number (if your system is equipped with a dialer).
- Share contact information with other people.
- Associate contacts with tasks and schedules.

I am always finding new uses for Outlook contacts — it's a great tool.

Scheduling

You say that you have a really busy life? That's a common complaint these days—everyone seems to have more and more to do. It's a lot easier if you can organize your time and find a way to keep track of important tasks. Outlook has two related features, the calendar and tasks, that can greatly simplify the job of managing your schedule.

Figure 1.2 shows Outlook's calendar display. This is a workweek display but you can customize it to show 7-day weeks, single days, or the entire month. The top section is the calendar per se, which shows appointments—items that have a specific start and end time. The lower section shows tasks, items on your to-do list that don't have a specific time frame associated with them (although they may have a due date).

FIGURE 1.2

Outlook's calendar displays both appointments and tasks.

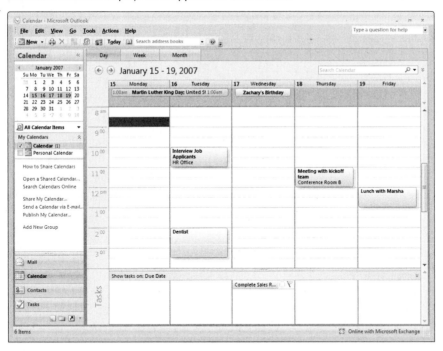

Outlook's calendar is much more than a day-timer or similar paper appointment book. Some of its features are

- You can easily schedule a recurring appointment such as the department meeting that is from 9:00 to 10:00 every 2nd Monday.
- You can have it remind you of appointments with a popup message on your screen.

- You can publish your calendar so that your coworkers can view your schedule and not plan meetings or other events when you are busy.

- You can view other people's published calendars when you are trying to schedule a meeting.

- You can use Outlook to invite people to meetings — and they can respond "yes" or "no" using Outlook as well.

- You can create a shared meeting workspace where you can share the agenda, other documents, and post meeting results.

Outlook's task feature is a really sophisticated to-do list. Each task has a start date and a due date and you can tell Outlook to remind you about the task if desired. Each task also has a priority — low, normal, or high — and a status that marks it as Not Started, In Progress, Completed, and so on. You can assign a task to someone else and receive a status report from them when the task is complete. You can view and organize tasks in almost any way you can imagine — overdue tasks, tasks due in the next week, active tasks, tasks assigned to a specific person or category, and so on. Figure 1.3 shows the Outlook task list with active tasks displayed.

FIGURE 1.3

Outlook can display your tasks in various ways.

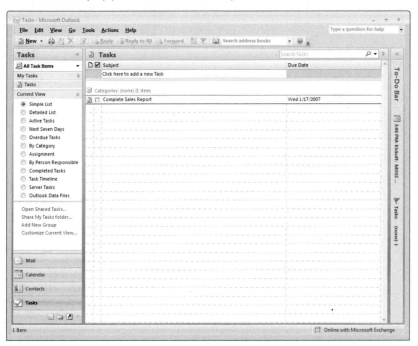

What's more, Outlook has the ability to connect to tasks you have stored in other programs such as Microsoft Project, OneNote, or on a SharePoint Services account.

Managing Information

In addition to contacts and scheduling, Outlook has two other tools for keeping track of information.

Notes are a very simple means for storing small bits of information. I think of them as the computer equivalent of the sticky notes that lots of people have pasted on their monitor and refrigerator. I use notes for things like frequent flier account numbers, to remind me of that mail-order source for great seafood, to make notes about restaurants, and the like. Figure 1.4 shows Outlook's notes display with one note open. It's easy to forward notes to other people using email so you can share the information as desired.

FIGURE 1.4

Outlook notes store small pieces of information.

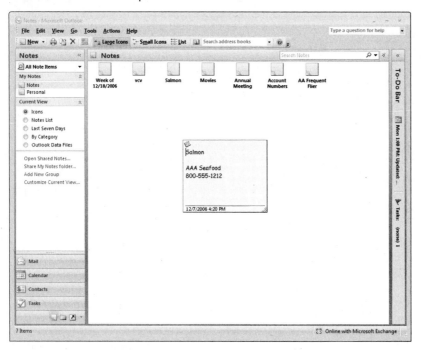

The journal is a sophisticated tool for keeping track of various kinds of information. More specifically, the journal is primarily designed for keeping track of your various activities and the time you spend on them. You can use it to track things like phone calls, working on Office documents, email, and meeting requests. The journal can record certain things automatically and also allows for manual entries. Figure 1.5 shows the Outlook journal display with two items tracked, a phone call and time spent working on a Word document.

FIGURE 1.5

Journal entries keep track of the time spent on various activities.

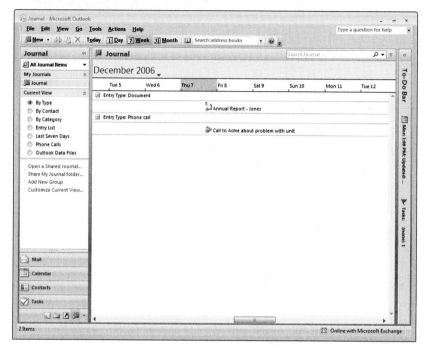

Mobile Service

It's hard to imagine life before the advent of mobile phones. No matter how much you love your cell, you may love it even more once you team it up with Outlook Mobile Service. In a nutshell, Mobile Service lets you send text messages between Outlook and your mobile phone. When you are away from your computer, you can have task reminders, contact information, and daily calendar information sent right to your phone. You'll have no reason to ever miss an appointment again — even though you might want to!

Mobile Service requires that you register with an Outlook 2007 Mobile Service provider that works with your mobile phone company.

Categories

Outlook categories are not so much a tool in their own right, like email or the calendar, but they are a feature that can greatly simplify your use of Outlook. Essentially any of the items that Outlook works with, such as email messages, appointments, and tasks, can be assigned to a category. You can use Outlook's predefined categories or, like most users, create your own such as Work, Personal, and so on. Assigning categories to these items makes organizing them and finding needed information a whole lot easier.

Searching

Knowing that you have some information is one thing — and finding it can be something quite different! Outlook provides sophisticated search capabilities within all the various types of information it works with. Outlook lets you search by category, keyword, date, and other flexible criteria to locate items in email, tasks, and all the other kinds of information Outlook works with. Instant Search is integrated into Outlook so it is always available right when you need it.

Getting News and Other Information

Really Simple Syndication, or RSS, is a method for content publishers to make information available to subscribers. News, sports, blogs, weather — you name it and it is probably available via an RSS feed. Some other terms for RSS feeds are XML feeds, Web feeds, RSS channels, and syndicated content. RSS feeds are not new but the ability to read them in Outlook is.

Figure 1.6 shows the MSNBC Headlines RSS feed displayed in Outlook. In some ways an RSS feed works like email. Each "message" has a subject and content, and can contain links to other material as well. Outlook provides you with a list of RSS feeds you can subscribe to. You can also subscribe to other feeds as long as you have the required information.

Security

Unfortunately, security is an important concern these days. The term security encompasses a number of different things including the following:

- Protecting messages from prying eyes.
- Using digital signatures to guarantee identity.
- Preventing problems caused by malicious attachments and macro code.
- Avoiding infection by viruses and worms.

Although there is no foolproof security solution, Outlook provides a full set of tools that can help you to minimize your risks.

FIGURE 1.6

Viewing RSS feeds in Outlook.

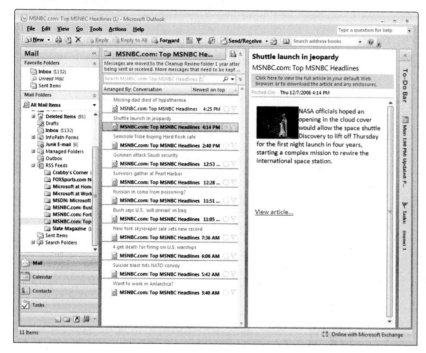

Custom Solutions

No matter how well designed it is, no application can be a perfect match for each user's individual needs. This is why Outlook provides several customization features that let you tailor it to the way you work and the tasks you need to perform.

One of these features is VBA programming. VBA stands for Visual Basic for Applications, sometimes just called Visual Basic. VBA is a powerful programming language that is built in to Outlook and the other Office programs such as Word and Excel. VBA provides the developer with access to all of Outlook's features and data. You can write programs, or macros, that automate tasks involving email, contacts, appointments, and so on. When there's an even modestly complex task that you perform regularly, automating it with a macro can save you both time and errors. Note that unlike some other Office programs Outlook does not allow you to record macros — you must program them manually — but once you understand the basic concepts it's not particularly difficult.

Another customization feature is userforms. A userform is, in essence, a dialog box that you have designed for the display and/or input of information. Used as part of a VBA macro, a userform provides data display and input that is customized for precisely what you need. Figure 1.7 shows a userform being designed in the form designer.

FIGURE 1.7

Designing a userform for custom data handling.

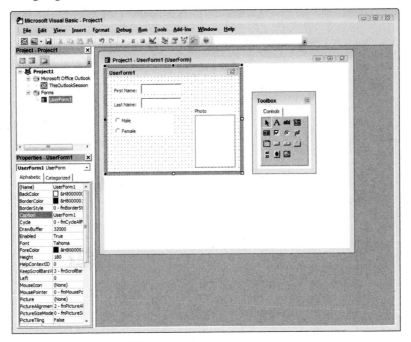

What's New

If you have used an earlier version of Outlook you will be glad to know that there have been no fundamental changes to the program. There is a new user interface, but most of the changes involve the addition of new features and enhancement of old ones. This section takes a look at the most important of these new and improved features.

New User Interface

Outlook's user interface has actually changed less than that of other Office programs. The main screen, shown in Figure 1.8, retains the main menu and the toolbar that were present in earlier versions of the program. The Outlook Today and folder views remain essentially unchanged as well.

Things are quite different, however, when you get to the windows you use to work with email messages, contacts, and so on. Microsoft has abandoned the menu and toolbar approach for a system of tabs and ribbons, as you can see in Figure 1.9. This figure shows an email window with four tabs across the top — Message, Insert, Options, and Format Text. Clicking a tab displays the associated ribbon, which provides access to buttons, menus, and dialog boxes for the related tasks.

The Outlook screen is covered in detail in Chapter 2.

FIGURE 1.8

The main Outlook screen retains the menu and toolbar of earlier versions.

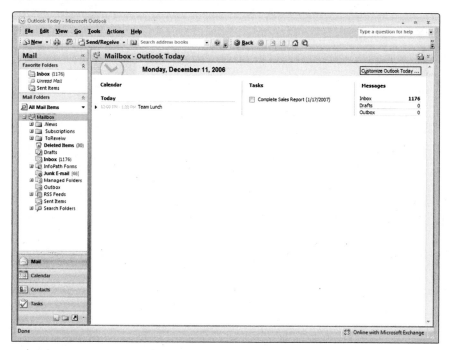

FIGURE 1.9

Other Outlook windows use the new tabs and ribbon look.

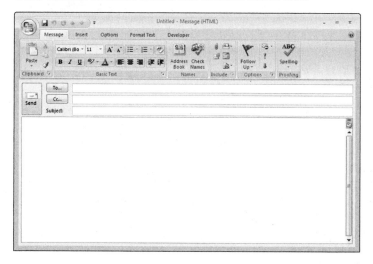

Instant Search

In a single step you can search through all your email messages, attachments, contacts, tasks, and calendars to find the information you are looking for.

To-Do Bar

The To-Do Bar, shown in Figure 1.10, provides a convenient, consolidated view of tasks, appointments, and emails that you have flagged for follow-up. You'll have no more excuses for forgetting something!

FIGURE 1.10

The To-Do Bar lets you view your daily priorities.

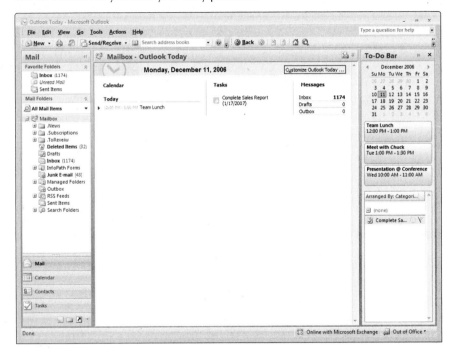

Color Categories

Outlook's categories are now coded by color. This makes it a lot easier to scan a list of items and pick out the high-priority ones.

Mail as Tasks

Outlook now lets you flag an email message as a task, greatly simplifying the process of defining a task based on a message you have received.

Attachment Previewer

No longer do you need to open an email attachment in its native application, such as Word or Excel, to see what it contains. This can save a lot of time because these native applications are often rather slow to open. In addition, the attachment previewer is safer because, unlike the native application, it cannot run any malicious macros that may be part of the document. Figure 1.11 shows an Excel workbook that was received as an email attachment being previewed.

FIGURE 1.11

The attachment previewer lets you view the content of email attachments without opening them.

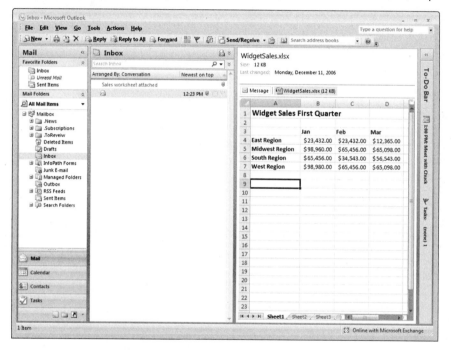

Calendar Features

Several new capabilities make Outlook's calendar even more useful:

- Calendar publishing makes it easy to share your calendar information with others.
- Calendar snapshots let you share your calendar information with people outside your organization.
- Calendar overlay mode makes it possible to view multiple calendars at the same time.

RSS Feeds

Outlook now provides integrated RSS (Really Simple Syndication) capabilities. You can view RSS information just like you would email messages.

Automated Account Setup

For certain kinds of email accounts, Outlook now offers an automated account setup process that lets you set up your account with only your email address and password — no more searching around to find the email server addresses!

Anti-Spam and Anti-Phishing

New and improved anti-spam and anti-phishing tools help protect you from junk email and malicious messages.

Email Postmarks

The new email postmark feature is an anti-spam tool. A message you receive that is postmarked is less likely to be from a spammer and more likely to be from a legitimate source, and Outlook can take that into account when deciding which messages are spam and which are not. Likewise, if you postmark messages that you send, the recipients may be able to use the postmark to determine that your message is probably not spam.

Summary

This chapter has provided you with a quick overview of what Outlook can do for you. You have also taken a look at some of the features that are new and improved in the most recent version of Outlook. I think you'll agree that Outlook is a jack-of-all-trades, providing capabilities that almost everyone needs on a regular basis. With all this power, Outlook is unavoidably somewhat complex. The remainder of this book shows you the ins and outs of Outlook so that you will soon be putting this powerful program to work to simplify and organize your own busy life.

Chapter 2 looks at the basics of installing and using Outlook.

Chapter 2

Installing and Using Outlook

The first thing required before you start using Outlook is, of course, to install the program on your computer. This may have already been done for you, but if not there's nothing to worry about because it's a simple process. Next you should become familiar with the Outlook screen and the way you use the screen elements to accomplish tasks. If you have some computer experience this may seem like old hat to you, but given the changes to the user interface it might still be worth your while to give this section a quick look-over. Finally, this chapter takes a look at how you can use Outlook's online help to get detailed information about program operation.

IN THIS CHAPTER

Installing and activating Outlook

Understanding the Outlook screen

Using Outlook help

Your Outlook Installation

Many users will already have Outlook installed on their computer. If you are using Outlook at your place of employment this will probably be the case, and even if it's not, you can be pretty sure that the IT department will want to do the installation themselves. Or perhaps you bought a new computer for use at home with Outlook already installed.

Seeing Whether Outlook Is Installed

If you are not sure whether Outlook is installed, follow these steps:

1. Click the Start button.
2. Click All Programs.
3. Click the Microsoft Office menu item.
4. On the final menu, look for a Microsoft Office Outlook 2007 menu item.

Office 2007 Already Installed?

If Office 2007 has already been installed, the first setup screen will offer these three options:

- **Add or Remove Features:** Select this option if you want to add features to or remove features from the Office installation.
- **Repair:** Select this option if one or more Office programs are not working properly. Repairing an Office installation fixes many, but not all, such problems.
- **Remove:** Removes the entire Office installation from the system.

If you can't find what you are looking for in step 3 or 4, Outlook has not been installed. The process is easy and is explained in the following section.

Installing Outlook

Outlook is almost always supplied on disks (CDs or DVDs) as part of a Microsoft Office System installation along with the other Office programs such as Word and Excel. Depending on your needs you can install just Outlook, the entire Office system, or any combination of programs you desire. This section deals specifically with the Outlook aspect of installation.

To begin installation, insert the Office 2007 CD into your CD drive. On most systems the setup program will start automatically. If it does not, follow these steps:

1. Open Windows Explorer.
2. Navigate to the CD drive.
3. Locate the file `setup.exe` in the root folder and double-click it.

The first setup screen, shown in Figure 2.1, asks you to enter your product key. You can skip this step and enter the key later if you wish.

Why Customize?

I recommend that you use a custom install only if you have a specific reason to do so and you are confident that you know how to make the correct choices. For example, you may not want to install all the Office programs to conserve disk space, or you may want to install program features that are not included in the default installation.

FIGURE 2.1

Entering the product key on the first setup screen.

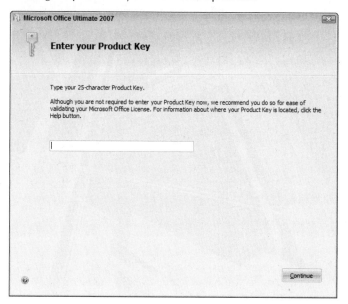

The next setup screen gives you two of the following three choices:

- **Install Now:** This option is available if you do not have an earlier version of Office installed on your computer. Selecting this option will install Office 2007 with the default settings, which includes all the Office programs and the most commonly needed options.

- **Upgrade:** This option is available if the setup program detects an earlier version of Office installed on your computer. It allows you to replace the earlier version with Office 2007, using the default install choices. Many of the settings from the previous version of Office, such as email accounts, will be retained.

- **Customize:** This option lets you customize your Office 2007 installation as explained in more detail in the following text.

If you choose Install Now or Upgrade, the install process will complete automatically and notify you when it is complete. If you choose Customize, you will see the dialog box that is shown in Figure 2.2.

The Installation Options tab, shown in the figure, lets you specify which Office programs, and which components of each program, are installed. The initial settings here are the same as would be in effect for a default installation. If an item has a plus sign to the left, click it to expand the display to show sub-components. For example, Figure 2.3 shows the sub-components available for Outlook.

FIGURE 2.2

Specifying custom install options.

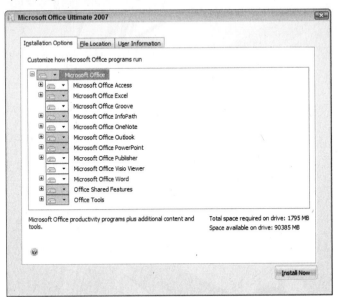

FIGURE 2.3

Installation options for Outlook.

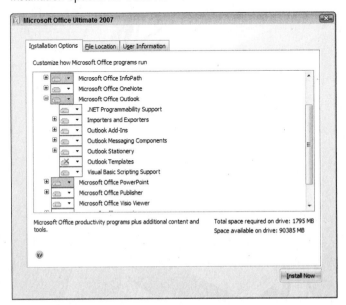

Each item has a down arrow that you can click to change the install options for that item. These options are

- **Run From My Computer:** The item will be installed on your computer.
- **Run All From My Computer:** The item and all the sub-items listed under it will be installed on your computer.
- **Installed on First Use:** The item will not be installed until you try to use it for the first time. You may be prompted for the Office 2007 CD in this situation.
- **Not Available:** The item will not be installed.

The other two tabs in this dialog box are

- **File Location:** Specify the location where Office will be installed. This is normally C:\ Program Files\Microsoft Office and should not be changed unless you have a definite reason to do so.
- **User Information:** Specify your name, initials, and organization for use by the Office programs.

Once you have finished customizing your Office installation, click the Install Now button to complete the installation.

Activating Outlook

Soon after you install Outlook, you must activate it in order to retain full functionality. Activation is Microsoft's way of preventing a single copy of Outlook from being installed and run on multiple systems in violation of the end-user license agreement.

To activate your Outlook installation, select Help, Activate Product and then follow the on-screen prompts. Activation requires an Internet connection. Though it's very unlikely that Outlook would ever be installed on a computer without an Internet connection, you can activate it by telephone if needed.

Checking for Updates

Microsoft makes product updates available for download from its web site. It's a good idea to stay current with updates because they can fix program bugs and security problems.

To check for updates, select Help, Check for Updates. This command will launch your web browser and navigate to Microsoft's update site. Follow the instructions on the update page to download and install updates.

Be aware that if you have the full Microsoft Office system installed, Outlook updates will be taken care of as part of Office updates. Also, if you have your Windows operating system configured for automatic updates, this process will be taken care of "behind the scenes" and you need not do it yourself. There's no harm in checking for updates, however — you will be informed if you already have the latest update installed.

The Outlook Screen

Outlook works with a lot of different kinds of information. There's no way that all the different kinds of information could be displayed on-screen at the same time, and anyway you would not want them to be — imagine the confusion! The Outlook user interface is designed to present information in a clear manner. Generally this means that only one or at most two kinds of information are displayed at a time. For example, if you are working with email, most of the Outlook screen will display email information such as message subjects and contents as well as buttons and commands for carrying out email-related tasks. When you switch to working with notes, the screen changes to show relevant information.

In addition, the Outlook screen can be customized to suit your preferences. This is covered in detail in Chapter 19. For now all you need to know is that the Outlook screen can take on many different appearances and that your screen may not look exactly like the images in this book. That's perfectly okay, and once you gain a little familiarity with the Outlook screen elements you will be able to find your way around like a pro.

The Menus

Like most Windows applications, Outlook has a menu bar at the top of the screen. It contains the top-level menus such as File, Edit, and View. You open a menu by clicking it or by pressing Alt + the access key, which is whatever letter is underlined in the menu name. A top-level menu command never performs an action on it own — rather, it displays a list of further commands from which you can choose — again, by clicking the item with the mouse or pressing the underlined access key (this time without Alt).

Figure 2.4 shows the open File menu. You can tell a lot about a menu command just by looking at it:

- If the item has a right-pointing arrow next to it, such as New in Figure 2.4, it means that selecting the menu item leads to yet another menu (which works just the same as the top-level menus).

- If the item has an ellipsis (...) next to it, like Save As, it means that selecting the menu item leads to a dialog box where you make entries and select options to complete the command.

- If the item has neither an arrow nor an ellipsis associated with it, it means that the command is carried out as soon as you select the menu item.

- If the item has a key combination next to it, such as Print, it means you can use this key combination — Ctrl+P in this case — to select the command without using the menus at all. This is sometimes called a *shortcut key*.

- If the item has an icon to the left, the icon identifies the toolbar button for the command.

Note that some menu commands turn something on or off. In this case the menu item will display a checkmark to its left when the item is on and no checkmark when it is off. If you have displayed a menu and then change your mind, press Esc or click anywhere outside the menu to close it.

FIGURE 2.4

Outlook's File menu.

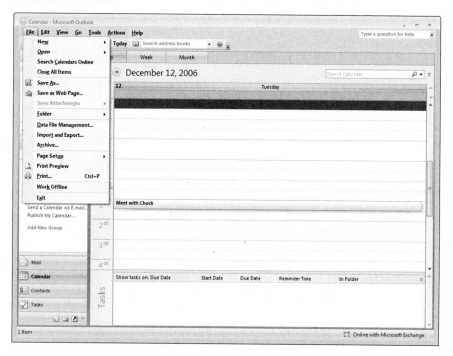

Menu Options

Outlook's menus can be customized to suit your preferences. You can add and remove items, move items to a different menu, and even rearrange the order in which menu items appear. This kind of customization is covered in Chapter 19. There is, however, one menu-related option you should know about now.

Outlook can display either full menus or short menus. A short menu contains a subset of the full menu commands. The commands that appear on the short menus consist of a few most important commands plus the commands you have used most frequently. That's right, Outlook keeps track of your command usage and configures the menus accordingly. This can help reduce screen clutter. After all, if you rarely or never use a particular command, why take up screen real estate with it?

When a short menu is displayed there is an arrow at the bottom of it — click this arrow to open the full menu. You can also tell Outlook to automatically display the full menu after the short menu has been open for a brief period. These options are set on the Options tab of the Customize dialog box, which you display by selecting Tools, Customize and clicking the Options tab (see Figure 2.5). The options of interest are near the top:

- **Always Show Full Menus:** Select this option if you want Outlook to always show all menu commands as soon as you open the menu.

- **Show Full Menus After a Short Delay:** Select this option if you want Outlook to show the short menu briefly and then show the full menu.

- **Reset Menu and Toolbar Usage Data:** Click this button to return the short menus to their default set of commands — in other words, to tell Outlook to forget which commands are your favorites.

The Toolbars

Outlook can display one or more toolbars directly below the main menu. Each toolbar contains buttons, lists, and other elements that provide access to commands that are relevant to the current situation. In other words, the content of the toolbars — some of them, anyway — changes as you move from task to task in Outlook. For example, when you are working on email there is a Reply button on the toolbar, but when you are working in the calendar there is not — because this command would not make sense. If you hover over a toolbar element — that is, rest the mouse pointer there without clicking — Outlook will display a *tooltip* at the mouse cursor describing the function of the element.

FIGURE 2.5

Customizing the way Outlook displays menus.

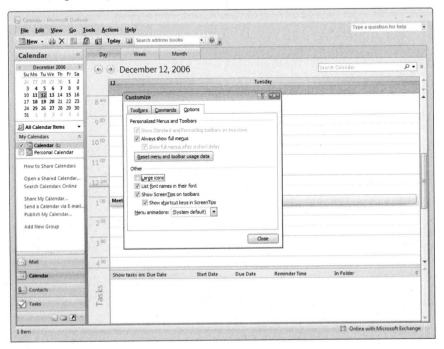

Menu Commands and This Book

The steps to carry out some action often involve menu commands. When I say *select File, Open* it means to open the File menu and then select the Open command. Whether you do this with the mouse or keyboard, or use the shortcut key instead of the menu, makes no difference.

Figure 2.6 shows Outlook's three toolbars. This is how the toolbars look when you are working on email. The toolbars are

- **Standard:** Displays buttons for most frequently used commands.
- **Advanced:** Displays buttons for advanced commands that are needed less often.
- **Web:** Displays buttons for Web-related commands.

If the Outlook window is too narrow to show the entire toolbar, some of the buttons will be hidden. You can access these hidden buttons by clicking the down arrow at the right end of the toolbar.

FIGURE 2.6

Outlook's three toolbars.

Standard toolbar

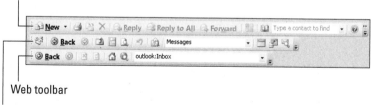

Web toolbar

Advanced toolbar

Note that at the left end of each toolbar is a vertical row of dots. You can point at these dots — the mouse cursor will change to a 4-headed arrow — and drag the toolbar to any desired location. You can dock the toolbar along any edge of the Outlook window. You can also display a toolbar as a free-floating window anywhere on the screen. Figure 2.7 shows the Web toolbar free-floating below the Outlook window. To move a free-floating toolbar, point at its title bar and drag.

To determine which toolbars are displayed, right-click any toolbar and on the menu that is displayed, shown in Figure 2.8, check or uncheck the toolbars as desired. The Customize command that you see on this menu is covered in Chapter 19.

FIGURE 2.7

Outlook can display its toolbars anywhere you want them.

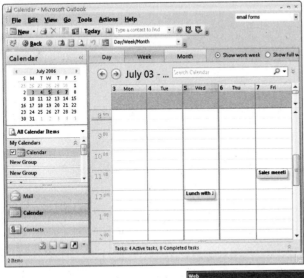

Ribbons

Although Outlook's main window has retained the traditional menu and toolbar structure, other windows, such as the one you use to compose an email message, now use *ribbons*. A ribbon is sort of a combination menu and toolbar, designed to provide fast and intuitive access to commands.

Figure 2.9 shows a ribbon, in this case one of the ribbons in the compose message window. You should note the following things about ribbons:

- In most windows, a series of tabs provides access to different ribbons, each containing related commands.

- On a ribbon, elements are organized into related groups—in Figure 2.9, for example, there are Names, Include, and Options groups (among others).

- As you increase or decrease the size of the window, the ribbon adjusts to fit by displaying more or fewer items. When an item is hidden you can access it by clicking its group.

- Some groups display a Dialog Box Launcher, which you click to display a dialog box containing related options and commands.

- The Quick Access Toolbar is always visible, and provides a few frequently needed commands such as for saving or printing.

- Click the File menu button to display a menu of commands including file-related actions (Save, Open for example).

FIGURE 2.8

Specifying which toolbars to display.

The Navigation Pane

The navigation pane is displayed at the left side of the Outlook window. It is shown in Figure 2.10 and contains two sections:

- The bottom section displays buttons that you click to move to a different part of Outlook such as Mail or Contacts.
- The top section displays information relevant to what you are doing. In Figure 2.10 for example, Calendar has been selected so the top section of the navigation pane displays calendar-related items.

A Menu Tip

I suggest that you set the menu option to always display full menus, at least at the beginning while you are learning Outlook. This is the best way to learn what commands are available on the menus, even if you don't use all of them or understand what they do. Once you have gained some familiarity with the menus you can switch to short menus if you prefer.

Using Context Menus

Outlook provides at least two ways for you to accomplish many tasks. For example, there will be a menu command and also a ribbon button for some tasks. Many commands are also found on the *context menus* (also called *popup menus*). A context menu is displayed when you right-click many of the elements on the Outlook screen. They are called context menus because the commands that are displayed are related to the object you clicked. I will generally not mention context menu commands when describing how to perform tasks in Outlook — rather, I will focus on the other means that Outlook provides for doing things. You should remember, however, that the context menus are available — you may prefer using them.

FIGURE 2.9

Most Outlook windows present commands and options on ribbons.

Office Button (File menu)

Quick Access Toolbar

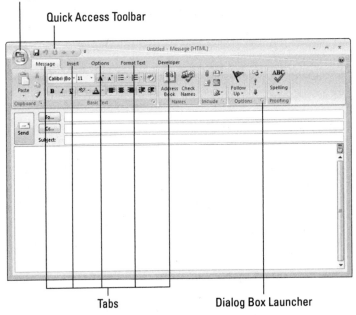

Tabs   Dialog Box Launcher

The lower section of the navigation pane normally displays buttons for the seven main parts of Outlook: Mail, Calendar, Contacts, Tasks, Notes, Folder List, and Shortcuts. If the Outlook window is not tall enough to display all seven buttons, some of them are shown as small icons instead. In the figure, for example, Mail, Calendar, Contacts, and Tasks are displayed as buttons and Notes, Folder List, and Shortcuts are displayed as icons just below the Tasks button.

FIGURE 2.10

Outlook's navigation pane.

At the top-right corner of the navigation pane you'll see a left-pointing arrow. If you click this arrow the navigation pane will collapse to a narrow bar along the left edge of the window. You still have icons in the lower section to move around in Outlook, but the upper section is not visible. You collapse the navigation pane to provide more room for other screen elements. Click the arrow again — it is a right-pointing arrow when the pane is collapsed — to return to the normal navigation pane display.

The To-Do Bar

The To-Do Bar can be displayed along the right edge of the Outlook window, as shown in Figure 2.11. If it is not visible, you can display it by selecting View, To-Do Bar, Normal.

The use of the To-Do Bar is covered as needed in later chapters. For now it's enough to know these basics:

- To collapse the To-Do Bar, click the right-pointing arrow at the top. To re-expand a collapsed To-Do Bar, click the left-pointing arrow at the top.

- To hide the To-Do Bar, click the X icon at the top.

FIGURE 2.11

The To-Do Bar summarizes tasks and appointments.

The Work Area

The remainder of the Outlook screen is the work area. This area displays a wide variety of information depending on what you are doing in Outlook. It's here that you'll read email messages, view your appointments, and so on. Use of the work area is covered in later chapters that deal with specific aspects of Outlook functionality.

Resizing Screen Elements

Many of the elements on the Outlook screen can be resized. For example, you can make the navigation pane larger, but only at the expense of making the work area smaller. To resize an element, point at the blue line that separates it from another screen element—the mouse pointer will become a 2-headed arrow. Then, drag the border to the desired position. If you point at a border and the mouse pointer does not become a 2-headed arrow, it means that you cannot resize at that location.

Using Outlook Help

Outlook has an extensive help system that provides information about all aspects of the program. I like to think that after reading this book you'll never need to use the help system, but that's not realistic! The help system makes use of both online information, obtained from Microsoft's Office Online web site, and offline information that is installed on your computer.

There are three ways to open help:

- Press F1.
- Click the ? icon displayed at the top right of many dialog boxes.
- Select Help, Microsoft Office Outlook Help.

The help window is shown in Figure 2.12 with the help home page displayed.

FIGURE 2.12

The Outlook help window.

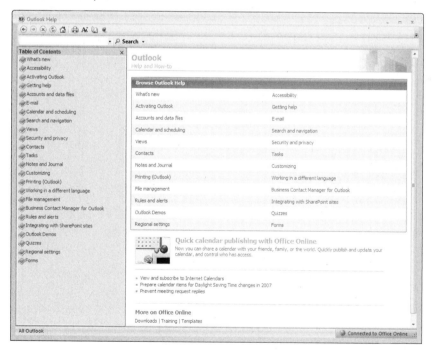

The help window toolbar displays buttons for the following commands (left to right on the toolbar):

- **Back:** Returns to the most recently viewed help topic.
- **Forward:** Moves forward to the next help topic.
- **Stop:** Stops transferring information from online help.
- **Refresh:** Refreshes information from online help.
- **Home:** Displays the help home page.
- **Print:** Prints the current help topic.
- **Change Font Size:** Changes the font size used to display and print help information.
- **Show/Hide Table of Contents:** Displays or hides the table of contents.
- **Keep on Top:** If selected, the help window remains visible when you return to Outlook, enabling you to read help while you work. If not selected, the Outlook window will cover the help window.

Working with Topics

Outlook help, and in fact all Office help, is based on *topics*. A topic can be thought of as a single page of help information on a specific topic (although the material in some topics is much longer than one page).

Topics make use of hyperlinks, just like the web pages you are probably used to surfing. Clicking a hyperlink takes you to a different location in the same topic or sometimes to a different topic. As you move around between topics you can use the Back and Forward buttons in the toolbar to retrace your steps.

Using the Table of Contents

The table of contents is organized into *books*. Each book can contain topics as well as other books. If the table of contents is not displayed, click the Show Table of Contents button on the toolbar.

To expand a book in the table of contents, click it. Figure 2.13 shows the table of contents with the Tasks book expanded and the To-Do Bar book expanded. You can see that the To-Do Bar book contains three topics. Click the topic that you want to view. Click an expanded book to collapse it.

Using Search

Outlook help has a search tool that lets you search for information. It can be very useful when you cannot locate what you need in the table of contents. It is located just below the help toolbar. All you need to do is enter the search term in the box and click the Search button. Outlook displays a list of relevant topics, as shown in Figure 2.14 for a search on "email format." Each item in this list is a link that you can click to view the topic.

FIGURE 2.13

The table of contents displays books and topic titles.

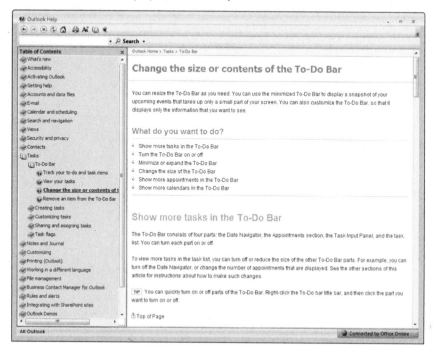

If you click the arrow next to the Search button you will see a list of search options. These options let you specify what will be searched. For the most complete and wide-ranging information you should keep the default All Outlook selected. In special situations you may want to select one of the other options to narrow the scope of the search.

FIGURE 2.14

Displaying the results of a help search.

Summary

This chapter has shown you how to install and activate Outlook, steps that are required before you can start using the program. If the program has not already been installed on your system, you'll find that the needed steps are easy to follow.

The Outlook screen packs a lot of information into a relatively small space. It's important that you understand the various screen elements, what they do, and how to use them, including the help system. There are lots more details to come, but this chapter gave you a good foundation to build on.

In Chapter 3 you really dive into Outlook, starting with the fundamentals of sending and receiving email.

Part II

Working with Email

Chapter 3

Working with Email Accounts

Before you can send and receive email using Outlook, you must set up at least one email account. When you set up an email account, you provide Outlook with the information it needs to connect to your online email account. Many people have just one account, but Outlook can work with multiple email accounts too.

Many people find that once their email account is set up they never have to make changes to the settings. Sometimes, however, making changes is required — and this chapter explains how to do this as well.

IN THIS CHAPTER

Understanding email accounts

Setting up your email accounts

Modifying account settings

Using profiles

Setting Up Your Email Accounts

Before you can use Outlook to send and receive email, you must set your email account. You can have more than one account — you'll follow the same steps for each one. There are two parts to this.

First, your account must be set up on the server or at your ISP. This is not done in Outlook. If your account is at your workplace it will likely have been set up by an IT person and he or she will have provided you with the required information such as your email address and password. If you are setting up a home or small business account, you may be doing this yourself. The details depend on your ISP so I cannot provide instructions, but as part of the process you will either specify or be given your email address and password.

Second, you must set up your account in Outlook. This process provides Outlook with the information, such as your email address and password, that it needs to connect to your email server and send and receive messages.

Hotmail Accounts and Outlook

As of this writing you cannot use Outlook to connect to a free Hotmail account — you must have one of its subscription accounts. You will have to access your free Hotmail account using your web browser, as usual.

If you are at work you may be lucky enough to have your IT guru set up Outlook for you, in which case you can skip this section. If you must do it yourself, the minimum information you'll need is your email address and your password. You may also need to know the address, or URL, of your email server. The URL looks a lot like a web page address and will be something like `mail.hosting.com`. Some mail accounts require two addresses, one for incoming mail and another for outgoing mail.

Outlook supports several different kinds of email accounts, including a Microsoft Exchange Server account. The account setup process differs depending on whether you have an Exchange account, an HTTP account such as Hotmail or MSN, or one of the other supported account types (POP and IMAP). All these procedures are covered in the following sections.

Automatic Email Account Setup

Outlook can automatically configure some email accounts. This works for some but not all POP, IMAP, Exchange Server, or HTTP accounts. To use the automated email account setup feature, you need to have your email address and your password. Then, here are the steps to follow:

1. From the menu, select Tools, Account Settings to display the Account Settings dialog box. Make sure the E-mail tab is selected, as shown in Figure 3.1. If there are any email accounts already set up they will be listed here. If you're just getting started the list will be blank.

2. Click the New button to display the Add New E-mail Account dialog box (Figure 3.2). Make sure the Microsoft Exchange Server, POP3, IMAP, or HTTP option is selected, then click Next.

3. The next dialog box, shown in Figure 3.3, asks for three pieces of information:

   - Your name.
   - Your email address.
   - Your password.

4. After entering the information click Next. Outlook will try to connect to your email server and set up the account.

FIGURE 3.1

The Account Settings dialog box.

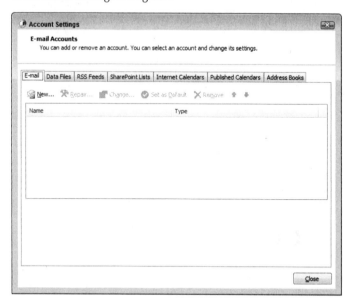

FIGURE 3.2

The Add New E-mail Account dialog box.

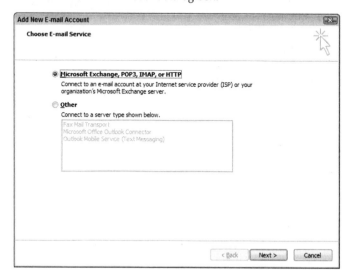

FIGURE 3.3

Entering your name, email address, and password during email account setup.

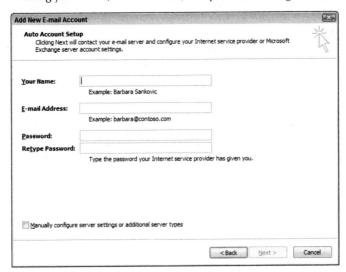

At step 3 you have the option of proceeding with manual account setup by selecting the Manually Configure Server Settings or Additional Server Types option and clicking Next. Manual email account setup is described for the various account types later in this chapter.

If you are continuing with automatic account setup, Outlook will attempt to connect to your email server and set up the account. In most cases this will work just as it is supposed to. The setup process will finish, the new account will be listed in the email accounts list, and you'll be able to start sending and receiving messages. However, this automated process does not always work. You may encounter one of the following situations:

- Outlook tells you that it cannot establish an encrypted connection to the server and offers to try again using an unencrypted connection. Click Next to proceed. The process will either complete properly or you'll encounter one of the other conditions in this list.

- Outlook cannot establish a connection to your account and asks you to verify the spelling of your email address. Make any needed corrections and click Next to try again. The process will either complete properly or you'll encounter the final condition in this list.

- If the preceding steps fail, Outlook will require that you manually configure the server settings. This option will be automatically selected in the Add New E-mail Account dialog box. Click Next to continue. The manual account setup steps differ for the various account types, and are covered in the following sections.

Email Terminology

All these acronyms can be confusing! POP stands for Post Office Protocol, a technology for receiving email. You'll also see POP3 used; they mean the same thing. IMAP is Internet Mail Access Protocol, another incoming mail technology. HTTP stands for Hypertext Transfer Protocol, which in addition to being a central technology for the Web is also used by some mail systems. SMTP is Simple Mail Transfer Protocol, the almost universally used technology for sending email.

Manual Email Account Setup (POP and IMAP)

If automatic account setup does not work for your POP or IMAP account, you will have to do it manually. It's a bit more involved but nothing to be afraid of. You will need some more information in addition to your email address and password. This information should be available from your ISP or your IT person:

- The addresses of your incoming mail server and outgoing mail server. These may be the same but are usually different.
- The username and password for your account login.

Once you have this information you are ready to begin. The first dialog box in the manual account setup process is shown in Figure 3.4. You will arrive at this dialog box either if automatic setup failed, or if you explicitly selected manual account setup. Both of these are explained in the previous section, "Automatic Email Account Setup."

FIGURE 3.4

The first step for manual email account setup.

41

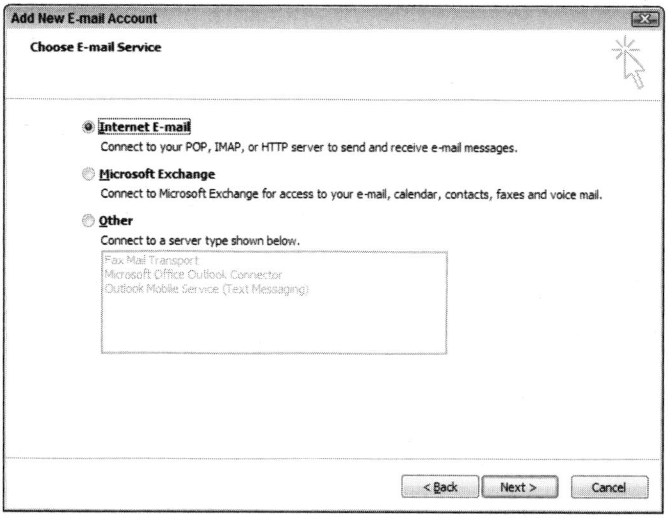

Here are the steps to follow:

1. Select the Internet E-mail option.

2. Click Next to display the dialog box shown in Figure 3.5. Enter all the requested information in the corresponding boxes, and be sure to select the type of email server from the Account Type list. The Remember Password option and Require Logon using Secure Password Authentication option are explained later in this chapter. Most people should leave these at their default settings. The More Settings button is also explained later in this chapter.

3. Once you have entered all the information, click the Test Account Settings button. If the test works, click Next and then Finish to complete the account setup. If the test does not work, please refer to the next section ("If Your Account Settings Don't Work") for steps to resolve the problem.

FIGURE 3.5

Entering required information for manual POP or IMAP email account setup.

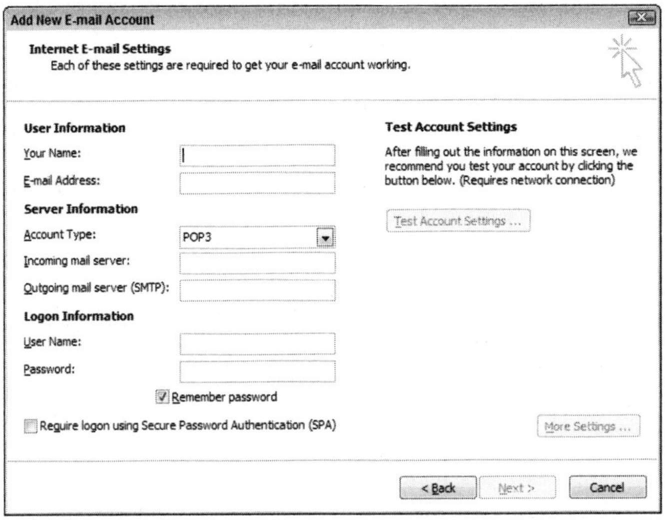

There are two options available in the account setup dialog box. If you select the Remember Password option, Outlook will be able to automatically log on to your email account as needed. Otherwise you will be prompted for the password each time.

Secure Password Authentication, or SPA, is an additional level of security that some mail servers have implemented. If your server requires this you should have been told this and also given any additional credentials required for login.

If Your Account Settings Don't Work

It's not uncommon for email account settings to not work at first. When you click the Test Account Settings button, Outlook tries to log on to your incoming mail server and also to send a test message via your outgoing mail server. One or both of these tests may fail, and the results shown in the Test Account Settings dialog box (shown in Figure 3.6 after a failed test) will tell you the results. Note also that this dialog box has an Errors tab, shown in Figure 3.7. The information on this tab may give you a clue as to where the problem lies. For example, if the problem is reported as The Server Rejected Your Login, the problem almost surely lies with the username or password that you entered.

FIGURE 3.6

This dialog box displays the results of testing your email account settings.

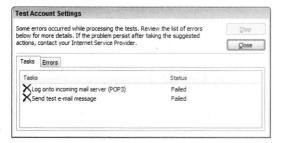

FIGURE 3.7

The Errors tab provides details on why the account settings test failed.

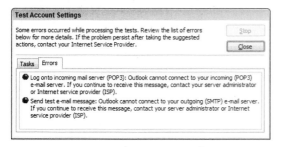

The most common cause of problems is simply mistyping some of the information required in the account setup dialog box. Everything must be 100% correct!

If the test failed in the outgoing mail server part, it most likely means that your outgoing mail server requires authentication. Setting this option is examined in the following section.

More Account Settings

The email account setup dialog box, shown in Figure 3.5, has a button labeled More Settings. You may not need to make any changes here, but if you do you can refer to this section for the details.

Clicking the More Settings button brings up the Internet E-mail Settings dialog box. This dialog box has four tabs for POP and IMAP accounts and a fifth for IMAP accounts only. The following sections look at these in turn.

General

The General tab, shown in Figure 3.8, has these three entries:

- **Mail Account:** This is the name Outlook uses to refer to the account, for example in the account list. The default is your email address but you can change it to anything you like such as Work Email or Yahoo Account.

- **Organization:** If you enter your organization name here it will be included in the headers of all email messages you send. Recipients normally do not see these headers, and Outlook does not make use of this information in any way. Other email programs may, however.

- **Reply E-mail:** When someone receives an email from you and replies by clicking the Reply button in their email program, their reply message will be sent to this address. By default it is the email address associated with the current email account, but if you have more than one email account you can enter another address here.

FIGURE 3.8

The General tab in the Internet E-mail Settings dialog box.

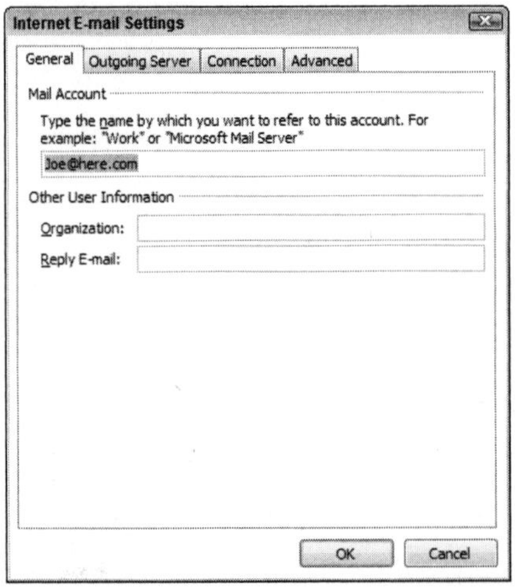

Outgoing Server

The Outgoing Server tab, shown in Figure 3.9, lets you specify authentication — that is, logon — settings for your outgoing mail server. By default this option is turned off because most outgoing mail servers do not require authentication. If yours does, put a check in the My Outgoing Server (SMTP) Requires Authentication box and then select other options and enter information as follows:

- **Use Same Settings as My Incoming Mail Server:** Outlook will log on to your outgoing mail server using the same username and password that you specified for your incoming mail server. This is the most commonly used setting.

- **Log On Using:** Select this option if your outgoing server requires its own log on. Then enter your username and password in the corresponding fields. The Remember Password option and the Require Secure Password Authentication (SPA) option work the same as was described for them in the previous section, "Manual Email Account Setup."

- **Log On to Incoming Mail Server before Sending Mail:** Select this option only if your incoming mail server is the same as your outgoing mail server. You will know this is the case when you are given the same address for both servers and enter this address for both during account setup.

FIGURE 3.9

The Outgoing Server tab in the Internet E-mail Settings dialog box.

Connection

The Connection tab, shown in Figure 3.10, lets you specify details of how Outlook connects to your email server. To set these options, you need to know how your computer is connected to the Internet. If you are at work, you almost surely connect via a local area network (LAN). If you are at home and have a cable modem or DSL connection, including wireless connections, this is also a LAN. A dial-up or phone line connection is an older connection technology that is still in use by a lot of people.

If you are connected via a LAN, select the Connect Using My Local Area Network (LAN) option. If you select this option you can also select the Connect Via Modem when Outlook Is Offline option. Doing so will cause Outlook to use a dial-up connection (assuming that one is available) to connect when the LAN is not available.

If you connect via a modem (phone line), select the Connect Using My Phone Line option. You may already have a dial-up connection defined in Windows. If not, you must define one before you can use Outlook for email. Defining a dial-up network connection is a process that is part of the Windows operating system, not Outlook, and is beyond the scope of this book. Please refer to Windows online help for more information. If you select this option, you then must select the defined dial-up connection you want to use in the Modem section of the dialog box. You can use the Add button to add a new dial-up connection, and the Properties button to examine and modify the properties of an existing connection.

FIGURE 3.10

The Connection tab in the Internet E-mail Settings dialog box.

Advanced

The Advanced tab contains options that most people will never need to change. You may not be "most people," however, so I explain these settings here. Note that the options available on this tab differ slightly for POP and IMAP accounts, as shown in Figures 3-11 and 3-12, respectively.

The Advanced tab for POP accounts in the Internet E-mail Settings dialog box.

The Advanced tab for IMAP accounts in the Internet E-mail Settings dialog box.

The advanced settings that are common to both POP and IMAP accounts are

■ **Server Port Numbers, Incoming Server:** The default values are 110 for POP servers and 143 for IMAP servers. It's rare for a server to be set up on different ports, but if yours is you can enter the correct port numbers here.

- **Server Port Numbers, Outgoing Server:** Regardless of whether your incoming server is POP or IMAP, your outgoing server will be SMTP and the default port number is 25. Do not change this unless you know that your outgoing mail server uses a different port, a rare occurrence.

- **This Server Requires an Encrypted Connection (SSL):** Turn this option on for the incoming and/or outgoing mail server if required.

- **Server Timeouts:** This is the amount of time that Outlook will wait for the mail server to respond when retrieving/sending email. The default setting of 1 minute works fine in most cases. If you find Outlook timing out, it probably means that you are working over a slow connection or that your server is often busy. Try a longer timeout setting to resolve this problem.

If you are working with a POP account, you have several settings available that control how Outlook handles messages on the server:

- **Leave a Copy of Messages on the Server:** By default, messages that you have received are removed from the server as soon as they are downloaded to Outlook. Turn this option on if you want Outlook to leave the messages on the server after download. This can be useful if you will want to later retrieve your messages from another computer.

- **Remove from Server after ... Days:** Specifies how long messages are to be retained on the server after they have been downloaded.

- **Remove from Server when Deleted from 'Deleted Items':** A message will be retained on the server until you permanently delete it in Outlook.

If you are working with an IMAP account there is one unique option, Root Folder Path, which specifies the root folder of the mailbox. Normally you will leave this blank and Outlook will use the default root folder on the server. If you need to specify a different root folder, enter it here.

Folders

The Folders tab is available in the Internet E-mail Settings dialog box only for IMAP accounts. It lets you specify whether copies of sent mail should be stored in the default Sent Items folder or somewhere else. If you choose the latter option you can select the folder to use or create a new folder.

Downloading an Exchange Profile

Some Exchange account providers give you the option of downloading an Exchange profile file to your computer. When you run this file, it sets up the Exchange profile for you. If available, this is an easy and error-free way to set up an Exchange profile.

Only One Exchange Account

Whereas Outlook can support multiple email accounts, you can have only one Exchange account set up.

Manual Email Account Setup (Exchange Server)

If automatic account setup does not work for your Exchange account, you will have to exit Outlook and set up the account through the Windows Control Panel. Though some of the dialog boxes look the same, you cannot set up an Exchange account manually while Outlook is running. In order to complete this setup you will need to know the address of your Exchange server (or its NETBIOS name), the username that has been set up for you, and your password.

These are the steps to set up an Exchange account:

1. Make sure Outlook is not running.
2. Select Control Panel from the Windows Start menu.
3. Double-click the Mail icon to display the Mail Setup dialog box.
4. Click the E-mail Accounts button to open the Account Settings dialog box. This is the same dialog box that you see when setting up accounts from within Outlook (shown earlier in Figure 3.1).
5. On the E-mail tab, click the New button to display the Add New E-mail Account dialog box.
6. Make sure that the Microsoft Exchange, POP3, IMAP, or HTTP option is selected and click Next.
7. In the next dialog box, select the Manually Configure Server Settings option and click Next.
8. In the next dialog box, select the Microsoft Exchange option and click Next.
9. In the next dialog box, shown in Figure 3.13, enter your Exchange server address and username.
10. If a dialog box appears asking whether you want to continue, click OK.
11. Click Finish.

After setting up your account you can start Outlook. You will be prompted for the Exchange account password. If the connection is established Outlook will display "Connected to Microsoft Exchange" at the right end of the status bar (which is at the bottom of the Outlook window).

You learn more about working with an Exchange account in Chapter 28.

FIGURE 3.13

Entering information about your Exchange server and username.

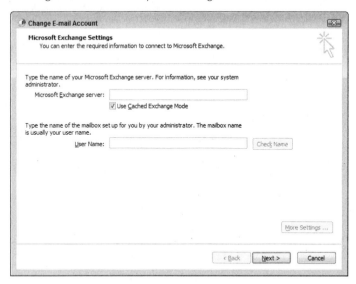

The preceding steps should set up your Exchange account with the default settings. This may be fine for you, but you may also want to make some changes to the settings. These settings are explained in Chapter 28, "Using Outlook with Exchange Server."

Manual Email Account Setup (HTTP)

You have an HTTP mail account if you have signed up for email with either Hotmail or Microsoft Network (MSN). Other email providers may also have HTTP accounts that are compatible with Outlook. If so, they will have provided you with the information you need to set up the account when you signed up.

HTTP mail accounts are designed primarily for Web use—that is, you will use a browser such as Internet Explorer to log on to your email account and read and send messages. However, it can be useful to set up an Outlook account too so you can download and read mail in Outlook and use the program's various features to organize your messages. Be aware that not all HTTP email accounts are compatible with Outlook.

To set up your HTTP email account in Outlook you need your email address and password. If you are setting up an HTTP account that is not Hotmail or MSN you will also need to know the address (URL) of the mail server and your username. Then, follow these steps:

1. Select the Manually Configure Server Settings option in the dialog box (refer to Figure 3.3) and click Next.

2. In the next dialog box make sure the Internet E-mail option is selected, then click Next.

3. In the next dialog box, shown in Figure 3.14, enter your name, email address, username, and password. Make sure HTTP is selected in the Account Type list.

4. Select Hotmail, MSN, or Other in the HTTP Service Provider list.

5. If you selected Other in the preceding step, enter the URL of your HTTP email server in the provided box.

6. Click Next to complete account setup.

FIGURE 3.14

Entering information for manual HTTP mail account setup.

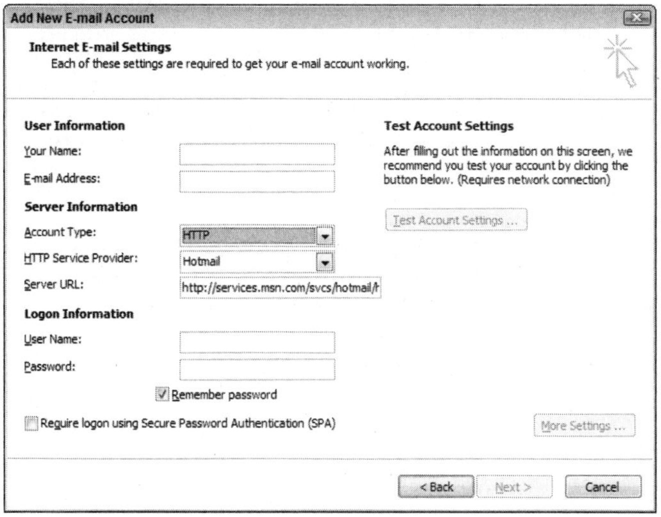

Modifying Account Settings

If you should need to change your account settings, the procedure is similar to setting up the account in the first place. Select Tools, Account Settings to display the Account Settings dialog box, and make sure the E-mail tab is displayed. Select the account of interest (necessary only if you have more than one) and click the Change button. You'll be taken through one or more dialog boxes where you can view and change the settings for this account. The settings will depend on the type of account and were explained earlier in this chapter in the section on setting up email accounts (Exchange server settings are covered in Chapter 28).

There are several other actions you can take with email accounts in the Account Settings dialog box:

- **Repair:** Outlook will try to connect to your email provider and refresh your account settings. This is the first step to try if an email account has suddenly stopped working.
- **Remove:** Deletes the account.
- **Set as Default:** If you have two or more email accounts, makes the selected account the default.

What exactly is the default email account? It's the account that is used to send email messages that you create from scratch. When you create an email message by replying to a message you have received, it will be sent using the account that the "reply to" message was received through. Note, however, that when you are composing an email message you can always change the account that the message will be sent through. This is explained in the next chapter.

Using Outlook Profiles

An Outlook profile stores information about a user's accounts and settings. All Outlook users have a single profile, and for most people that is all that is needed. In some circumstances, multiple profiles can be useful. This section explains how to create and use profiles in Outlook.

Understanding Profiles

In the first part of this chapter you learned how to set up your email accounts. Later chapters deal with configuring other aspects of Outlook such as RSS feeds and the screen appearance. All this information constitutes your profile. The vast majority of users never have a need for more than one profile, but there are situations where they can be useful:

- If you want to completely segregate two or more types of information, such as work and personal, you can create a profile for each.
- If you want to keep your regular POP and IMAP email accounts separate from an Exchange account.
- If more than one person uses the same computer, each person can have their own profile.

The third reason is usually a moot point because modern versions of Windows provide for different user accounts for logging on to Windows, which automatically gives each user their own Outlook profile. If, however, you want more than one person to use the same Windows logon and have separate Outlook data, you can use profiles.

Please note that creating an Outlook profile is not the same as creating a separate personal folders file. Although a given Outlook profile can have one or more personal folders files, each profile's folders are kept separate from other profiles.

Creating a New Profile

When you first install Outlook, a wizard walks you through the steps of creating a profile. To create a new profile you do not use Outlook but rather the Windows Control Panel, as follows:

1. Select Control Panel from the Windows Start menu.

2. Open Mail to display the Mail Setup - Outlook dialog box.

3. Click the Show Profiles button to open the Mail dialog box (Figure 3.15). This dialog box lists the existing profiles; the default profile is named Outlook.

FIGURE 3.15

The Mail dialog box.

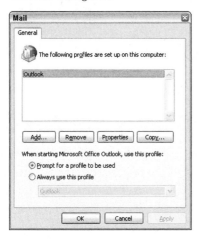

4. Click the Add button to open the New Profile dialog box (Figure 3.16).

FIGURE 3.16

Naming a new profile.

5. Enter a name for the new profile and click OK.

6. Follow the on-screen prompts to set up your email account. This procedure is covered earlier in this chapter.

Other actions you can take in the Mail dialog box are

- **Remove:** Removes the selected profile from the system.

- **Properties:** Lets you view and edit the properties of the profile, including the email account settings and data files. You learned how to work with email settings in Chapter ?? and data files in Chapter ??.

- **Copy:** Makes a copy of the selected profile under a new name. This is useful if you want a new profile that has some of the same settings as an existing one. Create a copy then edit it as needed.

- **Prompt for a Profile:** If this option is selected and you have more than one profile, Outlook will prompt you to select the profile you want to use each time the program starts.

- **Always use the Profile:** Select the profile that you want Outlook to use from the list.

Switching Profiles

You cannot switch from one profile to another while Outlook is running. If you selected the Prompt for a Profile option (as explained in the previous section), quit Outlook and restart it, then select the desired profile when prompted.

If you selected the Always Use this Profile option (also explained in the previous section), you must perform the following steps:

1. Quit Outlook.

2. Select Control Panel from the Windows Start menu.

3. From Control Panel, open Mail.

4. Click the Show Profiles button.

5. Select the Prompt for a Profile option.

6. Close all dialog boxes.

7. Start Outlook.

Summary

Setting up your email account — or accounts, as the case may be — is the first thing you must do if you want to use Outlook to send and receive email. Outlook supports several different kinds of accounts and you can be using one, two, or more different account types at the same time. Once you have your accounts set up and working, you can usually forget about them. Occasionally, however, you may need to modify some account settings and Outlook provides for that, too. Also, you can set up multiple Outlook profiles if you have the need.

Chapter 4

Fundamentals of Email

O utlook's email features are sophisticated and comprehensive. Underneath all that power, however, are the fundamental tasks of composing, sending, and reading messages. These basics are the subject of this chapter.

Composing and Sending Messages

This section explains the basics of composing and sending email messages.

Quick Compose and Send

Outlook provides a lot of flexibility when it comes to creating and formatting email messages. Often, however, all you want to do is to quickly create and send a basic message. Here's how:

1. If the Mail pane is displayed, click the New button on the toolbar or press Ctrl+N to create a new, blank email message. If another pane is displayed, click the down arrow to the right of the New button and select Mail Message from the list. The new message appears as shown in Figure 4.1.

2. Type the recipient's address in the To field, or click the To button and select a recipient from your address book.

3. Type the message subject in the Subject field.

IN THIS CHAPTER

Composing and sending email messages

Sending attachments

Reading and replying to messages

Working with received attachments

Understanding the Inbox display

4. Type the body of the message in the main section of the message window.

5. Click the Send button.

A blank email message ready to be composed and sent.

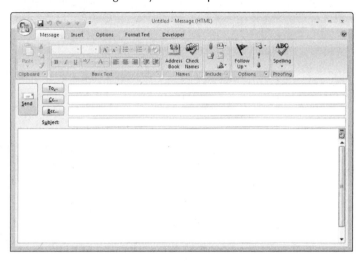

That's all there is to it. Depending on Outlook's Send/Receive options, your message will be sent immediately or will be placed in the Outbox to be sent the next time a send/receive is performed. If you want to be sure the message is sent immediately, press F9.

You can also create a new email message using settings other than the defaults by selecting New Mail Message Using from the Actions menu. Then, from the next menu:

■ To create a message based on stationery, select one of the recently used stationeries that are listed (if any) or select More Stationery to select from all available stationery. Stationery is covered in detail in Chapter 5.

■ To create a message in a format (HTML, Rich Text, or plain text) other than the default, select the desired format. Message format options are covered in detail in Chapter 5.

Message Addressing Options

An email message can have multiple recipients, and each recipient can be one of three types:

■ **To:** The main message recipient(s). Every message must have at least one recipient in the To field.

Sending a Message

When you click the Send button to send an email message, Outlook places the message in the Outbox. This is one of the mail folders displayed in the navigation pane. Depending on your connection status and Outlook option settings, the message may be transmitted to your email provider immediately or it may wait until your are online or until a timed send/receive occurs. In either case, once the message is sent it is removed from the Outbox folder and a copy is saved in the Sent Items folder.

- **CC (Carbon Copy)**: Generally you use CC when a person needs to be aware of the content of the message but is not a primary recipient — that is, does not need to respond or take action. All recipients of a message can see who is in the CC list.

- **BCC (Blind Carbon Copy)**: Like CC but the names and email addresses of BCC recipients are not visible to any other recipients of the message.

Changing the Reply To Address

By default, the reply to address that is part of every email message you send is the reply address that you specified when you set up the email account. There may be situations when you want replies to a message that you send directed to a different email address. To do so:

1. Click the Direct Replies To button in the More Options section of the Options ribbon. Outlook will open the Message Options dialog box.

2. Under Delivery Options, make sure the Have Replies Sent To option is checked.

3. Enter the desired reply address in the adjacent box, or click the Select Names button to choose from your address book.

4. Click OK.

Entering Recipients Manually

You can type recipients directly into the To, CC, and BCC fields. To enter more than one recipient in a field, use a semicolon as a separator between addresses.

Outlook's autocomplete feature is by default turned on for all recipient fields. As you start entering an address or name, Outlook displays suggestions based on what you have entered in the past. The suggestions come from a list of names and email addresses that you have entered previously. Outlook will narrow the list as you enter more of the name or address. If the recipient you want is displayed, select it by clicking. You can also highlight it with the up and down arrow keys and press Enter. Otherwise just continue typing in the full name or address.

Where's the BCC Field?

By default an email form does not display the BCC field in its header, just the To and CC fields. You can still add BCC recipients using the Contacts list, however. If you want the BCC field displayed, click the Options tab at the top of the message window and click the Show BCC button.

When Outlook is first installed the autocomplete list is empty so it may seem to not be working. As you continue to use Outlook, however, it will become a useful tool. Names that you use less frequently will move to the bottom of the list and eventually disappear.

Entering Recipients from Your Address Book

Any recipients who are listed in your address book can be added to an email message with a few clicks. If you refer back to Figure 4.1 you can see that the email window has To and CC buttons next to the corresponding fields. If the BCC field is visible it will have an adjacent BCC button. Click any of these buttons to open the Select Names dialog box, shown in Figure 4.2.

FIGURE 4.2

Selecting email recipients from your address book.

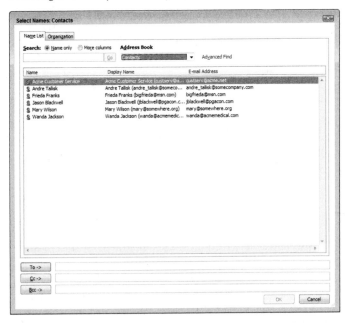

Deleting Autocomplete Items

If someone changes their email address you may find their old, invalid address still appearing on the autocomplete list. When the list is displayed and you see an address you no longer want, use the down arrow key to highlight it and then press Del.

If you have more than one address book you should select it in the Address Book list. The default address book, which is adequate for many Outlook users, is called Contacts. The entries in the selected address book are displayed in an alphabetized list. Then, add recipients to your message as follows:

- Select a single recipient by clicking it. Select multiple recipients by holding down Ctrl while clicking.

- Add the selected recipient(s) to the To, CC, or BCC field by clicking the corresponding button.

- Add the selected recipients to the active field by pressing Enter. The active field is the one corresponding to the button you clicked — To, CC, or BCC — to display the Select Names dialog box.

- Add a single recipient to the active field by double-clicking the recipient in the list.

- To remove a recipient from the To, CC, or BCC field, click it — the entire name will become highlighted — and press Del.

When you are finished adding recipients, click the OK button to return to the message.

Searching for Recipients

The Select Names dialog box lets you search for recipients by name or other information. Look at the upper-left corner of the Select Names dialog box (refer back to Figure 4.2). If you select the Name option and start typing in the box, Outlook will automatically highlight the first contact in the list that matches what you have typed so far. If there are no matches the highlight moves to the end of the list.

If you select the All Fields option, enter the desired search text in the box and click the Go button. Outlook will display any contacts that have a match in any of their fields, such as Company or Mailing Address. You learn about Outlook contacts and the various kinds of information that can be stored in Chapter 10.

Sending Attachments

An attachment is a file that you send along with an email message. When the recipient receives the message he or she can save the file to disk and open it. Attachments can be a very useful way to pass documents around — whether it's sending photos of the kids to other family members or distributing a Word document to your colleagues for review.

There are several concerns with attachments that you need to be aware of. One has to do with file size. Most email accounts limit the size of attachments that can accompany an email message. The limit varies between different accounts but 10MB is a common figure. Even if your account allows you to send large attachments, the recipient's account may not allow them to receive them.

The other concern I will mention has to do with security. Certain types of files have the potential to harm your computer by introducing a virus or by other means. Outlook and other email client programs block potentially harmful attachments based on the filename extension, which indicates the type of file. For example, executable program files use the .EXE extension and these are blocked by Outlook.

One approach to dealing with both of these concerns is to use a file archiving utility to compress your files into a ZIP or other kind of archive. This not only reduces the file size but also hides the extensions of files that might be blocked on the receiving end.

What kinds of files can you send and receive as attachments? Any image file is okay, including those with the .JPG, .GIF, .PNG, and .TIF extensions. So are text files (.TXT extension), XML files (.XML extension), and most Microsoft Office documents: Word (.DOC and .DOCX extensions), Excel (.XLS and .XLSX extensions), and PowerPoint (.PPT and .PPTX extensions). ZIP archives (.ZIP extension) are okay too.

You may want to review the section on attachment security in Chapter 20 if you will be sending and/or receiving a lot of attachments. The remainder of this section shows you how to add attachments to a message.

When you are composing an email message, you attach a file as follows:

1. If necessary, click the Message tab to display the Message ribbon.
2. Click the Attach File button (with a paper clip icon). Outlook opens the Insert File dialog box as shown in Figure 4.3. The initial display is the files in your My Documents folder.
3. If necessary, use the dialog box to navigate to the folder containing the file.
4. Click the name of the file to attach. To attach multiple files from the same folder, hold down the Ctrl key while clicking.
5. Click the Insert button.

Once you have attached one or more files, the message will display an Attached line in the header, as shown in Figure 4.4. The attached files are listed here along with the file size. If you change your mind and want to remove a file, click its name in the Attached box and press Delete.

FIGURE 4.3

Selecting files to attach to a message.

FIGURE 4.4

The names of attached files are displayed in the message header.

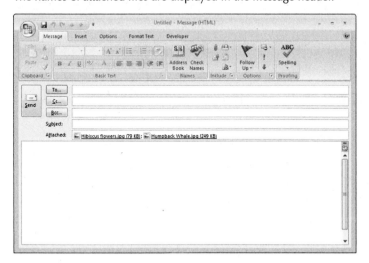

Sending and Receiving

Outlook's default is to send and receive messages on all accounts when the program first starts and then every 30 minutes. If you want to send/receive manually, click the Send/Receive button on the toolbar or press F9.

Saving Message Drafts

If you have started to compose a message and decide to complete it later, you can save a copy in the Drafts folder by clicking the Save icon — it looks like a diskette — on the Quick Access toolbar at the top left of the message window. You can also select Save from the menu that is displayed by clicking the Office button (the round icon in the top-left corner of the message window).

When you are ready to continue working on the message, open the Drafts folder by clicking it in the navigation pane, then double-click the message to open it. You can now complete and send the message as usual.

By default, Outlook saves copies of open items, including messages you are composing, every three minutes.

Reading and Replying to Messages

When Outlook receives an email message it is placed in your Inbox folder, as shown in Figure 4.5. By default, messages are sorted by the time and date they were received. You can see that the sender, the subject, the time/date received, and the message size are displayed. Please also note the following:

- A message that you have not yet read is displayed in bold type with a closed envelope icon — for example, the top message in the figure. A message that has been read is displayed in normal type with an open envelope icon — the bottom message in the figure.
- If the message includes one or more attachments, a paper clip icon is displayed.

Reading a Message

To read a message, double-click it in the Inbox. The message will open in its own window, as shown in Figure 4.6.

FIGURE 4.5

Messages that you receive are placed in your Inbox folder.

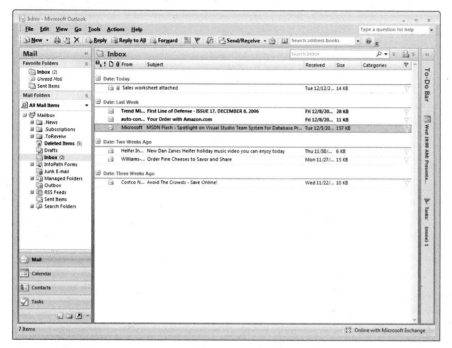

FIGURE 4.6

Reading an email message.

While you have an email message open, you can carry out the following actions:

- Print the message by clicking the Print button on the Quick Access toolbar.
- Close the message and delete it by clicking the Delete button on the ribbon. Outlook moves the message to the Deleted Items folder.
- Close the message without deleting it by clicking the X icon at the right end of the title bar.

Other actions that you can take with an email message are covered later in this chapter.

You can also move the message from the Inbox to another folder. This is useful when you want to organize received email messages. You learn more about working with Outlook folders in Chapter 18. The basic steps for moving an open message are as follows:

1. Click the Move to Folder button on the message window ribbon.
2. Select Other Folder from the menu. Outlook displays the Move Item To dialog box as shown in Figure 4.7.
3. Click the destination folder. Or, to create a new folder, click the New button. Details on creating a new folder are presented next.
4. Click OK. The message is closed and moved to the specified folder.

FIGURE 4.7

Moving an email message to another folder.

When you are moving an email message to another folder, you are given the opportunity to create a new folder. When you click the New button in the Move Item To dialog box, Outlook opens the Create New Folder dialog box, shown in Figure 4.8. Then:

1. Enter the name for the new folder in the Name box.
2. Make sure that Mail and Post Items is selected in the Folder Contains list.

3. Click the location for the new folder in the list. The new folder will be created as a sub-folder to the item you select here.

4. Click OK to close the dialog box and return to the Move Item To dialog box. The new folder will be selected in the list.

5. Click OK to complete moving the mail message.

FIGURE 4.8

Creating a new folder to move an email message to.

Marking Messages as Read or Unread

Messages that have not been read are displayed in bold font and with a closed envelope icon. When you open a message it is marked as read and will be displayed in normal font with an open envelope icon. You can control how a message is flagged. Perhaps you opened a message and then were called away — you might want to mark it as unread so you will be sure to look at it again later.

If the message is open, simply click the Mark as Unread button on the ribbon. If no message is open you can select a message in the Inbox (or whatever mail folder you are in) and then:

■ Select Edit, Mark as Read to mark the message as read.

■ Select Edit, Mark as Unread to mark the message as unread.

■ Select Edit, Mark All as Read to mark all messages in the folder as read.

Using the Reading Pane

Outlook's reading pane lets you view the contents of a message without opening it. When the reading pane is displayed, it shows the contents of whatever message is selected in the Inbox (or whatever other mail folder you are working in). This is shown in Figure 4.9.

FIGURE 4.9

Using the reading pane to view a message.

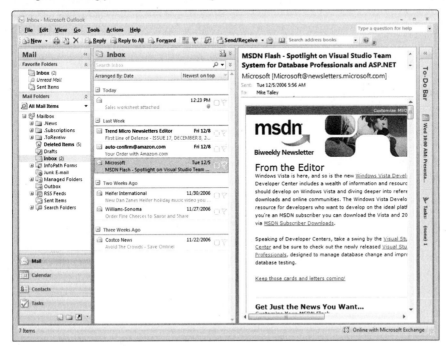

The reading pane can be displayed at the bottom of the screen or along the right edge. To control the display of the reading pane, select View, Reading Pane and then select Right, Bottom, or Off.

Normally, viewing a message in the reading pane will not mark it as read — this requires opening the message. However, you can tell Outlook to mark messages as read when they are viewed in the reading pane as follows:

1. Select Options from the Tools menu to open the Options dialog box.
2. Click the Other tab.
3. Click the Reading Pane button to open the Reading Pane dialog box.
4. Put a check in the box next to the Mark Items as Read When Viewed in Reading Pane option.
5. Click OK twice to close all dialog boxes.

Other Actions for Received Messages

When you are viewing a message that you have received, there are several other actions you can take with the message. Each of these actions corresponds to a button on the Message ribbon:

- **Create Rule:** Lets you create a rule for handling similar messages. Rules are covered in Chapter 9.

- **Block Sender:** Adds the message sender to your Blocked Senders list and moves the message to the Junk E-mail folder. You'll find more details on dealing with junk email in Chapter 8.

- **Safe Lists:** Adds the sender or the sender's domain to your safe list. See Chapter 8 for more details.

- **Categorize:** Assign the message to an Outlook category. See Chapter 17 for more information on using categories.

- **Follow Up:** Flag the message for follow-up and/or create a reminder associated with the message.

- **Related:** Find other messages from the same sender or that are related by subject or content.

Replying to and Forwarding Messages

Replying to and forwarding messages are two very useful things you can do with email using Outlook. When a mail message is open you have three buttons in the Respond section of the ribbon:

- **Reply:** Creates a new message addressed to the person who sent you the original message. The new message contains the entire original message, and the subject of the new message is "Re:" followed by the subject of the original message.

- **Reply to All:** Same as Reply except the new message is also addressed to any other people the original message was sent to.

- **Forward:** Creates a new, unaddressed message. The new message quotes the entire original message and the subject is "FW:" followed by the subject of the original message.

At this point the new message is ready for editing. You can add your own text to the body of the message, add or remove recipients (you must add at least one recipient when forwarding), add attachments, and so on. When you're finished, click Send.

Another message forwarding option is to select Forward As Attachment from the Actions menu. A new email message is created with the original message attached as a separate file rather than being inserted into the body of the new message.

What About Attachments?

When you reply (or reply all) to a message, any attachments that came with the original message are not included. When you forward a message, however, attachments are included.

Working with Received Attachments

Outlook lets you save attachments to disk and also lets you view attachments without opening them in their native application. The viewing option is available for many attachment types, including most image files, Word documents, and Excel workbooks.

Saving Attachments

When a received message includes one or more attachments, it will have a small paper clip icon displayed in the Inbox. There are two ways to save attachments. The first method lets you save attachments without opening the message:

1. Select the message in the Inbox (or whatever mail folder you are working in).
2. Select File, Save Attachments from the menu.
3. On the next menu, select the attachment to save. Outlook opens the Save Attachment dialog box.
4. Navigate to the folder where you want the attachment saved.
5. Edit the attachment filename, if desired. Warning: do not change the extension!
6. Click Save.

Repeat these steps, if necessary, for other attachments.

If the message has more than one attachment, the menu that Outlook displays in step 3 also has a Save All Attachments command. Selecting this command opens the Save All Attachments dialog box, as shown in Figure 4.10. Note that all attachments are listed and selected. Then:

1. If you want to save just some of the attachments, select them by clicking and Ctrl+Clicking (to select more than one individual attachment) or Shift+Clicking (to select a group of adjacent attachments).
2. Click OK. Outlook displays the Save All Attachments dialog box.
3. Select the folder to save the attachments in. You cannot edit attachment names — they will be saved under their original names.
4. Click OK.

The other way to save attachments can be used when the message is open or displayed in the reading pane:

1. In the message header, right-click an attachment name.
2. Select Save As from the context menu.
3. In the next dialog box, select a folder for the attachment and the attachment name if desired.
4. Click Save.

FIGURE 4.10

Saving all message attachments at once.

Viewing Attachments

When a message that you receive includes one or more attachments, they will be listed below the message head (both in the reading pane and when the message is open). You'll also see a Message button next to the attachment names.

- Click an attachment name to view the attachment.
- Click the Message button to return to the message.

Figure 4.11 shows these elements along with an attachment that is being viewed.

FIGURE 4.11

Viewing an attachment.

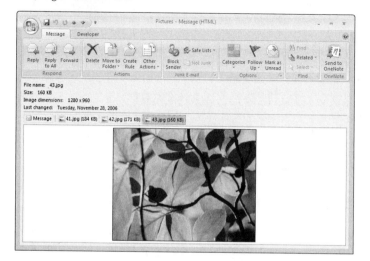

Native Applications

A native, or default, application is an application that is registered on your system for working with a particular kind of file. For some kinds of files there is only one application that can be "native," such as Microsoft Word for Word files and Excel for Excel files. For other kinds of files, such as image files, there are many possibilities and it will depend on what's installed on your system. For example, on my system PhotoShop is registered as the native application for most image files, but on your system it might be Paint Shop Pro or Corel Draw.

Opening Attachments

Opening an attachment in its native application is usually done by saving the attachment to disk, as described earlier, and then starting the application and opening the file as usual. You can, however, open an attachment directly from Outlook by following these steps:

1. Open the message or display it in the reading pane.

2. Right-click the attachment name.

3. Select Open from the context menu.

   Depending on the file type, Outlook may display a warning dialog box asking whether you want to open or save the file. Click Open.

4. The attachment will be opened in its native application.

The reason for the cautionary dialog box in step 3 is security. Some kinds of files, such as Word documents and Excel workbooks, have the potential to contain malicious macro code that could harm your system. This code is harmless unless the file is opened, so you may want to save it to disk first and run a virus scan before opening it.

If you do open an attachment this way, you can work with it in the application as you normally would, including saving to disk.

Understanding the Inbox Display

The Inbox, or any other Outlook folder that contains email messages, provides you with a lot of information about the messages it contains. The display is arranged in columns, or fields, with each field identified at the top of the display. You can customize this display by adding, removing, and rearranging columns. That topic is discussed in Chapter 19. For now it's important for you to understand the meaning of the fields in the default Inbox display. They are, from left to right in the default display (see Figure 4.12), as follows:

FIGURE 4.12

The field headings in the default Inbox display.

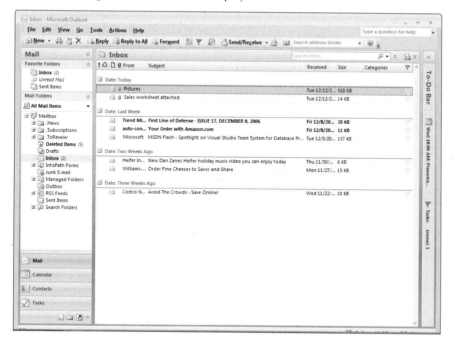

- **Importance (exclamation point icon):** A red exclamation point is displayed in this field if the sender marked the message as having high importance. Nothing is displayed for normal importance.

- **Reminder (bell icon):** A bell is displayed in this field if the message has been associated with a reminder.

- **Read (page icon):** Displays a closed or open envelope for unread and read messages, respectively. Also displays various icons for special messages such as alerts and meeting requests.

- **Attachment (paper clip icon):** Displays a paper clip icon if the message includes one or more attachments.

- **From:** The name or email address of the message sender.

- **Subject:** The message subject.

- **Received:** The time and date the message was received.

- **Size:** The size of the message and any attachments.

- **Categories:** If the message has been assigned to a category, the category name and icon are displayed here.

- **Follow-up (flag icon):** Displays a flag indicating the follow-up status of the message. A clear flag indicates no follow-up status. Various colored flags indicate other follow-up statuses such as due tomorrow or due next week. A checkmark indicates complete.

You can sort the messages in the Inbox by any of the fields that are displayed. Simply click the field heading to sort by that field in ascending order; click a second time to sort in descending order. If the field heading is wide enough it will display an upward or downward pointing arrow to show you that the messages are sorted by that field in ascending or descending order, respectively. For example, in Figure 4.12 you can see that the messages are sorted by the Received field in descending order.

Summary

This chapter explained the fundamentals of sending and receiving email messages. It also covered sending attachments and dealing with attachments that you receive. Finally, it provided a quick overview of the Inbox display.

There's a lot more to email, more options and flexibility that give you complete control over your messaging. These are covered in Chapter 5.

Chapter 5

Formatting Your Email Messages

An email message does not have to be limited to plain text. Outlook provides you with the ability to create messages with rich formatting, including different fonts, images, charts, and a variety of other elements. No longer is email just for sending simple messages — an email can be, in essence, a small document with all of the impact that is possible with advanced formatting.

Message Format Options

Outlook can create three types of email messages. The type of a message affects the extent to which you can apply formatting to the message. To a lesser extent the type of message also affects who can and cannot read the message. The three types of messages are

- **Plain text:** The most basic type of message, plain text can be read by everyone, no matter how old their email program, but cannot contain any formatting.

- **HTML:** This stands for Hypertext Markup Language, and is the same technique used to format web pages. HTML provides an excellent set of formatting options, and can be read by essentially any modern email client.

- **Rich text:** The rich text format, sometimes referred to as RTF, was developed for word processors. It provides more powerful formatting tools than HTML but can be read by a limited set of email clients, including Outlook and Exchange.

Which format should you use? There's rarely a reason to use plain text unless you believe that your message will be going to people who are using out-of-date software, for example in some third-world countries.

RTF is desirable because of its powerful formatting capabilities. There are just some things you can do in RTF that you cannot do in HTML, although to be honest they are all pretty specialized and the majority of users are unlikely to ever use them.

However, the limitations for reading RTF messages are an important consideration. Unless you know that all recipients will have a compatible email client you should avoid using RTF. If, for example, your company has standardized on Outlook for its email client, it is probably safe to use RTF for your internal company messages.

HTML is generally the best choice of message formats for most users. It provides all the formatting capability that most people will ever need, and it can be read by most email clients. For this reason, HTML is Outlook's default message type.

Changing Message

When you are composing a new message, you can change its type by clicking the Plain Text, HTML, or Rich Text button on the Options ribbon (see Figure 5.1). The highlighted button shows the message's current format — which is HTML in the figure.

FIGURE 5.1

Changing the format of an email message.

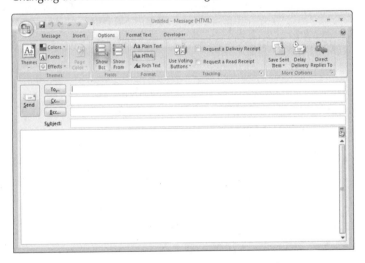

If you change an RTF or HTML message to plain text, any existing formatting will be lost.

As mentioned earlier, Outlook's default is to create messages in HTML format. If you want to change the default format, follow these steps:

1. Select Tools, Options to display the Options dialog box.
2. Click the Mail Format tab (shown in Figure 5.2).
3. In the Message Format section, select the desired default format in the list.
4. Click OK.

FIGURE 5.2

Changing the default message format.

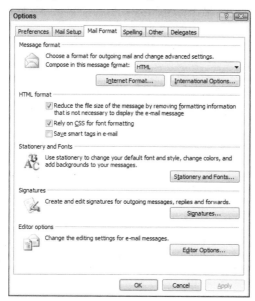

Now, every new email message that you create will have the specified format — although you can always change it for an individual message as described earlier.

Formatting Text

Tools for formatting message text are located on the Format Text ribbon in the email window. Some of the more frequently used text formatting tools are duplicated on the Message ribbon, for ease of access. Text formatting is divided into two categories: font and paragraph.

The Format Painter

The format painter lets you copy font and paragraph formatting from one location in the message and "paint" it onto other text. It works as follows:

1. Click anywhere in text that has the desired formatting.
2. Click the Format Painter button in the Clipboard section of the Message ribbon (it is also present on the Format Text ribbon). The mouse pointer will display a small paintbrush icon.
3. Drag the mouse over the target text.

If you want to paint more than one section of text, double-click the Format Painter button. It will remain active until you click it again.

Font Formatting

Font formatting affects individual characters in a message. It encompasses things such as underlining and italic, and can be applied to anything from a single character to an entire message. Most font formatting can be applied in two ways, either to selected text or to text you are about to type. Some formatting can be applied only to selected text. Selecting text is done as in most other applications:

- With the mouse, drag over the text.
- With the keyboard, hold down Shift and use the cursor movement keys.
- To unselect text, click anywhere outside the selected text or press any arrow key (without Shift).

The font formatting tools are located in the Font section of the Format Text ribbon. They are identified in Figure 5.3 and described here.

- **Font:** Select the font, or typeface.
- **Font size:** Select the font size, in points (1 point = 1/72 inch).
- **Increase/decrease font size:** Increases or decreases font size by one step.
- **Clear formatting:** Removes all formatting from text.
- **Bold:** Toggles boldface on and off.
- **Italic:** Toggles italic on and off.
- **Underline:** Click the button to toggle the default single underline. Click the adjacent arrow to select different underline styles and colors.
- **Superscript/subscript:** Click to toggle text between superscript or subscript and normal.

- **Change case:** Click then select from the menu to change the case of selected text.
- **Highlight:** Click the button then drag over text to apply highlighting in the default color (displayed on the button). Click the adjacent arrow to select a highlight color or turn highlighting off.
- **Font color:** Click the button to change font color to the color displayed on the button. Click the adjacent arrow to select a different font color.

FIGURE 5.3

Outlook's font formatting tools.

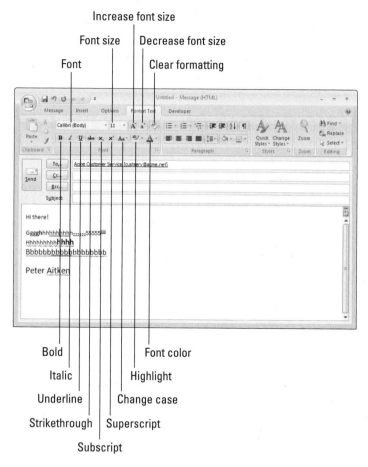

Paragraph Formatting

Outlook's paragraph formatting tools are located in the Paragraph section of the Format Text ribbon. These tools, or at least most of them, let you work with formatting that applies to entire paragraphs of text. This includes bulleted and numbered lists, line spacing, and background color. Some tools in this category are not for formatting *per se* but have other functions, which I describe here.

When you select paragraph formatting it will be applied to the paragraph that contains the insertion point (or editing cursor). If you first select text that spans two or more paragraphs, the formatting will be applied to all those paragraphs. A paragraph is created when you press Enter — this marks the end of the paragraph.

The paragraph formatting tools are shown in Figure 5.4 and described here. Additional explanation for some of the items is provided following the list.

FIGURE 5.4

Outlook's paragraph formatting tools.

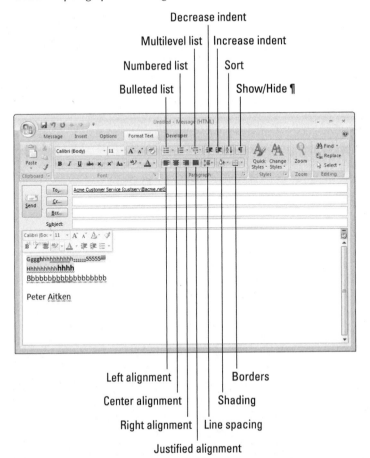

Soft Returns

Sometimes you may want to start a new line without starting a new paragraph. You do this with a *soft return*, created by pressing Shift+Enter. Text that is separated by a soft return is considered to be part of the same paragraph for formatting purposes.

- **Bullets:** Starts a bulleted list or converts existing paragraphs to a bulleted list. Click the button to apply the default bullet style. Click the adjacent arrow to select a different bullet style.

- **Numbering:** Starts a numbered list or converts existing paragraphs to a numbered list. Click the button to apply the default numbering style. Click the adjacent arrow to select a different numbering style.

- **Multilevel list:** Creates a multilevel list. See the "Multilevel Lists" section of this chapter for a fuller explanation.

- **Decrease/increase indent:** Changes the indent of the left edge of the paragraph.

- **Sort:** Sorts text alphabetically or numerically. See the "Sorting" section of this chapter for a full explanation.

- **Show/Hide ¶:** Shows or hides formatting marks. See the "Show/Hide ¶" section of this chapter for a full explanation.

- **Alignment:** Sets paragraph alignment to left, centered, right, or justified.

- **Line spacing:** Sets the spacing between lines of text. See the "Line Spacing" section of this chapter for a full explanation.

- **Shading:** Sets the shading displayed behind the paragraph. Click the button to apply the default shading displayed on the button. Click the adjacent arrow to select a different shading.

- **Borders:** Displays a border around paragraphs. See the "Borders" section of this chapter for a full explanation.

The following sections provide additional explanation for some of the paragraph formatting tools.

Multilevel Lists

A multilevel list contains items (paragraphs) at two or more levels. Each level is marked with a different system of numbering, lettering, or symbols and is usually indented with respect to the previous level. Figure 5.5 shows an example of a three-level multilevel list.

FIGURE 5.5

A multilevel list.

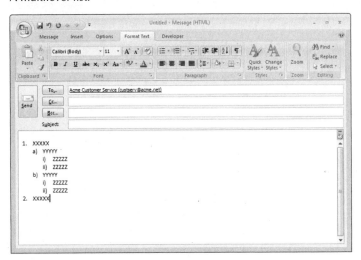

A multilevel list can contain a maximum of nine levels. You can create a multilevel list as you type, as described here:

1. Place the cursor where you want the list to begin.

2. Click the Multilevel List button on the Format Text ribbon to display the Multilevel List menu, shown in Figure 5.6.

3. Click the desired list style.

4. Type in the first list item. This will of course be at the top list level.

5. Press Enter to start the next list item. Press Tab one or more times to move it to a lower list level. Press Shift+Tab to move it to a higher list level.

6. Press Enter to start another list item. Each new list item is created at the same level as the one before it.

7. To change the level of an existing list item, place the editing cursor at the start of the item and press Tab or Shift+Tab.

8. To change the level of two or more list items, select the items and then select Change List Level from the Multilevel List menu.

9. To end the list, press Enter to start a new item, then open the Multilevel List and select None. Subsequent paragraphs will not be part of the list.

FIGURE 5.6

Selecting the multilevel list style.

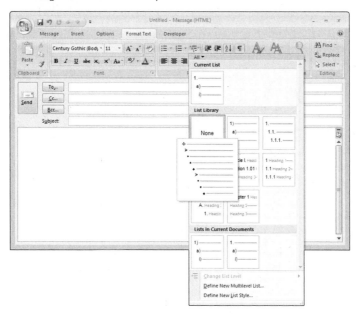

You can also create a multilevel list from existing text:

1. Select the paragraphs that you want to be in the list.

2. Open the Multilevel List menu and select the desired list style. Outlook will convert the selected paragraphs into a multilevel list.

3. To change the level of individual paragraphs, place the editing cursor at the start of the item and press Tab or Shift+Tab.

4. To change the level of two or more list items, select the items and then select Change List Level from the Multilevel List menu.

To change the style of an existing multilevel list, select the entire list and then select the desired new style from the Multilevel List menu. If you want to change a multilevel list back to normal text, select the entire list and then select None from the Multilevel List menu.

Sorting

The Sort command can be used to arrange paragraphs in alphabetical order, either ascending (A–Z) or descending (Z–A). To perform a sort:

1. Select the paragraphs that you want to sort.

2. Click the Sort button on the Format Text ribbon. Outlook displays the Sort Text dialog box (see Figure 5.7).

3. Select the Ascending or Descending option.

4. Click OK.

FIGURE 5.7

Sorting paragraphs alphabetically.

The additional settings that you see in the Sort Text dialog box are used when you are sorting a table. You learn about tables in Chapter 6.

Line Spacing

By default, lines of text in an Outlook email message are single spaced. You can change this as follows:

1. To change spacing for a single paragraph, place the cursor anywhere in the paragraph. To change spacing for multiple paragraphs, select them.

2. Click the Line Spacing button on the Format Text ribbon to display the Line Spacing menu.

3. Select the desired spacing: Single, 1.5, or Double.

4. For more control over spacing, select Paragraph from the Line Spacing menu to display the Paragraph dialog box (see Figure 5.8).

Points and Line Spacing

The default unit of measurement for line spacing (and also for font size) is *points*, a printer's measurement equal to 1/72 of an inch. Generally, single spacing is slightly larger than the size of the font in use. For example, line spacing of approximately 13 points would be considered single spacing for an 11 point font. You can enter spacing values in inches if you prefer. Simply enter a number followed by the " (double quote) symbol and Outlook will convert the inch value to points.

FIGURE 5.8

The Paragraph dialog box gives you complete control over line spacing.

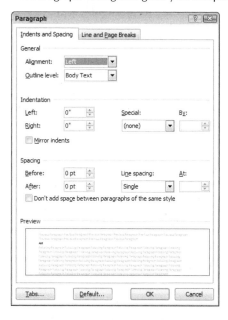

In the Paragraph dialog box, it is the Spacing area that is relevant to line spacing. You can precisely control spacing between lines in a paragraph as well as space before and after the paragraph. Your line spacing options, selected from the Line Spacing list, are

1. **Single, 1.5, or Double:** Single, one and a half, or double line spacing.

2. **At Least:** Line separation will be at least the value entered in the At box. It may be increased if needed to accommodate large fonts and so on.

3. **Exactly:** Line separation will be exactly the value entered in the At box and will never be adjusted.

4. **Multiple:** Spacing will be the number of lines entered in the At box.

To control space before and after a paragraph, enter the desired values in the Before and After boxes.

Show/Hide ¶

The Show/Hide ¶ button lets you display formatting marks in your text. Formatting marks indicate where normally invisible formatting elements are located. They are

- Paragraph marks (where you pressed Enter) are marked by the ¶ symbol.
- Soft returns (where you pressed Shift+Enter) are marked by the ↵ symbol.
- Tabs are marked with the → symbol.
- Spaces are marked by a dot.

Figure 5.9 shows an email message with formatting marks displayed. If you are having trouble getting the formatting to work just the way you want, displaying formatting marks can often help you locate the source of the problem.

FIGURE 5.9

Displaying formatting marks can help you to solve formatting problems.

Borders

Outlook's border feature is most frequently used with tables, a topic that is covered in Chapter 6. You can, however, use borders with regular text. For example, Figure 5.10 shows the use of a double border to call attention to a paragraph.

FIGURE 5.10

Using borders with paragraphs.

To apply borders:

1. Select the paragraph(s) that you want to apply borders to.
2. Click the arrow adjacent to the Borders button on the Format Text ribbon. Outlook displays the Borders menu (see Figure 5.11).
3. Click the style of border you want, or click No Border to remove existing border.

If you click the Borders button itself, or select Borders and Shading from the Borders menu, Outlook opens the Borders and Shading dialog box. This dialog box gives you more control over borders. It is covered in the section on tables in Chapter 6.

FIGURE 5.11

Selecting paragraph borders with the Borders menu.

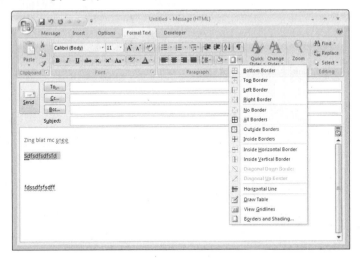

Using Quick Styles

Outlook quick styles, or just styles from here on, provide a quick and easy way to apply formatting to text. A style combines various aspects of formatting, such as font name and size, boldface, and text color, so you can apply all the formatting in a single step. You can use Outlook's defined styles and you can also define your own. Styles apply to entire paragraphs — remember, you define paragraphs by pressing Enter to end a paragraph and start another.

Applying a Style

To apply a style, place the cursor in the target paragraph or select multiple paragraphs. Then, click the Quick Styles button on the Format Text ribbon and select the desired style from the Quick Styles menu (shown in Figure 5.12). Note that as you move your mouse over the available styles, your text changes to preview each style. To remove a style, follow these steps but select Clear Formatting from the menu.

 If you create an email message based on a theme or stationery, as described later in this chapter, you will not be able to use quick styles with the message.

Defining a Style

If the styles that are already defined in Outlook do not suit your needs, you can create your own. Here are the steps to follow:

1. Format a paragraph in the message with the formatting that you want to be part of the new style (although you can make changes later in this process). Make sure the insertion point remains in that paragraph.

2. Click the Quick Styles button on the Format Text ribbon.

3. Select Save Selection as a New Quick Style from the menu. Outlook displays the Create New Style from Formatting dialog box, shown in Figure 5.13.

4. Enter a name for the new style in the Name box. You cannot use a name that is already assigned to a style.

5. Click OK.

If you want to make further changes to the style, click the Modify button in step 4. The dialog box will expand to allow you to change various aspects of the formatting.

FIGURE 5.12

Applying Quick Styles to message text.

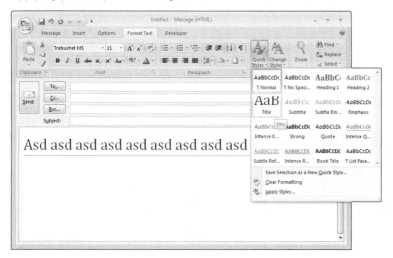

FIGURE 5.13

Creating a new style based on existing formatting.

Modifying, Renaming, and Deleting a Style

To modify an existing style, follow these steps:

1. Click the Quick Styles button on the Format Text ribbon.

2. Right-click the style you want to modify.

3. Select the command from the popup menu as follows:

   ▪ **Update XXXX to Match Selection:** Changes the style to match the formatting of the currently selected text.

   ▪ **Modify:** Opens the dialog box shown in Figure 5.14 where you can make changes to the style's formatting.

   ▪ **Rename:** Assigns a new name to the style.

   ▪ **Remove from Quick Style Gallery:** Removes the style from the Quick Styles menu (although the style remains available).

FIGURE 5.14

Modifying an existing style.

HTML Only for Themes

Themes and stationery are applicable only to HTML format messages.

Using Themes and Stationery

Themes and stationery are two related tools that let you provide a global design to an email message. Stationery includes a background color and/or pattern, and themes include backgrounds and other elements such as fonts, list styles, and effects. Using a theme or stationery does not mean the message formatting is fixed — you can use the theme formatting as it is defined or change it as desired.

Where do you get themes? There are several sources:

- Defined themes that are built into Outlook.
- Microsoft Word themes that are installed with Outlook.
- Themes you download from Office Online.
- Themes that you customize yourself.

The primary difference between Outlook themes and Word themes is that you can customize a Word theme but Outlook themes cannot be modified. There is also a difference in the way you apply them, as explained next.

Applying an Outlook Theme to All New Messages

You can select a default theme that will automatically be used for all new HTML email messages:

1. Select Tools, Options from the main Outlook menu to display the Options dialog box.
2. If necessary, click the Mail Format tab.
3. Click the Stationery and Fonts button to display the Signatures and Stationery dialog box.
4. Click the Theme button to display the Theme or Stationery dialog box (see Figure 5.15).
5. Click a theme or stationery name to see it previewed in the Sample area.
6. Depending on the theme selected, one or more of the following options may be available in the lower-left corner of the dialog box:
   - **Vivid Colors:** Use a brighter color scheme.
   - **Active Graphics:** Determines whether any active graphics that the theme contains are used.
   - **Background Image:** Turn this option off to use the theme without its background image.

   Click OK three times to exit all dialog boxes.

To remove the default theme so that new messages are created without a theme, follow the preceding steps and select No Theme in step 5.

FIGURE 5.15

Selecting a theme or stationery.

Applying an Outlook Theme to a Single New Message

You can also apply a theme or stationery to a single new message, overriding the default theme (if one is defined):

1. Select Actions, New Mail Message Using from Outlook's main menu.
2. Select More Stationery from the next menu. Outlook displays the Theme or Stationery dialog box as shown previously in Figure 5.15.
3. Select the desired theme.
4. Click OK.

Removing All Formatting

The quickest way to remove all formatting from an HTML or RTF format message is to convert it to a plain text message. You do this by clicking the Plain Text button in the Format section of the Options ribbon. Outlook will warn you that all formatting will be lost — click Continue to complete the process. Then you can change the message back to HTML or RTF format if desired. This technique works for removing a theme or stationery from a message as well.

Applying a Word Theme to a Message

To apply a Word theme to an email message, first create a new HTML format message. Then:

1. Click in the body of the message.

2. Click the Themes button on the Options ribbon and click Themes again on the menu. Outlook displays the Themes menu as shown in Figure 5.16. Built-in themes are listed in the Built-In section of the menu. If you have defined any custom themes they will be listed in the Custom section of the menu.

3. Click the desired theme.

FIGURE 5.16

Applying a Word theme to a message.

You'll note that there are several commands at the bottom of the Themes menu. Their functions are

- **Reset to Theme from Template:** If the selected theme has been customized, resets it to the original settings.

- **More Themes on Microsoft Office Online:** Look for additional themes on Office Online.

- **Browse for Themes:** Look for additional themes on your local computer or network.

- **Save Current Theme:** If you have customized the selected theme (covered in the next section), saves it to disk.

Customizing a Theme

Once you have applied a theme to a message, you can customize the theme by changing its fonts, its colors, and its effects. You can apply the changes to the current message only or save them for future use. There are three elements of a theme:

- **Fonts:** A theme's fonts consist of a heading font and a body font. A theme may use the same font in different sizes for both or it can use two distinct fonts.
- **Colors:** A theme's colors consist of a set of defined colors for various message elements.
- **Effects:** A theme's effects determine how various graphical elements of a message are drawn.

Each theme has assigned fonts, colors, and effects. Customizing a theme means to change the fonts, colors, and/or effects associated with the theme. To customize a theme:

1. Apply a theme to the message as described in the previous section.
2. Click one of the buttons next to the Themes button on the Options ribbon. There are three: Colors, Fonts, and Effects. Outlook displays the corresponding menu—Figure 5.17 shows the Effects menu.
3. Click the color, font, or effect that you want to apply to the theme.
4. Repeat steps 2 and 3 as needed for other theme elements.

FIGURE 5.17

Using the Effects menu to customize a Word theme.

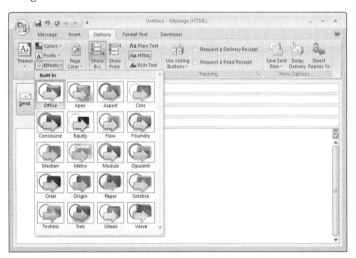

Creating Custom Font and Color Sets

Outlook provides a selection of defined font and color sets that you can use with Word themes. These sets are the selections you see on the Theme Colors and Theme Fonts menus when you customize a theme as described in the previous section. You can create custom color and font sets as well and have these available for use in Word themes. You cannot, however, create custom theme effects—you are limited to the effects that are supplied with Outlook. Any custom color or font sets that you create will be available in the Custom section of the Theme Colors or Theme Fonts menu.

To create a custom color set:

1. Click the Colors button in the Themes section of the Options ribbon.

2. Select Create New Theme Colors from the menu. Outlook displays the Create New Theme Colors dialog box as shown in Figure 5.18. The buttons on the left represent the colors that make up a color set.

3. Click the button for the color you want to change and select the new color from the palette that is displayed. The selected colors are previewed in the Sample section of the dialog box.

   Repeat step 3 for additional colors as desired.

   If you want to start over, click Reset to return all colors to their original values.

4. Assign a name for this color set in the Name box.

5. Click the Save button.

FIGURE 5.18

Creating a custom set of theme colors.

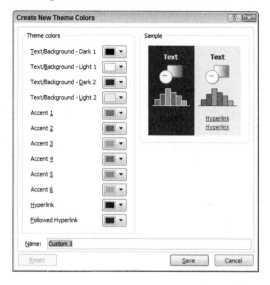

To create a custom font set:

1. Click the Fonts button in the Themes section of the Options ribbon.
2. Select Create New Theme Fonts from the menu. Outlook displays the Create New Theme Fonts dialog box as shown in Figure 5.19.
3. Select a new heading font and/or body font from the lists provided.
4. Enter a name for the font set in the Name box.
5. Click Save.

FIGURE 5.19

Creating a custom set of theme fonts.

Changing the Page Background

Sometimes you may not want to apply a theme or stationery to a message but only to change the message background. Outlook provides the ability to use a color, gradient, texture, pattern, or picture as the message background. You can also change the background that has been assigned to a message as part of a stationery or theme. To change the page background, click the Page Color button in the Themes section of the Options ribbon. Outlook displays the Theme Colors menu as shown in Figure 5.20. Then do one of the following:

- Click the desired color on the displayed palette.
- Click No Color to remove an existing background from the message.
- Click More Colors to select from a wider palette of colors.
- Click Fill Effects to use a gradient, texture, pattern, or image as the background.

If you select Fill Effects from the Theme Colors menu, Outlook displays the dialog box that is shown in Figure 5.21. You can see that this dialog has tabs for gradients, textures, patterns, and pictures. Select the appropriate tab and then make entries as needed to get the background you want.

FIGURE 5.20

Changing the message background.

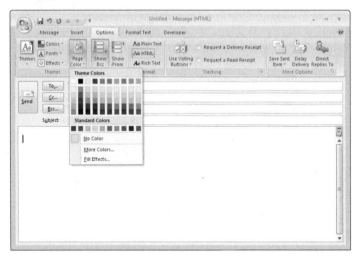

FIGURE 5.21

Applying fill effects to the message background.

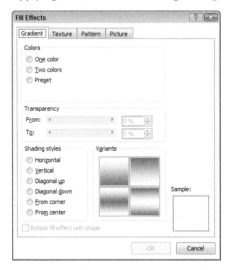

Creating and Using Signatures

A *signature* is a section of text that is added automatically to the end of email messages that you create. It can include your name, title, company name, and other information that you want to include with all messages. Note that this is distinct from a *digital signature*, a security device that is covered in Chapter 20.

Creating and Editing Signatures

You can define as many different email signatures as you need. To define a signature:

1. Select Options from the Tools menu to open the Options dialog box.

2. Click the Mail Format tab.

3. Click the Signatures button to open the Signatures and Stationery dialog box.

4. If necessary, click the E-mail Signature tab (shown in Figure 5.22).

5. Click the New button to open the New Signature dialog box.

6. Enter a name for the signature and click OK to return to the E-mail Signature tab.

7. Enter the desired text in the Edit Signature field, using the formatting tools that are provided to change font, alignment, and other aspects of formatting. You can also copy text from Word or another program and paste it here.

8. Click the Save button to save the signature.

FIGURE 5.22

Working with email signatures.

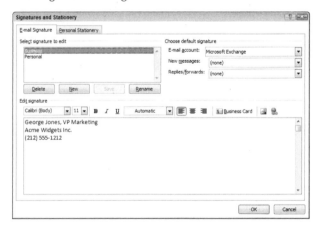

You also use this tab to edit an existing signature. Simply select the signature in the Select Signature to Edit list, edit it as desired, and click Save.

You can apply a signature manually to individual email messages. If you want a signature added automatically, use the Choose Default Signature options in the top-right corner of the dialog box:

- In the E-mail Account list, select the email account for which you want a signature used (this is relevant only if you have two or more email accounts).
- From the New Messages list, select the signature to use for new messages.
- From the Replies/Forwards list, select the signature to use when you reply to or forward a message.

Adding a Signature to a Message

If you want to add a signature to a message manually, click the Signature button on the Insert ribbon, then select the desired signature from the menu. The selected signature will be added to the end of the message.

Summary

Outlook provides you with a powerful set of formatting tools. No longer are you limited to sending boring, plain text messages. As long as your recipients can read HTML messages—and that's almost everyone these days—you can use fonts, borders, backgrounds, themes, and other elements to create visually appealing messages.

Chapter 6

Working with Advanced Email Message Components and Editing Tools

An Outlook email message is not limited to the formatting options covered in Chapter 5. Many of the most powerful things you can do with a message you are creating is to insert *objects*. This is a general term for all the various elements that Outlook lets you insert in a message — tables, pictures, clip art, and animations, just to name a few. This chapter also covers some of the advanced editing and proofing tools that Outlook provides.

If you have any experience using Word 2007, you will notice a lot of similarity between it and the Outlook editor. That's because the two programs share the same editing engine, so most of the editing capabilities you have in Word are also available in Outlook.

IN THIS CHAPTER

Inserting pictures and other objects in a message

Using hyperlinks and bookmarks

Working with tables

Using proofing and editing tools

Adding Objects to Messages

Email messages that you create with Outlook can be very sophisticated. They can include a variety of *objects* — a generic term for elements such as images and clip art. This section provides an overview of inserting these objects into your messages. It starts with an overview of what kinds of objects are available. Tables, which are a special kind of object, get their own section later in the chapter. You cannot add objects to plain text format messages.

Adding an object is not the same as attaching something to a message. When you add an object to a message, for example an image, it is displayed as part of the message. In contrast, an attachment does not display in the message.

Kinds of Email Message Objects

The following sections provide details on the variety of objects that you can use in your email messages. What objects are available? Here are brief descriptions:

- **Picture:** Any image, such as a digital photograph.
- **Clip Art:** Also images but tend to be small drawings.
- **Smart Art:** Flow charts, organizational charts, processes, and other types of diagrams.
- **Chart:** Bar, line, and other chart types to illustrate numerical data.
- **Shapes:** Various shapes such as rectangles, arrows, and triangles.
- **Hyperlink:** A link that the message recipient can click to navigate to another location.
- **Bookmark:** Identifies a location in a message that can be the target of a hyperlink.
- **Text Box:** A rectangular box for entering text.
- **Quick Part:** A selection of text and/or other message elements that you have saved for reuse.
- **WordArt:** Text with applied artistic effects.
- **Equation:** A mathematical equation.
- **Horizontal Line:** Just what it sounds like.

All objects have some things in common. After you insert it in the message the object will be *selected* as indicated by a border and handles, small circular or rectangular buttons on the border. You can see an example in Figure 6.1, which shows a selected clip art object.

A selected object displays a border and handles.

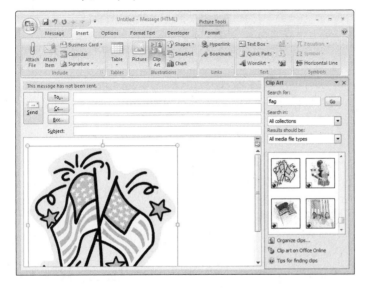

When an object is selected you can work with it as I soon describe. To work on other parts of the message, click away from the object. To select the object again, click it. When an object is selected here are some of the actions you can take (some actions may not be applicable to all types of objects):

- To delete the object, press Del.

- To move the object, point at it — the mouse pointer will change to a four-headed arrow. Then drag to the desired position.

- To change the object size, point at one of the handles at a corner or along an edge — the mouse pointer will change to a two-headed arrow. Then drag to the desired size.

- To rotate the object, point at the extra handle extending from the top of the object — the mouse pointer will change to a curved arrow. Then drag to the desired orientation.

When a message object is selected, Outlook displays a Format ribbon at the top of the message window. The content of this ribbon depends on the type of object selected, and includes tools and commands for working with that type of object. For example, Figure 6.2 shows the ribbon displayed when a picture object is inserted. Some of the tools offered help you with changing picture borders, modifying brightness and contrast, changing text wrapping (how text flows around the picture), and special effects.

Some objects, such as Smart Shapes, also display a Design ribbon when selected. This ribbon provides access to additional commands for working with the selected object.

The remainder of this section shows you how to insert the various kinds of objects that Outlook messages support. First you learn about graphical objects, then text objects.

FIGURE 6.2

When an object is selected, Outlook displays a ribbon for working with that type of object.

Don't Forget Undo

When you are working with objects in a message—or on most other aspects of a message for that matter—you can always press Ctrl+Z to undo your most recent action.

Graphical Elements

Some objects you can insert into an Outlook email message are graphical—that is, they are primarily visual in emphasis.

Images

You can insert essentially any kind of image in an email message, including digital photographs, scans, and drawings. To insert an image in your email message:

1. Click the Picture button on the Insert ribbon. Outlook displays the Insert Picture dialog box (see Figure 6.3).

2. Navigate to the folder where the desired image is located.

3. If you want to view thumbnails of the images, click the Views button at the top right of the dialog box and select Thumbnails from the menu displayed.

4. Click the desired image.

5. Click the Insert button.

FIGURE 6.3

Inserting a picture in an email message.

Clip Art

When most people hear "clip art" they think of small drawings used to illustrate or provide emphasis — for example, a flag, a dollar sign, a car, or a palm tree. This is indeed clip art, but the term has expanded to include photographs, sounds, and animations. Outlook lets you search for the clip art you want and then insert it in a message. To find and insert clip art:

1. Click the Clip Art button in the Illustrations section of the Insert ribbon. Outlook displays the Clip Art panel as shown in Figure 6.4.

2. In the Search For box, enter a term that describes what you are looking for.

3. Open the Search In list to select the clip art collections to be searched.

4. Open the Results Should Be list to select the types of clip art to be found.

5. Click the Go button. Outlook searches according to the parameters you entered and displays the results in the bottom part of the Clip Art panel.

6. Browse the results and double-click to insert a clip art item.

7. Click the X in the Clip Art panel title bar to close it.

FIGURE 6.4

Finding clip art to insert in an email message.

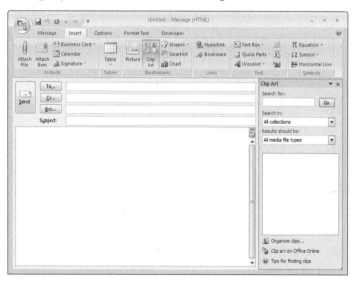

Smart Art

Outlook's Smart Art elements let you add a wide variety of diagrams to an email message. These diagrams are designed to illustrate processes, cycles, relationships, hierarchies, and so on. To add a Smart Art object:

1. Click the Smart Art button on the Insert toolbar. Outlook displays the Choose a SmartArt Graphic dialog box as shown in Figure 6.5.

2. On the left side of the dialog box, select the category of graphic you are interested in.

3. In the center of the dialog box, click the specific diagram you want. It will be previewed on the right.

4. Click OK.

FIGURE 6.5

Selecting a Smart Art diagram to insert in an email message.

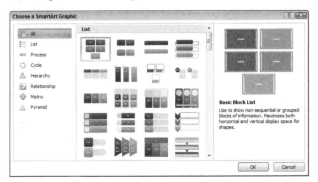

Once the Smart Art diagram has been inserted into the message, you edit it using the tools provided by Outlook. For example, Figure 6.6 shows a Bending List, one type of Smart Art diagram, selected for editing. Outlook provides a place for you to type in text as well as Design and Format ribbons for you to select commands related to the object.

Charts

Inserting a chart into a message requires that you have Microsoft Excel installed. To insert a chart into a message, click the Chart button on the Insert ribbon. Outlook displays the Insert Chart dialog box as shown in Figure 6.7. You use this dialog box to select the type of chart that you want by clicking the sample from the gallery on the right. Then, click the OK button.

FIGURE 6.6

Editing a Smart Art diagram.

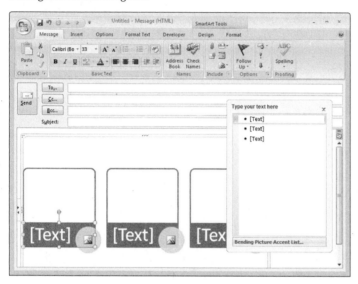

FIGURE 6.7

Choosing the type of chart to insert.

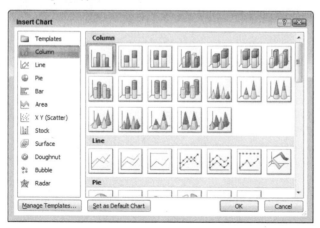

Next, Outlook inserts a chart in the message and opens, in Excel, a worksheet with some dummy data in it, as shown in Figure 6.8. At this point you can do one or more of the following:

- Delete the dummy data and type in your own data.
- Copy data from another workbook and paste it in.
- Expand or contract the data range by dragging the lower-right corner of the blue outline (only the data in the outlined range will be included in the chart).

As you work, the chart in the message will be updated to reflect your changes.

FIGURE 6.8

Editing the data for the chart.

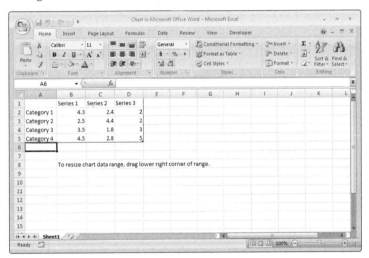

When have finished editing/entering your data, you can close Excel (with or without saving the data as your needs dictate). The chart will be in your message as shown in Figure 6.9. You can complete the message and send it, or you can make changes to the chart format and layout by right-clicking the chart and selecting commands from the popup menu (a topic beyond the scope of this book).

Shapes

Outlook's Shape feature lets you insert a wide variety of shapes into an email message. Each shape is inserted as an image, and that's how it will appear to the message recipient. Figure 6.10 shows an email message with a couple of shapes in it.

FIGURE 6.9

The chart is inserted into your email message and is ready to send.

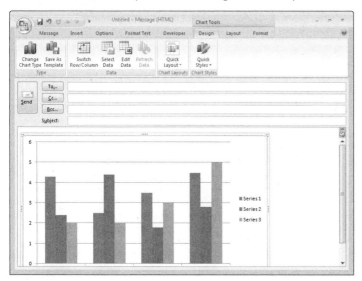

FIGURE 6.10

An email message containing two shapes.

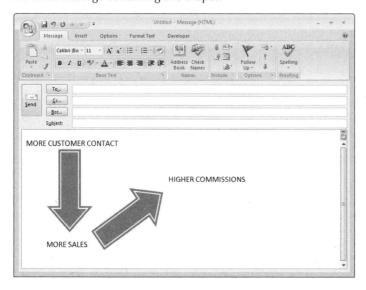

To insert a shape:

1. Click the Shapes button on the Insert ribbon. Outlook displays the Shapes menu as shown in Figure 6.11.

2. Click the shape you want to insert.

3. Drag in the message body to place the shape.

FIGURE 6.11

Selecting a shape to insert into an email message.

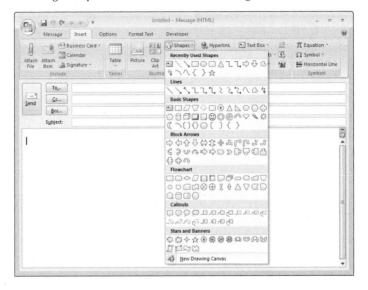

WordArt

WordArt is a tool for creating attractive banners and headings. It is called WordArt because it originated as part of the word processing program Microsoft Word. Figure 6.12 shows an example of a message heading created using WordArt.

To add WordArt to a message:

1. Click the WordArt button on the Insert ribbon. Outlook displays the WordArt menu as shown in Figure 6.13.

2. Click the desired style. Outlook displays the Edit WordArt Text dialog box as shown in Figure 6.14.

3. At the top of the dialog box, select the font and size for the WordArt.

4. In the box, type the text for the WordArt. Use the Bold and Italic buttons as desired to make some of the text boldface or italicized.

5. Click OK.

FIGURE 6.12

An example of WordArt in an email message.

FIGURE 6.13

Selecting the style of WordArt to insert in an email message.

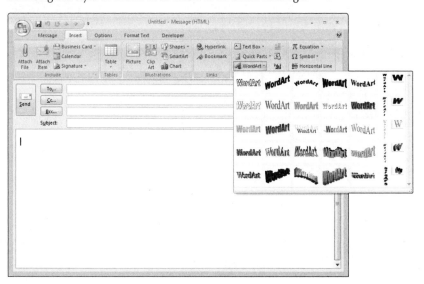

FIGURE 6.14

Entering the text for WordArt.

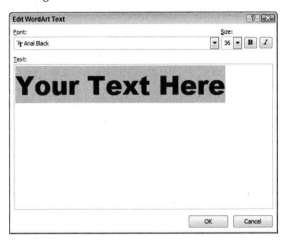

After you have inserted WordArt you can edit the text by right-clicking it and selecting Edit Text from the context menu.

Text Elements

Some of the objects you can insert into an email message are text-based. They are explained in this section.

Hyperlinks and Bookmarks

A hyperlink is a clickable link in an email message. It acts just like a hyperlink on a web page. A hyperlink can point to several types of targets:

- A bookmark that specifies a location in the current message. When the recipient clicks this kind of link, the message scrolls (if necessary) to bring the bookmark into view.

- A web page. When the recipient clicks this kind of link, the page opens in the default web browser (for example, Internet Explorer).

- An email address. When the recipient clicks this kind of link, a new email message is created with the address in the link inserted in the To field.

- A file. When the recipient clicks this kind of link, they are prompted to download the file. The file must be in an Internet or network location accessible to the recipient.

Inserting Symbols

Symbols are not objects like the other elements discussed in this section—they are simply text characters that do not happen to be available on the keyboard, such as Greek letters, monetary symbols such as Yen and Pound, and letters with diacritical marks such as é and ö. To insert a symbol, click the Symbol button on the Insert ribbon and then click the desired symbol.

To add a hyperlink to an email message:

1. If the text that will be the hyperlink is already in the message, select it. If not, place the editing cursor at the desired location in the message.

2. Click the Hyperlink button on the Insert ribbon. Outlook displays the Insert Hyperlink dialog box, shown in Figure 6.15.

FIGURE 6.15

Entering a hyperlink in an email message.

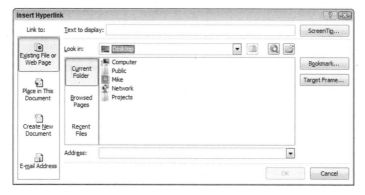

3. If you selected text in step 1 it will be displayed in the Text to Display field. If not, enter it now.

4. On the left side of the dialog box, click the button that corresponds to the type of hyperlink you want to insert. Then:

   ▪ If you select Existing File or Web Page, the dialog box will let you browse to the target file or page. You can also type in the address directly if you know it.

   ▪ If you select Place in This Document, Outlook will display a list of bookmarks in the current message, from which you select the link target. You can also choose to link to the top of the message or to any headings in the message.

- If you select New Document, Outlook lets you enter the name of the new document and to specify whether to edit the document now (as soon as the link is inserted) or later. In either case, Word opens for editing the new document.
- If you select E-mail Address, Outlook lets you enter the email address and an optional subject for the message that will be created when the recipient clicks the link.

5. Click OK.

Hyperlinks are displayed by default as blue underlined text. You can change the target of a hyperlink by right-clicking it and selecting Edit Hyperlink from the context menu. To remove the link while leaving the text in the message, select Remove Hyperlink from the context menu.

To link to a location in your message, you must insert a bookmark. Here's how:

1. Place the editing cursor at the desired location in the message. Optionally you can select text at the location.
2. Click the Bookmark button on the Insert ribbon. Outlook opens the Bookmark dialog box.
3. If you selected text in step 1, it will be entered in the Bookmark Name field. You can accept this as the bookmark name or enter something else. If you did not select text in step 1, enter a unique name for the bookmark in this field.
4. Click OK.

Text marked as a bookmark does not display in any special way. It is just labeled "behind the scenes" as a bookmark.

To manage bookmarks, click the Bookmark button to display the Bookmark dialog box. Using this dialog box you can view existing bookmarks and delete ones you no longer need.

Equations

Outlook incorporates a powerful equation editor. Most of us will never need this, but if you are mathematically inclined you may find it useful. When you create an equation by clicking the Equation button on the Insert ribbon, Outlook enters a blank equation and displays the Design ribbon for equations. You can type equation elements directly into the equation box and also use the tools and commands on the ribbon. Figure 6.16 shows an equation being created in an email message.

When you send a message that includes an equation, the equation is converted to an image. The recipient can view the equation but not edit it.

FIGURE 6.16

FIGURE 6.16

Entering an equation in an email message.

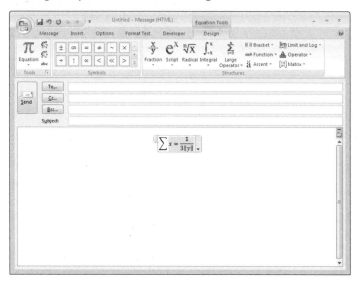

Working with Tables

A table can be very useful for organizing and presenting information. Outlook provides you with several ways to create a table in an email message. You access these by clicking the Table button on the Insert ribbon.

Drawing a Table

When you click the Table button on the Insert ribbon, Outlook displays the menu shown in Figure 6.17. The quickest way to insert a table is to drag your mouse over the grid to highlight the desired number of table rows and columns. Outlook inserts a blank table of the specified size and you can start entering data.

Another way to draw a table is to select the Draw Table command on the Table menu. This command gives you more flexibility in creating a table with an unconventional row/column structure as shown in Figure 6.18.

FIGURE 6.17

Use the Table menu to insert a table into an email message.

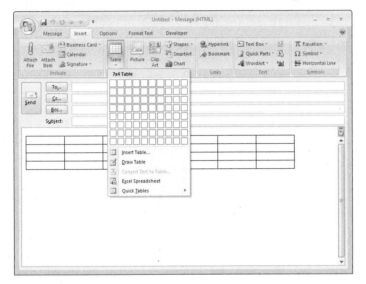

FIGURE 6.18

Use the Draw Table command to create a table with an unusual row/column structure.

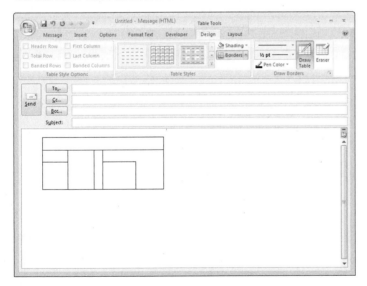

When you select this command, the mouse pointer changes to a pencil icon when over the message body. You start by dragging in the message to define the outer boundary of the table. Then drag within the table to place vertical and horizontal lines to define cells. When you are finished, press Esc to exit table drawing mode.

Inserting a Table

You can also create a table using the Insert Table command on the Table menu. This command brings up the Insert Table dialog box, shown in Figure 6.19. Specify the number of columns and rows in the Table Size section, and then select one of the AutoFit options:

- **Fixed Column Width:** Select Auto to have column width set automatically based on the number of columns and the window width, or select a specific column width.

- **AutoFit to Contents:** The width of each column in the table automatically increases or decreases to fit the data that the column contains.

- **AutoFit to Window:** The width of the entire table adjusts to fit in the window width, and individual columns change accordingly.

If you select the Remember Dimensions for New Tables option, the size of the table (number of rows and columns) that you specify will be the new default the next time you display the Insert Table dialog box.

FIGURE 6.19

Inserting a table into an email message using the Insert Table command.

Creating a Table in Excel

One of the commands on Outlook's Table menu is Excel Spreadsheet. When you select this command, Outlook inserts a small, blank Excel spreadsheet in your message, as shown in Figure 6.20. You will also notice that the ribbons at the top of the message have changed to Excel commands. You can add data, text, formulas, and other elements to the spreadsheet just as if you were working in Excel — which, in effect, you are. Using this command requires that you have Excel installed on your system.

FIGURE 6.20

Adding a table to a message using Excel.

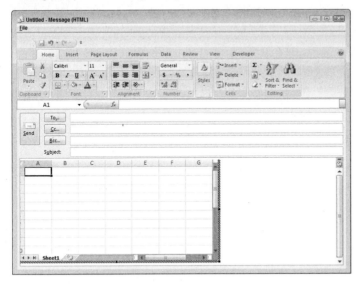

As soon as you click anywhere outside the spreadsheet, Outlook converts it to an image. You cannot change it in any way after this. You can add text and other elements to the message, address it, and so on. When you send the message the recipient receives the image as part of the message, as shown in Figure 6.21.

FIGURE 6.21

When you create a table using Excel, the message recipient gets an image of the table.

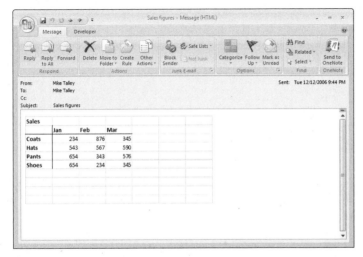

When you use this technique to create a table you cannot open an existing Excel spreadsheet inside the message — you are limited to what you can enter yourself. Nor can you save the spreadsheet that you create other than as an image. You can, however, open an existing spreadsheet in Excel and copy data to the spreadsheet in the message.

Converting Text to a Table

Outlook has the capability to look at regular — that is, non-table — text and convert it to a table. Each paragraph in the text becomes a row in the table. The text within the paragraph can be split up into columns based on tabs, commas, or another character that you specify. For example, Figure 6.22 shows text suitable for making into a table because the individual parts of each paragraph — last name, first name, and graduation year — are separated by commas. Figure 6.23 shows the table that was automatically created from this text.

FIGURE 6.22

Text suitable for automatic conversion to a table.

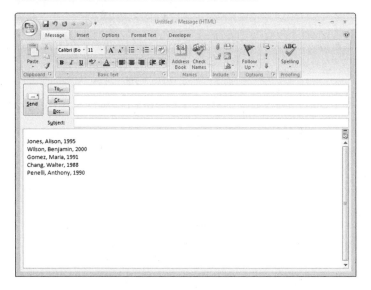

FIGURE 6.23

The table created from the text in Figure 6.22.

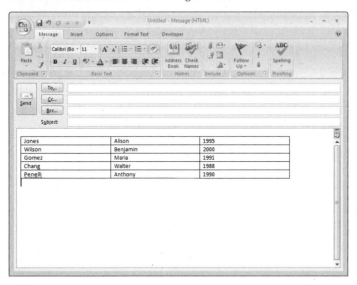

To convert text to a table:

1. Select the text.

2. Click the Table button on the Insert ribbon.

3. Select Convert Text to Table to display the Convert Text to Table dialog box (see Figure 6.24).

FIGURE 6.24

Specifying parameters for converting regular text to a table.

4. In the Separate Text At section, select the desired separator. If you select Other, enter the desired separator character in the adjacent box.

5. If the Number of Columns value is not correct, change it as needed. You cannot change the number of rows.

6. Select the desired AutoFit option. These options were explained earlier in the section "Inserting a Table."

7. Click OK.

Using Quick Tables

Outlook's Quick Tables feature lets you save tables you have created to a gallery. You can then insert the saved table into a message with a few clicks. A Quick Table is one of Outlook's *building blocks*, a feature that lets you save not only tables but sections of text and other message components for reuse.

Saving a Quick Table

To save a table as a Quick Table you must first create the table and apply all the formatting that you want saved with it, such as borders, shading, and column headers. Any data in a table is saved too, so you probably want to save the table before you add the data. Then:

1. Select the entire table by dragging over it with the mouse.

2. Click the Table button on the Insert ribbon.

3. Select the Quick Tables command from the Insert Table menu, then select Save Selection to Quick Tables Gallery from the next menu. Outlook displays the Create New Building Block dialog box as shown in Figure 6.25.

4. Enter a name for the saved table in the Name box.

5. Select the category for the table from the Category list, or select Create New Category to create a new category.

FIGURE 6.25

Saving a table as a Quick Table.

6. Optionally, enter a description of the table in the Description box.

7. From the Options list, select how the table will be inserted: as a separate paragraph, as a separate page, or on its own.

8. Click OK.

Inserting a Quick Table

If you have saved one or more Quick Tables, you can insert one by clicking the Table button on the Insert ribbon and selecting Quick Tables from the menu. The next menu previews the available Quick Tables — simply click the one you want to insert into your message.

Proofing and Editing Tools

Outlook provides several tools to help you avoid errors in your email messages.

Checking Spelling and Grammar

Outlook provides spelling and grammar checkers that can help you find errors in your messages. After composing a message, run these tools by clicking the Spelling button on the Message ribbon or by pressing F7. For each misspelled word, the Spelling and Grammar dialog box is displayed, as shown in Figure 6.26. The error — in this case the misspelled word "watter" — is highlighted in the top part of the box and suggested corrections, if any, are listed in the bottom. Actions you can take are

- **Ignore Once:** Ignore this instance of the error but catch any others.
- **Ignore All:** Ignore all occurrences of this error in the message.
- **Add to Dictionary:** Add the flagged word to the dictionary.
- **Change:** Change the flagged word to the correction selected in the Suggestions box.
- **Change All:** Change all occurrences of the flagged word to the selected correction.
- **AutoCorrect:** Change the flagged word to the selected correction and add the two words to the AutoCorrect list. AutoCorrect is covered later in this chapter.

When checking of grammar is enabled (I explain how to do this in a moment), sentence elements that Outlook thinks contain a grammar error are flagged and the Spelling and Grammar dialog box offers these options:

- **Ignore Once:** Ignore this instance of the error.
- **Ignore Rule:** Ignore the relevant grammar rule for the remainder of the grammar check.
- **Next Sentence:** Stop checking the current sentence and move to the next sentence.
- **Change:** Changes the text to the correction selected in the Suggestions box.
- **Explain:** Displays information about why this was flagged as a grammar error.

FIGURE 6.26

The spelling and grammar checker flags mistakes and suggests corrections.

If you are checking spelling only and want to enable grammar checking, select the Check Grammar option in the Spelling and Grammar dialog box. You can also turn this option on or off, along with other spelling and grammar options, as described in the next section.

Spelling and Grammar Options

To set spelling and grammar options, select Tools, Options from the main Outlook menu to open the Options dialog box and then click the Spelling tab. There are three elements on this tab:

- **Always Check Spelling before Sending:** Select this option if you want Outlook to check spelling (and grammar, if selected) each time a message is sent.

- **Ignore Original Message Text in Reply or Forward:** Select this option if you want the spelling/grammar checker to ignore quoted text when you reply to or forward a message.

- **Spelling and AutoCorrections:** Click this button to set additional spelling and grammar options. You can also display these other spelling and grammar options by clicking the Options button in the Spelling and Grammar dialog box.

Don't Rely on the Spelling and Grammar Checkers

Outlook's spelling and grammar checkers are useful tools, but they are not perfect—far from it, in fact. They can be a help but are no replacement for your own skills and knowledge. Given the complexity of English grammar it is not surprising that the grammar checker makes frequent mistakes. And though the spelling checker can catch a lot of misspellings it cannot tell when you have, for example, used "there" instead of "their" or misspelled "so" as "do."

The spelling and grammar options are set in the Editor Options window as shown in Figure 6.27. The options in the top part of this window relate to spelling and grammar checking throughout Office (Outlook uses the same checker as the other Office programs). These are self-explanatory and you can set them as desired.

FIGURE 6.27

Setting the spelling and grammar options.

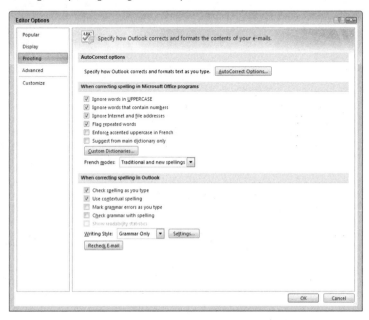

The other options relate to Outlook only and are as follows:

- **Check Spelling as You Type:** Outlook detects misspelled words as you type and marks them with a red wavy underline.

- **Use Contextual Spelling:** If you select this option, the spell checker will attempt to detect errors based on context. For example, "there" is a legitimate word but is wrong in this sentence (it should be "their"): "Linda told me that there vacation was a lot of fun."

- **Mark Grammar Errors as You Type:** Outlook detects grammar errors as you type and marks them with a green wavy underline.

- **Check Grammar with Spelling:** Always checks grammar when you do a spelling check.

- **Show Readability Statistics:** Select this option to view readability statistics that use the average number of syllables per word and the average number of words per sentence to determine the grade-level readability. For example, a score of 8 indicates that the document should be understandable by someone with an 8th grade education. You must select the Check Grammar with Spelling option to enable the Show Readability Statistics option.

- **Writing Style:** You can choose to check grammar only or both grammar and style. Click the Grammar Settings button to display the Grammar Settings dialog box (see Figure 6.28) where you specify the details of how grammar is checked.

- **Recheck E-mail:** If you have changed any options while in the midst of a spelling/grammar check, resets the checker to start over from scratch.

FIGURE 6.28

Setting options for how grammar and style are checked.

When you have turned on the options to check grammar and/or spelling as you type, Outlook underlines errors as it detects them in the message. When you right-click an error that's flagged in this manner, Outlook displays a context menu with commands relevant to the error. For example, the menu displayed when you right-click a misspelled word offers Ignore, Ignore All, and Add to Dictionary commands as well as any suggested replacements the spell checker has found.

The Writing Style Option

A known Outlook bug prevents you from setting Writing Style options when you display the Editor Options via the Tools, Options command (as described earlier). You have to open the item you want to check, click the Office button at the top-left corner, select Editor Options from the Office menu, and then select Proofing.

AutoCorrect

AutoCorrect is a feature that detects certain things in text you are typing and automatically changes them to something else. When enabled, AutoCorrect can:

- Correct typing errors, such as when you mistakenly start a word with TWo INitial CApitals.

- Insert symbols and other special characters automatically, such as replacing (c) with ©.

- Automatically correct spelling errors you make frequently, such as replacing "abuot" with "about."

- Ease entry of long words that you use frequently, such as replacing "Alb" with "Albuquerque."

AutoCorrect options are accessed as follows:

1. Select Tools, Options from the main Outlook menu to display the Options dialog box.

2. Click the Spelling tab.

3. Click the Spelling and AutoCorrection button to open the Editor Options window.

4. Click the AutoCorrect Options button.

The AutoCorrect options are shown in Figure 6.29. The options near the top of this dialog box are self-explanatory. Click the Exceptions button to view and define exceptions to the various AutoCorrect rules. For example, if you have the Correct TWo INitial CApitals option turned on, you can specify that "IDs" not be corrected.

Setting the AutoCorrect options.

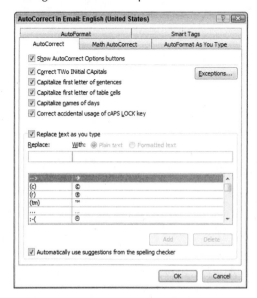

The lower section of the AutoCorrect dialog box deals with replacing text as you type. If the option is turned on, each text item in the left column of the list will automatically be replaced with the corresponding text item in the right column. You work with this list as follows:

- To add an item, enter the text to be replaced in the Replace field and the replacement text in the With box, then click Add.
- To remove an item, select it in the list by clicking and then click the Delete button.
- To modify an item, select it in the list by clicking and then edit the Replace and With fields as desired.

Other "Auto" Features

Outlook provides several other tools that can help you when you are composing the body of an email message.

Math AutoCorrect

Math AutoCorrect is like regular AutoCorrect but it works with mathematical and other symbols. It works mostly with keywords preceded by a backslash — for example, \approx is replaced with $\oplus$. By default, Math AutoCorrect works only within math regions, a section of a message designed specifically for entering mathematical equations. To insert an equation into a message:

1. Place the editing cursor at the location in the message where you want the equation.
2. Click the Symbols button on the Insert ribbon.
3. Select Equation from the menu. Outlook inserts a math region into the message and displays a Design ribbon that offers various tools for working with equations (see Figure 6.30).
4. Enter and edit the equation as needed.
5. Click outside the math region to work on other parts of the message. Click the math region again to edit the formula.

To set Math AutoCorrect options:

1. Select Tools, Options from the main Outlook menu to display the Options dialog box.
2. Click the Spelling tab.
3. Click the Spelling and AutoCorrection button to open the Editor Options window.
4. Click the AutoCorrect Options button to display the AutoCorrect dialog box.
5. Click the Math AutoCorrect tab (shown in Figure 6.31).

FIGURE 6.30

Entering an equation into an email message.

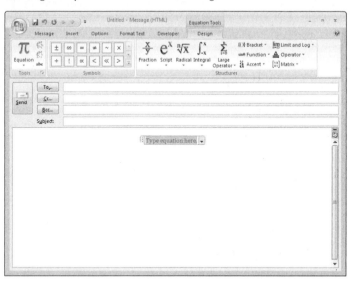

FIGURE 6.31

Setting Math AutoCorrect options.

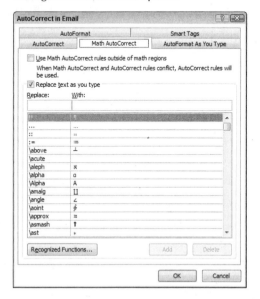

The first option, Use Math AutoCorrect Rules Outside of Math Regions, determines whether these rules apply just in math regions or throughout the entire message. The Replace Text as You Type option determines whether Math AutoCorrect is on or off. You add items to and delete items from the list as described for AutoCorrect in the previous section.

Smart Tags

Smart Tags is a tool that lets Outlook recognize certain types of information in your messages, such as dates and telephone numbers. Then, Outlook marks the item with a dotted underline and, when the mouse cursor is near the item, displays a Smart Tag, or small button, next to the item. Clicking the Smart Tag displays a menu of commands relevant to the type of data item. For example, if the item is a date, the commands on the Smart Tag menu let you schedule a meeting, open your calendar, and so on. This is shown in Figure 6.32.

FIGURE 6.32

Smart Tags provide quick access to commands for certain data items in a message.

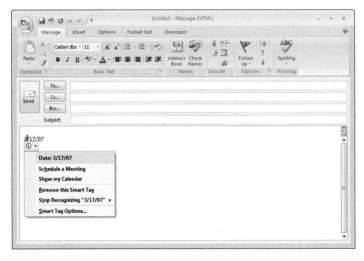

To set Smart Tag options:

1. Select Tools, Options from the main Outlook menu to display the Options dialog box.
2. Click the Spelling tab.
3. Click the Spelling and AutoCorrection button to open the Editor Options window.
4. Click the AutoCorrect Options button to display the AutoCorrect dialog box.
5. Click the Smart Tags tab (shown in Figure 6.33).

FIGURE 6.33

Setting Smart Tag options.

The option at the top of this dialog box, Label Text with Smart Tags, turns Smart Tags on or off. If this option is on, the types of data selected in the Recognizers list will be detected and marked with a tag.

AutoFormat

The AutoCorrect dialog box contains two tabs that control automatic formatting — the AutoFormat As You Type tab and the AutoFormat tab. The items on these tabs are similar in concept — Figure 6.34 shows the AutoFormat As You Type tab. You can turn these options on or off as suits your working style.

Checking Names

The Check Names command, located on the Message ribbon, verifies that the recipients of your message are all valid email addresses. *Valid* in this context does not mean that there is a working email account with the specified address, only that the address has the proper format (xxxx@yyyy.zzz). If all the recipients pass the test, no message is displayed. If possible, Outlook will correct the address. Otherwise you will see a dialog box in which you can select a recipient to make changes to the address.

FIGURE 6.34

Setting AutoFormat options.

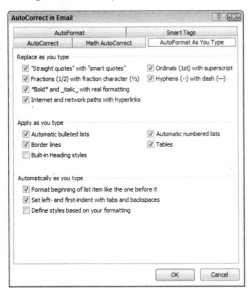

Other Tools

The Editing button on the Format Text ribbon gives you access to the following features.

Find, Replace, and Go To

Selecting Find from the Editing menu (click the Editing button on the Format Text ribbon) displays the dialog box shown in Figure 6.35. You can see it has three tabs, one for each of the three functions discussed in this section.

The Find tab lets you locate text in your message. Enter the search text in the Find What field and then:

- Click Find Next to highlight the next occurrence of the text in the message.
- Click Find All to highlight all occurrences of the text in the message.
- Click More to display additional search options such as matching case, finding whole words only, and finding formatting.

The Replace tab lets you locate specified text in the message and replace it with other text. It works the same as the Find tab except that in addition to a Find What field there is a Replace With field for you to enter the replacement text.

The Go To tab lets you quickly move to various locations in your message. This tool is useful primarily with long messages. You can, for example, move to a specified page number or table.

FIGURE 6.35

The Find and Replace dialog box.

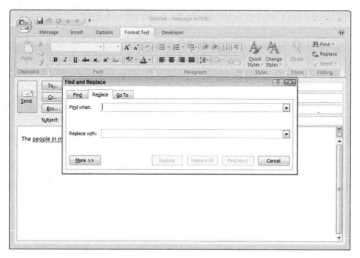

Summary

The days when email messages consisted of nothing but plain text are long gone. Outlook provides you with a rich set of tools for creating attractive email messages with complex formatting, embedded images and tables, and other elements to help you get your message across in the most effective way. Then, you can use Outlook's powerful proofing tools to catch errors before you send the message.

Chapter 7

Understanding Email Options

IN THIS CHAPTER

Setting options for individual messages

Setting global email options

Although it's possible to create and send email messages using all of Outlook's default settings, you would be missing a lot of flexibility and convenience if you did so. The various email options that Outlook offers let you use email in the way that is most convenient and productive for you. These options fall into two categories: those that apply to a single message and those that apply globally. These are covered in turn. A third category of options, those that apply to an individual email account, was covered in Chapter 3.

Setting Options for Individual Email Messages

This section explains a variety of options available for individual email messages that you create.

Changing the Send Account

This is relevant only if you have two or more email accounts. By default, messages are sent as follows:

- Messages you create from scratch are sent using the default email account.

- Messages that are replies to a message you received are sent using the account through which the original message was received.

- Messages you forward are sent using the account through which the original message was received.

Changing the Default Email Account

To change the default email account:

1. Select Tools, Account Settings from the main Outlook menu to display the Account Settings dialog box.
2. If necessary, click the E-mail tab.
3. The current default account is indicated in the account list by (send from this account by default).
4. Click another account in the list.
5. Click the Set as Default button.
6. Click Close.

To change the send account for a message:

1. Click the Account button on the Message ribbon. A menu is displayed with the current send account checked.
2. Select the desired account from the menu.

Saving Sent Items

By default, email messages that you send are saved in the Sent Items folder. You can change this location for an individual message as follows:

1. Click the Save Sent Item button on the Options ribbon.
2. To save the item to a folder other than the default, click Other Folder and select the folder.
3. To not save the item at all, click Do Not Save.

Sending Items with a Message

You learned in Chapter 4 how you can attach a file to a message. Outlook also lets you attach certain items, specifically calendars and business cards, to a message.

Sending a Calendar

Sending calendar information with a message can be useful to let colleagues know when you are and are not available for a meeting. To send calendar information with an email message, click the Calendar button in the Include section of the Message ribbon. Outlook displays the Send a Calendar via E-mail dialog box, shown in Figure 7.1. You make entries in this dialog box to specify the calendar information that will be sent, as follows:

1. If you have more than one calendar, select the calendar to use from the Calendar list.

2. Select the date range from the Date Range list. Predefined ranges include Today, Tomorrow, and Next 7 Days. Select Specify Dates from the list to enter a custom date range.

3. From the Detail list, select the level of calendar detail that you want included in the message. The choices are

   ▪ **Availability Only:** Time will be shown as Free, Busy, Tentative, or Out of Office.

   ▪ **Limited Details:** In addition to availability, this option includes the subjects of calendar items.

   ▪ **Full Details:** In addition to availability, this option includes the full detail of calendar items.

4. Select the Show Time within My Working Hours Only option to limit the sent calendar information to these hours. By default they are 8:00 AM to 5:00 PM Monday–Friday. Click the Set Working Hours link to change this.

5. Click the Show button to display three additional options. Two of them relate to what information is included in the message. These options are relevant only if you selected Limited Details or Full Details. The third option determines the format of the sent calendar: Daily Schedule or List of Events. See the main text for information on these two layouts.

6. Click OK to close the dialog box and insert the calendar information in the message.

FIGURE 7.1

Sending calendar information in an email message.

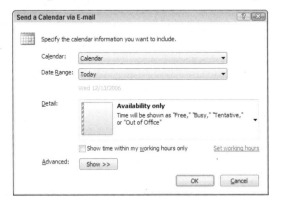

When calendar information is inserted in an email message, at the top is a calendar of the month or months involved with the relevant days highlighted and underlined, as shown for July 13–19 in Figure 7.2. The recipient can click these days to go to the detail section for that day.

FIGURE 7.2

This part of the calendar information includes links to individual days.

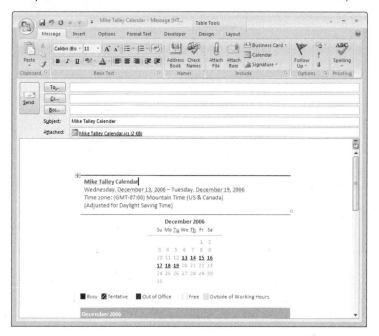

If the calendar information was sent using the Daily Schedule option, the details appear as shown in Figure 7.3. You can see that blocks of time during each day are marked as Free, Busy, and so on.

If the calendar information was sent using the List of Events option, the details appear as shown in Figure 7.4. This option lists specific calendar events only — free time is not explicitly marked.

Sending a Business Card

A business card is just what it sounds like — an electronic representation of the information normally found on a paper business card. Every entry in a contacts list automatically has a business card created for it. You can insert these cards into email messages to send contact information to email recipients. When you do so, a visual representation of the business card is added to the message and a VCF file is attached to the message. The recipient can use the VCF file to quickly add the contact information to his or her own contacts list.

FIGURE 7.3

Display of calendar details when the Daily Schedule option is used to send the calendar.

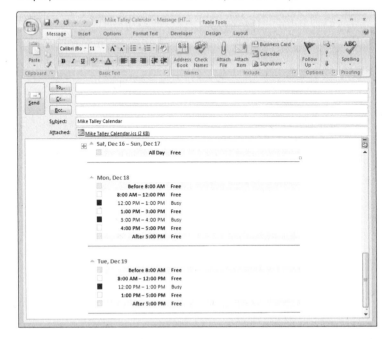

FIGURE 7.4

Display of calendar details when the List of Events option is used to send the calendar.

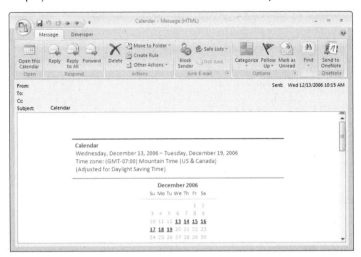

To send a business card with an email message:

1. Click the Business Card button in the Include section of the Message ribbon.

2. The menu that is displayed lists recently sent business cards. Select the one you want to send, or select Other Business Cards to select from your contacts list.

3. If you selected Other Business Cards, Outlook displays the Insert Business Card dialog box as shown in Figure 7.5.

4. If you have more than one address book, select the desired one from the Look In list.

5. Click the contact whose business card you want to include. The card is previewed in the lower part of the dialog box.

6. If you want to include more than one card, hold down Ctrl while clicking.

7. Click OK

FIGURE 7.5

Selecting a business card to include in an email message.

Your Own Business Card

If you create an entry for yourself in your contacts list, you can send your own business card with email messages.

Setting Message Importance and Sensitivity

An email message can be flagged as having low importance or high importance. Low is the default. The recipient's email program may indicate the importance of a message in some way. For example, Outlook displays an exclamation point next to the message in the Inbox if it is marked as having high importance. Many email clients, including Outlook, also allow recipients to sort their received messages by importance.

To mark a message with high importance, click the High Importance button (a red exclamation point) in the Options section of the Message ribbon. To return a message to the default setting of low importance, click the Low Importance button (a downward-pointing arrow).

Setting Message Restrictions

Message restrictions, or permissions, let you restrict who can view your email messages and what they can do with them (for example, can the message be forwarded?). This feature, which is applicable to all Office documents as well as email messages, is part of Information Rights Management, or IRM.

IRM is based on the concept of *credentials*. To create rights-restricted content, such as an email message, you must possess appropriate credentials to associate with the message. The recipient must also possess the appropriate credentials to view or take other actions with the content.

IRM requires that both the creator and the recipient of restricted content be subscribed to an IRM server. Many people use the Windows Right Management (WRM) service, which at present is free (but with no guarantee that Microsoft will continue the service indefinitely). WRM uses .Net Passport as a means of verifying identities and validating credentials. Some companies use their own IRM server or one provided by a third party.

The steps described in this section assume that you have a rights management client installed on your computer and have set up the necessary credentials.

By default, email messages are created with no restrictions. You can add a Do Not Forward restriction by clicking the Permissions button on the Message ribbon and selecting Do Not Forward from the menu. This button will be displayed only if you are set up for IRM. This restriction permits the recipient to view the message if they have the required credentials, but not to forward, print, or copy the message.

You may be asked which credentials to use for this message (it's possible for an individual to possess multiple credentials). When a message you are composing is restricted it displays a banner below the ribbon describing the restrictions, as shown in Figure 7.6.

If you attach a document, workbook, or presentation to a message, the restricted permissions of the message will be applied to the attachments as well. If the attachment has already had restrictions set in the originating program (Word, Excel, or PowerPoint) those restrictions also remain in effect.

A message that has restrictions applied displays a notification of that fact below the ribbon.

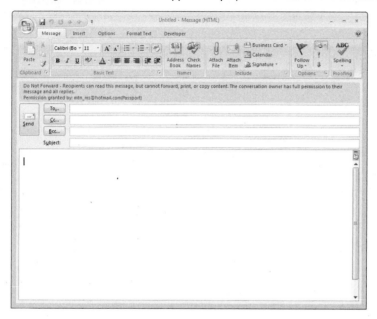

You may also have custom restrictions available to you. In a company, the IT department may have defined a restriction level that restricts contents to people on the company network. Your IT person can provide you with information on custom restrictions if they are in use in your organization.

Flagging a Message for Follow-Up

Sometimes, when you send a message, you would like to be reminded to follow up on the message — for example, to make sure that you have received a reply. You can flag a message for follow up and, optionally, have Outlook remind you. Here's how.

1. Click the Follow Up button on the Message ribbon. Outlook displays the menu shown in Figure 7.7.

2. To flag for follow up at one of the predefined times (for example, tomorrow or next week), click the corresponding command on the menu.

3. To specify a custom time, click the Custom command. Outlook displays the Custom dialog box as shown in Figure 7.8.

4. Make sure the Flag for Me option is selected.

5. From the Flag To list, select the type of follow up (for example, follow up, reply, and so on).

6. Enter the desired start and due dates in the corresponding fields. Click the down arrow next to each field to select from a calendar.

7. If you want Outlook to remind you of this item, select the Reminder option and enter the date and time in the adjacent fields.

8. Click OK.

FIGURE 7.7

Flagging a message for follow-up.

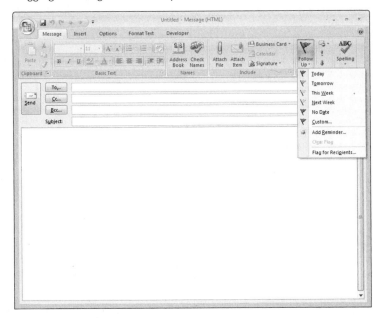

FIGURE 7.8

Specifying a custom follow-up interval.

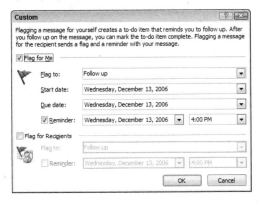

You can also flag a message for the recipient. All you need to do is select Flag for Recipients from the Follow Up menu (see Figure 7.7) and then enter the relevant information in the lower part of the Custom dialog box (see Figure 7.8).

When an Outlook user receives a message with such a flag, the flag status column in the Inbox will display a special icon indicating that there is follow-up information included with the message. The user can right-click this icon to add the message to his or her to-do list. Email programs other than Outlook may ignore this information or handle it differently.

Assigning a Message to a Category

Outlook's categories are a powerful tool for organizing all kinds of information. Categories are covered in more detail in Chapter 17. When you create a message, you can assign it to a category. Then you'll be able to find the message — the saved copy of the sent message, that is — based on this category. To assign a category to a message:

1. Click the dialog box launcher in the More Options section of the Options ribbon to display the Message Options dialog box.

2. At the lower left of the dialog box, click the Categories button.

3. Select the desired category from the menu. Or, click Clear All Categories to remove any category assignment from the message.

Requesting Delivery and Read Receipts

When you send a message you can request delivery and/or read receipts by selecting the corresponding option in the Tracking section of the Options ribbon. A delivery receipt is generated when the message is delivered to the recipient, and a read receipt is generated when the message is opened by the recipient. The receipt consists of an email message back to you that contains the date and time that the original message was delivered or read.

Delivery and read receipts sound like a great idea but their usefulness in practice is limited. The delivery receipt must be generated by the email server software, and sometimes this feature is turned off by the server administrator to reduce the load on the server. Even if you do receive a delivery receipt, there is no guarantee that the recipient has read the message. Likewise, the read receipt is sent by Outlook (or whatever other email program the recipient is using), and the user may have this feature turned off.

When you have sent a message and requested a receipt, Outlook automatically processes the receipt(s) when and if they arrive (unless you have turned this feature off under Tracking Options, as explained later in this chapter). When you open the message in the Sent Items folder, the ribbon displays a Show section with Message and Tracking buttons (see Figure 7.9). Click the Tracking button to view the details of the receipt(s) received for this message. Click the Message button to return to the message text.

Be aware that if Outlook has not yet received and processed any receipt for a message, the Tracking button will not be available on the ribbon.

FIGURE 7.9

Viewing the tracking status of a message.

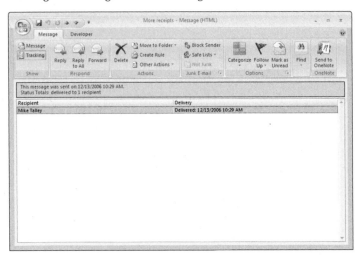

Delaying Delivery

If you do not want a message delivered right away, you can specify a "do not deliver before" date, as follows:

1. Click the Delay Delivery button in the More Options section of the Options ribbon. Outlook displays the Message Options dialog box (see Figure 7.10).

2. In the Delivery Options section, turn on the Do Not Deliver Before option.

3. Enter the desired date and time in the adjacent fields.

4. Click the Close button.

If you are using a Microsoft Exchange email account, the message will be sent to the server and held there until the specified date and time. If you are using another kind of email account, the message will be held in Outlook's outbox until the first send operation that occurs after the specified date and time.

Setting a Message Expiration Date

If you are sending a message relevant for only a limited period, you can set an expiration date for the message. When the recipient receives the message, it will behave normally until the expiration date, after which it will display in the Inbox (or whatever folder it is in) with a line through the header. The recipient can still open the message, but the strikethrough provides a visual indication that the message has expired. Other email programs may handle message expiration differently.

FIGURE 7.10

Delaying the delivery of a message.

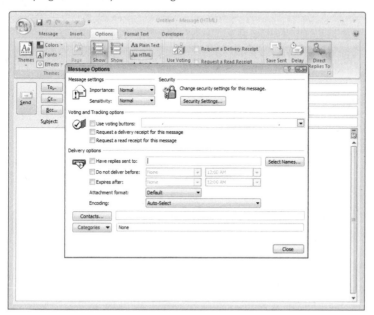

To set an expiration date:

1. Click the dialog box launcher in the Options section of the Message ribbon. Outlook displays the Message Options dialog box (shown previously in Figure 7.10).

2. In the Delivery Options section of the dialog box, turn on the Expires After option.

3. Enter the desired expiration date and time in the adjacent fields.

4. Click Close.

Using Signatures

Outlook lets you define signatures that can be quickly added to an email message. You can have multiple signatures; one for business use and another for personal messages, for example. Creating signatures is covered in Chapter 5, as is defining a default signature that is automatically added to all messages. To manually add a signature to a message, click the Signature button in the Include section of the Message ribbon and select the desired signature from the menu. If you have not defined any signatures, none will be listed here.

Setting Global Email Options

A number of Outlook's options apply globally to all messages and to email in general. You select these options using several dialog boxes, which display the options in related groups. This section follows the same organization.

Mail Preferences

To view and change email preferences:

1. Select Tools, Options from the main Outlook menu to display the Options dialog box.

2. If necessary, click the Preferences tab.

3. At the top of this dialog box, click the E-mail Options button. Outlook displays the E-mail Options dialog box (see Figure 7.11).

4. Set options in this dialog box as explained next.

5. Click OK.

FIGURE 7.11

Setting global email preferences.

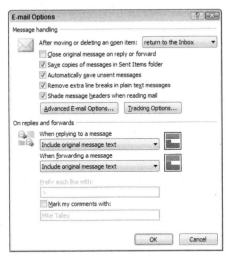

The options in the Message Handling section of this dialog box are as follows:

- **Close Original Message on Reply or Forward:** When you select Forward or Reply in a message that you received, the original message is closed.

- **Save Copies of Messages in Sent Items Folder:** When you send a message, a copy is saved in the Sent Items folder (recommended!).

- **Automatically Save Unsent Messages:** Messages you have started composing but not sent are saved in the Drafts folder.

- **Remove Extra Line Breaks in Plain Text Messages:** Unneeded line breaks are stripped from plain text messages.

- **Shade Message Headers when Reading Mail:** When you are reading a message that contains quoted components, Outlook will use subtle shading to mark the quoted section (this does not always work properly, I have found).

- **Advanced E-Mail Options:** Click this button to view and set advanced email options (explained in the following section).

- **Tracking Options:** Click this button to view and set tracking options (explained later in the chapter).

The On Replies and Forwards section of this dialog box determines what Outlook does when you reply to a message or forward a message. You set each independently but the options are essentially the same:

- **Do Not Include Original Message:** Replies are sent without the original message. Not applicable to forwarded messages.

- **Attach Original Message:** Replies and forwards are sent with the original message included as an attachment.

- **Include Original Message Text:** Replies and forwards are sent with the original message included as part of the new message.

- **Include and Indent Original Message Text:** Replies and forwards are sent with the original message included as part of the new message, indented with respect to the other parts of the message.

- **Prefix Each Line of the Original Message:** Replies and forwards are sent with the original message included as part of the new message, with each line of the original message prefixed by what is entered in the Prefix Each Line With field (by default this is >).

The final option in this dialog box is Mark My Comments With. You use this option when you prefer to reply to or forward messages with your comments included along with the original message text. When this option is selected, your comments are each preceded by your name (or whatever you specify) in brackets.

Advanced Email Options

When you click the Advanced Email Options button in the E-mail Options dialog box, Outlook displays the dialog box shown in Figure 7.12.

FIGURE 7.12

Setting advanced email options.

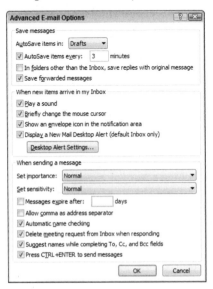

Most of these options are self-explanatory so I will not go into details. The few that may require explanation are

- **AutoSave Items In:** Specifies the folder when Outlook autosaves items (for example, messages you have started composing but not yet sent).

- **In Folders Other Than the Inbox...:** When you reply to a message that is located in any folder other than the Inbox, your reply is saved in that folder rather than in the Sent Items folder. This can help to keep related messages together.

- **Display a New Mail Desktop Alert:** When a new message arrives, Outlook displays a small, semitransparent preview of the message in the lower-right corner of your screen. Click the Desktop Alert Settings button to specify the details of how this alert appears.

- **Set Importance/Sensitivity:** Specifies the default importance and sensitivity levels for new messages you create.

Tracking Options

If you click the Tracking Options button in the E-mail Options dialog box, Outlook displays the dialog box shown in Figure 7.13.

Setting email tracking options.

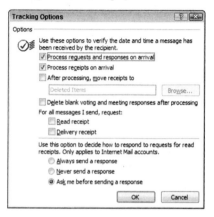

The options in the top portion of this dialog box determine how Outlook handles requests for read and delivery receipts and receipts that have been returned to you:

- **Process Requests and Responses on Arrival:** When a read or delivery receipt is received, Outlook records the receipt as part of the original item (the sent message).
- **Process Receipts on Arrival:** Receipts are deleted on arrival (after processing).
- **After Processing, Move Receipts To:** Specify a folder for saving processed receipts.

In the middle of this dialog box are options that you can set if you want every message you send to include a request for a delivery and/or read receipt.

At the bottom of the dialog box you can specify how Outlook handles requests for receipts that you receive.

Mail Setup

To access the Mail Setup dialog box, select Tools, Options from the main Outlook menu and click the Mail Setup tab in the Options dialog box. This tab is shown in Figure 7.14.

The E-mail Accounts button lets you access Outlook's email accounts to add, delete, or modify accounts. Working with email accounts was covered in Chapter 3.

FIGURE 7.14

The Mail Setup tab in the Options dialog box.

The Send Immediately When Connected option specifies that a message you create and send is sent immediately rather than being put in the Outbox and sent the next time a send/receive operation takes place. If you click the adjacent Send/Receive button, Outlook opens a dialog box where you can specify how often Outlook performs an automatic send/receive. The default is 30 minutes.

If you click the Data Files button on the Mail Setup tab, Outlook opens a dialog box where you can change settings related to the data files that Outlook uses to store information (messages, calendar, and so on). This topic is covered in Chapter 18.

The final group of options on the Mail Setup tab are relevant only if you are using a dial-up (modem) connection to the network. For most users, the default settings are fine and need not be changed.

Mail Format

To access the Mail Format dialog box, select Tools, Options from the main Outlook menu and click the Mail Format tab in the Options dialog box. This tab is shown in Figure 7.15.

FIGURE 7.15

The Mail Format tab in the Options dialog box.

The Message Format section of this dialog box has the following elements:

- **Compose in this Message Format:** Select the default format (HTML, Rich Text, or plain text) for new messages. See Chapter 5 for details.

- **Internet Format:** Click this button to specify that messages you create in RTF format are converted to HTML or plain text when being sent to Internet mail accounts (which generally cannot read RTF messages).

- **International Options:** Click this button to set language options for new messages.

The HTML Format section has these options:

- **Reduce the File Size...:** Make HTML messages as small as possible by removing unneeded formatting information.

- **Rely on CSS for Font Formatting:** Select this option if you want to use Cascading Style Sheets for font formatting.

- **Save Smart Tags in Email:** Smart Tags are sent as part of a message rather than being present only while you are composing the message.

The Stationery and Fonts button and the Signatures button give you access to the tools for creating and modifying these items, specifying the defaults to use with new messages, and so on. Stationery and signatures are covered in Chapter 5.

Click the Editor Options button to display the window shown in Figure 7.16. You use this window to set a variety of options that control how the email editor works. Note the list of categories on the left. Click each one to display a different set of related options.

Setting options for the email editor.

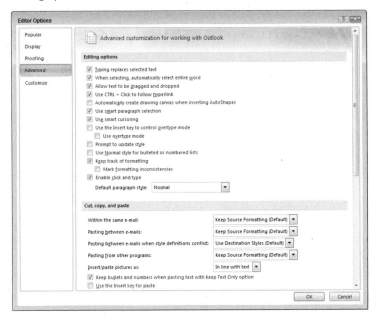

Many people use Outlook without ever making changes to any of these options, but they are available if you want to make the editor better suit your working style. If you have used the Microsoft Word word processing program, you may recognize a lot of overlap between Outlook's editor options and the options available in Word. There a good reason for this — Outlook's editor is in fact based on Word.

Summary

It seems that Outlook has an overwhelming number of email options — it can seem overwhelming to try to understand them all. Fortunately, most options can be left with their default settings and changed only when you have a specific reason to do so. As you become more familiar with Outlook, you gain a better understanding of how to set options to maximize your convenience and productivity.

Chapter 8

Dealing with Junk Email

J unk email, often called spam, is a problem for most email users. It can range from a minor annoyance for a home user to a major problem for a large organization, clogging mail servers and reducing the efficiency of employees. Fortunately, Outlook provides you with tools that greatly reduce the spam problem.

Understanding Junk Email Filtering

Junk email filtering works on two principles. The first is the content of the message — certain keywords and phrases are considered likely to be spam. The other is the identity of the sender. You can define a safe list — people whose messages are never treated as spam regardless of content. Likewise you can define a blocked list, people whose messages are always treated as spam regardless of content. In either case, messages that Outlook flags as spam are placed in the Junk E-mail folder rather than the Inbox.

Why doesn't Outlook just delete spam messages? The fact is that content-based spam filtering is not perfect, and it's possible that legitimate messages will sometimes be caught as spam. Some people like to quickly scan their Junk E-mail folder before permanently deleting the messages just to make sure that a legitimate message has not been caught. However, if you want spam to be deleted automatically, you can tell Outlook to do this. See the next section, "Setting Junk EMail Options," for details.

Third-Party Anti-Spam Software

There are several anti-spam programs on the market that work in conjunction with Outlook to catch spam. These programs may provide more sophisticated filtering options and other features. If you are using one of these programs you may want to turn Outlook's spam filtering off. You do not have to, however—leaving it on does no harm and may in fact catch spam that the other program misses.

Setting Junk Email Options

Settings for Outlook's filtering and handling of junk email are made in the Junk E-mail Options dialog box, as follows:

1. Select Tools, Options from the main Outlook menu to display the Options dialog box.

2. On the Preferences tab, click the Junk E-mail button. Outlook displays the Junk E-mail dialog box.

3. If necessary, click the Options tab (shown in Figure 8.1).

4. Make option settings as described next.

5. Click OK.

FIGURE 8.1

Setting options for junk email filtering.

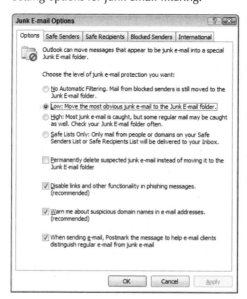

The first option in this dialog box determines the level of filtering based on message content. There are four levels to choose from:

- **No Automatic Filtering:** Messages are not filtered based on their content.

- **Low:** Only obvious spam is treated as such. Some spam will get through to your Inbox.

- **High:** More stringent spam rules are applied when scanning message content. Some legitimate messages may be treated as spam.

- **Safe Lists Only:** Only messages from senders on your safe lists (explained later in this chapter) are allowed through — all other messages are treated as spam regardless of their content.

The other options in this dialog box are as follows:

- **Permanently Delete...:** If this option is selected, messages that Outlook considers to be spam will be deleted rather than moved to the Junk E-mail folder. You may not want to use this option unless you are sure that legitimate messages are not mistakenly being tagged as spam.

- **Disable Links...:** Phishing messages (see sidebar) usually contain links to web pages where you will be asked for confidential information such as passwords. If this option is selected, Outlook will disable these links.

- **Warn Me About...:** A spoofed domain name is one that is not what it appears to be. For example, a link might display www.microsoft.com but actually be a link to another domain. If this option is selected, Outlook will warn you about possibly spoofed domain names in a message.

- **When Sending Email, Postmark...:** If this option is selected, all messages you send will be postmarked as an anti-spam measure. See the following section for more information on postmarking.

Understanding Postmarking

Postmarking is a new technique designed to help in the fight against spam. Postmarking a message adds to the time required to process and send it. For normal users who send dozens or even

Phishing

Phishing is a particularly dangerous kind of junk email. A phishing message pretends to be from a company you do business with, for example PayPal or eBay. The message asks you to take some seemingly legitimate action, such as resetting your password. When you follow the link to a web site, the site looks just like the real thing, but it is not — it's a fake web site set up by the phisher. The end result is that some unscrupulous person now has your password and you can imagine the possible consequences.

Spam and Viruses

Is spam related to viruses? Not directly, although viruses often arrive as part of a spam message (but can come with a legitimate message too). Virus protection in Outlook is covered in Chapter 20.

hundreds of emails a day, the extra time required is insignificant. For spammers who rely on being able to send millions of emails, however, the extra time results in an increase in costs. Therefore, a postmarked message is less likely to be spam than one that is not postmarked. Postmarks are just one of many factors that an email client can take into account when filtering spam.

Blocking and Allowing Specific Addresses

A very useful tool in the fight against spam is Outlook's capability to define lists of email addresses and domains that are always blocked or always allowed through.

Defining Safe Senders

A *safe sender* is a person, or more precisely an email address, whose email messages are always considered to be okay — not spam — regardless of the content. Sometimes a safe senders list is called a *white list*. You can create a safe senders list based on your contacts and also by entering individual addresses. You can also specify entire domains as safe — for example, all messages from www.microsoft.com would be considered to be safe. Here are the steps to follow:

1. Select Tools, Options from the main Outlook menu to display the Options dialog box.
2. On the Preferences tab, click the Junk E-mail button. Outlook displays the Junk E-mail dialog box.
3. If necessary, click the Safe Senders tab (shown in Figure 8.2).
4. To add an address or domain to the list, click the Add button.
5. Enter the address (for example, someone@microsoft.com) or the domain (for example, microsoft.com or @microsoft.com).
6. Click OK to add the address or domain to the safe list.
7. To edit or remove a safe list entry, highlight it in the list and click the Edit or Remove button.
8. Click OK.

The other two options in this dialog box are self-explanatory. It is recommended to have the Also Trust E-mail from My Contacts option selected, because this saves you the effort of entering these addresses manually.

FIGURE 8.2

Defining your safe senders list.

The Import and Export tools are useful if you want to transfer a safe list between Outlook and another email program, or pass your safe list to a friend or colleague. The import/export format is a plain text file with one address per line.

Defining Safe Recipients

The safe recipients list, located on another tab in the Junk E-mail Options dialog box, is similar to the safe senders list but it marks messages as okay based on their recipients rather than their sender. This is useful when you are on a distribution list or in another situation where you receive emails that are sent to a list of recipients including you. When an email address is on the safe recipients list, any message sent to you *and* to that address will never be treated as spam, regardless of the message sender and content. The Safe Recipients tab works exactly the same as the Safe Senders tab, described in the previous section.

Defining Blocked Senders

A blocked sender is an email address or domain whose messages are always treated as spam. The Blocked Senders tab in the Junk E-mail Options dialog box works exactly like the Safe Senders tab as described earlier.

Blocking/Allowing Individual Senders

The context menu is a fast way to add addresses to your safe and blocked lists. All you have to do is right-click the message in the Inbox (or whatever folder it is in), select Junk E-mail from the context menu, then select the desired action from the next menu. If you have opened a message, you can use the commands in the Junk E-mail section of the ribbon to perform related commands:

- **Block Sender:** Adds the message sender to your blocked senders list.
- **Safe Lists:** Choose from the menu to add the sender to your safe sender or safe recipient list or to add the sender's domain to the safe senders list.
- **Not Junk:** This command is available only if the message is in your Junk E-mail folder. Click to move the message to the Inbox and add the sender to your safe senders list.

International Junk E-mail Options

You may find that you receive some emails that appear to be gibberish, random meaningless characters. This is caused when someone sends you an email using a different character encoding than the one you are using. For example, a person in China will likely use Chinese encoding to create a message in Chinese characters. If your email reader is set to use, say, English encoding, the message will display as gibberish. Outlook lets you block messages that use specified character encodings. It also lets you block emails from certain countries based on the top-level domain of the sender's address. Here are the steps to follow:

1. Select Tools, Options from the main Outlook menu to display the Options dialog box.
2. On the Preferences tab, click the Junk E-mail button. Outlook displays the Junk E-mail dialog box.
3. If necessary, click the International tab.
4. To block top-level domains, click the Blocked Top-Level Domains button to display a list of domains (see Figure 8.3).
5. Put a checkmark next to the domains you want to block and click OK.
6. To block character encodings, click the Blocked Encodings List to display a list of encodings (see Figure 8.4).
7. Put a checkmark next to the character encodings you want to block and click OK.
8. Click OK to close the Junk E-mail Options dialog box.

FIGURE 8.3

Specifying top-level domains to block.

FIGURE 8.4

Specifying character encodings to block.

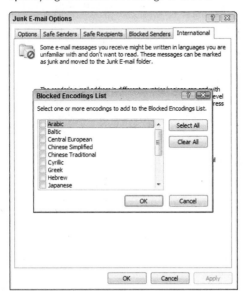

What's a Top-Level Domain?

The top-level domain of an email address is the part after the last period. In the United States we are used to seeing top-level domains such as .com, .org, and .edu that indicate the type or organization. In the rest of the world, however, the top-level domain usually identifies the country of origin — for example, .ca for Canada, .cn for China, and .fr for France. For the United States, .us is used although you rarely see it.

Summary

Spam, or junk email, is a serious problem for most email users. Outlook provides you with some powerful tools to detect and filter spam. By understanding these tools and using them efficiently, you can greatly reduce the negative impact spam has on your productivity.

Chapter 9

Processing Messages with Rules

utlook lets you automate the handling of email messages with *rules*. A rule can do things such as moving messages from a specific person to a designated folder or deleting messages with certain words in the subject. Rules can also display alerts, play sounds, and move InfoPath forms and RSS feed items. Rules can help you save time and stay organized.

Understanding Email Rule Basics

Outlook email rules are all similar in that they specify a *condition* and an *action*. A rule can be defined to apply to email messages when they arrive, which is most common, and also to messages as you send them. The Rules Wizard, where you create rules, provides a set of partially defined rules for commonly needed actions — all you need to do is fill in the details. It also provides the capability to define a rule completely from scratch, a feature you'll use if one of the existing rule templates does not meet your needs.

Creating a New Rule

To create a new email rule, select Rules and Alerts from the Tools menu. Outlook displays the Rules and Alerts dialog box where you should select the E-mail Rules tab. If you have any rules already defined they will be listed here. You can work with existing rules as described later in this chapter. To create a new rule, click the New Rule button to display the Rules Wizard, as shown in Figure 9.1.

FIGURE 9.1

The first step in defining a new rule.

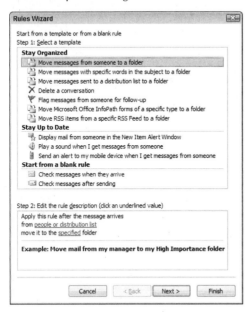

You can see that there are two parts to this dialog box, Select a Template at the top and Edit the Rule Description at the bottom. The following sections look at these in turn.

Selecting a Rule Template

The Select a Template portion of this dialog box is divided into three sections, each containing two or more templates:

- **Stay Organized:** Templates that move, delete, or flag messages or other items.
- **Stay Up to Date:** Templates for alerting you when messages arrive.
- **Start from a Blank Rule:** Templates that are empty and let you define a rule from scratch.

The remainder of this section deals with the first two of these categories. Starting from a blank rule is covered separately later in this chapter.

When you click an item in the Select a Template section, the Edit the Rule Description section displays the rule definition along with an example. Editing the definition is covered in the next section.

Editing a Rule Description

A rule definition contains underlined elements that represent the parts of the rule that you can edit. Figure 9.2, for example, shows a definition with two editable elements: "people or distribution list" and "specified." When you click such an underlined element, Outlook opens a dialog box where you can specify the details. In this example:

- Click "people or distribution list" to open a dialog box where you can select the people and/or distribution lists from your address book. The rule is applied to messages from the selected people.

- Click "specified" to select a folder to which matching messages will be moved.

FIGURE 9.2

The elements of a rule definition that can be edited are underlined.

After you have made selections for the editable rule items, the rule displays the selected information. An example is shown in Figure 9.3 where the rule is defined to move messages from specific people to a specific folder. Note that these elements of the rule are still underlined and can be clicked to make changes to the rule as needed.

A completed rule definition displays the details that you have specified.

Finishing the Rule

At this point the rule is ready to use. You can click Finish in the Rules Wizard dialog box to save the rule. In some cases you may want to fine-tune the rule, in which case click the Next button. Fine-tuning a rule is essentially the same as creating a rule from a blank template, covered in the next section.

Creating a Rule from a Blank Template

If the rule templates that Outlook provides do not suit your needs, you can create a rule from a blank template. In the first step of the Rules Wizard, shown earlier in Figure 9.1, you must select one of the following from the Start from a Blank Rule section:

- **Check Messages When They Arrive:** To create a rule that works with messages you receive.

- **Check Messages After Sending:** To create a rule that works with messages you send.

After making your selection, click the Next button. Outlook displays the next wizard step as shown in Figure 9.4. You use this dialog box to specify the conditions for the rule. You can have more than one condition for a rule. When you do, all conditions must be met for a message to be processed. The steps to follow are described next.

FIGURE 9.4

Selecting conditions for a rule.

1. Click the box next to a description to place a checkmark in the box and add the condition to the rule description.

2. If the condition requires it, click the underlined element in the description to specify the details.

3. Repeat steps 1 and 2 if needed to add additional conditions to the rule.

4. Click the Next button to proceed to the next wizard step where you will define the rule's action. This dialog box is shown in Figure 9.5.

5. Put a checkmark next to the action that you want to be part of the rule.

6. If necessary, click any underlined element in the action to specify the details.

7. Click Next to display the next wizard step where you specify any exceptions to the rule (see Figure 9.6). An exception lets you modify a rule as in this example: If the message subject contains the word "free" then delete it unless the sender is in my contacts list. Exceptions are optional, and they are added the same way as conditions and actions.

8. Click Next to go to the final step of the wizard (see Figure 9.7). In this dialog box you specify a name for the rule and have the opportunity to edit the rule by clicking under-lined elements in the rule description. You can also set the following options:

- **Run This Rule Now...:** Apply the rule to messages already in your mailbox.

- **Turn on this Rule:** Enable the rule for newly received or sent messages.

- **Create This Rule on All Accounts:** Apply the rule for all your email accounts (rele-vant only if you have multiple accounts).

9. Click Finish to complete the rule definition and return to the Rules and Alerts dialog box.

FIGURE 9.5

Selecting an action for a rule.

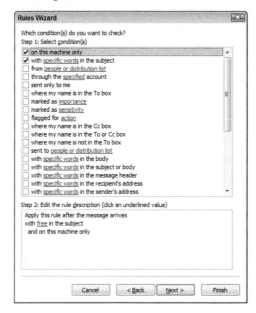

FIGURE 9.6

Specifying exceptions for a rule.

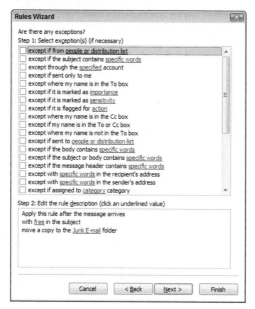

FIGURE 9.7

The final step of the Rules Wizard.

Some Rule Examples

Outlook email rules are admittedly rather complex. It may help you to understand them if you follow the steps required to define a few different kinds of rules.

Rule Example 1

This first rule example shows you how to define a rule that moves all messages from a certain domain to a specified folder. It would be useful if, for example, you are doing some contracting work for a company and are interacting with several people there. This rule moves all email that you receive from anyone at that company into one folder, helping you to stay organized.

The first step is to create the folder:

1. In the mail navigation pane, click the location where you want to place the new folder. You can click a mailbox if you want the new folder to be at the top level in that mailbox. You can also click an existing folder to create the new folder within that folder. See Figure 9.8.

FIGURE 9.8

Selecting where to create a new mail folder.

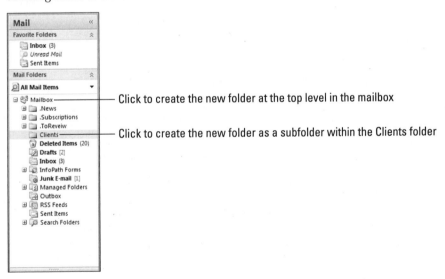

Click to create the new folder at the top level in the mailbox

Click to create the new folder as a subfolder within the Clients folder

2. Click the arrow next to the New button on the toolbar and select Folder from the menu. Outlook displays the Create New Folder dialog box, as shown in Figure 9.9.

FIGURE 9.9

Entering a name for the new folder.

3. Enter the new folder name in the Name box.

4. Make sure that Mail and Post Items is selected in the Folder Contains list.

5. Click OK.

Now that you have created the folder you can proceed to defining the rule:

1. Select Tools, Rules and Alerts from the Outlook menu to display the Rules and Alerts dialog box.

2. On the E-mail Rules tab, click the New Rule button. Outlook displays the Rules Wizard dialog box.

3. In the Stay Organized section, click the "Move messages from someone to a folder" template.

4. In the Edit the Rule Description section, click the "people or distribution list" link. Outlook displays the Rule Address dialog box (see Figure 9.10).

5. If you wanted to move messages from a single individual who is in your contacts list, you could click that person's entry in the list and then click the From button. Because you want to move all messages from a domain, enter "acme.com" in the From box (without the quotes, of course).

6. Click OK.

7. Outlook may display a dialog box claiming not to recognize "acme.com" because it is not a complete email address. This is okay—just click Cancel to close this dialog box and return to the Rules Wizard.

Specifying an address to be part of a new email rule.

8. In the Edit the Rule Description section, click the "specified" link. Outlook displays the dialog box shown in Figure 9.11.

Specifying the folder where messages are to be moved.

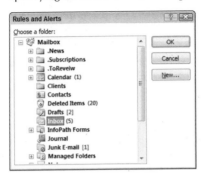

9. Select the desired destination folder and click OK. Note: If you had not created the new folder earlier, you could do it now by clicking the New button in this dialog box.

10. Back in the Rules Wizard dialog box, click the Finish button to close the Rules Wizard and return to the Rules and Alerts dialog box.

After you create a rule you will see it listed in the Rules and Alerts dialog box. It is assigned a default name based on the information in the rule. You can, if desired, change the rule name as explained later in this chapter in the section on managing rules.

Rule Example 2

This rule example shows you how you can use a rule to help guard against spam. Say you receive a lot of junk email offering to sell you prescription medication online. However, the subject of the message is often disguised, so you want to define a rule that looks for the word "prescription" in both the subject and the body of the message — if the word is found, delete the message.

But there's a wrinkle — you do in fact get some meds from a legitimate online drug store, and you do not want emails from them to be caught — so the rule will have to include an exception. Here are the steps for creating this rule:

1. Select Tools, Rules and Alerts from the Outlook menu to display the Rules and Alerts dialog box.

2. On the E-mail Rules tab, click the New Rule button. Outlook displays the Rules Wizard dialog box.

3. In the Start from a Blank Rule section, click the Check Messages When They Arrive template.

4. Click Next to display a list of conditions.

5. Put a checkmark next to "with specific words in the subject or body."

6. In the lower part of this dialog box, click the "specific words" link to open the Search Text dialog box (see Figure 9.12).

FIGURE 9.12

Specifying words that will be searched for in a message.

7. Enter the word "prescription" in the upper box and click Add to add the word to the list. If you wanted to search for more than one word you would repeat this step as needed.

8. Click OK to return to the Rules Wizard dialog box.

9. Click Next to display a list of actions.

10. Put a checkmark next to the Delete It action. This moves matching messages to the Deleted Items folder. You can also select the Permanently Delete It action, which does precisely what it says.

11. Click Next to display a list of exceptions.

12. Put a checkmark next to the "Except if from people or distribution list" exception.

13. In the lower part of the dialog box, click the "people or distribution list" link to display the Rule Address dialog box.

14. If the legitimate online pharmacy's address is in your contacts list you can add it using the From button. Otherwise just type it in the From box and click OK.

15. Back in the Rules Wizard dialog box, click Finish to complete your rule definition.

Rule Example 3

The final rule example shows you how to process messages that you send. Suppose your major client is Acme Corporation and you have created an Outlook category specifically for items related to Acme. You would like any and all messages you send to Acme to be placed in this category automatically. Here's how:

1. Select Tools, Rules and Alerts from the Outlook menu to display the Rules and Alerts dialog box.

2. On the E-mail Rules tab, click the New Rule button. Outlook displays the Rules Wizard dialog box.

3. In the Start from a Blank Rule section, click the Check Messages after Sending template.

4. Click Next to display a list of conditions.

5. Put a checkmark next to "sent to people or distribution list."

6. In the lower part of the dialog box, click the "people or distribution list" link to open the Rule Address dialog box.

7. Enter "acme.com" in the To box and click OK.

8. Outlook may display a dialog box claiming not to recognize "acme.com" because it is not a complete email address. This is okay — just click Cancel to close this dialog box and return to the Rules Wizard.

9. Click Next to display a list of actions.

10. Put a checkmark next to the Assign it to the Category Category option.

11. In the lower part of the dialog box, click the "category" link to open the Color Categories dialog box (see Figure 9.13).

12. Put a checkmark next to the desired category — in this case Acme — and click OK to return to the Rules Wizard dialog box.

13. Back in the Rules Wizard dialog box, click Finish to complete your rule definition.

FIGURE 9.13

Selecting a category to assign sent messages to.

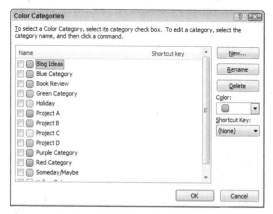

Managing Rules

When you select Rules and Alerts from the Tools menu, the E-mail Rules tab in the Rules and Alerts dialog box lists all the rules defined (see Figure 9.14). If you have more than one rule, they are applied in top-down order. The actions you can take in this dialog box are

- To edit a rule, click it and then click the Change Rule button. Then select Edit Rule Settings or Rename Rule from the menu.

- To change a rule's position in the list, click it and then click the up or down arrow button.

- To copy a rule, click it and then click the Copy button. Outlook makes a copy of the rule, which you can then rename and modify as desired.

- To delete a rule, click it and then click the Delete button.

- To run rules, click the Run Rules Now button. Then, in the dialog box displayed, select the rules to run and the folder(s) and messages to apply the rules to (see Figure 9.15).

- To inactivate a rule, click the adjacent box to remove the checkmark.

- To import or export your rules from/to other versions of Outlook, or for use by a friend or colleague, click the Options button.

FIGURE 9.14

You manage your email rules in the Rules and Alerts dialog box.

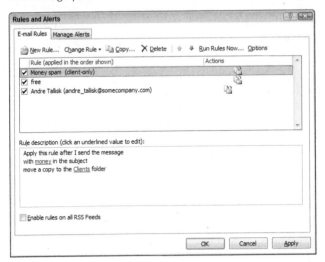

FIGURE 9.15

Running rules manually.

Summary

Email rules are another way that Outlook helps you save time and stay organized. You may be hesitant to spend the time to define a rule, but in the long run it will be well worth the effort. Of course, rules are probably not warranted for situations that arise only occasionally, but most people who rely on email in their work — and who doesn't these days — will find plenty of good uses for them.

Part III

Managing Information

Chapter 10

Managing Your Contacts

Outlook's contacts feature is much more than a simple address book. It provides you with powerful tools to not only store but to find and use information about your business and personal contacts.

Understanding Outlook Contacts

Outlook's contacts are one of its most powerful features. At heart, it is just an address book, but what an address book! Of course it covers the basics of organizing names, addresses, and phone numbers, but it can do so much more. Many people use contacts primarily as a way to store people's email addresses for ease of sending emails. This is important, but if that's all you use contacts for you are really missing out. For example, did you know that you can use Outlook contacts to do the following?

- Create electronic business cards so you can send your or other people's contact information by email.

- Store multiple phone numbers, email addresses, and postal address for an individual.

- Perform an automated mail merge, creating a mailing to some or all your contacts.

- Automatically dial a contact's phone number (if your computer is equipped with a modem).

- Store a photograph as part of a contact's information.

- Define custom fields to store whatever information you need as part of a contact.

- View a map of the location of a contact's address.

Once you understand all the power of Outlook contacts, you can use as many or as few of its features as you like.

Note that Personal Address Books, a feature available in earlier versions of Outlook, are no longer supported.

The Contacts Window

When you select Contacts in the navigation pane, the top part of the pane displays the name of your address book. Usually this is Contacts. If you have more than one address book, they will all be displayed here. Using multiple address books is covered later in this chapter — most people have and need only one.

Below the address book name is a section titled Current View (see Figure 10.1). Here you can select the way that information will be displayed in the Contacts window. There are several options, including business cards, phone list, by company, and by location. Simply click the view you want and the Contacts window changes immediately.

FIGURE 10.1

Outlook offers several different ways to view contacts.

At the bottom of the Current View section — you may need to scroll to bring these into view — are two commands: Add New Group and Customize Current View. The following sections look at these in turn.

Adding a New Contact Group

By default an address book is not subdivided. As the number of contacts grows, you may find it useful to define groups to organize contacts in a way that makes them easier to find and use. You might have Work, Personal, and Family groups, for example. To define a group, follow these steps:

1. Make sure that Contacts is selected in the navigation pane.
2. At the bottom of the Current View list, click the Add New Group link. Outlook adds a group called New Group under My Contacts (see Figure 10.2).

FIGURE 10.2

After adding a new group to your contacts.

3. Type in the group name and press Enter.

4. Repeat steps 2 and 3 as needed to create more groups.

Figure 10.3 shows how the navigation pane will look after you create three new groups.

FIGURE 10.3

After creating and renaming three new groups.

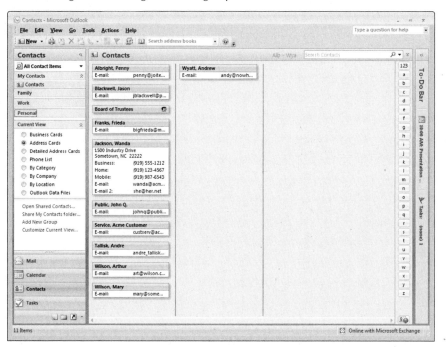

After you have created one or more additional groups, you can simply drag a contact from its current group to the group that you want it in. For example, Figure 10.4 shows how you would move Wanda Jackson from the Contacts group to the Work Contacts group. If you want a given contact to be in more than one group, follow these steps:

1. Select the contact.

2. Press Ctrl+C to copy the contact to the Clipboard.

3. Display the destination group.

4. Press Ctrl+V to paste the contact.

Customizing a Contacts View

The different views that Outlook provides for contacts can be customized to suit your needs. You cannot, however, create a new view from scratch. To customize a view:

FIGURE 10.4

Moving a contact from one group to another.

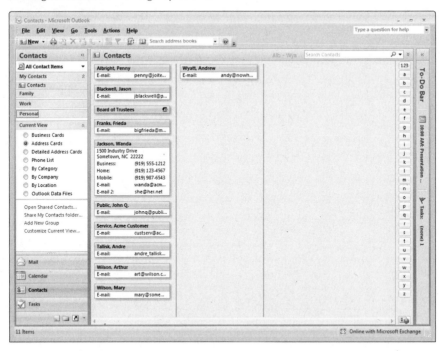

1. Select the view that you want to customize in the Current View list.

2. At the bottom of the Current View list, click the Customize Current View link. Outlook displays the Customize View dialog box (see Figure 10.5).

3. Click one of the buttons to change related view settings (explained in more detail in the text). The text next to each button describes the purpose of each.

4. If necessary, click Reset Current View to return the view to its original default settings.

5. Click OK to save your changes and close the dialog box.

Depending on the view you are customizing, you may have only some of the buttons in the Customize View dialog box available. This is because certain aspects of a view are not relevant to some views. The aspects of the view that you change with the different buttons are described in Table 10-1.

FIGURE 10.5

Customizing a contacts view.

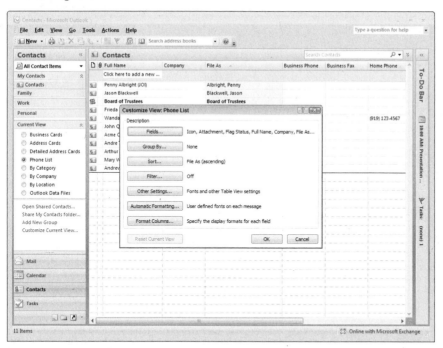

TABLE 10. 1

Components of Customizing a Contacts View

Button	Action
Fields	Specify which fields (items of information) are included in the view.
Group By	Define grouping for the displayed contacts based on one or more fields. For example, you could group contacts by company or state.
Sort	Define how contacts are sorted. You could sort by last name, for example.
Filter	Display only those contacts that meet your defined criteria.
Other Settings	Specify fonts, grid lines, and other details of contact view layout.
Automatic Formatting	Define special formatting for contacts that meet certain conditions such as an overdue task or have been flagged.
Format Columns	Define formatting for columns in the view.

Finding Contacts

As your contact list grows in size, you may find it helpful to search for contacts rather than simply look through the list hoping to find what you are looking for. At the top right of the Contacts window is a search field where you type the text you are looking for. Outlook automatically filters the contacts to show only those that match what you have entered. An example is shown in Figure 10.6. If there are no matches, a message to that effect is displayed.

After conducting a search, click the X next to the search box to clear the search and return to displaying all contacts.

The search I have just described searches all the contact fields for the text you entered. If you want to search in specific fields, you can perform an advanced search by clicking the double down arrow to the right of the search box. Outlook displays the advanced search tools as shown in Figure 10.7 (your screen may show different fields than are shown in the figure). To use these tools:

Enabling Instant Search

Instant Search is available by default in the Windows Vista operating system, but not in Windows XP. You may be prompted to download and install the search components when you start Outlook or another Office program. If you do not, and try to use Instant Search in Outlook, you will be prompted again. If you do not enable Instant Search, your search capabilities in Outlook will be limited compared to what is described here.

- Type in any of the search fields to search in that field only.

- Type in two or more search fields to display records that meet all your criteria.

- To include more fields in the search, click the Add Criteria button and then select the desired fields from the menu.

- To clear each criteria and return to display of all contacts, click the X next to the search box.

- To close the advanced search tools (while keeping the search active), click the double up arrow to the right of the search field.

FIGURE 10.6

Searching for contacts.

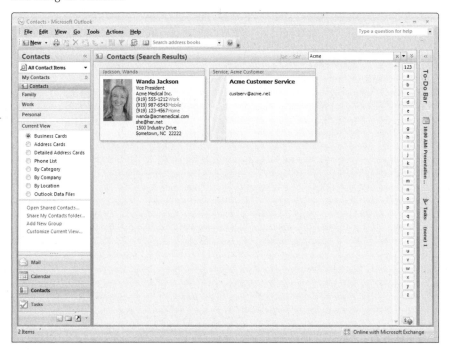

Searching by Category

Assigning your contacts to categories, as is explained later in this chapter, can make the advanced search tool even more useful. When you add criteria to the search, one of your choices is Categories. You can use this criterion to find all contacts that fall into a certain category. This can be particularly useful when you want to perform a mail merge, as described later in this chapter.

Finding Contacts Alphabetically

In some contact views, Outlook displays a column of index buttons at the right side of the Contacts window labeled 123 then A through Z. Click one of these buttons to scroll the contact display to entries that begin with the specified letter.

FIGURE 10.7

Performing an advanced search in Contacts.

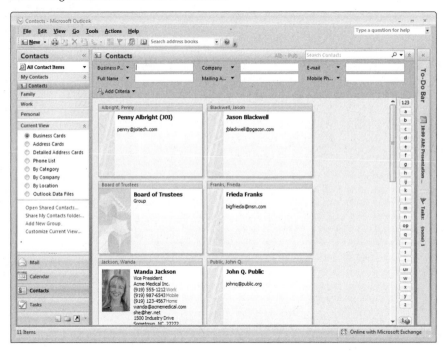

Adding Contacts to the Address Book

Outlook provides you with several ways to add information to an address book.

Adding a Contact Manually

To add a new contact to the address book:

- If Contacts are active in Outlook, click the New button on the toolbar or press Ctrl+N.

- If Contacts are not active in Outlook, click the arrow next to the New button on the toolbar and select Contact from the menu.

In either case, Outlook displays a new, blank contact form as shown in Figure 10.8. Type in the information — only a name is required and you can use or not use the other fields as you desire — and then click Save and Close on the ribbon. If you want to save this contact and enter another, click Save and New. Most of the fields on the contact form are self-explanatory, but I provide full details about the form later in this chapter.

FIGURE 10.8

A blank contact form.

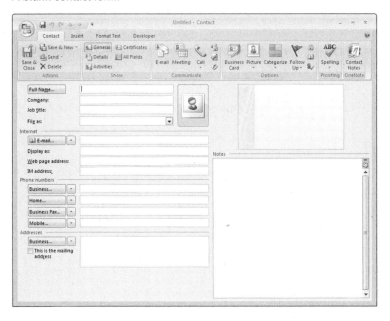

Adding a Contact from a Received Email

When you have opened a received email, the From field displays the name and/or the email address of the sender. It also displays any other recipients — other than you, that is — in the To and Cc fields. You can add the From person or any of the other To or Cc people to your contacts list by right-clicking the name or address and selecting Add to Outlook Contacts from the context menu. Outlook opens a new contact form with the available information filled in. This is only the person's email address and perhaps their name. You can add additional information to the contact, if desired, then click Save and Close.

Adding a Contact from an Outlook Contact

The heading of this section may seem confusing but it makes more sense when you understand that an Outlook user can send a contact as an attachment to an email message. The technique for doing this is covered later in this chapter in the section "Sending Contact Information by Email."

If you receive a contact in an email message, it will appear as an attachment identified by a small business card icon and the contact's name, as shown in Figure 10.9. If you double-click the attachment, Outlook will open a new contact form with the contact's information entered. You can edit the information if needed and then save it to your address book.

FIGURE 10.9

When you receive an Outlook contact attached to an email message, it is identified by a small business card icon.

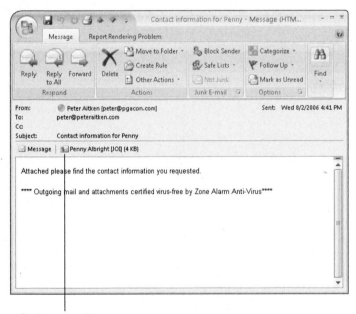

Business card icon

Adding a Contact from a vCard File

A vCard file is a special file format designed to send contact information. Although this is not Outlook's native format for sending and receiving contact information, Outlook can read vCard files that you may receive from people using other email software. They work the same way as Outlook contacts that were described in the previous section — double-click the attachment to add the information to your address book. Outlook users can also send vCards to other people — this is explained later in the chapter in the section "Sending Contact Information by Email."

Working with Distribution Lists

A distribution list is a collection of two or more contacts. You can easily send an email message to everyone on the list simply by selecting the list from your address book when addressing the message — there's no need to add each person individually to the message's To field.

Creating a Distribution List

To create a distribution list, click the down arrow next to the New button on the toolbar and select Distribution List from the menu. Outlook will open a distribution list form as shown in Figure 10.10. The form is initially empty, of course — this example shows some names that have been added.

FIGURE 10.10

A distribution list can contain two or more contacts.

To add contacts that are already in your address book, click the Select Members button. Outlook displays the Select Members dialog box as shown in Figure 10.11. If you have more than one address book you have to select the desired one in the Address Book list. Then select individual contacts by clicking (Ctrl+Click to select more than one) and click the Members button followed by the OK button. You can also select existing distribution lists to add to the new list.

FIGURE 10.11

Selecting contacts from your address book to add to a distribution list.

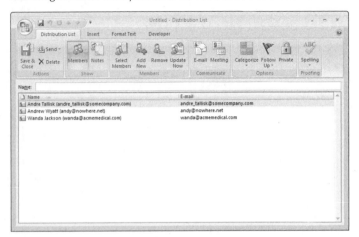

To add a contact that is not in your address book to the list, click the Add New button. Outlook displays the Add New Member dialog box (see Figure 10.12). Enter the new contact's name and email address and select the Add to Contacts option if you want the person added as an individual entry to your contacts list as well as to this distribution list. Then, click OK.

FIGURE 10.12

Adding a contact who is not in your address book to a distribution list.

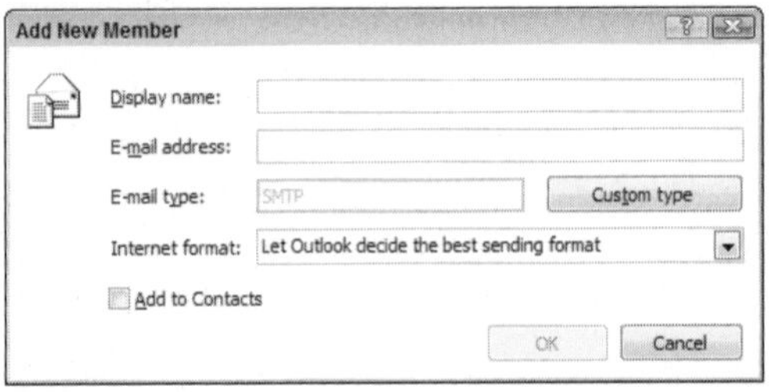

Updating a Distribution List

Suppose that one of your contacts changes her email address and you make the necessary edit in her entry in your address book. This change will *not* be reflected automatically in any distribution lists this person is part of. You must manually update the list by opening it and clicking the Update Now button on the ribbon.

Using Distribution Lists

In many ways, a distribution list is like an individual entry in your address book. When a distribution list is open, you can use the various buttons on the ribbon (E-mail, Meeting, Categorize, and so on) just like you do for an individual contact (these are described elsewhere in this chapter). You can also send a distribution list as an attachment to an email message as described in this chapter in the section "Sending Contact Information by Email."

When you address an email message to a distribution list, the list name is displayed in the To or Cc field of the message with an adjacent + sign, as shown in Figure 10.13. If you click this + sign, the list will be expanded to its individual members just as if you had added them individually to the To or Cc field. This can be useful if you want to send a message to everyone on the list except one or two people — you can expand the distribution list and delete those few individuals from the To or Cc field of the message.

FIGURE 10.13

A distribution list in the To field of an email message.

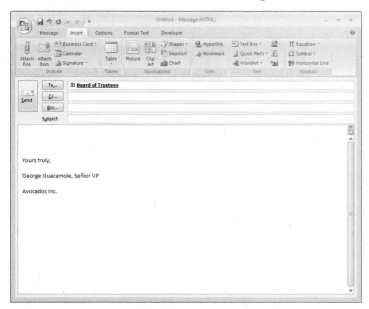

More About Contacts

Outlook contacts are much more than a simple address book. This section covers additional details and capabilities of Outlook contacts.

The Contact Form

The contact form, shown in Figure 10.14, provides places for you to enter many different kinds of information about a contact. The only field that is required is the name — you can use all, some, or none of the other fields as required. Some of the elements on the contact form may benefit from an explanation.

FIGURE 10.14

The contact form provides fields for a wide variety of information about the contact.

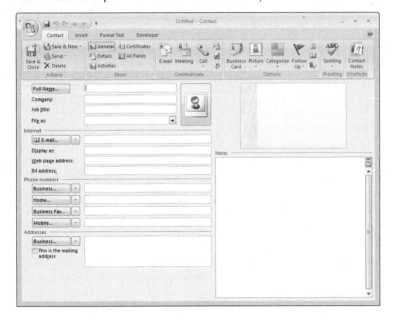

Full Name

You can simply enter a contact's name in the Full Name field in the usual way, for example John Q. Public. You can also click the adjacent Full Name button to bring up the Check Full Name dialog box as shown in Figure 10.15. Here you can specify a title such as Dr. or Mrs. and a suffix such as Jr. or Sr.

Quick Email

When a contact is open, click the E-mail button on the ribbon to create a new email message addressed to the contact.

FIGURE 10.15

The Check Full Name dialog box lets you enter more details for a contact's name.

Note the option in this dialog box: Show This Again When a Name Is Incomplete or Unclear. When this option is on (the default), Outlook will open this dialog box automatically when you enter an unclear name such as "Fred" in the Full Name field.

The File As field determines how a contact will be filed in the address book. The default is last name first (Public, John Q.) but you can also choose to file a contact first name first.

Phone Numbers

The Phone Numbers section of the contact form provides spaces for four numbers. By default these are labeled as Business, Home, Business Fax, and Mobile, but you can change which numbers are displayed in a particular phone number field by clicking the adjacent down arrow and selecting from the list. Some of the choices available are Home Fax, Pager, and Assistant. Outlook will save a phone number for each designation but only four numbers will be displayed on the contact form at one time. When you open the list of designations, those for which you have entered a phone number will be checked.

Next to each phone number field is a button with the field's designation on it. If you click one of these buttons, Outlook opens the Check Phone Number dialog box as shown in Figure 10.16. Here you can enter additional details for the phone number if desired.

FIGURE 10.16

The Check Phone Number dialog box lets you enter more details for a contact's phone number.

Addresses

The Addresses section of the contact form can store up to three addresses designated as Home, Business, and Other. Select the one to display by clicking the down arrow adjacent to the address box. Click the adjacent button to open the Check Address dialog box (see Figure 10.17) where you can enter or edit address details. By default, Outlook will display this dialog box automatically if you enter an address that appears to be incomplete or unclear.

FIGURE 10.17

The Check Address dialog box lets you enter more details for a contact's address.

One of the addresses for a contact can be designated as the mailing address by selecting the corresponding option. Outlook uses this address when you are doing a mail merge using Outlook contact data. Mail Merge is discussed later in this chapter.

Picture

You can associate a picture with a contact by clicking the Picture button on the contact form. Outlook displays a dialog box that lets you browse for the picture file. When you have associated a picture with a contact, it displays on the picture button and also on the contact's business card, as shown in Figure 10.18. To remove or change the picture, right-click it and choose from the context menu.

FIGURE 10.18

You can associate a picture with a contact.

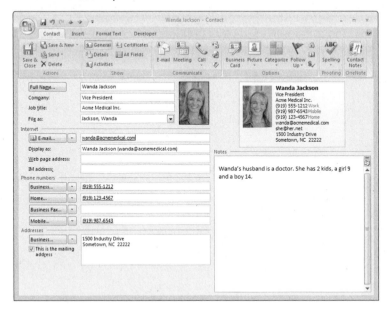

Email Addresses

Outlook can store as many as three email addresses for a contact, designated as E-Mail, E-Mail 2, and E-Mail 3. You select which one to display on the contact form using the arrow adjacent to the E-mail field.

If you create an email message to a contact by clicking the E-mail button on the ribbon on a contact form, Outlook will create a message addressed to all the email addresses for that contact. If you click the To button on an email message, the list of contacts will display each email separately and you can choose the one to use.

The Display As field determines how the contact is displayed in a message's To or Cc field. By default Outlook displays the contact's name followed by the email address in parentheses, but you can edit this to display as desired—for example, just the person's name.

Notes

The Notes section on a contact form is for entry of any arbitrary information that you want to save with the contact. Simply click in the box and enter/edit as usual. You can use the tools on the Format text ribbon to apply formatting to the notes text, if desired.

Other Contact Displays

The default contact display, called General, has been shown in the figures throughout this chapter so far. This is the display that you will probably use most often. There are several other displays, or views, available — you select the display to view from the Show section of the Contact ribbon.

Details

The Details view gives you access to secondary information about a contact. This display is shown in Figure 10.19. This information includes fields such as Department, Office, Nickname, Spouse/Partner, as well as details for the person's NetMeeting settings. You may never use this view but it's available if you need it.

FIGURE 10.19

The Details view for a contact.

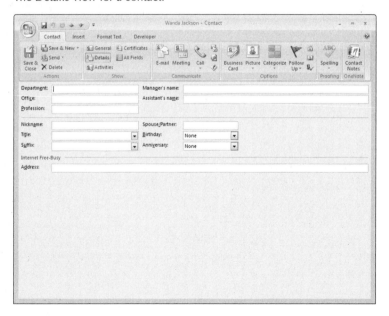

Certificates

One of the security features available in Outlook is digital certificates. A contact can send you a certificate. You can then use this certificate to send encrypted mail to that person. The Certificates display lets you view and work with the certificate(s) that you have for a contact. Digital certificates are covered in detail in the chapter on security (Chapter 20).

All Fields

The All Fields display lets you view all or selected subsets of the data associated with a contact. The amount of information — number of fields — that an individual contact can hold is quite impressive, way too much to display fully in any other contact view. The All Fields display also lets you define your own custom fields for a contact and to change the properties of some fields.

The All Fields display is shown in Figure 10.20. Near the top is the Select From list where you choose which fields to display in the window. You can display all fields and can also display one of several defined subsets such as All Contact Fields or All Mail Fields.

FIGURE 10.20

The All Fields view for a contact.

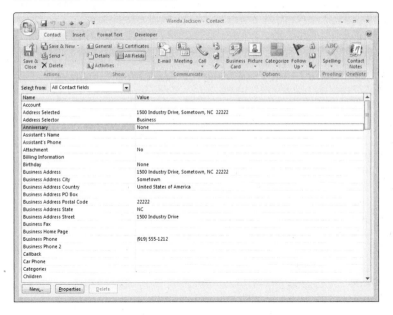

Some fields can be edited in this view by clicking in the Value column and making the desired changes. Other fields are generated internally by Outlook and cannot be edited.

You can add a custom field to the contact by clicking the New button at the bottom of the window. Outlook displays the New Field dialog box (see Figure 10.21) where you enter a name for the field (which cannot duplicate an existing field name). You also select the data type for the field. Your choices are Text, Number, Percent, Currency, Yes/No, and Date/Time. For certain data types you can also select a format from the Format list. When you are finished, click OK and the custom field will be added to the All Fields display.

FIGURE 10.21

Defining a new field for a contact.

You can change the properties of a field by clicking it in the list and then clicking the Properties button. This is relevant only for user-defined fields — the properties of Outlook's built-in fields are locked.

Editing the Business Card

Outlook creates a business card for each contact based on a default template. As you can see in Figure 10.22, this template includes name, company, title, phone numbers, email and postal addresses, and a photo (assuming these elements are part of the contact).

FIGURE 10.22

The default business card template includes the most often needed information.

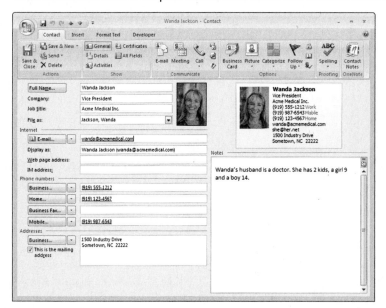

To edit the business card for a contact, click the Business Card button on the Contact ribbon. Outlook opens the Edit Business Card dialog box, shown in Figure 10.23.

FIGURE 10.23

Editing the business card for an individual contact.

The top-left section of this dialog previews how the business card will look with your edits. The top-right section defines the overall layout of the card:

- **Layout:** Specifies the image location. You can also omit the image or use it as the card background.
- **Background:** Lets you select a background color for the card.
- **Image:** Click the Change button to specify a different image.
- **Image Area:** Determines how much of the card is occupied by the image. The maximum is 50%.
- **Image Align:** Determines how the image is positioned within the image area.

The lower-left section of the Edit Business Card dialog box lets you specify the data fields that are included on the card and their order. You can:

- Click Add, then select from the menu to add a field to the card.
- Click Remove to remove the selected field from the card.
- Click the up or down arrow to change the position of the selected field.

The lower-right section of this dialog box is for text formatting. When a field is selected in the Fields list, use the tools here to:

- Increase or decrease font size.
- Make font bold, italic, or underlined.
- Align text left, center, or right.
- Change font color.

Oddly enough, you cannot change the font used on a business card, just its size.

The Label section lets you add a label to any data field. You can specify the text of the label, its color, and whether it is displayed to the left or right of the item.

Click the Reset Card button to undo any edits you have made and return the card to the default appearance. Click OK to save your changes and close the dialog box.

Dialing the Phone

If your computer is equipped with a modem, you can have Outlook dial the phone for you based on the number associated with a contact. Then you can pick up your handset and complete the call as usual. This requires that the modem and handset be on the same line, which can be inconvenient if you use the modem to access the Internet. If your Internet connection is via cable modem or DSL, or via a second telephone line, you may want to use an old modem as a dedicated dialer on your voice line. The speed of the modem is not relevant in this application.

When a contact is open, click the arrow on the Call button to display the menu shown in Figure 10.24. This menu lists all the phone numbers for the current contact. Select the one to dial and Outlook opens the New Call dialog box (see Figure 10.25) with the selected phone number entered. The settings and commands in this dialog box are

- **Dialing Properties:** Opens the dialing properties where you define rules for dialing from your computer. You should not have to change these because they are set up when you install and configure your modem.
- **Create New Journal Entry...:** Creates an Outlook journal entry for the call, noting the number called and the time and date of the call.
- **Dialing Options:** Lets you set speed dialer options and add names and numbers to the speed-dial list.
- **Start Call:** Dial the number.
- **End Call:** Hang up.

FIGURE 10.24

Using Outlook to dial the phone.

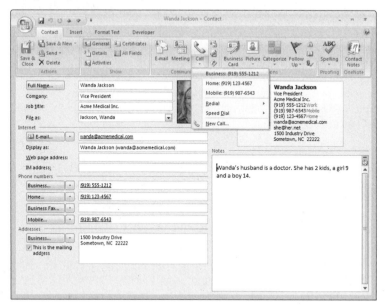

FIGURE 10.25

The New Call dialog box.

The Call menu has several other commands:

- **Redial:** Dial a recently called number.
- **Speed Dial:** Dial a number on your speed-dial list.
- **New Call:** Opens the New Call dialog box without any phone number entered.

Outlook can also make Instant Messenger calls. If you have specified an Instant Messenger address for the contact, this option will appear on the Call menu.

Sending Contact Information by Email

It can be very useful to send contact information attached to an email message. This lets recipients enter the information in their address book quickly and without errors. If you keep an entry for yourself in your address book, you can easily send your own information as well.

Sending Contact Information in Outlook Format

Outlook offers two formats for sending contact information. Outlook's native format is to send the information as an Outlook item. You can send individual contacts and distribution lists this way. Information sent this way can be used by other Outlook users and possibly by users of other email programs that support this format. To send contact information as an Outlook item:

1. Create and address the email message as usual.

2. On the Insert ribbon, click the Insert Item button. Outlook displays the Insert Item dialog box (see Figure 10.26).

3. In the Look In list at the top of the dialog box, click the Contacts folder.

4. In the Items list at the bottom of the dialog box, click the contact or distribution list to send. Hold down the Ctrl key while clicking to select more than one contact.

5. Make sure the Attachment option is selected. If you select the Text Only option, the information will be added to the body of the message but the recipient will not be able to automatically add it to their address book.

6. Click OK. The item, with a small business card icon, will be added to the message's attachment list.

FIGURE 10.26

Inserting an item into an email message.

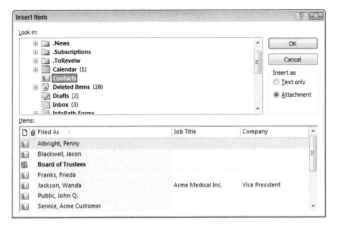

Sending Contact Information in vCard Format

The second format for sending contact information is vCard, a widely supported format for contact information. Most email programs support this format and you may want to use it when you are not sure that all the intended recipients use an email program that supports Outlook items. You can send only individual contacts using a vCard, not distribution lists. To send a vCard:

1. Open the contact that you want to send.
2. In the Contact window, click the File button and select Save As from the File menu. Outlook displays the Save As dialog box (see Figure 10.27).
3. Use the dialog box tools to navigate to the location where you want to save the vCard file.
4. In the Save as Type list, select vCard Files (*.vcf).
5. The default name for the file is the contact name. You can edit this if desired.
6. Click Save.
7. Create an email message and attach the vCard file that you just saved.

FIGURE 10.27

Saving a contact as a vCard file.

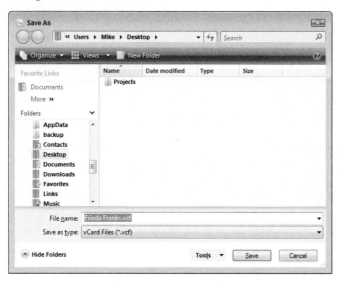

Sending Contact Information from the Contact Form

When you have a contact open, the Actions section of the ribbon includes a Send button. You can use this button to send the open contact in one of three ways by selecting the desired command from the associated menu:

- **Send as Business Card:** Outlook creates a new message with the contact inserted in the message body as a business card and attached to the message as a vCard file.

- **In Internet Format (vCard):** Outlook creates a new message with the contact attached to the message as a vCard file.

- **In Outlook Format:** Outlook creates a new message with the contact attached to the message as an Outlook item.

Other Contact Actions

This section describes some of the other actions you can perform with contacts.

Viewing a Map of the Contact's Address

If a contact has a valid address entered, you can click the Map button on the Contact ribbon to open a web browser and view a map of the specified location. This feature is powered by the Windows Live Local web site, which provides other services such as driving directions and business search.

Inviting the Contact to a Meeting

To invite the contact to a meeting, click the Meeting button on the Contact ribbon. Outlook creates a new meeting request addressed to the contact, as shown in Figure 10.28. You can specify the subject and location, enter the date, start and end times, and include a message. You can also add other recipients to the request. You learn all about meeting requests in Chapter 12.

FIGURE 10.28

Sending a meeting request to a contact.

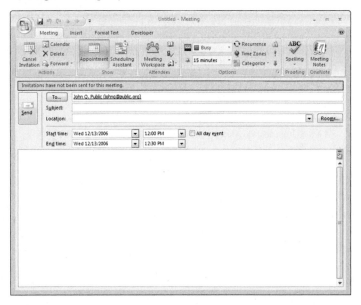

Use the Context Menus

Many of the actions that you can take with contacts that are described in this section can be accessed without opening the contact. In the Contacts window, simply right-click the contact and select from the context menu. You can use this technique to send a contact, call a contact, or assign a follow-up of category to a contact.

Assigning a Task to a Contact

To assign a new task to a contact, click the Assign Task button on the Contact ribbon. Outlook opens a task window, as shown in Figure 10.29, where you can enter details of the task and save it. You learn more about tasks, including assigning an existing task to a contact, in Chapter 15.

Viewing the Contact's Web Page

If you have entered a web page URL for a contact, clicking the Web Page button on the Contact ribbon launches your default web browser and displays the web page.

Tagging a Contact for Follow Up

To tag a contact for follow up, click the Follow Up button in the Options section of the Contact ribbon and select the desired follow-up interval from the menu.

FIGURE 10.29

Assigning a task to a contact.

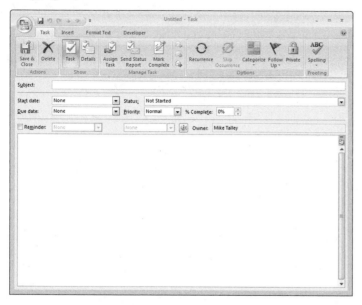

Performing a Mail Merge from Your Contacts

Mail merge is a technique that lets a form letter be addressed and sent to many different individuals. It can also be used to create mailing labels, envelopes, and catalogs such as a mailing list. Microsoft Office has merge tools built in to several of its applications, most notably Word, and Outlook is included in this list.

When would you use Outlook to perform a mail merge? Only when the names and addresses that you want to use are in your Outlook address book. In this situation, using Outlook is often the simplest approach. Even so, there are some factors that may mitigate against using Outlook for a merge and instead using the more advanced mail merge tools available in other Office applications. For example, Outlook cannot separate documents by ZIP code to get reduced mailing rates, and it would not be a good choice for a large merge that will create thousands of documents. You need to have Microsoft Word installed on your system to perform a mail merge.

The first step in performing a mail merge is usually to filter your contacts so that only the ones you want included are shown. You can do this by using Outlook's search capability or by customizing the Contacts view, both of which were covered earlier in this chapter. However, you can skip this step and select the contacts to include later. Then:

1. Make sure Contacts are active.

2. Select Mail Merge from the Tools menu. Outlook displays the Mail Merge dialog box as shown in Figure 10.30.

FIGURE 10.30

Performing a mail merge with Outlook contacts.

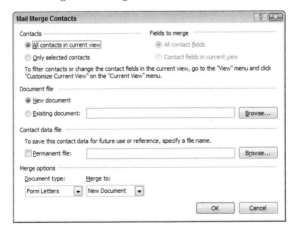

3. Make entries in this dialog box as described in the following list.

4. Click OK to open Word to complete the merge.

The options in the Mail Merge dialog box are as follows:

- **Contacts:** Select All Contacts in Current View to include all displayed contacts in the merge. Select Only Selected Contacts to select contacts to include later.

- **Fields to Merge:** Specifies whether only visible contact fields or all contact fields will be available for the merge. These options may or may not be available depending on the current Contacts view.

- **Document File:** Specifies whether the merge will use a new or an existing Word document. If you choose the latter option, use the Browse button to locate the document to use.

- **Contact Data File:** You can select this option to save the merge contact data in a separate Word document. Typically this option is used to create a record of the people who were included in the mailing.

- **Document Type:** You can merge to form letters, mailing labels, envelopes, or a catalog.

- **Merge To:** Specify whether the merge output goes to a Word document, to the printer, or to email:

  - **New Document:** Merge creates a Word document that you can edit as needed before creating the final output.

  - **Printer:** The merged document is created and sent directly to the default printer.

  - **E-mail:** The merged documents are created as email messages and placed in your Outbox.

In most situations the remainder of the merge process is carried out in Word. Please consult your Word documentation for information on how to do this.

Working with Multiple Address Books

The majority of Outlook users will have only a single address book. This is all that most people need, in fact. In some situations you may have two or more address books. This can happen if you create more than one Outlook data file. Each data file will have its own address book, and you will have access to the one in whichever Outlook data file is open. You might want to use more than one Outlook data file if you want to keep your personal email completely separate from your work email. You learn more about working with Outlook data files in Chapter 18.

Another situation where you will have more than one address book is if you have both a regular (that is, SMTP/POP) email account and a Microsoft Exchange account set up in Outlook. The regular account will have its own address book and the Exchange account will have another, separate one. You will have both available to you at the same time in Outlook—they will be listed at the top of the navigation pane when Contacts are active, and you can choose to view one or the other. When you add a contact it will be added to whichever address book is active. Exchange address books have some additional capabilities such as sharing—this is covered in Chapter 28.

Setting Contact Options

Outlook has some global options that affect the way contacts work. To view and change these options:

1. Select Options from the Tools menu to display the Options dialog box.

2. If necessary, click the Preferences tab.

3. Click the Contact Options button to display the Contact Options dialog box (see Figure 10.31).

4. Set options as described in the following list.

5. Click OK twice to exit all dialog boxes.

FIGURE 10.31

Setting global options for contacts.

The options that are available for contacts are described here:

- **Default "Full Name" Order:** Specifies how contacts are sorted when you order them based on full name. You can choose First Middle Last, Last First, or First Last1 Last2.

- **Default "File As" Order:** Specifies how contacts are sorted when you order them based on the File As field. Your choices are Last First, First Last, Company, Last First (Company), Company (Last, First).

- **Check for Duplicate Contacts:** If this option is selected, Outlook will warn you if you try to enter a new contact with the same name as an existing contact.

- **Show Contact Linking on All Forms:** Controls whether all information linked to a contact (tasks, for example) is displayed.

- **Show an Additional Contacts Index:** If this option is selected, Outlook will display a second set of index buttons at the right edge of the Contacts window using the language you select from the list.

Summary

Outlook contacts is a powerful tool for managing and using information about people. It goes way beyond the basic address book to store just about any kind of information about a person you can imagine. What's more, it makes it easy to find and use that information in various ways. Many people find contacts to be one of Outlook's most useful tools.

Chapter 11

Working with the Calendar

A calendar is something you hang on the wall, right? It has a page for each month and a picture of a puppy, lighthouse, or famous painting. If that's what you think, then you haven't used the Outlook Calendar! Outlook provides a sophisticated calendar that helps you manage your time efficiently. It can even do things such as remind you of an upcoming appointment, help you set up meetings, and let you share your calendar with others.

This chapter covers the Outlook Calendar itself. Some other Outlook tools related to the Calendar are covered in other chapters: scheduling and meetings in Chapter 12 and tasks in Chapter 15.

Understanding the Outlook Calendar

At its heart, the Outlook Calendar stores and displays appointments. An *appointment* is just what it sounds like — a scheduled event with a title and a time/date specified for the beginning and end of the appointment. Outlook distinguishes between two types of appointments:

- A regular appointment has a specific start time and stop time. They are usually on the same day but do not have to be.

- An all-day event does not have specific start and stop times but rather takes up all of one or more days.

Scheduling appointments may not sound so special, and in fact it's not. But it's the way that Outlook lets you organize, use, and share your appointments that makes the Calendar so useful.

Using the Calendar

To show the Calendar, click the Calendar button in the navigation pane. The view window shows the Calendar itself, and you'll get to that in a moment. The top section of the navigation pane shows a small calendar of the current month, called the *Date Navigator*, which has several useful features, as shown in Figure 11.1.

- Today's date is enclosed in a box—the 22nd in the figure.
- The days displayed in the larger Calendar view are highlighted in the small calendar. In the figure, this is the 21st through the 25th.
- Days on which there is at least one appointment are in bold.
- The arrows to the left and right of the month and year can be clicked to move to the previous or next month, updating the Calendar view as well.
- Click any day number to change the Calendar view accordingly.

FIGURE 11.1

In Calendar view, the navigation pane displays the Date Navigator.

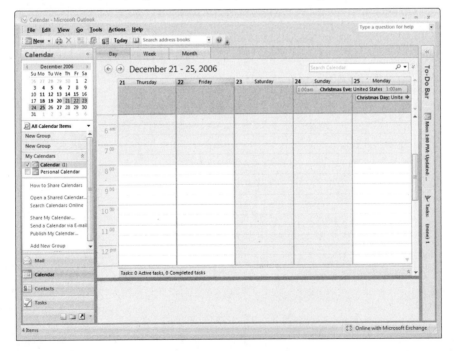

No Date Navigator?

If the Date Navigator is not displayed in the navigation pane, it is probably because it is displayed in the To-Do Bar. The Date Navigator is displayed in one place or the other, not both. You learn about the To-Do Bar later in this chapter.

Working with Calendar Views

When the Calendar is displayed, you can choose between viewing a single day, a week, or an entire month. In Week view, you can also choose to view the entire week or just the work week (Monday–Friday), and in Month view you can set the level of detail display to low, medium, or high. You select your view using the buttons at the top of the Calendar. In this area, Outlook also displays the date or date range displayed as well as buttons that move the calendar forward or back by one of whatever unit (day, week, or month) is displayed. This is shown in Figure 11.2.

FIGURE 11.2

The Outlook Calendar can display a day, a week, or a month at a time.

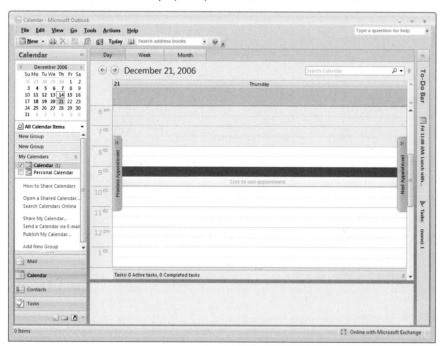

Finding Today

No matter what day, week, or month you are viewing in the Calendar, you can always go directly to the current day by clicking the Today button on the toolbar.

Using the Calendar Day View

When the Calendar is displaying a single day, it looks as shown in Figure 11.3. Times of the day are listed at the left edge of the window, and each appointment is displayed in its assigned time slot. Use the scroll bar to bring different times into view. Any all-day events for the day will be displayed at the top of the window.

FIGURE 11.3

The Outlook Calendar displaying a single day's appointments.

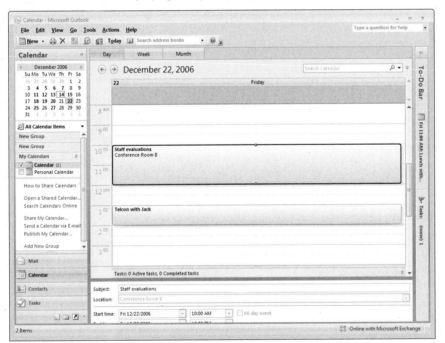

Click an appointment to select it — it will display with a black border and small handles (boxes) on the top and bottom border. You can:

- Point at the appointment and drag to move it to a different time slot.
- Point at one of the handles and drag it to change either the start or stop time.

If you double-click an appointment, it will open for editing, as explained later in this chapter.

Using the Calendar Week View

The Calendar Week view is shown in Figure 11.4. This example shows only the work week — you can display the full seven-day week by selecting the Show Full Week option at the top of the window.

In essence, the Week view is five or seven single-day views side-by-side and you can perform the same actions as described for the Day view. You can also drag an appointment to a different day.

NOTE You'll note in the figure that when an appointment is selected, its details are displayed at the bottom of the window in the reading pane. This can be useful when the Calendar itself is too crowded to show these details for each appointment.

FIGURE 11.4

The Outlook Calendar displaying an entire week's appointments.

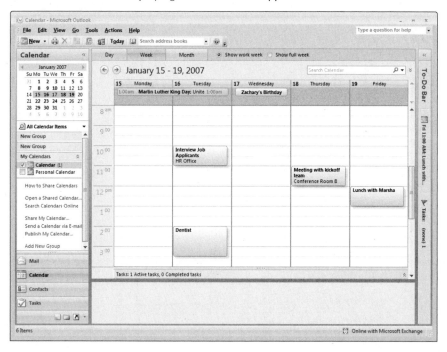

Displaying the Reading Pane

If the reading pane is not displayed, turn it on by selecting Reading Pane from the View menu and then selecting the desired position — bottom or right. You can also toggle the reading pane display with the Reading Pane button on the toolbar.

Using the Calendar Month View

Month view shows an entire month of appointments, as shown in Figure 11.5. Appointments for each day are displayed in order but without time details. If an all-day event exists for the day, it is displayed at the top with a line around it — for example, the "Meeting with Sales Staff" appointment in the figure on the 13th and 14th. If there are more appointments for a day than can be shown, a small down arrow is displayed. Click the arrow to open the single day display where you can view all appointments for that date.

FIGURE 11.5

The Outlook Calendar displaying a month's appointments.

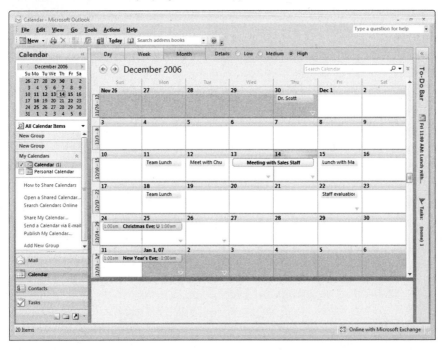

Customizing the Calendar View

If you open the Current View list on the toolbar you'll see an item called *Define Views*. This command lets you define a custom view for the Calendar, and is covered in Chapter 19.

The figure shows the month display with the High option selected for details. You can also select Low or Medium details:

- **Low:** Shows only all-day events. Appointments with specific start and stop times are not displayed.

- **Medium:** All-day events are displayed as usual. Appointments with specific start and stop times are displayed as shaded lines or rectangles with the position and thickness of the line or rectangle indicating the approximate time and duration of the appointment.

Using the To-Do Bar with Appointments

Outlook's To-Do Bar can be useful for working with Calendar items. To display the To-Do Bar, select To-Do Bar from the View menu and then select Normal. The To-Do Bar is shown in Figure 11.6.

FIGURE 11.6

The To-Do Bar can display the Date Navigator and upcoming appointments.

To-Do Bar Appointment Display

Y ou can specify how many appointments are displayed in the To-Do Bar—the default is three. However many you choose to display, the To-Do Bar always displays the appointments that are coming up the soonest.

The To-Do Bar can display three items:

- The Date Navigator, a small monthly calendar whose features were explained earlier in this chapter. If the Date Navigator is displayed in the To-Do Bar it will not be displayed in the navigation pane.
- A list of appointments for the current week.
- A list of tasks. Tasks are not directly related to the Calendar and are explained in Chapter 15.

You can control what is displayed on the To-Do Bar. You can display all, two, or one of the items in the preceding list. To change the To-Do Bar display, select To-Do Bar from the View menu and then check or uncheck the individual items—Date Navigator, Appointments, and Task List—on the next menu. You can also select Options from this menu to display the To-Do Bar Options dialog box, shown in Figure 11.7. Here you can turn the display of individual items on or off as well as specify how many months are displayed in the Date Navigator and how many appointments are displayed.

FIGURE 11.7

Setting To-Do Bar display options.

Working with Appointments

An Outlook appointment can be very simple, or you can use Outlook's tools to add various features and options to an appointment. Start with the basics of creating a simple appointment and then look at the various options.

Creating a Simple Appointment

To create a simple appointment, make sure that Outlook is displaying the Calendar. Then you do either of the following:

- Click the New button on the toolbar. Outlook opens a new appointment form for whatever day is selected in the Calendar.

- Double-click a day on the Calendar. Outlook opens a new appointment form for that day.

The appointment form is shown in Figure 11.8 before any information has been entered. Then:

FIGURE 11.8

An Outlook appointment form.

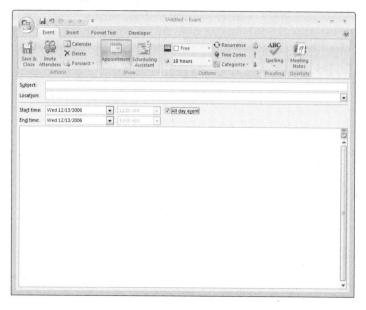

1. At a minimum, you must enter a subject for the appointment. This is the title of the appointment and is displayed in the Calendar — or at least part of it is, depending on the length.

2. Optionally, enter a location for the appointment. If you click the arrow adjacent to the Location field, Outlook will display a list of previously used locations from which you can select. Otherwise, just type the location into the field. Space allowing, the location displays along with the appointment subject in the Calendar.

3. If necessary, adjust the start and/or stop date by clicking the arrow next to the displayed date and selecting from the calendar that Outlook displays. An appointment could span two or more days, if needed.

4. If the appointment is an all-day event, make sure the All Day Event option is selected. An all-day event marks one or more entire days as busy with no specific start and stop times.

5. If the appointment is not an all-day event, make sure the All Day Event option is not checked. Outlook will display fields for the start and stop times.

6. To select a start or stop time, click the adjacent arrow and select from the list displayed (see Figure 11.9).

FIGURE 11.9

Selecting the stop time for an appointment.

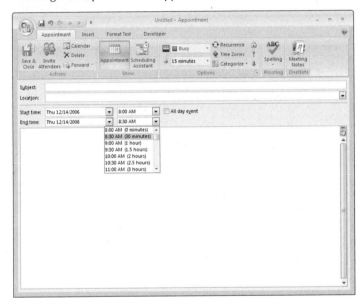

7. Optionally, enter any desired notes in the field provided.

8. Click the Save & Close button on the ribbon.

WARNING When you create an appointment that is an all-day event, Outlook does not mark the time as "busy" but rather keeps it marked as "free." If you want an all-day event to display on the Scheduling Page as either "tentative" or "busy" you must explicitly select this option in the Options section of the Event ribbon.

Editing and Deleting Appointments

To edit an appointment, double-click it in Calendar view to open the appointment form. Make any needed changes and click the Save & Close button on the ribbon.

Dealing with Conflicts

Outlook does not specifically warn you of potential conflicts — you are free to schedule overlapping appointments if you wish. When there's an overlap, Outlook displays a striped bar between the appointments in Week view and also in Day view.

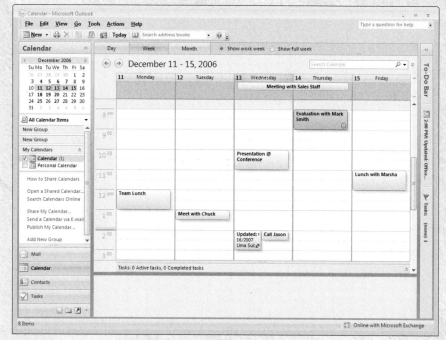

Outlook displays a striped bar between conflicting appointments.

To delete an appointment, click it in Calendar view to select it and press Del.

If you simply want to change the duration of an appointment, you can do so without opening the appointment form. When you select the appointment in the Calendar by clicking it, it will display small square handles on its border as shown in Figure 11.10. For a regular appointment, the handles will be at the top and bottom, as in the figure. Drag the top or bottom handle to change the appointment's start or stop time, respectively. For an all-day event the handles will be on the left and right edges, and can be dragged to change the start or stop time.

You can also change an appointment's time and/or date, without changing its duration, by pointing at the appointment and dragging it the new position on the Calendar.

FIGURE 11.10

Drag a selected appointment's handles to change its duration.

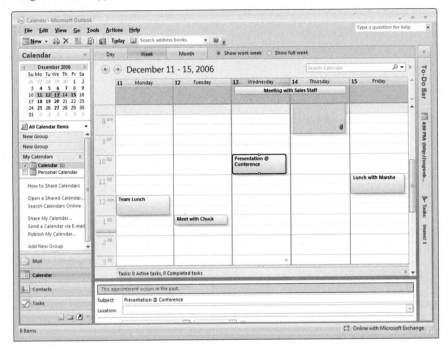

Appointment Options

When you create an appointment, there are several optional features you may want to use. They are described here.

Scheduling Recurring Events

Some events occur on a regular basis. Perhaps you have a chiropractor appointment at 10:00 AM every Monday, or a company strategy meeting on the first Tuesday of each month. You can enter such appointments only once and have Outlook create all the recurrences automatically. Here's how:

1. Use the techniques that you learned earlier in this chapter to create an appointment for the first instance, but do not save and close it.

2. In the appointment form, click the Recurrence button on the Appointment ribbon. Outlook displays the Appointment Recurrence dialog box as shown in Figure 11.11.

3. In the Appointment Time section of the dialog box, make sure that the start time and stop time are correct.

4. In the Recurrence Pattern section, select Daily, Weekly, Monthly, or Yearly.

5. Depending on the option selected in the previous step, enter other recurrence details:

   - **Daily:** Specify how often the appointment recurs (for example, every two days) or that it occurs every weekday.

   - **Weekly:** Specify how often the appointment recurs (for example, every week) and then on which day or days.

   - **Monthly:** Specify how often the appointment recurs (for example, every three months) and on which day. You can select a day by number, such as the 15th of every month. You can also select a day by day of week, such as the second Tuesday of the month.

6. Under Range of Recurrence, enter the starting date and then specify when the recurrences end. Your choices are

   - No end date.

   - End after a certain number of occurrences.

   - End by a specified date.

7. Click OK to return to the appointment form.

8. Complete any additional appointment details, as needed.

9. Click Save & Close.

FIGURE 11.11

Defining a recurring appointment.

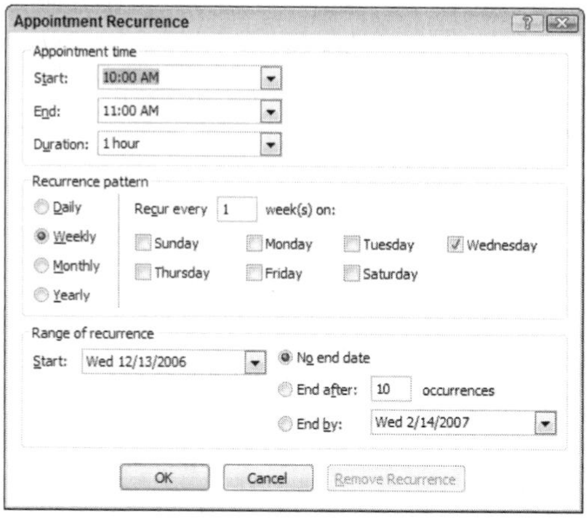

When you open an existing recurring appointment for editing, you can click the Recurrence button to open the Appointment Recurrence dialog box to modify the recurrence pattern. You can also remove the recurrence by clicking the Remove Recurrence button in this dialog box. Outlook will remove all instances of the appointment from the Calendar except the next one.

If you try to delete a recurring appointment, Outlook will give you the option of deleting all occurrences of the appointment or just the current one.

Using Appointment Reminders

Outlook can remind you of an appointment by displaying a dialog box and playing a sound. You can specify how much advance notice you get and also change the sound that is played. You can also turn reminders off. To set a reminder:

1. Create the appointment, or open an existing one for editing.

2. Click the Reminder list on the Appointment ribbon (see Figure 11.12).

3. Select the desired duration of the advance warning, from 0 minutes to 2 weeks. The default is 15 minutes before the start time, although you can change this in Calendar Options (covered later in this chapter). Select None for no reminder.

4. Select Sound to specify the sound played when a reminder is displayed. Turn off the Play This Sound option if you do not want a sound played (a dialog box is displayed).

5. Click OK to return to the appointment form.

FIGURE 11.12

Specifying the reminder interval for an appointment.

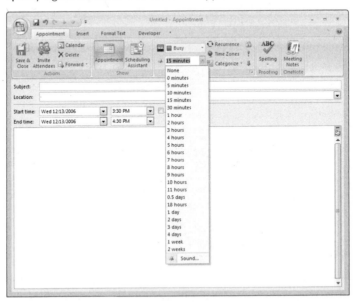

When a reminder comes due, Outlook plays the sound (if one was specified for the appointment) and displays the dialog box shown in Figure 11.13. If there is more than one reminder due, they will all be listed. The actions you can take are

- Click Dismiss to dismiss the selected reminder.

- If more than one reminder is listed, click Dismiss All to dismiss all the listed reminders.

- Click Open Item to open the corresponding appointment.

- Click Snooze to be reminded again in the specified time, selected from the adjacent list. You could, for example, choose to be reminded 5 minutes before the appointment's start time, or in 10 minutes from the current time.

FIGURE 11.13

The Appointment Reminder dialog box.

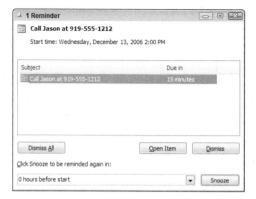

 When you dismiss a reminder, it does not affect the appointment itself, which will remain in your calendar.

Inviting Meeting Attendees

Outlook lets you invite other people to a meeting via email, and handle their responses automatically. Because this is a complex topic, it is covered in its own chapter along with tasks (Chapter 12).

Using Other Time Zones

By default, Outlook appointments use the time zone that your system is set up to use. At times you may want to use another time zone, for example if you are in New York and your client says "Call me at 8:00 AM, my time." You may not know the number of hours' difference, but as long as you know his time zone you are all set.

When you have the appointment form open, click the Time Zones button on the ribbon to display time zone selectors next to the start and stop time fields (see Figure 11.14). Change either the start or stop time zone to the desired setting; the other changes to the same thing. Now the start and stop times you enter are interpreted as being in the selected time zone, and the appointment is displayed in the correct local time slot. For example, if you are in the Eastern time zone and enter an appointment from 8:00 AM to 9:00 AM in the Pacific time zone, the appointment will display between 11:00 AM and 12:00 PM on your calendar because the Pacific zone is three hours behind the Eastern zone.

221

FIGURE 11.14

Basing an appointment on a different time zone than the one you are in.

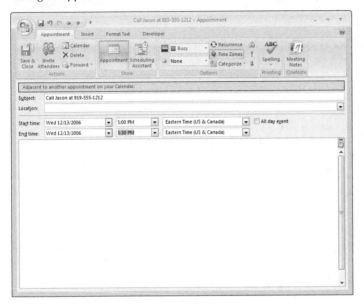

Forwarding an Appointment

Outlook lets you forward an appointment to an email recipient. Forwarding is different from inviting an attendee to a meeting (covered elsewhere in the next chapter). There are two ways to forward an Outlook appointment:

- Open the appointment and click the Forward button on the Appointment ribbon.
- Right-click the appointment in the Calendar and select Forward from the Context menu.

Another Way to Forward an Appointment

Forwarding an appointment as described here has exactly the same result as inserting an appointment item into an email message, as was described in Chapter 4. Briefly, you create the email message first, then use the Attach Item command to browse for the desired appointment in the Calendar folder.

In either case, Outlook creates a new email message with the appointment attached as an Outlook item and the title of the appointment inserted in the Subject field. You then address and complete the email message as usual. If you are using Outlook with an Exchange Server account, the appointment itself is forwarded without being attached to an email message.

When the recipient receives a forwarded appointment, he or she can double-click the attachment to open it. It will open in an appointment window, and the user can save it to his or her calendar or discard it as desired. Of course, the recipient must be using Outlook or another program that supports the Outlook appointment format.

Another forwarding option for appointments is the iCalendar format. This is a widely supported format for calendar information and is supported by Outlook as well as many other scheduling programs. If you are not sure that all your recipients are using Outlook, it may be a good idea to use this format when forwarding an appointment. To do so:

1. In an open appointment, click the arrow next to the Forward button.
2. Select Forward as iCalendar from the menu. Outlook creates a new email message with the iCalendar attached.
3. Complete and send the message as usual.

Assigning Appointments to Categories

As with most Outlook items, an appointment can be assigned to a category. Outlook comes with six predefined and color-coded categories. Initially they are named according to their color, but you can change this to more meaningful names such as "Work" or "Personal." You learn more about Outlook categories in Chapter 17.

There are two ways to assign an appointment to a category:

- With the appointment open, click the Categorize button and select the desired category from the list displayed. Select Clear All Categories to remove any assigned categories from the appointment.
- In the Calendar, right-click the appointment and select Categorize from the context menu. Then, select the desired category.

An appointment, like other Outlook items, can be assigned to more than one category. In the Calendar, a categorized appointment is displayed in the color of the assigned category.

Setting Appointment Importance

By default, all appointments you create are assigned normal importance. You can assign either low or high importance to an open appointment by clicking the corresponding button on the ribbon, as shown in Figure 11.15. Then you can use this importance level as a criterion when using the search feature in your Calendar, as discussed elsewhere in this chapter.

FIGURE 11.15

Assigning low or high importance to an appointment.

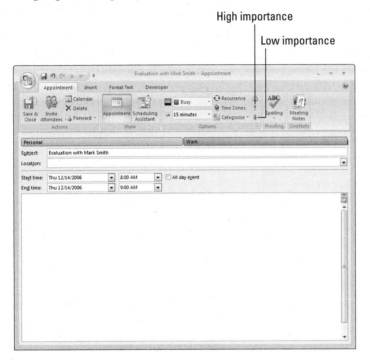

Marking an Appointment as Private

Outlook gives you the ability to publish your calendar so that other people can view your schedule. This topic is covered elsewhere in this chapter. You may at times want to mark an appointment as private so that other people viewing your calendar cannot see the details. They will still be able to see that you are busy during the period of the appointment but will not have access to details about the appointment.

To mark an open appointment as private, click the padlock button on the Appointment ribbon (see Figure 11.16).

FIGURE 11.16

Marking an appointment as private.

Click to mark private

Determining How an Appointment Displays on the Scheduling Page

Outlook's Scheduling Page provides a quick visual view of your schedule and the schedules of other people whose calendars you have imported. It is a very useful tool for finding time that is free for all the people you want to attend a meeting. Using the Scheduling Page is covered in detail in the next chapter.

An appointment in your calendar can display in one of several ways on the Scheduling Page — Busy, Tentative, Out of Office, or Free. This affects both your own Scheduling Page as well as that of other people with whom you are sharing your calendar. When you create an appointment, you can specify how it will display. The default is "busy" (except for all-day events as mentioned earlier in this chapter). To do so, click the Show As list on the Appointment ribbon and select from the list (see Figure 11.17).

Why Display an Appointment as "Free?"

It may seem strange that Outlook gives you the option of displaying an appointment as "free" on the Scheduling Page. It makes sense, however, when you realize that some appointments are not critical and can easily be changed. For example, you can just as well get that haircut tomorrow as today. By displaying such appointments as free, you will not prevent other people from scheduling a meeting at that time when they view your schedule.

FIGURE 11.17

Specifying how an appointment will display on the Scheduling Page.

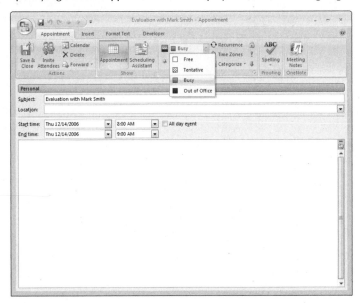

Searching the Calendar

As your calendar becomes filled with appointments past and future, it will become difficult if not impossible to find information by simply scrolling through the Calendar. You can use the search feature to filter the Calendar to show just the information you want. For example, you could filter to show only appointments within a certain month assigned to a specific category.

For a basic search, enter your search term in the Search Calendar box at the top right of the Calendar display (see Figure 11.18). You can also click the down arrow to select from previously used search terms. Outlook automatically searches as you enter the term and displays only matching appointments (or a message if there are no matching entries). Click the X adjacent to the Search box to cancel the search and return to displaying all Calendar items.

If you need more control over the search, click the double down arrow at the top-right corner of the Calendar display. Outlook displays additional criterion fields as shown in Figure 11.19. Each field lets you enter a search term or select from a drop-down list. As you make entries, the Calendar display is automatically filtered to show only matching entries. You can also take the following actions:

- To change a displayed criterion field — for example, from Categories to Sensitivity — click the arrow adjacent to the field name and select from the list displayed.

- To remove a criterion field, click the arrow adjacent to the field name and select Remove.

- To add a new criterion field, click Add Criteria and select from the list.

- To cancel the search and display all Calendar entries, click the X to the right of the Search Calendar box.

- To hide the additional criterion fields, click the double up arrow at the top-right corner of the Calendar display.

FIGURE 11.18

Performing a basic search of the Calendar.

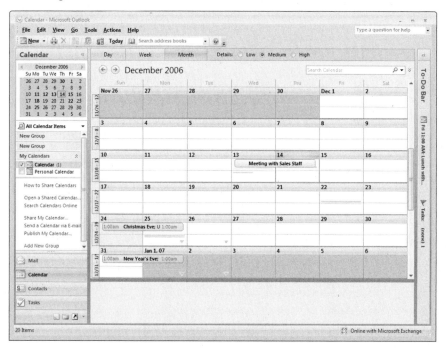

FIGURE 11.19

Performing an advanced search of the Calendar.

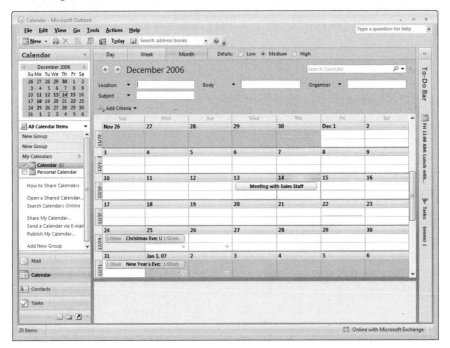

Sharing Your Calendar with Others

Outlook lets you publish your calendar so other people can have access to the information it contains. For example, if you manage a bowling team you can keep the team schedule in an Outlook calendar and publish it so team members can access it on the Internet.

You have two options as to how your calendar is shared:

- A *calendar snapshot* that is a static copy of your calendar at the time it is published.
- A *dynamic calendar* that can be automatically updated with changes you make to your calendar.

You also have two options as to where the calendar is published (these are applicable only to dynamic calendar sharing):

- To Microsoft Office Online, a Microsoft service that uses Windows Live ID credentials to control access to the information.
- To a web server that supports the WebDAV protocol.

Calendar Sharing with Exchange

Outlook users who have a Microsoft Exchange account have additional calendar sharing options available to them. These are covered in Chapter 28, which deals with Exchange accounts.

Sending a Calendar Snapshot

A calendar snapshot is sent as part of an email message. To send a calendar snapshot, make sure that you are in Calendar view. Then, click the Send a Calendar via E-Mail link on the navigation pane. Outlook will create a new email message and display the Send a Calendar via E-mail dialog box (Figure 11.20). Make entries in this dialog box as follows:

1. In the Calendar list, select the calendar to use. This is relevant only if you have more than one calendar.

2. In the Date Range list, select the range of dates to include.

3. In the Detail list, specify how much detail should be included. You can select Availability Only, Limited Details, or Full Details.

4. Select the Show Time Within My Working Hours Only option to limit the published information to the times defined in Outlook as working hours.

5. Click OK.

FIGURE 11.20

Sending a Calendar snapshot via email.

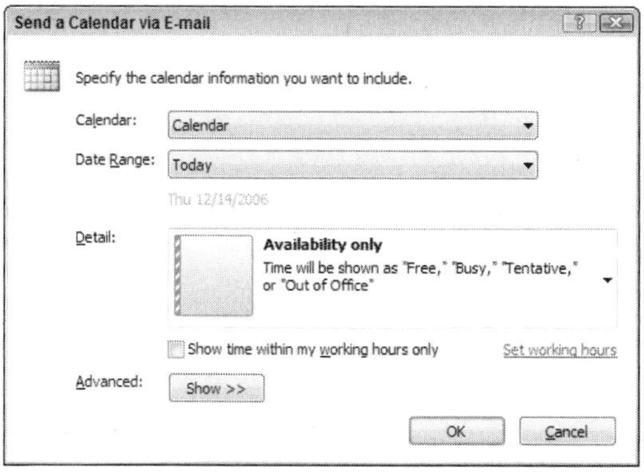

After you close this dialog box, you are returned to the new email message. The calendar will have been inserted into the body of the message and also added as an attachment. You can then address and send the message as usual. When the recipient gets the message, he can either view the calendar in the message or open the attached file to get information about your schedule.

Publishing a Calendar to Microsoft Office Online

Microsoft Office Online is a free service offered to Office users. One of its features is the capability to publish your Outlook Calendar so that other people can view it. To use Microsoft Office Online you need an account. If you already have a Microsoft Passport account you can use that login. If not, you will be prompted to create your account when you first publish your calendar.

To publish your calendar, you must be in Calendar view. Then, click the Publish My Calendar link in the navigation pane. Outlook will take you through the steps of signing into Office Online (or creating an account if needed) and will then display the dialog box shown in Figure 11.21. Fill in this dialog box as follows:

- **Time Span:** Select the span of time to be published.

- **Detail:** Specify how much detail should be included. You can select Availability Only, Limited Details, or Complete Details.

- **Show Time Within My Working Hours Only:** Select this option to limit the published information to the times defined in Outlook as working hours. Click the adjacent Set Working Hours link if you want to view or modify the working hours.

- **Permissions:** Select whether the calendar will be restricted to people you invite or accessible by anyone.

- **Description:** Depending on where you are publishing to, you may be able to enter a description of the calendar that will help other people to find it.

- **Advanced:** Click this button to specify the upload method. You can specify whether or not changes to your calendar will be uploaded automatically. Automatic is the default and is suitable for most situations. If you do not select automatic updating, you will have to publish the calendar again to make changes available.

When you click OK, Outlook publishes your calendar and asks you whether you want to invite others to share the calendar. If you select Yes, Outlook will create an email message that contains a link to the just-published calendar. Send the message to the people you want to invite to share your calendar. If you published the calendar with restricted access, people will need a Microsoft Passport account associated with the email address you sent the invitation to in order to view the calendar.

FIGURE 11.21

Publishing your calendar to Microsoft Office Online.

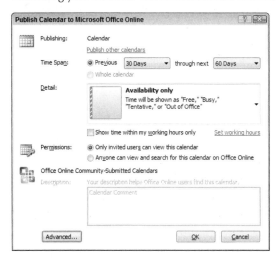

Publishing a Calendar to a Web Server

Another way to make your calendar available to others is to publish it to a web server. Then, anyone with access to that server can view your schedule using a web browser such as Internet Explorer. You cannot publish a calendar to just any web server but only to one that supports the WebDAV protocol (World Wide Web Distributed Authoring and Versioning). If a server is available to you, your IT department will provide you with its location (URL) and your login information. Once you have this information, you can publish your calendar as follows:

1. Make sure that you are in Calendar view.

2. In the navigation pane, right-click the calendar that you want to publish.

3. From the menu, select Publish to Internet.

4. From the next menu, select Publish to WebDAV Server. Outlook displays the Publish Calendar to Custom Server dialog box as shown in Figure 11.22.

5. In the Location box, enter the location (URL) of the server.

6. Under Time Span, select the span of time that you want to be published.

7. From the Detail list, select the amount of detail to be included in the published calendar. You can select Availability Only, Limited Details, or Full Details.

8. Select the Show Time Within My Working Hours Only option to limit the published information to the times defined in Outlook as working hours.

9. Click the Advanced button to specify whether changes to your calendar will be uploaded automatically.

10. Click OK.

FIGURE 11.22

Publishing your calendar to a web server.

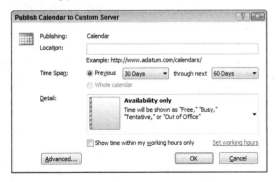

At this point, depending on how the server is set up, you may be asked for your login and password. Once you have entered this information correctly, the calendar will be published and will be available for others to view.

WARNING When you publish a calendar to a web server, you do not have any control over who can view it. Rather, restrictions (if any) are set by the web site administrator.

Inviting Others to View Your Calendar

Once you have published your calendar to a web server, you need to let your colleagues and friends know about it so they can view it. When publishing to Microsoft Office Online, you can do this as the last step of the publishing process, as described earlier. You can also invite people at a later time, whether for a calendar published on Office Online or on a web server. Here's how:

1. In the navigation pane, right-click the calendar.

2. From the menu, select Share Calendar (or whatever the name of the calendar is). Outlook creates an email message containing a link to the calendar. Note: The Share Calendar command will be available only if the calendar has been published.

3. Address the message to the people you want to invite.

4. If desired, add text to the body of the message.

5. Click Send.

Other Actions with Published Calendars

Once you have published a calendar, there are several other actions you can take with it. These commands are all accessed by right-clicking the calendar in the navigation pane and selecting Publish to Internet from the menu. Then, on the next menu:

- Select Change Publishing Options if you want to change access restrictions, upload method, or any other detail of how the calendar is published.

- Select Stop Sharing to make the calendar unavailable. It will remain on the server and sharing can be re-enabled at a later date.

- Select Change Sharing Permissions if you want to change who can access the published calendar.

- Select Remove from Server to delete the calendar from the server.

Subscribing to Internet Calendars

Outlook supports *Internet calendars*, a way for people and organizations to publish a calendar you can subscribe to in Outlook. For example, your employer might publish a calendar of company holidays, or the local soccer team can publish its game schedule. By subscribing to an Internet calendar you can view the information in Outlook—and, it will be updated automatically as needed.

When an Internet calendar is made available, you will be informed of its location by the publisher. Navigate to that location in your web browser and you'll see a link for each published calendar. Click the link and Outlook displays the dialog box shown in Figure 11.23. If you want to change the name that Outlook will display for the calendar, click the Advanced button and make the change. Then click Yes to complete the subscription process.

FIGURE 11.23

Subscribing to an Internet calendar.

When you have subscribed to one or more Internet calendars, they will be displayed in the navigation pane under Other Calendars, as shown in Figure 11.24. Click a calendar name to display or hide it (as indicated by the adjacent checkmark).

If you right-click a subscribed calendar in the navigation pane, Outlook displays a menu with various commands, including renaming the calendar and deleting it — which also unsubscribes you from the calendar.

FIGURE 11.24

Internet calendars are listed under Other Calendars.

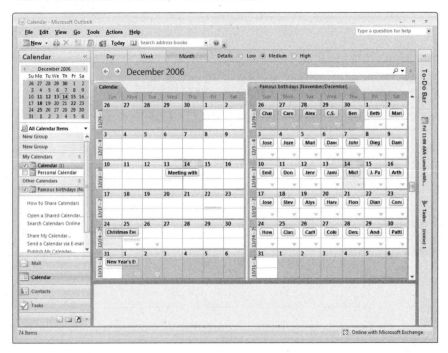

Using Overlay Mode

When you have two or more calendars displayed, they are normally displayed side-by-side as shown in Figure 11.25. Outlook also offers Overlay mode, which can be very useful. In *Overlay mode*, the two calendars are overlapped so that events from both calendars are displayed together, as shown in Figure 11.26. This makes it easy to locate potential conflicts between the two calendars.

To switch Calendar View mode, open the View menu and select View in Side-By-Side Mode or View in Overlay Mode.

FIGURE 11.25

Calendars displayed in Side-by-Side mode.

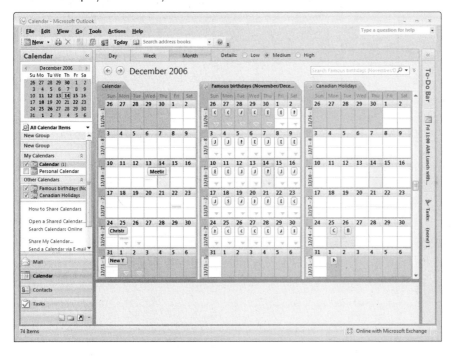

FIGURE 11.26

Calendars displayed in Overlay mode.

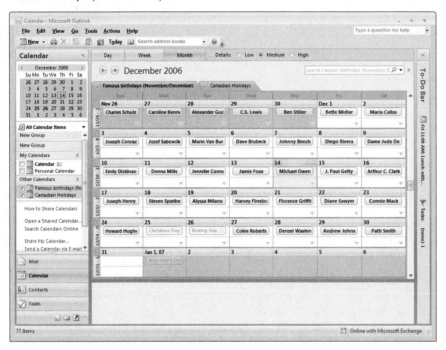

Setting Calendar Options

The Outlook Calendar comes with default settings for many aspects of its operation. As you become familiar with the Calendar you may want to make changes to these settings to customize the Calendar for the way you work. You access Calendar options by selecting Options from the Tools menu and then, in the Options dialog box, clicking the Preferences tab. The Calendar section of this tab is shown in Figure 11.27.

The one option shown here has to do with reminders for appointments. By default, Outlook reminds you of appointments 15 minutes before the start time (you can change this for individual appointments, of course). To change the default lead time, select it from the drop-down list. You can select any time from 0 minutes to 2 weeks. If you do not want a default reminder for messages, uncheck the Default Reminder option.

FIGURE 11.27

The Calendar section of the Preferences tab in the Options dialog box.

Other Calendar options are accessed by clicking the Calendar Options button to display the Calendar Options dialog box, shown in Figure 11.28. The various options available here are divided into several sections. The first section has to do with how Outlook defines the work week:

- **Calendar Work Week:** Check those days that you want to be considered part of the work week, and uncheck those that you do not.

- **First Day of Week:** Select the day that Outlook will use as the first day of the week for calendar displays.

- **Start Time/End Time:** Select the times of day that Outlook will use for the start and stop of the work day.

- **First Week of Year:** Select how Outlook will determine the first week of the year. The options are Starts on Jan 1 (the week that contains Jan 1), the first week with four days in the new year, and the first week that is entirely in the new year.

FIGURE 11.28

The Calendar Options dialog box.

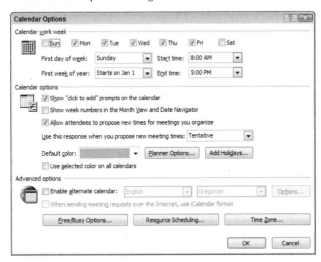

The next section of the Calendar Options dialog box includes options for a variety of things:

- **Show "Click to Add" Prompts on the Calendar:** If this option is selected, Outlook will display prompts on the calendar where you can click to add an appointment.

- **Show Week Numbers...:** If this option is selected, Outlook will display week numbers (the week of the year) where indicated. An example is shown in Figure 11.29.

- **Allow Attendees to Propose...:** If this option is selected, people whom you invite to meetings are allowed to respond by proposing a new time for the meeting.

- **Use This Response...:** Select from the list to specify whether new meeting times that you propose are marked as Tentative, Accept, or Decline.

- **Default Color:** Select the color to use for the calendar display.

- **Use Selected Color...:** If this option is selected, the color you choose will be used for all calendars you view, not just your own calendar.

- **Planner Options:** Click this button to display the Planner Options dialog box where you can set options for the Meeting Planner and Group Schedule features. These options were discussed earlier in this chapter .

- **Add Holidays:** Lets you copy holidays for one or more specific countries onto your calendar. You select the country or countries from a list.

Finally there are a few advanced options in this dialog box:

- **Enable Alternate Calendar:** Lets you display an alternate calendar in parallel with the default one using the language and calendar structure you select.

- **When Sending Meeting Requests…:** Sends meeting requests in the more widely supported iCalendar format instead of Outlook's proprietary format.

- **Free/Busy Options:** Sets options for publishing your calendar. These options were covered earlier in the chapter.

- **Resource Scheduling:** Sets options for working with meeting requests. These options were covered earlier in the chapter.

- **Time Zone:** Sets the default time zone for your calendar and also permits you to display a second, alternate time zone in the Calendar.

FIGURE 11.29

Outlook can display week numbers in the Date Navigator, shown here, and also in the Month view.

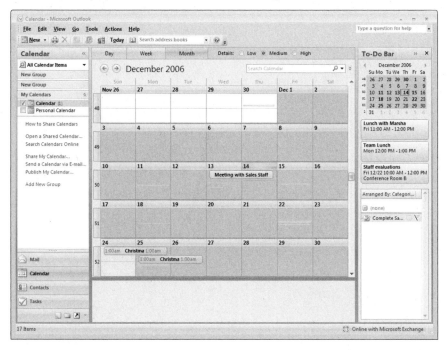

Summary

Outlook's Calendar is a powerful and flexible tool for keeping track of your appointments and other time commitments. Much more than a simple date book, the Outlook Calendar can do things such as reminding you of an upcoming appointment and sharing your schedule with others.

Chapter 12

Working with Schedules and Meetings

In the previous chapter, you learned how you can use Outlook to keep track of appointments. As useful as this is, it is only one of the tools Outlook provides to help you organize and manage your time. Scheduling goes a step further. In a nutshell, *scheduling* refers to arranging your time commitments so they do not conflict with other commitments you may have or with commitments that other people have. For example, scanning your calendar to find a mutually agreeable night to go to dinner with friends is scheduling, as is choosing a meeting time at work that will permit the whole project team to attend.

Understanding Scheduling

An *appointment* is an event that lasts less than a full day and does not require coordination with anyone else's time. A *meeting*, on the other hand, is an event that must be coordinated with one or more people's schedules. Outlook provides two tools that help to automate the task of setting up meetings:

- Viewing other people's calendars to see when they are free.
- Sending meeting requests via email allowing the recipients to accept or decline.

You may use just one of these tools to schedule a meeting, or you may use both. The following section takes a look at how this is done.

Creating a Meeting

In many ways, creating a meeting is the same as creating an appointment, as you learned how to do in the previous chapter. As with an appointment, you can assign a meeting to a category, associate it with one or more contacts, and so on. This section focuses on those aspects unique to creating a meeting.

To create a new meeting, select Meeting Request from the New menu or press Ctrl+Shift+Q. Outlook opens a new, blank meeting form as shown in Figure 12.1. This form is very similar to the new appointment form. The differences are

- It has a Send button instead of a Save & Close button.
- It has a To field.
- It has a Cancel Invitation button in place of an Invite Attendees button.

You see how these new elements are used soon.

FIGURE 12.1

Creating a new meeting.

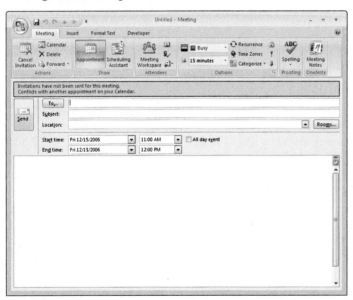

To continue creating the meeting, follow these steps:

> **NOTE** **Please note that these steps do not all have to be performed in this precise order.**

1. Enter a subject for the meeting in the Subject field.

2. Enter the meeting location in the Location field, or click the adjacent down arrow to select from a list of recently used locations. This is important so the meeting invitees will know where the meeting is.

3. Specify the date of the meeting and the start and end time in the corresponding fields.

4. Look at the message just above the To field. It will tell you that invitations for this meeting have not been sent yet. If the time and date you selected conflict with an existing appointment, it will also inform you of this fact, as shown in Figure 12.2. If there is a conflict you can use the Scheduling tab to resolve it, as described in the next section. If not, continue with step 5.

5. Click the To button to display the Select Attendees and Resources dialog box as shown in Figure 12.3. Resources can be scheduled only if you are using an Exchange Server account.

6. Select individual attendees and click the appropriate button to place them in the Required or Optional field depending on whether their attendance at the meeting is required or optional.

7. Click OK to return to the meeting form. You'll see the selected attendees are now listed in the To field.

8. Click the Send button to send the invitation to the invitees and add the meeting to your Calendar.

When an invitee receives your meeting invitation, she can accept, tentatively accept, decline, or propose a new time for the meeting. Her response is sent back to you and automatically registered by Outlook, as described later in the chapter.

FIGURE 12.2

Outlook tells you whether a proposed meeting time conflicts with an existing appointment.

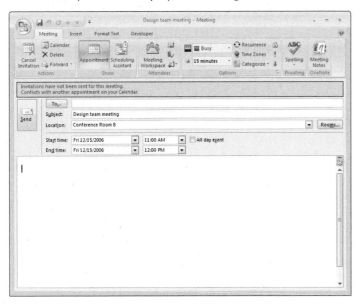

Meeting Request Options

There are two options that you can change before sending a meeting request. You access them by clicking the Responses button in the Attendees section of the ribbon:

- **Request Responses:** This is on by default. If you turn it off, your meeting invitation will be an informative message with the time, date, subject, and place of the meeting, but no request for a response. If the recipient accepts the meeting, it will be added to his calendar but no response will be sent to the meeting organizer.

- **Allow New Time Proposals:** This option determines whether meeting invitees are allowed to respond by proposing a new time for the meeting. Its default setting is on or off depending on the setting of the calendar option Allow Attendees to Propose New Times for Meetings You Organize, as described later in this chapter in the section "Setting Meeting Options." This option is not available if the Request Responses option is turned off.

FIGURE 12.3

FIGURE 12.3

Selecting attendees for a meeting.

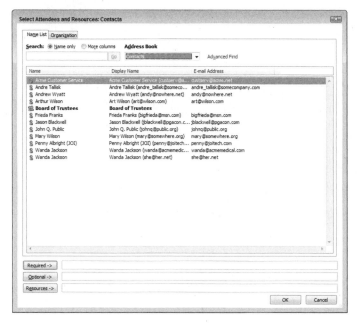

Using the Plan a Meeting Command

When the Calendar is active, you'll find the Plan a Meeting command on Outlook's Actions menu. This command provides you with another way to plan a meeting and invite attendees. The steps you'll carry out are the same, but are in a different order. The process starts with the Scheduling window (covered in the next section) where you can view your calendar and those of any of your contacts whose calendar information is available. Once you have selected the meeting time, you click the Make Meeting button, which creates a new meeting at the scheduled date and time. You then proceed as described elsewhere to complete the meeting request.

Using the Scheduling Window

The *Scheduling window*, available from the meeting form, provides a visual tool that lets you schedule a meeting so that it does not conflict with existing appointments on your schedule. After you have entered the date and time for a meeting on a meeting form, click the Scheduling button on the ribbon to display the Scheduling window as shown in Figure 12.4.

FIGURE 12.4

The Scheduling window lets you view conflicts with your schedule and optionally other people's schedules.

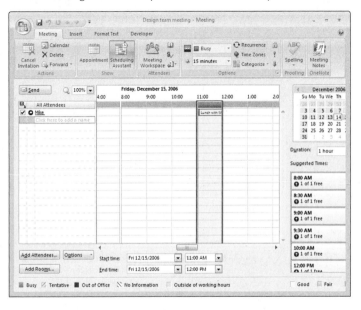

The elements in this window are

- The Zoom list lets you select how much time is displayed across the window. You can zoom out to show a whole week or zoom in to show just a couple of hours.

- The Attendees list contains your name and the names of any people that you have added to the To field on the meeting form. To add additional attendees, click at the bottom of the list where it says Click Here to Add a Name, or click the Add Others button. People who you add here will be added to the To field for the meeting.

- The row to the right of each attendee's name provides information about their availability, as explained in more detail later.

- The All Attendees row at the top displays free/busy information based on the schedules of all attendees.

- The vertical green and red lines show the start and end of the meeting, respectively.

Viewing Group Schedules

Outlook's Group Schedule feature, which (among other things) allows you to view the schedules of other people when creating a meeting, is available only if you are using a Microsoft Exchange account. You learn more about group schedules in Chapter 28.

The Scheduling window lists availability information for meeting attendees other than yourself only if you are using a Microsoft Exchange Server. Otherwise, the Scheduling window lists attendees' time as "No Information," indicated by diagonal hatching.

If the meeting time you have specified conflicts with one or more schedules — or even if it does not — you can use the AutoPick feature to find another time free for all attendees. Click the AutoPick Next >> button to select the next time period free for all attendees whose schedule information is available; click the << button to look for the nearest earlier time slot. You can also change the meeting time and date manually using the corresponding fields at the bottom of the window.

When you are finished with the Scheduling window, you can do one of the following:

- Click the Appointment button to return to the meeting form and finish setting up the meeting.
- Click the Send button to save the meeting and send requests to all attendees.

Setting Scheduling Options

You can see that the Scheduling window has an Options button. Click this button to do any of the following:

- Specify whether only your working hours, as defined in Outlook, are displayed.
- Specify whether calendar details are displayed.
- Select how the AutoPick feature works in identifying free time. For example, you can specify that all attendees must be free or only that required attendees be free.
- Update the schedule display of other attendees to reflect any changes they may have made to their calendars.

Responding to Meeting Invitations

When a recipient receives a meeting invitation and opens it, it appears as shown in Figure 12.5. They can respond in various ways to an invitation. Responding lets them add the meeting to their own calendar (unless they decline the meeting) and also sends a message to the person who originally proposed the meeting. This lets them keep track of who can and who cannot attend the meeting, and to change the time if needed.

FIGURE 12.5

Responding to a meeting invitation.

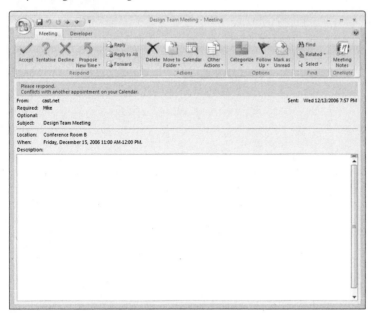

In some respects, a meeting invitation is like a regular email message — you can reply to it, forward it, categorize it, and so on. Note that Outlook displays a message just below the ribbon if the meeting conflicts with something already on your calendar. There are four special buttons on the ribbon that let you respond to the invitation.

- **Accept:** Accept the invitation and add the meeting to your calendar. Outlook displays the dialog box shown in Figure 12.6. The options have to do with the response, if any, that is sent to the person who sent you the invitation:
- **Edit the Response Before Sending:** Lets you add text or otherwise edit the response before sending it.
- **Send the Response Now:** Sends the response immediately.
- **Don't Send a Response:** No response is sent.

Click the Tentative button to accept the invitation and add the meeting to your calendar as "tentative." Outlook displays the same dialog box as shown in Figure 12.6, where you select response options.

FIGURE 12.6

Options when responding to a meeting invitation.

Click the Decline button to decline the invitation. Nothing is added to your calendar. You are offered the same response options as described earlier for Accept.

Click the Propose New Time button if you want to either decline the meeting or accept tentatively while proposing a new time. Outlook opens the Scheduling window and displays your free/busy time as well as the free/busy time of other invitees for whom the information is available. Select the time you want to propose and click the Propose Time button. Outlook creates a new email message with the proposed time information, addressed to the person who sent you the invitation.

Tracking Meeting Invitations

When you have requested responses to a meeting invitation, each response sent will appear in your Inbox. In addition, Outlook automatically registers the response and keeps track of all responses to a particular meeting. You can view this information by opening the meeting (double-click it in Calendar view) and then clicking the Tracking button in the Show section of the ribbon. The Tracking window, shown in Figure 12.7, lists all the people who were invited to the meeting, whether they are a required or an optional attendee, and their response (if any). In the figure, for example, you can see that Wanda Jackson has not yet responded to the invitation.

Meeting Response Handling Options

The behavior described in this section for handling responses to meeting requests is based on Outlook's default settings. You can change how responses to meeting requests are handled as described later in this chapter in the section "Setting Meeting Options."

FIGURE 12.7

Tracking responses to a meeting invitation.

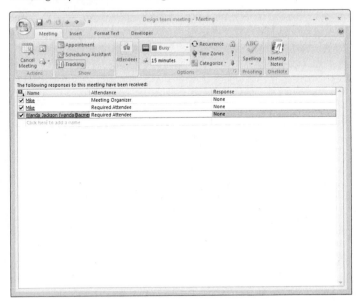

Working with Existing Meetings

A meeting on your calendar can be either a meeting that you organized or a meeting that someone else organized and invited you to.

When you open a meeting that you organized, you can modify various aspects of the meeting including the subject, time, and location. Then, click the Send Update button to send the revised information to all attendees. Other actions you can take are

- Click the Cancel Meeting button in the Actions section of the ribbon to cancel the meeting and send a cancellation message to all attendees. The recipient can open the message and click the Remove from Calendar button to remove the cancelled meeting from her calendar.

- Click the Add or Remove Attendees button in the Attendees section of the ribbon to add or remove attendees. Then, click the Send Update button. You have the option of sending updates only to added and deleted attendees or to all attendees. Attendees you add receive a regular meeting invitation, and deleted attendees receive a message saying the meeting was cancelled.

- Click the Message to Attendees button to create a regular email message or reply addressed to all meeting attendees.

Removing Meeting Attendees

When you remove a previously invited attendee from a meeting, the message he receives says the meeting was cancelled, which is not the case. Also, you are not able to include a note with the message explaining why he has been uninvited. This has the unfortunate potential to cause misunderstandings when a person finds out that a meeting was not actually cancelled but was held without them. Sending a separate email explaining the situation may be advisable in some situations.

When you open a meeting that someone else invited you to, a message is displayed just below the ribbon with information about whether you have responded. For example, the meeting shown in Figure 12.8 indicates the meeting was accepted on December 14.

FIGURE 12.8

Setting options for meeting requests.

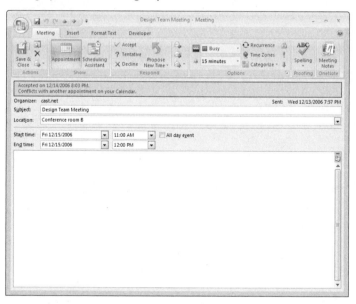

When the meeting is open, you can change the subject, location, and date/time, although doing so makes little sense seeing that you are not the meeting organizer. You can also change your response. For example, suppose that you had initially accepted the meeting but something important has come up that will prevent you from attending. You can click Decline to send another response to the organizer informing her of your change in plans.

Setting Meeting Options

Outlook has several options that affect the way meeting requests and responses work. Some of these options are found in the Calendar Options dialog box. To view and change these options:

1. Select Options from the Tools menu to display the Options dialog box.

2. If necessary, click the Preferences tab.

3. Click the Calendar Options button to display the Calendar Options dialog box (see Figure 12.9).

4. Set options as described next.

5. Click OK twice to close all dialog boxes.

FIGURE 12.9

Setting options for meeting requests.

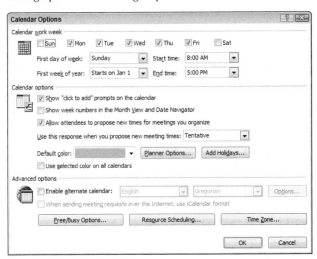

Two of the meeting-related options are in the Calendar Options section of this dialog box:

- **Allow Attendees to Propose New Times for Meetings You Organize:** If this option is turned on, people to whom you send meeting invitations can propose new times for the meeting. If not, they will not have this option available to them.

- **Use This Response When You Propose New Meeting Times:** If this option is selected, the widely supported iCalendar format is used for the response when you propose a new meeting time. If not, the less widely supported Outlook format is used. You should leave this option on unless you have a specific reason for turning it off.

The third option is in the Advanced Options section, and determines the format used for sending meeting requests. Again, unless you have a specific reason to do otherwise, you should leave this option turned on so that the more widely supported iCalendar format will be used.

Other options are located in the Tracking Options dialog box. To display this dialog box (which is shown in Figure 12.10):

1. Select Options from the Tools menu to display the Options dialog box.
2. If necessary, click the Preferences tab.
3. Click the E-mail Options button to display the E-mail Options dialog box.
4. Click the Tracking Options button.

The relevant options are

- **Process Requests and Responses on Arrival:** If this option is selected, Outlook automatically processes responses to invitations when they arrive — that is, records the response in the tracking section of the meeting request. If not, you will have to open the response message and manually process it.

- **Delete Blank Voting and Meeting Responses After Processing:** If this option is selected, Outlook automatically deletes blank meeting responses after processing. A blank response is one to which the sender has not added text.

FIGURE 12.10

Setting options for handling responses to meeting requests.

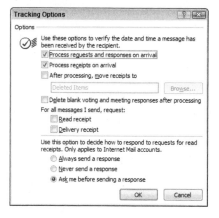

Creating and Using a Meeting Workplace

A *Meeting Workplace* is a web site linked to a meeting or project that you are organizing. By giving other meeting attendees access to the Meeting Workspace, you enable a variety of collaboration tools that let everyone share information and meeting materials. A Workspace can be created for a project and then linked to each meeting that you organize for the project. Meeting Workspaces are available only when you are using Outlook in conjunction with a Microsoft SharePoint Services server, which is covered in Chapter 29.

Summary

Outlook may not be able to reduce the number of meetings you have to attend, but it can make it a lot easier to keep track of them and to manage your schedule. Whether you are organizing a meeting or are being invited to one, Outlook's meeting and schedule tools can be a huge help.

Chapter 13

Working with Outlook Notes

Notes is an Outlook feature designed specifically for quick and easy jotting down of those small bits of information we all seem to be inundated with. You can think of them as the electronic equivalent of the sticky notes that most people have pasted all over their monitor, desk, and refrigerator. They are easy to use and understand.

Understanding Outlook Notes

Notes are designed to be as easy as possible to use. They are not designed for storing large amounts of information or for organizing information in any sophisticated way. They can contain text only — no pictures or similar items — and do not permit any formatting. I use notes for things like:

- Airline frequent flier account numbers
- Descriptions of favorite restaurants
- Software installation keys
- A list of movies to see

Figure 13.1 shows an open note. The form is very simple and — aside from the content — contains only four elements:

FIGURE 13.1

An Outlook note.

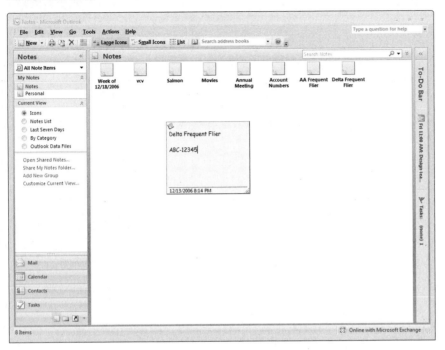

■ A close button (the X at the top-right corner) used to close the note

■ A menu button (at the top-left corner) used to open a menu with note-related commands

■ The time and date the note was created or last modified

■ A handle (lower-right corner) used to change the size of the note form

Two features contribute to the ease of use of notes:

■ You never have to save a note — they are always saved automatically by Outlook.

■ You never have to name a note — the first line of the note is automatically used for the name.

By default, Outlook displays notes as small icons with the title underneath, as shown in Figure 13.2. You can change the note view in various ways as described later in this chapter.

Notes and the Desktop

You can drag a note from Outlook and drop it on the Windows Desktop. The note will remain functional even when Outlook is not running. Such a note will display on the Desktop as well as in Outlook Notes view.

FIGURE 13.2

By default, Outlook displays notes as small icons with a title.

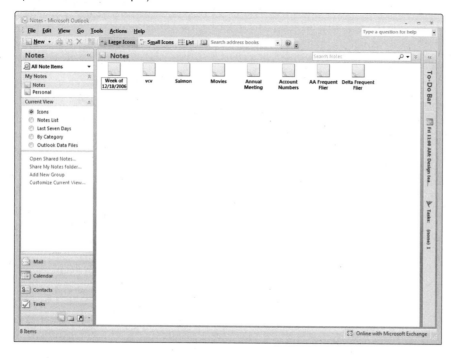

Creating a Note

You can create a new note in several ways:

- If Notes are displayed in Outlook, click the New button or press Ctrl+N.
- If some other view is displayed, display the New menu and select Note, or press Ctrl+Shift+N.

Outlook displays a new, blank note. All you need to do is type in the note title as the first line, hit Enter, and type the rest of the note. Then, click the note's close button or click anywhere outside the note to close and save it.

Opening and Editing a Note

To open a note, double-click it. You can then edit the note and save your changes by closing the note. If you want to change the note's title, you must change the first line in the note.

When a note is open, you can take the following actions by clicking the menu icon in the top-left corner of the note and selecting from the menu (see Figure 13.3):

- **Save As:** Save the note as an RTF file. The original note is not affected.
- **Delete:** Delete the note.
- **Forward:** Creates a new email message with the note attached. You then address and send the message as usual.
- **Categorize:** Assign the note to an Outlook category or remove any previously assigned categories.
- **Contacts:** Associate one or more contacts with the note.
- **Print:** Print the note.

FIGURE 13.3

Using the Note menu.

Using Notes View

Outlook's Notes view displays your notes as icons with the note titles. You can change the way your notes are displayed and also perform various actions with notes from Notes view.

Changing Notes Display

By default, notes are displayed as large icons with the note title underneath, as you saw earlier in Figure 13.2. Outlook provides two other Notes views, selected by clicking the Small Icons or List button on the toolbar:

- **Small Icons view** displays each note as a small icon with the title next to it, as shown in Figure 13.4.

- **List view** is similar to Small Icons view except that the notes and icons are displayed as a list (see Figure 13.5).

Whichever view you are using, you can customize it further by right-clicking a blank area in Notes view and selecting either Sort, Filter, or Other Settings from the context menu.

FIGURE 13.4

Notes displayed in Small Icons view.

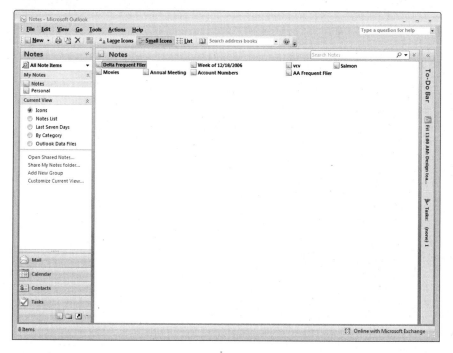

Finding the Icon Buttons

The Large Icons, Small Icons, and List buttons are available on the toolbar only when Icons is selected in the Current View list. This list, covered in the next section, makes some additional views available to you.

FIGURE 13.5

Notes displayed in List view.

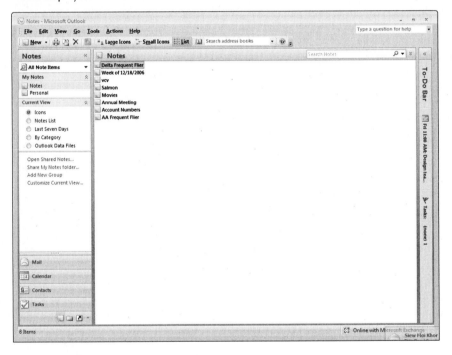

If you select Sort, Outlook displays the dialog box shown in Figure 13.6. You can sort notes on as many as four fields. By default, they are sorted only by Subject (the title). You can sort in ascending or descending order by creation date/time, last modified date/time, contacts associated with the note, color (that is, category), and a few others. To specify how notes are sorted:

1. Select the primary sort field in the Sort Items By list.

2. Select either the Ascending or the Descending option.

3. If you want a secondary sort field for breaking ties in the primary field, select the second-ary sort field in the top Then By list and select either the Ascending or the Descending option.

4. If desired, define a third and fourth sort field in the other Then By sections.

5. Click OK.

Sorting can be particularly useful when you have a lot of notes.

FIGURE 13.6

Specifying how notes should be sorted.

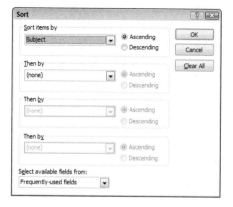

If you select Filter from the context menu, Outlook displays the Filter dialog box as shown in Figure 13.7. Only the Notes tab is relevant. To define a filter:

1. Enter one or more words of interest in the Search for the Word(s) field. Click the adjacent arrow to select from recently used search words.

2. Open the In list and select where Outlook should search. You can choose Contents Only (the entire note) or Subject Field Only (the note's first line).

3. If you want to filter by date/time, pull down the Time list and select Created or Modified. Then open the adjacent list and select your criterion (for example, yesterday, last week, and so on).

4. Click OK.

If you want to remove a filter from Notes view:

1. Open the Filter dialog box.

2. Click the Clear All button.

3. Click OK.

FIGURE 13.7

Defining a filter for Notes view.

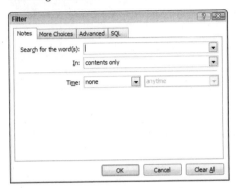

The final command on the context menu, Other Options, brings up the dialog box shown in Figure 13.8. This dialog box lets you specify the kind of icon displayed for the notes and how they are arranged.

FIGURE 13.8

Setting other Notes view options.

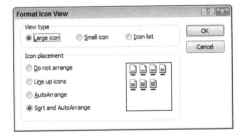

Using the Current View List

You can select additional ways to display notes from the Current View list on the toolbar or the navigation pane. This is shown on the toolbar in Figure 13.9 and on the navigation pane in Figure 13.10. There are several predefined views on this list:

Selecting a view from the Current View list.

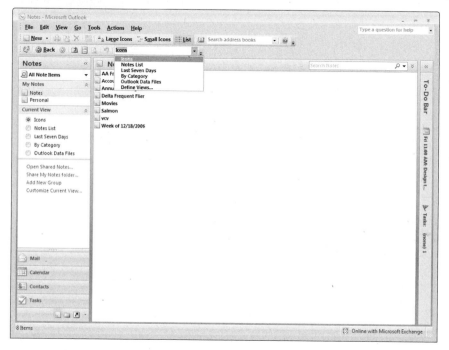

FIGURE 13.10

You can also select a view on the navigation pane.

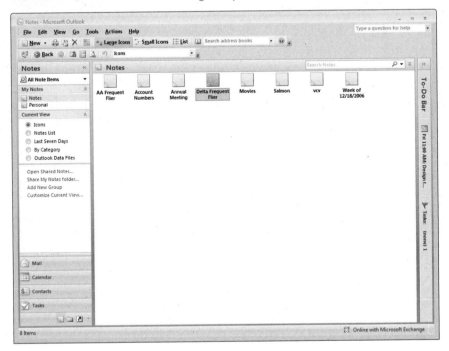

- **Icons:** Lets you choose Large Icons, Small Icons, or List using toolbar buttons as was described in the previous section.

- **Notes List:** Displays a list of notes showing the title, content, and creation/modification date and time. This is shown in Figure 13.11.

- **Last Seven Days:** Displays only those notes that were created or modified within the past seven days. Uses the same display format as Notes List.

- **By Category:** Displays notes in list format organized by assigned category.

- **Outlook Data Files:** Displays notes in list format organized by Outlook data file. This is relevant only if you have two or more Outlook data files, a topic that is covered in Chapter 18.

FIGURE 13.11

Notes displayed in Notes List view.

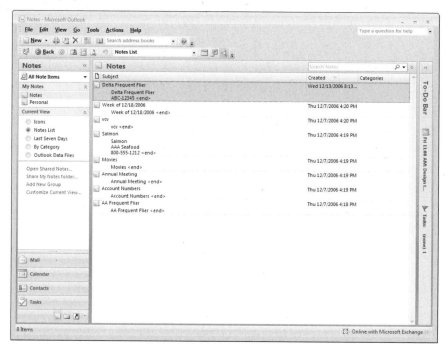

The last item on the Current View list in the toolbar is Define Views. Selecting this command lets you define custom views for notes. This feature is explained in full in Chapter 19.

Searching Notes

As your collection of notes grows, you'll find it useful to be able to search your notes to find just the information that you are looking for. Searching is similar in some respects to defining a filter for Notes view, as was discussed in the previous section. It provides additional power and flexibility, however, and the two used together are even more powerful.

To perform a basic search that matches your search words to the content of the notes, type the search term into the search box (see Figure 13.12) or click the adjacent down arrow to select from previous searches. Outlook searches your notes and displays any notes that contain a match, with the search term highlighted, as shown in the figure. If you have a filter applied to your notes, the search will look only in notes that the filter displays.

FIGURE 13.12

Performing a simple Notes search.

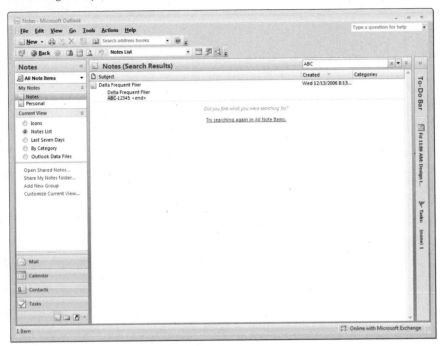

When you are done, click the X adjacent to the search box to delete the search term and return to display of all notes.

For a more advanced search, click the down arrow at the top right of the Notes window. Outlook expands the search panel to show more criteria fields, as shown in Figure 13.13. Four criteria fields are by default available: Categories, Color, Body, and Subject (or title). Enter your search term in the adjacent box, or select from the list, to search. You can also fine-tune your search as follows:

- Click the down arrow next to a field name to change to a different criterion. For example, you could change the Categories field to Created if you want to search based on note creation date/time.

- Click the Add Criteria button to add additional criteria to the search if you need more than four.

- Click the X next to the search box to clear all criteria and cancel the search.

- Click the up arrow to hide the advanced search fields.

FIGURE 13.13

Performing an advanced Notes search.

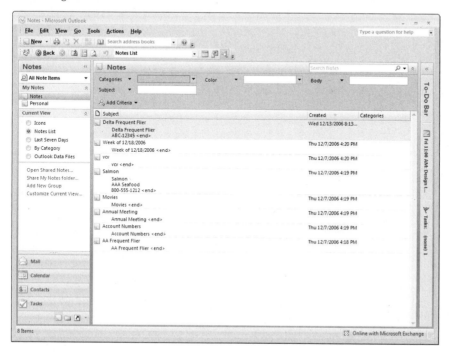

Setting Notes Options

Outlook has only a few general options for notes. They control the default color and size for notes and the font used to display them. You set these options in the Notes Options dialog box, shown in Figure 13.14. To open this dialog box:

1. Select Options from the Tools menu to open the Options dialog box.

2. If necessary, click the Preferences tab.

3. In the Contacts and Notes section, click the Note Options button.

FIGURE 13.14

Setting global options for notes.

The final option for notes determines whether the time stamp is displayed at the bottom of the note. By default this is turned on, but you can turn it off or back on as follows:

1. Select Options from the Tools menu to open the Options dialog box.
2. Click the Other tab.
3. Click the Advanced Options button to open the Advanced Options dialog box.
4. Click the When Viewing Notes, Show the Time and Date option.

Summary

Notes may be Outlook's simplest feature but they can be a very valuable tool. They provide an easy way to store and organize all those little bits of information that we all have to deal with. When combined with Outlook's categories and search tools, their usefulness becomes even greater.

Chapter 14

Using the Journal

Many people need to keep track of their time. You know that you spent eight hours at work today, but how much of that time was spent on which tasks? You may need this information for something specific such as client billing — or you may just want to know how you spend your time in order to work more efficiently. Outlook's Journal is designed for just this purpose.

Understanding the Journal

Fundamentally, the Journal is a log of how you spend your time. An individual Journal entry contains, at a minimum, the following information:

- A start date and time
- A duration
- An identification of the task: phone call, email, document, conversation, and so on
- Information linking the entry to a project, contact, or client company

Journal entries can be created two ways: automatically and manually. Outlook can automatically create Journal entries for certain activities that you carry out in Outlook, such as working on email messages and meeting requests. Outlook can also automatically create entries for activities that you perform in other Microsoft Office programs (Word, Excel, PowerPoint, Access, and Project).

Journal entries can also be created manually. This is useful for tracking tasks that Outlook cannot track automatically, such as working in non-Office programs or talking on the phone.

269

Using Journal View

To view your Journal, select Journal from the Go menu or press Ctrl+8. The default Journal view lists entries by type — Word document, phone call, and so on. This is shown in Figure 14.1. You can see that:

- An automatic entry for an email message is listed by the message subject.

- An automatic entry for an Office document is listed by the document name.

- A manual entry — the two phone call entries in the figure — is listed by the subject that you assigned to the Journal entry.

In the By Type view, Journal entries are displayed on a timeline. In the figure, for example, you can see that the Journal entries for a single day — Monday, December 11 — are displayed with the hours of the day across the top of the display. You can scroll the display to bring earlier or later time periods into view using the horizontal scroll bar at the bottom of the Journal display. You can also display different time periods by clicking the Today, Day, Week, or Month button on the toolbar.

FIGURE 14.1

The default Journal view lists entries by type.

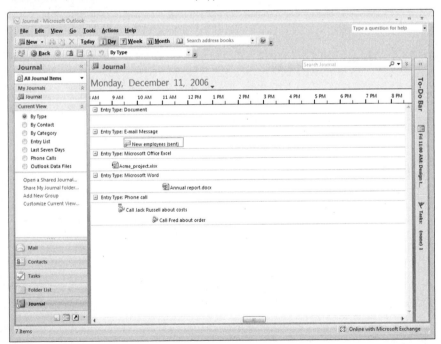

Create a Journal Button

By default, the Journal is not available from the navigation pane — that is, there is no Journal button displayed. You open the Journal by selecting Journal from the Go menu or by pressing Ctrl+8. You can add a Journal button to the navigation pane if you wish, as follows:

1. Click the down arrow at the bottom of the navigation pane.
2. Select Add or Remove Buttons from the menu.
3. Select Journal from the next menu.

Changing Journal View

Outlook offers several other ways for you to view your Journal entries. To switch views, you can use the Current View list on the toolbar, shown in Figure 14.2, or the Current View options on the navigation pane.

FIGURE 14.2

Selecting a Journal view from the toolbar.

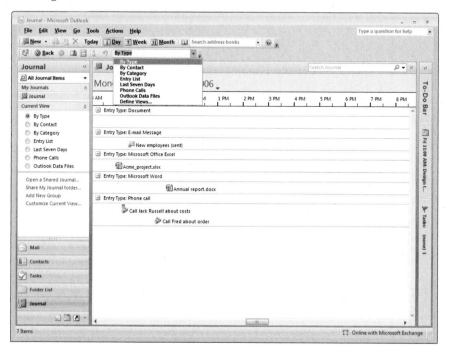

By Contact View

When you select the By Contact view, Outlook organizes your Journal entries according to the contact that is associated with them. This is shown in Figure 14.3. Some entries may not have an associated contact, and they will be listed at the top.

Some Journal entries are associated with a contact automatically. For example, if you are tracking email messages in the Journal using the Automatic Tracking feature, each entry is associated with the recipient of the email message. You can also manually assign a contact to a Journal entry, as explained later in this chapter.

Entry List View

Entry List view provides a sortable list of all Journal entries, as shown in Figure 14.4. The type of each entry is indicated by the icon in the left column. You can sort the list on any column by clicking the column heading once (for ascending order) or twice (for descending order). The current sort column is marked by an arrow in the column heading (the Start column in the figure).

FIGURE 14.3

Viewing Journal entries by contact.

FIGURE 14.4

Viewing Journal entries as a list.

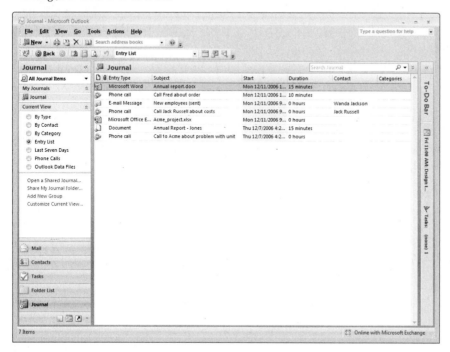

You can see that in Entry List view, some entries have an attachment icon (paper clip) displayed in the second column. This indicates that the entry has a document associated with it. For example, an automatic entry for a Word session will be associated with the document you worked on, and an entry for an email message will have the message linked to it. Other Journal entries, such as for a phone call, do not have an associated document.

Other Journal Views

There are several other Journal views you can select. They are explained briefly here:

- **By Category:** Organizes entries by the category (if any) they are assigned to.
- **Last Seven Days:** Displays only those entries for the past seven days.
- **Phone Calls:** Displays only entries of type phone call.
- **Outlook Data File:** Organizes entries by the Outlook data file they are in. This is relevant only if you have two or more Outlook data files.

Creating a Custom Journal View

On the Current View list on the toolbar, the last selection is Define Views. This command lets you define a custom view for whatever you are viewing — in this case, Journal entries. The process of defining a custom view is covered in Chapter 19.

Creating a Manual Journal Entry

To keep track of activities that Outlook cannot track automatically, you must create a Journal entry manually. To create a new Journal entry manually:

- If you are currently in Journal view, click the New button or press Ctrl+N.

- If you are not in Journal view, click the arrow next to the New button and select Journal Entry from the menu, or press Ctrl+Shift+J.

Outlook opens a new, blank Journal entry form as shown in Figure 14.5. The current date and time are filled in, and the timer is stopped. Then:

FIGURE 14.5

Creating a new Journal entry manually.

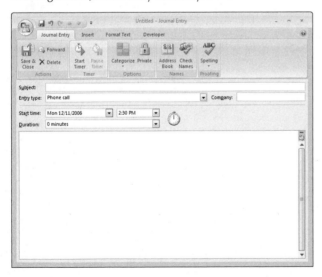

1. Enter a subject for the Journal entry in the Subject field.

2. Select a type for the entry from the Entry Type pull-down list.

3. If desired, enter a company name in the Company field. If you have entered company names in previous Journal entries, you can click the adjacent arrow to select from a list of these names.

4. If desired, click the Contacts button to associate the entry with one or more contacts from your address book.

5. Optionally, click the Categorize button to assign a category to the entry.

6. Optionally, enter any notes in the large box in the middle of the form.

At this point, the Journal entry is almost complete. There are two ways you can use it. One is to time an event that you are about to start. For example, perhaps you are about to join a teleconference and want a Journal entry for your participation. Here's how to do this:

1. Click the Start Timer button. The stopwatch icon will become animated to show that the timer is running.

2. If there's a pause in your activity, click the Pause Timer button. When the activity resumes, click Start Timer again.

3. When the activity is completed, click Save & Close to stop the timer and save the entry.

The other way to create a Journal entry is for an activity that is already over. Perhaps Joe from Marketing came by your office and you talked about strategy for half an hour. Now you want to log that time in the Journal. Then:

1. Create the new Journal entry as described previously, but do not start the timer.

2. If necessary, change the start date by clicking the arrow next to the date field and selecting from the calendar that Outlook displays.

3. Click the arrow next to the time field and select a start time. They are listed in 30-minute increments. If you need a more precise time entry, for example 10:40, select a time that is close from the list and then edit the time in the field.

4. Click the arrow next to the Duration field and select the duration of the event. Again, if the precise duration is not listed you can edit the field directly.

5. Click Save & Close.

Sharing Your Journal

Like many other aspects of Outlook data, you can share your Journal with other people. This can be useful in various situations such as when you are part of a team working on a large project. Being able to view each others' Journals can help keep the project on track. Sharing Journal entries and other kinds of Outlook data is covered in Chapter 28.

Searching the Journal

As you use the Journal, the number of entries will grow to the point where it's hard to find information by simply scrolling through it. You can use the Search feature to filter the Journal to show just the information you want. For example, you could filter to show only Journal entries where the Company field is "Acme Widgets" and the Start field is last month — enabling you to total the time spent on the Acme Widget project last month.

For a basic search, enter your search term in the Search Journal box at the top right of the Journal display (see Figure 14.6). You can also click the down arrow to select from previously used search terms. Outlook will automatically search as you enter the term and display only matching Journal entries (or a message if there are no matching entries). Click the X that is adjacent to the Search box to cancel the search and return to displaying all Journal items.

FIGURE 14.6

Performing a basic search of the Journal.

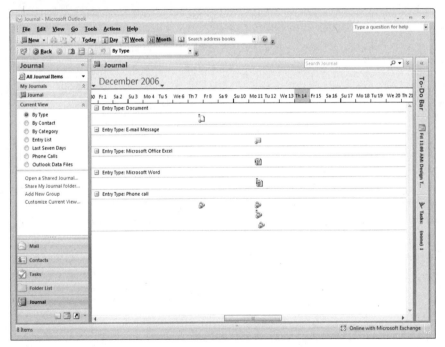

If you need more control over the search, click the double down arrow at the top-right corner of the Journal display. Outlook displays additional criterion fields as shown in Figure 14.7. Each field lets you enter a search term or select from a drop-down list. As you make entries, the Journal display is automatically filtered to show only matching entries. You can also take the following actions:

- To change a displayed criterion field — for example, from Categories to Start — click the arrow adjacent to the field name and select from the list that is displayed.

- To remove a criterion field, click the arrow adjacent to the field name and select Remove.

- To add a new criterion field, click Add Criteria and select from the list.

- To cancel the search and display all Journal entries, click the X to the right of the Search Journal box.

- To hide the additional criterion fields, click the double up arrow at the top-right corner of the Journal display.

FIGURE 14.7

Performing an advanced search of the Journal.

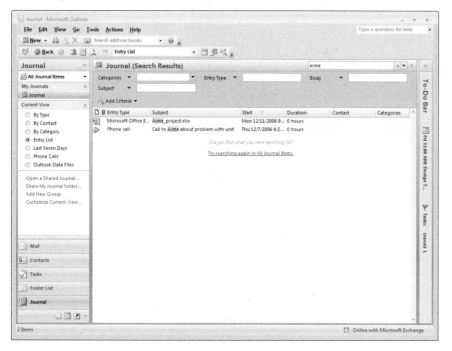

Specifying What's Saved in Journal Entries

Outlook's automatic Journal entry feature can be useful, but you may not want it to save everything you do. You can customize Outlook to specify precisely which types of items are automatically saved as Journal entries. Here's how:

1. Select Options from the Tools menu to display the Options dialog box.

2. If necessary, click the Preferences tab.

3. In the Contacts and Notes section, click the Journal Options button to open the Journal Options dialog box (see Figure 14.8).

4. In the Automatically Record These Items list, place a checkmark next to the Outlook items for which you want automatic Journal entries created.

5. In the For These Contacts list, place a checkmark next to the contacts for which you want automatic Journal entries created.

6. In the Also Record Files From list, place a checkmark next to the Microsoft Office applications for which you want automatic Journal entries created.

7. Click OK twice to close all dialog boxes.

FIGURE 14.8

Setting Journal options.

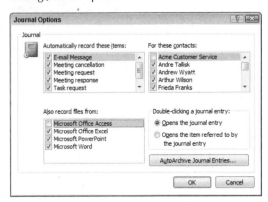

There are two other elements in the Journal Options dialog box. One option determines what happens when you double-click a Journal entry that has a file associated with it, such as an email message or a Word document. You can choose to open either the Journal entry itself or the linked document.

Finally, the AutoArchive Journal Entries button lets you set AutoArchive options. These options are covered in Chapter 18.

Summary

Outlook's Journal lets you keep track of the time you spend on various activities. Some activities, such as working on email messages and Microsoft Office documents, can be tracked automatically. Other activities can be tracked manually. You can choose between several Journal displays to view the information in the way you need. You can also use the powerful search tool to narrow the Journal display to show only the entries of interest. The Journal is a useful tool for keeping track of and managing your time.

Chapter 15

Keeping Track of Tasks

I n today's busy world, few of us have any shortage of things to do. There always seems to be a list of tasks waiting for our attention. Particularly in a high-pressure business or professional environment, it can be very important to keep track of your tasks so that you can organize your time efficiently. Outlook's Task feature is a powerful tool that can greatly simplify this.

Understanding Tasks

A *task* is similar to an appointment in that it is something you must attend to. It is different in that it does not have a specific date or time associated with it, although it may well have a due date by which it is supposed to be completed. In this sense, Outlook tasks are pretty much like a paper to-do list that you stick on the fridge. When you look a little deeper, however, you'll find they can do so much more:

- You can be reminded of a task at a specified time and date.

- You can specify different priorities for different tasks.

- You can assign a task to someone else and send them a message with the required information.

- You can assign a status to a task (not started, in progress, and so on) as well as a percent completed value.

- You can send a status report on a task to other people.

I find that Outlook's Task feature is something I use all the time.

Using the Task View

To switch to Task view in Outlook, click the Tasks button in the navigation pane or select Tasks from the Go menu. The default Tasks view is shown in Figure 15.1. This view shows active tasks—those not yet completed. They are arranged by due date initially, although you can change the sort order by clicking the column headings (To-Do Title, Status, and so on) at the top of the list.

Strictly speaking, the display shown in Figure 15.1 is the *To-Do List*—that is, uncompleted tasks. If you want to display all tasks, including completed ones, click the Tasks item under My Tasks in the navigation pane (see Figure 15.2). This view shows all tasks, with completed ones displayed at the bottom and crossed out.

FIGURE 15.1

The default Tasks view displays a list of all your active tasks.

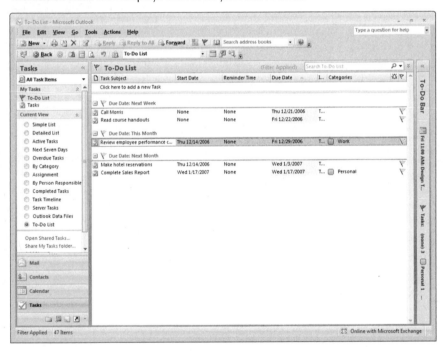

No Due Date?

Though most tasks have a due date, it is not required. Tasks that do not have a due date are displayed in their own section, No Due Date, when tasks are organized by due date.

FIGURE 15.2

You can also display all tasks, including completed ones.

View all tasks

View active tasks

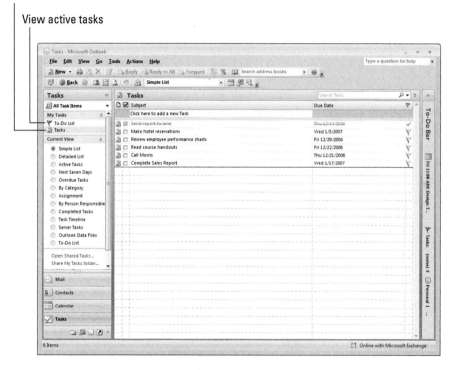

While you are viewing tasks, you can open a single task by double-clicking it. You can also perform certain actions with the task by right-clicking it and selecting from the context menu. These actions are

- Mark a task as complete
- Assign the task to someone
- Add a follow-up to the task
- Assign a category to the task

You learn more about these actions later in the chapter when I show you how to create a new task.

Outlook provides you with several other ways to view your tasks. You can switch to a different view by selecting the desired view in the navigation pane. The views are:

- **Simple List:** A list of all tasks including completed ones (same as clicking Tasks as described earlier).
- **Detailed List:** Similar to Simple List but with more details about each task.
- **Active Tasks:** Tasks not marked as completed.
- **Next Seven Days:** Tasks due within the next seven days.
- **Overdue Tasks:** Tasks whose due date has passed but are not marked as completed.
- **By Category:** All tasks organized by assigned category.
- **Assignment:** Tasks organized by the person they are assigned to.
- **By Person Responsible:** Tasks organized by owner (the person who created the task).
- **Completed Tasks:** Tasks that have been marked as completed.
- **Task Timeline:** Displays tasks arranged on a timeline according to due date.
- **Outlook Data Files:** Displays tasks organized by the Outlook data file they are in. This is relevant only if you have more than one Personal Folders file.
- **To-Do List:** Displays active tasks in a simplified, easy-to-use format. See the section "To-Do List View," later in this Chapter, for more details.

Task Timeline View

Task Timeline view arranges tasks on a timeline according to their due date, as shown in Figure 15.3. This visual representation can be useful for finding time periods when a lot of tasks are due, or for locating relatively free periods on your schedule.

What About Start Dates?

A task can have a start date assigned to it as well as a due date. A start date can be useful when there is a reason that you cannot start a task before that date. When displayed in Timeline view, a task with a start date is displayed at the start date with a line extending to the due date.

FIGURE 15.3

Tasks displayed on a timeline.

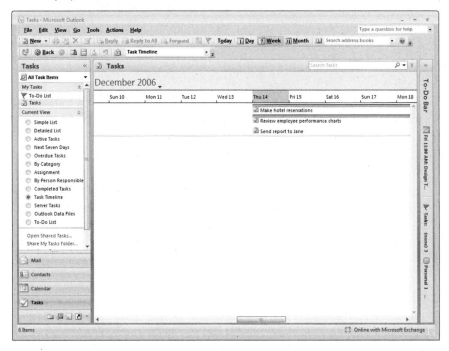

In the figure, the Task Timeline view is displaying a week, with the days listed across the top of the display. You can switch between day, week, and month views by clicking the corresponding button on the toolbar. You can also quickly scroll to today by clicking the Today button. To scroll forward and backward in time, use the horizontal scroll bar at the bottom of the window.

To-Do List View

The To-Do List view displays a simplified list of active tasks. It is not the same thing as the To-Do Bar, which is covered later in the chapter. The To-Do List is shown in Figure 15.4. In the figure, the tasks are arranged by due date, as indicated by the heading at the top of the list. Click this heading to arrange the tasks by other fields such as Category or Importance.

FIGURE 15.4

Viewing the To-Do List.

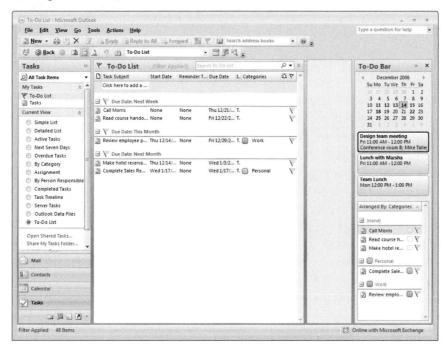

At the top of the To-Do List is a box labeled Click here to add. You can click here and type a new task title. When you press Enter, the task is automatically created with a due date of today and default settings for other task data such as importance. Double-click the newly created task to change the due date or any other aspects of the task.

Creating a New Task

To create a new task, click the New button when you are in Task view, or select Task from the New menu when in any other view (you can also press Ctrl+Shift+K). Outlook will create a new task and display it as shown in Figure 15.5.

The only required entry on this form is the subject, which will be the title of the task displayed in Task view. The other task information on this form is explained here and in the following sections:

- **Start Date:** If you want to specify a start date for the task, click the adjacent down arrow and select the date from the calendar.

- **Due Date:** Click the adjacent down arrow and select the task's due date from the calendar.

- **Status:** By default this is Not Started. If necessary, you can open this list and select In Progress, Completed, Waiting on Someone Else, or Deferred.

- **Priority:** The default is Normal; you can also select Low or High.

- **% Complete:** If the task is already partially complete, use the up and down arrows to specify the correct value in this field.

- **Categorize:** Click this button to assign the task to an Outlook category.

- **Follow Up:** Click this button to assign a follow-up to the task.

- **Private:** Click this button to make the task private so it will not be viewable by other people when you share your calendar.

- **Reminder:** Check this option if you want to be reminded of the task, then use the adjacent fields to specify the date and time of the reminder. Click the speaker icon to change the sound played at the reminder time.

- **Contacts:** Click this button to associate the task with one or more of your contacts.

- **Save & Close:** Click this button when you are finished defining the task.

Other aspects of creating a new task are explained in the following sections.

FIGURE 15.5

Creating a new task.

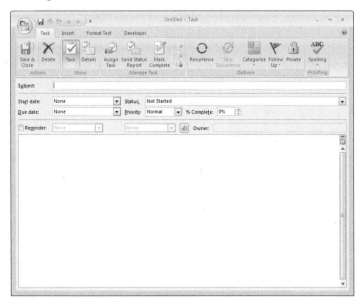

Entering Task Details

If you click the Details button in the Show section of the ribbon, Outlook displays the Details window for the task. This window is shown in Figure 15.6.

Entering details for a new task.

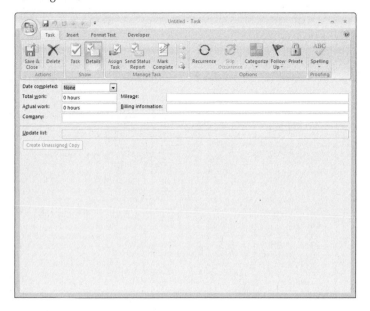

The fields available in the Details window let you keep track of additional information related to a task. You can specify the completion date, enter information about the time spent on the task, identify a company associated with the task, track mileage, and enter billing information. Outlook does not track this information for you, but just provides these detail fields for you to enter it in.

The lower section of the Details window is relevant only if the task has been assigned to someone and is explained in the next section.

When you have finished entering details for the task, click the Task button on the ribbon to return to the regular task window. You can also click Save & Close if you have finished defining the task.

Assigning a Task

Outlook lets you assign a task to someone else. This can be useful in a variety of situations such as when you are heading a committee and need to delegate various jobs to the committee members. By using Outlook's Assign Task command you can track progress and be notified when each task has been completed.

To assign a task, create the task as described earlier in this chapter. You can also open an existing task and, as long as you are the owner of the task, assign it to someone else. Here's how:

1. Click the Assign Task button on the ribbon. Outlook displays the form shown in Figure 15.7. This is actually just the regular task form with a few extra elements.

2. In the To field, enter the email address of the person you are assigning the task. You can also click the To button and select from your contacts.

3. Enter additional information about the task, such as subject and due date, if it has not already been entered.

4. Check or uncheck the two available options (explained next).

5. Click the Send button.

FIGURE 15.7

Assigning a task to someone.

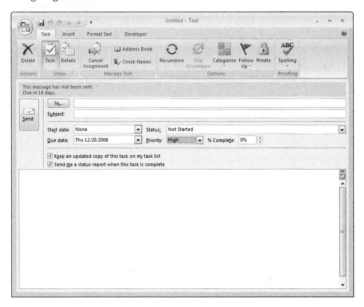

There are two options available when you assign a task to someone. They are

- **Keep an Updated Copy of This Task on My Task List:** If this option is selected, you will receive automatic updates when the person whom you assign the task to updates its status.

- **Send Me a Status Report When This Task Is Complete:** If this option is selected, you will receive an automatic notification when the person whom you assign the task to marks it as completed.

When you send a task assignment, the recipient receives an email message containing information about the assignment and permitting them to either accept or decline the assignment. You learn more about this and other aspects of task assignments later in this chapter in the section "Working with Assigned Tasks."

Specifying Task Recurrence

Like appointments, a task can have a defined recurrence. For example, you may have to review each month's sales figures by the end of the next month. Rather than entering a new task each month, you can define a task that recurs each month.

To define a recurring task, create the task as usual and before saving and closing it click the Recurrence button on the ribbon. Outlook opens the Task Recurrence dialog box as shown in Figure 15.8.

FIGURE 15.8

Defining a recurring task.

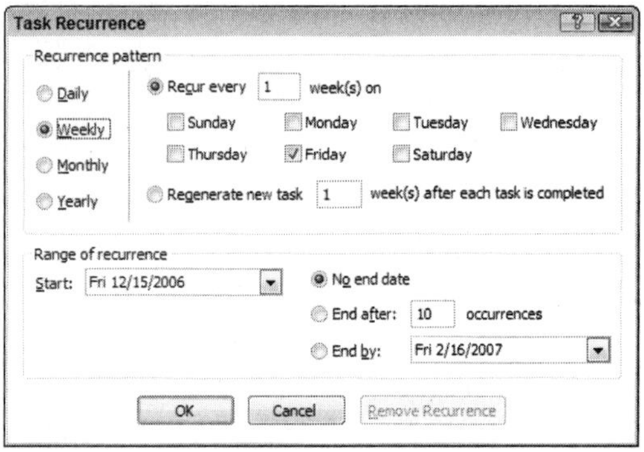

You can see that there are four basic patterns of recurrence: Daily, Weekly, Monthly, and Yearly. When you choose the basic pattern in the top left of the dialog box, the remainder of the options will change to reflect what's available:

- **Daily:** You can choose every so many days or every weekday.
- **Weekly:** You specify how often (every week, every two weeks, and so on) and the day or days of the week.
- **Monthly:** You specify which day of the month, either as a number (the 25th of each month, for example) or a day of the week (the first Thursday, for example).
- **Yearly:** You specify a specific date (June 12, for example) or a day of a month (the first Monday in June, for example).

In all cases, you also specify a start date and when the recurring tasks will end.

Assigning Recurring Tasks

When you assign a recurring task, a copy of the task will remain in your task list but cannot be updated automatically. However, if you requested a status report when the task is complete, you will receive a status report for each occurrence of the task that is completed.

Working with Assigned Tasks

Working with assigned tasks, whether you are the person doing the assigning or the person accepting the assignment, can be a bit confusing. Once you understand it, however, I think you'll find the tool very useful.

Receiving a Task Assignment

When someone sends you a task assignment, you receive an email that looks as shown in Figure 15.9. There are three buttons of importance on the ribbon:

FIGURE 15.9

Receiving a task assignment from someone else.

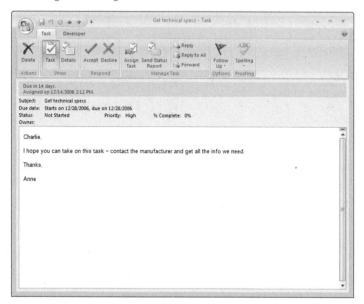

- **Accept:** Accepts the assignment, adds it to your task list, and notifies the person who sent you the assignment that you have accepted.

- **Decline:** Declines the assignment and notifies the person who sent you the assignment that you have declined.

- **Assign Task:** Lets you assign the task to a third person who will receive the same notification and can accept, decline, or assign the task to yet another person. The person who originally assigned the task to you will be notified of the reassignment.

Receiving Accept/Decline Notifications

When you send a task assignment to someone, one of three things will happen (assuming that the assignment is not simply ignored!):

- First, the person may accept the task. You'll receive a message to that effect, and the task will automatically be updated to reflect that the task was accepted and is now owned by that person.

- Second, the person may decline the task. You'll receive an email notification. When you open this email you can take one of two actions by clicking the corresponding button on the toolbar:

  - **Return the Task to Your Task List:** You regain ownership of the task.

  - **Assign Task:** Assign the task to someone else.

- Finally, the person you assigned the task to may assign it to someone else. That person can accept, decline, or reassign the task.

About Task Ownership

A task has, at any given moment, one and only one owner. Owning a task means that you can assign it to someone else. Here's how ownership works:

- When you create a task, you are the original owner.

- When you assign the task to someone, they become the temporary owner.

- The person who receives the assignment can do one of three things: (1) Accept the task and become the owner, (2) Decline the task and return ownership to you, or (3) Assign the task to a third person who then becomes the temporary owner.

If you assign a task to someone and that person declines, ownership passes back to you only when you reclaim ownership by returning the task to your task list — it does not happen automatically.

Assigning a Task to Multiple People

Though Outlook does not prevent you from assigning a task to two or more people, you cannot keep an updated copy of the task in your task list. For this reason, it is better to divide a multi-person task into parts and assign each part, as a separate task, to an individual person.

Task Status Reports

When you have accepted a task assignment, you own that task, and no one but you can change the task even though it may be on their task list. You can then, as you work on the task, open it and update the status and percentage completed of the task and you can also mark it as completed. When you do so, and save the modified task, an update will be sent to the person who assigned you the task (assuming that the Keep an Updated Copy of This Task on My Task List option was selected when you were sent the assignment). By default, this update will not appear in the task assigner's Inbox but will be processed automatically and the updated information will be available the next time they view the task.

Likewise, if the Send Me a Status Report When This Task Is Complete option was selected when you were sent the assignment, the person who assigned the task will receive an automatic update when you mark the task as complete. While task complete updates are processed automatically, they will appear in the person's Inbox.

A task can have more than one prior owner. Suppose, for example, that person A created the task and sent a task request to person B. Then, person B sent a task request to person C, who accepted the task. C is the owner of the task and both A and B are prior owners and will receive status updates.

Sending a Status Report Manually

There may be times when you want to manually send a status report or comments about a task. There are two situations when this might be desirable:

- The original task request (when you were assigned the task) did not include a request for automatic status updates.

- You were not assigned the task—it is simply a task that you created but want to keep other people updated about.

To do so, open the task and click the Send Status Report button. Outlook creates an email message with information about the task status in the body of the message. You can add text as needed. If the task was assigned to you, the To field will already contain the addresses of the task's prior owners. You can add additional recipients if desired.

Other Ways of Viewing Tasks

The most flexible way to view your tasks is using Task view, as explained earlier in this chapter. You can also have Outlook display tasks on the To-Do Bar and in Calendar view.

Viewing Tasks on the To-Do Bar

You can display active tasks on the To-Do Bar along with the Date Navigator and upcoming appointments. They are displayed at the bottom as shown in Figure 15.10.

If you do not see your tasks on the To-Do Bar, you may need to change the To-Do Bar display by right-clicking it and then selecting Task List from the context menu.

FIGURE 15.10

Viewing the daily task list on the To-Do Bar.

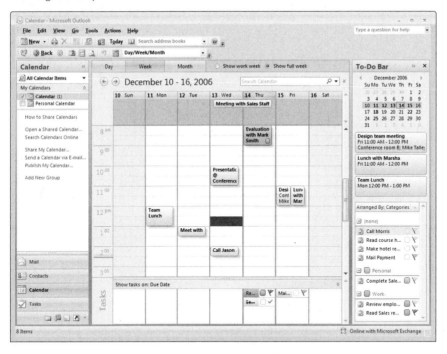

Viewing Tasks on the Calendar

The Outlook Calendar can display the daily task list along with your appointments. The daily task list is displayed below the appointment section of the Calendar as shown in Figure 15.11. You have three options as to how the daily task list is displayed:

- **Normal**, as shown in the figure, with task subjects, categories, and follow-up flags.
- **Minimized**, which displays the number of active tasks for the displayed time period without any details.
- **Off**, which does not display the list.

To switch between daily task list views, display the Outlook Calendar, choose Daily Task List from the View menu, and then select the desired view from the next menu. This menu also lets you specify whether to display tasks by due date (the default) or start date, and whether to show completed tasks.

FIGURE 15.11

Viewing the daily task list on the Outlook Calendar.

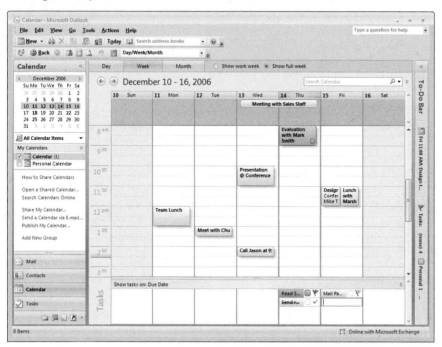

Setting Task Options

Outlook offers several options that relate to the way tasks and task assignments work. To view and change these options, select Options from the Tools menu to display the Options dialog box. One task option is located on the Preferences tab, as shown in Figure 15.12. It specifies what time of day a reminder is displayed for a task that is due today (only for tasks with a reminder set, of course).

FIGURE 15.12

The Task Options section of the Preferences tab in the Options dialog box.

The other task options are accessed by clicking the Task Options button on the Preferences tab to open the Task Options dialog box, shown in Figure 15.13. The first two options determine the colors used to display overdue tasks and completed tasks — the default colors are red and dark gray, respectively. The other options are

- **Keep Updated Copies**...: If selected, Outlook maintains updated copies of tasks you have assigned on your task list.

- **Send Status Reports**...: If selected, Outlook automatically sends a status report when you mark as completed a task that you have been assigned.

- **Set Reminders**...: If selected, Outlook automatically sets a reminder for all tasks that you create with a due date.

The Task Options dialog box.

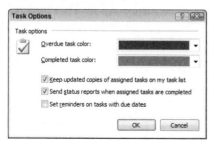

Summary

Outlook provides some powerful tools for keeping track of your tasks. Though a task does not have a specific period of time associated with it (unlike an appointment), it can have a due date. By listing your tasks and optionally reminding you of when they are due, Outlook can greatly reduce the chance that you'll forget to do something important. Outlook even lets you assign tasks to other people and track their progress, a really valuable tool for a manager or team leader.

Chapter 16

Making Use of RSS Feeds

RSS stands for *Really Simple Syndication*, a family of web feed formats that are used to deliver content over the Internet. The term *syndication* refers to the fact that you subscribe to one or more specific feeds and your software — Outlook in this case — automatically receives the files and displays the information they contain. You can subscribe to RSS feeds on just about any topic you can imagine — news, sports, finance, weather...you name it.

Understanding RSS

Though most people interpret RSS to stand for Really Simple Syndication, the fact is that it is a whole family of syndication formats that includes Really Simple Syndication as well as Rich Site Summary and RDF Site Summary. But in reality, the precise syndication format is irrelevant to you, the end user, as long as you get the information you want.

RSS is particularly useful because it lets you combine information from a variety of sources in one location. No longer do you have to visit separate web sites for news, weather, stock reports, and so on. Instead you can subscribe to the RSS feed from each of the web sites and then have titles or brief summaries displayed in your RSS reader. When a title catches your interest, click the link to read the entire article.

Most modern web browsers support RSS feeds, and there are also many stand-alone programs, many of them free, for this purpose. Why then use Outlook? For me, it's a matter of having one place where I go for all sorts of information. I go to Outlook for email, appointments, contact information, tasks, and so on — why not for news and other RSS feeds?

> ## RSS Aggregators?
>
> You may have heard the term *RSS aggregator* and wondered what it is. Nothing special — it just refers to a program, such as Outlook, that lets you subscribe to and view RSS feeds.

Subscribing to an RSS Feed

In Outlook, an RSS feed is considered to be a kind of account. Accordingly, you subscribe to feeds and edit or delete existing subscriptions in the Account Settings dialog box. To display RSS feed accounts, select Account Settings from the Tools menu and click the RSS Feeds tab. The dialog box is shown in Figure 16.1. In the figure, there are several RSS feeds listed, but if you are just getting started the list will be empty.

FIGURE 16.1

You use the Account Settings dialog box to work with RSS feed accounts.

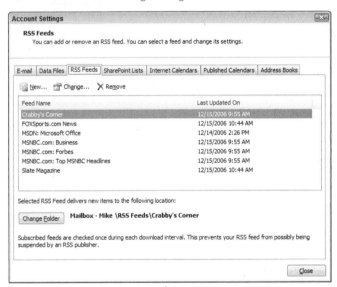

To subscribe to an RSS feed you must know its URL. This is similar to the URL for a web page and will have this general form:

```
http://rss.somesite.com/rss/news.rss
```

The file extension may be .RSS as in this example or it may be .XML. There are two ways to get the URL for an RSS feed. In one situation, the URL may be listed on the web site that offers the subscription, and you can simply copy and paste it into Outlook or just type it in. However, some web sites display small buttons that visitors can click to subscribe their browser to the feed. The most commonly used icons are shown in Figure 16.2.

When only an RSS button is displayed on a web site and not the URL of the feed, here's how to get the URL:

1. Right-click the button to display a context menu.

2. From the menu select Copy Shortcut (in Internet Explorer) or Copy Link Location (in Firefox) to copy the URL to the Windows Clipboard.

FIGURE 16.2

These icons are used on web sites to identify RSS feeds.

Once you have the URL of the RSS feed, here's how to subscribe Outlook to the feed:

1. On the RSS Feeds tab of the Account Settings dialog box, click the New button to display the New RSS Feed dialog box (see Figure 16.3).

2. Paste or type the feed URL into the box.

3. Select Add to display the RSS Feed Options dialog box as shown in Figure 16.4.

4. Set options as described here (although these options rarely need changing):

   ▪ **Feed Name:** You can accept the default feed name or enter your own. This name is displayed in Outlook to identify the feed.

   ▪ **Change Folder:** If you want to change the folder where download feed items are kept, click this button. There is rarely a reason to do this.

   ▪ **Automatically Download Enclosures...:** If you select this option, any enclosures that the RSS feed provides will be downloaded automatically when the feed is updated and not just when you view the feed.

   ▪ **Download the Full Article...:** If you select this option, full articles will be downloaded automatically when the feed is updated rather than just on demand when you open them. This increases update time but lets you read articles when you are offline.

   ▪ **Update Limit:** If this option is selected (recommended), the RSS feed will be updated at the publisher's recommended interval. If you turn this option off, Outlook may try to update the feed more often, which can cause your subscription to be cancelled.

5. Click OK to return to the Account Settings dialog box.

6. Click Close to close the Account Settings dialog box.

FIGURE 16.3

Subscribing to a new RSS feed.

FIGURE 16.4

Setting options for a new RSS feed.

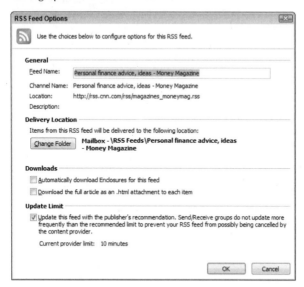

Displaying RSS Feeds

RSS feeds that you are subscribed to are displayed in the Outlook folder display in the navigation pane, as shown in Figure 16.5. The number next to each feed tells you the number of unread items in the feed.

To display a list of the items in a feed, click it. The items are displayed in a list in Outlook's main window, as shown in Figure 16.6. Each item's title is displayed, although you can change this as I explain soon. In many ways, feed items are like email messages — you can assign them to categories, flag them for follow up, forward an item to an email recipient, and so on.

FIGURE 16.5

Subscribed RSS feeds are displayed in the folder list.

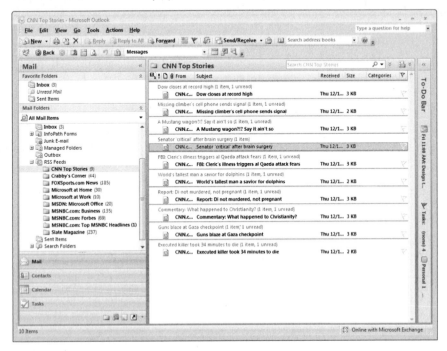

Renaming an RSS Feed

I f you want to rename an RSS feed, right-click it in the folder list and select Rename from the context menu. You can then edit the name directly in the folder list.

FIGURE 16.6

The titles of the items in the selected RSS feed are displayed in the main window.

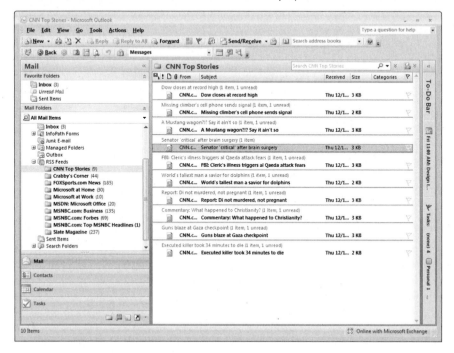

By default, RSS feed items are arranged by date received, with the newest at the top of the list. You can change this by selecting Arrange By from the View menu and then selecting the desired arrangement from the next menu.

You can also change the item display to show not only the title of each item but a brief synopsis (if provided by the feed publisher). To do so, select AutoPreview from the View menu. The display of RSS feed items with AutoPreview is shown in Figure 16.7. Select the same command again to turn AutoPreview off.

FIGURE 16.7

Use AutoPreview to display titles and summaries of RSS feed items.

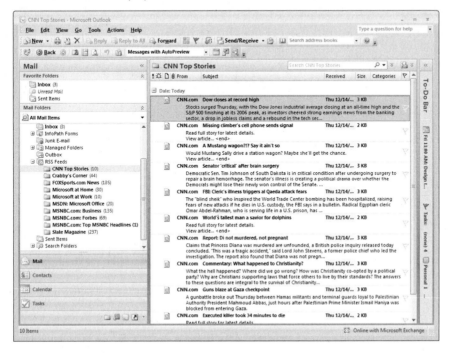

When you open an RSS item by double-clicking it, it opens it its own window as shown in Figure 16.8. You can see that a summary of the article is displayed as well as a link to the full article (the link says "View Article"). At this point there are two slightly different things that you can do to read the article and any associated content:

- **View the article:** By clicking the View Article link you display the article in your default browser. This is just like viewing a web page.

- **Download the article and any content:** By clicking the Download Content button on the ribbon and then selecting Download Article, you download a copy of the article to your computer. It displays as an attachment to the RSS item, as shown in Figure 16.9. You can open this attachment to view in your browser.

The difference here is that in the second case you have a local copy of the article on your computer, whereas in the first case you do not. Note that if you select the Download the Full Article option when setting up the RSS feed account, this download happens automatically.

FIGURE 16.8

When you open an RSS item it appears in its own window.

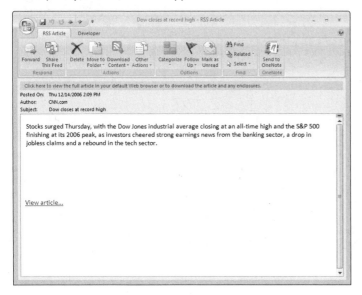

FIGURE 16.9

After you download an article, it is displayed as an attachment to the item.

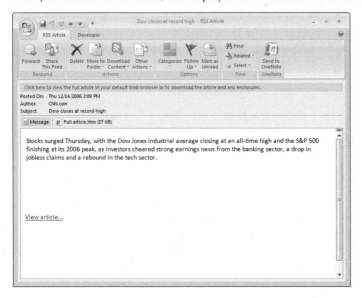

Sharing Feeds with Other Outlook 2007 Users

When someone receives a Share This Feed invitation from you, the message contains the URL of the feed. Most people will have to add this URL to their RSS feed program manually, but Outlook 2007 users can click an Add This RSS Feed link to quickly add the feed to their RSS accounts list.

Other actions you can take with an open RSS item include:

- **Forward:** Click the Forward button on the ribbon to create a new email message with the article summary in the body and the full article attached. You can edit the message, address it, and send it to other people.

- **Share This Feed:** Click the Share This Feed button on the toolbar to create a new email message that contains information about the RSS feed. Then, address and send the message to whomever you desire. The recipients can then subscribe to the feed if they find it interesting.

Deleting and Changing RSS Feeds

To delete an RSS feed, you can right-click it in the folders list and select Delete from the context menu. You can also display the RSS Feeds tab of the Account Settings dialog box (select Account Settings from the Tools menu), click the RSS Feeds tab, click the feed you want to delete, and click Remove.

You can also modify the settings for a feed by selecting it in on the RSS Feeds tab of the Account Settings dialog box and clicking Change. The RSS Feed Options dialog box is displayed (shown earlier in Figure 16.4) where you can make the desired changes.

Importing or Exporting Groups of RSS Feeds

Outlook supports the ability to import and export collections of RSS feed configuration information. This information is stored in an XML file that has the .opml extension (which stands for Outline Processor Markup Language). This file can be forwarded by email or stored on a central server and made available to employees. For example, a stock brokerage firm could put together a list of RSS feeds that it thinks would be useful to its brokers.

Exporting RSS Feed Information

To export an RSS feed collection:

1. Select Import and Export from the File menu to display the Import and Export Wizard (see Figure 16.10).

2. Select Export RSS Feeds to an OPML File.

3. Click Next. Outlook displays a list of RSS feeds that are defined in Outlook — in other words, feeds that you have subscribed to (see Figure 16.11).

4. Put checkmarks next to the RSS feeds you want to export and clear those that you do not want to export.

5. Click Next.

6. Enter the name of the file to export to, or click the Browse button to change folders and specify a name, then click Save.

7. Click Next to complete the export process.

FIGURE 16.10

Exporting RSS feed information to an OPML file.

FIGURE 16.11

Selecting which RSS feeds to include in the OPML file.

Importing RSS Feed Information from an OPML File

Importing RSS information from an OPML file is essentially the reverse of the previous process:

1. Select Import and Export from the File menu to display the Import and Export Wizard.

2. Select Import RSS Feeds from an OPML File.

3. Click Next.

4. Enter the name of the file, or use the Browse button to find it.

5. Click Next.

6. In the next dialog box, put a checkmark next to the feeds that you want to import and clear those that you do not want to import.

7. Click Next.

Backing Up Your RSS Settings

Even if you do not need to share your RSS feed information with others, you can export it to an OPML file to serve as a backup.

Importing RSS Feed Information from the Common Feed List

Microsoft's web browser, Internet Explorer, can also be used as an RSS aggregator. If you have version 7 or later of the browser, it has the capability to share RSS feed information with Outlook — this is called the *common feed list*. In other words, RSS feeds you have subscribed to in Internet Explorer are available in Outlook, and vice versa.

When Outlook detects a compatible version of Internet Explorer, it asks you whether you want to combine and synchronize the lists. Select Yes if you want to be able to view all your RSS feeds in either program, both existing feeds and ones you add in the future. Select No to keep a separate list of RSS subscriptions in each program.

If you decide not to combine the RSS subscriptions for Outlook and Internet Explorer, you can always import subscriptions from the common feed list at a later time. The process is very similar to importing from an OPML file except that there is no file involved:

1. Select Import and Export from the File menu to display the Import and Export Wizard.
2. Select Import RSS Feeds from the Common Feed List.
3. Click Next.
4. In the next dialog box, put a checkmark next to the feeds that you want to import and clear those that you do not want to import.
5. Click Next.
6. Click Finish.

Summary

Really Simple Syndication, or RSS, is an excellent way to keep track of updated information from a wide variety of sources. Many different web sites publish RSS feeds on just about any topic you can imagine. Outlook's RSS aggregator tools let you subscribe to and view RSS feeds in the same program that you use for email, contacts, and appointments.

Part IV

Getting the Most Out of Outlook

Chapter 17

Making the Most of Outlook Categories

One of Outlook's most useful but underutilized features is categories. By using categories consistently, you can greatly simplify the task of using Outlook and finding the information you need. This is particularly true after you have been using Outlook for a while and the amount of information in Outlook has grown to a size that is hard to manage without categories.

Understanding Categories

We all use categories in our daily lives whether or not we are aware of it. At work, do you devote one file cabinet drawer to suppliers and another to customers? If so, you are using categories. At home, do you keep soups on one shelf in the pantry and vegetables on another? Again, categories. How about your CD collection — are your rock-and-roll CDs kept separate from your jazz and classical? It's hard to imagine getting by without using categories.

In Outlook, you can assign a category — or more than one category — to essentially every kind of item that Outlook has: email messages, tasks, appointments, notes, and so on. Then you can use various Outlook tools to organize and locate information based on category. There are three main ways to do this:

- In any item view, such as messages, tasks, or calendar, you can tell Outlook to organize the display by category making it easy to find related items.

- In any item view you can also use the search tool to display only those items assigned to a specific category.

IN THIS CHAPTER

Understanding categories

Working with the category list

Assigning categories to items

Organizing items by category

Filtering items by category

Sending messages with categories

Using a Quick Click category

315

■ You can use the Advanced Search tool to locate all items of any type assigned to a specific category.

The way you use categories depends on your specific situation. For some people, dividing items between Work and Personal categories is enough. A lawyer might create an Outlook category for each of his clients. A corporate vice president might create a category for each department that she oversees.

In Outlook, categories are sometimes called *color categories* because each category is associated with a color. This color is used to mark an item for quick identification. For example, Figure 17.1 shows how a categorized email message is marked in the Categories column. In this example, both the category color and category name are displayed, but if the Categories column were narrower, only the identifying color would appear. If an item has not been assigned to a category, the Category column will be blank.

FIGURE 17.1

Items are identified by the category color.

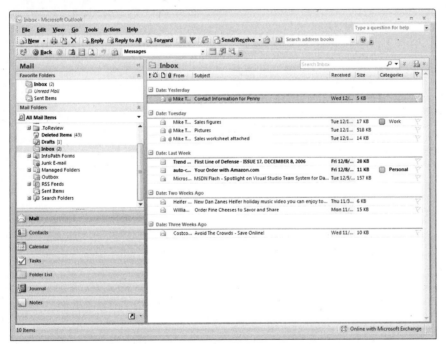

Working with the Category List

Outlook comes with a small set of defined categories. Each is named after its color — blue category, orange category, and so on. These names aren't too useful, so you'll want to rename them. You can also create new categories if the existing ones are not enough.

To work with the category list, click the Categorize button on Outlook's toolbar, as shown in Figure 17.2, and select All Categories from the menu. Outlook displays the Color Categories dialog box as shown in Figure 17.3. All defined categories are listed here. In the figure, you can see that two of the color categories have already been renamed. You can take various actions with categories in this dialog box, as described next.

FIGURE 17.2

The Categorize button.

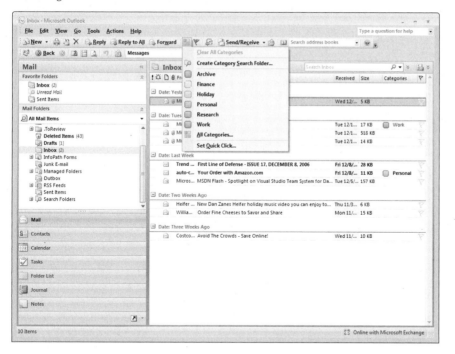

No Categorize Button?

If the Categorize button is not visible or is grayed out, it is probably because you do not have an item, such as an email message or task, selected. Because this button is also used to assign categories to items, it makes no sense to have it available if an item is not selected.

FIGURE 17.3

The Color Categories dialog box.

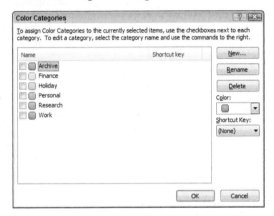

- To rename a category, click it and then click the Rename button. Edit the name as desired and press Enter. The new name applies to all items that have already been assigned this category as well as to new items.

- To delete a category, select it and click Delete.

- To create a new category, click the New button to display the Add New Category dialog box (see Figure 17.4). Enter a name for the category, select its color, and if desired select a shortcut key, then click OK.

- To change an existing category's color, select the category and choose from the Color list. Though Outlook does not prevent you from using the same color with two or more categories, it is not recommended.

- To assign a shortcut key to a category, select the category and choose a shortcut key from the list. The available shortcut keys are Ctrl in combination with the function keys F2 through F12. You can use a shortcut key to assign a category to a selected Outlook item without using the menus or toolbar. To unassign a shortcut key, select (none) from the list.

When finished, click OK.

FIGURE 17.4

Creating a new category.

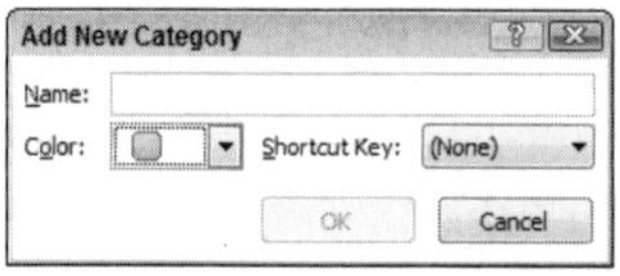

Assigning Categories to Items

Assigning a category to an Outlook item is done the same way regardless of the type of item. You can assign one or more categories to an item, or remove a category assignment, when it is selected but not open—for example, if you have clicked a message in the Inbox:

- If you have assigned a shortcut key to the desired category, simply press the shortcut (for example, Ctrl+F3).

- To assign a single category, click the Categorize button on the toolbar and select the desired category from the menu. You can access the same menu by right-clicking the selected item in the Categories column.

- To assign multiple categories, click the Categorize button on the toolbar and select All Categories from the menu to display the Color Categories dialog box (shown earlier in Figure 17.3). Put a checkmark next to the categories that you want to assign to the item, then click OK.

You can assign categories to multiple items at once using the previous steps. All you need to do is select the items first:

- To select a continuous range of items, click the first item and then hold down the Shift key and click the last item.

- To select individual items, click the first item and then hold down the Ctrl key while clicking other items.

You can also assign a category to an open item. Simply click the Categorize button on the ribbon and select from the menu.

An open item displays its assigned categories, if any, as colored bars just below the ribbon. For instance, Figure 17.5 shows an email message that has been assigned to the "Personal" and "Holiday" categories. Right-click a category bar to access a context menu that lets you work with categories.

FIGURE 17.5

An open item displays assigned categories just below the ribbon.

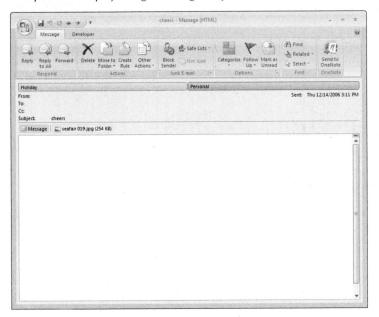

Organizing Items by Category

Each Outlook view — Mail, Contacts, Tasks, and so on — gives you the option of organizing the items in various ways. One of these options is to organize the view by category. Using the Task view for an example (other views work in much the same way), you can see in Figure 17.6 that the default organization is by due date — which makes sense for tasks. But you may want to organize them by category. You do so by selecting Current View from the View menu and then selecting By Category from the next menu. The resulting display is shown in Figure 17.7. If you have any items not assigned a category, they will have their own group.

FIGURE 17.6

The default Task view organizes tasks by due date.

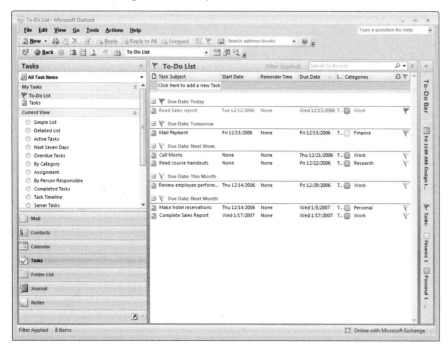

FIGURE 17.7

FIGURE 17.7

You can also display tasks and other items organized by category.

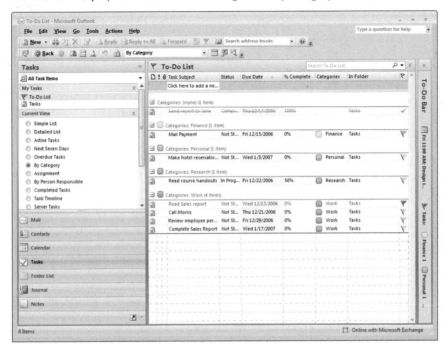

Filtering Items by Category

A *filter*, or search, goes beyond organizing items by category to display only those items assigned to one or more specified categories. Non-matching items are temporarily hidden. The search feature works in essentially the same way for all views and can be used for messages, appointments, contacts, and so on. I will use tasks to illustrate.

At the top right of the View window is a search field with an adjacent arrow. When you click the arrow, the search area expands to display more fields, as shown in Figure 17.8. Click the arrow again to hide these details.

FIGURE 17.8

Searching for items in a specified category.

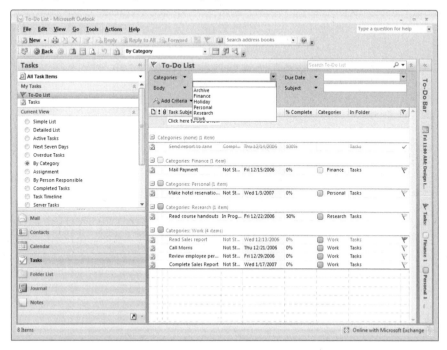

You can see that one of the search fields is Categories. If you click the arrow to the right of this field, you can select from a list of all Outlook categories. As soon as you do so, the display changes to show only those items that have been assigned that category, as shown in Figure 17.9. To cancel the filter and return to displaying all categories, click the X as shown in the figure.

Of course, you can combine a category filter with other filters. You could, for example, search for all tasks in the Personal category that have a due date next week. If the criterion you want to use is not shown, click the Add Criteria button to display a list of additional criteria from which you can select.

FIGURE 17.9

Displaying only those tasks in the Personal category.

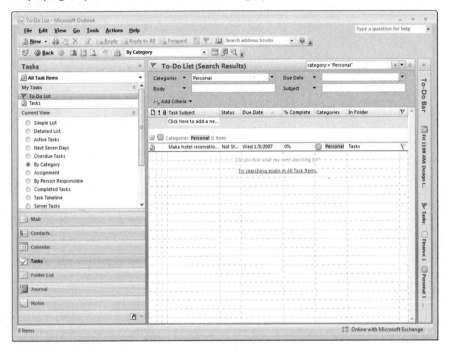

Sending Messages with Categories

You can easily assign email messages that you have received to a category, as explained earlier in this chapter. You can also assign messages that you send to a category before you send them. There are three reasons you might want to do this:

■ The copy of the message in your Sent Items folder are assigned to that category and can be organized and filtered based on category, as described earlier in this chapter.

■ The message the recipient gets is assigned to that category without their having to do anything.

■ The category is added to the recipient's category list (if not already there).

There's a potential fly in the ointment, however. Many installations of Outlook have a rule defined that automatically removes any categories from received messages (Outlook rules are covered in Chapter 9). If this rule is active, you'll never know if someone sends you a message with a category assigned. For reasons that are not clear, Microsoft recommends that you keep this rule active. If you choose, however, you can turn it off as follows:

1. Select Rules and Alerts from the Tools menu to display the Rules and Alerts dialog box.

2. If necessary, click the E-mail Rules tab (see Figure 17.10).

3. If the Clear Categories on Mail rule is listed and checked, it is active. Clear the checkmark to turn the rule off (you can always turn it back on later).

4. Click OK.

Turning off the Clear Categories rule.

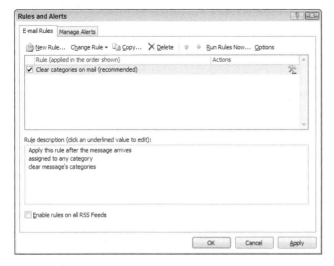

Using a Quick Click Category

Usually you have to select from a list or a dialog box to assign an Outlook item to a category. If there is one category you use more than any other, you can make it your Quick Click category and then assign it to any item by clicking once in the category column. Click again to remove the category. Other categories can still be assigned in the usual manner.

To set or change the Quick Click category:

1. Click the Categorize button on the toolbar.

2. Select Set Quick Click from the menu. Outlook displays the Set Quick Click dialog box (see Figure 17.11).

3. Select the desired category from the list, or select No Category if you do not want to have a Quick Click category.

4. Click OK.

FIGURE 17.11

Specifying the Quick Click category.

Summary

Though many Outlook users do not make use of categories, they can be a very useful feature. This is particularly true when you have been using Outlook for a while and have accumulated a large amount of information. Having information is one thing, but being able to use it efficiently is another! Categories let you organize and view your Outlook items as you see fit.

Chapter 18

Working with Outlook Folders and Data Files

Outlook stores all its data in one or more files on your hard disk (with the exception of certain Exchange account configurations). Within those files, some items are organized into folders. To use Outlook with maximum efficiency, you may want to know how to work with these folders and files.

You should be aware, however, that most users never need to be concerned with Outlook's files and folders — the default arrangement is just fine for their purposes. I recommend that you do not change Outlook's file and folder settings unless you have a real need to do so.

Understanding Files and Folders

All computer users are familiar with the idea of a *file*. It's a unit of storage on a disk that contains data, such as a word processing document, a spreadsheet, or a digital photograph. Outlook uses files to store all its information, ranging from email account settings and user options to all its email messages, appointments, tasks, and other items. In fact, Outlook uses a single file called an *Outlook Personal Folders file* to store just about everything.

Most computer users are also familiar with the concept of a *folder* (sometimes called a *directory*). Folders are used to divide a hard disk into discrete storage areas — can you imagine the confusion if all your files were stored in the same location? Outlook uses folders, too, but they are not the same as disk folders. They serve the same purpose — to help organize the items stored — but they exist within the Outlook Personal Folders file and not as separate folders on your hard disk.

Outlook folders come in different types based on the kind of item they are designed to hold. For example, your Inbox is a folder and it is intended to hold email messages, but you cannot store a contact there.

Outlook Data Files

For most Outlook users, program data and items are stored in an Outlook Personal Folders file. This is true if you are using a POP, IMAP, or HTML email account. The file has the .PST extension and is by default named OUTLOOK.PST. The folder on your hard disk where this file is normally kept is

- **Windows XP and Windows Server 2003:** X:\Documents and Settings*user*\Local Settings\Application Data\Microsoft\Outlook
- **Windows Vista:** X:\ *user*\Local Settings\AppData\Microsoft\Outlook

Here, X is the drive letter, usually C, where the operating system stores user settings, and *user* is the name you have used to log on to Windows. If the computer is configured for more than one user, each will have their own separate and independent Outlook Personal Folders file.

You can have more than one Personal Folders file, but only one is designated as the default, which means Outlook uses it to store account settings, messages, and other items. Additional PST files are used for special purposes such as archiving old items. You cannot change the storage location of the default PST file.

Outlook Data File Compatibility

Beginning with Outlook 2003 and continuing with the current version, Microsoft changed the internal format of PST files to allow for storage of more items and folders and to support multilingual Unicode data. This format is not compatible with Outlook versions 97 through 2002. If you install a new Outlook over one of these older versions, the old format PST file will be automatically converted to the new format. If, however, you want your PST file to be compatible with Outlook 2002 and earlier, you must create a PST file in the older format. This is explained later in this chapter in the section "Creating a New Personal Folders File."

Hidden Folders?

The folder where the Outlook data file is kept may be *hidden*, which means that it normally does not show up in Windows Explorer or My Computer. To see hidden folders and files, you must change a view option by selecting Options from the Tools menu (in My Computer or Explorer, not Outlook) and then on the View tab, selecting the Show Hidden Files and Folders option.

Offline Folders File

If you use a Microsoft Exchange email account rather than, or in addition to, an IMAP, POP, or HTML account, you may have an Offline Folders file (which has the .OST extension). Normally, Exchange keeps copies of your messages and other items on the server, but you can configure Outlook to keep a local copy of the items on your system, in the Offline Folders file. Doing this allows you to work with your Outlook items when a connection to the Exchange server is not available. You can find more details on OST files in Chapter 28.

Working with Outlook Folders

Outlook folders let you organize all the myriad items that you work with in Outlook. Outlook comes with a default set of folders that is a good starting point, but many users find these folders to not be enough. This section shows you how to create new folders and work with folders and folder items.

As I mentioned earlier, Outlook folders are designed to hold a specific type of item. The choices are

- **Calendar folders** hold appointments and other scheduling items.
- **Mail folders** hold email messages.
- **Contacts folders** hold contact information.
- **Journal folders** hold journal entries.
- **Task folders** hold task items.
- **Notes folders** hold notes.

You cannot move an item into a folder of the wrong type, such as moving an email message into a contacts folder. The one exception to this rule is the Deleted Items folder, which can hold any type of item.

 Note that RSS feed items are treated like email messages by Outlook when it comes to folder types.

Outlook's Default Folders

When installed, Outlook has a set of default folders located at the top level in your Personal Folders file. You cannot rename, move, or delete these default folders. They are

- **Calendar:** Holds calendar items (appointments, and so on).
- **Contacts:** Holds your contacts.

- **Deleted Items:** Holds any and all items you have deleted before they are permanently deleted. See the section "Using the Deleted Items Folder" later in this chapter.

- **Drafts:** Holds email messages you have started composing but not yet sent.

- **Inbox:** Holds received emails.

- **Journal:** Holds your journal items.

- **Junk E-mail:** Holds email that has been flagged as junk (spam).

- **Notes:** Holds your notes.

- **Outbox:** Holds emails that you have sent but that have not yet been transferred to your email server.

- **Quarantine:** Holds emails that have been flagged as containing a virus, worm, or other malicious element.

- **RSS Feeds:** Holds content from your subscribed RSS feeds.

- **Sent Items:** Holds copies of email messages you have sent.

Creating a New Email Folder

Email folders get their own section because Outlook treats them a bit differently from other folders. To be more specific, you cannot organize email folders into groups, but rather have to organize them hierarchically when you create them.

When you create a new email folder, you can place it at the top level under Personal Folders — the same level as Outlook's default folders. You can also put it in an existing folder. You can put folders within folders to essentially any level and thereby organize your email messages in the way that best suits you.

Take a look at an example. Figure 18.1 shows Outlook's default email folders. You can see that they are all at the same level within Personal folders.

FIGURE 18.1

The organization of Outlook's default email folders.

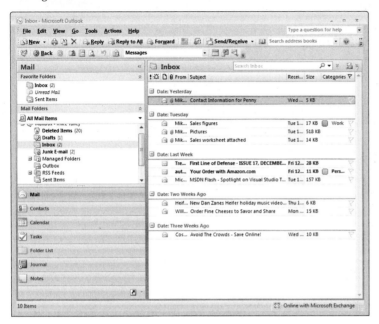

Suppose you want to organize emails from your clients by creating an email folder for each client. For this example, assume that you have three clients: Acme, Consolidated, and National. One approach would be to create three new folders at the top level. The resulting structure is shown in Figure 18.2.

FIGURE 18.2

New email folders can be created at the top level of the folder hierarchy.

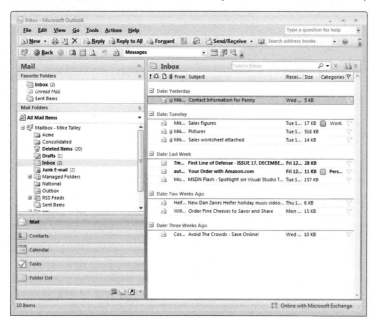

Another approach, one that I prefer, is to use the capability to create folders within other folders, resulting in a hierarchy of folders structured according to the folder contents. This approach could be implemented by creating a Clients folder at the top level and then creating Acme, Consolidated, and National folders in the Clients folder. This structure is shown in Figure 18.3. Note that a folder that contains other folders — Clients in this case — displays an adjacent plus or minus icon that you can click to show or hide the subfolders.

In any event, you do not have to decide all the details of your email folder structure ahead of time because you can always move the folders around if needed.

FIGURE 18.3

New email folders can also be created in a hierarchical structure by placing folders within other folders.

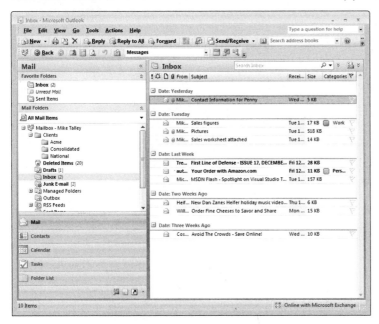

Now you can get to the details of creating a new email folder. Here are the steps to follow:

1. If necessary, click the Mail button on the navigation pane to display the mail folders.

2. If you want the new folder at the top level, right-click Personal Folders (or whatever name you have assigned to the top level). Otherwise, right-click the folder that you want the new folder in.

3. Select New Folder from the context menu. Outlook displays the Create New Folder dialog box (see Figure 18.4). The location for the new folder is shaded in the folder display — Inbox in the figure, for example. You can, if necessary, change the location at this point.

4. Type the name of the new folder in the Name box.

5. Make sure that Mail and Post Items is selected in the Folder Contains list.

6. Click OK.

The new folder is created and you can start using it to store mail items.

FIGURE 18.4

Creating a new folder to hold email items.

Creating a New Non-Email Folder

Non-mail folders — those for tasks, calendar, journal, and contacts — are handled a bit differently than mail folders. Rather than organize folders by placing them in other folders, as you do with mail folders, you use *groups*. First, here are the steps to create a non-mail folder:

1. Click the appropriate button in the navigation pane corresponding to where you want to add a new folder — Calendar, Contacts, and so on.

2. Select Folder from the File menu, then select New Folder from the next menu. Outlook displays the Create New Folder dialog box (see Figure 18.5). The folder for the type of item you selected in step 1 — Tasks in the figure, for example — will be highlighted in the folder list.

3. Enter the name of the new folder in the Name box.

4. Make sure that the Folder Contains list displays the appropriate type of item for the folder you are creating.

5. Click OK.

After you create a non-email folder, it is displayed near the top of the navigation pane along with other folders, including the default one, for that type of item. Figure 18.6 shows an example for Tasks after creating two new task folders called Work-related and Personal.

FIGURE 18.5

Creating a new folder to hold non-email items, Tasks in this case.

FIGURE 18.6

User-created folders for non-email items are displayed along with the default folder in the navigation pane.

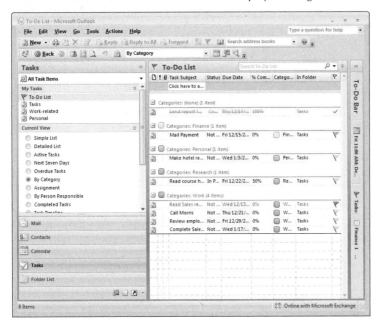

WARNING You can create new Task folders if you wish, but be forewarned that task items you move from the default task folder to a new folder will not be updated if you have assigned the task to someone else and receive accept, decline, or progress update messages.

Organizing Folders in Groups

Outlook folders that are not email folders can be organized into groups. This is similar in concept to organizing email folders by their location in the folder hierarchy, but the procedures are a bit different.

By default, every category of non-email item has a single group with a name such as My Contacts, My Tasks, and so on. If you create new folders, they are displayed as part of this default group. For example, Figure 18.7 shows the contact folders after adding four new folders to the default Contacts folder. They are all part of the default My Contacts group (which can be expanded or collapsed using the adjacent arrow).

FIGURE 18.7

All folders for non-email items are initially part of the default group, My Contacts in this figure.

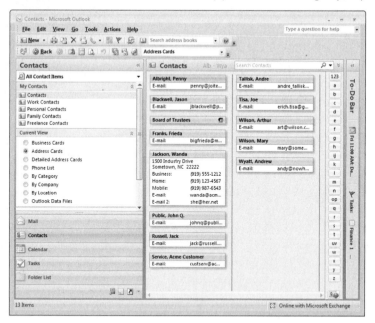

By creating new groups you can organize these folders as desired. In this example, there are five contact folders and you might want to arrange them as follows:

- The Contacts folder, for miscellaneous contacts, remains in the My Contacts group.
- The Personal Contacts and Family Contacts goes into a new group named Personal.
- The Work Contacts and Freelance Contacts folders goes into a new group called Work.

The result of this reorganization (which you learn how to do in a moment) is shown in Figure 18.8. Now, you can expand and contract individual groups to find just the items you need.

FIGURE 18.8

Folders can be organized into separate groups.

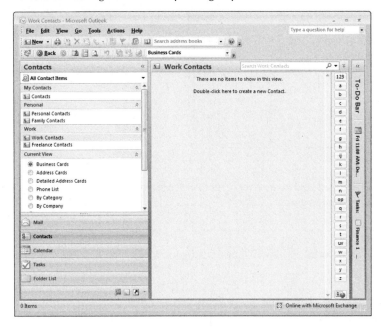

Creating a New Group

To create a new group, right-click an existing group (for example, My Contacts in Figure 18.9) and select New Group from the context menu. Then, type in the name for the group and press Enter.

A newly created group is empty, as you might well expect. To move a folder to it, point at the folder, press and hold the left mouse button, and drag it to the destination folder. Figure 18.9 shows how you would move the Personal Contacts folder to the My Contacts group.

FIGURE 18.9

Moving a folder to a different group.

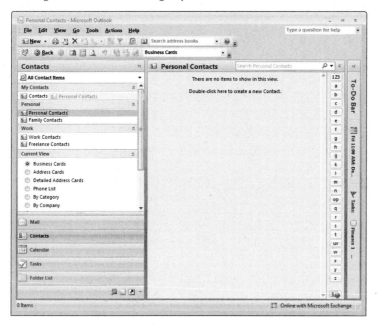

To create a new folder within a group, follow the procedures earlier in this chapter for creating a new folder, then move it to the desired group.

Working with Groups

You can take the following actions with a group by right-clicking it and selecting from the context menu:

- Rename the group.
- Remove the group (and any folders it contains).
- Arrange by Name — order the folders in the group alphabetically.
- Move Up/Down in List — change the position of the group in the list.

Additional actions you can take with groups are covered in the next section.

Working with Folders, Groups, and Items

This section covers the everyday tasks that you'll need to perform with your folders, groups, and Outlook items in order to keep them organized.

Viewing Folder Contents

When you switch from one type of item to another—for example, from viewing mail items to viewing contact items—Outlook automatically displays the contents of one folder, usually the default one, in the main Outlook window. To view the contents of another folder (also called opening the folder):

- Click the folder to display its contents in the main window.
- Right-click the folder and select Open in New Window to view the folder's contents in a new window.

You can open as many new windows as you want. When you close a window, Outlook remains running as long as at least one window is open.

Moving or Copying Items

Outlook lets you move or copy items between folders. For some types of items, only moving is allowed, not copying. To move or copy one or more items, you must first select them:

- **To select a single item**, click it.
- **To select multiple contiguous items**, click the first item then hold down the Shift key and click the last item.
- **To select multiple non-contiguous items**, click the first item then hold down the Ctrl key and click each additional item.
- **To select all items in the folder**, press Ctrl+A. You can then deselect individual items with Shift+Click.
- **To deselect multiple items**, release any key and click any non-selected item.

Now you can move/copy the selected items in one of several ways:

- Drag the item or group of items to the destination folder and drop.
- Select Cut (to move) or Copy from the Edit menu. Then, open the destination folder and select Paste from the Edit menu.
- Select Move to Folder from the Edit menu. Outlook opens the Move Items dialog box, shown in Figure 18.10. Select the destination folder from the list and click OK. You can also click the New button in this dialog box to create a new folder.

Shortcut Keys for Copy, Cut, and Paste

The standard Windows shortcut keys work in Outlook: Ctrl+C for copy, Ctrl+X for cut, and Ctrl+V for paste.

FIGURE 18.10

Moving an item or items to a different folder.

Moving, Copying, Deleting, and Renaming Folders

As you fine-tune your Outlook organization, you may want to move folders to new locations. Depending on the type of folder, you may be able to copy a folder as well. Email folders can be moved to a new location in the folder hierarchy, and other folders can be moved from one group to another.

To move an email folder, point at it and drag it to the new location. For example, Figure 18.11 shows how you would move the National folder from its location in the Clients folder to a new location in the Work Stuff folder.

FIGURE 18.11

Moving an email folder to a new location.

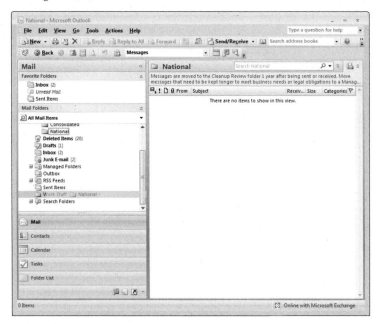

To move a non-email folder, point at it and drag it from the current group to the new group. Figure 18.12 shows how you would move the Freelance Contacts folder from the Work group to the My Contacts group.

You can also use the Copy (when allowed), Cut, and Paste commands on the Edit menu to copy and move folders.

To delete a folder, right-click it and select Delete *XXXX* (where *XXXX* is the name of the folder) from the context menu.

To rename a folder, right-click it and select Rename *XXXX* (where *XXXX* is the name of the folder) from the context menu, and then type in the new name and press Enter.

FIGURE 18.12

Moving a contacts folder to a new location.

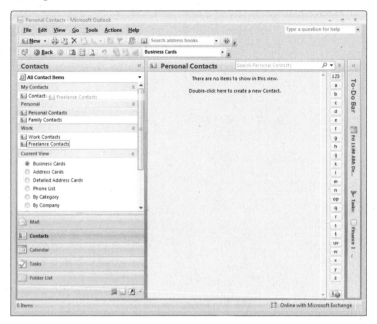

Creating a New Personal Folders File

By default, Outlook has a single personal folders file called *Personal Folders* and with the filename Outlook.PST. In many cases, there will be a second personal folders file named Archive.PST used for archiving expired items (archiving is explained later in this chapter). You can also create additional personal folders files if you wish.

Why would you want to have more than one personal folders file? Here are a few reasons that people use multiple personal folder files:

- **For backup and archiving.** You can create a second personal folders file and move items to it for backup. This reduces clutter in your main Personal Folders file while keeping the items in case you should need them at some future date.

- **For organization.** You may want to keep all items for a large project in their own file and use the default file for all other items.

- **For transfer.** If you use a desktop computer as well as a laptop, you can have your default PST file as well as a second one that is transferred between the two computers.

To create a new personal folders file:

1. Select New from the File menu, then select Outlook Data File. Outlook displays the dialog box shown in Figure 18.13 where you select the format of the file.

2. Most users should select Office Outlook Personal Folders File. Select Outlook 97-2002 Personal Folders File only if you need the new file to be compatible with these older versions of Outlook.

3. Click OK. Outlook displays the Create or Open Outlook Data File dialog box, shown in Figure 18.14.

4. The default location is the same folder where the default Personal Folders file is kept (as explained earlier in this chapter). You can accept this location or select another one.

5. Enter a descriptive name in the File Name box.

6. Click OK. Outlook displays the Create Microsoft Personal Folders dialog box (see Figure 18.15).

7. Enter the display name for the file in the Name box. This is not the filename but the name displayed in Outlook.

8. If you want to password-protect the file, enter the password in the Password and Verify Password boxes.

9. Select the Save This Password option if you want Outlook to remember your password so you do not have to enter it each time you open the file.

10. Click OK.

 When you password-protect an Outlook data file, having Outlook remember your password may be convenient but it sort of defeats the purpose of password protection.

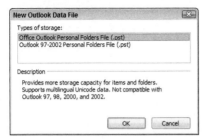

FIGURE 18.13

Selecting the format for a new personal folders file.

FIGURE 18.14

Specifying the name and location for a new personal folders file.

FIGURE 18.15

Specifying the display name and password for a new personal folders file.

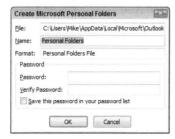

What's a Personal Folders File?

Outlook terminology on this point can be confusing. Any Outlook data file with the .PST extension is a personal folders file, no matter what it is named. However you have only one Personal Folders file — this is the default personal folders file and is listed as "Personal Folders" in the navigation pane.

After you have created a new personal folders file, it is displayed in the navigation pane along with your Personal Folders file and archive file (if you have one) as shown in Figure 18.16. You can close the file by right-clicking it and selecting Close from the context menu. To open a personal folders file, select Open from the File menu, then select Outlook Data File from the next menu.

FIGURE 18.16

Additional personal folder files are displayed in the navigation pane.

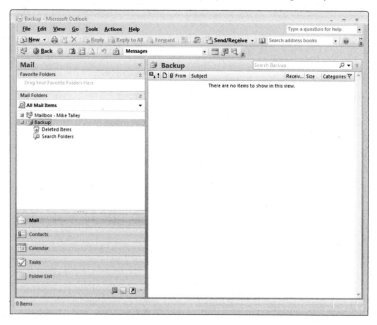

Setting Personal Folder File Options

Each personal file folder has a few options, or *properties*, that you can change if desired. To access these properties, right-click the file in the navigation pane and select Properties from the context menu. Outlook will display the *XXXX* Properties dialog box as shown in Figure 18.17 (where *XXXX* is the name of the file). The items on the General tab are

FIGURE 18.17

Setting properties for a personal folders file.

- **Name:** The display name of the personal folders file. You cannot change this here but must use the Advanced button as described later in this list.

- **Description:** Enter an optional description for the file.

- **Show...:** Select whether the folders in the file display the number of unread items or the total number of items in parentheses after the folder name.

- **When Posting to This Folder Use:** Use this option to select a form that will be used as the default for postings to this folder.

- **Automatically Generate Microsoft Exchange Views:** Select this option if you want Outlook to automatically create views of public folders that can be viewed by other Exchange users. Relevant for Exchange accounts only.

- **Folder Size:** Click this button to view information about the overall size of the file and the size of each of its subfolders.

- **Upgrade to Color Categories:** Click this button if you want to upgrade mutli-colored For Follow Up Flags and Calendar Labels to Color Categories (these items may be present in a PST file imported from an earlier version of Outlook).

- **Advanced:** Click this button to open a dialog box where you can change the display name for the file, change or assign a password, and compact the file to save disk space.

The properties dialog box for a personal folders file also has a Home Page tab, shown in Figure 18.18. The settings here determine what Outlook displays in its main window when the Personal Folders file (not one of its folders) is selected in the navigation pane. There are three options:

FIGURE 18.18

Setting the home page for a personal folders file.

- **Turn the Show Home Page option off:** The main window displays blank when the file is selected.
- **Turn the Show Home Page option on and use the default address:** The main window displays Outlook Today with a summary of tasks and messages.
- **Turn the Show Home Page option on and enter another address:** The main window displays the page, which can be local or remote. You can type in a URL or use the Browse button to find a local file.

Click the Restore Defaults button to return to the default address of the Outlook Today page.

 You can customize the Outlook Today page to meet your needs. This topic is covered in Chapter 19.

Using the Search Folders

Search folders are an Outlook tool that lets you automate the process of finding certain email messages. A search folder is a virtual folder that displays messages that meet certain criteria. You can display messages from certain people, messages with specified words in the subject or body, messages with attachments, messages with importance marked as high — the possibilities are seemingly endless.

What do I mean by *virtual*? It means that the search folder does not actually contain the message but only displays it — the message itself remains in its original folder such as the Inbox.

The Default Search Folders

Outlook is installed with three default search folders, located in the folder Search Folders. They are

- **Categorized Mail** displays all mail items that have been assigned a color category.
- **Large Mail** displays all messages larger than 100 KB.
- **Unread Mail** displays messages that have not been read.

The default folders are not set in stone — you can delete them, rename them, and redefine their criteria, as explained next. You cannot, however, move them.

Adding a Predefined Search Folder

Outlook comes with a number of predefined search folders (including the default search folders). You can add any of these folders as follows:

1. In Mail view, select New from the File menu, then select Search Folder. Outlook displays the New Search Folder dialog box (see Figure 18.19).
2. Click the search folder you want to add.
3. For some search folders, a Choose button is displayed. Click this button to specify additional criteria for the search folder. For example, if you select the Mail from Specific People, you will click the Choose button to select the people whose messages will be displayed in the search folder.
4. Use the Search Mail In list to select the personal folders file the search folder will search. A search folder can be associated with only one source PST file.
5. Click OK.

FIGURE 18.19

Adding a predefined search folder.

The new search folder is added to the Search Folders folder.

Adding a Custom Search Folder

If the predefined search folders do not meet your needs, you can define a custom search folder:

1. In Mail view, select New from the File menu, then select Search Folder. Outlook displays the New Search Folder dialog box (shown earlier in Figure 18.19).

2. Scroll down and select Create a Custom Search Folder.

3. Click the Choose button to display the Custom Search Folder dialog box (see Figure 18.20).

4. Enter a name for the search folder in the Name box. It is advisable to use a descriptive name.

5. If necessary, click the Browse button to select the personal folders file that this search folder will be connected to.

6. Click the Criteria button to display the Search Folder Criteria dialog box (see Figure 18.21).

7. Use the three tabs in this dialog box to define criteria as follows:

    ▦ On the Messages tab, define criteria that involve words in the message subject or body, the person the message is from or is sent to, and the time of the message.

    ▦ On the More Choices tab, define criteria that involve the message's read status, attachments, importance level, flag status, or size.

    ▦ On the Advanced tab, define criteria that involve custom message fields.

8. When you are finished defining criteria, click OK twice to close all dialog boxes.

FIGURE 18.20

Defining a custom search folder.

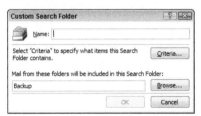

Customizing a Search Folder

To customize an existing search folder, right-click it and select Customize from the context menu.

FIGURE 18.21

Setting criteria for a custom search folder.

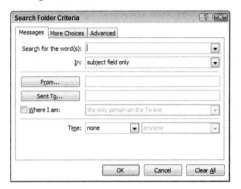

Using Favorite Folders

Many Outlook users have a large number of mail folders, but use only a few of them regularly. To make it easy to get at these frequently used folders, Outlook lets you define Favorite Folders displayed in a separate section of the navigation pane, as shown in Figure 18.22.

FIGURE 18.22

Use the Favorite Folders section to display the mail folders that you use most often.

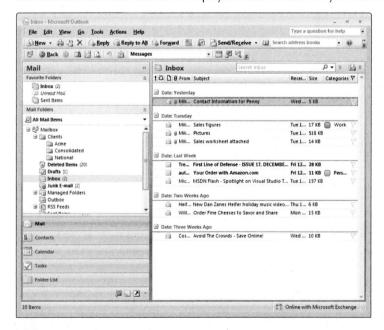

Can't View Favorite Folders?

Some Outlook users have reported a bug that causes their Favorite Folders and the menu command to display them to both vanish. There is no fix for this at present other than reinstalling Outlook. It should be addressed when Microsoft makes Office updates available.

Actions you can take with Favorite Folders are as follows:

- To turn Favorite Folders display on or off, select Navigation Pane from the View menu and click Favorite Folders on the next menu.

- To add a folder to Favorite Folders, right-click the folder and select Add to Favorite Folders from the popup menu.

- To remove a folder from Favorite Folders, right-click the folder and select Remove From Favorite Folders from the popup menu.

- To change the order of folders in the Favorite Folders list, right-click a folder and select Move Up in List or Move Down in List from the popup menu.

Remember that folders in the Favorite Folders list are not separate from the folders in the regular list. For example, in Figure 18.22 there is still only one Inbox folder but you have two ways to get to it.

Using the Deleted Items Folder

When you delete a folder or an Outlook item, it does not vanish permanently — at least not immediately. Rather, it goes to the Deleted Items folder. This is a safety feature that allows users to recover from accidental deletions. You can "delete" items in the usual way (select them and press Del) or you can drag them to the Deleted Items folder.

When you delete an item from the Deleted Items folder, it is truly gone. Most people prefer to delete items from this folder manually, by selecting one or more items and pressing Del. To delete all items from the Deleted Items folder, select Empty "Deleted Items" Folder from the Tools menu. You can also tell Outlook to automatically empty the Deleted Items folder whenever the program exits as follows:

1. Select Options from the Tools menu to open the Options dialog box.
2. Click the Other tab (shown in Figure 18.23).
3. Select the Empty Deleted Items Folder Upon Exiting option.
4. Click OK.

"Undeleting" Items

I f an item has not been permanently deleted — that is, if it is still in the Deleted Items folder — you can "undelete" it by moving it back to its original folder (or another folder of the same type).

FIGURE 18.23

Setting options for emptying the Deleted Items folder.

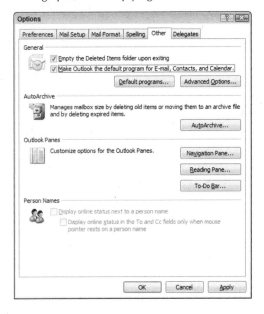

AutoArchiving Outlook Items

AutoArchive is an Outlook tool that can automatically archive mail messages and other items based on their age. It is based on the premise that there are many Outlook items that you will probably never need but don't want to permanently delete just in case. By moving these items to an archive, they no longer clog up your personal folders but are available when and if you need them. AutoArchive can also permanently delete items that you are sure you will not need again.

Items archived are kept in a separate PST file called, appropriately enough, Archive.PST. It is kept in the same location on your disk as your personal PST file as described earlier in this chapter —

although, unlike the Personal Folders file, you can change this location. After archiving items for the first time, the archive file appears in your folder list along with your personal folders, as shown in Figure 18.24.

FIGURE 18.24

Archived items are stored in their own PST file.

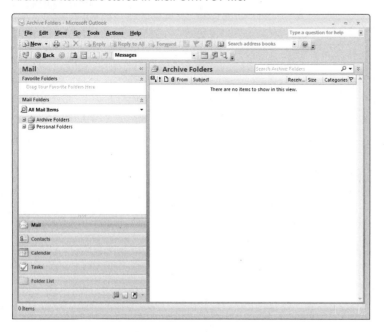

An archive file retains the folder structure of your personal folders file, making it easy to find things.

Deciding What Gets Archived, and When

The archiving process is completely under your control. You do not have to use it at all, but if you do you can decide which folders are archived, how often the archiving process is run, how old an item has to be in order to be archived, and so on. Many of these settings are made in the AutoArchive dialog box, shown in Figure 18.25. To display this dialog box:

1. Select Options from the Tools menu.
2. Click the Other tab.
3. Click the AutoArchive button.

FIGURE 18.25

The AutoArchive dialog box.

Here are the options available in this dialog box:

- **Run AutoArchive Every:** If this option is selected, Outlook will run AutoArchive automatically at the selected interval—the default is 14 days. If this option is not selected, you can run AutoArchive when desired by selecting Archive from the File menu (more on this soon).

- **Prompt Before AutoArchive Runs:** If this option is selected, Outlook will prompt you before AutoArchive runs. Otherwise it will run without notification.

- **Delete Expired Items (E-mail Folders Only):** Specifies that expired email items will be deleted and not moved to the archive file.

- **Archive or Delete Old Items:** Determines whether remaining options in the dialog box are available.

- **Clean Out Items Older Than:** Specifies the age at which items are archived. The default is 6 months.

- **Move Old Items To:** If selected, old items (other than email items) are archived to the specified archive file.

- **Permanently Delete Old Items:** If selected, old items are deleted and not archived.

- **Apply These Settings to All Folders Now:** Use your selected settings for all folders (as opposed to individual archive settings for each folder, as described soon).

- **Retention Policy Information:** Some organizations set retention policies for Outlook items when you are using an Exchange server. See Chapter 28 for more information on using Outlook with an Exchange server.

Setting AutoArchive Options for Individual Folders

You may not want all your Outlook items treated the same as regard to archiving. For example, you may want to keep work-related emails for a longer period than personal emails. You can set AutoArchive options for individual folders (other than Contacts folders) as follows:

1. Right-click the folder.

2. Select Properties from the context menu to display the Properties dialog box for the folder.

3. Click the AutoArchive tab (see Figure 18.26).

4. Set options as described in the previous section.

FIGURE 18.26

Setting AutoArchive options for a single folder.

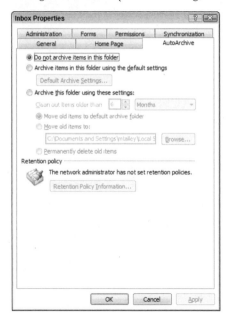

> **TIP** It's easy for your PST file to grow to a huge size. In and of itself this is not a problem, but it does slow things down. Deleting unneeded items on a regular basis is a good idea — and I mean permanently deleting them, not just moving them to the Deleted Items folder. But suppose you received a message with a large attachment. You want to keep the message but no longer need the attachment. You can remove the attachment and save space in your PST file by opening the message, right-clicking the attachment, and selecting Remove from the context menu.

Manually Archiving Outlook Items

You do not have to rely on Outlook's AutoArchive tool to archive your items. You can manually move mail messages and other items from your personal folders to the archive folders, using the techniques explained earlier in this chapter in the section "Moving or Copying Items." Nor do you have to use the archive folders — you can create a separate PST file specifically for backup purposes and move items to it.

Setting Other Folder Options

Each Outlook folder has a set of options, or properties, that determine certain aspects of the folder's display and operation. Each folder's properties are accessed by right-clicking the folder in the navigation pane and selecting Properties from the context menu. There are some slight differences in the properties you can change depending on the folder. For example, you can change the name of folders that you have created but not of Outlook's default folders such as Inbox and Contacts.

The Properties dialog box has five tabs. The General tab, shown in Figure 18.27, has these settings:

FIGURE 18.27

Setting General properties for a folder.

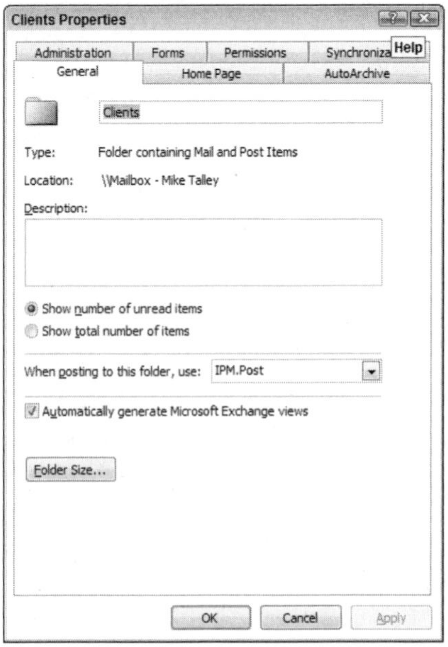

- **Name:** At the top of the dialog box the folder's name is displayed. You can change this for non-default folders.

- **Description:** Enter an optional description for the folder.

- **Show...:** Select whether the folder displays the number of unread items or the total number of items in parentheses next to its name.

- **When Posting to This Folder, Use:** Use this option to select a form that will be used as the default for postings to this folder.

- **Automatically Generate Microsoft Exchange Views:** Select this option if you want Outlook to automatically create views of public folders that can be viewed by other Exchange users. Relevant for Exchange accounts only.

- **Folder Size:** Click this button to view information on the size of the folder and any sub-folders it contains.

The Home Page tab lets you specify a web page that will be displayed as the default view for this folder.

The AutoArchive tab lets you set AutoArchive options for this folder. These are explained elsewhere in this chapter in the section "Setting AutoArchive Options for Individual Folders."

The Administration tab is mostly relevant for Exchange accounts and is covered in detail in Chapter 28. For non-Exchange accounts, most of the items will be grayed out (as in the figure). The one item you can set for non-Exchange folders is the Initial View On Folder, which determines how the folder contents are displayed when the folder is first opened. For example, for a Mail folder you can use the default Normal view or you can select to have items displayed by From, by Subject, and so on.

The Forms tab lets you specify which forms are used with this folder. Forms and setting form options for a folder are covered in detail in Chapter 26.

Backing Up Outlook Data

Losing data is the worst nightmare of most computer users, and given the importance of all the information stored in Outlook, losing your Outlook data is a particularly terrifying possibility. Unless you or your employer has an integrated backup solution in place, I advise you to make the effort to back up your Outlook data regularly. You have several ways to do this.

Internet Calendar Subscriptions

Information about your Internet Calendar subscriptions is kept separately from your Personal Folders file in a file named Internet Calendar Subscriptions.PST.

Automating Backup

Advanced users can write batch files or Windows script files that automate the process of backing up Outlook data. These topics are beyond the scope of this book, but you may want to explore them further on your own. When you automate a task such as backup, you are much less likely to avoid doing it.

Back Up Your Entire PST File

As mentioned previously, all your Outlook data — email messages, contacts, tasks, appointments, account settings, and so on — is by default stored in a personal folders file named Outlook.PST. This file is kept in the following location (where *user* is your Windows logon):

- **Windows XP and Windows Server 2003:** X:\Documents and Settings*user*\Local Settings\Application Data\Microsoft\Outlook

- **Windows Vista:** X:\ *user*\Local Settings\AppData\Microsoft\Outlook

You may have additional PST files as well — Archive.PST if you are using the AutoArchive feature as well as any other personal folders files that you created. Archive.PST is kept in the same default location as Outlook.PST, and any additional personal folders files are stored where you specified.

Backing up these files is simply a matter of making copies in a secure location. Be aware, however, that before you can copy these files you must exit Outlook and any other programs that might access them, such as Windows Messaging or a remote connection to Microsoft Exchange. Then use Windows Explorer or another means to make the copy.

Where should you copy these files to? That depends on your setup and resources. If you are on a network, there may be a location on the network server that you can use for backup. If you have a CD burner, creating backups on CD is an excellent choice. Other options that may be open to you include flash drives and external hard disks.

Summary

Outlook data consists of items such as email messages, appointments, and contacts. These items are organized into folders that are, in most cases, specialized to hold a single type of item. Folders in turn are stored in a Personal Folders file that also contains your account information and other Outlook settings. This chapter showed you how to work with items, folders, and data files to keep your Outlook information organized, accessible, and backed up.

Chapter 19

Customizing Outlook to Suit the Way You Work

IN THIS CHAPTER

Customizing the screen

Customizing toolbars

Customizing the menus

Defining custom views

Customizing Outlook Today

No matter how clever a software company is — and Microsoft is plenty clever — there's no way they can design a program that works just the way everyone wants it to. Recognizing this, Microsoft has made Outlook very flexible so that you can change many aspects of how it looks and works to suit you. This is the topic of this chapter.

Please note that customizing Outlook is not the same as setting program options, a topic covered Chapter 7 for email-related options and in other individual chapters as needed. Options affect how the program operates, whereas customization deals primarily with the screen appearance of the program and how you enter commands.

Customizing the Outlook Screen

Outlook provides you with many ways to customize the appearance of the screen.

Changing the Size of Screen Elements

Like any Windows program, you can change the size of the main Outlook window (assuming that it is not maximized to full-screen size) by pointing at a border or corner of the window and dragging to the desired size. You can also change the size of certain elements within the window. When you point at an element that can be dragged to change size, the mouse cursor will change to two parallel lines with arrow heads:

■ Drag the right border of the navigation pane to change its width.

■ Drag the horizontal border within the navigation pane to allow more or less space for the Mail, Calendar, and other buttons.

■ Drag the border between the reading pane and the main window to change their relative sizes.

When the main window is displaying a view that uses columns, you can change the width of a column by pointing at its right border, as shown in Figure 19.1, and dragging to the desired width.

FIGURE 19.1

You can change the width of columns in the main window.

Drag to change column width

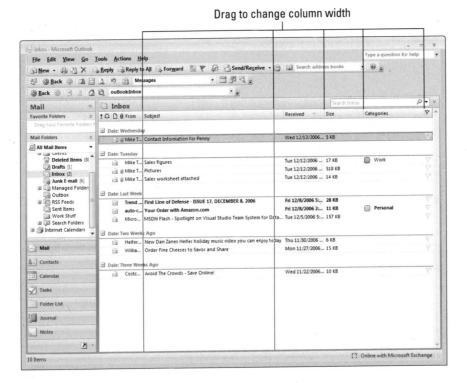

An Easy Switch Between Normal and Minimized

At its top-right corner, the navigation pane displays an arrow that looks like << when the pane is displayed normally and like >> when the pane is minimized. Click this arrow to switch between these two display states.

Customizing the Navigation Pane

The navigation pane can be displayed normal size, minimized, or not at all by selecting Navigation Pane from the View menu and then selecting Normal, Minimized, or Off. On this same menu you can also choose to display or hide two parts of the navigation pane:

- **Current View Pane:** Displays view options you can select (rather than using the menus).
- **Favorite Folders:** Displays your favorite folders (as explained in Chapter 18). Available in Mail view only.

Customizing Other Screen Elements

You can customize the display of other Outlook screen elements as described here:

- The **reading pane** can be displayed at the right or the bottom of the screen or turned off altogether by selecting Reading Pane from the View menu.
- The **To-Do Bar** can be displayed at normal size, minimized, or not displayed at all by selecting To-Do Bar from the View menu. This menu also lets you specify which elements (Date Navigator, Appointments, Task List) are displayed on the To-Do Bar and to set display options.
- The **daily task list** can be displayed at normal size, minimized, or not displayed at all by selecting Daily Task List from the View menu. You can also use this command to specify how the displayed tasks are arranged.

Customizing Toolbars

The applications in the Microsoft Office 2007 suite have almost all gotten away from the traditional menus-and-toolbars user interface in favor of *ribbons*, which I consider to be sort of a sophisticated hybrid between menus and toolbars. Outlook is lagging behind, and for reasons unknown still uses the traditional menus and toolbars in its main screen. Other Outlook windows, such as the ones you see when you open an email message or a task, use ribbons, so Outlook is sort of a mongrel—but it all works perfectly well.

Outlook has three toolbars called the *Standard*, *Web*, and *Advanced* toolbars. They are identified in Figure 19.2. The Standard and Advanced toolbars are *adaptive*, which means the buttons they display change depending on what you are doing in Outlook. Most toolbar buttons are identified by an icon, and if you cannot figure out what the icon means, rest the mouse cursor over a button for a moment to view an informative *ScreenTip*, also shown in the figure.

If you don't need or want the ScreenTips, turn them off as follows:

1. Select Customize from the Tools menu to display the Customize dialog box.
2. Click the Options tab.
3. Turn off the Show ScreenTips on Toolbars option.
4. Click OK.

FIGURE 19.2

Outlook's three toolbars and a ScreenTip.

Advanced toolbar   Standard toolbar

Screen Tip

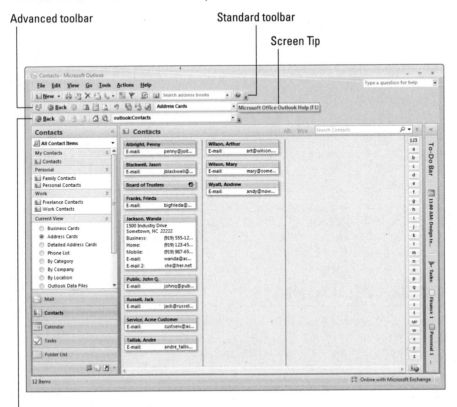

Web toolbar

Hiding and Displaying Toolbars

If you do not want all three — or any — toolbars displayed, right-click any toolbar or in the toolbar area to display the menu shown in Figure 19.3. Click the toolbar names to check (display) or uncheck (hide) them.

Positioning the Toolbars

The toolbars are normally displayed near the top of the screen just under the main menu. You can move a toolbar to another screen location by pointing at the vertical row of dots at the left end of the toolbar. You'll see the mouse cursor change to a four-headed arrow. You can position a toolbar in one of two ways:

- **Docked:** If you drag the toolbar to any of the four edges of the Outlook window, it will dock in position along that edge.

- **Floating:** If you drag the toolbar to any other screen location, it will "float" at that position. You move a floating toolbar by dragging its title bar.

Figure 19.4 shows Outlook with the Web toolbar floating and the Advanced toolbar docked at the top of the Outlook window.

FIGURE 19.3

You can display or hide Outlook's toolbars as desired.

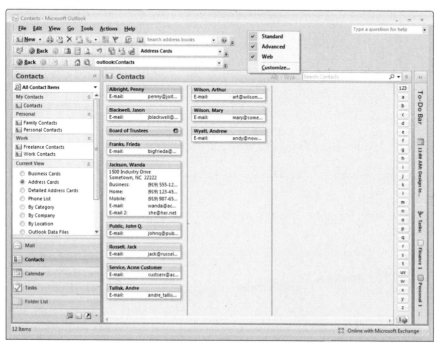

FIGURE 19.4

Outlook's toolbars can float or be docked along any edge of the program window.

Docked   Floating

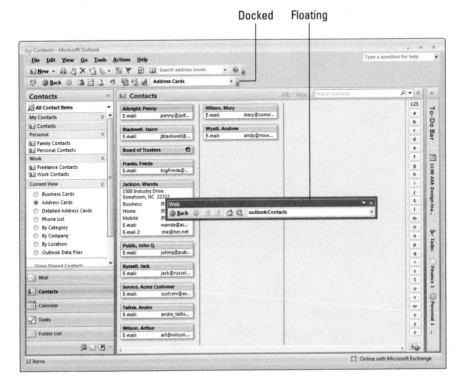

Adding and Removing Toolbar Buttons

Each of the three Outlook toolbars has a set of buttons it can display. When first installed, Outlook displays all these buttons on each toolbar. If there's a button you never use, you can remove it to save screen space. You can always add it back later. Here are the steps to follow:

1. Click the arrow at the right end of the toolbar that you want to customize.

2. Select Add or Remove Buttons.

3. Select the name of the toolbar. Outlook displays a list of available buttons as shown in Figure 19.5.

4. Click a button in this list to check or uncheck it. Click Reset Toolbar to return the toolbar to its default set of buttons.

5. When finished, press Esc or click anywhere outside the button list.

Viewing Hidden Toolbar Buttons

If the Outlook window is narrower than a toolbar, some of the toolbar buttons will be hidden. To access these buttons, click the arrow at the right end of the toolbar. Two small dots will be displayed above this arrow if there are any hidden buttons.

FIGURE 19.5

Specifying which buttons a toolbar displays.

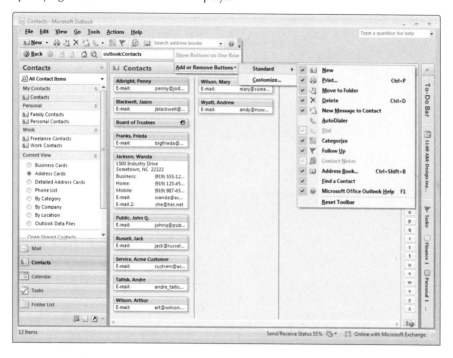

Advanced Toolbar Customization

You can go beyond hiding or showing a toolbar's default buttons to adding essentially any Outlook command to a toolbar and even creating new, custom toolbars. To do so, click the arrow at the right end of any toolbar, select Add or Remove Buttons, and then select Customize. You can also select Customize from the Tools menu. Outlook displays the Customize dialog box. The Toolbars tab of this dialog box is shown in Figure 19.6. It lists the three default toolbars, the Menu Bar (which corresponds to the main menu), and any custom toolbars that exist.

FIGURE 19.6

The Toolbars tab of the Customize dialog box.

On the Toolbars tab you can:

- Hide or display a toolbar by checking or unchecking it (but you cannot hide the Menu Bar).
- Create a new toolbar by clicking New and typing in the name of the toolbar. Outlook displays the new toolbar, which is empty, and you add commands to it as I describe soon.
- Delete or rename a custom toolbar.
- Reset a default toolbar to its original complement of buttons.

While the Customize dialog box is open, you can add, remove, and move toolbar buttons using drag and drop. If you want to add new buttons, you must display the Commands tab of this dialog box, shown in Figure 19.7. This dialog box lists all of Outlook's commands, organized by category. Here's what you can do; these actions include any new, empty toolbar that you may have created:

- **To move a button from one toolbar to another**, drag it from the old toolbar and drop it on the new toolbar. A vertical black line shows where the button will be placed before you drop it.
- **To move a button to a new location on the same toolbar**, drag and drop it.
- **To place a new command on a toolbar**, drag it from the list of commands in the Customize dialog box and drop it in the desired location.
- **To remove a command from a toolbar**, drag it off the toolbar and drop it anywhere away from the toolbars.

When you are finished, click the Close button to close the Customize dialog box.

FIGURE 19.7

The Commands tab of the Customize dialog box.

Customizing Menus

Outlook's main menu is a special type of toolbar, called the *Menu Bar*. It too can be customized although the procedures are slightly different than for toolbars:

1. Display the Customize dialog box by selecting Customize from the Tools menu.

2. Click the Commands tab.

3. Click the menu you want to customize (on the actual Menu Bar, not in the dialog box). The menu opens. Then:

    ■ To move a command from one menu to another, drag it from the old menu to the new (which opens) and then drop it in the desired position.

    ■ To move a command to a new position on the same menu, drag it to the new position.

    ■ To place a new command on the menu, drag it from the Commands list in the Customize dialog box to the desired position on the menu.

    ■ To remove a command from the menu, drag it off the menu and drop it somewhere else away from the menus.

4. When finished, click Close to close the Customize dialog box.

Another Way to Rearrange Commands

You can also rearrange commands on menus and toolbars by clicking the Rearrange Commands button on the Commands tab of the Customize dialog box. Outlook displays the Rearrange Commands dialog box. Then:

1. If you want to rearrange commands on a menu, select the Menu Bar option then select the desired menu in the adjacent list. If you want to rearrange commands on a toolbar, select the Toolbar option then select the desired toolbar in the adjacent list. The commands on the selected element are displayed in the Controls list.

2. Select an existing command.

3. Use the buttons to add a new command, delete the selected command, or move the selected command up or down in the list.

4. Click Reset to return the toolbar or menu to its default set and order of commands.

5. Click Close when you are finished.

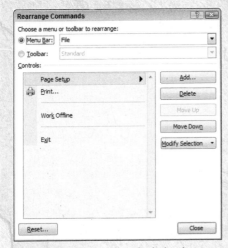

The Rearrange Commands dialog box.

WARNING Given that Outlook provides you with great flexibility when it comes to customizing your menus, it can be tempting to spend a lot of time doing so. But is this really a good idea? Windows programs, particularly those from Microsoft, tend to follow the same general menu organization. Of course, different programs do not have the same menu commands, but there are quite a few common commands that people expect to find in a certain location within the menu structure. Do you want your copy of Outlook to be different? Also, what will happen if you have to use Outlook on another system? The menus will be different from your customized ones and may be hard to use. Think twice before making any significant changes to the menus.

Other Customization Options

When you display the Customize dialog box (select Customize from the Tools menu), there is a third tab called *Options*, as shown in Figure 19.8. The options on this tab are as follows:

- **Always Show Full Menus:** If this option is selected, Outlook always shows the full menu as soon as the menu title is clicked on the Menu Bar. Otherwise, Outlook displays an abbreviated menu with the most frequently used commands and shows the full menu only if you click the arrow at the bottom of the abbreviated menu (see Figure 19.9).

- **Show Full Menus After a Short Delay:** If Always Show Full Menus is turned off, you can select this option to have Outlook display the full menu after a short delay.

- **Reset Menu and Toolbar Usage Data:** Outlook keeps track of which menu commands you use most often and uses this information to determine which commands are displayed on abbreviated menus. Click this button to reset your usage data.

- **Large Icons:** Select this option to display larger icons on toolbars.

- **List Font Names in Their Font:** If this option is selected, then when selecting fonts, the font names will be displayed in the actual font.

- **Show ScreenTips on Toolbars:** This option determines whether a ScreenTip displays when the mouse cursor is hovered over a toolbar button.

- **Show Shortcut Keys in ScreenTips:** If this option is selected, a ScreenTip for a toolbar button will also display the shortcut key (if there is one) assigned to that command.

- **Menu Animations:** Use this option to select how Outlook animates opening and closing menus.

FIGURE 19.8

Setting other customization options.

FIGURE 19.9

Click the arrow to display the full menu.

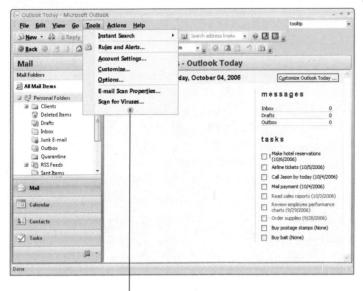

Click here to display full menu

Defining Custom Views

In Outlook, you may be viewing mail, contacts, tasks, or any of the other kinds of information that Outlook supports. Regardless of what you are viewing, the Current View command on the View menu lists a selection of predefined views you can use. For example, when viewing mail you can view mail for the last seven days, unread messages, and so on.

In addition to the predefined views, the Current View menu also has two other commands, Customize Current View and Define Views. These commands let you make modifications to the predefined views and also to define your own custom views.

Customizing the Current View

When you select Current View from the View menu and then select Customize Current View, Outlook displays the dialog box shown in Figure 19.10. The title of the dialog box displays "Customize View *XXXX*", where *XXXX* is the name of the current view — By Category in the figure.

FIGURE 19.10

The Customize View dialog box.

You can see there are seven buttons that provide access to additional dialog boxes that let you customize specific aspects of the view. Be aware that for some views, not all these buttons are available (they are grayed out). This is because some views are more flexible than others and allow for greater customization. The following sections look at these choices in turn. Remember the examples shown in the figures are for a specific view — the By Category view for Tasks. When you are customizing a different view things are likely to look different.

Fields

The Show Fields dialog box, shown in Figure 19.11, lets you specify which *fields*, or pieces of information, are included in the view. The left side of the dialog box lists the fields that are available, and the right side lists those that are part of the view definition. You use the Add and Remove buttons to move fields from one list to the other, and the Move Up and Move Down buttons to change the order of fields in the view.

Group By

The Group By dialog box, shown in Figure 19.12, lets you determine how items are grouped in the view. Most views that use grouping will group on a single field — for example, Category. You can also define subgroups if you want to use the Then By section of this dialog box.

FIGURE 19.11

The Show Fields dialog box lets you specify which fields are included in the view.

FIGURE 19.12

The Group By dialog box lets you specify how items are grouped in the view.

Sort

The Sort dialog box (see Figure 19.13) lets you specify how items are sorted in the view. If the items are grouped, the sorting is applied within each defined group.

FIGURE 19.13

The Sort dialog box lets you specify how items are sorted in the view.

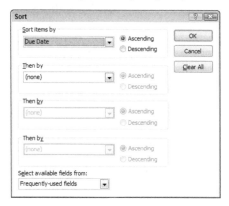

Filter

The Filter dialog box, shown in Figure 19.14, lets you define a filter that will be applied to the view. When a filter is in effect, only those items that meet your defined criteria are displayed.

FIGURE 19.14

The Filter dialog box lets you define criteria for which items are shown in the view.

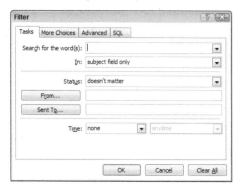

Other Settings

The Other Settings dialog box, shown in Figure 19.15, is used to control miscellaneous settings for the view, such as the font used, the appearance of gridlines, and the way AutoPreview works.

FIGURE 19.15

The Other Settings dialog box controls fonts, gridlines, and other miscellaneous aspects of the view.

Automatic Formatting

The Automatic Formatting dialog box, shown in Figure 19.16, lets you define automatic formatting that will be applied to items in the view. You can, for example, specify that completed tasks are displayed using a strikethrough font and that overdue tasks are displayed in a red font.

FIGURE 19.16

The Automatic Formatting dialog box lets you define automatic formatting that will be applied to items in the view.

Format Columns

The Format Columns dialog box, shown in Figure 19.17, is used to specify the display format for columns in the view. For example, a column that displays a date could be formatted to display as 12/22/06, 22-Dec-06, or December 22, 2006 (among others). You can also specify the alignment and label for each column.

The Format Columns dialog box lets you specify the display format for individual columns in the view.

Reset Current View

Click this button to return the current view to its default settings.

Customizing Outlook Today

Outlook Today is the default home page for Personal Folders (you learned about specifying a home page for folders in Chapter 18). It provides a summary of important information, such as unread mail messages, tasks with upcoming due dates, and the next few days in your calendar. You can customize Outlook Today as follows:

1. Display Outlook Today.

2. Click the Customize Outlook Today button at the top right of the window. Outlook opens Customize Outlook Today in the main window (see Figure 19.18).

3. Make changes as follows:

   - **When Starting . . . :** If this option is selected, Outlook automatically displays Outlook Today when the program starts.

   - **Messages:** Click Choose Folders to specify which folders have their messages summarized in Outlook Today.

- ■ **Calendar:** Specify how many days of your calendar are shown in Outlook Today.
- ■ **Tasks:** Specify which tasks are shown and how they are sorted.
- ■ **Styles:** Choose a display style for Outlook Today.

4. Click Save Changes.

FIGURE 19.18

Customizing Outlook Today.

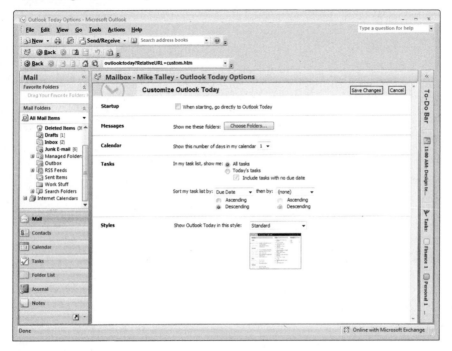

Summary

No two people are alike, or so they say, so why should we all have to use exactly the same Outlook? With the many customization options available to you, you can set up Outlook's screen, toolbars, menus, and views to suit you and the way you work.

Chapter 20

Managing Security Issues

omputer security has unfortunately become a very important topic. With the almost universal use of the Internet and email, it's easier than ever for various kinds of malicious software such as viruses to spread. Security issues also include message privacy and verification of people's identities. Because email is the favored means of spreading such malware, Outlook users have to be particularly vigilant. This chapter explains the various tools that Outlook provides to enhance your security.

Protecting Against Viruses

Everyone has heard about *viruses*, those malicious software elements that infect and harm computer systems. Viruses range from the merely annoying to the truly disastrous, but they all have one thing in common — you do not want them on your system! Because viruses often spread by means of email, Outlook provides you with some defenses against them.

It's important to understand that Outlook itself does not have any anti-virus capabilities. An *anti-virus program* is specialized to detect and remove viruses and will have a way to automatically download the latest virus definitions so it can stay up to date. Symantec, Zone Alarm, and McAfee are three of the better-known publishers of anti-virus software. Most systems have anti-virus software installed, and part of protecting yourself against viruses that come with email is to make sure your anti-virus program is configured properly. Specifically, you should set the anti-virus program's options so that it always scans incoming email and attachments for viruses before they get to Outlook. It's also advisable to set the program to scan outgoing email and attachments to prevent you from inadvertently spreading a virus that you have been infected with through other means (such as a floppy disk).

A Virus By Any Other Name

Technically, a *virus* is a piece of software that not only infects a computer system but actively spreads itself to other systems by means of a host file, much like the biological viruses that cause colds and other human illnesses. The term is often used more broadly to include other kinds of "malware"—a generic term for harmful software—that do not fit the strict definition of a virus, such as worms and Trojan horses.

On-Demand Email Scan

If you have an Outlook-compatible anti-virus program installed, you will find two virus-related commands on Outlook's Tools menu:

- **Scan for Viruses:** Opens your anti-virus program and performs an immediate virus scan of email items according to the program options. Use this command when you are not sure that the anti-virus program's automatic scanning is enough.

- **Email Scan Properties:** Opens your anti-virus program's Options dialog box where you can specify the details of how the program scans email items for viruses.

The details of how the virus scan works and how you set options will depend on the specific anti-virus program that you have installed. Please refer to that program's documentation for more information.

Dealing with Attachments

One of the most common ways for viruses to spread is by means of email attachments. However, all attachments are not equal in their ability to spread a virus. Certain file types are potentially very dangerous, such as executable programs, batch files, and installation files. Others, such as image and music files, are generally safe.

Reassuring Email Recipients

People worry about getting viruses via email, and I think it's a good idea to reassure them messages from you are safe. I include a brief note at the bottom of every email I send that states "This email message and any attachments have been scanned for viruses by XXX" (where XXX is the name of the anti-virus program that I use.

Protection Against Phishing Attacks

*P*hishing is a technique where you receive an email that appears to be from a legitimate company that you do business with, perhaps an online payment service such as PayPal. The message asks you to click a link to go to the company's web site to renew your password or some such thing. Though the site looks legitimate, it is in fact a cleverly designed front that lets unscrupulous people get hold of your password. Outlook provides anti-phishing protections that are covered in Chapter 8 along with other methods for dealing with junk email.

Automatically Blocked Attachments

Because of the potential danger posed by some file types, Outlook blocks certain kinds of attachments sent to you — you receive the message with a notification that an unsafe attachment has been blocked. This blocking is built in to Outlook and cannot be turned off or changed. The blocked file types are listed in Table 20.1.

Outlook also catches these file types on the way out — that is, if you try to send them as an attachment. They aren't necessarily blocked, but Outlook reminds you that the recipient — particularly if they too use Outlook — will not be able to receive them and asks you if you want to proceed.

TABLE 20.1

File Types Blocked by Outlook

Extension	File Type
.ADE	Access Project Extension (Microsoft)
.ADP	Access project (Microsoft)
.APP	Executable application
.ASP	Active Server Page
.BAS	BASIC source code
.BAT	Batch processing
.CER	Internet Security Certificate file
.CHM	Compiled HTML help
.CMD	DOS CP/M command file, or a command file for Windows NT
.COM	Command
.CPL	Windows Control Panel Extension (Microsoft)
.CRT	Certificate file

continued

TABLE 20.1	*(continued)*
Extension	**File Type**
.CSH	csh script
.DER	DER encoded X509 certificate file
.EXE	Executable file
.FXP	FoxPro compiled source (Microsoft)
.HLP	Windows Help file
.HTA	Hypertext application
.INF	Information or Setup file
.INS	IIS Internet Communications settings (Microsoft)
.ISP	IIS Internet Service Provider settings (Microsoft)
.ITS	Internet Document Set, Internet Translation
.JS	JavaScript source code
.JSE	JScript encoded script file
.KSH	UNIX shell script
.LNK	Windows Shortcut file
.MAD	Access Module shortcut (Microsoft)
.MAF	Access (Microsoft)
.MAG	Access diagram shortcut (Microsoft)
.MAM	Access macro shortcut (Microsoft)
.MAQ	Access query shortcut (Microsoft)
.MAR	Access report shortcut (Microsoft)
.MAS	Access Stored Procedures (Microsoft)
.MAT	Access table shortcut (Microsoft)
.MAU	Media Attachment Unit
.MAV	Access view shortcut (Microsoft)
.MAW	Access Data Access Page (Microsoft)
.MDA	Access Add-in (Microsoft), MDA Access 2 Workgroup (Microsoft)
.MDB	Access Application (Microsoft), MDB Access Database (Microsoft)
.MDE	Access MDE database file (Microsoft)
.MDT	Access Add-in Data (Microsoft)
.MDW	Access Workgroup Information (Microsoft)
.MDZ	Access Wizard Template (Microsoft)
.MSC	Microsoft Management Console Snap-in control file (Microsoft)

Extension	File Type
.MSH	Microsoft Shell
.MSH1	Microsoft Shell
.MSH2	Microsoft Shell
.MSHXML	Microsoft Shell
.MSH1XML	Microsoft Shell
.MSH2XML	Microsoft Shell
.MSI	Windows Installer File (Microsoft)
.MSP	Windows Installer Update
.MST	Windows SDK Setup Transform Script
.OPS	Office Profile settings file
.PCD	Visual Test (Microsoft)
.PIF	Windows Program Information file (Microsoft)
.PLG	Developer Studio Build Log
.PRF	Windows System file
.PRG	Program file
.PST	Exchange Address Book file, Outlook Personal Folder File (Microsoft)
.REG	Registration Information/Key for Registry Data File
.SCF	Windows Explorer command
.SCR	Windows screen saver
.SCT	Windows Script component, FoxPro screen (Microsoft)
.SHB	Windows Shortcut into a document
.SHS	Shell Scrap Object file
.TMP	Temporary file/folder
.URL	Internet location
.VB	VBScript file or any VisualBasic source
.VBE	VBScript encoded script file
.VBS	VBScript script file, Visual Basic for Applications script
.VSMACROS	Visual Studio .NET binary-based macro project (Microsoft)
.VSW	Visio workspace file (Microsoft)
.WS	Windows script file
.WSC	Windows script component
.WSF	Windows script file
.WSH	Windows Script Host settings file

Blocked File Types and Exchange

If you use an Exchange account for email, these same file types are blocked by default. However, the Exchange administrator can modify the list if needed.

Other Attachment Types

Some other file types are not on the blocked list even though they have the potential to carry viruses. The reason these file types are not blocked is because they are very commonly sent as attachments. They include Microsoft Word documents (*.DOC), Excel workbooks (*.XLS), and PowerPoint files (*.PPT). When you receive this kind of file as an attachment, it's important for you to be aware of the potential for harm. Even if you have anti-virus software, you cannot be sure it will catch every virus, particularly because new ones are being created regularly.

The general rule of thumb is to not open any such file unless you trust the source. It is also wise to have macro security set to a safe level, as described elsewhere in this chapter.

Sending Blocked File Types

Many people have perfectly legitimate reasons for sending blocked file types as attachments. There are two ways you can get around Outlook's restrictions to do this:

- **Change the file's extension.** For example, if you want to forward a compiled HTML help file named MyHelp.CHM, change the file extension to something that Outlook will not block, such as MyHelp.TXT. In your message, instruct the file recipient to change the file extension back before using the file.

- **Put the file in a ZIP or other kind of archive.** This kind of file is permitted by Outlook. You need to instruct the recipient as to how the file can be extracted, of course.

Sending ZIP Files as Attachments

When you create a ZIP file, you have the option of protecting it with a password. Although this can provide security against unauthorized access to the ZIP file's contents, it can prevent anti-virus software from checking the ZIP file's contents for viruses.

Macro Security

A *macro* is a sequence of program commands that have been recorded and saved and can be executed with a single command. Outlook has its own macro capabilities, as is covered in Chapter 22. More germane to the topic of security, however, are the macros in programs such as Microsoft Word and Excel. Such macros are part of the document file and as such will be included when the file is sent as an email attachment. A malicious macro can be set to execute automatically when the file is opened, and has the potential to wreak havoc on your system and data files. Such viruses are called *macro viruses*.

Anti-virus programs catch most macro viruses, and the precaution of not opening attachments from unknown sources is another layer of protection. The final layer of protection against macro viruses is the macro security level in your programs.

Macro security applies to all Office programs, and it is set in the Trust Center. The *Trust Center* is an Office component, not specifically part of Outlook or any other any program. On Outlook, you access the Trust Center by selecting Trust Center from the Tools menu. Then, in the list on the left, click Macro Security. The Macro Security screen is shown in Figure 20.1.

FIGURE 20.1

Setting macro security in the Trust Center.

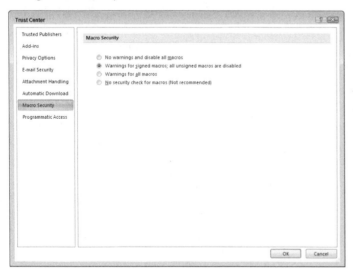

You can see that the options mention signed macros. *Digital signing* is a way that the person who creates a macro can "sign" it so the recipient can be assured that it comes from a trusted source. You learn more about digital signatures later in this chapter. You can choose from four levels of macro security, described here from the strictest to the least strict:

- **No Warnings and Disable All Macros:** No macros, whether signed or not, are ever run.

- **Warnings for Signed Macros; Unsigned Macros Are Disabled:** For a signed macro, the program displays a warning and asks you if it should be run. Unsigned macros are never run. This is the default macro security level.

- **Warnings for All Macros:** The program displays a warning for any macro, signed or unsigned, and asks you if it should be run.

- **No Security Check for Macros:** All macros are run without a warning. For reasons probably obvious, this level is not recommended.

It is recommended to maintain the default level of macro security for all Office programs. You can always set a lower level temporarily if you want to run some unsigned macros from a trusted source.

Using Certificates and Digital Signatures

A *certificate*, also known as a *digital ID*, provides a higher level of security with Outlook. You can use a certificate to send encrypted emails so that only the intended recipient can view the contents. You can also use them to sign messages to prevent tampering and prove your identity. Finally, you can use a digital ID in lieu of a username and password to access certain restricted web sites, although this use is not relevant to Outlook.

Digital IDs are based on the technique of a *public/private key pair*. These are two long numbers related to each other. You can use either key of the pair to encrypt data, and only people who have the other key of the pair are able to unencrypt the data. When you have a digital signature, you keep your private key secret and make your public key freely available. Then, here's how it works:

- To send an encrypted message to someone, you use their public key to encrypt it. Only they can unencrypt the message because no one else has their private key.

- To prove your identity, encrypt some data using your private key. When the recipient of a message decrypts the data using your public key, if the data is intact they will know you must have encrypted it because nobody else has your private key.

Digital certificates have expiration dates, typically one year after they are issued.

Obtaining a Digital ID

If you are using Outlook at work, your employer may provide a digital ID to you which you'll import as described in the next section. Otherwise, you can get your own. Digital IDs are provided by independent companies for a small fee. A digital ID is linked to a specific email address and cannot be used with other addresses.

To get your own digital ID:

1. Select Trust Center from the Tools menu to open the Trust Center.

2. Click Email Security in the list on the left to display the E-mail Security page (see Figure 20.2).

3. Click the Get a Digital ID button. Your web browser opens and displays a Microsoft page listing companies selling digital IDs.

4. Select the company you want and follow the prompts to register for and pay for your digital ID.

FIGURE 20.2

Using the Trust Center to get a digital ID.

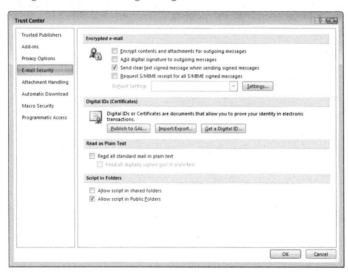

After you complete the ordering process, the issuing company will send you an email containing instructions for installing the digital ID.

Importing/Exporting Digital IDs

Digital IDs can be provided to you in a file as well as obtained over the Web as described in the previous section. Your employer may provide you with an ID in a file, and you can also export an existing ID to a file for backup purposes. These files are password-protected for security reasons.

To import a digital ID:

1. Select Trust Center from the Tools menu to open the Trust Center.

2. Select E-mail Security from the list on the left.

3. Under Digital IDs, click the Import/Export button to display the Import/Export Digital ID dialog box (see Figure 20.3).

4. Select the Import Existing Digital ID option.

5. Enter the name of the file in the Import File box, or use the Browse button to locate it. Digital ID files have the .EPF, PFX, or .P12 extension.

6. Enter the file password in the Password box.

7. Enter a name of your choosing for the certificate in the Digital ID Name box.

8. Click OK.

FIGURE 20.3

The Import/Export Digital ID dialog box.

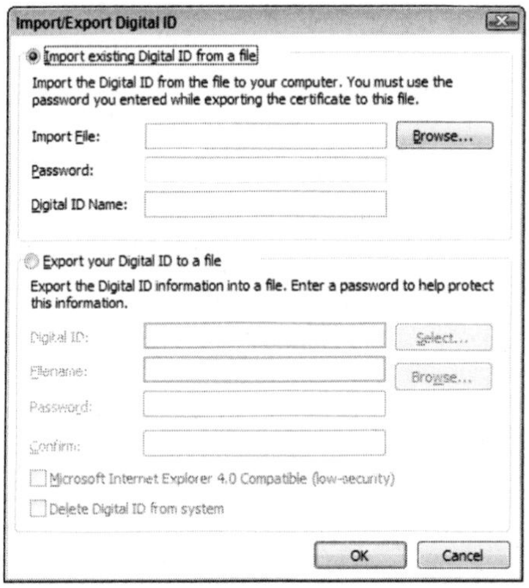

Exporting a digital ID uses the same dialog box except that you must select the Export option. Then:

1. If you have more than one digital ID, use the Select button to choose the ID to export.

2. Enter the export filename in the Filename box, or use the Browse button to select an export location.

3. Enter and confirm the password in the boxes provided.

4. Select the Microsoft Internet Explorer 4.0 Compatible option only if you will use the exported ID with older versions of Internet Explorer.

5. Select Delete Digital ID from System if you want to completely delete the ID rather than export it.

6. Click OK.

Receiving Digitally Signed Messages

When you receive a digitally signed message, the only difference is that the message says "Signed By *XXXX*" (where *XXXX* is the sender's email address) in the header, just below the subject line. You can use such a message to add the sender's public key to your Contacts list, as explained in the next section.

Just because a message is signed does not mean that the signature is legitimate. On the same line as the "Signed By *XXXX*" is displayed, Outlook displays a red ribbon icon as shown in Figure 20.4 to indicate the signature is valid. If the signature is not valid, the message "There are problems with the signature" is displayed, and you can click a button to view the details. A digital signature could be invalid because it has expired, the issuing authority has revoked it, or the server that verifies the certificate is invalid.

FIGURE 20.4

This icon indicates that the digital signature in a message is valid.

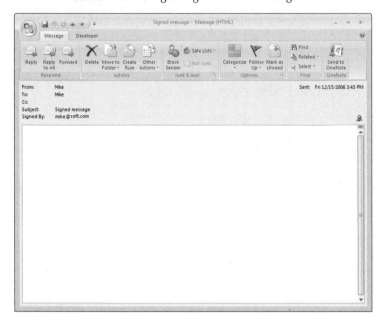

Obtaining Other People's Public Keys

To send an encrypted message to someone, you must have their public key. You can get this from a signed message the person sent you. Their certificate is added to their entry in Contacts, and is available for you to use to send encrypted email:

1. Open the digitally signed message.

2. Right-click the sender's name or address in the From box.

3. Select Add to Outlook Contacts from the context menu.

4. If the contact already exists in your Contacts folder, Outlook will notify you. Select Update Information of Selected Contact.

You can view a contact's certificates by opening the contact and clicking the Certificates button in the Show section of the ribbon. Outlook displays a list of the contact's certificates, if there are any, as shown in Figure 20.5. You can take the following actions by clicking the buttons at the right side of this window:

- **Properties:** View the certificate details, including the name of the issuing company and its expiration date.

- **Set as Default:** If the contact has more than one certificate, this command sets the one that will be used as the default for encrypting messages to the contact.

- **Import:** This option lets you import a person's certificate from a file. Certificate files have the .P7C or .CER extension.

- **Export:** This option lets you export the certificate to a file. This can be useful when you want to transfer a contact's certificate to another computer.

- **Remove:** This option deletes the certificate from the contact information.

Encrypting and Digitally Signing Messages

It's important to understand that encrypting a message and signing a message are two different things:

- **Encrypting** uses the recipient's public key to encrypt the message and attachments so that only the recipient can read them.

- **Signing** uses your digital ID to mark a message so that recipients can verify that it really came from you.

A message can be signed, encrypted, or both.

FIGURE 20.5

Viewing a contact's digital certificates.

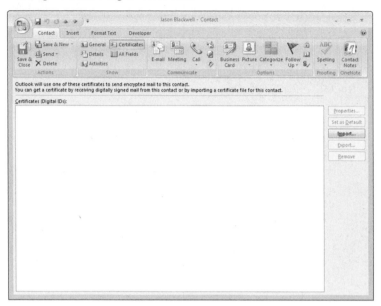

Encrypting Messages

You can send an encrypted message to anyone for whom you have the public key — in other words, you have their certificate as part of their contact information. You can encrypt single messages or specify that all messages be encrypted (when possible).

To encrypt a single message:

1. Create the new message.

2. Click the arrow in the Options section of the Message ribbon to display the Message Options dialog box.

3. Click the Security Settings button to open the Security Properties dialog box (see Figure 20.6).

4. Select the Encrypt Message Contents and Attachments option.

5. Click OK, then click Close, to return to the message.

6. Compose and send the message as usual.

FIGURE 20.6

The Security Properties dialog box.

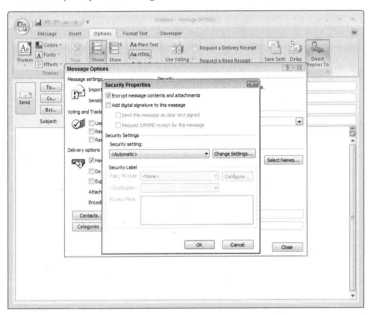

Of course, a message can be encrypted only when it is going to one or more recipients for whom you have a certificate. If you request encryption for a message going to people for whom you do not have a certificate, Outlook displays a message and gives you the option of sending the message without encryption.

You can also tell Outlook to encrypt all outgoing messages and attachments. Of course, this affects only messages that you send to people whose public key you have.

1. Select Trust Center from the Tools menu to open the Trust Center window.
2. Select E-mail Security from the list on the left.
3. Select the option Encrypt Contents and Attachments for Outgoing Messages.

Digitally Signing Messages

As with encryption, you can apply digital signatures to individual outgoing messages or to all of them.

To add a digital signature to an individual message:

1. Create, compose, and address a new email message as usual.

2. Click the arrow in the Options section of the Message ribbon to display the Message Options dialog box.

3. Click the Security Settings button to open the Security Properties dialog box (shown earlier in Figure 20.6).

4. Select the Add Digital Signature to the Message option.

5. Click OK, then click Close, to return to the message.

To add a digital signature to all outgoing messages:

1. Select Trust Center from the Tools menu.

2. Click E-mail Security.

3. In the Encrypted E-mail section, select the Add Digital Signature to Outgoing Messages option.

4. Click OK.

HTML Message Dangers

Because HTML messages can contain script and ActiveX controls, they are a potential source of virus attacks. To guard against any HTML viruses that make it past your anti-virus software, you can tell Outlook to display HTML messages as plain text. Because scripts and ActiveX controls are not activated until the HTML is displayed, this prevents them from doing harm.

To guard against malicious HTML messages:

1. Select Trust Center from the Tools menu.

2. Click E-mail Security.

3. Under Read as Plain Text, select the Read All Standard Mail in Plain Text (this means unsigned messages).

4. If you want to include digitally signed messages, select the Read All Digitally Signed Mail in Plain Text option.

5. Click OK.

Switching from Plain Text to HTML Display

If you have set your options to read HTML messages as plain text, you can switch an individual open message to HTML display by clicking the Info bar and selecting Display as HTML.

Summary

You ignore email security at your own peril. In today's interconnected world, it is all too easy for viruses and other malicious software to spread. Fortunately, Outlook provides you with a number of tools that help you to protect yourself against these threats.

Chapter 21

Using Outlook with Other Applications

O utlook is part of the Microsoft Office suite of productivity programs. Microsoft has designed these programs to work with each other, sharing data to make your work easier. Outlook can also work with other non-Office applications. This chapter explores some of the ways you can integrate Outlook with your other programs.

Sending Email from Office Applications

Office users often need to send various documents via email, such as sending a Word document or an Excel workbook to a client or colleague for review. The usual procedure is as follows:

1. Create the document, for example a report written in Word.
2. Save it to disk.
3. Start Outlook if necessary, or switch to it.
4. Create a new email message.
5. Click the Attach File button in the message.
6. Locate and select the document.
7. Complete the message and send it.

There's an easier way, however. On the Office menu in other Office applications (you open this menu by clicking the Office button at the top left of the application screen), you'll find a Send command, and on the next menu an

IN THIS CHAPTER

Sending email from Office applications

Pasting data into email messages

Creating mailings using Outlook contacts

Exporting data from Outlook

E-mail command, as shown for Word in Figure 21.1. When you select this command, Office creates a new email message with the document attached. All you need to do is compose and address the message, and then send it.

Using the Send E-mail command in other Office applications to send a document as an email attachment.

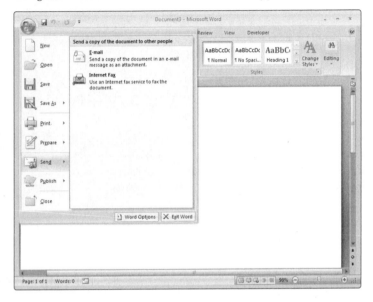

Pasting Office Application Data into Email Messages

An alternative to attaching Office documents to email messages is to include the document, or part of it, right in the body of the email message. There are a couple of reasons why you might want to do this:

- You can easily send part of the document rather than the whole thing.
- The content is immediately visible when the recipient opens the message — he does not have to open, or even have, the parent application to view it.

A potential disadvantage is that the recipient will not have a complete document that he can open and edit. Sometimes, however, that's just what you want: to let someone view and perhaps approve something without having access to an editable document.

Exploring Paste Special

In some situations, the Paste Special command gives you additional options for pasting data. It is accessible by clicking the arrow at the bottom of the Paste button on the Message ribbon. The Paste Special command will be available only when the Clipboard contains appropriate data.

 **NOTE**   Please note that you cannot paste formatted content into plain text email messages, only HTML and RTF format messages.

The procedure is simple — simply select the content in the parent application and select the Copy command (or press Ctrl+C). Then switch to the email message you are composing, position the cursor at the desired location, and select Paste (or press Ctrl+V).

What can you paste into an email message? The possibilities are almost endless. You can paste formatted text from Word, and the fonts, colors, and other formatting details will all be retained. You can copy and paste a table created in Word, and your email message will have the same table. Charts created in Excel are another example of a data element you can paste into an email message.

Figures 21.2 and 21.3 show an example of a formatted Word document and the results when you paste the text into an email message. Figures 21.4 and 21.5 show an example using an Excel chart.

FIGURE 21.2

A formatted Word document can be copied and pasted into an email message.

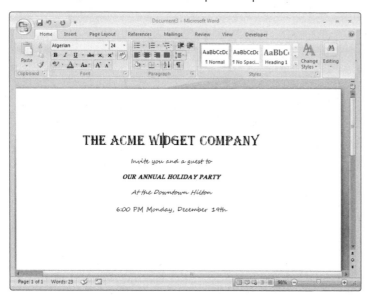

FIGURE 21.3

An email message after pasting the formatted text from the Word document in Figure 21.2 into it.

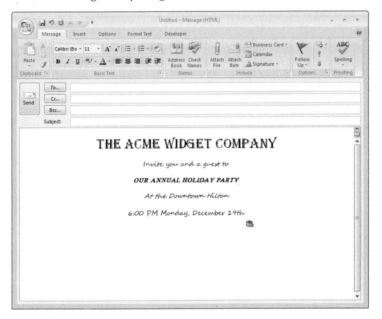

FIGURE 21.4

A chart created in Excel is also a candidate for pasting into an email message.

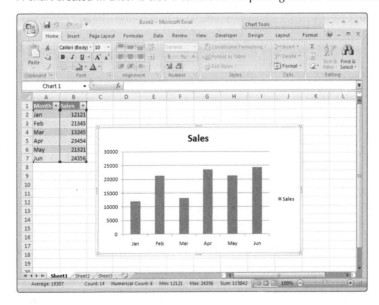

FIGURE 21.5

A chart pasted from Excel into an email message looks exactly the same as the original.

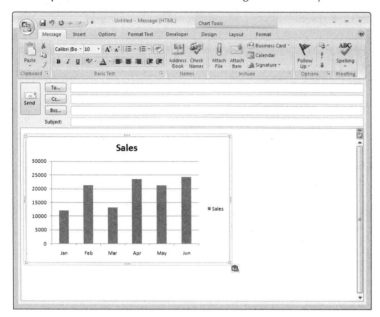

Can you edit text or other data after pasting it into a message? Generally speaking, yes. Pasted text and tables can be edited just as if you had typed them directly into the message. Other pasted items, such as charts, will be more or less editable depending on the program they came from. Right-click such a pasted object to view a context menu that will contain any available editing commands. However, it is almost always preferable to perform necessary editing in the parent application before copying to the message.

Note that copy and paste is a two-way street — you can copy data from Outlook and paste it into other programs as well.

Not Just Office Programs

You are not limited to pasting data into messages from only Microsoft Office programs. Essentially any Windows application has the ability to copy data to the Clipboard from where you can paste it into a message.

Creating Mailings Using Outlook Contacts

Outlook Contacts is a great place to keep all the information about your friends, family, and business associates, including their postal addresses. You can use this information to create a mail merge using Microsoft Word. In a *mail merge*, you create a form letter and then Word creates one copy of the letter, along with an envelope or mailing label, for each name and address in a list. Outlook Contacts is one possible source for this list. Of course, this will work only for those contacts whose postal address is included in their Contacts entry.

This is not a book about Word, so I will not go into the complete details of performing a mail merge using Outlook Contacts, just the basics.

A mail merge document is created using two kinds of elements. One element is normal text that you type in as usual. Sometimes this is called *boilerplate* text because it will be the same in every document or message. The other element is fields that specify where in the document information from the recipient list is to be placed. For example, suppose you want to start each letter with "Dear" followed by the recipient's first name. You would type "Dear " (note the space!) and then insert the first name field; it will look like this in your document:

Dear <<first>>,

To perform a merge in Word using Outlook Contacts:

1. Start a new document in Word.
2. Click the Mailings tab to display the Mailings ribbon.
3. In the Start Mail Merge section, click Start Mail Merge.
4. Select the type of document you want to create from the menu (see Figure 21.6).
5. Click the Select Recipients button on the ribbon.
6. Choose Select from Outlook Contacts from the menu. If you have more than one Contacts folder, you will be prompted to select the folder to use.

Email Merge

Word also has the capability to perform a merge whose output is email messages. This may seem unnecessary — after all, it's easy enough to create a message and send it to multiple recipients using Outlook alone. However, a merge lets you personalize the messages, such as starting each one with "Dear Alice" or whatever the recipient's first name is.

7. Word displays a list of all contacts in the selected folder, as shown in Figure 21.7. Actions that you can take here include:

   - Remove the checkmark from any recipients that you do not want included in the merge.

   - Click the Sort link to specify the order of the merge (for example, ZIP code order, last name order, and so on).

   - Click the Filter link to filter the recipient list (for example, only recipients in California).

   - Click the Find Duplicates link to scan the recipient list for possible duplicates.

8. Click OK.

At this point, you are ready to start composing your document. Enter and format text as usual. When you come to a place where you want the document personalized with information from the recipient's list, click Insert Merge Field on the ribbon. Word displays a list of all the available fields, as shown in Figure 21.8.

FIGURE 21.6

Selecting the type of output document for a mail merge.

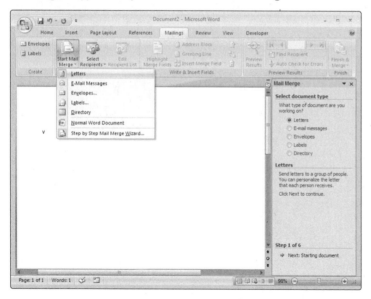

FIGURE 21.7

Selecting the contacts to include in a mail merge.

FIGURE 21.8

Inserting a merge field into a mail merge document.

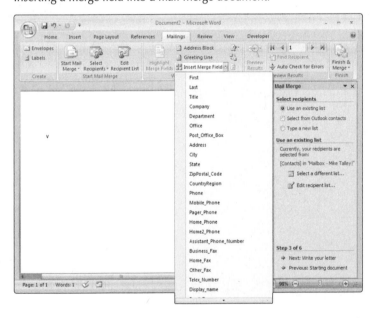

Using the Mail Merge Wizard

When you are selecting the type of document for your merge, one of the menu choices is Step By Step Mail Merge Wizard. If you select this command, the wizard will walk you through all the steps of creating your mail merge.

As you work on the document, you can preview what the end result will look like by clicking the Preview Results button. All merge fields in the document are replaced with data from the first contact in the recipient list. Click the button again to return to the display of merge fields.

When the document is complete, click the Finish & Merge button. The options available on this menu depend on the type of merge you are performing. For example, if you are creating an email merge, you can select Send Emails to generate and send the merged email messages.

Summary

Outlook is one of several programs in Microsoft's Office productivity suite. These programs are designed to work with each other, sharing data and completing tasks in an efficient manner. This chapter showed you some of the ways you can use Outlook with other Office programs.

Part V

Programming Outlook

Chapter 22

Writing Macros and Visual Basic Code in Outlook

A macro is a sequence of program commands and keyboard input that has been saved. At any time, you can play the macro back and the result is exactly the same as if you had entered the same commands and input using the keyboard and mouse. Macros are terrific for automatic tasks that you perform regularly, and they can also help prevent errors.

Understanding Macros

Outlook (along with other Office programs) has a built-in programming language called *Visual Basic for Applications*, or *VBA* for short, that lets you write programs, called *macros*, to automate program operations. A macro may do something as simple as inserting a signature into an email message, or something as complex as sorting all incoming email into folders based on the sender. Macros offer two important benefits:

- **They save time.** A sequence of actions that might take you a minute or more to perform manually can be executed essentially instantly with a macro.

- **They prevent errors.** A properly written macro does not make mistakes. It performs the exact same sequence of commands each time it is run without typos or other errors.

You are not limited to using macros that you write. You may be able to get useful macros from your friends and colleagues, and some commercial products that add functionality to Outlook do so by means of macros. In any situation where you are considering a macro from an outside source, you must be aware of the issues surrounding macro security as discussed later in this chapter.

Recording Macros? Sorry, No.

Many programs (including Word and Excel) let you record macros. In other words, you perform the desired series of actions, and the macro recorder saves the corresponding VBA commands. You can then use the recorded macro as-is or modify it. Unfortunately, Outlook does not have a macro recorder—the only way to create a macro is to write it yourself.

Many people use Outlook for years without ever wanting or needing to create or use macros. The fact is, however, that macros are an extremely powerful tool, and you may be missing a lot of time savings and error prevention if you ignore them.

The Macros Dialog Box

Outlook's macro command center is the Macros dialog box, shown in Figure 22.1. You open this dialog box by pressing Alt+F8 or selecting Macro from the Tools menu and then selecting Macros.

FIGURE 22.1

The Macros dialog box is Outlook's macro "command center."

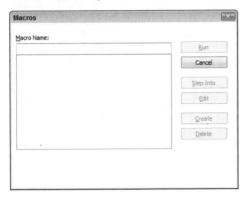

If you have any macros defined they will be listed here, otherwise the list will be empty. If you select an existing macro from the list, you can take the following actions by clicking the buttons in the dialog box:

- **Run:** Execute the macro.
- **Step Into:** Debug the macro. Debugging macros is covered later in this chapter.

Other Ways to Run Macros

In addition to running a macro from the Macros dialog box, you can assign macros to your menus and toolbars for easier access. This is explained later in this chapter.

- **Edit:** Open the VBA editor to edit the macro.
- **Delete:** Delete the macro.

To create a new macro, enter its name in the Macro Name box (the name must be unique for obvious reasons) and click the Create button. Outlook opens the VBA Editor with the shell — that is, the first and last lines — of the new macro in place, ready for you to add code.

The VBA Editor

The VBA Editor is where you create, edit, and debug macros. The editor is a powerful programming tool and is designed to make your programming efforts as easy as possible. You can open the editor from Outlook in several ways:

- Press Alt+F11 (press Alt+F11 again to return to Outlook).
- Select Macro from the Tools menu and then select Visual Basic Editor.
- From the Macros dialog box, select the Edit or Create command (as explained in the previous section).

The VBA Editor is shown in Figure 22.2. You learn more about the editor's various tools and commands in subsequent chapters; for now it's enough for you to become familiar with the parts of the editor screen:

- At the top left of the screen is the *Project Explorer*, where the editor lists the various components of the Outlook VBA project.
- At the bottom left of the screen is the *Properties window*, where you view and edit the properties of whatever object is currently selected. In the figure, there is only a single property, but in other situations there will be dozens of properties listed here.
- The main part of the screen, at the top right, displays one or more editing windows. It's here that you enter and edit VBA code.
- At the bottom of the screen is the *Immediate window*, which you can use to debug macros.

FIGURE 22.2

The VBA Editor.

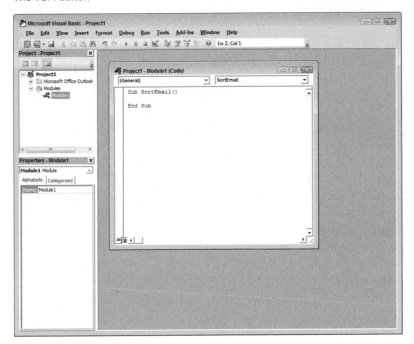

Security and Macros

VBA is a powerful programming language. As such, it has the potential to do great harm to your data and files. So-called *macro viruses* have become more common, and are typically spread when Office documents are passed around as email attachments.

Outlook-based macro viruses are rarely if ever a problem because of the way its macros are stored. With other Office programs, such as Word and Excel, macros can be a part of an individual document and will go along with the document when it is forwarded as an attachment, thus permitting a malicious macro to be spread. In contrast, Outlook macros are not part of any document but are associated and stored with the Outlook program itself. In other words, you cannot pass an Outlook macro to someone else by sending them an email or any other Outlook data (you can specifically export an Outlook macro to send to someone else, but in that case it's obvious what's happening).

Does this mean that you need not be concerned with macro security? Absolutely not! Chapter 20 explains a variety of measures that Outlook users should take with regards to security.

WARNING Even when it comes to Outlook macros, you must use caution. Just because you cannot be infected with a malicious Outlook virus by means of an email attachment does not mean you are safe. If you plan to use macros from any outside source, you should use macros from trusted sources only, and when in doubt look over the macro source code to look for potential problems.

Assigning Macros to Menus and Toolbars

When you have a few macros that you use a lot, you may not want to open the Macros dialog box to run them each time. You can place a macro on a menu or a toolbar to make it more readily available. The procedures are similar to those for customizing menus and toolbars that were covered in Chapter 19. You may want to create a new toolbar, as explained in that chapter, specifically for macro commands:

1. In Outlook, select Customize from the Tools menu to display the Customize dialog box.

2. If necessary, click the Commands tab.

3. Select Macros in the Categories list. As shown in Figure 22.3, the Commands list displays the names of all macros.

4. To place a macro on a toolbar or menu, drag it from the list and drop it at the desired position on the toolbar or menu.

5. When finished placing commands, click Close to close the Customize dialog box.

FIGURE 22.3

Assigning macros to menus and toolbars.

By default, a macro is displayed on a menu or toolbar with the macro name and the generic Macro icon, as shown in Figure 22.4.

FIGURE 22.4

A toolbar or menu initially displays a macro's name and a default icon.

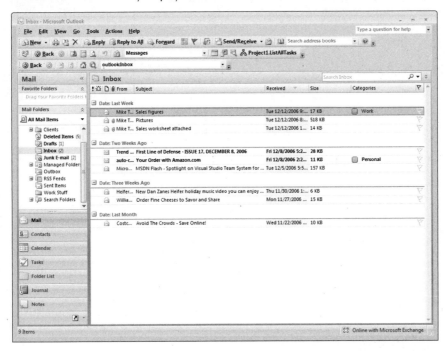

You can change how a macro is displayed on a toolbar or menu. First, you have to open the Customize dialog box by selecting Customize from the Tools menu. You do not actually use the dialog box in these procedures, but it must be open for the menus and toolbars to be in edit mode. Then, right-click the macro item on the menu or toolbar to display the context menu shown in Figure 22.5. The commands are

- **Reset:** Resets the button to the default appearance.
- **Delete:** Deletes the button from the toolbar or menu.
- **Name:** In the adjacent box, edit the text that is displayed on the button.
- **Copy Button Image:** Copy the button's image so you can paste it into another button.
- **Paste Button Image:** Use the image copied from another button.
- **Reset Button Image:** Resets the button to the default "macro" icon.

■ **Edit Button Image:** Opens an icon or button editor, shown in Figure 22.6, where you can edit the button's image.

■ **Change Button Image:** Lets you select from a gallery of button designs, as shown in Figure 22.7.

■ **Default Style:** Sets the button to display an icon only (no text).

■ **Text Only (Always):** Sets the button to display text only both in toolbars and on menus.

■ **Text Only (in Menus):** Sets the button to display text only on menus.

■ **Image and Text:** Sets the button to display both text and an image.

■ **Begin a Group:** Adds a vertical (on toolbars) or horizontal (on menus) divider before the button.

■ **Assign Hyperlink:** Lets you assign a hyperlink to a toolbar item.

FIGURE 22.5

This context menu provides commands for changing how macros are displayed on toolbars and menus.

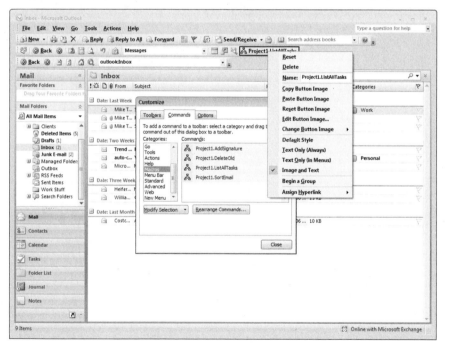

The Button Editor lets you customize the appearance of toolbar buttons.

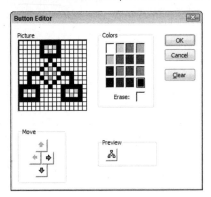

Selecting a button design from the button gallery.

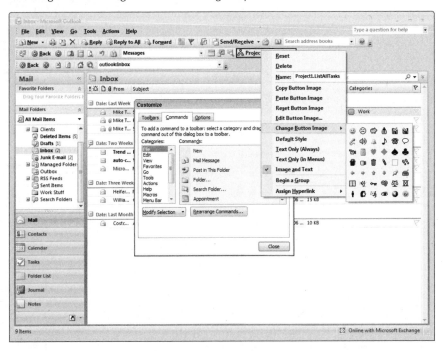

Assigning Macros to Shortcut Keys

Sorry, no can do. It would be a nice feature to be able to assign frequently used macros to shortcut keys, but Outlook does not permit this.

Debugging Macros

When you create a macro, you may find that it does not do exactly what you wanted it to do. This is called a *bug* and the Outlook VBA Editor provides you with some tools for finding and fixing bugs. Generally, bugs are almost always the result of one or both of the following problems:

- A program variable takes on the wrong value.

- Program execution takes the wrong path through the macro code.

The debugging tools let you address both of these problems as follows:

- Breakpoints let you temporarily suspend the macro's execution at specified lines of code or when specified conditions are met.

- Watches let you examine and change the value of variables during macro execution.

- Controlling execution lets you execute a program one line at a time and control the path execution takes.

Working with Breakpoints

When a macro is executing inside the VBA Editor, you can temporarily pause macro execution—in other words, put the macro in *break mode*. You do this by setting one or more breakpoints, which specify that the program should pause either when a specified line of code is reached or when a certain condition is met. When a program is in break mode, the next statement to be executed is highlighted in the editor window (if possible—the next statement may not be known), and you can carry out various actions to help track down the cause of a bug. Then, you can continue execution normally or terminate the program.

When in break mode, you can rest the mouse pointer over a variable name in your code and the VBA Editor will display the current value of the variable in a small window. You can also edit your code, with some limitations. The other tools described in this section are also available in break mode.

To enter break mode when execution reaches a certain location in your macro code, set a breakpoint on that line. Before you start execution, or while in break mode, move the editing cursor to the line and press F9. A line that has a breakpoint set is displayed in a different color and with a dot in the left margin, as shown in Figure 22.8. Execution pauses just before executing the line with the breakpoint. You can set breakpoints on as many lines as you want. Press F9 again to remove the breakpoint from a line. Press Ctrl+Shift+F9 to remove all breakpoints.

The Debug.Print Statement

The Debug.Print statement is a very useful tool for debugging macros. All it does is display the specified data in the Immediate window of the VBA editor. There are all sorts of uses for Debug.Print during program development and debugging, such as verifying the value of variables, seeing where program execution goes, and so on. The beauty of Debug.Print is that the statement has no effect outside of the VBA environment, when your macro is being run by the end user. All you do is include the Debug.Print statement in your macro code followed by the name of the variable whose value you want to see. For example,

```
Debug.Print "The value of X is " & X
```

displays a message and the value of the variable X.

FIGURE 22.8

A breakpoint displays as shown in the VBA Editor.

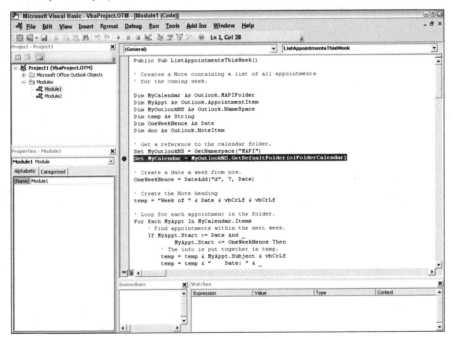

You can also enter break mode based on the value of variables in your program. For example, you could specify that the program enters break mode when the variable `Count` has the value `100`. You learn about this technique in the next section, "Using Watches."

When you are finished working in break mode, press F5 to continue macro execution. Other options for controlling program execution are covered in the section "Controlling Program Execution" later in this chapter.

Using Watches

While you are debugging a macro you can use watch expressions to keep track of the data your macro is working with. A *watch* can be any expression — variables, properties, functions, and so on. Because many program bugs are caused by variables and properties taking on unexpected values, the use of watches is an important debugging tool.

VBA supports two types of watches and you can choose the one that's right for your needs. Regular watches are displayed in the Watches window, which you open by selecting Watch Window from the View menu. You can have multiple watch expressions in the window, and VBA displays the following for each one:

- **Value:** The current value of the watch expression.
- **Type:** The data type of the watch expression.
- **Context:** The names of the module and macro where execution is paused.

The Watches window is shown in Figure 22.9. It indicates the variable `Count` is type Integer and has the value `45`, and the variable `temp` is type String as has the value `"Week of 12/12/2006"`.

FIGURE 22.9

Use the Watches window to view the value of variables and expressions during macro debugging.

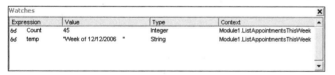

A watch expression can be a single variable or an expression made up of variables and any of VBA's operators and functions. You would create watch expressions when you are interested in the relationship between variables rather than their exact values. For instance, you might need to keep track of whether the variable `Count` is greater than the variable `Max` without regard to their actual values. The watch expression `Count >Max` displays a result of either `True` or `False` depending on the data. Likewise, if you want to see whether a string's length is less than 10, you would use the watch expression `Len(SomeString)<10`.

To add a variable to the Watches window, right-click the variable name in your code and select Add Watch from the popup menu. To add an expression to the Watches window:

1. Move the editing cursor to any location in the code you are debugging.

2. Select Add Watch from the Debug menu. VBA displays the Add Watch dialog box (see Figure 22.10).

3. Enter the desired watch expression in the Expression box.

4. Make sure the Watch Expression option is selected.

5. Click OK.

Each time the program enters break mode the display in the Watches window is updated. Then, you can examine the values of your watch expressions to determine whether they reveal anything about the bug you are working on. You can also edit a watch expression, or delete it from the window, by right-clicking it and selecting from the popup menu.

FIGURE 22.10

Adding a watch expression to the Watches window.

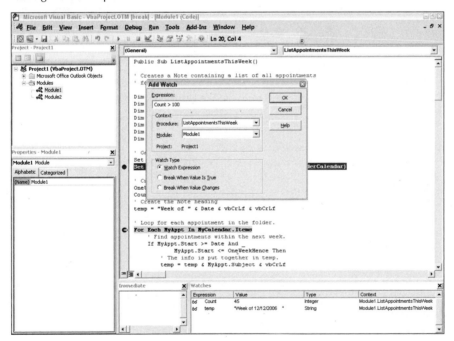

The second type of watch is called a Quick Watch. When the macro is in break mode, highlight an expression in your code and select Quick Watch from the Debug menu (or press Shift+F9). VBA displays a box containing the current value of the expression as well as its data type and context. Figure 21.11 shows a Quick Watch display.

Watches can also be used to control break mode. For example, you can specify that the macro break either when a watch expression is True or when a watch expression changes value. You add this type of watch using the Add Watch dialog box (see Figure 22.10), and is displayed in the Watches window along with other watches. Type the expression in the Expression box of the Add Watch dialog box, then select either the Break When Value Is True or Break When Value Changes option. In the Watches window, the three types of watches — regular, break on true, and break when changes — are displayed with different symbols in the left column. When a program breaks based on a watch expression, the corresponding watch expression is highlighted in the Watches window.

FIGURE 22.11

Displaying Quick Watch information about an expression.

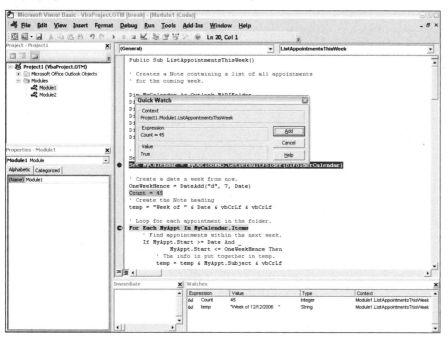

Watches and Scope

To be available for a watch, a variable must currently be in scope. If you are debugging code in one procedure, the local variables in a second procedure will not be available because they are out of scope. Out of scope variables in a watch expression display as Out Of Context until the variable comes back into scope.

The Locals Window

VBA provides yet another useful way of keeping track of the values of program variables — the Locals window. To display this window, shown in Figure 22.12, select Locals Window from the View menu. You cannot specify what is shown in this window — it always displays the values and types of all variables, properties, objects, and constants that are in scope at the time the program enters break mode.

FIGURE 22.12

The Locals window.

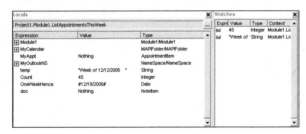

Controlling Macro Execution

The ability to control the execution of your macro can be an essential part of debugging. Earlier in this section you have seen how to pause macro execution, entering break mode based on code location or on the value of program variables. Once you are finished working in break mode, you have several choices on the Debug menu:

- **Continue (F5):** Continues macro execution normally.
- **Step Into (F8):** Executes the next statement then pauses in break mode. If the next statement is a procedure call, pauses at the first statement in the procedure.

Other Uses for the Immediate Window

You have already seen how to use the `Debug.Print` statement to display information in the Immediate window. This window has other uses as well. When a macro is in break mode, the Immediate window has the same scope as the current procedure. You can change the value of a variable by simply typing the new value in the Immediate window. For example, if the current procedure has a variable `Count`, then by typing

```
Count = 100
```

in the Immediate window (on its own line) and pressing Enter you assign the new value to the variable. When you continue program execution you can see the effects of the new value.

- **Step Over (Shift+F8):** Executes the next statement then pauses in break mode. If the next statement is a procedure call, executes the entire procedure then pauses after exiting the procedure. This command has the same effect as Step Into if the next statement is not a procedure call.

- **Step Out (Ctrl+Shift+F8):** Executes to the end of the current procedure, then pauses in break mode.

- **Run to Cursor (Ctrl+F8):** Executes to the line of code containing the cursor, then pauses in break mode.

The Step Into and Run to Cursor commands are available even when you are not in break mode. By using one of these commands to start the macro, rather than the usual Run Sub/User Form command (or pressing F5), you can start the project and run it one line at a time, or up to the cursor.

What's Next?

This chapter has just scratched the surface of Outlook macros and VBA programming. Here's a brief look at what's coming up. The next three chapters deal with macros and VBA programming in more detail:

- Chapter 23 deals with the VBA language and how it is used to write macros. You need an understanding of VBA structure and syntax before you can proceed.

- Chapter 24 explores the Outlook Object Model, which provides the VBA programmer with a rich set of objects that represent various elements in Outlook, such as messages, contacts, and tasks. Macro programming is mostly a matter of manipulating these objects to accomplish your task.

- Chapter 25 walks you through some complete, real-world examples of Outlook macros.

Summary

This chapter has introduced you to Outlook macros and VBA programming. Macros let you automate repetitive, commonly performed tasks and can save you time and errors. Though you cannot record macros in Outlook, you can create your own and import macros from friends and colleagues. There's a lot more to learn, so stay tuned.

Chapter 23

Getting Started with VBA

V BA, or Visual Basic for Applications, is the programming language built in to the programs in the Microsoft Office suite, including Outlook. To be able write and edit Outlook macros, you must have a decent understanding of the VBA language. Fortunately, it is a fairly easy language, having been designed from the very beginning to be accessible not just to computer geeks but also to us ordinary mortals.

This chapter provides an introduction to the VBA language, giving you an overview of the most essential language elements. It is by no means a complete treatment of VBA — that would require an entire book in itself! With the information provided in this chapter, you can start writing useful macros. As your needs and interest dictate, you can find more information on VBA in the online help, books, and other sources.

Basic VBA Syntax

A VBA program, or *macro*, is made up of a series of VBA statements. Each *statement* is an instruction that tells Outlook to perform an action such as adding two numbers or opening an email message. Each statement is on its own line in the source code, although long lines can be split with a space followed by an underscore in order to make them easier to read in the editor. Thus, the following is treated as a single line of code:

```
ActiveWorkbook.CustomDocumentProperties.Add _
    Name:="Part number", LinkToContent:=False, _
    Type:=msoPropertyTypeNumber, Value:=566
```

Outlook is very literal when it comes to running VBA code. It can do only what you specify in the code — it has no way of knowing what you really meant. Even the slightest misspelling or punctuation error will cause problems, so you need to be careful. Fortunately, the case of words does not matter.

Code Comments

A *comment* is text in your macro code that is for information only — it has no effect on how the macro operates. Comments are useful — in fact they are recommended — for describing how your code operates. Then, when you or someone else needs to edit the code sometime down the road, its operation will be clear and not a matter of guesswork.

To create a comment, start a line with either an apostrophe or REM. You can put a comment at the end of a line of code using the apostrophe but not REM:

```
Rem This is a comment.
' This is another comment.
Dim S As String ' This too is a comment.
Dim S As String Rem But this is not permitted.
```

Storing Data

Many macros need some way to store data while they are running. This is temporary storage and lasts only while the macro is running — it is not permanent such as saving something to disk. VBA gives you a full range of options for storing data.

Variables

A *variable* is a place where you can store a single piece of information, such as a number of a segment of text. The name "variable" comes from the fact that the information can change while the macro is executing — it is not fixed. When you create a variable, you assign it a name, and then you use that name to refer to the variable in your source code. VBA variable names must follow these rules:

- Do not use one of VBA's keywords.
- The maximum length is 255 characters.
- The first character must be a letter.
- The name cannot contain a period, space, or any of these characters: ! @ # & % $.

The case of names is irrelevant, although the VBA Editor automatically adjusts case to be the same for all instances of a given variable name. For example, if the first time you use a variable you call it Count, and the second time you type in COUNT, the second entry will be changed to Count by the editor.

You should use *descriptive variable names* — that is, names that describe the data the variable holds. For instance, a variable that holds an interest rate might be called IntRate or InterestRate. You could call it MickeyMouse or Q99 and VBA would not care, but descriptive names make your code a lot easier to read and debug.

It is common practice, although not required, to use a combination of upper- and lowercase letters for variable names as shown in these examples:

- TotalOfIncome
- AverageSize
- RecipientEmailAddress

All variables should be *declared* before being used for the first time. This tells VBA about the variable, specifically its name and the kind of data it will hold. A variable declaration takes this form:

```
Dim varname As type
```

varname is the name of the variable, and type is the name of the variable's data type (as explained in the following sections). You can place multiple declarations on the same line:

```
Dim varname1 As type1, varname2 As type2, varname3 As type3
```

I say that variables *should be* declared, not that they *must be* declared. VBA gives you the option of not requiring variable declaration — you simply use new variable names as needed in your code. This may sound like a good idea, but in fact it is not. When variable declaration is required, misspelling a variable name results in an error message when you run the program, because the (misspelled) variable has not been declared, and the misspelling can be easily corrected. If variable declaration is not required, misspellings go undetected and can cause lots of problems. To make sure variable declaration is required, select Tools, Options in the VBA Editor and select the Require Variable Declaration option on the Editor tab. You can obtain the same effect by placing the Option Explicit statement at the start of every VBA module.

Numeric Variables

Numeric variables hold number data. VBA has six different numeric variable types that differ in whether they hold integer data (numbers without a decimal part such as 2, –145, and 32,190) or floating-point data (numbers with a decimal part such as –1.143, 0.0045, and 123,900.5). These six numeric variable types are summarized in Table 23.1.

TABLE 23.1

VBA's Numeric Data Types

Name	Type	Range	Precision	Size
Byte	Integer	0 to 255	N/A	1 byte
Integer	Integer	−32,768 to 32,767	N/A	2 bytes
Long	Integer	−2,147,483,648 to 2,147,483,647	N/A	4 bytes
Single	Floating point	-3.4×10^{38} to 3.4×10^{38} *	6 digits	4 bytes
Double	Floating point	-1.79×10^{308} to 1.79×10^{308} *	14 digits	8 bytes
Currency	Floating point	-9.22×10^{11} to 9.22×10^{11} *	4 digits	8 bytes

* Approximate values

Why have three integer types and three floating-point types? You can see that the types differ in terms of the range of values they can hold and, for the floating-point types, their precision or accuracy. They also differ in the amount of memory they consume. It's also true that certain operations, such as division, are faster with the integer types. To be honest, these memory and speed differences are rarely relevant with today's fast, memory-laden computers. Choose a numeric data type based on the range of values the variable will hold. When in doubt, it is always advisable to err on the side of caution, using a type Long rather than a type Integer, for example. If you try to store an out-of-range value in a variable, VBA generates an Overflow error.

String Variables

Strings, which is just programmer-talk for text data, represent the second main class of data that VBA programs work with. VBA provides two types of string variables. A *variable-length* string can hold any amount of text up to about 2 billion characters. A variable-length string expands and contracts automatically to fit the data you put in it, so you do not need to specify the size when declaring it:

```
Dim City As String
```

A *fixed-length string*, on the other hand, has a fixed size you specify when the variable is declared. This can range from 1 to as many as approximately 64,000 characters. The declaration syntax is as follows:

```
Dim FirstName As String * 15
Dim  LastName As String * 15
```

If you assign text that is too long to a fixed-length string variable, the extra part of the text is cut off and lost.

VBA can figure out that you mean to use s as a number even though it was declared as a string, so the division is performed properly with the result that i is equal to 8.

Numbers Versus Strings

You need to be aware of the difference between a number and a text representation of a number. In a VBA program, 12345 (without quotes) is a number, whereas "12345" is text. VBA is actually pretty clever when it comes to figuring out what you mean. For example, look at this code:

```
Dim s As String
Dim i As Integer
s = "16"
i = s / 2
```

Constants

As its name implies, a *constant* is program data whose value does not change. VBA has two types of constants, literal and symbolic. A *literal constant* is a number or string typed directly into your code. String literals are typed in double quotation marks. Numeric literal constants are typed without special formatting. In this code, `"Jackson"` and `0.75` are literal constants:

```
Dim Ratio As Single
Dim Name As String
Max = 0.75
Name = "Jackson"
```

A *symbolic constant* has a name. To create a symbolic constant, use the `Const` keyword:

```
Const CONSTNAME As Type = value
```

The rules for constant names are the same as for variables. I like to use all uppercase names with underscore separators for constants, which makes them easily distinguishable from variables in the code (which are commonly written with a combination of upper- and lowercase). Thus, `PRIME_RATE` is easily identified as a constant, and `PrimeRate` is clearly a variable. The `As type` part of the declaration is optional and is required only if you want the constant to be stored as a specific data type. `value` is the constant value.

Here are two examples:

```
Const PRIME_RATE As Double = 0.042

Const FILE_SAVE_PATH = "c:\my documents\databases\"
```

A big advantage of using symbolic constants is that you can change the value of a constant throughout the program simply by editing its declaration statement. Another advantage is that the constant's name can help in making the program easier to read.

Boolean Variables

Boolean variables can hold only the two values `True` and `False`. They are widely used in all areas of programming because you'll find that you often need to store values that are true/false, yes/no, or on/off. You assign values to Boolean variables using the VBA keywords `True` and `False`. Here's an example:

```
Dim TaskDueToday As Boolean
TaskDueToday = True
```

Behind the scenes, VBA represents `True` and `False` by the values –1 and 0, respectively. When treated as a Boolean, any numeric expression will evaluate as `True` if its value is non-zero.

Date Variables

In VBA, the term "`date`" refers to the time of day as well as the calendar date. Dates are stored internally as floating-point numbers in which the part to the left of the decimal point represents the number of days since December 30, 1899, with negative numbers representing prior dates. The part to the right of the decimal point represents the time as a fraction of a day, so that `.25` is 6 A.M., `.5` is noon, and so on.

The `Date` data type is designed to hold date values. When you display a date value, the display format is determined by the system's short date format setting, and times are displayed as either 12- or 24-hour times, again in accordance with the system settings.

You write literal date values in just about any recognizable format, enclosed in # signs. Here are some examples:

```
Dim d1 as Date, d2 As Date, d3 As Date

d1 = #January 31, 2005#
d2 = #31 Jan 05#
d3 = #1/31/2005#
```

The VBA Editor will automatically convert date literals to a standard format. VBA has a wide range of tools for working with dates and times. They are beyond the scope of this chapter, but you can find detailed information on the VBA online documentation.

The Variant Type

The `Variant` data type is VBA's default variable type, and also its most flexible. *Default* means that if you declare a variable without specifying a type, it is created as a `Variant`. These declarations create two type `Variant` variables:

```
Dim x

Dim y As Variant
```

This data type's flexibility comes from its ability to hold almost any type of data (with the single exception of fixed-length strings). Thus, a type `Variant` can hold numbers, text, object references, user-defined types, and arrays. One common use for this data type is when data needs to be treated either as text or as a number depending on circumstances. Another use is as an argument to procedures that can take different kinds of data. You should not, however, simply use type `Variant` as a convenience to avoid the necessity of thinking about what data type should be used for specific variables. The `Variant` data type requires more memory to store, and more processor time to manipulate, than other data types.

Object Variables

Another type of variable holds a reference to an object. *Objects*, which represent the various parts of the Outlook program (among other things), are a central part of VBA programming. You learn more about object variables when you look at Outlook's Object Model in Chapter 24.

Arrays

An *array* is a group of two or more variables that have the same name and are distinguished by a numeric index. VBA offers two types of arrays: static and dynamic.

Static Arrays

A *static array* is created with a specified number of elements and this number does not change while the program is executing. To declare a static array, use the following syntax:

```
Dim ArrayName(n) As type
```

`ArrayName` is the name of the array, which follows the same naming rule as regular VBA variables. n is the number of elements in the array, and `type` can be any of VBA's data types. Here's an example:

```
Dim NewArray(100) As Long
```

This statement creates an array of type `Long` variables. VBA starts array indexes at 0; this array actually contains 101 elements, at indexes 0 through 100. You access an array's elements using any expression to specify the index. For example:

```
NewArray(1) = 25
x = 15
NewArray(x) = 99   ' Same as NewArray(15)
NewArray(MyArray(1)) = 5   ' Same as NewArray(25)
```

You can also create arrays where the index does not start at 0 by using the `To` keyword, which lets you specify any starting index you like. The format is as follows:

```
Dim NewArray(start To stop)
```

start and stop are the starting and ending indexes for the array. Here's an example:

```
Dim Months(1 To 12)
```

The arrays you have seen so far have a single index — they are one-dimensional. VBA also supports multidimensional arrays that have two or more indexes by including the information about the additional indexes in the Dim statement. Here's an example that creates a two-dimensional array:

```
Dim ChessBoard(1 To 8, 1 To 8) As Integer
```

Dynamic Arrays

A *dynamic array* does not have a fixed size — it can be enlarged or shrunk while the program is running. The syntax for declaring a dynamic array is the same as for static arrays except that no indexes are specified — the parentheses are left blank:

```
Dim MyDynamicArray() As type
```

Before you can use the array, you must set its size using the ReDim statement:

```
ReDim MyDynamicArray(indexes)
```

The indexes argument specifies both the number of dimensions and the number of elements, using the same syntax as you learned about earlier for declaring static arrays. Here are some examples of declaring and sizing dynamic arrays:

```
Dim DynamicArray1()
Dim DynamicArray2()
Dim DynamicArray3()
' 1 dimension, 21 elements 0-20.
Redim DynamicArray1(20)
' 1 dimension, 26 elements 5-30.
Redim DynamicArray2(5 to 20)
' 2 dimensions, 40 total elements.
ReDim DynamicArray3(1 To 4, 1 to 10)
```

You can change the array size while the program is running as many times as needed using this syntax:

```
ReDim [Preserve] arrayname(indexes)
```

indexes specifies the new array size, as shown here. Use the optional Preserve keyword if you want the existing data in the array to be kept. If you omit Preserve, the array will be reinitialized and existing data lost when you execute ReDim. There are some limitations on the use of Preserve:

■ When you make an array smaller, the data in the part of the array that is "trimmed off" will be lost.

■ You cannot change the number of dimensions of the array.

■ For multidimensional arrays, you can change only the upper bound of the last dimension.

User-Defined Types

A *user-defined type*, or *UDT*, can be used to define your own data structures. A UDT contains two or more elements and is designed to meet specific data storage needs of your macro. To define a UDT, use the `Type ... End Type` statement:

```
Type UDTName
    Element1 As type
    Element2 As type
    ....
    Elementn As type
End Type
```

Each element can be any of VBA's data types: `Byte`, `Boolean`, `Integer`, `Long`, `Currency`, `Single`, `Double`, `Date`, variable-length or fixed-length `String`, `Object`, `Variant`, another UDT, or an object type. Each element can be a single variable or an array. The rules for naming the UDT itself and it elements are the same as the rules for naming VBA variables as described earlier in this chapter.

Once you have defined a UDT, you declare it using the `Dim` statement. A UDT must be declared in a module but not within any procedure. Here's a UDT definition:

```
Type Person
    FirstName As String
    LastName As String
    EmailAddress As String
End Type
```

Then declare in a variable of this type:

```
Dim MyBestFriend As Person
```

Finally, access the elements of the UDT using the `VariableName.ElementName` syntax:

```
MyBestFriend.FirstName = "Alice"
MyBestFriend.LastName = "Wilson"
MyBestFriend.EmailAddress = "alice@somewhere.net"
```

You can create arrays of UDTs as well:

```
Dim AllMyFriends(100) As Person
```

Enumerations

An *enumeration* is a user-defined data type that consists of a defined set of symbolic constants. You use the `Enum` keyword to create an enumeration as shown in this example:

```
Enum Flavors
    Vanilla
```

```
        Chocolate
        Strawberry
        Banana
    End Enum
```

This creates an enumeration called `Flavors` with the constants `Vanilla` equal to 0, `Chocolate` equal to 1, and so on. If you do not want the enumeration values assigned sequentially starting at 0, you can specify the values:

```
Enum Flavors
    Vanilla = 2
    Chocolate = 3
    Strawberry = 5
    Banana = 10
End Enum
```

Enumerations can be defined only at the module level. Once an `Enum` is defined, it becomes available as a data type you can use to declare variables:

```
Dim IceCreamCone As Flavors
```

A variable declared as an enumerated type can only take on the set of values defined in the enumeration. A real convenience is that VBA displays autolist members for enumerated types, permitting you to select from a list of the enumeration's constants.

Using Operators

Operators are symbols that instruct VBA to manipulate data in some manner, for example multiplying two numbers. The operators available in VBA fall into several categories.

The Assignment Operator

The *assignment operator* (=) tells VBA to assign a value to a variable. Specifically, the value of the expression on the right side of the operator is assigned to the variable on the left side of the operator. For example, the statement

```
x = 15
```

assigns the value 15 to x.

The Mathematical Operators

The mathematical operators perform the common operations such as addition and division. There are the four common arithmetic operations as follows:

- \+ Addition
- – Subtraction
- * Multiplication
- / Division

There are three others that are perhaps less common:

\\: Integer division without rounding. For example, 15 \\ 4 evaluates to 3.

^: Exponentiation (to the power of). For example, 2 ^ 4 evaluates to 16.

mod: Modulus (remainder after division). For example, 33 mod 6 evaluates to 3.

For both division operators, a `Divide by Zero` error occurs if the divisor is 0.

The String Operator

There is one string operation called *concatenation*, which simply joins two strings together. The operator for this is &. For example, after this code:

```
Dessert = "Chocolate " & "cake"
```

the variable `Dessert` contains `"Chocolate cake"`. There are lots of other things you can do with strings, but they involve functions rather than operators. You can find information on these functions in VBA's online documentation.

The Comparison Operators

You use *comparison operators* to perform comparisons between two expressions. The result of a comparison is either `True` or `False` depending on whether or not the comparison was true. The most commonly used comparison operators, which are used primarily with numeric expressions, are

- = Is equal to?
- > Is greater than?
- < Is less than?
- >= Is greater than or equal to?
- <= Is less than or equal to?
- <> Is not equal to?

For example, the expression

```
a < b
```

asks the question "is a less than b?" and returns either True or False depending on the values of a and b.

The Logical Operators

You use *logical operators* to manipulate logical (True/False) expressions. Most of the logical operators combine two logical expressions into a single logical value. The logical operators are described in Table 23.2.

TABLE 23.2

The Logical Operators

Operator	Example	Evaluation
And	X And Y	True if both X and Y are True; False otherwise.
Or	X Or Y	True if X or Y, or both of them, are True; False only if both X and Y are False.
Xor (exclusive Or)	X Xor Y	True if X and Y are different (one True and the other False); False if both are True or both are False.
Eqv (Equivalence)	X Eqv Y	True if X and Y are the same (both True or both False); False otherwise.
Imp (Implication)	X Imp Y	False only if X is True and Y is False; True otherwise.
Not	Not X	True if X is False, False if X is True.

The logical operators are often used in conjunction with the comparison operators. For example, the following expression evaluates as True only if x is equal to 5 and y is not equal to 0:

```
(x = 5) And (y <> 0)
```

Operator Precedence and Parentheses

When an expression contains more than one operator, it may not always be clear how the expression evaluates. For example, look at this expression:

```
20 / 4 + 6
```

How should you read this?

■ If the addition is performed first, the expression evaluates to 2 (4 plus 6 is 10, 20 divided by 10 is 2)

■ If the division is performed first, the result is 11 (20 divided by 4 is 5, 5 plus 6 is 11).

Potentially ambiguous expressions such as this one are resolved by VBA's rules of *operator precedence*, which determine the order in which operations are performed. The precedence of VBA's operators is given in Table 23.3. Operators with lower precedence numbers are performed first.

TABLE 23.3

VBA Operator Precedence

Operator	Precedence
Exponentiation ^	1
Multiplication (*), division (/)	2
Integer division (\)	3
Modulus (Mod)	4
Addition (+), subtraction (–)	5
String concatenation (&)	6

Operators that have the same precedence level, such as multiplication and division, are executed in left-to-right order.

With this information on the precedence rules, you can see that the previous example will evaluate to 11 because the division will be performed before the addition.

You can use parentheses in an expression to modify the order of execution. Those parts of an expression enclosed in parentheses are always evaluated first regardless of operator precedence. Therefore,

```
20 / (4 + 6)
```

evaluates to 2 because the parentheses force the addition to be performed before the division. You can use as many parentheses in an expression as you like as long as they always come in pairs with each left parenthesis having a matching right parenthesis. *Nested parentheses* — when one set is inside another set — execute starting with the innermost set and proceed outward.

Writing Conditional and Loop Statements

An important part of VBA programming is controlling which VBA statements execute and when. VBA has several tools for this purpose, the two most important being loop statements and conditional statements.

Using Loop Statements

A *loop statement* is used to execute a block of VBA statements a certain number of times. There are three loop statements.

For...Next

The `For...Next` statement executes a block of statements a prespecified number of times. It is written like this:

```
For index = start To stop Step step
...
statements
...
Next index
```

- `index` is a numeric variable that serves as the loop counter.

- `start` and `stop` are the starting and ending values of index.

- `step` is the amount that `index` is incremented with each repetition of the loop. If you omit the `step` value, the default increment of 1 is used.

When a `For...Next` loop is encountered, here's what happens:

1. `index` is set to the value of `start`.

2. `index` is compared to `stop`.

3. If `index` is less than or equal to `stop`, the statements in the loop are executed. If not, the loop terminates.

4. `index` is incremented by the value of `step` (or by 1 if `step` is not specified).

5. Return to step 2.

This `For...Next` loop sets the values of the array to 0, 4, 8, ... 200:

```
Dim NewArray(50) As Integer
Dim j As Integer
For j = 0 To 50
    NewArray(j) = j * 4
Next j
```

Code inside the loop should never change the value of the counter variable.

It is possible to use a `For...Next` loop to count down by making `step` negative. When you do this, `start` must be greater than `stop`, and the loop terminates when counter is less than `stop`. In this example, the `For...Next` loop fills the elements of the array with the values 100, 99, ... 0.

```
Dim NewArray(100) As Integer
Dim j As Integer

For j = 100 To 0 Step -1
    NewArray(j) = 100 - j
Next j
```

If you want to exit from a `For...Next` loop early — that is, before the index variable reaches its final value — use the `Exit For` statement.

VBA permits you to nest `For...Next` loops within each other. Each inner loop must be totally within the outer loop.

For Each...Next

You use the `For Each...Next` loop to execute a group of statements once for each member of a collection. It is used to go through a collection and do something to or with each member. The syntax is

```
For Each item in collection
...
statements
...
Next item
```

- `item` is the variable used to iterate through the collection and must be declared as a data type appropriate for the members of the collection. This is usually the same data type as the collection contains, although you can use type `Object` or `Variant` as well.

- `collection` is the name of the collection. The statements are executed once for each element in the collection.

Here's an example that sets the `Color` property of all objects in the collection to `Blue`:

```
Dim o As Object
For Each o In SomeCollection
    o.Color = Blue
Next o
```

You'll see plenty of examples of using `For Each...Next` when you start looking at the Outlook Object Model.

Do...Loop

The `Do...Loop` statement executes a block of statements repeatedly as long as a specified logical condition is met. Depending on how the `Do...Loop` statement is written and where the logical condition is placed, the statements may be executed no times, a single time, or multiple times.

This statement has several slightly different syntaxes. To execute statements repeatedly as long as a logical condition is True, use the `While` keyword:

```
Do While condition
...
statements
...
Loop
```

You can also execute statements repeatedly as long as a condition is False by using the `Until` keyword:

```
Do Until condition
...
statements
...
Loop
```

When program execution reaches the `Do` statement, `condition` is evaluated. If it is True (if using `While`) or False (if using `Until`), the statements are executed and then `condition` is evaluated again. This continues until the value of `condition` changes. Depending on the initial value of `condition`, the statements in the loop may not be executed even once.

You can also write a `Do...Loop` statement that tests `condition` at the end of the loop. As before, you can use either `While` or `Until`:

```
Do
...
statements
...
Loop While condition
```

```
Do
...
statements
...
Loop Until condition
```

When you use this syntax, the statements are executed once and then `condition` is evaluated. By testing `condition` at the end of the loop, you ensure that the statements in the loop will be executed at least once.

To exit a `Do...Loop` early, use the `Exit Do` statement.

Using Conditional Statements

VBA's *conditional statements* are used to execute or not execute a block of statements depending on a program condition. The statements are executed once or not at all. There are two conditional statements in VBA.

If...Then...Else

The `If...Then...Else` statement executes a block of statements if a specified condition is True. Optionally, a second block of statements is executed if the condition is False. The syntax is

```
If condition Then
    block1
Else
```

```
        block2
    End If
```

condition is a logical expression. If it is True, the statements in block1 are executed. If condition is False, the statements in block2 are executed. The Else keyword and the second block of statements are optional. If they are omitted, no statements are executed if condition is False.

You can test multiple conditions in an If...Then...Else statement by using the ElseIf keyword. Here's how this is written:

```
If condition1 Then
    block1
ElseIf condition2 Then
    block2
ElseIf condition3 Then
    block3
....
Else
    block4
End If
```

There's no limit to the number of ElseIfs. The testing of the various conditions starts at the top and works downward. As soon as a True condition is found, the corresponding block of statements is executed and execution exits the If statement. One block of statements at most will be executed regardless of how many of the conditions are True.

When you need to test multiple conditions, it is usually easier to use the Select Case statement, covered next.

Select Case

The Select Case statement evaluates a single expression and compares the result with a series of templates. If it finds a match, the associated block of statements is executed. The syntax is

```
Select Case expression
    Case template-1
        statements-1
    Case template-2
        statements-2
    ....
    Case template-n
        statements-n
    Case Else
        statements-else
End Select
```

expression is evaluated and the result is matched against the various templates, in order from top to bottom. When a match is found, the following block of statements is executed. If no match is found, the statements following the `Case Else` are executed. The `Case Else` keyword is optional. Even if more than one template matches, only a single block of statements will be executed — the block that follows the first matching template.

Each template in a `Select Case` statement can contain one or more of the following elements:

- **Any expression.** The test expression must match the template exactly.
- **Two expressions separated by the `To` keyword.** The test expression must fall within the range specified by the two expressions. For example, `0 To 50`.
- **The `Is` keyword followed by a comparison operator and an expression.** For example, `Is > 10`.

You can use multiple elements in a template, separating them by commas. This example defines a template that would match if the test expression evaluated to 0, to any value between 5 and 10, or to any value greater than 25:

```
Case 0, 5 To 10, Is > 25
```

Writing Procedures

A *procedure* is a section of VBA code that is independent and has been assigned a name. In fact, every Outlook macro is a procedure, and it is the procedure names that you see listed in the Macros dialog box. However, whereas all macros are procedures, not all procedures are macros. This kind of procedure can be very useful in your VBA programming.

Say you have written a number of macros that manipulate and organize your email, tasks, and so on. Each macro, as part of its operation, needs to sort a list of items into alphabetical order. Rather than including the VBA code that performs the sort in each and every macro, you can place the code in a separate procedure and then call the procedure as needed from each macro.

Subs versus Functions

VBA supports two kinds of procedures, Subs and Functions. They are identical except for the fact that a Function returns data to the calling program, whereas a Sub does not.

To define a Sub procedure, the basic syntax is

```
Sub subname(argumentlist)
...
' Code is placed here
...
End Sub
```

The syntax to define a Function is similar:

```
Function functionname(argumentlist) As type
...
' Code is placed here
functionname = returnvalue

End Function
```

For both types of procedures, the name must follow VBA variable naming rules and also must be unique within the module where the procedure is located. `argumentlist` is an optional list of data passed to the procedure when it is called (as explained in the next section). For a function, the `As type` clause specifies the data type of the function's return value, and the `functionname = returnvalue` statement sets the value of that return value.

Passing Arguments to Procedures

Many procedures have arguments that permit data to be passed to the procedure when it is called. The argument list can include as many arguments as are needed, and has the following syntax:

```
argname1 As type, argname2 As type, .....
```

Here's an example of a function procedure that is passed three numbers and returns the largest one:

```
Function Largest(n1 as Double, n2 As Double, n3 As Double) _
    As Double

    Dim temp as Double
    If n1 > n2 Then
        temp = n1
    Else
        temp = n2
    End If
    If n3 > temp Then
        Largest = n3
    Else
        Largest = temp
    End If

End Function
```

Each argument can be any of VBA's data types, including UDTs, arrays, or enumerations. To specify an array argument, use an empty set of parentheses:

```
Sub ProcessArray(array() As String)
...
End Sub
```

Calling Procedures

Calling a procedure requires a different syntax for Sub and Function procedures. For Sub procedures you have two choices: You can use the `Call` keyword, in which case the argument list must be in parentheses:

```
Call ProcedureName(ArgumentList)
```

Or, you can omit the `Call` keyword and the parentheses as well:

```
ProcedureName ArgumentList
```

Because a function returns a value, it can be treated as an expression and used — that is, called — any place an expression could go. For example:

```
result = Largest(x, y, z)
```

Understanding Procedure Variables

You learned earlier in this chapter how to declare variables in your VBA programs. Most of the variables you use will in fact be declared within procedures. These are called *local variables* and they have some special characteristics that relate to scope.

Scope refers to the parts of a program where a variable is visible. You can use a variable only where it is in scope. In other parts of the program, it is out of scope and might as well not exist. In your VBA programs, you control a variable's scope by where the variable is declared:

- A variable declared within a procedure is visible only within that procedure.
- A variable declared at the *module level* — that is, outside any procedure — is visible in all procedures in that module.

This has implications for the programmer. You can use the same variable name in two or more procedures and they will be totally independent of each other. But what if you have a variable declared within a procedure and also use the same name for a variable declared at the module level? If a procedure contains a variable with the same name as a module-level variable, the local copy takes precedence. Otherwise, the module-level variable is visible within the procedure.

Creating a Procedure

Now that you have learned something about how to write procedures, how do you actually go about it? The VBA Editor makes it easy:

1. In Outlook, press Alt+F11 to open the VBA Editor.
2. If necessary, double-click Module 1 in the Project Explorer to open that module for editing.
3. Select Procedure from the Insert menu to open the Add Procedure dialog box (see Figure 23.1).

4. In the Type section, select either Sub or Function depending on the type of procedure you want.

5. Type the procedure name in the Name box.

6. Click OK. The editor creates the shell of the Sub or Function procedure, ready for you to edit.

Procedures versus Macros

What is it that differentiates a macro procedure from a non-macro procedure? The main difference is whether you intend the user to execute the procedure directly from the Macros dialog box. In order to be considered a macro by Outlook and to be listed in the Macros dialog box, a procedure must meet two criteria:

■ It must not return a value — that is, it must be a Sub procedure and not a Function procedure.

■ It must not take any arguments.

FIGURE 23.1

Adding a Sub or Function procedure to a VBA module.

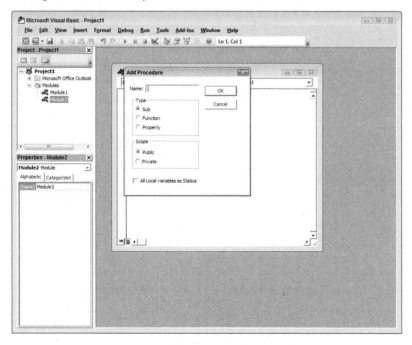

Suppose, however, that you wrote a Sub procedure that takes no arguments, yet you do not want it listed in the Macros dialog box. You can "hide" it by using the `Private` keyword:

```
Private MySub()
...
End Sub
```

Now your other macro code will be able to call this Sub, but the user will not be able to execute it from the Macros dialog box.

Interacting with the User

Sometimes your macro will need to get some information from the user. Perhaps it needs to prompt for a name, or to get a Yes/No answer. VBA provides two tools for this purpose, `MsgBox` and `InputBox`.

The MsgBox Function

The `MsgBox` function displays a dialog box with a message and one or more buttons. The function's return value indicates which of the buttons the user clicked. You use this function as follows (I have omitted a couple of optional and rarely used arguments):

`MsgBox(prompt, buttons, title)`

- `prompt` is a string expression specifying the message to display in the dialog box.

- `buttons` is an optional argument specifying what buttons and/or icons to display in the dialog box and, when there is more than one button, which one is the default (the default is the one selected if the user presses Enter). If this argument is omitted, only an OK button is displayed. The possible settings for this argument are given in Table 23.4. To combine settings, use the Or operator.

- `title` is an optional argument that specifies the title displayed in the dialog box's title bar. If this argument is omitted, the application name is used as the title.

TABLE 23.4

Defined Constants for the MsgBox Function's buttons Argument

Constant	Value	Description
vbOKCancel	1	Display OK and Cancel buttons
vbAbortRetryIgnore	2	Display Abort, Retry, and Ignore buttons
vbYesNoCancel	3	Display Yes, No, and Cancel buttons

Constant	Value	Description
vbYesNo	4	Display Yes and No buttons
vbRetryCancel	5	Display Retry and Cancel buttons
vbCritical	16	Display Critical Message icon
vbQuestion	32	Display Warning Query icon
vbExclamation	48	Display Warning Message icon
vbInformation	64	Display Information Message icon
vbDefaultButton2	256	Second button is default
vbDefaultButton3	512	Third button is default

As mentioned, the function's return value indicates which of the buttons the user selected. The possible return values are represented by the constants shown in Table 23.5.

TABLE 23.5

Defined Constants for the MsgBox Function's Return Value

Constant	Value	Button Selected
vbOK	1	OK
vbCancel	2	Cancel
vbAbort	3	Abort
vbRetry	4	Retry
vbIgnore	5	Ignore
vbYes	6	Yes
vbNo	7	No

To use the MsgBox function, call it with the appropriate arguments and then test the return value. Here's an example, with the displayed dialog box shown in Figure 23.2:

```
Dim retval As Integer
retval = MsgBox("Delete file - are you sure?", vbYesNo, _
    "Confirm delete")
If retval = vbYes Then
    ' Code to delete file goes here.
End If
```

FIGURE 23.2

An example of a dialog box displayed by the MsgBox function.

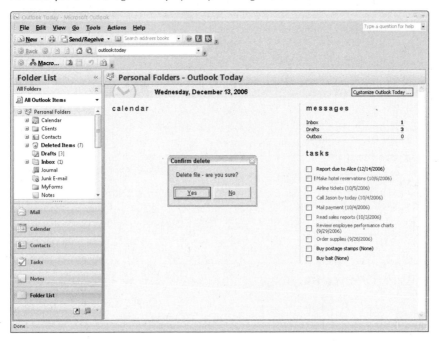

The InputBox Function

You use the `InputBox` function to return a string entered by the user. The syntax for this function is (I have omitted some optional and rarely used arguments):

```
InputBox(prompt, title, default,)
```

- `prompt` is the text displayed as the prompt in the dialog box.

- `title` is an optional argument that specifies the title displayed in the dialog box's title bar. If this argument is omitted, the application name is used as the title.

- `default` is an optional string expression that specifies the default response if the user does not enter one. If this argument is omitted, the default response is an empty string.

This code uses the `InputBox` function to get the user's country of residence, with "United States" being the default response. The displayed dialog box is shown in Figure 23.3.

```
Dim Country As String
Country = InputBox("Your country of residence?", "Country", _
    "United States")
```

FIGURE 23.3

Getting user input with the InputBox function.

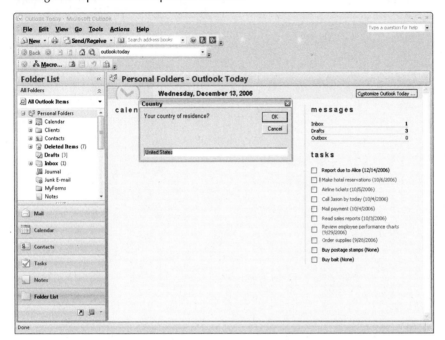

Summary

This chapter has provided you with a quick introduction to programming macros with the VBA language. This information is sufficient to get you started writing your own macros (although you should read the next chapter before getting started). There's lots more to the VBA language, aspects that could not be covered here due to space limitations. You can further explore VBA on your own using the VBA Editor documentation, online resources, or books published on the subject.

Chapter 24

Understanding the Outlook Object Model

I n order to program Outlook with macros, it is necessary to have some understanding of the Outlook Object Model. Though this may sound intimidating, it is actually a great help to the macro programmer and makes your job much easier.

This chapter gives you an overview of programming the Outlook Object Model and presents numerous examples. The focus is on programming mail items and calendar items because it is these two aspects of Outlook that benefit the most from macro programming. The next chapter develops a few of the programming concepts presented here into full VBA applications you can use or modify.

Understanding Office Objects

All Office programs operate on the principle of objects. This means that internally, all the various components of the program are represented by their own kind of object. In Word, for example, a paragraph is an object, a table is an object, and an entire document is an object. In Excel, a worksheet is an object, and charts and cells are objects, too. Outlook works the same way.

From the perspective of the end user, the fact that a program is structured as objects does not make any practical difference. For the macro programmer, however, it makes a world of difference because all the objects are available for you to use in your macros. Each type of object has a great deal of functionality built in, and that functionality is all ready for you to use with very little programming effort. To be an effective macro programmer, therefore, you need to know about the Outlook Object Model.

Creating Object References

Before you can work with an object in your VBA code, you must have a reference to it. A *reference* is simply a variable name. Instead of holding data, however, an object reference lets you work with an object in your code.

There are two parts to obtaining an object reference. First, you must create a variable that is of the proper type to hold a reference to the specific kind of object you are dealing with. The preferred way to do this is as follows:

```
Din RefName As type
```

This looks like a regular `Dim` statement for declaring a variable—and in fact, it is the same except that `type` refers to the specific type of object and not to a data type. For example, in the Outlook Object Model the object type `MailItem` represents an email message. To declare a variable that can reference a message, you would write the following:

```
Dim MyMessage As Outlook.MailItem
```

Note that the Outlook prefix to the object name is used to ensure that you are referencing the Outlook Object Model, because some object names are duplicated between programs.

At this point you have a name that can refer to the specified type of object—`Outlook.MailItem` in this case—but it does not yet refer to an actual object. Your next step will take one of two paths depending on your needs.

First, you can create a new object of the specified type and set the variable name to refer to it. You do this with the `Set` and `New` keywords:

```
Set RefName = New type
```

Object Creation Shortcut

Rather than using separate `Dim` and `Set` statements, you can combine them using the following syntax:

```
Dim RefName As New Type
```

As before, however, this works only for some types of objects.

The Nothing Keyword

VBA has a special keyword, Nothing, that indicates that an object reference does not contain a valid reference to an object. When an object reference has been declared but not initialized, it contains Nothing. You can also explicitly set an object reference to Nothing when you are finished using the object or to make sure the reference does not point at a valid object:

```
Set objRef = Nothing
```

The Is Nothing operator lets you test for this value:

```
If objRef Is Nothing Then
   ' Actions to take if the reference is not valid.
Else
   ' Actions to take if the reference points to a valid object.
End If
```

However, this technique cannot be used with many kinds of objects, including MailItem. Rather, you must get a reference to an instance of the object using the Outlook Object Model. For example, you cannot create a new MailItem object with the following code:

```
Set MyMessage = New Outlook.MailItem
```

You see exactly how to create references to Outlook objects throughout the chapter.

Working with Collections

Collections are an important part of Outlook macro programming. Whenever the Object Model requires more than one of something, it uses a collection to keep track of them. For example, in Outlook each mail folder, such as the Inbox, is represented by an object. A folder can contain any number of email messages, and these messages are represented as a collection. Collections are designed with built-in tools that make is easy to find an individual object in the collection or to do something with all of the objects in the collection. Every collection has the Count property, which tells you the number of elements in the collection.

The most common use for collections is when you want to process every item in the collection. For example, suppose you want to write a macro that looks at every email message in the Inbox and moves those messages from a certain sender to another folder. By looping through the collection of email messages in this folder, the task is easily accomplished no matter how many or few messages there are in the folder. You use the For Each...Next loop, introduced in Chapter 23, for this purpose.

Collection Naming Conventions

By tradition, a collection is named with the plural of the object it contains. For example, a collection that holds `Folder` objects will be called `Folders`. Unfortunately there are a few exceptions to this rule that you'll encounter as you explore the Outlook Object Model.

First, you must declare an object variable of the same type as the objects in the collection. Continuing with the email example:

```
Dim msg As Outlook.MailItem
```

Then create a reference to the object that contains the collection — in this case, an Outlook folder — specifically, the Inbox:

```
Dim f As Outlook.Folder
Dim MyOutlookNamespace As Outlook.NameSpace
Set MyOutlookNameSpace = GetNameSpace("MAPI")
Set f = MyOutlookNameSpace.GetDefaultFolder(olFolderInbox)
```

Finally, loop through the collection as follows:

```
For Each msg in f.Items
  ' With each repetition of the loop, msg refers to the   ' next
message in the collection.
Next
```

The previous code examples are missing a couple of details and will not actually run, but they serve to illustrate the principle of collections. You'll note that this is one of those exceptions where a collection — `Items` in this case — is not named as the plural of the kind of object it contains, `MailItems`.

Using Named Constants

If you examine the previous code snippet, you'll see this line of code:

```
Set f = GetDefaultFolder(olFolderInbox)
```

What is `olFolderInbox`? It's not a variable that you have declared. Rather it's one of the named constants in the Object Model. Some methods (a procedure that is part of an object) require an argument to tell them what to do. Rather than use hard-to-remember numbers, the Object Model provides these descriptive constants that are a lot easier to remember. What's more, the VBA Editor's IntelliSense feature will list the available constants as you are typing in your code, as shown in Figure 24.1.

FIGURE 24.1

The editor's IntelliSense feature lets you select from a list of named constants.

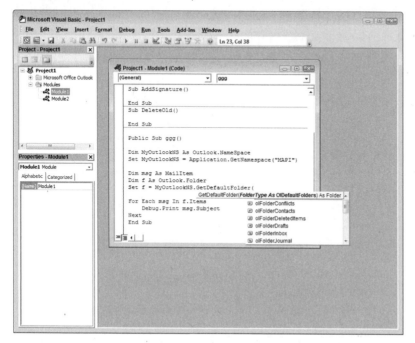

The Outlook Object Model Hierarchy

The Object Models for all Office applications are arranged in a hierarchical structure. Two of the top-level objects in this arrangement are `Application` and `Namespace`.

The Application Object

At the very top of the Outlook Object Model is the `Application` object. As you might have already guessed, this object represents the Outlook application itself. All other objects in the hierarchy are subsidiary to the `Application` object. Often, when you are trying to locate data in Outlook, you start with the `Application` object and work down to levels of greater detail.

The `Application` object is available as an implicit reference for VBA code in Outlook. This means that you do not have to use the term in your code — it is understood automatically. If you were writing VBA code to run in another Office application, such as Word, you would have to explicitly reference the Outlook `Application` object.

For example, the GetNamespace() method is part of the Outlook Application object. Full syntax for this would be

```
Application.GetNamespace()
```

but because of the implicit availability of the Application reference, you can write it like this:

```
GetNamespace()
```

The Namespace Object

Another high-level object in the Outlook Object Model is the Namespace object. It exists because Outlook was designed to be usable with different kinds of data, each of which would be identified by its own namespace. So far, only one kind of data is supported in Outlook, MAPI data (MAPI stands for Messaging Application Programming Interface). Therefore there is only one namespace. Though it seems like unnecessary effort, you must use this namespace when accessing email and other items in Outlook. In many of the code examples in this and later chapters, you'll see a few lines of code like this:

```
Dim MyOutlookNamespace As Outlook.Namespace
Set MyOutlookNamespace = GetNamespace("MAPI")
```

Then, the Namespace object is used when accessing mail and other folders:

```
Set f = MyOutlookNS.GetDefaultFolder(olFolderInbox)
```

Getting References to Outlook Folders

Outlook items are all stored in folders, and before you can work with items you need to get a reference to the containing folder. Outlook has two types of folders: the default folders and user-created folders.

Referencing Default Folders

A *default folder* is one of the folders that is part of Outlook and cannot be deleted, such as the Inbox, the Deleted Items folder, and the Notes folder. To get a reference to one of these folders, which are represented by the Folder object, you use the GetDefaultFolder() method. This method takes one argument that specifies the folder you are interested in:

```
Dim folder As Outlook.Folder
Set folder = MyOutlookNamespace.GetDefaultFolder(foldertype)
```

The foldertype argument can be one of the named constants listed in Table 24.1, along with the folder each returns. This table lists only those constants used frequently; you can refer to online help for the complete list.

Referencing the MAPI Namespace

In some of the code examples in this and following chapters, you'll see code that explicitly gets the MAPI namespace. In other code, particularly short snippets, it will be assumed that this has already been done.

TABLE 24.1

Constants for the GetDefaultFolder Method's *foldertype* Argument

Constant	Folder Containing
olFolderCalendar	Calendar items
olFolderContacts	Contacts
olFolderDeletedItems	Items that have been deleted
olFolderDrafts	Drafts of incompleted items
olFolderInbox	Received email messages
olFolderJournal	Journal entries
olFolderNotes	Note entries
olFolderOutbox	Email messages waiting to be sent
olFolderSentMail	Email messages that have been sent
olFolderTasks	Task entries

Referencing User-Created Folders

Folders that the user has created are not default Outlook folders and references to them are obtained from the Folders collection. Because folders can themselves be organized in a hierarchy, things are arranged as follows:

- Each top-level folder is a member of the NameSpace object's Folders collection.
- Each of these top-level folders has its own Folders collection, which contains any sub-folders that the folder contains.
- Each folder in turn has its own Folders collection.

User-created folders are identified by name, which is obtained from the Folder object's name property. To get a reference to a folder, assuming that you do not know exactly where it is located, you must look through all folders until you either find it or run out of places to look. This technique can locate the default folders as well, based on their name, but the technique using the `GetDefaultFolder()` method, described in the previous section, is easier to use.

In the folder hierarchy, what the user considers a top-level folder is in fact a second-level folder. Thus, for example, in the folder structure shown in Figure 24.2, Clients is considered a second-level folder and Acme, Consolidated, and National are third-level folders. The top-level folders are Personal Folders, Archive Folders, Internet Calendar, and similar items.

To get a reference to a specific folder, you can use the function in Listing 24.1. This function is passed the name of the desired folder and returns a reference to the desired folder, if it exists, or else the value `Nothing`. Be aware that folder names in Outlook are case-sensitive. If the folder does not exist, the value `Nothing` is returned. You can check for the `Nothing` value using `Is Nothing` as explained earlier in this chapter.

This function looks at second- and third-level folders but does not go any deeper. Thus, looking at the folder structure in Figure 24.2 the function would find Clients, and it would find Acme, Consolidated, and National, but it would not find any folders nested deeper than that. It could easily be modified to do so, however, and that would be a good programming exercise for you.

FIGURE 24.2

Understanding Outlook folder levels.

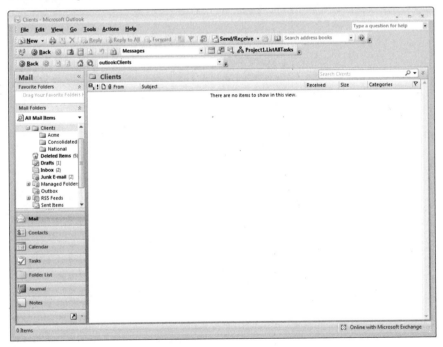

LISTING 24.1

A Function to Obtain a Reference to a User-Created Folder

```
Public Function FindFolder(FolderName As String) _
    As Outlook.Folder

Dim folder1 As Outlook.Folder
Dim folder2 As Outlook.Folder
Dim folder3 As Outlook.Folder
Dim FoundFolder As Outlook.Folder
Dim MyOutlookNamespace As Outlook.NameSpace

Set MyOutlookNamespace = GetNamespace("MAPI")
Set FindFolder = Nothing

For Each folder1 In MyOutlookNamespace.Folders
    ' We know that top-level folders will not match
    ' so no comparison is needed here.
    For Each folder2 In folder1.Folders
        If folder2.Name = FolderName Then
            Set FindFolder = folder2
            Exit Function
        End If
        For Each folder3 In folder2.Folders
            If folder3.Name = FolderName Then
                Set FindFolder = folder3
                Exit Function
            End If
        Next
    Next
Next

End Function
```

Working with Folder Items

Every folder can contain items, and the purpose for getting a reference to an Outlook folder is almost always to do something with the items that it contains. With user-defined folders, you specify the type of Outlook item the folder will contain when you create the folder. When you are working with a folder in VBA, you may want to determine its default type of item. For example, perhaps you are writing a macro that will look for certain information in all email messages in all folders. You can iterate through all Outlook folders using the techniques described earlier in this chapter, and then process the folder items only if its default item type is email.

To determine a folder's default item type, look at its `DefaultItemType` property. The values that can be returned are represented by named constants as described in Table 24.2. This property is read-only, which means that you cannot change it.

TABLE 24.2

Named Constants for the Folder Object's DefaultItemType Property

Constant	Value	Meaning
olAppointmentItem	1	Appointment items
olContactItem	2	Contact items
olDistributionListItem	3	Exchange distribution list items (relevant to Exchange Server accounts only)
olJournalItem	4	Journal items
olMailItem	5	Mail items (email messages)
olNoteItem	6	Note items
olPostItems	7	Post items (an item posted to a public folder)
olTaskItems	8	Task items

Programming Email Items

In Outlook, an email message is represented by the MailItem object. Once you have a reference to a folder containing email items, you can loop through the folder's Items collection to access each email in turn. You can also create macros that compose and send email messages.

Working with Received Messages

Many of the things you'll do with email messages that you have received involve message properties that provide information about the subject, recipients, sender, and other aspects of the message. The MailItem properties used most often when working with received messages are described in Table 24.3.

TABLE 24.3

MailItem Properties Used When Working with Received Messages

Property	Description
Attachments	A collection of Attachment objects, each representing a document or link attached to the message.
Body	Text of the message (if the message is in plain text format).
CreationTime	The date when the message was created (as a type Date).

Property	Description
HTMLBody	The text of the message (if the message is in HTML format).
Importance	Returns the importance level of the message as one of the following values: olImportanceHigh, olImportanceLow, and olImportanceNormal.
ReceivedTime	Returns the date specifying when the message was received (as a type Date).
Recipients	A collection of Recipient objects representing the message recipients.
Saved	True if the message has been saved since it was last modified, False otherwise.
SenderName	The display name of the message sender.
SentOn	The date when the message was sent (as a type Date).
Subject	The message subject.
To	A semicolon-delimited list of the message recipients' display names.
UnRead	Returns True if the message has not been opened. False if it has been.

Next look at some examples of writing macros to perform useful, everyday tasks in Outlook.

Moving Selected Messages

One way you can use macros is to go through any folder containing email messages, typically the Inbox, and move messages to various other folders depending on their sender, subject, or other characteristics.

The first step in doing this is to get a reference to both folders. You have already seen how to get a reference to the Inbox using the GetDefaultFolder() method, and how to get a reference to a user-created folder using the FindFolder() procedure presented earlier in this chapter.

Next you must loop through all the messages in the Inbox, checking each one to see whether it meets the criterion for being moved. You use a For Each...Next loop for this purpose. For this code snippet, assume that:

- fInbox is a reference to the Inbox.
- The variable m has been declared as type Outlook.MailItem.
- The variable Subject holds the text you want to look for.

```
For Each m In fInbox.Items
    If InStr(m.Subject, Subject) > 0 Then
        ' Move the message here.
    End If
Next
```

Note the use of the Instr() function. This is one of VBA's built-in string functions. It looks for one string in another and returns a value greater than 0 if it is found. In this example you use Instr() to see whether the subject text you are looking for, in the variable Subject, is found in the message's subject, obtained as the m.Subject property.

The final step is moving the message. This is easily done with the Move method. If fDestination is the folder you want to move the message to, and m is a reference to the message, you would write:

```
m.Move fDestination
```

There's a small wrinkle, however. If you move a message out of the Inbox before you have completed looping through all the messages, the For Each...Next loop can sometimes be thrown off and the process will not be completed properly. For this reason, it is necessary to keep a list of the messages to be moved without actually moving them until the For Each...Next loop has finished looking through the Inbox. You see how this is done in the full application presented in Chapter 25.

Dealing with Attachments

An email message can contain one or more attachments. An *attachment* can be either an actual file or a link to the file location. A MailItem object, representing an email message, has the Attachments collection, which contains one Attachment object for each attachment associated with the message.

When you are dealing with a received message, you can determine how many attachments the message has from the MailItems.Attachments.Count property. If this property returns a non-zero value, you can loop through the attachments using a For Each...Next loop:

```
Dim at As Outlook.Attachment
For Each at in MyMailItem.Attachments
  ' Deal with each attachment here.
Next
```

The Attachment object has the following properties that you can use to work with it:

- DisplayName: The name that Outlook displays below the attachment's icon when the message is displayed on-screen. This is often, but not necessarily, the same as the attachment's filename.

- FileName: The filename of the attachment.

- PathName: The full path to an attached linked file. This property is valid only for linked attachments.

- Type: The type of the attachment. Possible settings are olByValue (an attached file), and olByReference (a link to a file).

To save an attached file (but not a linked file) to disk, call its SaveAsFile method. This method's one argument is the path and filename for the file. You can, but do not have to, use the original attachment filename when saving, as shown in this example, which saves all attachments to disk under their original name and using the specified path:

```
Dim at As Outlook.Attachment

For Each at in MyMailItem.Attachments
    If at.Type = olByValue Then
        at.SaveAsFile("c:\data\" & at.FileName)
    End If
Next
```

Creating and Sending Messages

In addition to processing received messages, you can write macros that create and send email messages. Outlook's Object Model makes the task relatively simple. The MailItem object has some properties mostly relevant when you are creating a new message to send. These properties are described in Table 24.4.

TABLE 24.4

Properties of the MailItem Object for Creating and Sending Messages

Property	Description
Attachments	A collection that contains one Attachment object for each file attached to the message.
BCC	A semicolon-delimited list of display names for the blind carbon copy (BCC) recipients.
Body	The text of the message for plain text messages.
CC	A semicolon-delimited list of display names for the carbon copy (CC) recipients.
HTMLBody	The text of the message for HTML format messages.
ReadReceiptRequested	Set to True in order to request a read receipt for the message, False by default.
Recipients	A collection that contains one Recipient object for each message recipient.
SaveSentMessageFolder	The Outlook folder where a copy of the message will be saved when it is sent. The default is the Sent Items folder.
Sent	True if the message has been sent, otherwise False.
To	A semicolon-delimited list of display names for the message recipients.

The general procedure for creating and sending an email message is as follows:

1. Create a new `MailItem` object.

2. Put the message text in the `Body` property (for plain text messages) or `HTMLBody` property (for HTML format messages).

3. Put the message subject in the `Subject` property.

4. Put one or more recipients in the `Recipients` collection.

5. Call the `MailItem` object's `Send()` method.

The following sections look at some details.

Creating a New Message

As mentioned, creating a new message means creating a new `MailItem` object. However, you cannot do this in the usual way using the `New` keyword. Rather, you must use the `CreateItem()` method as shown here:

```
Dim msg As Outlook.MailItem
Set msg = CreateItem(olMailItem)
```

Once you have the new `MailItem`, you can address, compose, and send it.

Addressing the Message

Each recipient of a message is represented by a `Recipient` object. All message recipients are placed in the `MailItem` object's `Recipients` collection. This is true for regular "To" recipients as well as CC and BCC recipients. Whether a given recipient is To, CC, or BCC is controlled by its `Type` property.

To add a recipient to message, call the `Add()` method of the `MailItem.Recipients` collection and pass it the recipient's email address. This method returns a reference to the new recipient, which you'll need as I soon show you. Assume that `msg` refers to the new `MailItem` object created as described in the previous section:

```
Dim recip As Outlook.Recipient
Set recip = msg.Recipients.Add("someone@somewhere.net")
```

By default, new recipients are considered "To" recipients. To change a recipient to CC or BCC, set the `Recipient.Type` property to either of the named constants `olCC` or `olBCC`:

```
recip.Type = olCC
```

You can also add a recipient based on his or her display name as shown here:

```
Dim recip As Outlook.Recipient
Set recip = msg.Recipients.Add("Jane Austin")
```

No Need to Resolve?

You do not need to resolve a recipient if you specified the actual email address when you added the recipient to the message's `Recipients` collection.

When you use this approach, the recipient must be *resolved* before you can send the message. This procedure looks through the Outlook address book for the specified display name. If it is found, the corresponding email address is added to the recipient and you can send the message. If a message has one or more unresolved recipients, trying to send it will cause an error.

To resolve a recipient, call the `Resolve()` method. The method returns True if the resolution was successful, False if not. Here's an example:

```
Dim recip As Outlook.Recipient
Set recip = msg.Recipients.Add("Jane Austin")
If recip.Resolve Then
   ' Resolved OK - safe to send.
Else
   ' Resolution failed - take steps to correct.
End If
```

Adding Attachments to a Message

When you are writing VBA code to create email messages, you can add attachments to each message as desired. You use the `Attachments` collection's `Add()` method, which has the following syntax:

```
MailItem.Attachments.Add(Source, Type, Position, DisplayName)
```

- `Source` is a required argument specifying the path and name of the file to attach.

- `Type` is an optional argument specifying the type of the attachment: `olByValue` (for an attached file) or `olByReference` for a link (shortcut) to a file. The default is `olByValue`.

- `Position` is an optional argument specifying the position of the attachment in the message. The default is for attachments to be placed at the end of the message.

- `DisplayName` is an optional argument giving the attachment's display name. If this argument is omitted, the name of the file will be used as the display name.

It is recommended to save a message before adding or removing attachments. Here's a code example that attaches two file attachments to a message:

Using Your Address Book

Your macro code can also get email addresses from the address book. You see an example of this in Chapter 25 when I present a VBA application that sends a message to all contacts in a specified address book.

```
MyMailMessage.Save
With MyMailMessage.Attachments
    .Add "c:\data\TechnologyWhitePaper.doc", olByValue, , _
        "White Paper"
    .Add "c:\data\MedicalExpenses.xls"
End With
```

Completing and Sending a Message

Other than addressing an email message, a message needs a subject line and a body. The subject is set by assigning text to the `MailItem.Subject` property.

The body is not quite so simple because you have the option of sending a plain text format message, a Rich Text Format (RTF) message, or an HTML format message. When you create a new `MailItem` object, the format is set to the default message format as specified in Outlook's mail options (refer to Chapter 5 for more information). To change the format for an individual message, set the `MailItem.BodyFormat` property to one of these constants: `olFormatHTML`, `olFormatPlain`, or `olFormatRichText`.

You assign the actual body of the message to either the `Body` property or the `HTMLBody` property depending on whether or not the text includes HTML formatting tags. Of course, the `HTMLBody` property is irrelevant for a plain text format message.

Finally, call the `MailItem.Send()` method to send the message.

Programming Calendar Items

The first thing you must do to work programmatically with calendar items is to get a reference to the Calendar folder. Because this is one of Outlook's default folders, you obtain this reference using the `GetDefaultFolder()` method just like you learned earlier in this chapter for the Inbox folder:

```
Dim MAPINameSpace As Outlook.NameSpace
Dim CalendarFolder As Outlook.Folder
Set MAPINameSpace = GetNameSpace("MAPI")
Set CalendarFolder = _
    MAPINameSpace.GetDefaultFolder(olFolderCalendar)
```

Once you have this reference, you can start accessing the individual calendar items. Though several kinds of objects can be present in the Calendar folder, the most important one is the `AppointmentItem` object, which represents one-time appointments, recurring appointments, all-day events, and multi-day events. This object has a set of properties that hold information about the appointment. The `AppointmentItem` properties that you are most likely to need in your macro programming are described in Table 24.5.

TABLE 24.5

Properties of the AppointmentItem Object

Property	Description
AllDayEvent	True if the appointment is an all-day event, in which case the start and stop times are ignored.
Body	The main body of the appointment.
Categories	Holds information about the appointment category, if any.
CreationTime	Returns a date value indicating the date and time when the appointment was created.
Duration	The duration of the appointment, in minutes.
End	A date value specifying the ending date/time for the appointment.
Importance	Specifies the importance of the appointment. Possible values are indicated by the constants `olImportanceLow`, `olImportanceNormal`, and `olImportanceHigh`.
IsRecurring	True if the appointment is recurring.
Location	Specifies the location of the event.
ReminderMinutes BeforeStart	The number of minutes before the start of the appointment that the reminder is to be displayed.
ReminderSet	A True/False value specifying whether a reminder will be displayed before the appointment start time.
Start	A date specifying the starting date/time for the appointment.
Subject	The subject of the appointment.

Creating a New Appointment

To create a new appointment, you use the `CreateItem()` method. The syntax is

```
Dim NewAppt As Outlook.AppointmentItem
Set NewAppt = CreateItem(olAppointmentItem)
```

The new appointment is, of course, blank — you must fill in the various details such as subject, start/stop times, and whether a reminder will be displayed. A new appointment created in code is not visible on the screen. There are two approaches to filling in the details of a new appointment.

You can do it all in code without ever making the appointment visible to the user. In this case you must save the appointment by calling the `Save()` method:

```
Dim NewAppt As Outlook.AppointmentItem
Set NewAppt = CreateItem(olAppointmentItem)
NewAppt.Subject = "Sales review meeting"
NewAppt.Location = " Conference Room B"
NewAppt.Start = #9/26/2006 1:00:00 PM#
NewAppt.End = #9/26/2006 3:00:00 PM#
NewAppt.Body = "Make sure to bring the worksheet."
NewAppt.Save
```

The other approach is to display the appointment to the user by calling its `Display()` method. The user fills in the appointment details and saves it by clicking the Save & Close button, as usual.

Accessing Existing Appointments

You access existing appointments using the Calendar folder's `Items` collection. You can retrieve an appointment based on its subject. Here's how to retrieve an appointment by its subject, in this case "New Employee Training" (assume that `CalendarFolder` is a reference to Outlook's Calendar folder):

```
Dim MyAppt As Outlook.AppointmentItem
Set MyAppt = CalendarFolder.Items("New Employee Training")
```

The problem with this approach is that if there are multiple appointments with the same subject, it retrieves only the first one. It is preferable to loop through all the appointments in the folder with a `For Each...Next` statement, looking for one or more appointments of interest. Here's an example that sets the variable `MyAppt` to point at the first appointment that has "New Employee Training" as its subject. If there is no such appointment, a message is displayed alerting the user.

> **WARNING** If you try to retrieve an appointment by subject and there is no matching appointment, a runtime error occurs. This error can be trapped, but it is better to avoid trying to retrieve individual appointments in this manner.

```
Dim MyAppt As Outlook.AppointmentItem
Dim Appt As Outlook.AppointmentItem
Dim Found As Boolean

Found = False
For Each Appt In CalendarFolder.Items
    If Appt.Subject = "New Employee Training" Then
        Found = True
        Set MyAppt = Appt
```

```
        End If
Next

If Found Then
        ' Process the matching appointment here.
Else
        MsgBox "Appointment 'New Employee Training' not found."
End If
```

A Calendar Demonstration

Chapter 25 presents a complete calendar application that creates and prints a document listing all the appointments for the upcoming week. This demonstration also shows you how an Outlook VBA program can control other Office applications.

Summary

The Outlook Object Model is central to any macros or VBA applications that you create in Outlook. The objects represent all the various components in Outlook — folders, messages, appointments, and so on. The functionality built in to these objects is available for you to use in your VBA code.

Chapter 25

Programming Outlook with VBA: Some Examples

I n the previous two chapters, you learned a lot of details about the VBA programming language and the Outlook Object Model. This information is essential, but it can also be a terrific learning aid to see these concepts put into use in a real-world situation. To this end, this chapter presents two complete and tested Outlook VBA applications that perform tasks that Outlook users really might want to perform. You can use these projects as-is, modify them to suit your specific needs, or simply use them as learning aids.

IN THIS CHAPTER

Organizing email messages by subject

Listing the next week's appointments

Organizing Email Messages Based on Subject

You had an introduction to this project in Chapter 24. This chapter goes into a lot more detail and presents a complete, working application.

At the heart of this application is a VBA function called `MoveMessagesBySubject()`. It takes two arguments:

- The text that you are searching for
- The name of the destination folder

The function's return value is type Boolean. It returns True if the code completes successfully and False if there was a problem. The most likely problem that might occur is that the destination folder cannot be found. However, the function includes error handling code to deal with unforeseen errors.

The function MoveMessagesBySubject() is presented in Listing 25.1. Note that this function calls the function FindFolder(), which was presented in Chapter 24. In other words, FindFolder() must be in the same module as MoveMessagesBySubject() or you will get an error message.

LISTING 25.1

The MoveMessagesBySubject() Function

```
Public Function MoveMessagesBySubject(Subject As String, _
    DestinationFolder As String) As Boolean

' Moves all messages from the Inbox to the specified folder
' if the message subject contains the text in the Subject
' argument.
' Returns True on success, False on error.

' Requires access to the function FindFolder() to run.

    Dim fInbox As Outlook.Folder
    Dim fDestination As Outlook.Folder
    Dim m As Outlook.MailItem
    Dim MyOutlookNamespace As Outlook.NameSpace
    Dim FoldersToMove As New Collection

    'Obtain the required MAPI namespace.
    Set MyOutlookNamespace = GetNamespace("MAPI")

    ' Set up error handling.
    On Error GoTo ErrorHandler

    ' Get the references to the Inbox and destination folders.
    Set fInbox = MyOutlookNamespace.GetDefaultFolder(olFolderInbox)
    Set fDestination = FindFolder(DestinationFolder)

    ' If destination folder not found, display
    ' message and exit.
    If fDestination Is Nothing Then
        MsgBox ("The destination folder could not be found.")
        MoveMessagesBySubject = False
        Exit Function
    End If

    ' Now loop through the Inbox looking at each mesasage.
    For Each m In fInbox.Items
        If InStr(m.Subject, Subject) > 0 Then
            ' Add message to the "to be moved" collection.
            FoldersToMove.Add m
        End If
```

```
   Next

   ' If any matching messages were found, move them.
   If FoldersToMove.Count > 0 Then
       For Each m In FoldersToMove
           m.Move fDestination
       Next
   Else
       MsgBox "There are no messages to move."
   End If

   MoveMessagesBySubject = True

ErrorExit:
   Exit Function

ErrorHandler:
   MoveMessagesBySubject = False
   Resume ErrorExit

End Function
```

You should note two things about this function. First, it uses the function FindFolder() to obtain a reference to the destination folder. This function was presented in Chapter 24. It must be available in your Outlook project.

Second, you can see how the code uses a collection to move folders. As mentioned in Chapter 24, it can cause problems if you move an item out of the Inbox (or any other folder) while the For Each...Next loop is still looping through the folder. Instead, you should keep track of which items are to be moved, and the Collection object is ideal for this purpose. Then, after the For Each...Next loop has completed, you can move the items by going through the collection.

Some Possible Changes

As written, the function moves any message in which the message subject contains the specified text. This is done using the Instr() function, which compares two strings:

```
Instr(String1, String2)
```

If String2 is found anywhere within String1, the function returns a value greater than 0 (in fact, it returns the position at which String2 is found). Otherwise it returns 0. You could also move messages only if the message subject exactly matches the specified text by changing that line of code to:

```
If StrComp(m.Subject, Subject, vbTextCompare) = 0
```

The StrComp function compares two strings and returns:

- 0 if the two strings are the same.
- −1 if the first string is less than (before alphabetically) the second string.
- 1 if the first string is more than (after alphabetically) the second string.

The vbTextCompare argument tells StrComp() to ignore the case of letters. Other options are explained in the VBA documentation.

There are lots of other criteria you can use to move or process messages, such as receipt date, sender name, whether the message has been read, and so on. Table 24.3 described the various message properties that may be useful when processing messages.

Using the Application

There's one more element needed to complete this application. You cannot run MoveMessages BySubject() directly. You need a macro that can be run from the Macros dialog box and also lets the user enter the required information — subject text to search for and destination folder name. This is accomplished by the macro MoveFolder(), shown in Listing 25.2.

LISTING 25.2
_____

The MoveMessages () Macro

```
Public Sub MoveMessages()

Dim Subject As String, DestinationFolder As String
Dim result As Boolean

Do
    Subject = InputBox("Enter the subject text to look for", _
      "Move Folders By Subject")
Loop Until Len(Subject) > 0

Do
    DestinationFolder = InputBox("Enter the name of the destination folder", _
      "Move Folders By Subject")
Loop Until Len(DestinationFolder) > 0

result = MoveMessagesBySubject(Subject, DestinationFolder)

If result Then
    MsgBox "Messages moved successfully"
Else
    MsgBox "An unknown error occurred"
End If

End Sub
```

Why a Macro and Not a Procedure?

Why do I call this a macro and not a procedure? It is technically a procedure, but there are three factors, mentioned earlier in Chapter 24, that make it a macro (that is, it will be listed in the Macros dialog box):

- It is a `Sub` and not a Function.
- It takes no arguments.
- It is not marked with the `Private` keyword.

This macro uses the `InputBox` statement to prompt the user for the text to search for and the name of the destination folder. Note that the two `InputBox` statements are enclosed in `Do...Until` loops. This is for data validation purposes — to guard against the possibility that the user accidentally enters a blank string. The `Len()` function returns the length of a string (number of characters it contains), and the loops continue prompting the user until a non-empty string is entered.

Adding the Code to Your Outlook Project

The steps required to add this code to your Outlook installation are simple:

1. In Outlook, press Alt+F11 to open the VBA Editor.
2. In the Project Explorer, double-click Module1 to open it.
3. If there is any code in the module, move the editing cursor to the end of the module.
4. Copy the code for the macro `MoveMessages()` and the procedures `FindFolder()` and `MoveMessagesBySubject()` and paste them into the module.
5. Click the Save button on the VBA Editor's toolbar.

After you perform these steps, the macro `MoveMessages` will be listed in the Macros dialog box from where you can run it (see Figure 25.1).

FIGURE 25.1

The macro MoveMessages is listed in the Macros dialog box.

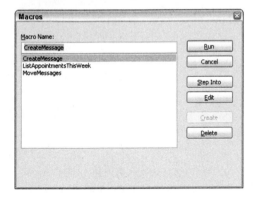

Creating a Summary of Upcoming Appointments

The demonstration that is presented here serves two purposes. First, it presents a useful example of using VBA to work with your calendar items. Second, it shows how to work with Outlook Notes programmatically. In addition, it shows you some of the things you can do with dates in VBA.

This application is a macro—that is, it is a Sub procedure with no arguments. I have named it ListAppointmentsThisWeek. Its operation proceeds as follows:

1. Get a reference to the default Calendar folder (as was described in Chapter 24).

2. Create a date that is one week from the present.

3. Create the note heading (the first line of the note) that consists of the text Week of followed by today's date. You'll recall from Chapter 13 that the first line of a note is automatically used as its subject.

4. Loop through all appointments in the folder using a For Each...Next loop.

5. Examine each appointment's start date—it must be greater than or equal to today's date and less than or equal to the date you created one week hence.

6. If the appointment meets these criteria, extract the required information from it.

7. When all appointments have been processed, create and display the note.

The technique used here to compile all the information from all matching appointments is to create a string variable and add each additional bit of information to the end of the string. Note the use of the constant vbCrLf, which is the newline character—it moves everything that follows to the next line.

Be aware that this macro will find appointments only in the default Calendar folder. If you have created additional calendar folders, and want the macro to look in them, you will have to modify the code to get a reference to these additional folders and process the appointments they contain as well. You saw how to get a reference to a user-created folder in Chapter 24.

Figure 25.2 shows a note created by this macro. The code for the macro is presented in Listing 25.3.

FIGURE 25.2

The macro ListAppointmentsThisWeek creates a note containing all your appointments for the next week.

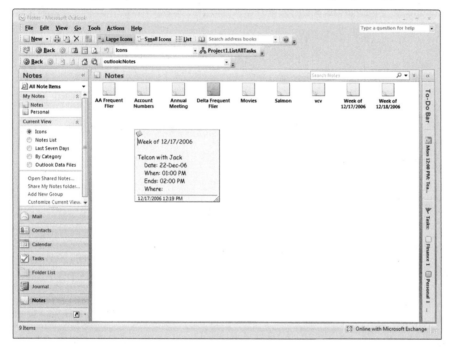

LISTING 25.3

The ListAppointmentsThisWeek Macro

```
Public Sub ListAppointmentsThisWeek()

' Creates a Note containing a list of all appointments
' for the coming week.

Dim MyCalendar As Outlook.MAPIFolder
Dim MyAppt As Outlook.AppointmentItem
```

continued

LISTING 25.3 *(continued)*

```
Dim MyOutlookNS As Outlook.NameSpace
Dim temp As String
Dim OneWeekHence As Date
Dim doc As Outlook.NoteItem

' Get a reference to the calendar folder.
Set MyOutlookNS = GetNamespace("MAPI")
Set MyCalendar = MyOutlookNS.GetDefaultFolder(olFolderCalendar)

' Create a date a week from now.
OneWeekHence = DateAdd("d", 7, Date)

' Create the Note heading
temp = "Week of " & Date & vbCrLf & vbCrLf

' Loop for each appointment in the folder.
For Each MyAppt In MyCalendar.Items
    ' Find appointments within the next week.
    If MyAppt.Start >= Date And _
            MyAppt.Start <= OneWeekHence Then
        ' The info is put together in temp.
        temp = temp & MyAppt.Subject & vbCrLf
        temp = temp & "    Date: " & _
            Format(MyAppt.Start, "Medium Date") & vbCrLf
        temp = temp & "    When: " & Format(MyAppt.Start, "Medium Time") _
            & vbCrLf
        temp = temp & "    Ends: " & Format(MyAppt.End, "Medium Time") _
            & vbCrLf
        temp = temp & "    Where: " & MyAppt.Location & vbCrLf & vbCrLf

    End If
Next
        ' Create a new note.
        Set doc = CreateItem(olNoteItem)
        ' Add the compiled text to the Note.
        doc.Body = temp
        ' Display the note.
        doc.Display

End Sub
```

Summary

Macros and VBA programming let you automate commonly performed tasks in Outlook. Although it takes some time and effort to create the macros, you'll often find that this investment is generously repaid in saved time and reduced errors. This chapter presented two real-world examples of VBA code that performs useful, real-world tasks. These applications can serve as the basis for your own projects.

Chapter 26

Working with Outlook Forms

Almost everything you do in Outlook is based on a form. When you create or read an email message, you use a message form. When you read an appointment, you use an appointment form. The same goes for contacts, journal entries, and tasks. Outlook provides you with all these predefined forms, but you do not have to limit yourself to these — you can create your own custom forms and publish them for others to use. This chapter takes you through the basics of creating and using forms in Outlook. The next chapter goes beyond the basics to cover more advanced form topics.

Understanding Outlook Forms

An *Outlook form* provides a way to collect and distribute information. In addition to all the standard things you can do with forms in Outlook, such as creating email messages, you can use custom forms for tasks such as posting information to public folders, gathering requests from meeting attendees, and the like. The term *form application* is sometimes used for a collection of one or more Outlook forms designed to serve a particular purpose.

Custom forms in Outlook are based on existing form templates. All Outlook installations include the basic set of templates that correspond to the forms that Outlook itself uses. These are

- Appointment
- Contact
- Journal Entry
- Message
- Task

IN THIS CHAPTER

Understanding Outlook forms

Creating a custom form

Working with fields, controls, and pages

Understanding control and page properties

Testing and publishing a form

Forms and Microsoft Exchange

Though not strictly required, it is true that almost all Outlook forms applications use Microsoft Exchange for public folders. This is covered in Chapter 28.

There are some other form templates that may require some explanation:

- **Post:** This form is intended for collecting information for posting to a public folder.
- **RSS Article (hidden):** This form is designed for use with RSS feeds.
- **Meeting Request (hidden):** This form is used to send a meeting request.
- **Task Request (hidden):** This form is used to send a task request.

Note that three of these forms are marked as hidden. This is because during normal Outlook operation you never see these forms — they are used behind the scenes. They are still available for use as a template, however.

When you decide which template to base your custom form on, think about the purpose of the application. If the functionality requires sending information between recipients, the Message form is likely your best bet. If the functionality requires posting information to public or private folders, a Contact, Appointment, Task, or Post template would be suitable depending on the nature of the information.

In practice, two of Outlook's forms are used most often as templates: Message and Post. This chapter focuses on using these form templates, but the principles are the same for the other templates.

Creating a custom form involves two fundamental steps:

1. Design the form to work with the information required by your application.
2. Publish the form to make it available.

These topics are covered in the remainder of this chapter and in the next chapter.

Designing a Form

You create custom forms in the *Forms Designer*, a powerful tool that lets you customize a form to precisely meet your needs. This section explains the procedures you use in the Forms Designer, then later in the chapter I present some step-by-step examples of creating custom forms.

In Outlook, a *field* represents a single piece of information, such as the subject of an email message or the phone number of a contact. Forms use fields, too — in fact, all the information a form

Different Types of Custom Forms

Outlook supports three categories of custom forms. The most basic, called simply *Outlook Forms*, are the most widely used because they are compatible with other versions of Outlook and provide all the power and flexibility that most people require. The other two types are *Outlook Form Regions* and *InfoPath Forms*, which are more advanced and are beyond the scope of this book.

contains is represented by fields. Each form template starts with a set of default fields. When you design the form, you can add additional fields from Outlook's list of predefined fields, and you can also create you own custom fields.

Starting a New Form

To open the Forms Designer and create a new custom form, select Forms from the Tools menu and then select Design a Form. The Design Form dialog box, shown in Figure 26.1, lets you select the form that your custom form will be based on (as explained earlier in this chapter). By default, this dialog box displays the form templates in the Standard Forms Library. This section uses the Message template for illustration purposes, but the procedures and principles are the same for other form templates.

FIGURE 26.1

Selecting the template for a custom form.

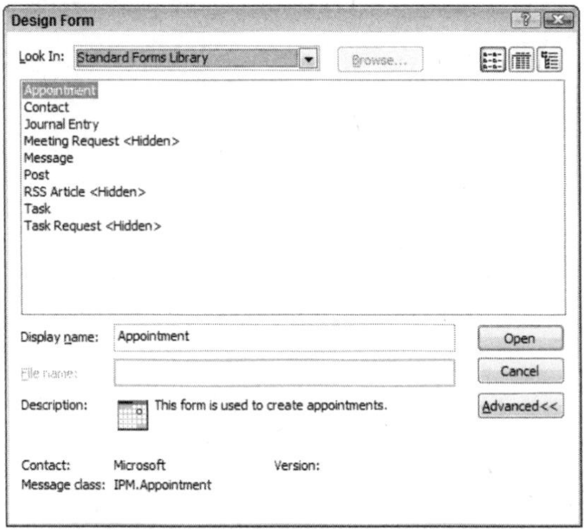

After selecting the desired template and clicking OK, the template opens in the Forms Designer as shown in Figure 26.2.

FIGURE 26.2

The selected template — in this case, the Message template — is ready for editing.

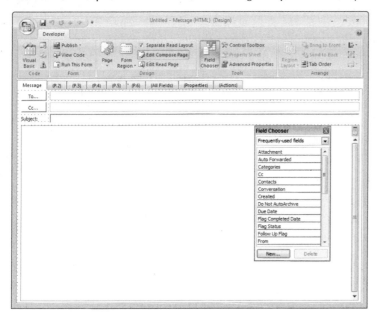

When you first look at the form in the Forms Designer, it may look like the form it is based on — in this case, the Message form. You see the To and CC and Subject fields and a large field to enter the message body. But a moment's observation will reveal that it is very different:

- The ribbon, named the *Developer ribbon*, displays an assortment of tools you use in designing your form. It is not the usual ribbon that you see displayed on the Message form.

- The Field Chooser lists the various fields available for the form.

- The form itself has nine tabs, some of which have meaningless names such as P.2 and P.3.

- The background of the form — although perhaps not clearly visible in the figure — displays a grid of dots.

These factors show you that the form is in design mode, ready to be modified as needed.

Using Other Form Templates

You are not limited to using the form templates in the Standard Forms Library. There may be other templates available, installed by your IT department, and you can also use custom forms that you have designed previously as a template.

Can't Edit a Page?

Some form templates have one or more of their pages locked, which means you cannot edit them. For example, the Task page in the Task template is locked. Creating a custom form based on one of these templates means working with the other pages in the template.

Modifying a Form

If you want to modify a form that you designed previously:

1. Open the Design Form dialog box (shown earlier in Figure 26.1).

2. Open the Look In list at the top of the dialog box and select the folder where you originally published the form.

3. Select the form from the list.

4. Click Open.

You can now use the techniques explained in this chapter to modify the form and publish it.

Form Structure

A form is made up of one or more tabs, called *pages* in Outlook. If you refer back to the Message form template in Figure 26.2, you can see that it has nine pages. Some pages are defined as part of the template — for example, the Message, All Fields, Properties, and Actions tabs in this example. Others — P.2, P.3, and so on — are blank to start with so that you can design them exactly as you see fit. You do not have to use all the available pages. A custom form has at least one visible page, of course, and as many more as the application requires. In the Forms Designer, pages whose name is displayed in parentheses are be displayed when the form is used.

Each tab can be thought of as a page on which you place elements or controls. The Forms Designer has a set of controls to perform specific tasks. Look at Figure 26.3, which shows part of the Message template with the controls called out. There are three types of controls on this form:

- **Textbox:** For user entry and editing of text.
- **Label:** For displaying text that the user cannot edit.
- **CommandButton:** For carrying out an action when the user clicks it.

A form usually has actions associated with it as well. Actions are defined in *VBScript*, a lightweight version of the VBA programming language that can be included with a form. VBScript is usually associated with a `CommandButton` control because that is the control designed for the user to click to perform some action.

FIGURE 26.3

Each tab on a form contains controls, three of which are identified here.

CommandButton   TextBox

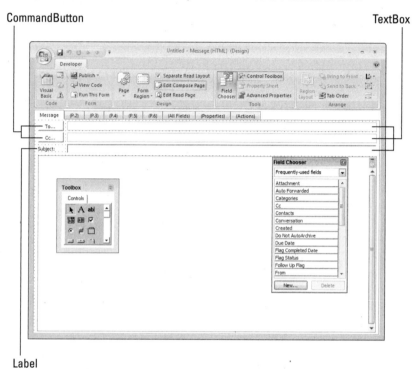

Label

In a nutshell, designing a custom form consists of arranging controls on the pages of the form. The controls are selected and arranged to accommodate the information the form is designed to work with. A form also has actions defined in VBScript.

Working with Pages

Every form template has a certain number of built-in pages. You cannot add pages to or delete pages from a form, but you can control which ones are shown when the form is used. Pages whose names are in parentheses are not displayed. To specify that a page should be displayed when the form is run, or to change a page name, click the page's tab, click the Page button on the ribbon, and select either Display This Page or Rename This Page from the menu.

When a form is run, the pages you specified to be displayed will be listed in the Show section of the ribbon. For example, in Figure 26.4 you can see the Show section for a form that has three pages named Message, Names, and Deadlines. The user clicks the name of the page she wants to view.

When a form is run, the user selects from the available form pages in the Show section of the ribbon.

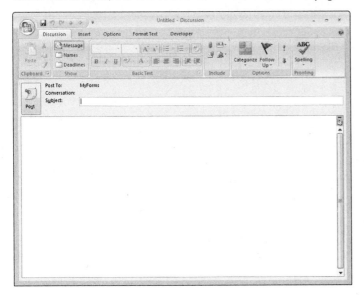

Page Properties

Each page of a form has a set of properties. To display the Properties dialog box for a page (shown in Figure 26.5), select the page by clicking its tab (make sure that no control on the page is selected). Then, click the Advanced Properties button in the Tools section of the ribbon.

To set a property, click its name in the list and select the desired value from the list at the top of the dialog box. For some properties, a small button with ... on it is displayed at the top right of the dialog box — click this button to open a dialog box where you set the property.

Click the Apply button to apply new property settings to the page without closing the dialog box. To close the Properties dialog box, click the Advanced Properties button again or click the close button (the red X at the top right of the dialog box).

FIGURE 26.5

Displaying the Properties dialog box for a page.

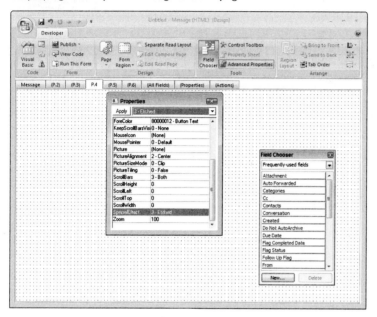

Adding Fields to a Form

As has already been mentioned, a form uses fields to hold its data. A form template contains its own default set of fields; you can add more fields to a form and delete some of the default ones until the new custom form contains just the fields you need.

Every field on a form is represented by a control. The type of control is appropriate for the data the field contains. By adding a field to a form you are automatically adding the corresponding control. This is the easiest and recommended way to add controls to a form, although it is not appropriate in all situations.

You add fields to a form using the Field Chooser. This is usually displayed by default when you create a new form, but if necessary click the Field Chooser button in the Tools section of the ribbon to display it. The Field Chooser is shown in Figure 26.6.

At the top of the Field Chooser is a pull-down list where you select the category of fields to be displayed in the Chooser. The default is Frequently Used Fields. To add a field to the form, drag it from the Field Chooser and drop it at the desired location on the page (although you can change the position later).

FIGURE 26.6

FIGURE 26.6

You use the Field Chooser to add fields to a form.

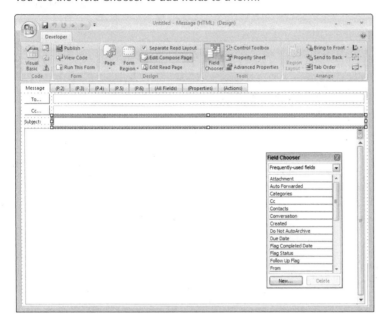

To illustrate, look at Figure 26.7. To create this example, four fields were dragged from the Field Chooser to the form. From top to bottom they are

- **Due Date:** The Forms Designer has created a TextBox control to hold the date as well as an adjacent Label control to identify the field.

- **Importance:** This field can take three values: Low, Normal, and High. The Forms Designer has created a ComboBox control from which the user can select one of these values. Again, an adjacent Label serves to identify the field.

- **Read:** This field is a yes/no, true/false value, and the appropriate control is a CheckBox, which includes its own identifying label.

- **Icon:** The last control/field represents the icon associated with the form data — in this case a message (envelope) icon because the form is based on the Message template. The Image control, designed specifically for displaying digital images, is used here.

After you have added one or more fields to a page, you can work with them as described in the following sections — changing their size and position on the page, modifying their properties, and so on.

When you add a field to a page, the Forms Designer automatically adds the appropriate control(s).

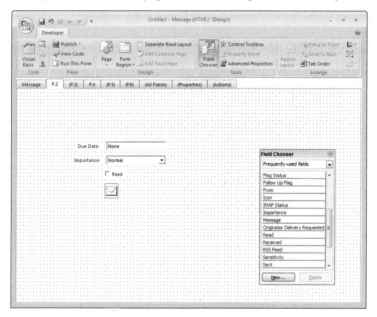

Working with Controls

Controls are the foundation of form design. The Forms Designer provides you with a toolbox of 14 controls you can place on a form. Each control has a set of properties that determine its appearance and, in some cases, its behavior. A control that holds information is *linked*, or bound, to the corresponding form field. The techniques described in this chapter can be used to add new controls to a page or to modify or delete controls that are part of the template.

Adding Controls Manually

The usual way to add most controls to a page is by adding fields, as was described in the previous section. When you add a field, the Forms Designer automatically adds a control of the appropriate type to the page, saving you time and effort.

There are times, however, when you will want to add controls manually. For example, some forms use controls not linked to a field so you will have to use the manual method. You can also add a control manually and then later link it to a field.

You use the Toolbox to manually add controls to a page. The Toolbox, shown in Figure 26.8, is displayed or hidden by clicking the Control Toolbox button in the Tools section of the ribbon.

FIGURE 26.8

You manually add controls to a page from the Toolbox.

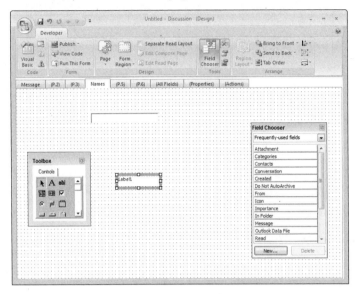

The arrow icon at the top left of the Toolbox is not a control — you select it when you want to manipulate controls already placed on a page. The other icons in the Toolbox represent the controls. In order across and then down, they represent:

- **Label:** Displays text that the user cannot edit. Usually used to identify other page elements.

- **TextBox:** Used for user entry/editing of text.

- **ComboBox:** Combines an editable text field with a list of items from which the user can select.

- **ListBox:** Displays a list of items from which the user can select.

- **CheckBox:** Represents an on/off option.

- **OptionButton:** Represents one in a set of two or more options. Within a set, one and only one option can be selected at a time.

- **ToggleButton:** Represents an on/off option.

- **Frame:** Used to group controls, for example to define a set of two or more OptionButtons.

- **CommandButton:** Used to carry out an action (defined in VBScript).

TabStrip and Multi-Page Controls

These controls are rarely used in Outlook forms because the multi-page structure of the form itself provides the same functionality. They are not covered further in this book.

- **TabStrip:** Used to display two or more tabs or pages.
- **MultiPage:** Similar to a TabStrip but easier to use.
- **ScrollBar:** Displays a vertical or horizontal scroll bar that the user can use to scroll with the mouse.
- **SpinButton:** Displays a pair of up/down arrows that the user can click to increment or decrement a numerical value.
- **Image:** Displays a digital image.

To add a control to a page manually, click the desired icon in the Toolbox and then drag on the page to place the control. Don't worry about the precise size or placement of the control — you can always change them later.

Selecting, Sizing, and Moving Controls

After placing one or more controls on a page, you can select an individual control by clicking it. A selected control displays a hatched border and small squares, called *handles*, on its corners and sides. In Figure 26.9, the upper TextBox is selected and the lower one is not.

Adding OptionButtons

This is the only control that requires a special technique when adding it to a page. You must first place a Frame control on the page and then draw the individual OptionButton controls on the Frame. This is how a group of OptionButtons is defined, and within a group only one OptionButton can be selected at a time. When the user selects one, any other in the group that is selected is automatically turned off. You cannot define a group of OptionButtons by placing them on the page and then moving them onto a Frame — you must draw them directly on the Frame.

Control Names

Every control has a name that identifies it. The name must be unique on the page. When you add a control to a page, the Forms Designer assigns a default name that consists of the type of control followed by a number. Thus, adding two TextBox controls will result in the controls named `TextBox1` and `TextBox2`. You will often want to change the name of a control to describe its function. This is explained in the section on control properties later in this chapter.

FIGURE 26.9

A selected control displays a border and handles.

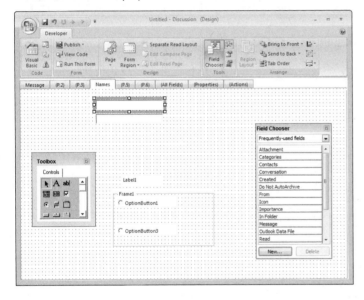

When a control is selected, you can perform the following actions with it:

- To move it, point at the border — the mouse cursor will change to a 4-headed arrow — and drag to the new location.
- To resize it, point at one of the handles — the mouse cursor will change to a two-headed arrow — and drag to the desired size.
- To delete it, press Del.

Aligning Controls

By default, all controls align to the grid of dots displayed on the page background. This alignment affects both the control position and size — in other words, the top-left corner is always at a grid boundary, and the height and width are always multiples of the grid size. This default behavior simplifies the task of creating neat-looking forms with controls that are aligned. You can modify this behavior if desired by clicking the Align button in the Arrange section of the ribbon and then selecting these commands from the menu:

- **Snap to Grid:** Turn this option off if you want to be able to position and size controls freely, without reference to the grid.

- **Show Grid:** Toggles the grid display on or off. Snap to Grid will still operate even when the grid is not displayed.

- **Set Grid Size:** Opens a dialog box where you can set the size of the grid (the default is 8). Changing the grid size does not affect controls already on the form.

Automatic Alignment and Sizing of Controls

The Forms Designer provides commands to automatically adjust the size and/or position of two or more controls to be the same. To use these commands you must first select two or more controls to adjust:

1. Click the first control to select it. This is the reference control whose size and/or position is applied to the other controls.

2. Hold down the Shift key while clicking the other control(s).

When you select two or more controls in this manner, you'll see that all selected controls display handles and a border, but the reference control has white handles while all other selected controls have black handles. This is shown in Figure 26.10.

Once you have selected the controls, you size them by clicking the Size button on the ribbon, clicking the Make Same Size command, and then selecting Width, Height, or Both from the next menu.

To align the selected controls, click the Align button on the ribbon, then from the menu:

- Select Left, Middle, or Right to align the controls horizontally by their left edges, centers, or right edges.

- Select Top, Center, or Bottom to align the controls vertically by their top edges, centers, or bottom edges.

FIGURE 26.10

When multiple controls are selected, the reference control displays white handles.

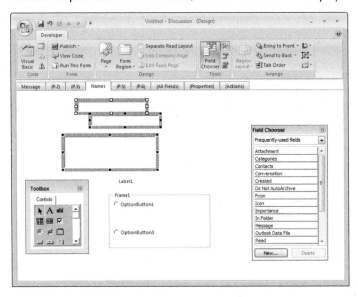

Other Size and Position Tools

The Size and Align menus have a few additional commands that simplify the task of arranging controls on a page. On the Size menu:

- **Size to Fit:** Changes the size of the selected control(s) to fit between other controls on the page.

- **Size to Grid:** Changes the size of the control to match the closest grid points.

On the Align menu:

- **Distribute Horizontally:** Displays a submenu with commands for arranging selected controls horizontally.

- **Distribute Vertically:** Displays a submenu with commands for arranging selected controls vertically.

- **Center in Form:** Positions the selected control(s) either vertically or horizontally at the center of the form.

- **Arrange:** Displays a submenu with commands for arranging selected controls.

Working with the Z-Order

The Z-order of controls is relevant when one control overlaps another. You can think of it like overlapping sheets of paper on your desk — there's one on top, one on the bottom, and the ones in between in a certain order. With controls, this is the *Z-order*. For example, Figure 26.11 shows a label control that overlaps a TextBox control. You can see that the Label control hides the portion of the TextBox that is behind it — this means that the Label is at the front of the Z-order.

FIGURE 26.11

When controls overlap, the Z-order determines which one — the Label control in this figure — is on top.

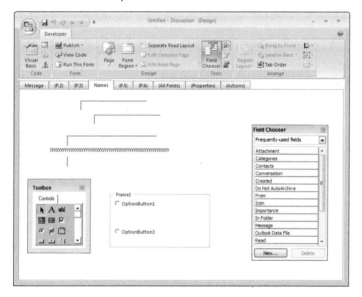

More Precise Z-Order Control

When there are more than two controls overlapping, you can precisely control their position in the Z-order rather than simply sending them to the front or back. Click the arrow next to the Bring to Front or Send to Back button on the ribbon and you'll see Bring Forward and Send Backward commands. These commands move the selected control one position in the indicated order. For example, if you had three overlapping controls, selecting the one at the top of the Z-order and using the Send Backward command would result in that control being at position 2 and the control that was at position 2 being at the top of the Z-order.

By selecting a control and clicking either the Bring to Front or the Send to Back button on the ribbon, you can change the position of the selected control in the Z-order. Figure 26.12 shows the same controls as in Figure 26.11 after either sending the Label control to the back or bringing the TextBox control to the front.

FIGURE 26.12

By changing the Z-order, you can modify which control is displayed on top.

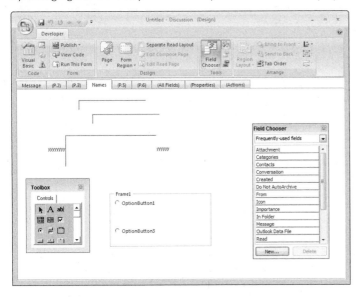

Changing the Tab Order

When a form is being used, only one control is *active* — that is, has the focus — at a given time. The active control is indicated visually in some way. For example, when a TextBox is active it will display a blinking cursor.

The user can move the focus by clicking with the mouse or by pressing Tab or Shift+Tab to move the focus forward or backward in the tab order. Also, when the form is first opened, the control that is first in the tab order gets the focus.

By default, controls are added to the tab order in the same sequence they are placed on the page (each page has its own tab order). To change the tab order, click the Tab Order button on the ribbon to open the Tab Order dialog box, shown in Figure 26.13. To change the order, click a control name and use the Move Up and Move Down buttons to change its position in the list.

Removing a Control from the Tab Order

If you do not want the user to be able to tab to a control, set its `TabStop` property to False (as explained later in this chapter in the control properties section).

FIGURE 26.13

Changing the tab order of the controls on a page.

The tab order on a form should reflect the logical structure of the form and how a user would normally move from control to control.

Working with Control Properties

As mentioned earlier, every control has a set of properties. Some properties are common to all or most controls, whereas others are relevant to only one or two controls. This section starts by describing the most important common properties and then discusses some individual controls in detail.

Control properties are accessible to the person designing the form. Some of them can also be changed in VBScript code while the form is running.

Accessing Control Properties

Each control's properties are divided, simply for convenience, into two groups. The more commonly used properties are grouped together on the control's property sheet, whereas the less frequently needed advanced properties have their own dialog box.

To view a control's property sheet, select the control and click the Property Sheet button in the Tools section of the ribbon. You can also right-click the control and select Properties from the context menu. Advanced properties are also accessed from the context menu by selecting the Advanced Properties command.

Common Control Properties

Some of the common control properties are found on the property sheet. The property sheet is essentially the same for most controls. It is shown, for a TextBox control, in Figure 26.14.

The property sheet provides access to the most often needed control properties.

The Display tab, shown in the figure, contains these properties. Note that some of these properties will not be available for some controls:

- **Name:** The control name, which must be unique on its page. You may want to change this from the default name to something more descriptive such as `FirstName` or `ZIPCode`, particularly if you will be manipulating the control in VBA code.
- **Caption:** The text of the control's caption, where applicable.
- **Font:** The font used for the control.
- **Foreground Color:** The color of the control's text.
- **Background Color:** The color of the control's background.
- **Visible:** If selected, the control will be visible when the form runs.
- **Enabled:** If selected, the control will be enabled (can be accessed by the user) when the form runs.
- **Read Only:** If selected, the data in the control cannot be changed by the user.
- **Sunken:** If selected, the control displays with a 3-D sunken appearance.
- **Multi-line:** If selected, the control can display multiple lines of text. Applicable to TextBox controls only.

The Foreground Color and Background Color properties let you choose from a set of predefined Windows operating system colors. For more choices you must use the `BackColor` and `ForeColor` properties in the Advanced Properties dialog box.

The Layout tab of the property sheet is shown in Figure 26.15. The `Top`, `Left`, `Height`, and `Width` properties specify the size and position of the control. You can change these here, but usually size and position of controls is modified in the designer.

The Resize with Form option determines whether the control always keeps its set size (option off) or grows and shrinks with the form.

FIGURE 26.15

The Layout tab of the property sheet.

The Validation tab is used to define data validation rules for a control/field and is covered in the next chapter.

A control's advanced properties are listed alphabetically in the Properties dialog box as shown in Figure 26.16. The property names are in the left column and the values are in the right column. The properties listed here duplicate some of the properties found in the property sheet, and you can change them in either place. Other properties listed here can only be accessed via the Advanced Properties command.

FIGURE 26.16

The advanced properties for a control are listed in the Properties dialog box.

Some of the advanced properties that you are most likely to need to change are described here. To change a property, click its name in the list and then select a value at the top of the dialog box:

- **BackColor, ForeColor:** Same as Background Color and Foreground Color in the property sheet, but provide a greater selection of colors to choose from.

- **BackStyle:** Sets the control background to Opaque or Transparent.

- **BorderStyle:** Sets the style of the control's border to Single or None.

- **Locked:** If True, the control is read-only.

- **MousePointer:** Specifies the shape of the mouse pointer when it is over the control.

- **TabStop:** If True (the default), the control is part of the tab order. Set to False if you do not want the user to be able to tab to the control.

The Value Properties

The Value tab of the property sheet is related to the field that the control corresponds to. This tab is shown in Figure 26.17. If the control is already associated with a field, the property values will be filled in (as in the figure). Otherwise they will be blank.

WARNING To associate a control with a field, or to change its association to a different field, click the Choose Field button and follow the prompts to select a field. Be careful doing this because not all control types are appropriate for certain field data types — although the Forms Designer will let you make inappropriate associations, the resulting form is likely to be less useful.

FIGURE 26.17

The Value tab of a control's property sheet specifies the field the control represents.

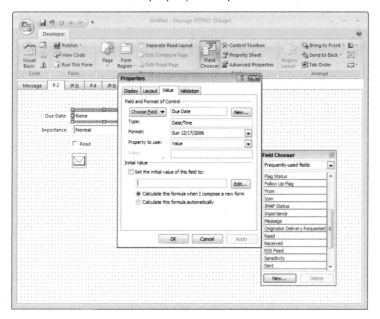

The other properties are

■ **Type:** Displays the data type of the field. This is a read-only property — you cannot change it because the data type is a characteristic of the field.

■ **Format:** Depending on the data type, you can select the format it should be displayed in.

■ **Property to Use:** Specifies the control property linked to the field. This is almost always the `Value` property and generally should not be changed unless you have a good reason to.

Testing a Form

While you are designing a form, you can test, or run, the form to see how it works. To do so, click the Run This Form button on the ribbon. The form opens and you can use it just as if you were using it "for real." You can test your tab orders, make sure controls display as desired, check default data values, and so on. If it's a form that can be sent, you can send it (which closes the form as well). If it's a form to be posted, you can post it. Otherwise, after testing close the form and return to the Forms Designer by clicking the X at the top right of the form.

Publishing a Form

You must publish a form to make it available for use. You have three options:

- Publish the form to the Personal Forms Library, where it will be available for use as a template.

- Publish the form to a personal folder, where it will be available for your use only.

- Publish the form to a public folder (Microsoft Exchange only), where it will be available for use by anyone who has permission to access that folder.

The true power of Outlook forms can only be realized when you are using them with an Exchange Server account. This topic, including publishing forms to public folders, is covered in Chapter 28. For now I will explain the fundamentals of publishing a form.

After you have completed form design, click the Publish button on the ribbon. The Forms Designer displays a menu with two choices: Publish Form and Publish Form As.

If your form was created based on one of Outlook's default templates, these commands are equivalent—either command opens the Publish Form As dialog box (see Figure 26.18). Then:

1. Open the Look In list and select the folder where you want to publish the form. If the folder you want is not on this list, click the Browse button to locate it.

2. Enter a descriptive name for the form in the Display Name box. This is the name Outlook uses for the form.

3. By default, the Form Name box—which is the name that the form's file will be given— is the same as the display name. There is rarely a reason to change this but you can if needed.

4. Click Publish.

Creating Folders for Forms

In most situations you will publish a form to a folder created specifically for that form (or for two or more forms of the same type). When you create such a folder, you will specify the type of item it will contain. Be sure to specify the same type of item as the template your form is based on.

FIGURE 26.18

Selecting a folder and name for a published form.

Summary

Outlook forms provide a powerful tool for creating custom solutions, or applications, that require the collection and/or distribution of data. You can create a custom form based on any of Outlook's built-in forms, adding controls and fields to perfectly suit your application's needs. This chapter covered the fundamentals of designing and publishing custom forms. In the next chapter, you learn some more advanced aspects of Outlook forms.

Chapter 27

Going Beyond Basic Forms

In the previous chapter, you learned the fundamentals of designing and publishing custom Outlook forms. This chapter goes beyond the basics to cover some more advanced aspect of custom form design.

Using Custom Fields

Given the wide array of form fields provided by Outlook, you might think you would never need a custom field. This would be a mistake — it is fairly common for a form design to require one or more custom fields to meet the needs of the application. This section shows you how to define custom fields and add them to a page on a form.

Planning a Custom Field

Once you have determined that none of Outlook's built-in fields are appropriate for your data, your next step is to do a little planning. Two factors come into play:

- Is the custom field a good match for the type of data it will contain?
- Does the custom field provide flexibility for further changes to the form?

For example, suppose you are designing a form for employee data, and one of the pieces of information is gender. There are only two mutually exclusive choices, Male and Female, and the list of choices will never expand, so using an OptionButton control — two of them to be precise — makes sense.

But suppose another piece of information is health plan — which of the three company health plans is the employee enrolled in? Again you have mutually exclusive choices, so why not use OptionButtons again? But you cannot be guaranteed that your company will always offer only three health plans. Suppose they expand the offering to eight plans — modifying the form to include eight OptionButton controls would be a hassle, not to mention that the form's visual appearance would suffer. Better in cases like this to use a ComboBox, which offers an easily expandable list of mutually exclusive choices.

Creating a Custom Field

Once you have decided how to implement your custom field, there are two ways to go about it. The end result is the same, but one technique gives you more flexibility in selecting the control type that will be used.

Using the Field Chooser to Define a New Field

The Field Chooser has a New button that you click to define a new field. It brings up the New Field dialog box, shown in Figure 27.1. Enter information about the field as follows:

- **Name:** The name of the field.
- **Type:** The data type of the field (text, number, date, yes/no, and so on).
- **Format:** Select the display format for the field.

FIGURE 27.1

Defining a custom field for a form.

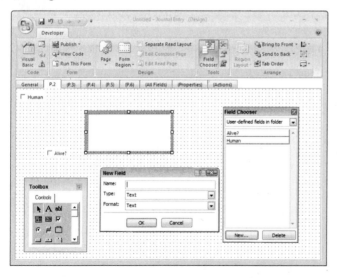

Some types of fields do not offer formatting options. For example, if the data type is Text there are no formatting choices, but if the type is Number you can select format options such as the number of decimal places displayed.

After you click OK to close the New Field dialog box, the new field appears in the User-Defined Fields section of the Field Chooser. From here you can drag the field onto a form page just like with the built-in fields.

Adding a Control First

The other way to define a new field involves adding the control to the page first and then creating the field for it:

1. If necessary, display the Toolbox.
2. Click the desired control icon in the Toolbox.
3. Draw the control at the desired location on the page.
4. With the control selected, click the Property Sheet button on the ribbon to open the control's property sheet.
5. In the property sheet, click the Value tab (see Figure 27.2). If this tab is not available, it means that you have selected a type of control that cannot be associated with a field. Delete the control and choose another one.
6. Click the New button to display the New Field dialog box (shown earlier in Figure 27.1).
7. In the New Field dialog box, enter the new field name and select its data type and format.
8. Click OK to return to the property sheet. The details of the new field are now displayed on the Value tab (see Figure 27.3).
9. Click OK to close the property sheet.

FIGURE 27.2

Before associating a new field with a control, the Value tab is blank.

FIGURE 27.3

After associating a new field with a control, the Value tab displays the field details.

Using Read and Compose Modes

For certain types of forms, the person who composes the form (when using it, not designing it) has different needs from the person who receives and reads the form. Email messages are a perfect example.

- The person who composes the message needs to have To and CC fields that can be edited.

- The person who receives the message needs to have To and CC fields, but they need not be editable. The reader also needs a From field and a Sent field.

To handle situations such as this, Outlook forms — at least some of them — can have two display modes: Read and Compose. This is illustrated in Figures 27.4 and 27.5, which show a message form in the Forms Designer in Compose and in Read modes, respectively.

FIGURE 27.4

In Compose mode, a message form displays editable To, CC, and Subject fields.

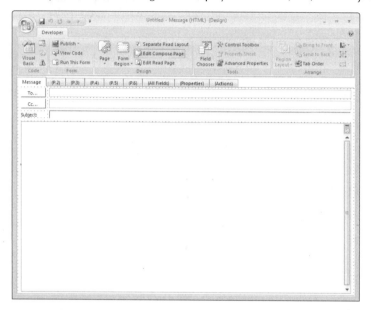

FIGURE 27.5

In Read mode, a message form's To, CC, and Subject fields are not editable, and there are also From and Sent fields displayed.

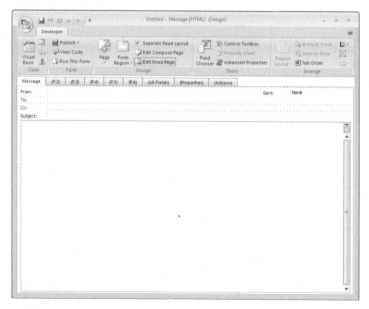

Some form templates do not support Read and Compose modes. In this situation, the Separate Read Layout option is available in the Design section of the ribbon (see Figure 27.6). Turn this option on if you want separate Read and Compose modes for a particular form page, or turn it off if you do not. If the option is selected, you use the adjacent Edit Compose Page and Edit Read Page buttons to switch the Forms Designer between modes.

FIGURE 27.6

You choose Read/Compose mode options on the ribbon.

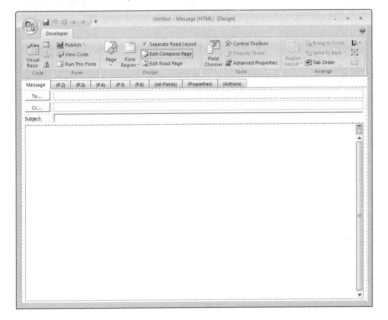

Working with Fields

This section covers some of the details and options that are applicable to working with fields on an Outlook form.

Shared Fields

A *shared field* is one present on both the Compose and Read views of a page (Compose and Read modes were explained earlier in this chapter). A shared field is linked to two controls, one on the Read view of a page and the other on the Compose view. The two controls can have different properties. For example, in the Compose view you might use a TextBox with the Enabled property set to True so the user can edit the data, whereas in the Read view you use a TextBox with Enabled set to False so the data is not editable. You can even have two different types of controls linked to the same field, for example a TextBox on the Compose view and a Label on the Read view.

To create a shared field, you can simply drag the field from the Field Chooser to the Read view and then switch to the Compose page and drag it there. This works only if you want the same type of control in both locations. You can edit each control's properties independently as needed.

If you want different types of controls on the Read and Compose pages:

1. Display the Compose page.
2. Using the Toolbox, add the desired kind of control to the page.
3. Use the Value tab in the control's property sheet to associate the control with the field.
4. Display the Read page and repeat steps 2 and 3.

Creating Combination Fields

A *combination field* is one that combines data from two or more fields and treats it as a unit. For example, if your form has FirstName, MiddleName, and LastName fields you can create a combination field for full name.

To create a combination field, display the Field Chooser and click the New button to open the New Field dialog box. Enter a name for the custom field and select Combination in the Type list. You can see that the dialog box now displays a Formula field and an Edit button (see Figure 27.7).

FIGURE 27.7

Defining a combination field.

To define the field, click the Edit button to open the Combination Formula Field dialog box, shown in Figure 27.8. For most combinations fields, you want to select the Joining Fields... option at the top, which works by combining two or more fields into a single data item. The second option, Showing Only..., is used when you want the custom combination field to display data from the first non-empty field in a list you specify.

FIGURE 27.8

Creating the formula for a combination field.

To define the formula for the combination field, click the Field button. You can choose from all available fields including user-defined ones. Repeat this action to select all of the fields that you want combined in the combination field, in the desired order. Each field is added to the formula as a field name enclosed in brackets, with a space between fields, as shown in Figure 27.9. If you want to add punctuation or other elements, add it as needed between the field names.

FIGURE 27.9

A combination field formula displays the source field names in brackets.

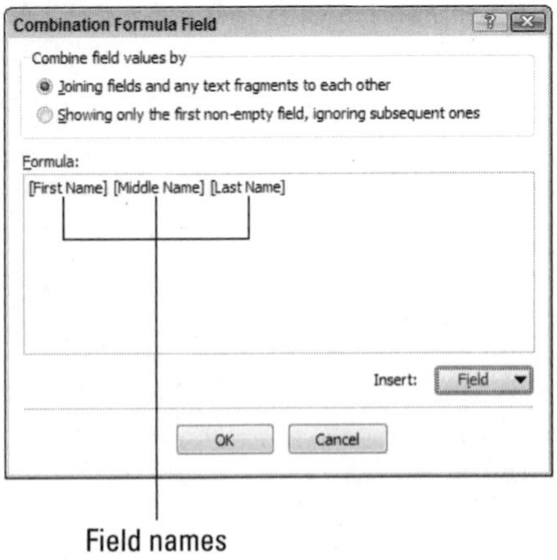

Field names

When the formula is complete, click OK to return to the New Field dialog box, which now displays the formula in the Formula box. Click OK to close the New Field dialog box and the new combination field is available, as a user-defined field, in the Field Chooser. You use it on your forms like any other field.

Using Formula Fields

A *formula field* displays the result of a calculation using data in other fields. This kind of field is usually used to work with numbers, but it can also perform operations on text data that are more complex than simply combining fields as with a combination field. For example, suppose you are designing an order form that already has fields for OrderTotal and SalesTaxRate. You could define a formula field that calculates the sales tax amount by multiplying these two fields together.

To define a formula field:

1. If necessary, display the Field Chooser.

2. Click the New button to display the New Field dialog box (shown earlier in Figure 27.7).

3. Enter a name for the new field in the Name box.

4. Select Formula from the Type list.

5. Click the Edit button to open the Formula Field dialog box (see Figure 27.10).

6. Click the Field button to select each field that you want to use in the formula. Each field name is entered into the Formula box enclosed in brackets.

7. Edit the formula, adding the standard mathematical operators + (addition), – (subtraction), / (division), and * (multiplication) to define the formula.

8. If desired, click the Function button to select from the built-in functions for use in your field formula.

9. When finished, click OK.

FIGURE 27.10

Defining a formula field.

Validating User Input

Many of the problems that arise when a form-based application is used result from the entry of incorrect data. Some errors are impossible to catch, for example if someone mistypes an email address as bill_gates@microsift.com. But you can catch other errors such as:

- An email address without the @ character
- A ZIP code only four digits long
- A data field left blank when an entry is required
- A percentage value way out of range

With the data validation feature available for Outlook forms, you can catch many errors before they cause a problem.

Data validation is performed at the field level. When you add a field to a form, you can define validation rules for it. When a user adds data to the form and then posts or sends it, the rules are evaluated and if a violation is encountered, a message is displayed to the user who can then make the necessary corrections.

You define validation rules on the Validation tab of a field's properties sheet. This is shown in Figure 27.11.

Use the Validation tab of the properties sheet to create validation rules for a field.

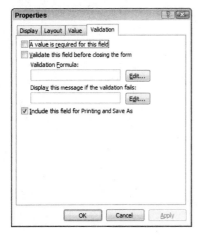

Two types of validation are available, and either one or both can be applied to a field. The first, implemented by selecting the A Value Is Required for This Field option, is used simply to ensure that a field is not left blank.

The second type of validation looks at the data in the field and makes sure that it meets a defined criterion. To implement this type of validation, select the Validate This Field Before Closing the Form option and click the Edit button to define the validation formula. The procedure for this is very similar to that for defining a formula for a formula field as covered earlier in this chapter, and is not repeated here. The one essential difference is that you will create a logical formula, one that evaluates to True (validation successful) or False (validation failed). The syntax for these formulas are the same as for the VBA logical formulas that were covered in Chapter 23.

The final step in defining validation rules is to specify the message to display when the validation fails. You can simply type the message in the Display This Message... box or use the Edit button to define a more complex message.

Setting Form Properties

The properties for a form are located on the Properties page when the form is open in the Forms Designer. This page is shown in Figure 27.12. These properties apply to the form as a whole rather than to a specific page or control.

FIGURE 27.12

Setting form properties on the Properties page.

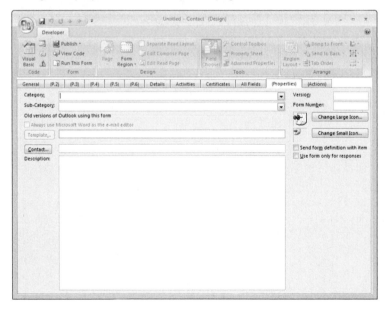

The properties are

- **Category and Sub-Category:** Lets you assign a category and subcategory to the form. These are not the same as Outlook categories, but rather are arbitrary categories that you can use to organize your forms.

- **Contact:** Click this button to associate the form with a contact from your address book.

- **Version and Form Number:** You can use these properties to keep track of changes to the form. For example, when the form is first designed you could assign the version number 1, then when you make modifications you could change the version number to 2.

- **Change Icon:** Use these buttons to change either the small icon or the large icon displayed for the form in Outlook.

- **Send Form Definition with Item:** If you will be sending the form to people who do not have access to the form in the Organizational Forms Library — for example, sending a message to someone outside your company — check this option so the form definition is sent along with the data. This enables people to view the form as it was designed.

- **Use Form Only for Responses:** If this option is selected, people who receive the form and then respond are forced to use the form for their response.

Understanding the Actions Page

The Actions page, shown in Figure 27.13, defines the routing capabilities that the form has. In other words, it specifies what a recipient can do with the form:

- **Reply:** Reply to the original sender with the message subject prefixed by "Re:".

- **Reply to All:** Reply to the original sender and all recipients with the message subject prefixed by "Re:".

- **Forward:** Forward the message with the message subject prefixed by "FW:".

- **Reply to Folder:** Post to a folder without adding anything to the subject.

To modify any of these actions, double-click the action you want to change to open the Form Action Properties dialog box for that action. This is shown in Figure 27.14. The options are

- **Enabled:** This option must be selected for the action to be available to a recipient.

- **Form Name:** Specifies the form used for the action. Normally this is the same form but you can specify that another form be used for replies and forwards if desired.

- **When Responding:** This option determines certain aspects of how a response is created, such as whether the original text is included in the response. Normally this is set to Respective User's Default, which means that the response settings that are in effect on the recipient's system will be used.

- **This Action Will:** Specifies what happens when the recipient chooses the action.

- **Subject Prefix:** Specifies any prefix that will be added to the subject line.

FIGURE 27.13

The Actions page specifies a form's routing capabilities.

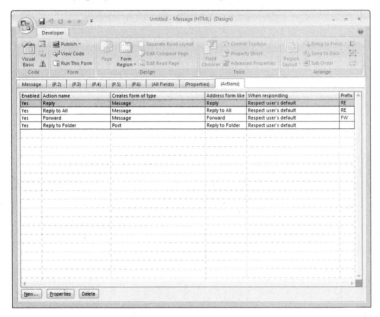

FIGURE 27.14

Setting options for an individual form action.

You can also define new actions for a form. An *action* in this context means that a form will be created. To define a new action, click the New button at the bottom left of the Actions page. Outlook will open the dialog box shown in Figure 27.15. This is essentially identical to setting properties for an existing action with these additions:

- **Name:** Enter a name for the action.
- **Form Name:** Specify the name of the form that the action will open either by clicking the down arrow and selecting a form or by typing in the form name.
- **Check:** If you type in a form name, click this button to verify that the specified form is available in the Forms Library.
- **Show Action On:** Specify where on the form the action should be displayed.

FIGURE 27.15

Defining a new action for a form.

Using VBScript in Your Forms

VBScript is a programming language that can be used to add functionality to Outlook forms. It is a lightweight version of the VBA language you use in Outlook macros. Unlike VBA macro code, however, VBScript code is part of the form and its functionality goes wherever the form goes. Furthermore, VBScript was designed to be safe, lacking many of the programming commands that could be damaging if used in a malicious manner. Examples of things you can do with VBScript are to create a form that interacts with an external database, write form data to an XML file, and manipulate controls on the form.

To work with a form's VBScript, click the View Code button in the Form section of the ribbon. This opens the Script Editor, shown in Figure 27.16 (with no code visible). You enter and edit your code here, then when finished close the Script Editor to return to the form — the code is automatically saved with the form.

FIGURE 27.16

The Script Editor.

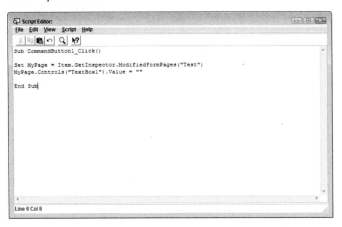

Many of the syntax elements of VBScript are identical to those in VBA (refer to Chapter 23). A detailed treatment of VBScript is beyond the scope of this book, but I will present an example to give you a feel of how it is used.

Suppose you have designed a custom form with a page that contains several TextBox controls for the user to enter data. You want to provide an easy way for the user to clear all the TextBox controls and start over. VBScript is perfect for this.

First, add a CommandButton to the form and use its property sheet to change its caption to `Clear`. Then, open the Script Editor and enter the code shown here. This assumes that the page the controls are on is named PageName and that the TextBox controls you want to clear are named TextBox1, TextBox2, and TextBox3:

```
Sub CommandButton1_Click()

Set MyPage = Item.GetInspector.ModifiedFormPages("PageName")
MyPage.Controls("TextBox1").Value = ""
MyPage.Controls("TextBox2").Value = ""
MyPage.Controls("TextBox3").Value = ""

End Sub
```

The first line of code gets a reference to the form page that you want to work with. The other lines each get a reference to a TextBox and set its `Value` property to a blank string.

Summary

This chapter has shown you some of the more advanced aspects of creating custom forms in Outlook. You learn more about publishing and using custom forms when you explore Microsoft Exchange Server in Chapter 28.

Part VI

Additional Topics

Chapter 28

Using Outlook with Exchange Server

Microsoft Exchange Server is designed to facilitate communication and collaboration among groups of people. It works in conjunction with client applications such as Outlook, and provides services such as email, instant messaging, sharing of calendars and tasks, thin-client (that is, browser) based access to email, and support for mobile devices.

This chapter shows you how to get the most out of Outlook when you are using it with an Exchange account. It does not cover aspects of Exchange not specifically related to Outlook, such as Exchange Server administration.

Be aware that Exchange Server is a complex piece of software with lots of options, which may be set differently by the Exchange administrator. There are also different versions of Exchange Server in use at different organizations. For these reasons you cannot be sure that each Exchange Server account will work exactly the same as all the others.

Understanding Exchange Server

Exchange Server is designed to facilitate the exchange of information between users. An Exchange Server account may have just a few users, dozens, or even hundreds. Each individual user has his own username and password that he uses to log on to the account. The username and password are part of the information that must be specified when setting up your Exchange account in Outlook, as was covered in Chapter 3.

Central to the concept of Exchange is the fact that all information — your received emails, your calendar, your tasks, and so on — is stored on the server. Most Outlook users will have a local copy of this information, stored in an Offline Folders File regularly synchronized with the information on the server. It is this fact — that all users' information is stored centrally — that gives Exchange Server its power in terms of collaborating and sharing information with others.

In many ways, using Outlook with an Exchange Server account is no different from using it with a regular — that is, non-Exchange — email account. You'll have an email address and can send and receive messages. You'll have all the usual folders — Inbox, Contacts, Tasks, Search Folders, and so on. You also have some other folders, called public folders that are central to the way Exchange Server works, as is explained soon. You can see the folder structure of a typical Exchange account in Figure 28.1.

What's different in Exchange is that you can give other Exchange users the rights to use your folders. For example, if you have an assistant, you could give him the rights to view your Calendar folder and to schedule meetings for you. Or, while you are away on vacation, you could give a colleague permission to view and respond to emails you receive so that important messages are not ignored until you come back.

FIGURE 28.1

An Exchange account includes the same folders present in a non-Exchange account.

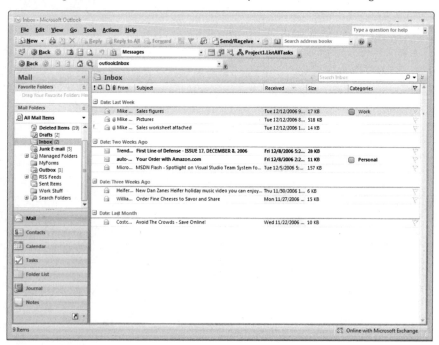

A fundamental part of Exchange is its *public folders*, which are also displayed in Outlook as shown in Figure 28.2. As the name suggests, these are folders that do not belong to any individual but are accessible to any user (although the Exchange administrator can restrict availability of public folders as needed). When you keep information, such as your contacts or calendar, in a public folder it can easily be used by others. Public folders are also central to the full use of forms-based applications.

Many aspects of using Outlook with an Exchange account are identical to using a non-Outlook email account. There are some differences, however, as well as added capability, and these are the topic of this chapter.

FIGURE 28.2

Public folders are an important aspect of an Exchange account.

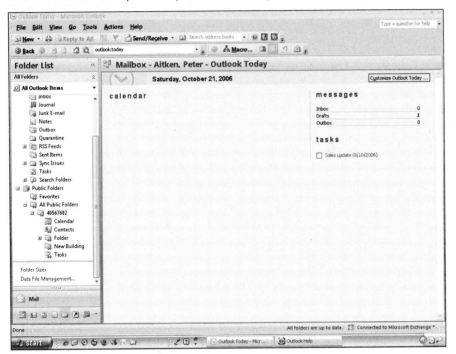

Understanding Offline Folders Files

Exchange stores all your information — messages, appointments, tasks, and so on — on the server. After all, this is a main function of Exchange: to provide a central and sharable repository for information. Does this mean you cannot work with this information when you are not connected to the server? No, because you can use Offline Folders.

An *Offline Folders File* is a local copy of all your Exchange information. When you are not connected you can work with this information, then when you reconnect the Offline Folders File is synchronized with the Exchange server. Changes you made while working offline are copied to the server and new information on the server, such as email messages you received while offline, are downloaded.

From the perspective of the user, an Offline Folders File is exactly like a Personal Folders File (PST). The folders display in the navigation pane in the same way, and you create, edit, and move items in the same way. The difference is that a PST file remains local and is never synchronized with any server.

When you set up Outlook to work with an Exchange server, the Offline Folders File is set up automatically. It is named Outlook.ost by default and for Windows XP users is located in C:\Documents and Settings*username*\Local Settings\Application Data\Microsoft\Outlook (the location may be different if you are using Vista). The location of this file is rarely of any interest to the user. However, you must attend to details of when synchronization occurs and which folders are synchronized.

By default, Outlook uses Cached Exchange Mode, explained in the next section, to keep your offline folders synchronized with the server. Though you can turn Cached Exchange Mode off, there is rarely any reason to do so and I do not recommend it.

Using Cached Exchange Mode

Cached Exchange Mode is the default way that Outlook synchronizes offline folders with the server. When using this mode, Outlook always uses the local copy of your data — that is, the offline folders — and automatically synchronizes the local copy with the Exchange server. To make sure that Outlook is using Cached Exchange Mode:

1. Select Account Settings from the Tools menu to display the Account Settings dialog box.
2. If necessary, click the E-mail tab.
3. Select your Exchange account in this list (it may be the only entry in the list).
4. Click the Change button to display the Change E-mail Account dialog box.
5. Make sure that the Used Cached Exchange Mode option is selected.

If you change the setting, you will have to exit and then restart Outlook to put the new setting into effect.

Exchange and Other Email Accounts

It is possible to have both an Exchange account and a POP/IMAP email account defined as part of the same Outlook profile. In this situation, both sets of folders will be displayed in the navigation pane. However, some people who have both kinds of accounts prefer to set up a separate Outlook profile for each account, to avoid confusion. Setting up profiles was covered in Chapter 3.

When using Cached Exchange Mode, all folders are kept synchronized. You can also perform a manual synchronization by pressing F9. This is useful when, for example, you want to ensure that your local data is completely up to date. You may want to specify which folders are synchronized when a manual synchronization is performed. For example, you may want to manually synchronize only mail items and let your other folders be synchronized during the automatic updates. To change manual send/receive settings:

1. Select Send/Receive from the Tools menu.

2. Select Send Receive Settings and then select Define Send/Receive Groups. Outlook displays the Send/Receive Groups dialog box, shown in Figure 28.3. (Note: To quickly open this dialog box without using the menus, press Ctrl+Alt+S.)

3. If you have more than one group name, select the one that includes your Exchange account.

FIGURE 28.3

Changing manual send/receive settings for your Exchange account.

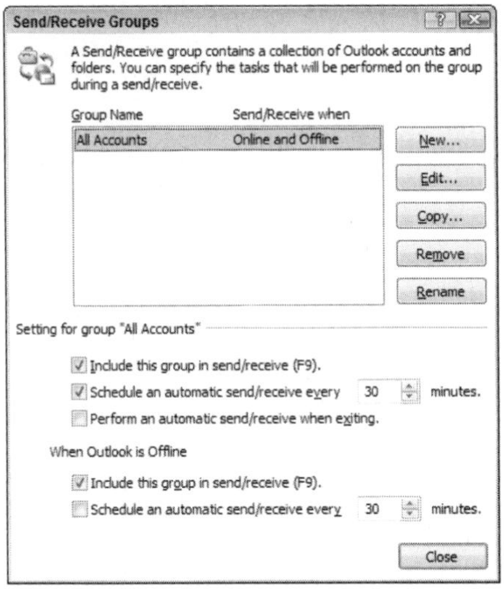

4. Click the Edit button to open the Send/Receive Settings dialog box (see Figure 28.4):

5. In the Accounts list on the left, click your Exchange account.

6. Make sure that the Include the Selected Account in This Group option is selected.

7. In the Folder Options section, select the send/receive options — these are all self-explanatory.

8. In the Account Options section, select which individual folders are synchronized by placing a checkmark in the adjacent box. These are the folders that will be available offline.

NOTE For some types of folders, such as the Inbox, you can use the options on the right (grayed out in the figure) to specify whether headers only or complete items are downloaded. The latter option results in longer synchronization times, but lets you read items immediately.

9. Click OK to return to the Send/Receive Groups dialog box.

10. Click Close.

FIGURE 28.4

Specifying the send/receive details.

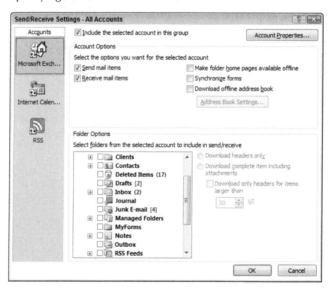

Quick Offline Use

To quickly change whether an individual folder is available offline, select the folder in the navigation pane and then select Tools, Send/Receive, Send/Receive Settings.

Working Offline

In Outlook, *offline* does not mean that a connection to the server is not available. Of course, if this connection is not available you have no choice but to work offline, but you can also work offline when the connection is available.

When you are online, Outlook is connected to your Exchange server. Mail you receive is available immediately, and mail you send is sent immediately. You can also work offline even when the server connection is available, perhaps to avoid connection fees.

If you are using Cached Exchange Mode, as explained in the previous section, Outlook automatically switches between online and offline modes depending on the availability of the server connection. Cached Exchange Mode is recommended because the state of the server connection is essentially transparent to the user. Information about the connection state and the status of synchronized folders is displayed in the status bar, as shown in Figure 28.5.

If you click the arrow next to the connection state, Outlook displays a small popup menu. You can use this menu to manually switch to offline mode and, when in offline mode, to try to reconnect to the server. The other commands on this menu let you control certain aspects of the synchronization process.

FIGURE 28.5

Connection state and folder status are displayed in the status bar.

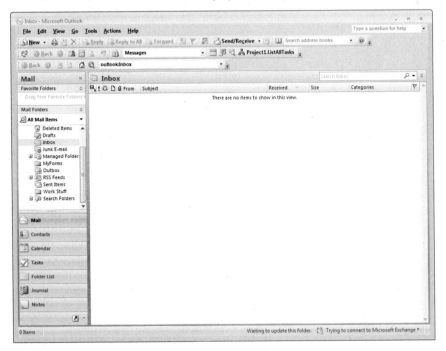

Configuring Outlook for Exchange Server

In Chapter 3, you learned the fundamentals of setting up an Exchange Server account in Outlook. There are some additional settings that relate to how Outlook and Exchange work together. Most users will not need to change these settings, but they are explained here just in case. To access these settings:

1. Select Account Settings from the Tools menu to display the Account Settings dialog box.

2. Make sure that the E-mail tab is displayed.

3. If you have more than one email account, click your Exchange account.

4. Click Change to open the Change E-mail Account Settings dialog box.

5. Click the More Settings button to open the Microsoft Exchange dialog box. This dialog box has several tabs, which are covered in the following sections.

Setting General Properties

The General tab in the Microsoft Exchange dialog box, shown in Figure 28.6, displays these options:

- **Name:** The name Outlook displays for this account.

- **Automatically Detect Connection State:** This option tells Outlook to detect the *connection state* — that is, online or offline — when the program starts and to run in the appropriate mode. Use this setting when you connect to Exchange Server with a network connection always available (for example, a LAN).

- **Manually Control Connection State:** Lets the user control the connection state when the program starts. Use when you are not always connected to the network, such as a dial-up connection or a notebook computer. The following three settings are relevant when you select this option.

  - **Choose the Connection Type When Starting:** Select this option if you want to be able to choose whether Outlook works online or offline each time it starts. If this option is not selected, Outlook automatically makes this determination (this is the default).

  - **Connect with the Network:** Choose this option to connect to Exchange through a network rather than a dial-up connection. This option is appropriate when your computer is connected to an always-on network (LAN or DSL, for example).

  - **Work Offline and Use Dial-Up:** Select this option if you connect to Exchange using dial-up networking.

- **Seconds Until Server Connection Timeout:** This is the amount of time Outlook waits for a connection to Exchange before timing out. If you are using a slow network connection you might want to increase this value.

FIGURE 28.6

Setting general properties for an Exchange Server account.

Setting Advanced Properties

The Advanced tab of the Microsoft Exchange dialog box, shown in Figure 28.7, presents options related to mailboxes, security, and the Offline Folders File.

FIGURE 28.7

Setting advanced properties for an Exchange Server account.

The Mailboxes section of this dialog box lets you add additional mailboxes that will be opened along with your own default mailbox. This may be desirable if you own more than one mailbox on the server or if you have been granted delegate permission (as explained later in this chapter) for one or more other users' mailboxes. To add a mailbox, click the Add button and type in the mailbox name.

The other options on this tab are

- **Use Cached Exchange Mode:** Cached Exchange Mode was explained earlier in this chapter. You can turn this mode on or off here as well as in the Change E-mail Account dialog box as described earlier.

- **Download Shared Folders:** Select this option if you want Outlook to automatically download any shared folders. If this option is not selected, a shared folder will be downloaded only when you open it.

- **Download Public Folder Favorites:** If this option is selected, Outlook will cache any public folders you have added to Favorites under Public Folders. Be aware, however, that this can slow down the synchronization process if these folders contain a lot of items and are very active.

- **Offline Folder File Settings:** Click this button to verify the name and location of your Offline Folders File (although it is rare that you will need to change either of these). You can also compact the file to reduce its size — something that's good to do once in a while.

Setting Security Properties

The Security tab, shown in Figure 28.8, displays these three options:

- **Encrypt Data...:** If this option is selected, data transmitted between Outlook and Exchange is encrypted for greater security with a small speed penalty.

- **Always Prompt for Logon Credentials:** If this option is selected, Outlook will prompt you for your username and password each time it tries to connect to the Exchange server. If other people have access to your computer, you may want to select this option to prevent them from accessing your mailbox.

- **Logon Network Security:** This option specifies the kind of authentication that Outlook uses when connecting to Exchange. There are three options available: You can select NTLM Password Authentication (NTLM stands for Windows NT LAN Manager) and Kerberos Password Authentication to specify that Outlook should use that security model. You can also select Negotiate Authentication (the default), which tells Outlook to use whichever type of security the server is using. You rarely, if ever, need to change this setting.

FIGURE 28.8

Setting security properties for an Exchange Server account.

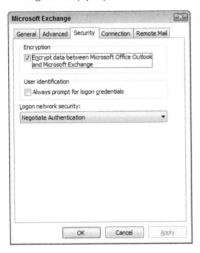

Setting Connection Properties

The Connection tab in the Microsoft Exchange dialog box, shown in Figure 28.9, specifies how Outlook connects to Exchange. The options available here are

- **Connect Using My LAN:** Select this option if your computer is permanently connected to an always-on network, such as a LAN, a cable modem, or DSL.

- **Connect Using My Phone Line:** Select this option to use an existing dial-up connection to connect to the network via your phone line.

- **Connect Using Internet Explorer's or a 3rd Party Dialer:** Select this option if you use a dialer, either Internet Explorer's or another one, to connect.

- **Modem:** The settings in this section are relevant only if you select the Connect Using My Phone Line option. You can choose an existing dial-up connection from the list, modify its properties, or add a new dial-up connection.

- **Connect to Microsoft Exchange Using HTTP:** Set this option as your Exchange administrator or setup guide instructs you. If you select it, use the Exchange Proxy Settings button to enter detailed HTTP settings—these will be provided to you by your Exchange administrator.

Setting Remote Mail Properties

You set Remote Mail properties on the Remote Mail tab (see Figure 28.10). When using Remote Mail, which is explained later in this chapter, you have the option of downloading message headers only without the body or any attachments, which can speed the download process if you have a slow connection. You can review message headers and then download only those you need. The settings are

- **Process Marked Items:** Retrieve only those items that you have marked for download.
- **Retrieve Only Items That Meet the Following Conditions:** Retrieve only those items that meet the filter conditions you define.
- **Filter:** Click this button to define a Remote Mail filter. You can filter based on who messages are from, the subject, the size, the presence of attachments, and various other criteria.

FIGURE 28.9

Setting connection properties for an Exchange Server account.

FIGURE 28.10

Setting Remote Mail properties for an Exchange Server account.

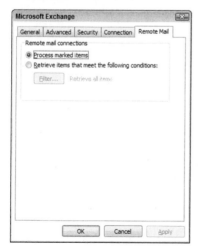

Voting

Exchange Server lets you conduct polls by sending email messages with a question and voting buttons. You can then tally the responses and use the information as needed. The people you send a voting message to must be using Exchange, too. Other people will receive the message but will not have the voting buttons available.

Requesting a Vote

To send a message for people to vote on, create and address the message as usual. On the Options ribbon, click the Use Voting Buttons button and select the kind of buttons you want:

- Approve and Reject buttons
- Yes and No buttons
- Yes, No, and Maybe buttons
- Custom: Opens the Message Options dialog box where you can specify the buttons separated by semicolons. For example, Figure 28.11 shows how to specify Red, Green, and Blue buttons.

When finished, complete and send the message as usual.

FIGURE 28.11

Specifying custom voting buttons.

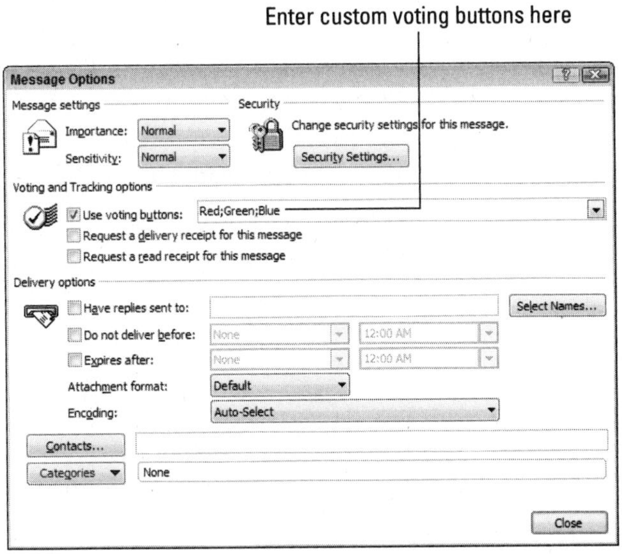

Enter custom voting buttons here

Responding to a Voting Request

When you receive a voting message, you will be prompted to vote by a message in the header and can click the Vote button to select your response (see Figure 28.12). You have the choice of sending the response immediately or editing it first.

FIGURE 28.12

Cast your vote by clicking these buttons.

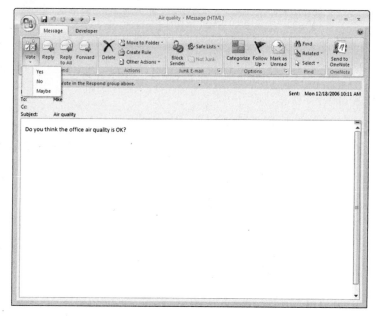

It's possible to vote more than once, but don't bother — if you do, Outlook ignores all but your first vote.

WARNING Think before you vote! Once your vote has been sent you cannot change it.

Tallying the Votes

Replies to voting requests go to the original sender as regular messages that can be opened and read as usual. The vote is displayed in the Info Bar just below the ribbon, as shown in Figure 28.13. Outlook keeps track of all responses, and you can view the results by opening any voting response message, clicking the Info Bar, and selecting View Voting Responses. Outlook displays a list of all the voting messages you sent, the response to each one (or a blank if the response has not been received), and the totals, as shown in Figure 28.14.

FIGURE 28.13

A voting response message displays the vote in the Info Bar.

Voting response

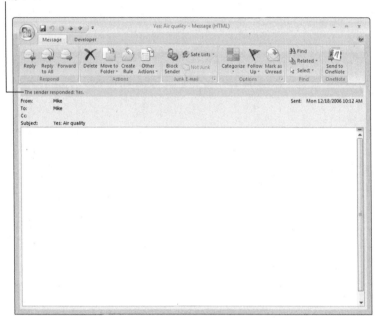

FIGURE 28.14

Viewing a summary of voting responses.

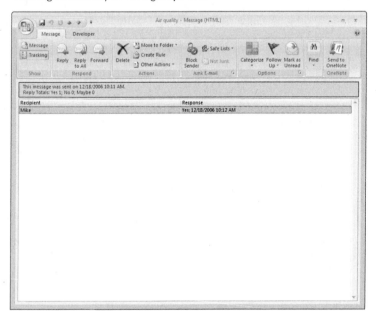

Setting Vote Tracking Options

Outlook has two options that affect the way Outlook deals with voting responses. These options are in the Tracking Options dialog box, shown in Figure 28.15. You access this dialog box as follows:

1. Select Options from the Tools menu to open the Options dialog box.

2. On the Preferences tab, click E-mail Options to open the E-mail Options dialog box.

3. Click the Tracking Options button to open the Tracking Options dialog box.

The two options in this dialog box related to voting are

■ **Process Requests and Responses on Arrival:** If this option is selected, Outlook tallies votes automatically as each response is received. Otherwise, you must explicitly open each response in order for Outlook to tally it.

■ **Delete Blank Voting and Meeting Responses After Processing:** If this option is selected, Outlook automatically deletes voting responses (and meeting responses too) after they are tallied if they have no additional comments added by the responder.

FIGURE 28.15

Setting tracking options related to voting.

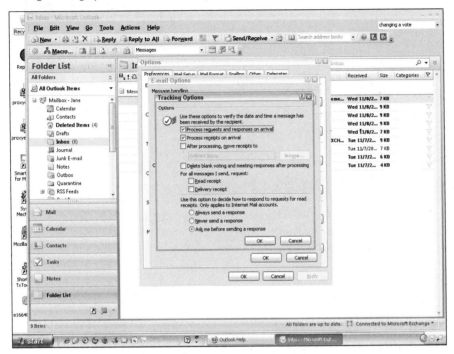

Recalling Sent Messages

Exchange gives you the option of recalling a message you sent to another Exchange user as long as that person has not yet read it. To do so:

1. Open the Sent Items folder.

2. Double-click the message you want to recall to open it.

3. Click Other Actions and select Recall This Message to open the Recall This Message dialog box (see Figure 28.16).

4. Select options as described here:

   ■ **Delete Unread Copies of This Message:** Recall the message without creating a replacement message.

   ■ **Delete Unread Copies of This Message and Replace with a New Message:** Recall the message and open a new message to create a replacement message.

   ■ **Tell Me...:** Select this option if you want to be notified whether or not the recall was successful for each message recipient.

5. Click OK.

FIGURE 28.16

Recalling an unread message.

Using Forms with Exchange

You learned about designing custom Outlook forms in Chapters 26 and 27. As mentioned earlier, Outlook custom forms really come into their own when used with an Exchange server. This is because you can publish a form to Exchange so that it becomes available to all users of the Exchange server.

Publishing a Form

Basically, there are two options for publishing a form:

- Publish it to a forms library where it will be available to all users.
- Publish it to the public folder where it is meant to be used.

After completing the design of your form, publish it as follows:

1. Click the Publish Form button on the ribbon to open the Publish Form As dialog box.
2. Enter a descriptive display name for the form.
3. If desired, change the form name — but usually this is left as the default, which is the same as the display name.
4. Open the Look In list (see Figure 28.17) and select the destination folder for the form.
5. Click Publish.

Using a Form

To use a form, select Forms from the Tools menu and select Choose Form from the next menu. Navigate to the folder containing the form and open it — that's all there is to it.

Keep Unfinished Forms Separate

It's a good idea to keep forms that are in the process of being designed separate from forms that have been completed and tested. You can do this by creating a folder accessible only to you or the members of the form design team and publishing forms not complete to that location. Only when the form has been completely tested should you publish it to a public folder for general use.

FIGURE 28.17

Selecting the folder to publish a form to.

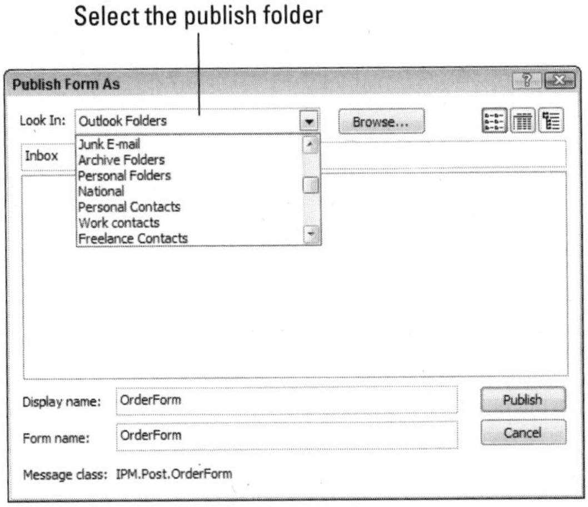

Select the publish folder

Working with Outlook's Group Schedules

A *group schedule* is just what is sounds like — a calendar that shows busy and free time for multiple people. Group schedules can greatly simplify the task of scheduling a meeting for members of a team, to allow a supervisor to get an overview of how employees are spending their time, or to permit a receptionist to locate specific individuals.

Creating a Group Schedule

To create a new group schedule, select View Group Schedules from Outlook's Actions menu. Outlook opens the Group Schedules dialog box, as shown in Figure 28.18. Any existing group schedules are listed here. Then:

1. Click the New button to open the Create New Group Schedule dialog box.

2. Enter a name for the new group schedule and click OK.

3. Outlook opens a blank schedule as shown in Figure 28.19. You can add members in three ways:

   ▪ To enter a name manually, click where it says Click Here to Add a Name, then type in the member's name. The name must be something that Exchange recognizes as a user.

   ▪ To select a member from your address book, click the Add Others button and select Address Book from the menu. Outlook opens a dialog box where you can select from the available address books and then select one or more members.

   ▪ To select a member from a public folder, click the Add Others button and select Public Folder from the menu. Outlook will open a dialog box where you can navigate to the public folder and select members.

4. When all group members have been added, click Save and Close.

FIGURE 28.18

The Group Schedules dialog box.

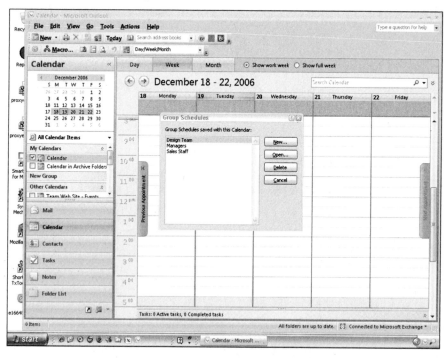

A blank group schedule before any members are added.

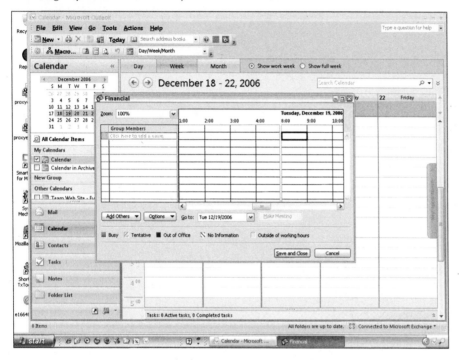

Using Group Schedules

To use a group schedule, select View Group Schedules from Outlook's Actions menu. Outlook opens the Group Schedules dialog box (shown earlier in Figure 28.18). Click the schedule you want to use, then click Open. Outlook displays the schedule with each member's schedule indicated in the row next to his or her name, as shown in Figure 28.20. Blocks of time are marked as one of the following according to the legend at the bottom of the dialog box:

- **Busy:** The member is busy and cannot be scheduled for anything else.

- **Tentative:** The member has tentatively scheduled this block of time, for example if they have an unconfirmed appointment. You can schedule over a tentative block of time and the member will have to decide between the conflicting events.

- **Out of Office:** The member is away from the office and therefore not available.

- **Open:** The member has nothing scheduled. You can schedule over these blocks of time.

- **No Information:** If Exchange has no information about the member's schedule it is marked this way. It might indicate that the member does not use Outlook or that there is a problem with their account.

FIGURE 28.20

A group schedule shows the members' free and busy time.

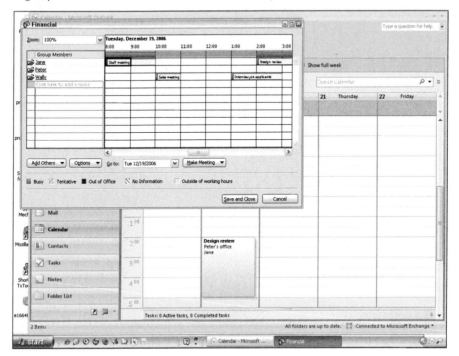

Scheduling Meetings

You can schedule a meeting with individual members of the group or with the entire group. When you schedule a meeting, a meeting request is sent to the attendees, and they can respond by accepting the meeting, tentatively accepting it, or declining.

To schedule a meeting with the entire group:

1. On the schedule, click the block of time when you want to hold the meeting. This step is optional but convenient.
2. Click the Make Meeting button.
3. Select New Meeting with All from the menu. Outlook opens a meeting request form addressed to all group members, as shown in Figure 28.21.
4. Enter the subject and, optionally, a location for the meeting.
5. If necessary, adjust the date and/or time of the meeting.
6. If desired, add a message to the request.
7. Click the Send button.

FIGURE 28.21

Sending a meeting request to all group members.

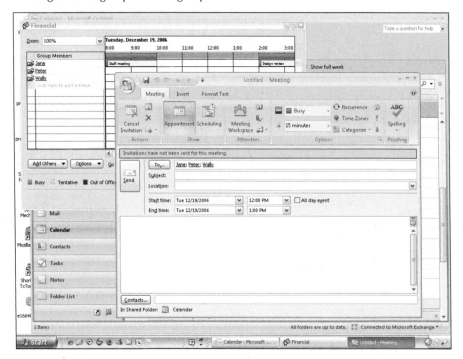

To schedule a meeting with one or more group members:

1. On the schedule, click the block of time when you want to hold the meeting in the row of the person you want to invite.

2. Click the Make Meeting button.

3. Select New Meeting from the menu. Outlook opens a meeting request form addressed to the selected member (this form was shown earlier in Figure 28.21).

4. To invite additional people to the meeting, click the To button and select from your address book.

5. Complete the subject and other elements of the meeting request.

6. Click Send.

Sending Email to Group Members

You can easily send email to the entire group or to single selected members. To do so, click the Make Meeting button and select one of these commands from the menu:

- **New Mail Message:** Creates an email message addressed to the selected group member (select a member by clicking their row in the schedule).
- **New Mail Message with All:** Creates an email message addressed to all group members.

Setting Group Schedule Options

The Options button in the Group Schedule dialog box provides you with the following options:

- **Show Only My Working Hours:** If this option is selected, the group schedule will display only the days and times that you have designated as working hours.
- **Show Calendar Details:** If this option is selected, the group schedule will display the meeting subject for each block of time in which you have scheduled an appointment.
- **AutoPick:** Lets you configure how the AutoPick feature works. AutoPick was covered in Chapter 12.
- **Refresh Free/Busy:** Select this command to update the group schedule with the latest information from the members' calendars. Though the group schedule is updated automatically on a regular basis, selecting this command ensures you can see information that other members may have entered very recently.

Other Group Schedule Actions

There are several other actions that you can take when a group schedule is open:

- To view an individual member's calendar, double-click the small folder icon to the left of the member's name.
- To remove members from the group, right-click their name and select Cut from the popup menu.
- To view information about members, double-click their name.

Delegating Outlook Tasks

When you work in a group — which is usually the case when you are using Outlook with an Exchange server — you may want to let certain other people perform specified tasks for you. For example, you could permit your assistant to access your Inbox to review your received messages before you see them, or you could permit your manager access to your task list to assign you tasks. In Outlook, this process is called *delegation*, and the person to whom you give access to Outlook

Delegation Versus Folder Permissions

In some situations, you may be able to accomplish the desired sharing by granting folder access rather than creating a delegate. What sets a delegate apart is that this person can send items on your behalf including creating and responding to meeting requests. See the section "Granting Folder Access" later in this chapter.

data is a *delegate*. Delegation is done on a per-folder basis and is available with these folders: Calendar, Tasks, Inbox, Contacts, Notes, and Journal. A user who has been granted delegate permissions is sometimes referred to as an *assistant*.

When you use delegation, you can assign one of the following levels of permission to an assistant:

- **None:** This is the default — it does not let the assistant access the folder at all.
- **Reviewer:** This level of permission allows the assistant to read items but not add new items or edit existing items.
- **Author:** This level of permission allows the assistant to read items and add new items but not to edit existing items.
- **Editor:** This level of permission allows the assistant full access to read, create, and edit items.

Creating Delegates

This section shows you how to create a delegate and define his/her permissions:

1. Select Options from the Tools menu to open the Options dialog box.
2. Click the Delegates tab (shown in Figure 28.22). If you have not yet created any delegates, this list will be empty, as shown in the figure.
3. Click Add to open the Add Users dialog box (see Figure 28.23).
4. If necessary, select the desired address book in the Address Book list.
5. Double-click the desired user. You can select more than one user if you want each to have the same delegate permissions.
6. Click OK to open the Delegate Permissions dialog box (see Figure 28.24).
7. For each of the folders listed in this dialog box, use the adjacent list to select the permission that you want the delegate to have: Reviewer, Author, Editor, or None.

8. Select other options as follows:

   - **Delegate Receives Copies...**: If you select this option, the delegate will receive a copy of any meeting-related messages sent to you.

   - **Automatically Send a Message...**: If you select this message, the delegate(s) you define will be sent a message detailing the delegate permissions that they have been granted.

   - **Delegate Can See My Private Items**: If you select this option, the delegate will be able to see items that you have marked as Private.

9. Click OK to complete the process.

FIGURE 28.22

The first step in creating a delegate.

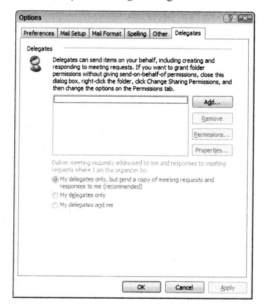

FIGURE 28.23

Selecting users to be given delegate permissions.

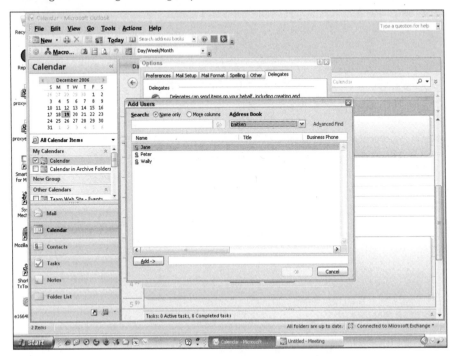

To remove or modify a delegate, display the Delegates tab as just described. Select a delegate in this list and then do one of the following:

- Click Remove to remove the delegate.
- Click Permissions to view and change the delegate's permissions.
- Click Properties to see information about the delegate.

FIGURE 28.24

Specifying permissions for a new delegate.

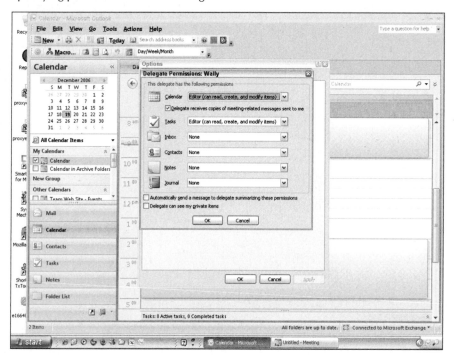

Working as an Assistant

If you have been granted delegate permission to another user's folders, you will be able to open and use them according to the specific permissions you have.

Opening Another User's Folder

To open a folder to which you have been granted permission, follow these steps:

1. Select Open from the File menu, then select Other User's Folder. Outlook displays the Open Other User's Folder dialog box as shown in Figure 28.25.

2. Type the person's name in the Name box or click the Name button to select from a list of users.

3. Select the folder that you want to open from the Folder Type list.

4. Click OK.

At this point one of two things will happen: the folder will open, or Outlook will display an error message if you do not have the required permission to open the folder.

FIGURE 28.25

Opening another user's folder when you have delegate permissions.

Sending Email on Behalf of Another User

If you have been given delegate permission for another user's Inbox, you can send email on behalf of that person:

1. Create a new email message.

2. If necessary, display the From field by clicking the Show From button on the Options ribbon.

3. In the From field, type the name of the person on whose behalf you are sending the message.

4. Compose, address, and send the message as usual.

Scheduling on Behalf of Another User

If you have been given delegate permission for another user's calendar, you can schedule appointments and meetings on behalf of that person. All you need to do is open that person's Calendar folder as described earlier and then create the item as you normally would in your own Calendar folder.

When you send a meeting request on behalf of someone else, the message will appear to the recipient as having come from the calendar owner, not the assistant. When the message is opened, however, the header will reveal that the request was sent by the assistant on behalf of the calendar owner.

Granting Folder Access

Granting other users access to your folders is similar to delegation in some ways. The primary difference is that delegation permits other users to send items on your behalf whereas granting folder access does not. Folder access also provides a finer level of control over what people can and cannot do in individual folders.

To grant another user access to a folder, or to change access rights, right-click the folder and select Change Sharing Permissions from the context menu. Outlook opens the Properties dialog box for that folder with the Permissions tab displayed, as shown in Figure 28.26. Then:

- **To add permissions for a new user:** Click the Add button and select the user from the Add User dialog box.
- **To change permissions for an existing user:** Click that user in the list.

FIGURE 28.26

Defining sharing permissions for a folder.

The lower section of the Permissions tab lists the individual folder access options that you can set (although usually you will not set them individually, as explained later). They are

■ **Read:** Select whether the user can read either full details of items in the folder or none.

■ **Write:** Select whether the user can create items and/or subfolders. Also select whether the user can edit only items he owns (that is, items that person created) or all items in the folder.

■ **Delete Items:** Specify which items the user can delete.

■ **Other:** There are three options here:

    ■ **Folder Owner:** The folder owner has all permissions.

    ■ **Folder Contact:** A folder contact receives automated messages from the folder including requests from users for additional permissions and resolution conflict messages. This is a read-only setting and is set automatically based on other permission settings.

    ■ **Folder Visible:** Users can see the folder (but not necessarily its contents).

Setting Default Folder Permissions

Every folder has default permissions that apply to all users. Normally these are set to None, which means that all users can see the folder but can view or manipulate its contents. If you want to change the default permissions for a folder, display the Permissions tab in the folder's Properties dialog box, click Default in the Name list, and set permissions as desired.

Rather than setting folder permissions individually, you will almost always use one of the predefined permission levels available in the Permission Level list. These are, in order from least to most permission:

- **None:** User can see the folder but not view or manipulate items it contains.

- **Contributor:** User can create new items in the folder but not view or manipulate existing items or create subfolders.

- **Reviewer:** User can view existing items but not create, edit, or delete them or create subfolders.

- **Non-editing Author:** User can create new items and can read all items; he cannot edit or delete any items or create subfolders.

- **Author:** Same as Editing Author with the addition of the ability to edit items he owns.

- **Publishing Author:** Same as Author with the addition of the ability to create subfolders.

- **Editor:** User has all permissions except the ability to create subfolders.

- **Publishing Editor:** User has all permissions but is not the folder owner.

- **Owner:** User has all permissions and is the folder owner.

Using Remote Mail

The *Remote Mail* feature allows you to manage your email messages without downloading them from the Exchange server. You connect to the server and download just the message headers, then disconnect. You can then review the message headers at your leisure and decide which ones you need to download in their entirety. Other messages remain on the server. Remote Mail is particularly useful when using a slow connection or if you receive messages with very large attachments. It is also handy when a corrupted message aborts the normal download process — you can view the corrupted message's header and delete it from the server.

To use Remote Mail, you must be using Outlook with an Offline Folders File.

Remote Mail and Exchange Versions

Exchange Server 2003 and later versions handle Remote Mail somewhat differently than earlier versions. With earlier versions, Remote Mail is available only if you are working offline. When you are online, the related commands are not available. Exchange Server 2003 and later also let you preview the first few lines of a message before downloading the entire thing.

To use Remote Mail, Outlook must be configured so that it does not perform automatic send/receives, which would download all the messages, not just the headers, and would defeat the purpose of Remote Mail. To check this:

1. Select Options from the Tools menu to open the Options dialog box.

2. Click the Mail Setup tab.

3. Click the Send/Receive button to open the Send/Receive Groups dialog box (see Figure 28.27).

4. Uncheck all three of the options related to automatic send/receive.

FIGURE 28.27

Setting automatic send/receive options.

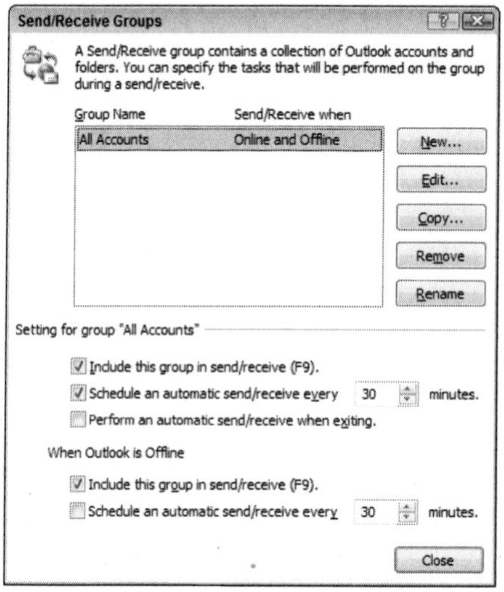

Then, you download headers by opening the desired folder (usually the Inbox) and selecting Send/Receive from the Tools menu and from the next menu selecting Download Headers in This Folder. Once the headers are downloaded, they are displayed in the folder and you can preview each message as shown in Figure 28.28.

Other Remote Mail–related commands are also found on the Send/Receive menu, including marking and unmarking headers and downloading marked messages.

Using Remote Mail on a LAN

When you connect to Exchange using a LAN, Remote Mail does not make a lot of sense because even if you use the Download Headers command to download headers for a folder, the full items will be downloaded automatically shortly thereafter. Of course, with a fast LAN connection there is rarely any reason to use Remote Mail, but there are two ways you can force it.

The first is to put Outlook into offline mode by clicking the connection status indicator at the bottom right of the Outlook window and selecting Work Offline from the menu (see Figure 28.29). When you are finished using Remote Mail, repeat the same steps to unselect Work Offline.

FIGURE 28.28

Previewing a message with Remote Mail.

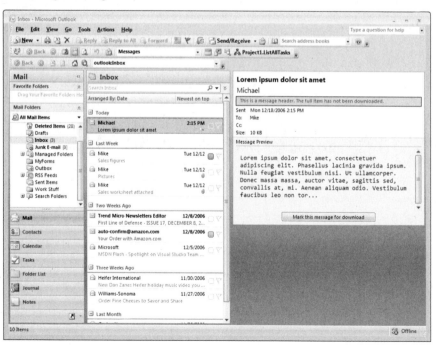

FIGURE 28.29

Working offline when using a LAN to connect to Exchange.

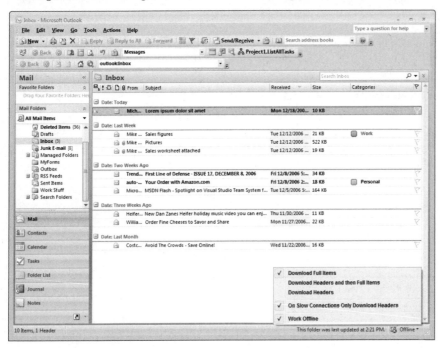

The other approach is to use the same menu shown in Figure 28.29 and select the Download Headers option for how Cached Exchange Mode synchronizes the server with the Offline Folders File. The available options are

- **Download Full Items:** Complete items, including attachments, are synchronized.

- **Download Headers and Then Full Items:** All headers are downloaded after which the full items are downloaded.

- **Download Headers:** Only the message headers are downloaded.

- **On Slow Connections...:** If Outlook detects a slow connection to Exchange, it downloads only headers. On fast connections the selected option is applied.

Summary

The combination of Outlook and Exchange Server provides you with unprecedented power and flexibility when you are working with a group of people. This chapter covered the details of setting up Outlook to work with Exchange and using the various tools available.

Chapter 29

Using Outlook with SharePoint Services

Microsoft SharePoint Services is designed to allow you to share your Microsoft Office information with others. This includes Outlook information as well as documents from Word, Excel, and other Office applications. SharePoint Services is relatively easy to install and use and, as a result, has achieved a good deal of popularity.

This chapter covers the details of using a SharePoint Services installation with Outlook. It does not deal with the other Office applications, and assumes that you have an existing SharePoint Services account — it does not cover installation or administration of SharePoint Services itself.

Understanding SharePoint Services

SharePoint Services, or *SPS*, provides a remote location, or server, that you can access over the Internet. Sometimes people refer to this type of service as a *portal*. It is designed for collaboration and document management within a team. Typically, each team within an organization will have its own SPS portal. When you have access to SPS, you can do a variety of things, such as:

- Share Office documents
- Participate in threaded discussions
- Share lists of important information, such as contacts

SharePoint Portal Server

A closely related product is *SharePoint Portal Server*, which is in essence SharePoint Services on steroids. Whereas SPS is designed for workgroup-level collaboration, SharePoint Portal Server has the power for enterprise-wide collaboration by permitting the creation of multiple SPSs — such as sites for the individual workgroups and departments and then linking them together. If you are using SharePoint Portal Server instead of SPS, many of the concepts and techniques presented in this chapter will still be applicable.

One thing that SPS does not do is email. Though SPS can be configured to send email notification messages to users, it does not act as an email client that lets you receive and send email messages yourself. Note, however, that some service providers bundle standard POP/IMAP or Exchange email accounts with SharePoint Services hosting.

Working with Shared Contacts

One of the features of SPS is the ability to share contacts. SPS can maintain a shared contacts list that lets all team members access those contacts that are needed for the team to operate. This shared contacts list can interact with your Outlook contacts in various useful ways.

Viewing Shared Contacts

To view the shared contacts list on your SPS server, log in to the SPS site using your web browser. On the left, click the Contacts link under Lists, as shown in Figure 29.1. Your browser displays the shared contacts list as shown in Figure 29.2.

SharePoint Services Permissions

When the SPS administrator creates your account, he will give you certain permissions that will determine what you can do on the site. You may be limited to viewing information, or you may have more extensive permissions that allow you to edit and delete items. Some of the actions described in this chapter may not be available to you depending on your permissions level.

FIGURE 29.1

Accessing shared contacts on an SPS site.

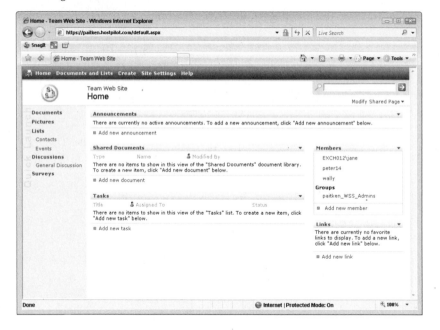

FIGURE 29.2

The shared contacts list.

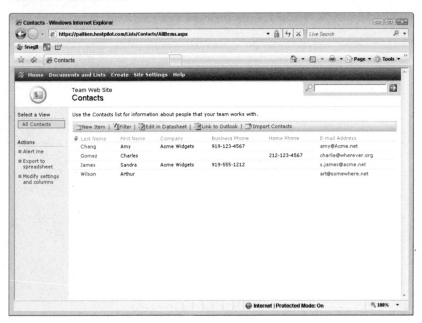

When this list is displayed, you can take the following actions by clicking the buttons at the top of the list:

- **New Item:** Opens a form where you can add a new contact to the list.

- **Filter:** Displays drop-down lists at the top of each column (see Figure 29.3) that let you filter the contacts list to display only certain entries.

- **Edit in Datasheet:** Displays the entire list in a datasheet format where you can edit multiple entries at once.

- **Link to Outlook:** Lets you link the shared contacts list to your local Outlook address book. This is explained in more detail later.

- **Import Contacts:** Lets you import contacts from a local Outlook address book to the shared contacts list.

FIGURE 29.3

Filtering the shared contacts list.

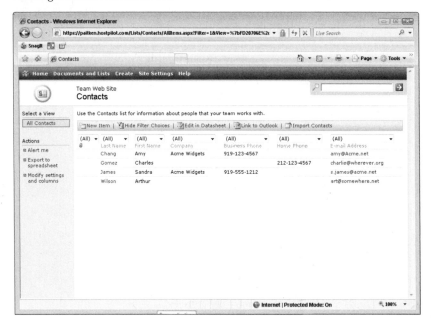

To send an email to a person on the shared contacts list, click the person's email address in the list. A new message form is displayed, addressed to that person. Complete the message and send it as usual.

You can also take the following actions in the shared contacts list by resting the mouse cursor over a contact's last name to display an adjacent down arrow. Click the arrow to select from the following actions (see Figure 29.4):

- **View Item:** View all details for this contact.
- **Edit Item:** Edit this contact's information.
- **Delete Item:** Delete this contact.
- **Export Contact:** Exports the contact's information as a VCF file, which you can then import into your Outlook address book.
- **Alert Me:** Displays the page shown in Figure 29.5 where you can set up an alert that will notify you by email when the item is changed.

Actions available for a contact in the shared contacts list.

Linking the Shared Contacts List to Outlook

If you use the shared contacts list frequently, you may want to have these contacts available in your Outlook address book rather than having to go to the SharePointSPS site each time you need an address from the list. Of course you can export individual contacts to Outlook as described in the previous section, but you may find it easier to link the shared list to your local Outlook address book.

To create the link, click the Link to Outlook button at the top of the shared contacts list. Outlook warns you about linking only to lists from trusted sources. Click Yes to create the link, or click the Advanced button to set advanced linking options (these rarely need to be changed).

Once the link is established, the shared contacts list will be available in Outlook as a separate address book. It is read-only — you have to go to the SharePointSPS site to make new entries or edit existing ones. Changes that are made to the shared list are reflected in your local linked copy.

FIGURE 29.5

Setting up an alert for changes to a shared contact.

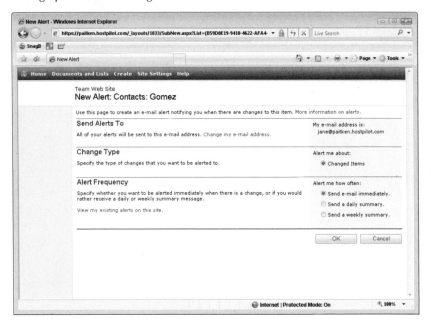

Working with the Shared Calendar

SharePointSPS supports a list called *Events*, which is a calendar used to maintain a schedule of events the entire team needs to know about. You access the Events list by clicking the Events link on the left side of the SharePointSPS home page. The default event display, which is called All Events, is shown in Figure 29.6. It lists all events in order with the title, location (if specified), and start/stop date and time. Two other views can be selected using the links on the left:

- **Calendar:** Displays events on a traditional calendar display that can show a single day, a week, or a month at a time.

- **Current Events:** Displays, in list format, only those events that are in the near future.

FIGURE 29.6

The default Events list display.

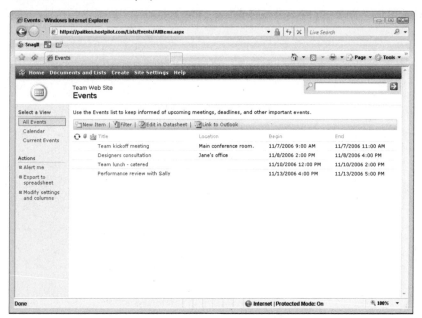

You can take various actions with the Events list by clicking the buttons at the top of the list or the links at the left:

- **New Item:** Adds a new event to the list.
- **Filter:** Defines a filter to display only certain events.
- **Edit in Datasheet:** Displays the list of events in a datasheet where you can edit multiple events at one time.
- **Alert Me:** Lets you define an email alert that will be sent to you when the Events list changes.
- **Export to Spreadsheet:** Exports a Microsoft Excel Web Query file that lets you view the event list in a linked worksheet.
- **Modify Settings and Columns:** Opens a page where you can set options for how the Events list is displayed.

Linking a Shared Calendar to Outlook

If you want to be able to view the shared events calendar without going to the SharePointSPS site, you can link it to Outlook. Then it is available like any other calendar in Outlook, although it is read-only. Changes to the shared Events list are automatically reflected in the local Outlook version.

To create the link, click the Link to Outlook button at the top of the Events list. Outlook warns you about linking only to lists from trusted sources. Click Yes to create the link, or click the Advanced button to set advanced linking options (these rarely need to be changed).

Working with Alerts

You have seen, earlier in this chapter, how you can configure SharePointSPS to send you an email alert whenever a contact or the Events list has changed. You can also configure SharePointSPS to send alerts when other kinds of documents are changed, although this is beyond the scope of this chapter.

Once an alert has been set up on the SharePointSPS site, and you have received at least one alert in Outlook, you can manage alerts from within Outlook. Here are the steps to follow to create a new alert:

1. Open the Inbox or any other mail folder.
2. Select Rules and Alerts from the Tools menu to display the Rules and Alerts dialog box.
3. If necessary, click the Manage Alerts tab (see Figure 29.7).
4. Click the New Alert button to open the New Alert dialog box (see Figure 29.8).
5. Expand the Source Currently Sending Me Alerts branch. You should see the SharePointSPS web site listed there.
6. Click the SharePointSPS web site link to open the SharePointSPS site's New Alert page in your browser (see Figure 29.9).
7. Select the list or document for which to set the alert.
8. Click Next.
9. Specify the type and frequency of the alert.
10. Click OK to complete the alert definition.

FIGURE 29.7

Managing alerts from within Outlook.

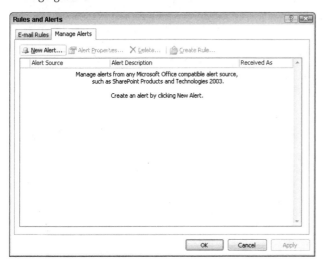

FIGURE 29.8

Selecting the source for a new alert.

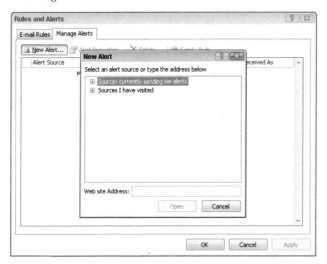

FIGURE 29.9

Defining a new alert.

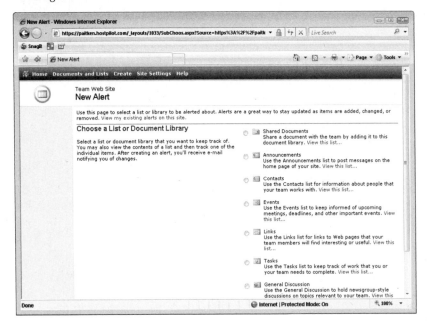

After the alert is completed you can continue working on the SharePointSPS site or close your browser.

You can also modify and delete alerts from within Outlook:

1. Display the Manage Alerts tab as described earlier. This tab lists the alerts you have defined.

2. Click the alert of interest.

3. Click the Delete button to delete the alert. Click the Alert Properties button to go to the SharePointSPS site where you can modify the alert.

Summary

SharePoint Services is an easy-to-use portal that permits members of a team to share documents and other information such as contacts and an events calendar. Some of the SPS features integrate with Outlook, helping you to get the most out of both of these tools.

Index

RSS feed articles as attachments, 308

setting restrictions blocking, 137

free indication for calendar time, 216, 225–226

free-floating toolbars, 25, 26, 363

full menus

defined, 23

opening from short menus, 23, 369, 370

options for, 23–24, 369

recommended to start with, 27

functions. *See also* procedures; *specific functions*

basic syntax, 439

naming, 439

referencing user-created folders, 454–455

Subs versus, 438–439

G

`GetDefaultFolder()` method

for Calendar folder, 462

overview, 452–453

for user-created folders, 454

`GetNamespace()` method, 452

Go To feature, 130

gradients for message background, 94–95

grammar checking. *See* spelling and grammar checking

graphics

adding to messages, 102–110

animations, 103, 369

associating with contacts, 190–191

on business cards, 195

charts, 100, 104–106, 107

clip art, 100, 103

equations, 100, 112–113

horizontal lines, 100

images, 94–95, 102, 190–191, 195

for message background, 94–95

shapes, 101, 106–108

Smart Art diagrams, 100, 104, 105

WordArt, 100, 108–110

Group Schedule feature (Exchange)

creating a group schedule, 535–537

described, 247

group schedule, defined, 535

indications for blocks of time, 537

removing members, 540

scheduling meetings, 538–539

sending messages to group messages, 540

setting options for, 540

using group schedules, 537–540

viewing member information, 540

viewing members' calendars, 540

grouping in views, specifying, 371–372

groups for non-mail folders

creating folders, 334–336, 338

creating new groups, 337–338

overview, 336–337

working with, 338

H

help window

books, 32, 33

opening, 31

search tool, 32–34

table of contents, 32, 33

toolbar buttons, 32

topics, 32

hidden forms, 476

hiding. *See also* collapsing and expanding; turning off

daily task list, 361

displaying hidden files and folders, 328

formatting marks in messages, 79, 84

reading pane, 361

To-Do Bar, 29, 361

toolbars, 363, 366

Toolbox, 484

hierarchical structure for folders, 332–333

highlighting message text in color, 77

holidays, adding to Calendar, 238

home page for personal folders, 346–347, 375–376

horizontal lines, 100

Hotmail email accounts, 38, 50–51, 148

HTML format for email

advantages of, 73, 74

changing the format type, 74–75

converting to plain text, 90

creating messages in, 56

as default, 74, 75

described, 73

Personal Folders file location with, 328

reducing file size, 148

removing all formatting, 90

security concerns, 391

switching display from plain text to, 391

themes and stationery, 56, 88–95

using CSS for fonts, 148

Notes view
  By Category view, 264
  Current View list, 263–265
  defining views for notes, 265
  described, 258
  filtering notes, 261–262
  Large Icons view, 264
  Last Seven Days view, 264
  List view, 259, 260, 264
  Notes List view, 264, 265
  Outlook Data Files view, 264
  removing filters, 261
  Small Icons view, 259, 260, 264
  sorting notes, 260–261
  specifying icons for notes, 262
Nothing keyword, 449
numbered lists for email, 79
numeric variables, 423–424

O

object variables, 427
objects. *See also* adding objects to messages; Outlook
        Object Model; *specific objects*
  defined, 99, 427
  deleting from messages, 101
  Design ribbon for, 101
  filtering by categories, 322–324
  Format ribbon for, 101
  graphic, adding to messages, 108–110
  kinds available for messages, 100
  moving, 101
  organizing by categories, 320–322
  overview, 447
  referencing, 448–449, 450
  resizing, 101
  rotating, 101
  selecting in messages, 101
  setting variable names for, 448
  text, adding to messages, 110–113
  undoing changes to, 102
Office applications. *See* Microsoft Office applications;
        specific applications
Office Online. *See* Microsoft Office Online
Offline Folders Files
  Cached Exchange Mode with, 520–522
  defined, 520

as local copy of server information, 517–518, 520
  manual send/receive settings, 521–522
  overview, 329, 520
  synchronizing folders, 521
  working offline, 523
opening. *See also* collapsing and expanding; running;
        viewing or displaying
  appointment form, 215
  appointments, 211, 216, 221
  Calendar, 208
  email attachments, 70
  email messages, 62
  Events list (SPS), 557
  folders, 339
  full menus from short menus, 23, 369, 370
  help, 31
  Journal entries, options for, 278
  message drafts, 62
  notes, 258
  RSS feed items, 306, 307
  Rules Wizard, 159
  Scheduling window, 246
  tasks, 283
  VBA Editor, 406
operators
  assignment, 430
  comparison, 431
  defined, 430
  logical, 432
  mathematical, 430–431
  parentheses with, 433
  precedence, 432–433
  string, 431
OPML files, 308, 309–310
OptionButtons, adding to forms, 486
organizing. *See also* categories; filtering; sorting
  email by subject, programmatically, 467–472
  email in folders, 64–65, 330–334
  Favorite Folders list, 351
  filtering versus, 322
  items by categories, 320–322
  personal folders files for, 342
OST files. *See* Offline Folders Files
out of office indication for calendar time, 225
Outbox folder, 57, 330
outgoing mail server. *See* mail server

Remote Mail feature (Exchange)
   configuring Outlook for using, 548–549
   described, 547
   Exchange versions with, 548
   setting properties for, 527–528
   using on a LAN, 549–550
removing. *See* deleting or removing
renaming. *See also* naming
   categories, 317, 318
   custom toolbars, 366
   folders, 341, 357
   form pages, 480
   groups for non-mail folders, 338
   personal folders file display name, 346
   quick styles, 88
   RSS feeds, 302, 304
   subscribed Internet calendars, 234
repairing
   email account settings, 52
   Outlook, 18
replacing text in email, 129, 130
replying to messages
   all meeting attendees, 250
   attachments not sent when, 67
   changing send account, 132
   default send account, 131
   form capabilities for, 510–511
   ignoring reply text when spell checking, 121
   options on ribbon for, 67
   preferences for, 144
   responding to meeting invitations, 247–249
   responding to voting request (Exchange), 530
resetting
   custom theme to original settings, 91
   menu and toolbar usage data, 369
   menus to defaults, 368
   toolbars to defaults, 366, 368
   views to default settings, 375
resizing. *See also* collapsing and expanding
   controls on forms, 487, 488–489
   fonts in email messages, 76
   fonts on business cards, 196
   HTML format messages, reducing, 148
   navigation pane, 360
   objects in messages, 101
   reading pane, 360
   screen elements, 30, 359–360

restrictions for email messages, 137–138
ribbons
   defined, 26
   Dialog Box Launchers, 26
   for objects in messages, 101
   overview, 26–27, 28
   viewing hidden items, 26
rich text format. *See* RTF
right-pointing arrows after menu commands, 22
rotating objects in messages, 101
RSS (Really Simple Syndication)
   accounts for feeds, 300, 302–303
   aggregators, 300
   AutoPreview for feeds, 305–306
   backing up settings, 310
   changing feed settings, 308
   common feed list, 311
   defined, 299
   deleting feeds, 308
   displaying feeds, 303–308
   downloading articles, 302, 306–307
   downloading enclosures, 302
   email folders for feeds, 329
   exporting feeds, 308–310
   finding URLs for feeds, 300–301
   folders for feeds, 302
   forwarding articles, 308
   importing feeds, 308–309, 310–311
   new feature for, 16
   opening items, 306, 307
   options for feeds, 302–303
   overview, 10, 11, 299
   renaming feeds, 302, 304
   sharing feeds with other Outlook users, 308
   sorting feeds, 305
   subscribing to feeds, 300–303
   syndication, defined, 299
   update limit for feeds, 302
   uses for, 299
RSS Feeds folder, 330
RTF (rich text format)
   advantages and disadvantages of, 73, 74
   changing default format to, 75
   changing the format type, 74–75
   converting for Internet mail accounts, 148
   converting to plain text, 90
   creating messages in, 56

W

The books you
read to succeed.

**Get the most out of the latest software and leading-edge technologies
with a Wiley Bible—your one-stop reference.**

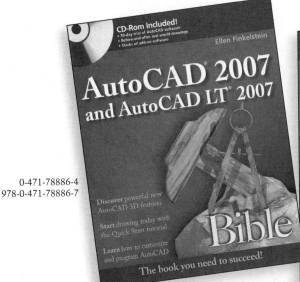

0-471-78886-4
978-0-471-78886-7

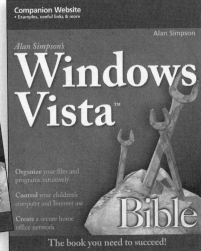

0-470-04030-0
978-0-470-04030-0

0-7645-4256-7
978-0-7645-4256-5

0-470-10089-3
978-0-470-10089-9

Office heaven.

Get the first and last word on Microsoft® Office 2007 with our comprehensive Bibles and expert authors. These are the books you need to succeed!

978-0-470-04691-3

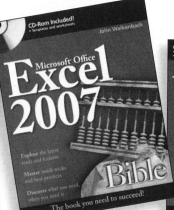

978-0-470-04403-2

978-0-470-04689-0

978-0-470-04368-4

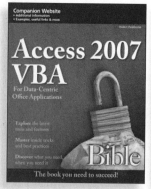

978-0-470-04702-6

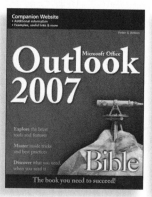

978-0-470-04645-6

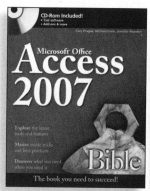

978-0-470-04673-9

978-0-470-00861-4

WILEY
Now you know.

Available wherever books are sold

Wireless

ALL-IN-ONE

FOR

DUMMIES®

2ND EDITION

Wireless
ALL-IN-ONE
FOR
DUMMIES®
2ND EDITION

**Sean Walberg, Loyd Case,
Joel Durham, Jr.
and
Derek Torres**

WILEY

Wiley Publishing, Inc.

Wireless All-in-One For Dummies,® 2nd Edition

Published by
Wiley Publishing, Inc.
10475 Crosspoint Boulevard
Indianapolis, IN 46256

www.wiley.com

Copyright © 2010 by Wiley Publishing, Inc., Indianapolis, Indiana

Published by Wiley Publishing, Inc., Indianapolis, Indiana

Published simultaneously in Canada

For general information on our other products and services or to obtain technical support, please contact our Customer Care Department within the U.S. at (877) 762-2974, outside the U.S. at (317) 572-3993 or fax (317) 572-4002.

Library of Congress Control Number: 2009939356

ISBN: 978-0-470-49013-6

Manufactured in the United States of America

10 9 8 7 6 5 4 3 2 1

Wiley also publishes its books in a variety of electronic formats. Some content that appears in print may not be available in electronic books.

WILEY

Dedication

To Rebecca, my wonderful and supportive wife — Sean Walberg

To Pablo, Victor-Emmanuel, and Anne-Claire — Derek Torres

I dedicate my portion of this book to Matt Firme — Joel Durham

About the Authors

Sean Walberg has been a network engineer for nine years. He's been in the information technology field since 1994 and has worked on development, technical support, systems administration, and network engineering.

When not working, you can find Sean playing with his three energetic sons or in the kitchen cooking.

You can find Sean's contact information and links to other writing at http://seanwalberg.com.

Derek Torres is an author and technical communicator. He has extensive experience working for software companies in the United States and in Europe. He has authored or coauthored several books on Windows operating systems and, most recently, BusinessObjects XI Release 2 For Dummies. He is currently based in Paris, France.

Joel Durham is passionate for all things technological. Whether it's a multimillion transistor integrated circuit or a really cool mouse, Joel has a deep desire to check it out. This personality trait at various times delights, amuses, and sometimes even infuriates Joel's wife and two children, with whom he lives in upstate New York. Joel worked on this particular book for the simple reason that wires infuriate him. The battle to clear out and ultimately eliminate the nests of thin, black, metal-wrapped-in-rubber snakes behind the desks and tables in Joel's house has become a top priority. The mice that drive the cursors of Joel's computers are wireless, as are the keyboards. Joel's PDA and MP3 players sync sans cables. If he could, Joel would also get rid of video, audio, and even power wires—but that last one appears to be a long way from becoming reality.

Loyd Case is a technology writer and analyst covering PC platform, graphics, digital media and gaming technologies. He's written extensively for a wide array of publications, including Maximum PC, PC Magazine, PC World and others. He began writing for Computer Gaming World back in the 1990s, when no one wrote about technology for gamers. When not working, you can find him playing board games, PC games or behind the viewfinder of his digital SLR. Loyd is married, with two daughters.

Publisher's Acknowledgments

We're proud of this book; please send us your comments through our Dummies Online Registration Form located at www.dummies.com. Some of the people who helped bring this book to market include the following:

Acquisitions, Editorial, and Media Development

Senior Acquisitions Editor: Stephanie McComb

Project Editor: Beth Taylor

Technical Editor: Jason Cross

Copy Editor: Beth Taylor

Editorial Director: Robyn Siesky

Editorial Manager: Cricket Krengel

Business Manager: Amy Knies

Senior Marketing Manager: Sandy Smith

Cartoons: Rich Tennant, (www.the5thwave.com)

Production

Project Coordinator: Katherine Crocker

Layout and Graphics: Joyce Haughey, Melissa K. Jester

Proofreaders: Melissa Cossell, Christine Sabooni

Indexer: BMI Indexing & Proofreading Services

Wiley Publishing Technology Publishing Group

Richard Swadley, Vice President and Executive Group Publisher

Bob Ipsen, Vice President and Group Publisher

Joseph Wikert, Vice President and Publisher

Barry Pruett, Vice President and Publisher

Mary Bednarek, Editorial Director

Mary C. Corder, Editorial Director

Andy Cummings, Editorial Director

Wiley Publishing Manufacturing

Ivor Parker, Vice President, Manufacturing

Wiley Publishing Marketing:

John Helmus, Assistant Vice President, Director of Marketing

Wiley Publishing Composition for Branded Press

Debbie Stailey, Composition Director

Wiley Publishing Sales

Michael Violano, Vice President, International Sales and Sub Rights

Contents at a Glance

Table of Contents

Introduction

Istill remember when I got my first cordless phone. Suddenly, I didn't
have to run to the kitchen when the phone rang, I just carried the phone
with me. I could make a phone call from wherever I was. Wireless meant
freedom, and this is just a phone that I'm talking about!

Wireless technology can make your life easier, and it's not just limited to
saving you from getting up to answer the phone. You can free up space on
your desk with a wireless keyboard and mouse, and you can even move
your laptop around the house and stay on the Internet with a wireless network. You can be productive wherever you want to now.

Cellular technology is another area of wireless growth. A phone that once
had to be carried over your shoulder now fits on your belt and offers a
video camera, location tracking, and Internet access. With Bluetooth, you
can have a wireless headset, which eliminates a lot of embarrassing fum-
bling when a call comes in.

Most types of devices have embraced wireless functionality in some form
or another, and given how convenient it is to get rid of wires, you should be
looking to do so whenever possible.

This book covers the whole spectrum of personal wireless technology,
from your computer to your cell phone, and even your home entertainment
system. There's not much we can do about those pesky power cords, but
that's what batteries are for! Read on and find out all the ways your life can
get easier by using wireless.

About This Book

Wireless All-In-One Desk Reference For Dummies is all about wireless technologies. It covers just about everything, from networking to digital TV
broadcasting to cell phones.

If that sounds like a hodgepodge for one book, think again. The book is separated into topic specific minibooks, each written by an author who is an
expert in the field.

With this book in hand, you can do all kinds of cool things:

+ Choose the right wireless networking hardware

+ Install and configure a wireless network in your home or small office

+ Troubleshoot your networking hardware

✦ Configure printers so you can use them across your network

✦ Plug security leaks and keep them plugged

✦ Connect your laptop computer to wireless networks while on the road, as well as keep it constantly supplied with power

✦ Connect and synchronize smartphones and handheld devices with wireless networks

✦ Purchase, configure, and use a BlackBerry e-mail device

✦ Choose and use cellular telephones

✦ Use media servers to play your music and view photos on your home entertainment center

✦ Set up your own weather station

✦ Use GPS technology for things like finding your way home and locating cemeteries for genealogy research

The first time a technical phrase is used in the book, it is italicized, so look out for that.

System Requirements

For the sections about wireless networking, we assume you are running Windows XP or Windows Vista (or perhaps you're an early adopter to Windows 7) on your computer. Earlier versions of Windows don't let you connect to a wireless network with the ease of later editions of Windows, so we recommend upgrading to one of these three Windows versions before setting up your network.

We don't cover Mac OS X or Linux in this book. It's not because they aren't wonderful operating systems conducive to wireless networking. Instead, whole books are devoted to both operating systems and wireless networking, so I focus on what most people are running these days. Whatever your view on monopolies, Microsoft still dominates the market.

Not everything in this book is about Windows-based computers. You find chapters on new third-generation smartphones and other handheld devices — and even an entire minibook on GPS. Obviously, you need some of that equipment to get the most from those chapters.

What You Don't Have to Read

Actually, you don't have to read anything if you don't want to. It's a free country. But I bet you didn't pay to not read this book. Assume you want to read everything that's precisely on topic and not a sentence more.

That's okay. You can skip two types of information without losing the big picture:

◆ Information marked by a Technical Stuff icon, which I discuss a little later in this introduction. This information appeals to your inner geek, but it's not absolutely necessary reading.

◆ Sidebars. These bits and bytes are off the beaten path. They're interesting (I hope!), but not essential.

Still, these two groups of information make up a small portion of the book. Reading them won't consume that much time. Plus, you will make me happy for having read them. (This book contains a hidden wireless transmitter that reports back to me what you have and have not read, so don't think I don't know.)

How This Book Is Organized

Wireless All-In-One Desk Reference For Dummies contains eight minibooks, each of which focuses on a general wireless topic. We wrote in a way that lets you easily find the topic you want to read about, skipping the others for the time being. For example, one minibook focuses on wireless networking, while another contains information about cell phones and other wireless technologies. When feasible, we've kept an entire minibook about one topic, such as networking or GPS. This is what the eight minibooks contain.

Book 1: Pulling the Plugs

I tell you about all the ways to cut your cords and live in a wireless world. Wireless technology has an advantage to its wired counterpart in that you can move anywhere and stay in touch. There's the rub: You're always in touch. Do you really want that? I also talk about some wireless Internet access technologies and how to choose one.

Book II: Planning Your Network

The nitty-gritty starts here, with talk of hardware such as routers and adapters. If and when you're ready to network wirelessly in your jammies, from the safety of your own den, you should take a crack at these chapters. Or at least take a peek. Already there and wrestling with some of your products? Hardware troubleshooting advice to the rescue.

Book III: Configuring Networks

First, I start off with the basics — you've got to crawl before you can walk, so what better place to start than by explaining Windows' wireless networking capabilities. That would, of course, include a look at an old Windows favorite called plug and play technology. From there, we'll learn how to use some of the more advanced networking features, especially Windows Vista's new Network and Sharing Center. We'll also lean how to manage your wireless networks both at home and on the road. Did we forget to mention that we'll cover other important features, such as creating a bridge between wired and wireless networks, as well as how to share a printer? Finally, we'll help you make sure that your network is busy doing its thing.

Book IV: Security and Troubleshooting

This brief but power-packed minibook makes you aware of the dark side of wireless computing and lets you know what you can do to best protect yourself. You can begin by getting a grip on the accounts that are available on your home network, and those instructions are here. These troubleshooting ideas are another way I help you keep your system running smoothly.

Book V: On the Road Again — But Without Wires

This book covers a wide variety of wireless technologies. It starts innocuously enough with your laptop, but moves on to handheld devices. It also covers how to strike the right balance when using your laptop on the road, so that you can take advantage of wireless technology while still thinking about battery life. You'll also learn how to synchronize your wireless devices — both laptops and handheld devices, such as mobile phones and PDAs. Speaking of wireless handheld devices, we'll also take a look at smartphones running Windows Mobile and check in on our old friend, the BlackBerry, and see how it is doing as it is rivaled by high-end mobile phones, including the iPhone. Finally, we'll take a look at how to stay connected on the road, using both hotspots in public places or using a wireless broadband card, which allows you to connect securely from just about anywhere on the planet.

Oh, before we forget, we'll take a look at another cool gadget called the Slingbox. This relatively new gadget allows you to watch your television or DVD player from anywhere in the world — provided that you've got a high-speed connection and your host has the proper Sling Media equipment installed.

Book VI: Other Networking Technologies

Starting with cell phones, this book discusses selecting a service plan and choosing a phone. It also talks about some other important issues, like health concerns and number portability. A second chapter talks about a similar topic: cordless phones. Which cordless phone technology should you choose? The technologies of both cellular and cordless telephony are evolving, and they're getting better all the time.

Another wireless technology, but one that gets less attention, is the Family Radio Service (FRS). With two or more FRS radios, you can stay in contact with people within a mile or so of each other while on vacation and elsewhere. This book also covers the heavily popular short-range networking technology called Bluetooth and the wider range and infinitely useful Wi-Fi technology. Finally, I go through some wireless peripherals you may want to include on your desk to help get rid of that snake's nest of cords behind your computer.

Book VII: Wireless Home Technology

Wireless in the home means a broad array of gear oriented toward entertainment and leisure activities. We'll show you what it takes to start streaming video and audio that lives on your PC to your living room entertainment center. If all you care about is getting your music where you want it in your house, we show you how to do that, using products like Logitech's Squeezeebox or the Sonos ZonePlayer.

If you want to see HDTV you've recorded on your PC, we show you how to do that as well, using media center extenders and even game consoles.

In today's Web-oriented world, though, you're not limited to media that lives on your local PC. There's a wealth of video and music content available through streaming services on a wide array of Web sites. Watching or listening on your PC is easy, but we show you the hard stuff: watching Web-based TV and listening to Web radio in your living room. We say "hard," but it's easier than you think.

Wireless technology has even invaded that seemingly nondigital technology, reading books. Amazon's new Kindle eBook readers are connected to Amazon.com's online service wirelessly, allowing you to buy an electronic version of a bestseller and be reading it minutes later on your Kindle 2 or Kindle DX — no PC needed.

So while wireless is great for on the go portability and for business, it's also terrific for improving your home entertainment experience. So kick back, get some tunes on, and fire up your eBook reader.

Book VIII: The Global Positioning System

The global positioning system (GPS) is the U.S. government's gift to all of humankind. It's a series of geosynchronous satellites that tell wireless GPS receivers exactly where they are at all times — and exactly how to get where they are going! Read about the technology behind it and how you can use it, but be sure to check out my tips regarding what to look for and what options to think about when you choose a GPS unit. After that, I describe some common GPS terminology that helps you in your quest, whatever it may be. Finally, you discover a couple of ways to use GPS technology that go beyond simple navigation, including an amazing and growing game called geocaching.

Icons

I point out some issues or topics to you with the use of icons.

A tip is a helpful bit of information that hopefully helps you accomplish a specific task a little easier. By flagging tips with icons, you can quickly find nuggets of helpful information.

Everyone needs a reminder now and then about something that's already been mentioned. That's where the Remember icon comes into play. Sometimes, the icon indicates something that's common sense or that you already know, but I point it out just in case.

Whoa, Betsy! You should know some important things, and I point out these with a Warning icon. Heed these or proceed at your own risk. I keep these to a minimum so that when you see one, you know it really is important.

Are you a geek? There's nothing wrong with that, as geeks now rule the world. If you see a Technical Stuff icon, it's likely the content is something you'll enjoy reading because of its technical bent. Geeks aren't dummies, but Dummies books are for geeks, too. Even if you're not a geek, it can't hurt to discover something new.

Where to Go from Here

Scissors ready? The next step is to begin cutting the wires that constrain your lifestyle. Instead, embrace radio waves and all things wireless! (Don't actually embrace them, as that effort is futile. They also can fry you; just look inside your microwave oven while it's running. But you know what I mean.) Lie upon the psychiatrist's sofa, as it were, and reject your old, constrained, wired life. Free those demons.

See you in the wireless world!

Book I
Pulling the Plugs

The 5th Wave   By Rich Tennant

"Frankly, the idea of an entirely wireless future
scares me to death."

Contents at a Glance

Chapter 1: Living Without Wires

*P*repare to do away with wires. Technology is terrific, but until recently the term has also been synonymous with *snakes* nests of cables under every table, counter, and desk in the whole darn house. No longer must this be the case.

This chapter introduces you to the ways of wireless. Wires have all kinds of downsides and few positives, and we take a look at the good parts of removing as many cords, cables, and technological tethers as you possibly can and still have your gizmos function the way they should. I cover wireless broadband, clearing cable clutter from beneath your household surfaces, and always knowing exactly where you are with a GPS device. Moreover, I talk about keeping connected to the world while on the go and the wonderful world of Wi-Fi.

There are downsides to living wirelessly, and you can glance at them, too. Wireless stuff is usually "always on," and that can be a hindrance. Find out why, and much more, in this introductory chapter.

Bidding Adieu to Wired Life

When you think about it, wires can be a real hassle. They limit your ability to move freely and to place things where you want them. A very good example of this is the ordinary everyday telephone. If you use a wired telephone, you have to sit at your desk or stand next to the wall phone to have a conversation. If the doorbell rings, you have to tell the person on the other end of the line to hold on while you go see who's at the door. If you're using a cordless phone or a cell phone, you can simply continue your conversation while you walk to the door.

A whole world of wireless possibilities

Now multiply the convenience provided by your wireless phone to include the whole multitude of gadgets that fill your home. Just imagine how these additional examples might apply to your situation:

✦ You're stuck with a slow dial-up connection to the Internet. Broadband is tempting, however, even if you're out of range of your phone company for a DSL connection or cable and fiber connections are unavailable. Consider a satellite connection. Even though the latency of such a hookup is worse than that with the aforementioned broadband solutions, you can still download big files, stream rich multimedia content, and perform other bandwidth-intensive tasks far more efficiently than you could with dial-up.

✦ You're pretty much solo at your computer. By adding a wireless network to your home, you can share files, printers, your Internet connection, music you've downloaded, and multiplayer games without the hassle of running wires. If you want to move a PC from one place to another, you can do it and not worry whether a handy network outlet is nearby. Why, you can even take your wireless laptop out into the backyard and surf the Internet in a lawn chair under your favorite tree.

✦ You're stuck at home waiting on messages and phone calls. With a wireless PDA, you are within reach of e-mail at your favorite coffee shop — you don't have to worry about missing that important message from a potential new client. You may even listen to an Internet radio station, so you don't have to listen to the rants from a fanatical talk radio show host. Figure 1-1 shows an example of a text message using a Pocket PC. Book V talks more about PDAs.

Figure 1-1:
My wireless
Pocket PC
can send
and receive
messages
with the
built-in
messaging
application.

✦ You're sans cell phone. It's hard to imagine another device that can help you keep in touch nearly as well as a cell phone. With it, you can quickly check to see what someone's scribbled notes on your shopping list really mean. Don't take a chance that what looks like sour cream in someone's poor handwriting is actually whipping cream!

✦ You're sick of the wiry clutter at your desk. Cutting the wires to your keyboard, mouse, printer, and other devices sounds like a sure way to kill your computer, but wireless peripherals are simply so much more convenient than their wired counterparts — especially if your desk is such a mess that you haven't seen the top of it in years. You can use a proprietary wireless standard, Bluetooth devices, or even the forthcoming WUSB (wireless universal serial bus) to connect peripherals without wires.

✦ You're a home entertainment technology junkie. Now, you can set up one computer to hold all of your music from your CDs or from Internet downloads, and play that music on your home entertainment system without putting an ugly PC in the living room and without running another tangled mess of wires.

✦ You love radio but hate commercials, and the terrestrial stations don't play the type of songs or talk shows you enjoy. With satellite radio, the choices are much more numerous, and many shows are commercial-free!

✦ Your family vacations seem more like battles over who can or cannot read a map. You're going to love how GPS technology can keep you from ever having to ask directions again. Figure 1-2 shows my GPS receiver as it determines my exact position.

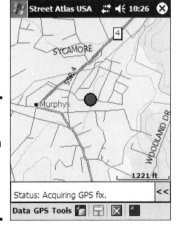

Figure 1-2:
With a GPS receiver you never have to wonder where you are.

I guess if that list doesn't have you thinking about the possibilities for a wireless life, nothing will — but even this list only scratches the surface.

Cutting the cords

Now that you've seen some of the ways that you can go wireless, what's next? Actually, that depends. You probably have to do some shopping, either to replace existing wired equipment or to add wireless equipment. In either case, it helps to plan ahead because so many different types of wireless equipment exist, and you want to make sure the things you buy work together. That's where this book helps.

Consider the example of the wireless home computer network. As you discover in Book III, home computer networks adhere to several different standards, and it's important to make sure that all the equipment you buy for your home computer network works with the same standard. As you discover in Book VII, the type of equipment you choose for your home computer network can have a great impact on how useful your network is in supplying entertainment options.

When buying wireless equipment, go for the highest performance you can afford. That way you won't close off your future options because the equipment you bought can't handle the demands of the need to process more data. Also, you can postpone the inevitable need to upgrade your equipment in the future.

Keeping your options open

Once you get the wireless bug, it can be awfully tempting to want to get rid of every cord. As tempting as that may be, just remember that you probably want to keep your options open. You might, for example, want to make sure that you have at least one wired phone in your home because cordless phones typically won't work if there is a power failure — unlike wired phones, which generally don't need a separate power supply. (Even though the handset on a cordless telephone runs off rechargeable batteries, the base station that it uses to connect to the phone line must be plugged into a power outlet to function.) Of course, if you have a digital cable phone system, all bets are off; the cable system needs power to supply phone service whether or not your phones are corded.

Remember, too, that just because some of your old, existing equipment is wired doesn't mean that it no longer serves any purpose. Sure, you probably prefer the convenience of playing music through your home entertainment system, which is connected to your computer, but that won't do you much good if you want to listen to some old, vinyl records. (I've never seen a PC with a built-in turntable.)

Don't forget to stock up on batteries when you go wireless. While some wireless devices come with built-in rechargeable batteries, others don't. Some wireless devices run through batteries at an amazing rate; consider buying a battery charger and rechargeable batteries for your devices. They're expensive at first, but they certainly save money in the long run. You may want to check out iGo (www.igo.com) or Batteries.com to find just the battery you need.

Connecting to the World on the Go

Wireless devices really do open up a whole new world for you, and not just when you're at home, either. Sure, it's pretty obvious that a cell phone enables you to connect to the world when you're on the go, but other wireless devices offer plenty of on-the-go options, too.

Connecting your PC on the go

To successfully communicate with someone, you generally have to both be using the same language. It doesn't really matter what language that happens to be, as long as you both understand it.

Likewise, computers need to use a common language to communicate. Modern wireless home networking equipment uses one of several standardized methods of communication that were developed to enable different brands of computers and networking equipment to successfully interact. You may have heard of these standards — especially if you've tried wading into the sometimes confusing world of wireless networking. These standards go by names like 802.11n, 802.11b, 802.11g, and 802.11a, but they also are known by the slightly less precise Wi-Fi label.

Even though the Wi-Fi label is applied to all four wireless networking standards doesn't mean those standards are identical. Of the four, 802.11b is the slowest but also the least expensive when you're buying hardware. 802.11g and 802.11a are rated for similar speeds (about five times as fast as 802.11b) but are incompatible with each other because they operate on different radio frequencies. 802.11b and 802.11g are generally compatible with each other, but can only communicate at the slower 802.11b speed. Just how fast are these different standards? That's impossible to say because your results vary greatly, depending on dozens of factors (which you discover in Books II and III). Then, of course, there's 802.11n, the newest and fastest standard, which is still emerging as this book is being written.

What does all of this have to do with connecting your PC on the go? Wi-Fi isn't limited to use on home networks. Wi-Fi is also for wireless office networks and is becoming widely available in other places, too. Want some Internet along with your coffee? Every Starbucks coffee shop now offers customers a Wi-Fi connection. (This type of connection is often called a hotspot.) If you'd rather have a Big Mac and fries while you surf, head on over to McDonald's — most of their stores have free Wi-Fi connections, too. Look for hotspots in airports, book shops, and lots of other places as well.

Head on over to the Wi-Fi-FreeSpot Directory (www.wififreespot.com) to find free high-speed Internet access hotspots.

Wi-Fi hotspots generally have a very limited range. In most cases you need to be within the building to get a reliable connection (and some hotspots are specifically designed to limit the range so that you can only connect if you're inside, where you are expected to be patronizing the store). Even those hotspots specifically set up to cover a broader area typically only spread their signal a few hundred feet from the hotspot's antenna, though, so Wi-Fi isn't a good option if you can't settle in one place close to the hotspot.

What can you do if you want a wireless Internet connection but aren't always within range of a Wi-Fi hotspot? One option is an AirCard from Sierra Wireless (www.sierrawireless.com). The AirCard comes in several models — each one designed for a specific type of service. Some models connect via the Sprint PCS Network, some with the AT&T Wireless Network, and some with other flavors of cellular service, too. Generally you should do your homework, choose the service plan that's right for you, and then buy the AirCard that works with that service. Sometimes cellular service providers even offer special pricing on the AirCard because they know that once you're hooked, you're probably going to spend a lot of money on your monthly service plan.

Connecting for voice and messages

Even though most people think of computers when they think about connecting on the go, sometimes a PC is overkill. Sometimes all you need is simply the ability to send and receive text messages. A couple of different types of wireless devices easily handle this duty:

✦ Wireless PDAs, including some models of the Palm and the Pocket PC, can easily send and receive text messages.

✦ The BlackBerry is a wireless device specifically designed for various types of electronic messaging, including e-mail and instant text messaging. It has a small, but serviceable keyboard for entering messages.

✦ Most cell phones now support short messaging service (SMS) so you can send and receive text messages. Apple's iPhone is a very popular PDA/smartphone.

You read more about connecting on the go in Book V.

Addressing the Downside: You're Always On

If the wireless world has one big problem, it's that always being connected means that people can contact you at any time. Sure, it's convenient to flip open your cell phone to quickly ask someone a question, but don't forget that it is just as convenient for someone to dial your cell phone number and interrupt whatever you're doing.

But once again, you shouldn't limit your concerns simply to the fact that anyone can call your cell phone at any time — that is, unless you're on vacation and you're trying to get away from it all!

Your wireless network is always on

Wireless home networks are awfully convenient because you can simply fire up your PC anywhere within range and connect. This convenience has its dark side, too. As long as your wireless network is working, a neighbor or a stranger driving by can conveniently try to connect to your home network. Remember, the fact that your wireless network doesn't require someone to connect using a physical network cable means it's much easier for someone you don't want on your network to gain access.

You can, of course, apply some security measures to make it harder for people to break into your wireless home network. In fact, it's not only possible, but it's also essential that you enable your wireless network's security features if you don't want to run into serious problems. See Book IV for more information on this very important topic.

Your wireless gadgets are probably open, too

Imagine how difficult it would be to keep your automobile safe if the manufacturers were in the habit of delivering cars without locks because they felt that locks were too complicated for the average driver. In most major cities you'd probably be able to measure in minutes (or hours, at the most) the time before your car was stolen.

Unfortunately, the manufacturers of many wireless devices do something similar to building cars without locks. Rather than building in advanced security features (or, as is the case with wireless home networking gear, leaving the security features turned off by default), manufacturers often opt for dumbing down their products so they work as soon as you take them out of the box. Bluetooth-equipped cell phones present an easy target for snoopers for this reason. (See Book VI for more information on Bluetooth technology and the security risks that are involved.)

In reality, the manufacturers probably are correct; so few people bother to read the technical sections of their product manuals that enabling features that increase security would result in many calls for help from new users. Or, even worse from the manufacturer's perspective, it could result in products being returned to the stores because "it doesn't work."

You can go a long way toward protecting your wireless world by taking a few minutes to understand (and use) whatever security measures are offered by your wireless devices. Remember, the harder you make it for a thief or a snoop, the more likely he'll move on and find an easier target. Even the simplest security measures often deter thieves unless they're specifically looking to get at your data. Thieves looking to score any data, or leech any Internet connection, typically skip the security-enabled devices and continue on their way.

Taking back control

Yes, going wireless does make life more convenient, and often a lot more fun, too. Keeping things in perspective is important, as well as making sure that the convenience isn't overshadowed by letting the wireless devices control your life, rather than the other way around. You do have the ultimate weapon if you're willing to use it, and that's the on/off switch.

Chapter 2: Choosing Internet Access

In This Chapter

✔ Using satellites for Internet access

✔ Microwaving without food

✔ Maximizing access with WiMax

You probably connect to the Internet using DSL or cable modem service, both of which deliver data over fat broadband connections, meaning they feature fairly wide bandwidth and allow data to download fairly quickly. (If you're going online via a dial-up connection, I hope you're considering switching to broadband access before venturing much farther into this book. Speedier broadband access is practically required for connecting to the Internet nowadays, if you don't want to spend your life in front of your computer, waiting for Web pages to load and programs to download.)

But what if you live in an area that doesn't have either DSL or cable modem broadband service? What's a computer user to do? (Thank goodness you at least have access to Dummies books!) If you live someplace where the local telecommunications providers haven't gotten around to offering broadband service, or if you live too far out of range of them to be able to offer you a high-bandwidth pipe, you can always turn to at least one other option.

In many cases this option is satellite Internet access. In some areas, you might be able to subscribe to something called fixed wireless, which means the company broadcasts a signal directly to your home (and you back to them). Both of these options can be expensive, but they are options.

In even fewer areas, entire cities or city centers are covered by Wi-Fi access, a topic I also talk about in Book V, Chapter 5.

I cover another wireless Internet technology that uses the cellular telephone network elsewhere in the book. You can find information about cellular-based packet data networks in Book VI, Chapter 1. In addition, some cellular carriers have launched so-called 3G (third-generation) networks that provide mobile data services, and 4G is on the way. I cover this in Book VI, Chapter 1, too.

Using Satellite Service

Just like satellite TV services deliver television programming directly to your home, satellite Internet providers provide you with broadband access that you can use to do anything you would do on the Internet over DSL and cable modem services.

Satellite service is great for folks who are off the beaten path (or don't even have a path nearby). The service might also be an alternative if you simply dislike your current DSL or cable modem provider, but beware some downsides:

- ✦ You need a clear view to the south, as that's where the satellite is in geosynchronous orbit — right over the equator.

- ✦ Bad weather can slow or cut off your Internet access, just like heavy rain and snow tend to disrupt satellite TV service.

- ✦ Trees that grow in your satellite path are not your friends. And as I learned the hard way, don't set up service in winter, when the trees have no leaves. As soon as spring comes, those leaves will grow back and obstruct your once-great, clear view to the south.

- ✦ Expect more latency than you experience with a typical cable, DSL, or fiber broadband connection. It takes time for the signal to get from the satellite to a receiver/transmitter dish, and a similar amount of time for the signal to get from the dish to the satellite. Thus, some time-sensitive Internet activities such as gaming and VOIP (voice over internet protocol) don't work well with a satellite connection.

StarBand by Spacenet

StarBand by Spacenet satellite service is available throughout the entire United States (yes, even Alaska and Hawaii), Puerto Rico, and the U.S. Virgin Islands. It's a two-way, always-on broadband service similar to DSL and cable modem service. It works with PC and Mac, Linux, and Unix, although tech support only provides help with Windows 2000 Professional, Windows XP Home, and Windows XP Professional and Mac OS X — that's according to the FAQ on the company's page.

Traveling with connections

StarBand evidently used to have a service that let you mount a satellite antenna on your RV so you could stay connected no matter where you traveled in the United States. Now, according to the FAQ on the Web site, that's not possible. The antenna both transmits and receives information to and from the satellite, and such a connection requires too precise an installation to allow travel.

Fair use policies

Both StarBand and HughesNet employ something they call fair use or fair access policies. In a nutshell, the policies may limit how much bandwidth you can consume in a given time period. They're designed to keep a small number of users from monopolizing the services.

StarBand "reserves the right, and will take necessary steps, to prevent improper or excessive consumption of bandwidth used," according to its fair access policy. It does, however, relax the policy during the wee hours of the morning. As for HughesNet, it too relaxes its fair access policy in the middle of the night. "Currently, you can use your HughesNet service for several hours during the middle of the night (the "Download Period") with relaxed application of the Fair Access Policy. The hours of unrestricted use shall begin no later than 2:00 AM and end no earlier than 7:00 AM eastern time."

Monthly service fees start at $69.99 for Nova 1000, a tier with download speeds up to 1 Mbps and upload speeds up to 128 Kbps. A one-time equipment fee includes the satellite dish and satellite modem, and that costs $299.99. An installation fee also applies, as StarBand requires that a professional install the equipment. Self-installation is not allowed.

A second tier of service, called Nova 1500, offers download speeds up to 1.5 Mbps and upload speeds up to 256 Kbps, and it starts at a monthly rate of $99.99 (plus equipment and installation charges).

HughesNet

HughesNet, formerly DirectWay, which itself was formerly called DirecPC, offers a satellite Internet service very similar to StarBand's. For its home package, it advertises up to 1.0 Mpbs for download and 128 Kbps for upload.

The service provider also limits to 22 the number of concurrent Internet connections. Unlikely a problem for simple Web surfing, but once you have a Web browser, e-mail program, music download software, and other Internet applications working all at the same time, the 22 connections begin to want for more.

HughesNet has many pricing plans, offering Home, Pro, ProPlus, Elite, and more, each of which has different tiers of bandwidth both upstream and down. Furthermore, you can choose whether to purchase or lease the necessary equipment. The sheer number of possibilities makes it impossible to list all the prices you might pay for HughesNet service, but expect to pay between $99 and $299 upfront for equipment and $59 to $349 monthly for bandwidth.

Maxing Out with WiMax

A lot of people in the wireless arena are asking, "Whatever happened to WiMax?" WiMaxstands for world interoperability for microwave access. It's a broadband wireless service that has the capability to provide service for people who get around.

One firm predicted that by 2009, more than 7 million subscribers worldwide would be using the fixed version of WiMax (not including mobile uses). What's so great about WiMax is that it's like having ubiquitous Wi-Fi access. Whether you're in your home, in your backyard, or in your car, you would have constant Internet access. Somehow, WiMax didn't jump into the center of the arena like many people thought it would.

WiMax had, and still has, the possibility of providing fast Internet access throughout a metropolitan area (unlike a local multipoint distribution system, which I describe next). Think about cell phones and how they continue to work as you move around. You don't have to turn off your cell phone when you leave your house and then turn it on again when you get in your car, so why should you have to do that with wireless Internet access? If WiMax ever makes the kind of splash that pundits once predicted, you won't need to do that.

WiMax requires new access adapters in desktop and laptop computers because it's incompatible with Wi-Fi technology. While it's been slow to catch on, there are a few WiMax devices on the market — it will be interesting to see if they take off or simply fizzle out.

Book II
Planning Your Network

The 5th Wave   By Rich Tennant

"That's it! We're getting a wireless network for the house."

Contents at a Glance

Chapter 1: Getting Started

In This Chapter

✓ **Figuring out your needs**

✓ **Surveying your wireless network**

✓ **Understanding radios**

✓ **Making a shopping list**

*J*ust five years ago, wireless networking was expensive and difficult to set up. Fortunately advances in technology have lowered costs and increased features, resulting in something that's both affordable and easy to set up. In fact, it's hard to ignore wireless networking now because it's everywhere!

Wireless networking has many benefits, including:

✦ **Mobility:** If you can drag your computer somewhere, you can get on your network from there. You don't even have to shut it down! Take your computer from the kitchen to the bedroom without having to close your work or tell your chat buddy "BRB" (that's "be right back" for those who were wondering).

✦ **Fewer cables:** Technically, there's only one less cable, but I've found that the network and power cables are the most bothersome. Now all you have to worry about is power, and I'm sure you've got more power outlets than network drops in your house.

✦ **Expandability:** Adding a computer to a wireless network takes a few mouse clicks. Adding a computer to a wired network often takes a drill and a lot of cable. Plus, you have to make sure you've got enough network ports. Guess which is faster to get up and running?

This chapter gets you started building your own wireless network. First, you need to determine what it is that you want to get out of your wireless network. Next, you find out how wireless networks work, and apply this to finding any potential trouble spots in your house. Finally, we get you ready to go shopping!

Figuring Out What You Want to Do

Before you even think about how to build your wireless network, take some time to figure out what you want to do with it. Hey, maybe you don't even need wireless. Would this be a bad time to mention your bookstore's "no refunds" policy?

When it comes down to it, networks connect people. You might connect to gain access to a service such as e-mail or the Web, or you might connect to share some files between two computers. Wired or wireless, a network's value is in the connections it provides.

You can do pretty much anything on a wireless network that you can on a wired network. Your requirements affect the kind of equipment you need, so it's important that you think about what you want to do before you open your wallet.

Think about which of the following you'd like to be able to do:

✦ **Access the Internet.** The Internet's a big place, and to see it you have to connect your network somehow.

✦ **Share files.** Do you have more than one computer in your home? Do you want to be able to get files between the two? Or maybe you're looking for a separate device to store files on, and you need to connect to that. Are these small files, large files, or huge files? Even though USB key fobs are cheap, you can't beat the convenience of being able to copy files by the drag-and-drop method.

✦ **Watch video.** Services are available that let you watch video over the Internet. You may also have a device that will let you watch TV over your home network. Either way, video introduces some demands that not every piece of wireless equipment can accommodate.

✦ **Play video games.** If you're a gamer, then you know how network conditions can affect your game. You can't control much on the Internet, but you can make sure that your network's not the problem.

✦ **Print.** Printers are coming with wireless capabilities now, so you can put your printer wherever you want, or move it whenever you need.

Give some thought to devices you have that may already be wireless capable. They may need an upgrade, or alter your plans slightly, depending on their age. You don't want that old PC you got from your aunt dragging down the speed of your network if you can avoid it.

Finally, think about where in your house you want to use your computer and wireless peripherals. We get into the details about range shortly, but a wireless solution for a living room will be different for a 30-room mansion, especially if you also need Internet access down in the guest mansion. What's that? Your guest mansion's empty? When can I move in?

Going the Distance

Just like your favorite radio station, the radio waves from your wireless network can't travel forever. And even if they could, your computer doesn't have the power to talk back.

Unlike your favorite radio station, the distances involved are much smaller. A radio station's coverage is measured in miles; your network is measured in feet.

Why, you ask? Isn't all radio the same? Not by a long shot! A radio station's power output is around 100,000 watts; your wireless devices are under a tenth of a watt. Frequency plays a part in it, too — higher frequencies travel shorter distances. Your wireless network's frequencies are at least 20 times as high as your radio's.

The wireless engineers at the IEEE are constantly updating their standards to give you faster speeds and better distance. (Incidentally, IEEE used to stand for Institute of Electrical and Electronics Engineers, but taking a page from a famous fried chicken chain, they have rebranded themselves just as IEEE, which is pronounced "Eye-triple-E") These standards are supposed to ensure that if you buy two products from two different vendors, they can work together.

IEEE standards for wireless have a name starting with 802.11 and ending with a letter. Each letter is a different standard that may or may not be interoperable with other standards. We talk about the standards in the next chapter, but just so you have an idea, here are some of the ranges of the various standards.

Table 1-1 shows ranges you can expect in a typical indoor environment. Note the use of the word typical. Depending on your hardware, your environment, and where you place your devices, you may see better or worse distances.

Table 1-1:	Comparing Wireless Radio Ranges
Standard	*Typical Indoor Range*
802.11a	100 feet
802.11b	150 feet
802.11g	150 feet
802.11n (draft)	300 feet

It's Wireless, Not Magic!

In the previous section, you learned that your wireless network has a limited range, and that it's hard to place a finger on what that range will be. In this section, you find out what kind of things cause problems with wireless signals.

A simple wireless network consists of a central radio, called an *access point,* that connects to a wireless transmitter/receiver in your computer, game console, or portable device. The access point is responsible for everything on the wireless network, so it's important that your equipment and the access point have no problems communicating.

Wireless isn't magic. It's a radio wave. Radio waves follow the laws of physics, some of which have the end result of damaging radio signals to the point where they can't be decoded. A signal that can't be decoded is useless to all involved; the result is a slow (or nonexistent) network.

In general, wireless problems fall into two categories: interference from other radio waves, and interference from physical objects.

Interference from other radio waves

Whatever country you're from, your government likely regulates which wireless frequencies can be used, by issuing licenses to people for certain parts (bands) of the radio waves. The governments do this in part to make sure that multiple people don't try to use the same frequency and step all over each other. (They also do it because they get large sums of money out of the deal.) Have you ever played with remote control cars when two people pick up a transmitter with the same frequency? Oh, what fun that is, when the single car tries to respond to two sets of commands.

Wireless network devices operate in unlicensed bands. Unlicensed bands are free for anyone to use as long as they abide by the rules the government set out. These rules, for one, limit the power output of a device so that your transmitter doesn't interfere with your whole block.

Anything transmitting in the ranges that wireless radios use (2.4 GHz and 5 GHz) is a potential source of interference. Other wireless networking devices can cause problems. This is why the IEEE specified several channels within the 2.4 GHz and 5 GHz bands. These channels are on slightly different frequencies so that two devices can coexist. We go over a lot more information about adjusting your channels later in this chapter, but for now, remember that having two access points on the same channel is a bad thing.

Microwave ovens emit interference in the 2.4 GHz range, which as you now know is the same as what your computer's trying to use. Playing with your access point's channels is not going to do much here, because microwave ovens interfere with all of them.

Your best bet for dealing with microwave ovens is to get them as far away from your computer and access point as possible. For example, I've got my microwave oven in one corner of the house and my access point on the opposite corner on a different level. This arrangement usually works unless I'm trying to use my computer in the kitchen with the microwave on.

Another source of interference is from cordless phones. Phones generally come in 900 MHz models, and, you guessed it, 2.4 GHz. Cordless phones bounce around from frequency to frequency to try to avoid interference. You'll probably find that the wireless network causes you more problems while talking on the phone than the other way around, though. However, if you're having periodic network problems and can't pin a cause on it, you might want to check and see if someone's talking on a cordless phone at the time.

Interference from other items

Radio waves can be interrupted in flight by almost any solid object. Walls, doors, furniture, and even glass can degrade your wireless signal.

Walls are likely to be your biggest concern. In general, the bigger and thicker the wall, the worse it's going to make the signal. Simple drywall walls may not cause a problem, but brick or stone walls, or metal (such as a concrete wall reinforced with rebar), are going to cause problems.

If your house has several levels, then try to determine what kind of material is between the floors. In a house, it's usually wood, which is only a mild barrier to radio waves.

The easiest approach to dealing with interference is to place your access point as close as possible to the places you want to use wireless. If you find some dead areas, you can try moving your access point. In the worst case, you buy a second access point or a repeater to give service to the dead zone. It's a lot cheaper than knocking down walls, after all.

Radio engineers have also found other problems caused by walls and furniture that have to do with the way radio waves bounce off of things. The 802.11n standard has features to deal with these.

Preparing to Shop

When wireless standards were first introduced, the cost of wireless was obscene. Access points ran in the thousands of dollars and were marketed to big companies with buckets of cash. Unsurprisingly, the technology was much slower and difficult to manage.

The technology life cycle

If you've followed any area of technology, you'll know that stuff keeps on getting better. Cameras get smaller, computers get faster, and televisions get bigger. You might expect that you'd have more options and be able to choose how fast you want your computer to be, but that is rarely the case.

When making parts for electronics devices, it's in the manufacturer's best interest to make as few versions as possible. Over the past couple of decades, Intel has made chips for computers that run from 4 MHz to over 3 GHz. Digital cameras started out well under a megapixel but have now blown past 12 megapixels. USB memory keys started out at megabyte, and now they're replacing your hard drive. But try to go to a store and find the full array of products? Not going to happen.

Part of it is that people are buying the higher end gear, but it's also that it costs more to make the old stuff. Chip-making machines have already been retooled for the newest chips. The chips to make a computer's wired network card run at the original 10 megabits per second cost a lot more than the ones that let them run 100 times faster.

At the same time, manufacturers shoot for certain price points. In the 1980s, a new computer cost around $2,000. The next model was faster and had more space, but it still cost around $2,000. Once the old model was sold out, it wasn't being made anymore.

This $2,000 price point carried on for a while. Then the introduction of the Internet drove demand for computers up, and advances in manufacturing (and the increased demand) drove the manufacturer's cost down. Now that $2,000 price point is much closer to $400.

The same goes with cellular phones. The price of phones has stayed the same, but you just get more features. Phones now have cameras and built-in MP3 players and can play video games. It's hard to find a basic cell phone now. The demand is low, and it's getting so cheap to add the phone or MP3 player that it makes more economic sense to not offer the bare-bones version.

Every so often something disruptive comes to a product that makes the current technology less desirable. Plasma and LCD televisions made older tube televisions cheap, for a while, as manufacturers tried to get rid of their parts inventory and to make a profit off their soon-to-be obsolete technology while they could. When a new wireless standard is on the horizon, the current technology drops in price. The popularity of wireless made the price of wired network equipment take a nosedive as manufacturers tried to keep the sales coming in.

Now, competition in consumer-grade computer equipment has driven down prices, and advances in manufacturing have allowed engineers to do more with less.

Prices in consumer electronics tend to follow an interesting pattern. First, the cost is high as a new technology is introduced. As the technology gains ground, the price drops as competition enters the market. This should not be a surprise.

However, as the technology matures, the cost stays within the same range; you just tend to get something that's smaller, faster, or more feature rich than the device that came out the month before. Instead of staying on the market, older equipment just goes away as it gets replaced. Prices fall only after something really innovative happens, usually because the manufacturers want you to stay with that technology instead of the new thing.

Within the price range of a particular technology, you find that the latest and greatest model costs the most. If you want to save a fair bit of money, you can get something with 90 percent of the features and speed of the device that happened to be new just a little while ago. You can also go really cheap and get a knock-off device made by a company you've never heard of. Each has their advantages and disadvantages.

All that said, the next section has a list of the types of equipment you'll be looking at, along with the expected price range.

Putting Together Your Shopping List

Here's where you get familiar with the types of equipment you might need and devise the list of what you need.

✦ A wireless access point connects your wireless network to your wired network. The access point's job is to manage the wireless network and relay messages between the wireless and wired devices. An access point costs between $50 and $150, depending on the technology.

✦ A wireless router is really a few devices in one box. It's a firewall that connects your network to the Internet and provides some network services and safety along the way. We go over these features later. The router also has a built-in access point. Optionally, the router can have a few wired network ports.

Wireless routers, like the one in Figure 1-1, go for $50 and up, depending on what extra features are on them and how fast they go. Most quality routers are in the $100 range, though. A wireless router can also be used only as an access point by plugging it in a certain way and not configuring all the features.

✦ A wireless range extender (shown in Figure 1-2) is used to boost a wireless signal for areas where the signal is weak. These, too, are like access points (some can double as an access point). As long as the extender can receive the signal well, it can rebroadcast at a higher power to extend the range. You should be able to find range extenders for $50–$100.

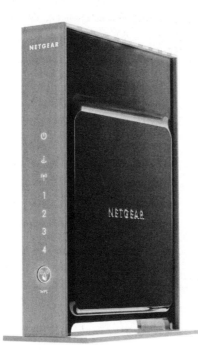

Figure 1-1:
A wireless
router.

Figure 1-2:
A wireless
range
extender.

+ On the computer side of things is the wireless NIC. For laptops that don't have wireless built in, you need a notebook adapter, sometimes called a PC card for your computer. These devices cost from $50 to $150, depending on features and the standards the card supports. Figure 1-3 shows such an adapter.

Book II
Chapter 1

Getting Started

Figure 1-3:
PC card
adapter.

+ If you are upgrading a desktop machine, you have a couple of options. You may buy either a PCI card that goes inside the computer or a USB-based one that plugs into a free USB slot. Note in Figure 1-4 that the PCI-based card has an external antenna, which is helpful in obtaining the best signal, especially if your desktop is in a tight spot.

Figure 1-4:
PCI wireless
adapter with
external
antenna.

Nothing says you can't use a USB adapter with a laptop. You'll find the PC card is probably more convenient because part of the card is inside your computer.

Wireless cards for PCs cost about the same as their laptop counterparts, though you may pay slightly more for the benefits of an external antenna.

To get your shopping list started, you'll want an access point or a router, plus a wireless card for each device you want to get on the network. Take stock of your existing computers; they may already have a wireless NIC built in.

Don't pull out your wallet just yet. We've yet to get into the various options you have underneath the wireless umbrella. There are different radio standards, frequencies, antennas, and routers . . . I'm getting excited just thinking about the possibilities!

Chapter 2: Choosing Hardware

*B*rowse the aisles of your favorite electronics store, and you will find a dizzying number of equipment choices at all price levels. You've got to choose between the various 802.11 standards, whether you need a router or an access point, which brand to buy, and which optional features you want. Did you need wired ports? So many choices, what do you do?

In this chapter, you find out what hardware you need to get on the Internet and to build your wireless network. After you read this chapter, you can confidently make a purchase. You'll also want to make sure your Internet connection is up to par. You are likely to have a few Internet access options available to you, so you'll want to make sure you know what each option offers.

The information in this chapter can help you form the foundation of your wireless network, so the best place to start is where the Internet meets your house.

Exploring Your Options: DSL or Cable

If you watch television for a while, you can see lots of ads for Internet access. Several companies are vying for your business, and they're all offering something slightly different. How do you cut through this noise and buy the right product for you?

Before you get much further on the topic, though, your decision might already be made for you. Maybe you're in a location where you've only got one option. Maybe you already have something. In that case, feel free to skip this section, or read on if you're interested.

Look at the flyers that come in your mailbox or newspaper. Look at your telephone and cable bills. Chances are you're being offered a choice between digital subscriber line (DSL) and cable. Usually both options are called "High Speed Internet," or some flavor of that. But read the fine print, it's probably one of those. If it comes from the phone company, it's DSL. If it comes from the cable company, it's cable.

Depending on where you live, you might be offered a satellite service, or even a fiber-based service. You also should have the option of dial-up. So many options! My head is spinning!

All other things being equal, your decision comes down to comparing speed and cost. How fast do you need your Internet to be, and how much do you want to spend?

Sharing the road

Even though the term *information superhighway* died a merciful death many years back, it's sometimes helpful to think of the Internet as a road system.

When you browse the Web, or receive e-mail, your computer sends information in the form of *packets* to the other end, which can be a Web server or an e-mail system. The other end looks at these packets and sends the response back to you in a new series of packets. These streams of packets are often called *traffic*.

It might help to think of these packets as cars on a road. Your Internet connection is a small road that can carry so many cars. This road connects to bigger roads that eventually lead to superhighways that are many lanes wide. Depending on who you're trying to talk to, they may be located right off the highway in the case of a busy Web site, or they may be on a road much like yours in the case of a small Web site or home user.

Just like cars on a road, Internet traffic sometimes gets congested if too many cars try to use the road. Only so many cars can fit on a single lane, which means information takes longer to get between the two sides.

Dealing with DSL

DSL is an Internet service that is delivered over your regular phone line. The frequencies that make up voice fall within a small range, so a DSL modem throws the Internet signals into the space that's left. At the phone company, these Internet signals are pulled out by a device called a DSLAM (what it means isn't important, but it's one of the coolest acronyms in the networking field).

The Internet goes on the higher frequencies, which means every phone jack in your house needs a filter placed on it so that you don't hear the noise generated by the high frequencies, and your phone doesn't affect the quality of the data transmissions.

You can choose from a wide variety of DSL, and only your Internet service provider knows which ones are being used. You can find that you usually get the appropriate DSL modem provided as part of the service, so don't worry

too much about buying one of your own. However, do make sure this is
the case if you are looking at DSL. You then plug your network into the DSL
modem.

The advantages of DSL are that you have a dedicated connection between
your computer and the service provider, rather than sharing it with your
neighbors. However, your Internet traffic eventually merges with your neighbors in the provider's high-speed core, anyway. DSL offers good speeds,
and because it's delivered over your phone line, you can usually get a price
break by bundling your DSL and phone service.

DSL is usually offered in different grades, such as 1 Mbps down and 384K up.
This means you can download files at 1 million bits per second, or roughly a
compact disc's worth of files in an hour and a half. The upstream speed isn't
as important because the bulk of your Internet usage is downloading. Having
1 Mbps down is adequate for Web browsing, but having 3–5 Mbps is more
desirable. (It goes up from there, so if you plan on downloading a lot of files,
then look at higher plans.)

Book II
Chapter 2

Choosing Hardware

Contemplating cable

Cable-based Internet uses some TV channels for sending and receiving the
Internet signals. A cable modem plugs into your TV jack, you plug your network into the cable modem, and you're off to the races.

Cable is a shared medium, so the connection between you and the service
provider is shared, usually with your neighborhood. Cable is capable of
higher speeds than DSL, so this tends to even out.

Like DSL, you require a modem (but not a DSL modem). The usual practice
of cable companies seems to be to charge a rental fee for the modem or to
allow you to buy your own. Cable modems tend to follow only one standard
called DOCSIS, so finding a compatible cable modem is easier. If you want to
go down this road, ask your cable company for a list of supported modems
and follow it to the letter!

Cable, too, is often sold in various grades. These grades are likely to be faster
than DSL, but remember, you are sharing your connection. Usually the basic
package is good enough to get you started, and you can easily upgrade later.

Don't forget to ask about bundling opportunities if you're a cable subscriber.

Debating dial-up

I only mention dial-up in here to tell you to avoid it. It's slow. It doesn't cost
much less than a basic high-speed DSL or cable package. You can't use your
phone when you're on the Internet because your computer is using it, which
defeats the purpose of wireless. Did I mention it's slow?

Just remember that both DSL and dial-up are delivered over the same phone service. Dial-up requires you to use a modem in your computer to make a call to another modem at your provider, while DSL injects the Internet signals on top of your voice calls (which you don't notice). DSL is good, dial-up is bad.

Oh, yeah, and dial-up is slow.

Exploring FIOS or FTTH options

Depending on where you live, you might have the option of getting fiber optic cable delivered to your home. You might see it called FIOS (Fiber Optic Service) or FTTH (Fiber to the Home). Pronouncing the two might get messy, though.

Fiber optic cable can deliver a lot of speed. It's reliable, too. This extra speed will cost from "slightly more than cable" to "a lot more than cable," depending on how fast you want to go. But, if the option is available to you, it's worth looking at. You will be able to get speeds much faster than cable or DSL. Depending on the provider of the fiber, you may be able to get better entertainment offerings, such as high-definition television and video on demand over the same fiber.

Going over the Letters

Getting set up with Internet access (if you don't have it already) takes a few days, which gives you time to think about the kind of wireless network you want.

The eggheads . . . I mean engineers . . . at the IEEE have been improving wireless standards to make them faster and more reliable. The IEEE 802.11 standards describe how wireless signals are transmitted and decided and in traditional geeky fashion have names such as 802.11a, 802.11b, and so forth. Over 20 standards exist in the 802.11 family, although consumer products only advertise support for a handful of them.

The Original — 802.11

The first one didn't have a letter after it, but it provided 1 or 2 megabit service at 2.4 GHz. It worked, but given the state of industry in 1997, it was expensive and bulky. They were the size of a shoebox!

The other standards out there are amendments to 802.11.

Improving on things — 802.11a and b

Despite coming out at nearly the same time, 802.11a and 802.11b are very different. The 802.11b improves on the original standard by giving up to 11 megabits over the same 2.4 GHz frequency. This increase in speed drove adoption of 802.11b networks, which pushed manufacturers to build smaller and cheaper devices.

802.11a on the other hand runs at 54 megabits per second, and at the 5 GHz frequency. You get a lot of noise at 2.4 GHz, so the IEEE thought it best to get out of that band. There's also more room up there, which means you can have more radios operating in the same area without stepping on each other. The downside is a slightly decreased range; indoor networks are usually rated at around 100 feet for 802.11a and at 150 feet for 802.11b. Needless to say, unless your gear has both a and b radios in them, you have to choose one or the other.

Mass market appeal and low prices made 802.11b the winner here, so you won't find much 802.11a gear out there. The market for 802.11a is mostly companies that are willing to spend some extra money for the benefits of 802.11a.

802.11b has been superseded by 802.11g. You can still find some 802.11a gear out there if you're buying for a company, but you're likely not going to find it on the shelves of a store.

Giving you 1999 speeds in 2003, it's 802.11g!

802.11g got the 2.4 GHz radios to the speed of the 5 GHz radios, only a few years later. 802.11g is also backward compatible with the b standard, so you can use an older network card on your g network, albeit at the lower speed.

There is a significant downside to running an older b radio on a g network, though, which is that the whole network's performance is degraded even if one b radio is joined up. In the worst case you get 802.11b performance, so it's worthwhile to upgrade any legacy 802.11b clients if you're going to run 802.11g.

That aside, 802.11g provides good speeds, good coverage, and it's cheap. Despite being released in 2003, this version is still current. If you look at what's on your store shelves, or if you already have a network card, chances are it's 802.11g (or n, but I cover that next).

802.11g is a good choice for the price conscious buyer, or the user that doesn't need anything fancy. At 54 mbps, 802.11g is still faster than your Internet connection, and still lets you shuffle files between computers with ease. If you already have 802.11g adapters built into your laptop, then this is the most straightforward option for you.

802.11n. Or is it pre-n? Or draft 2?

As of the writing of this book, there's no 802.11n. Although 802.11n has been worked on for years, it's still in draft form. But look in the stores, and you'll see 802.11n devices for sale, how does that happen?

A patent problem with a part of 802.11n is preventing the standard from being completed.

In the meantime, an industry group called the Wi-Fi Alliance has developed a certification program for devices to ensure that they comply with draft 2.0 of the 802.11n standard. This means that any device that's branded Wi-Fi CERTIFIED™ 802.11n draft 2.0 is interoperable with another device with the same brand. The logo is shown in Figure 2-1.

Figure 2-1:
The Wi-Fi
CERTIFIED®
802.11n draft
2.0 logo.

A device that is certified to draft 2 of the 802.11n standard can be upgraded to the final 802.11n standard by only a change in software. I talk about upgrading your router later, but for now, just understand that if you buy a certified product, you shouldn't have to buy anything else to upgrade once those lawyers get finished.

802.11n operates in both the 2.4 GHz and 5 GHz bands, and is backward compatible to a, b, and g radios. It also doubles the range of 802.11g to 300 feet and can operate at speeds of up to 600 Mbps. That's fast!

Behind those impressive numbers, though, is some marketing magic. You only get the benefits of 5 GHz if your equipment has 5 GHz radios (that means both your access point and wireless card). Such devices are labeled *dual band*, meaning that they have both the 2.4 GHz and 5 GHz capability. In the interests of dropping costs, though, many 802.11n devices only have the 2.4 GHz radios.

802.11n gets most of its speed from running larger channels and running them in parallel. For this to happen, the frequency has to be clear and the device has to have multiple antennas. At the 2.4 GHz range you probably have interference from other networks that causes 802.11n to degrade to smaller channels. Most consumer devices have two antennas, which is twice as good as one, but only half as good as the four that are required to get up to 600 Mbps.

It's not all bad news for 802.11n. There are still improvements on 802.11g that make 802.11n faster than g, even in the worst case. If you have a need for speed, then 5 GHz 802.11n is where you want to be.

Another benefit to the dual band radios is that you can run your 802.11n clients in the 5 GHz range and leave the 2.4 GHz band to the 802.11b/g clients. This way you can make sure your speed-hungry devices aren't slowed down by legacy adapters.

Compatibility concerns

Wireless devices are generally downward compatible with other devices in the same frequency. Therefore, you can mix 802.11b and 802.11g because they're both running at 2.4 GHz, but not with 802.11a at 5 GHz.

Keep in mind that just because something's compatible doesn't mean that it's going to run as well as it could. Even with an 802.11g card (54 Mbit/s, remember?), you're limited to 11 Mbps on an 802.11b network.

When your access point's capabilities exceed that of the clients, you still have problems. An 802.11g access point will instruct all clients to operate in a slower compatibility mode if even one 802.11b client is connected. 802.11n has some protections to prevent this problem with legacy clients but still is not as fast as an 802.11n only network.

802.11n will coexist with 802.11a, as long as you've got a dual band network card in your computer. This limitation isn't too much to worry about because 802.11a network cards aren't terribly popular.

Table 2-1 helps you make sense of the information in this section.

Table 2-1:	802.11 Frequencies, Speed, and Ranges			
Standard	*Frequency*	*Speed*	*Range*	*Should I Look at It?*
802.11	2.4 GHz	1–2 Mbps	100'	No
802.11a	5 GHz	54 Mbps	100'	No
802.11b	2.4 GHz	11 Mbps	150'	No
802.11g	2.4 GHz	54 Mbps	150'	Yes
802.11n Draft 2†	2.4 GHz	54–300 Mbps	300'	Yes*
	5 GHz	54–600 Mbps	300'	Yes*

If you go down the 802.11n path, do your best to get dual band (2.4 GHz and 5 GHz) equipment.

Make sure any 802.11n gear you buy is certified by the Wi-Fi alliance. Check www.wi-fi.org/ for the latest version of the standard.

At the moment, 802.11g provides good speed and coverage, and 802.11n expands on that. If speed is a concern, go with n. If your laptops already have a b or g radio, then consider starting out with 802.11g and then upgrading in a year or so after 802.11n is finalized and the gear comes down in price.

Purchasing a Brand Name

Go to the store and you're going to see an assortment of products, all by different manufacturers. The first part of the selection process is finding which of these boxes have the features you want, followed by picking a manufacturer.

You're going to see a few manufacturers, some you recognize, some you don't. I recommend going with a name-brand product instead of a cheap, white, box knockoff, especially if you're choosing 802.11n. Have a look for the following:

+ Do you recognize the manufacturer? Do you see the same manufacturer being advertised by different stores? If so, chances are it's a reputable brand that different stores are willing to stand behind. Also consider that an established brand has the resources and desire to maintain the software that makes your wireless card work.

+ Does the manufacturer offer a toll-free support line? You may need to call for help at some point.

+ Does the deal seem too good to be true? Cheap equipment is made cheaply.

+ Do you see certification logos? This is your guarantee that the device will interoperate with other vendors' equipment.

+ Do you need to supply other parts? Read the fine print carefully; sometimes items shown on the box aren't inside the box.

A few bucks extra on a name-brand device will almost certainly save you frustration down the road. Talk to some friends, neighbors, or coworkers to find out the brands that they like or dislike.

Routing and Bridging

You're going to have a network in your house, and it's going to connect to your service provider's network. To get between networks, you have to route. These networks are connected by a device called a router. This router is the part that lets you get out on the Internet. Routers also incorporate a firewall, which is a protection mechanism from the bad guys out there on the Internet. Pretty much every wireless router out there has a built-in firewall.

If you're connecting parts of your own network, you want to bridge. Maybe you're making your wired network bigger by adding more ports. Maybe you're adding a new wireless access point to an existing wireless network.

Take a look at Figure 2-2. The connection from the Internet service provider (which is drawn as a cloud, because you can't have a good network drawing with at least one cloud) comes in to the router. Anything to the right of the router is part of the internal network. On the internal network is a device called a *switch*, which allows you to add wired ports to a network. One of those ports connects to an access point, which brings in the wireless computers.

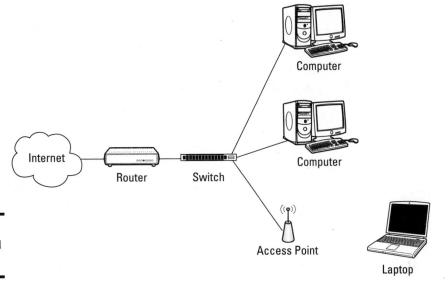

Figure 2-2:
Routing and
bridging.

Computer

Computer

Internet

Router   Switch

Access Point

Laptop

The router is routing between the stuff on the left and the stuff on the right. The network on the right is made up of the switch, the access point, and all the computers. The switch and the access point bridge all their connections to each other, which is how a small network grows.

Thankfully, you rarely have to worry about this because most routers you buy combine the router, the switch, and the wireless access point. If you need to connect some wired computers in, then make sure your router has enough ports, or that you've got an extra switch that you can connect to the router to add the ports.

Expanding Your Wireless Network

Before you go thinking "my house is so big, one access point will never be enough," give it a try. You might be surprised at what one access point will do, especially if you're using 802.11n.

If that one access point leaves you with dead spots in your house, try moving the access point around (if you can), to see if that helps. Turning an access point 90 degrees can make a difference. If that doesn't clean up those pesky dead spots, then you have to look at alternatives.

Upgrading your antenna

Your access point may have removable antennas, in which case you can try to find a better antenna. The short, plastic antennas that are what you probably got with your access point (the highly technical term for these are a *rubber ducky antenna*) are optimized to spray radio energy in all directions such as a big sphere. Other antennas are made to spray in one direction, or in a doughnut shape.

Changing your antenna is becoming a less attractive option as time goes on. Some access points have moved to internal antennae, and with the multiple antennas in 802.11n, replacing several antennae is just a pain. Adding more devices is becoming so cheap that worrying about your antenna is probably not worth it.

Repeaters and range extenders

The easiest approach is to add repeaters, or range extenders, to your network. These devices listen to the existing wireless network and rebroadcast the signal. Because of this, you can expect a repeater to increase your wireless range by about 150 percent in one direction, as shown in Figure 2-3.

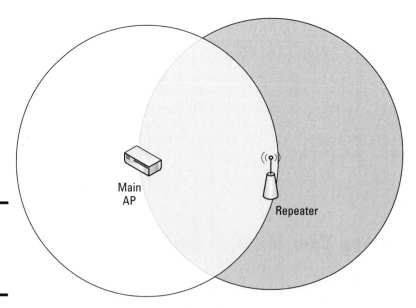

Figure 2-3: A wireless range extender in action.

Main AP

Repeater

Wireless range extenders are the easiest way to get what you want, even though they're not the most efficient way about going about it. As you can see from Figure 2-3, the range extender has to be inside the coverage area of the main access point (white circle). This scenario has a fair bit of overlap between the two radios: a large part of the extended coverage area (dark circle) is already covered by the main access point.

When shopping for range extenders, also remember that some wireless access points can be configured as a repeater, which is the same thing. They both do a fine job of extending the signal, but knowing that you have the two options helps you comparison shop.

Creating multiple access points

The solution that gives you the best range is to use multiple access points and then to bridge them together. Figure 2-4 shows how this works.

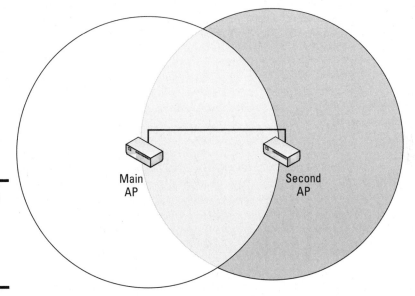

Figure 2-4:
How to
connect
multiple
access
points.

Main
AP

Second
AP

This option reduces the overlap between the two wireless zones because the two access points don't have to *see* each other over the wireless network. However, the two access points must somehow be connected over the wired network. Given that the benefit of wireless is avoiding wires, this option is cumbersome to set up. Figure 2-4 does show some overlap between the two access points, so that there is no dead zone between the two.

Multiple access points can also be helpful if an entire floor is inaccessible from the main access point. A repeater won't work in your basement if the signal isn't strong enough, and your only option might be to run a cable between two access points.

Dealing with Wired Devices

After all this talk about wireless, you still have to deal with some wires. You may have a PC or a video game console that doesn't have a wireless adapter.

Consider replacing your computer with one that has built-in wireless capability. But if you can't do that, you got three options:

Wire it, upgrade it, or bridge it.

Wiring a computer

The first option is to simply embrace your device's lack of wireless and run a cable from your router to computer. Your router probably has a switch built in, which is a device that's there to provide several wired ports. Figure 2-5 shows the switch ports on the back of a router.

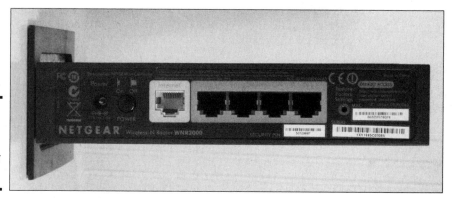

Figure 2-5: Switch ports on the back of your router.

In theory, wiring a computer is easy. If your computer is in the same room as the router, then run a cable of appropriate length between the two devices, and you're set. If your computer is in another room, you'll have to think of the least disruptive way to get there. The cable simply plugs into one of the switch ports on the router on one end, and into the Ethernet port of your computer on the other.

Run the cable along the baseboard of your wall if you can, or under a strategically placed rug. Avoid bare cable, it just looks bad and people tend to trip over them, especially when carrying fragile things. If you do have to drill, try to drill in closets to avoid an ugly mess.

Speaking of cable, you want Ethernet cable rated at category 5e. You may also see category 6 cable or some fancy thing with connectors coated in precious metals, but for a home network you'd just be throwing your money away. Even better, find a friend with cabling experience to do the work for you in exchange for dinner.

Wiring up your computer works, but you bought a book on wireless networking, not wired networking. Unless your computer is really close to your router, avoid the mess and pick one of the other options.

Upgrading a computer

Most computers have some expansion slots that let you add peripherals, such as network cards, to your computer without having to buy a completely new computer. With this option, you go out and buy the appropriate adapter for your computer, and then install it.

The key here is to make sure that you've got the right adapter for your computer. Computers are getting faster and smaller, and the expansion cards follow the trend.

Desktops

Desktop computers have two options, depending on the capabilities of your computer and how much work you feel like doing.

The traditional method is to install a PCI card (that's peripheral component interconnect, for those of you who need to know these things), which is a card that goes into specially designed slots right on the motherboard of your computer. The slots are aligned such that one edge of your card sticks outside your computer's case, which allows for easy connection of an antenna. (Chapter 1 of this minibook shows a PCI-based network card.)

Most computers that you buy will have a free PCI slot, but the only way to make certain is to check. You should see at least one blank panel on the back of your computer (it's about 4 inches high and slightly over half an inch wide). If you open your case, you can see an empty slot for the card.

Opening the case isn't for everyone, and improvements in the Universal Serial Bus (USB) have made it possible to get the same speeds without the hassle. If your computer has a free USB 2.0 slot then you can buy a USB-based card for around the same cost as an internal one.

Figure 2-6 shows the USB slot from a typical desktop computer.

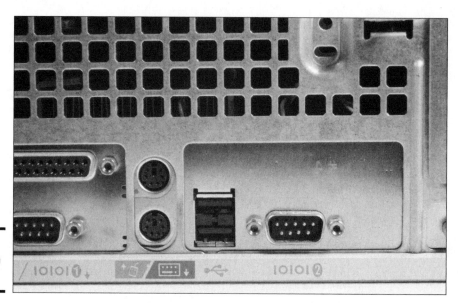

Figure 2-6:
USB slot on
a desktop.

When buying an adapter for a desktop machine, be it USB or PCI, keep in mind where your computer is and where the antenna would be. An antenna that's buried under a pile of books, or is stuck in a cabinet, will not perform as well as one that's got room to breathe. I'd recommend an external antenna with a cable for PCI cards.

USB adapters are also used with laptops, so are often designed to be small. You can take a USB adapter with an integrated antenna and attach a USB extension cable to it if your desk layout hides the antenna. Your adapter might come with this cable — check the box to make sure.

Laptops

Laptops follow the same idea as desktops; however, the technologies are different. If your laptop doesn't have wireless built in (or it's an older technology and you want to update), then you can go down the USB route, or an adapter.

USB devices for laptops work the same way as they do on desktops, except that you want something that's small and unobtrusive. Before you buy, look at where your USB ports are. If you dock your laptop, consider whether or not you need wireless while docked.

The other option for laptops is a peripheral card, much like the PCI card from a desktop. Laptops are a bit more refined, though; they have standard card types that plug into the side of the computer.

There are currently two popular types of laptop cards — the PC Card (sometimes called CardBus) and the ExpressCard. ExpressCards are a newer (and by newer I mean faster) version of PC Cards. The name is also better, don't you think?

Laptops have been shipping with ExpressCard since at least 2005, so chances are you already have an ExpressCard slot. You might also have a PC Card slot. The two types of cards are available in the same width (and not compatible), so it's not obvious from looking which one you have.

If you look at the pins inside the slot for the card (you might need a flashlight, and will certainly need to pop out the plastic holder), you find that PC Cards have a wide connector, almost 2 inches wide, and have protruding pins. The ExpressCard's connector is slightly over an inch wide and has more of a card interface.

To make things even more confusing, ExpressCards come in two widths. One is the ExpressCard/34 which is slightly over an inch wide (34 millimeters for those of you who understand metric), and ExpressCard/54, which is about 2 inches wide. The connector is the same, but you can't use the 54mm card in a 34mm slot! There should be a plastic guide inside the slot, though, that allows you to use the 34mm card in the 54mm adapter. Figure 2-7 shows the two ExpressCard variants.

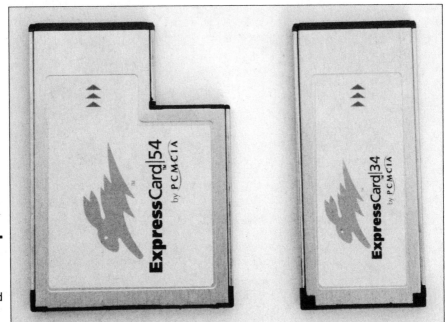

Figure 2-7:
PC Card
and PC
ExpressCard
compared.

When in doubt, check out the documentation that came with your computer, especially the sales brochure.

Bridging a computer

Bridging is remarkably simple — you buy a device that speaks wireless on one side and has a network jack on the other. This device bridges the wireless to the wired, so that the computer thinks it's on a wired network, but everything it sends goes out to the wireless network.

This option is great for video game consoles, where you may not have flexibility in what you can add. Some models can behave as a bridge for use at home and a standalone access point if you and a bunch of friends decide to get together with your consoles or computers and play multiplayer games.

Chapter 3: Setting Up Routers

In This Chapter

✔ **Unpacking your hardware**

✔ **Plugging equipment together**

✔ **Configuring your router**

*I*f you're ready to set up your router, you likely have all the equipment you need. For most of you, this will be the most foreign part of the whole process. Don't worry! In terms of difficulty, I rank this as easier than setting up a home entertainment system and slightly harder than falling off a log.

In this chapter, I discuss the router. If you bought some network adapters, you can set those aside for now. First, you get acquainted with the equipment, and then I explain how to put it together and get it going!

For those of you with foggy memories, or who skipped ahead, the router is the device that connects your home network to the Internet. The router hides all your internal computers and acts as a firewall, which helps to protect you from the bad guys out there. Your router probably has wireless built in, so it's going to take care of getting your wireless computers connected.

Unpacking the Box

Clear off a table and start unpacking the router box. You should see

✦ A router (if you don't see this, then pack everything up and take it back to the store)

✦ A power supply

✦ A network cable (3-inch to 6-inch long, with a square plug on each end)

✦ CDs and documentation

✦ Antennae, depending on the router you bought

Your box might come with some other goodies, such as a network card, if you bought a combination package, or some other odds and ends that the manufacturer threw in.

Handle with care

If your cable or DSL modem isn't in a good spot, then you might consider moving it somewhere better.

Moving a cable modem means that you have to find another cable jack in the house and plug the cable modem into that jack. Be careful, though, especially if you had someone from the cable company come out and set up your equipment. The installers for cable modems optimize your house wiring to give the best signal to the modem, so changing jacks might hurt your Internet speeds. Thankfully, you can just move things back if something goes wrong, or call your provider for a signal check if you're unsure.

For ADSL setups, you can move your modem to any phone jack. You have to make sure that all the other phones in your house have a filter on them, which prevents noise from the phone from interfering with the Internet signal.

Figuring Out Where to Put the Router

The router needs to be placed close to where your Internet service provider's equipment (such as a cable modem or an ADSL modem) is located. Ideally, this area is as close to the center of your house as possible, to maximize the wireless range.

So, you've found a central location with a bit of breathing room for the router. It's near a power outlet, and is out of the way enough that you're not going to trip over it.

Grab some masking tape and a marker before you start setting things up. Tag your cables as you go along so that someone looking for a free outlet doesn't pull your cable modem's plug, or you don't forget which port plugs into what, should they get separated.

Plugging Everything Together

Before you start hooking equipment up, throw together a quick picture of what you're trying to build. Figure 3-1 shows an example of a network.

Starting on the left, you have your cable modem, which is probably already plugged into your phone or cable line. The cable modem hooks into the external side of your router. Your router connects wirelessly to your workstations, and optionally through a wired interface to any devices that need it.

While you're configuring your network, you can connect your PC to the router using an Ethernet cable. After you've set up the router, you can begin using your wireless network.

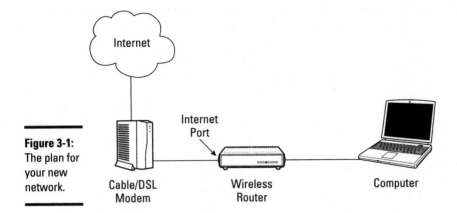

Figure 3-1:
The plan for
your new
network.

Cable/DSL
Modem

Internet
Port

Wireless
Router

Computer

Connecting the router to the Internet

Your cable or DSL modem will have one Ethernet cable coming out the back of it. To help you find it, I've taken a picture of my cable modem in Figure 3-2. An Ethernet jack looks a lot like a regular telephone jack, except the Ethernet jack is wider than the phone jack.

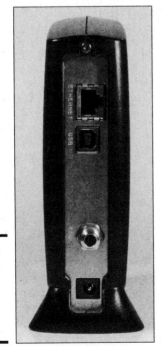

Figure 3-2:
Finding the
Ethernet
jack on
a cable
modem.

Your router has several Ethernet jacks on it. Your router connects your internal network to the Internet. It's expecting the Internet to be on a certain port. This port might be labeled:

✦ Internet

✦ Outside

✦ WAN

✦ External

Whatever it's called, this port is marked differently than the other ports.

1. **Plug the router's Internet port into your cable or DSL modem's Ethernet port.**

2. **Hook up the power adapter to your router and give it a few minutes to get started.**

   You should see lights on both your cable or DSL modem and the router, indicating that a connection was made. Sometimes the light is right underneath the port itself, sometimes it's on the front of the device.

3. **Unplug the power from your router until you're ready to set it up.**

When plugging in an Ethernet cable, it should click. Give the cable a gentle tug. It should not fall out of the port that it's plugged in.

Plugging your computer into the router

Now that you've found the Internet port on the router, the inside ports should be pretty easy. They are likely numbered and in a group, possibly with a label like Ethernet.

Plug a cable from your computer's Ethernet port into the first Ethernet port on the router. Now you should have something like Figure 3-3.

Congratulations, the hardest part is over! It's time to configure the router.

Figure 3-3:
The laptop, router, and cable modem all hooked up.

Configuring the Router

With your router at default settings, you might be able to turn your router on and be on the Internet in a matter of minutes. Even if everything works for you, going through the configuration steps is a good idea. Doing so improves your security, you can upgrade your router's software to the latest version, and you might even find it fun!

Depending on the router you buy, it may come with a CD that takes you through the configuration section. Feel free to use it, because they generally do a good job. You should still read through this section because it describes the settings you want to look at, and you may have to resort to the method we describe below.

I'm also using a Netgear router. If you have something different, the screens will look different but the process will be similar.

If you are having problems with a step here, jump over to Chapter 8 for some troubleshooting information.

Logging into the router

Your router is configured by using your Web browser by entering a URL pointing to the gateway. The URL you enter is either printed on the router or is in the manual that came with your router.

Maybe your dog ate your instruction manual before you got a chance to copy down the URL, and it's not on your router. That's fine — there's a way to find it.

1. **From the Windows Start menu, click on Run.**

A pop-up box appears above the Start button, asking which program you want to run.

2. **Type in cmd and press the Enter key.**

A black window opens.

3. **Type ipconfig and press the Enter key.**

I've pasted what I see.

Your window should look something like Figure 3-4. Look for the line starting with Default Gateway. The gateway is 192.168.1.1, which is the address of my router.

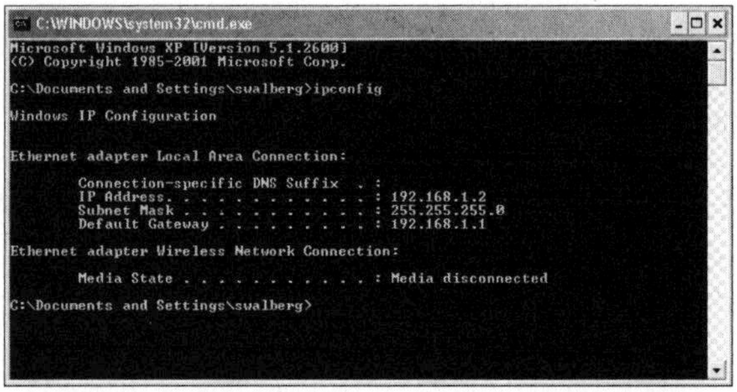

Figure 3-4: Determining your IP address and gateway.

If you don't have an address, or it starts with 169.254, then make sure that your computer is properly connected to the router. You see a status light on both the router and the computer's Ethernet port if you have a connection.

Whichever way you find it, open up your Web browser and enter the address of your router. On my Netgear router it is `http://routerlogin.net`, but it works just as well with `http://192.168.1.1` that I learned earlier from the ipconfig command.

After connecting, you are challenged to log in, as shown in Figure 3-5.

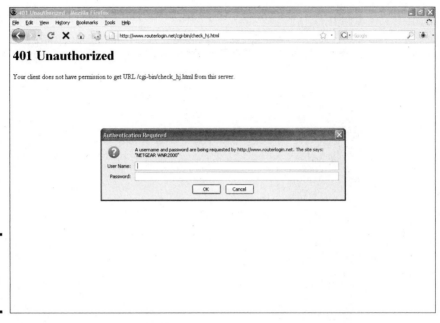

Figure 3-5:
The login
screen from
a router.

The password is printed on the router or in the manual. You can also try a username of *admin* and a password of *password* for many models.

If you lost your manual, the site www.routerpasswords.com has the default username and password for many models of routers.

After you've logged in, your router will probably check for software updates. If you are prompted to upgrade your router, you should do so. If you got an error that no Internet connection could be found, don't panic! You might need to make the changes in the next section.

After the router upgrade completes, for better or worse, you are sent to the wizard (no, not the pointy hat kind! I mean the menus that help you set up your Internet connection).

Setting up the Internet connection

The first stage of the configuration wizard is the Internet setup. Figure 3-6 shows the initial question that asks if you want the router to determine the Internet connection type.

Let the detection process proceed, because it can save you some time. After the detection runs, you are given an option to review your settings and to fill in any missing information about your Internet connection. Figure 3-7 shows the configuration screen for the Internet connection.

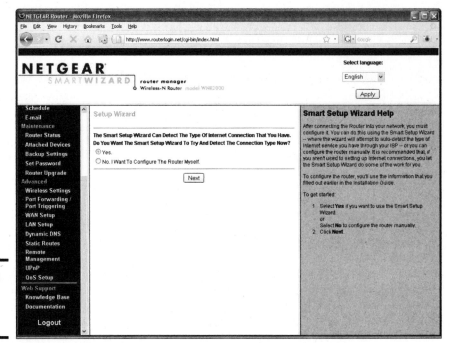

Figure 3-6:
To auto-
configure,
or not?

Figure 3-7:
Internet
configura-
tion screen.

The Does Your Internet Connection Require A Login option is set to No. The Internet IP address is filled in (but grayed out) because the router detected the Internet connection properly.

Do you need to log in?

Cable Internet generally doesn't require a login. If you have ADSL, it depends on your provider. If your ISP gave you a username and password when you signed up, or if the detection failed, then you probably need a login. If you had to run software such as the WinPoET on your computer to get on the Internet, then you need a login.

If you do need a login, follow these steps.

1. **Select Yes at the Does Your Internet Connection Require a Login question.**

Your screen changes to something such as Figure 3-8.

2. **If your ISP is listed in the ISP section, select it.**

North American users typically use the PPP over Ethernet (PPPoE) protocol to log in, which means you select Other for your ISP. For those in Europe or Australia, you probably use PPTP (Point to Point Tunneling Protocol). When in doubt, call your ISP and ask.

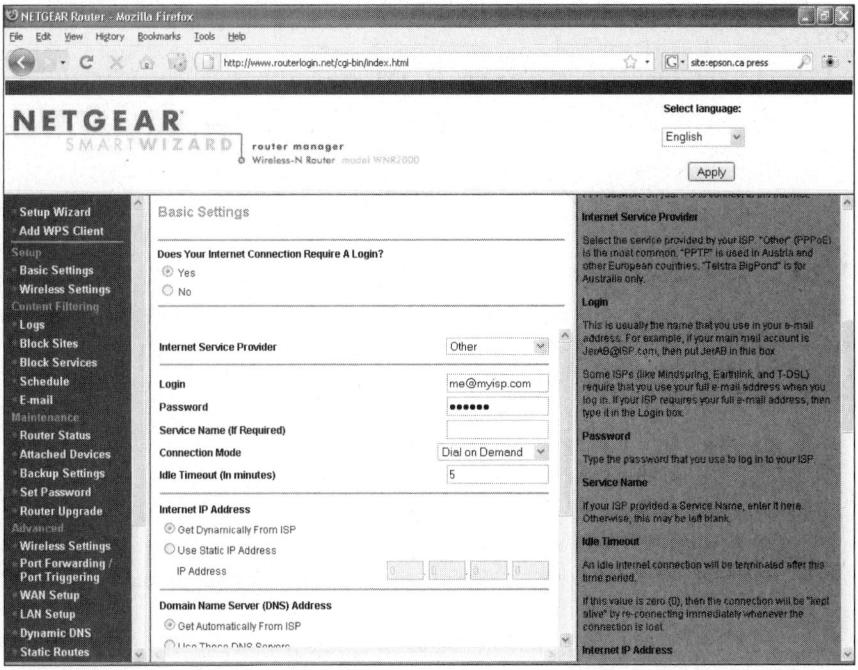

Figure 3-8:
Entering
your login
information.

3. **Enter the login information your Internet service provider gave you, and then scroll to the bottom and select Apply.**

   Doing so resets your router.

4. **Confirm you have an Internet address by selecting Router Status from the main menu.**

   If all went well you see an address on the Internet port. The status light on the router corresponding to the Internet port also changes to green.

If you ran software on your PC to log in to your ISP, then you can uninstall it now. Your router is taking care of logging in for you.

Congratulations, you're on the Internet!

Working with your ISP

Some Internet service providers are picky about who they let on the Internet and will not let you on from a different computer. This situation is most often the case with cable modems, because the ADSL service with a login identifies people by the login. From the ISP's perspective, your router is now the only person using the Internet because all your local devices are hidden behind it.

The first thing to do is to reboot your cable modem. Doing this clears out any computer associations should the restriction be made on the cable modem.

If that doesn't work, try plugging your computer directly into the cable modem (another reason I told you to label your cables!). If your computer works but the modem doesn't, then you need your ISP to intervene.

Give your ISP a call and tell them that you just installed a new router and are having problems connecting. Ask if you're being restricted based on your computer. Also let them know the outcome of plugging in the computer.

If you aren't getting anywhere with your ISP, and your computer works but the router doesn't, you can tell the router to act like your computer. Go back to the Basic Settings menu and scroll all the way to the bottom to the Router MAC Address section shown in Figure 3-9.

Increasing security

Security is a tradeoff between the risk of something bad happening and the frustration you're going to encounter trying to prevent it. We could talk for hours about all the things you could do to keep bad guys out, but in the next couple of sections, I focus on some simple fixes that can make a big difference.

Remember, you're never truly secure; all you can do is make your network hard enough to break into that the bad guys go somewhere else.

Figure 3-9:
Changing
your router's
MAC
address.

Changing the router login information

Most routers come with a default username and password of admin and
password, respectively. Want to guess the first thing someone is going to
try? That's right . . . "password" is a good way to describe what the word is,
but as a password, it makes a bad one.

Change that admin password!

The screen to change your password is found under the Set Password menu
item, as shown in Figure 3-10. You are prompted for your old password,
which is probably "password" in case you've forgot.

Here's my advice for choosing a good password:

✦ Make it at least 8 characters.

✦ Put at least one number and one uppercase character in your password.
Passwords are case-sensitive, so *G* and *g* are not the same.

✦ Make it memorable, but not obvious. If your name is Sarah, you might
try something like saraH500. Maybe you like cats, so try 100Meows.

✦ Avoid too many letters that look the same, such a zero and a capital O,
or the number 1 and a lowercase l.

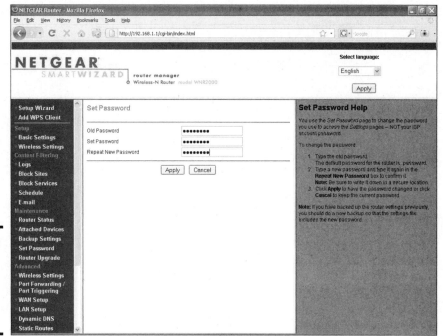

Figure 3-10:
Changing your adminis-trator password.

Finally, write the password down and put it somewhere safe (and some-where that you'll remember). That's right, I told you to write the password down! Doing this is often frowned upon, but think of it this way:

✦ You're not protecting Fort Knox, it's your home network. That's not saying your personal stuff isn't important, but with a password that's good enough, you're still making it harder to get in. Remember that security is a tradeoff between safety and convenience.

✦ You're going to store the password somewhere safe, like a filing cabinet. You're not going to tape a sign to your front window with the password on it.

✦ Someone has to first get on your network before they're going to be able to log in to the router.

✦ If you're still paranoid, ignore my advice and make up a complex pass-word. I won't be offended, really.

Keeping others out of your network

If someone could connect to your wireless network, he can surf the Internet from your ISP. That's not such a big deal, but you're now responsible for what they do. If something bad happens, the police will track the perpetrator back to your house. Then you get to explain to the police why it wasn't you.

Secondly, software is available that can intercept your network traffic. At best they see which Web sites you browse to, at worst they pretend to be your bank and rob you blind.

Protect your Network!

Figure 3-11 shows the Wireless Settings screen. At the top is the name of the wireless network called the SSID (Service Set Identifier). This makes your network unique. When you start off, it's usually set to the name of the manufacturer, such as Linksys or Netgear. Not only is a default SSID a magnet for hackers, it could cause conflicts if your neighbor is at the defaults, too. This setting is not a secret, so choose something obvious enough that if you saw it in a list, you'd recognize it.

Leave the channel at Auto — your router will choose the best channel to use.

For the mode, pick one of the higher ones. The options I get are 45 Mbps, 145 Mbps, and 300 Mbps. This is a wireless-N router, so it's capable of the full 300, but I'm in an area with some interference from neighbors so I dialed it back to 145. Try different settings and see which one works the best for you.

The security options dictate what sort of encryption level is used. None is the default and means that anyone can connect without a password. We know that's a bad thing.

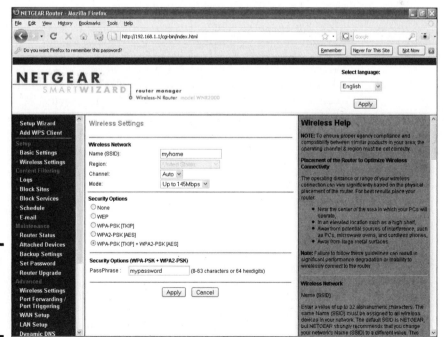

Figure 3-11: Protecting your wireless network.

WEP (Wired Equivalent Privacy) is old and broken. Someone sitting outside your house could break your password in a matter of a few minutes. I'm not even sure why vendors bother offering it; only ancient computers don't support anything better.

WPA and WPA2 (Wi-Fi Protected Access versions 1 and 2, respectively) are the current standards. WPA2 is newer and somewhat better, but some computers only support the original WPA. I recommend enabling both WPA and WPA2 — clients that support WPA2 will use it, and others will use WPA.

You see the box for the passphrase when you select one of the WPA options. A good password is the key to your network's security. You can write it down, but this Netgear router leaves it as plain text so you can look it up easily. (You have changed the admin password for your router, right?)

Dispelling a couple of myths

Wireless has come a long way since it first came out, and people have learned a lot about security over the years. The following list explains what not to do.

✦ Don't use WEP, use WPA2, or WPA if your computer doesn't support WPA2.

✦ Don't bother with restricting clients by MAC address. These addresses can easily be spoofed by bad guys.

✦ Don't hide your SSID; you just make it harder on yourself, and it's still easy for someone parked outside your house to find your SSID. Even the credit card companies have taken this restriction out of their requirements for businesses that take credit cards.

Chapter 4: Deciphering DHCP

In This Chapter

✔ **Discovering what a DHCP server is**

✔ **Configuring your DHCP server**

✔ **Finding out about the other settings that DHCP provides**

In Chapter 3, I explain how to set up your wireless router. And in Chapters 6 and 7, you discover how to set up wireless printers, computers, and even network-attached storage. But, before you can do this, you must first find out about addressing — the topic of this chapter.

The Internet works because everything on it has a unique address, and the devices that run the Internet are very good at getting information between two addresses. Before your computers and printers are ready to talk on your network, you have to make sure they have an address.

There's a protocol called DHCP, the Dynamic Host Configuration Protocol, that not only is the way to automatically address the computers on your network, but knowing the acronym is a great way to impress your geek friends.

Later in the chapter, I go over other related services that might come in handy some day.

Understanding DHCP

To first understand DHCP, you must know a bit about addresses. The most popular analogy is the snail mail system.

Through rain, sleet, or snow

To send a letter, you first put your message in an envelope, then you write your return address on the corner of the envelope and your recipient's address in the middle, and finally drop it in a mailbox. There's a stamp involved in there, too, but the Internet doesn't need stamps; they gum up all the gears.

Someone comes by and empties all the mailboxes into a truck. Trucks are emptied into a collection center. The mail is sorted based on the destination: envelopes are sent on trucks or planes at a facility that's closer to the destination, eventually working their way into a postal carrier's bag and in your friend's mailbox.

Finally, we talk about Internet addresses

As I said earlier, each computer on the Internet has a unique address, which is a number instead of a street name. Each time data (such as an e-mail) is sent over the Internet, the data is wrapped in a *packet* that has the addresses of the sender and the receiver of the packet. The devices that run the Internet look at that destination address and get the packet one hop closer to its destination. The next hop device does the same thing until the final hop — the destination — processes the message.

Incidentally, those devices that run the Internet are called *routers* and are similar to the one you have at home. The major difference is that the routers that run the Internet are more powerful because they have a lot more addresses to deal with, and yours only needs to worry about the one that your ISP gave you.

So, what does an address look like? You already saw one in the last chapter, where you ran the Windows ipconfig command. My address was 192.168.1.2, and I could see that the router's address on the wireless side was 192.168.1.1. My router also had a second (external) address that the ISP gave it, such as 24.79.42.159, which belongs to the cable or DSL side. The router's job is to send packets between these two networks, and it needs an address on each network to do that.

Hiding addresses

Earlier in this chapter, I said that every device on the Internet has a unique address. But you may have noticed that both your router and mine have an address of 192.168.1.1, which makes it not unique. What gives?

Your router also does something special called *address translation*. The networks starting with 192.168.x.x are meant to be private, that is, never seen on the Internet. Your router takes its address on the ISP side (such as 24.79.42.159, in my case) and uses that instead of your computer's address (such as 192.168.1.2) when relaying your packets to the Internet.

When responses come back, the destination is the router. The router remembers who was actually talking and changes the destination back to 192.168.1.2 or whoever was talking.

From your ISP's perspective, there's only one person using their service — your router. Clever, eh?

I still remember my first job out of school, which involved managing a small network. About 40 computers were on the network, and every time I added a new one, I went to a spreadsheet, picked the next available address, made a note in the spreadsheet, and then set up the computer with that address.

Manually specifying addresses is time consuming and error prone. If two devices on the same network try to use the same address, neither of them can talk. Additionally, some of the possible addresses are invalid, and using one will cause problems on your network. Addressing is clearly a job for a computer, not humans.

DHCP solves these problems by letting a computer hand out the addresses. This computer keeps track of who has which address and periodically makes sure the addresses are still in use. DHCP is simple enough that it's built into almost every router on the market, so you can probably start using DHCP right away.

At a high level, when your computer starts up, it sends a message to all the computers on the network that says "I need an address!" If there's a DHCP server on the network, it finds a free address and responds with, "Here, have this address!" Your computer responds with, "Thanks!"

Sounds like a breeze, eh? Of course, it's more complicated than that, but you don't have to worry about the gory details. Understand, though, that DHCP is an ongoing thing. Your computer must periodically remind the router it's still there, otherwise the router will reclaim the address for someone else. This usually happens every 12 to 24 hours and is handled automatically by your computer.

The last thing to remember is that it generally doesn't matter what address your computer has, as long as all the rules are followed. DHCP makes sure you follow the rules, so it doesn't matter if one day you're 192.168.1.2 and when you boot up the next day you're 192.168.1.50.

Your DHCP server

By default, your router almost certainly has DHCP turned on; otherwise, you wouldn't have been able to connect to your router in the first place!

Jump over to the Advanced LAN settings of your router, which I've shown in Figure 4-1.

In Figure 4-1, you see that familiar 192.168.1.1 address, which is the IP address of the internal side of your router. That address stays constant even though the rest of the addresses on your network will be dynamic. The reason is that the computers need to find your router by its address in order to get out on the Internet.

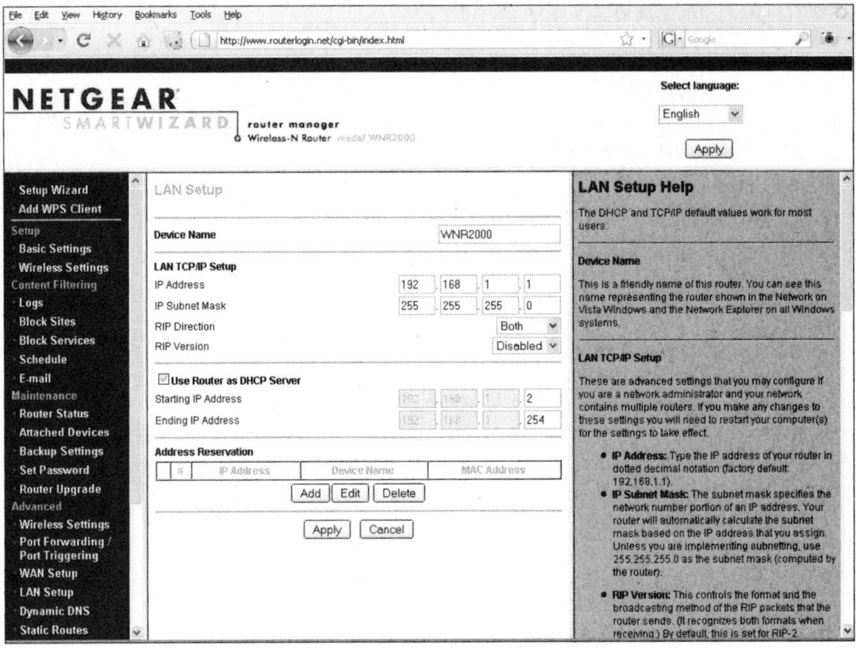

Figure 4-1:
Advanced
LAN
settings.

Don't worry about the subnet mask; it just tells your computer how big the network can get (big enough). And that RIP stuff, pretend it's not there.

What you're really after is the configuration on the second half of LAN setup, starting with Use Router as DHCP Server. This option is selected, and it turns on and off the DHCP functionality. If for some reason you want to turn it off, you deselect this button and click Apply.

Underneath the DHCP on/off switch are two lines that let you set the range of addresses that DHCP uses. You can see that the first three boxes are grayed out, and they happen to have the same values as the IP address of the LAN interface. This is intentional; if you were to change one of those values, you'd be handing out invalid addresses.

You can only change the last value, which can be a number from 1 to 254. Number 1 is already taken by the router itself, so this router is already handing out the maximum number of addresses. These addresses start at 192.168.1.2 and go up to 192.168.1.254, for a total of 253 possible addresses.

Underneath the starting and ending address fields is a place where you can reserve addresses for computers, so the same computer will always get the same address. Just hold on to that thought.

Turning off DHCP

After all that talk about the great things DHCP does, why would you want to turn it off? You probably don't *need* to, but DHCP can get in your way. Int the following sections, I go over some ways to make your new life with DHCP work for the best.

Reserving your spot on the network

Sometimes you've got some software that needs you to do something called *port forwarding*. This means that the router is going to let some connections from the Internet directly into your computer. I'm not going to get into port forwarding in this book, but your software manual has more detailed instructions on what's needed to make it work. Port forwarding needs an address on your network to which to forward the packet.

DHCP gives out addresses that can change. If your router is trying to send a packet to one address, and you've got a different one, what do you do? Turn off DHCP? No!

What if you could still use DHCP but be guaranteed the same known address all the time? No one else would be handed out that address. That's called a reservation. You're simply reserving the address from the DHCP server.

Go back to Advanced LAN Setup and click Add. A screen like the one shown in Figure 4-2 appears.

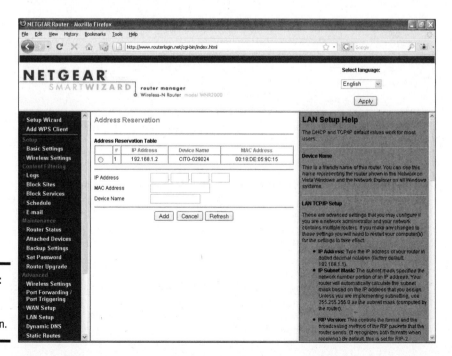

Figure 4-2: Adding a DHCP reservation.

**Book II
Chapter 4**

Deciphering DHCP

You need the IP address you want to give your machine, your computer's MAC address, and your computer's name to complete this form. *MAC* stands for Media Access Control, and it is part of a protocol that defines how networks work. It's also something you'll be able to forget about except for this one trick: To find out your MAC address, open a command window (Start⇨Run⇨cmd) and then type `ipconfig /all`. Figure 4-3 shows the result.

Figure 4-3:
Results of
ipconfig /all.

Look for the line that says Physical Address. Mine is 00-18-DE-05-9C-15 Type that address in the MAC address field, along with your IP address and name, and click Add. Presto! That address is yours forever.

You may be noticing in Figure 4-2 that my MAC is listed right above the field. In fact, if you click the radio button on the left side of that table, it'll even be prefilled in the form, effectively letting you make any dynamic address permanent with two clicks.

It's good to know how to reserve an address the long way, because not all routers support that shortcut.

Just give me static!

In the context of computers, static electricity is usually bad. Static addresses, though, aren't. Sure, they're harder to manage, but if only there were some way we could make them work without having to turn off DHCP.

This one is fairly easy to solve. When looking at the DHCP configuration, you saw that you could change the range of DHCP assigned addresses. Change it to give some space on one side, such as lowering the upper limit to 199. DHCP still offers addresses from 192.168.1.2 to 192.168.1.199, and anyone that wants to put their address in manually can use 192.168.1.200 to 192.168.1.254.

Some network-attached printers don't understand DHCP and need to be addressed statically. The same goes for much older computers, especially computers designed to be servers and not for daily personal use. Fair enough, just give them an address in your static range.

If you do break out a separate area for statically addressed machines, it's a good idea to make a note of it somewhere.

DHCP, get out of my hair!

Sometimes you just want to turn off DHCP. You only want one DHCP server on your home network. If you have another device that's doing the job of DHCP and you plug in your device, then you'll have two devices handing out addresses.

DHCP is so simple that most devices come with it turned on. As you add more pieces to your network, you'll probably come across the situation where you get two DHCP servers. Make sure to turn that second (or third, or fourth) server off.

As a case in point, these combination router–access point–switch devices are roughly the same price as an access point, so you might just come home one day with a second router to expand your new wireless network. Configure wireless, turn off DHCP, and give the new router a different static address, and you can plug it into the rest of your network as if it were an access point. Just remember to leave the Internet port unplugged, because your first router is providing the path out to the Internet, and the new one is bridging your computer between the wireless and wired inside networks.

But wait, there's more!

Looking back at the results of *ipconfig /all* from Figure 4-3, a bunch of other information is there. Most of it isn't that noteworthy, but tl discuss two in the following sections.

Default gateway

The Internet is one big game of Hot Potato. One guy throws his packet to a router, who throws it to the next router down the line, all the way until it lands at its destination. To join in, you have to know where to throw your packet.

Your default gateway is the place that your computer sends all the packets it doesn't know what to do with (for people on your local network, you can talk directly to them). DHCP tells you the address of your gateway when handing out the address. You can see that this address is 192.168.1.1, which is your router.

Without a default gateway, you're not going to get on the Internet.

DNS servers

This chapter has talked a lot about addresses like 192.168.1.1, but you've probably never typed one into your browser. You've always typed URLs like `http://example.com/`, right?

DNS, the Domain Name System, is what translates those names that you understand into the numbers that computers understand. It's like the phone book of the Internet.

Most routers make themselves the DNS server and relay your requests to your ISP's DNS servers. Sometimes they just tell you to talk to your ISP's name servers directly by handing out those addresses. Either way is good.

The funny thing about DNS is that you can be connected to the Internet, but without DNS, you'll get nothing but errors when you try to do anything. That's because your computer has no way to figure out how to convert the names to IP addresses, and you probably don't know the addresses off the top of your head, either. The address is required for your computer to connect to your destination, such as a Web server: a name won't cut it.

Troubleshooting DHCP

If you get an address through DHCP, then DHCP is working great. It's pretty simple that way.

With DHCP, you usually don't end up without an address. If there's a problem, your computer will assign itself an address starting with 169.254, which is called the *autoconfigure address range*. This address isn't helpful, because it's not one of yours and therefore can't be used to talk to the Internet.

If you get this autoconfigure address, then make sure you're within range of your access point. Sometimes you get enough strength from the wireless signal to see the other side, but not enough to have any meaningful conversation, such as the whole, "Hey, I need an address" song and dance that starts things off.

Other times, the problem is related to your wireless drivers, especially if you're trying to get equipment from two different vendors to play nicely together. You need to check to see if you can hookup using a wired connection, and download some updated drivers.

Of course, if you've turned off DHCP on your network, or never had it in the first place, you'll see a lot of those 169.254.x.x addresses until you set up a static address or turn on DHCP.

Chapter 5: Installing Your Wireless Adapter

In This Chapter

✔ Installing PCI-based network adapters

✔ Installing laptop expansion cards

✔ Installing USB adapters

✔ Configuring drivers and wireless utilities

After your wireless router is up and running, you are ready to install the wireless network adapters. Unless you were fortunate enough to have wireless functionality built into your computer, you're going to have to plug something into your computer so that you can get on the wireless network. That something is a wireless adapter, and they come in all shapes and sizes. In this chapter, you find out how to install different kinds of network adapters.

Installing a USB Adapter

USB adapters can be used in both laptops and desktops. Some USB adapters are sleek, little numbers that are designed to be unobtrusive in a laptop, and some are larger but flatter and are designed to be hidden on a desk. They're easy to install in either case, which is why we're looking at them first.

The USB adapter I've been working with is from NETGEAR and is of the laptop variety. However, it includes a USB extension cable and a simple bracket designed to be Velcroed to the wall, so it'll work equally well on a desktop. Have a look at Figure 5-1 to see what I mean.

A spare USB port is, of course, a prerequisite for a USB adapter. If you have USB ports but none are free, consider an inexpensive USB hub that splits one port into four (or more). If your computer doesn't have USB, the only way to get a port would be to add a PCI expansion card.

USB devices are *hot swappable*, meaning you can insert and remove them without powering down your computer. Be careful about the removal part, though; if you're storing anything on the USB device, it might get lost unless shut down properly!

Figure 5-1:
A laptop
USB dongle
that's
attached to
a desktop.

Installing the drivers first

As magical as it might seem, your computer needs to be told how to do everything through software. You're probably familiar with installing application software such as a word processor, spreadsheet, or games. Another class of software is called *drivers*, which are smaller pieces of code that tell Windows how to work with hardware. Chances are the piece of equipment you just bought came out after Microsoft released your version of the operating system, so Windows probably doesn't know how to deal with your new card without the right drivers.

In some cases the hardware is generic enough that Windows will work fine using its default set of drivers. If the hardware I'm installing includes its own drivers, I always use those. Vendor-supplied drivers are going to have the latest fixes and are usually faster than a generic version. After all, if the vendor made the hardware, I trust its drivers.

When installing the vendor's drivers, you usually get the opportunity to install the vendor's wireless management software, which is much better than the software built into Windows. It's a win-win situation.

1. **Load the CD that came with the adapter into your computer.**

After you load the CD, the setup wizard starts. (See Figure 5-2.)

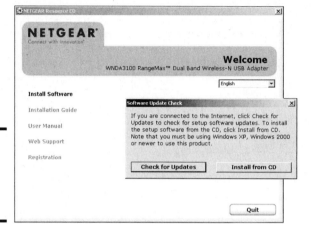

**Book II
Chapter 5**

**Installing Your
Wireless Adapter**

Figure 5-2:
Starting
the USB
wireless
wizard.

2. **Select the Install from CD option.**

The wizard is helpfully offering to check for a newer version of the drivers. Because this computer doesn't have any Internet connectivity (yet), the check would fail.

3. **Accept the license agreement and default installation path.**

The wizard reports that the software is installed, as shown in Figure 5-3.

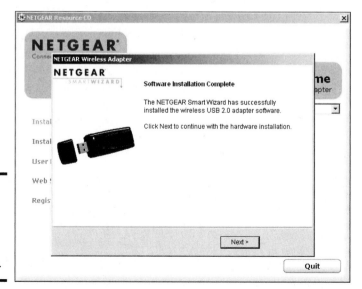

Figure 5-3:
The driver
software
has
completed
installation.

4. **Click Next to confirm that the software has been installed, and proceed to the next step.**

   You are asked to plug in your USB wireless adapter. If you got ahead of the game and did this earlier, don't worry, things can still work!

5. **Plug your USB wireless adapter in now. If you need help, see the next section, "Plug in the adapter."**

6. **Click Next.**

   A legal message appears, as shown in Figure 5-4.

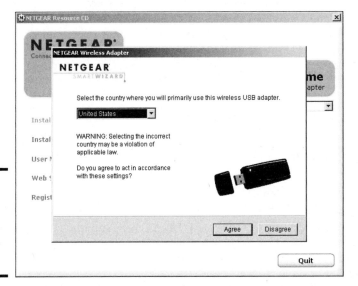

Figure 5-4: You're not going to use that in Japan, are you?

7. **After you agree not to engage in any radio warfare, you're asked if you want to use the built-in Windows configuration (Figure 5-5) or to install the vendor's package (NETGEAR Smart Wizard in this case). I always install the vendor's, so select that option and click Next.**

Understanding legal restrictions

Despite the various 802.11 standards being agreed upon internationally, some federal governments have slightly different limits on which frequencies can be used. As a result you get some oddities where some of the higher 2.4 GHz frequencies are legal in Japan, but not the United States, so they get a couple of extra channels than us.

If you're prompted with a legal message like the above, it's best just to fill in the proper country and rely on the software you just installed to know which frequencies can be used.

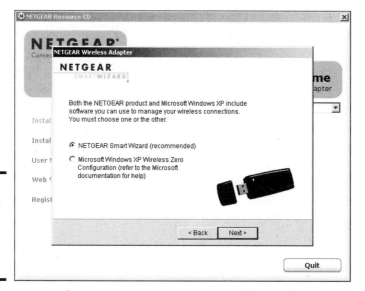

Figure 5-5:
Choose the
vendor's
manage-
ment
software.

At this point your wireless card is installed and ready to go. If you continue along with the wizard, you'll be able to get online right away. I'm going to stop here and pick it up again in Chapter 6, though.

Plug in the adapter

Identify the USB port on the back of your computer and plug in the USB adapter (or the cable, if you're using the cable.) It should take only slight pressure, so if it's not going in right, try flipping the adapter over. If you think pliers might solve your problem, you're probably wrong.

Figure 5-6 shows me plugging in the cable to a USB port on my desktop.

Your computer will probably emit a satisfying beep indicating the adapter was inserted correctly, and then you're off to the races. The next chapter tells you how to log in to your wireless network.

Using USB

USB is a pretty nice technology. You can pull the adapter from one computer and move it to another if you want, or only have it plugged in when you need to use wireless (like any peripheral, a USB wireless adapter uses power even when you're not using it).

Keep in mind that if you move the adapter from one computer to another, you need to install the drivers on both computers, but only once. The configuration is stored on the computer, not the adapter, so you'll have to set up the wireless networks separately.

Figure 5-6:
Plug in the
USB cable.

Finally, be careful! Although the adapter is pretty resilient, after you plug it into the computer it's not too happy being pulled at or bent. If there's a downside to USB, it's that it sticks out of the side of your computer. People who worry about bashing their adapter might be wise to use the desktop adapter and stick it to their monitor; the worst that happens is the cable breaks.

People Can't Memorize Computer Industry Acronyms

Laptop users have another option called PCMCIA cards, PC Cards, or ExpressCards. PCMCIA stands for the Personal Computer Memory Card International Association, though I always remember it as "People can't memorize computer industry acronyms."

ExpressCards are the newer standard, and replace PC Cards. Depending on how old your computer is, you may have one of each or only ExpressCard slots. Either way, these cards slide inside the base of your laptop, leaving only an antenna sticking out.

PC Cards might also be a good choice for older laptops with the slower USB 1.1 ports, which run a lot slower than the PC Card interface.

The D-Link DWL-G630 card I'm using here follows a similar setup process to the other hardware we've looked at.

1. **Make sure your PC Card isn't plugged in. Just like the USB installation procedure, you install the drivers before the card.**

2. **Start the installation program by inserting the CD that came with the card into your CD drive.**

3. **Click Next.**

   A dialog box appears, as shown in Figure 5-7.

Figure 5-7:
The D-Link
installation
starts with a
warning.

4. **Insert the PC Card into one of the slots in the side of your computer, like in Figure 5-8.**

   Do this gently because you don't want to bend any pins inside your computer. If the card doesn't fit, check to see if you are trying to plug an older PCMCIA card into an ExpressCard slot (you will see a small piece of plastic inside the slot which is designed to prevent you from plugging the wrong type of card). A hardware detection dialog box opens, as shown in Figure 5-9.

5. **Select Cancel to return back to the manufacturer's installation process.**

   You may see a screen like the one shown in Figure 5-10 that indicates that the driver hasn't passed logo testing.

6. **You are using the manufacturer's driver, so you can safely select Continue Anyway.**

7. **Wait while your computer installs the software.**

8. **After the installation quits, click the Exit button to exit the process.**

9. **Reboot your computer with the wireless card still inside.**

Figure 5-8:
A PC Card
that's been
inserted into
a laptop.

Figure 5-9:
The
Windows
hardware
detection
dialog box.

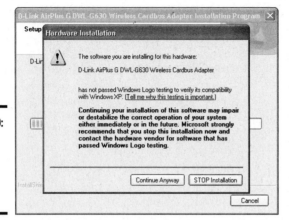

Figure 5-10:
Ignore the
warning
about
unverified
software.

Cracking Open That Case!

PCI Cards are a reliable way of getting a desktop onto the wireless network. To add a new card to your machine's motherboard, you must open up your PC. After everything's closed up, the network card becomes a permanent part of your computer. The PCI Card has no risk of getting unhooked accidentally, lost, or having coffee spilled on it. Well, maybe you're not safe from the coffee, but I think you get my drift.

Going over some ground rules

You're going to be opening up your computer and working inside it. I'd suggest it's turned off while you do that. No, actually, I insist that your computer is turned off while you work inside it. Humans and electricity don't mix well.

Like a fuzzy cat, you're a natural collector of electric charge in the form of electrons. Collect enough electrons by shuffling your feet on carpet, rubbing a sweater against other items, or just picking a bad day to work, and you can turn those excess electrons into lightning bolts known as static electric shocks.

Those lightning bolts find their way to ground through the most efficient path possible, and all those electronics in your case provide such a path. The problem is that your computer is made to run on 12 volts, and those shocks that you're throwing around like Zeus run in the tens of thousands. Shock the wrong part and you'll be an unhappy computer owner.

Fortunately, protecting yourself while working inside your computer is quite easy. Follow these suggestions:

✦ Don't wear a heavy sweater, sweat pants, or dangly jewelry.

✦ Keep all parts in their protective bags until you need them.

✦ Keep a hand on the computer case at all times to ground yourself.

✦ Get your tools ready in advance so that you're not building up charge as you run around the house.

✦ Hold on to cards by the edges and don't touch the contacts or components.

Also, keep a small dish handy to hold any screws you might have to remove. That's got nothing to do with static electricity — those screws are small!

Installing the drivers

Just like the other devices we installed, you want to install the CD that came with the card before actually installing the card. It's remarkably similar to the USB and PC Card procedure; in fact, it's so similar that I'm just going to point you back to Step 2 in the previous section instead of reproducing it here.

Opening the case

Unplug everything from your computer's case and put it on your desk. The goal here is to separate the lid from the rest of the computer so that you can access the components inside.

Every computer is different, though. Rest the computer on its feet and have the buttons facing you. Look on the sides of the computer for buttons that you can push in to release the top. Push these in while rotating the lid upward, and it should open like a clam.

Failing that, look at the back of your computer for screws that hold the lid to the rest of the chassis. Some computers require that you turn a thumbscrew to release the lid, which slides back to reveal the parts inside.

Figure 5-11 is what my computer looks like. The button visible on the side releases the back of the cover, which swings upward to reveal the inside.

Accessing the PCI slots

Figure 5-12 shows the edge of the wireless card. This is a standard PCI card (Peripheral Component Interconnect) that you can use to expand your computer.

1. **Peer into you open computer case and look for some slots that would fit this card.**

You should see between two and five in parallel against the back edge of your computer. Some computer designs have a riser board that comes out of the computer's motherboard at a 90 degree angle.

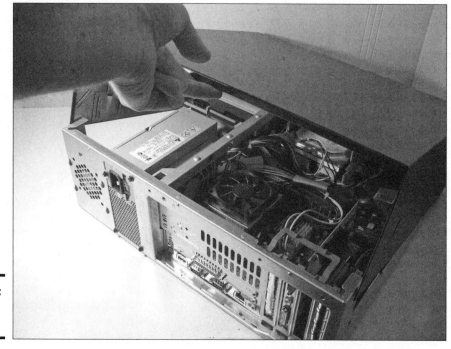

Figure 5-11:
Open the
case.

Figure 5-12:
The edge
connectors
on a
wireless
card.

Figure 5-13 shows the PCI slots in my desktop. You may see slots that
look similar but are offset somewhat. These are generally not PCI, and
you want to avoid them.

Figure 5-13:
PCI slots in
a standard
desktop.

2. **Notice that the case of the computer has openings to the outside but
are probably covered up at this point (you can see such an opening
back in Figure 5-13).**

When properly plugged in, one edge of the PCI card shows to the outside of the computer through one of these openings. Take a moment to
figure out which PCI slot you're going to use and which opening on the
case corresponds to that slot. The two don't line up perfectly, though,
so you can use your card as a guide to figure out which port is to be
used.

3. **Depending on your computer, you might have to undo a screw on the
case to allow the card to go in.** You replace the screw later to hold the
card down. You may also have to punch out part of the case to make
room for the card — be careful! Other computers might use a clamp
mechanism to hold down all the PCI cards at once.

4. **Gently line up the PCI card with the slot, and then make sure it's
straight against the case so that the connectors on the card show
through the outside.**

Figure 5-14 shows the card all ready to go.

Figure 5-14:
A PCI
network
adapter
ready to be
seated.

5. **Push down with your fingers on the edge of the card until the card is properly seated.**

   The card should be level in the case, that is, both sides of the connectors should be in the slots to the same depth. The edge of the card that shows outside the computer should also be seated snugly against the case, with the notched edge flush with the case and ready to be fastened.

6. **Screw the card down to the case or replace the clamp as appropriate.**

   Take a last look for forgotten tools and replace the top of the case.

Attaching the antenna

You will see some connectors protruding from your wireless card when looking at the back of your computer, as in Figure 5-15. Screw the connectors from the antenna onto those connectors. Make sure they fit snuggly, but hand-tighten only, please. Your card might indicate which cables go to which ports, so follow those directions. In the Linksys PCI card I'm using, the middle port is marked in blue, but it corresponds to a blue tag on the antenna cable. The other two ports can go in any order.

Figure 5-15:
Antenna
connectors
on the
wireless
card.

Finally, put your computer back in its spot and hook up all the cables. Make sure the antenna cord is free of the other cords, and put the antenna somewhere where it will be unobstructed. That's it!

By now you've got your USB or PCMCIA network adapter plugged into your laptop and the drivers installed. If you're a desktop person, then you've conquered your computer's case and installed a PCI card, or you took the USB route.

Either way, you've got a functioning network card and a wireless network that's just begging to be used. The next chapter looks at getting your computer online.

Chapter 6: Getting Your PC On the Net

In This Chapter

✓ Configuring Windows XP and Vista

✓ Using your wireless utilities

✓ Measuring your signal strength

✓ Using your laptop on the road

This chapter covers how to get your computer on a wireless network. First, you take a look at how to configure a wireless network within Windows XP without the benefit of your wireless utilities. Sometimes those utilities just don't work as well as you'd like, and you have to resort to the old standard.

After looking at using the default wireless configuration, you see how life can be made easier by using the manufacturer's utilities. For those that are still running Windows 2000 or earlier, you need to use the manufacturer's utilities in any case.

Vista is the latest release from Microsoft, so after looking at Windows XP, you find out how wireless is configured in Vista. A lot has changed in Vista, so it's worthwhile looking at it separately.

Finally, you discover what else you can see in the wireless world. If you're ever on the road, this information can come in handy, because you'll have to find a different network to connect to.

Configuring Windows XP

Before you can configure wireless networking in Windows XP, you need to find out some information about the network you're currently connected to. You may think that I'm putting the cart before the horse, but knowing what a properly configured network looks like makes it easier to follow along when configuring your own network.

Microsoft developed the Wireless Zero Configuration system (WZC) short) for configuring wireless inside Windows XP. The name implies that there's no configuration for you to do; unfortunately, that's not necessarily true.

You put a password on your wireless network, so you know that at some point you'll have to type it in. But WZC for short tries to make most of the other choices on your behalf.

Figuring out if you are connected

The system tray, way down in the bottom right of your screen, contains a bunch of icons that give you both a status indicator of some aspect of your system as well a quick way to access options.

Figure 6-1 shows my system tray when I'm connected to the wireless network. The icon of the computer with the radio waves refers to wireless network adapter.

Figure 6-1: Hovering over the network icon shows the network status.

If a red X shows, you know that you aren't connected to your wireless network. But if an X does not appear, you know you must be connected to some network. Hovering the mouse over the icon brings up the network status. From there, you can find out some information, such as

✦ This computer is connected to the *myhome* network.

✦ The connection speed is 54 Mbps (Wireless G or A).

✦ The signal strength is excellent, which is the best you can get.

✦ The computer is connected to the network (but you already knew that!).

The example in this section shows a signal strength of excellent. Other options are very good, good, low, and very low. As you can imagine, those are fairly subjective. I look at some better ways to measure the strength but in the meantime shoot for excellent through good.

Checking status

That information from the hover was nice, but you can find more help by clicking your mouse a few more times.

Right-click on the wireless adapter icon in the system tray and select Status. Something like Figure 6-2 appears.

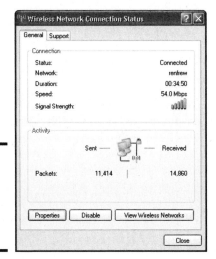

Figure 6-2:
The Status page for a wireless network adapter.

At the very top you see two tabs, General and Support. The General tab gives a lot more information than you had before. You can see the status, name, and connection speed of the network. The duration tells you how long you've been connected, and instead of the nondescript signal strength, you get a display from 0 to 5 bars (which really maps to the same scale as before, but looks a lot nicer!).

In the section marked Activity, you can get an idea of how much data you've sent and received. The actual numbers aren't important, other than for curiosity's sake, but sometimes you want to make sure that you're able to transmit and receive. If your computer is supposed to be working, but the received packets counter isn't increasing, you are having a problem receiving data.

The final point of interest on this tab is the three buttons along the bottom (right above the Close button, which closes the window, and is not at all interesting). You've got three options here that you can use later:

✦ **Properties:** This button takes you to the adapter's property configuration window, which has everything from IP addressing to firewalls.

✦ **Disable:** Pressing this button disables your adapter and then changes to an Enable button. Pressing the button again re-enables the adapter.

✦ **View Wireless Networks:** You use this later to show all the wireless networks that your computer can see. You can then pick the one that you want to connect to.

The Support tab, shown in Figure 6-3 has more information about your connection.

The Support tab shows you your IP address, mask, and gateway. Recall from Chapter 4 that if you see an IP address starting with 169.254 that something is wrong with your computer or network, because those addresses are only used when DHCP fails to work.

You can click on the Details button to get even more details, but usually knowing your IP address is enough.

The most important button on this page is the Repair button. If you click this button, Windows disables your adapter, re-enables it, and then goes through the connection sequence again. Often, if everything else looks right but things still aren't working, using the Repair button fixes the problem.

Configuring wireless, the zero configuration way

Ideally, Windows will take care of all the technical details behind wireless configuration. All you need to know is the name of the network and the password.

With that in mind, open up a list of the available wireless networks. You get there either by right-clicking on the adapter icon in the system tray and selecting View Available Wireless Networks or by double-clicking on the same icon and pressing the button marked View Wireless Networks. Either way you go, you see a dialog box as in the one shown in Figure 6-4.

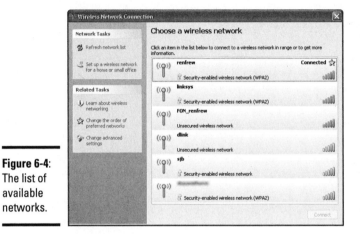

Figure 6-4:
The list of available networks.

When you pull up the list of available networks, your computer stops transmitting and receiving on the wireless network and starts listening for any networks that might be in range. This list is then displayed to you.

Several pieces of information in Figure 6-4 help to find the right network to connect to. First, the SSID (Service Set Identifier) is displayed in bold. The SSID is the technical term for the name of the network. Here I can see *renfrew*, which is the name of the network I configured earlier on. Off to the right is the now-familiar signal strength icon. Along the bottom of each row is a description of the type of security the network uses. Anything with a padlock requires a password to join. The text to the right of the padlock describes the exact protection being used, which Windows takes care of on your behalf.

Finally, the gold star on the rightmost side of some rows indicates that this is a so-called preferred network. A *preferred network* is one that Windows will automatically try and connect to. In addition to the star is a behavior, such as Connected for the network you're currently connected to, and Automatic for networks that Windows has been told to automatically connect to.

If you think that a network should be on the list, but it isn't, click the Refresh network list under Network Tasks.

Joining the network

Join the network you want by double-clicking on the row for that network. If the network is secured then you are prompted for a password.

In the dialog box shown in Figure 6-5, you must enter the same password you entered when you configured WPA protection on your router. Type the password twice and click the Connect button. After you've connected to the network, you are returned to the list of available networks.

Figure 6-5: Entering the network key.

Wireless Network Connection

The network 'linksys' requires a network key (also called a WEP key or WPA key). A network key helps prevent unknown intruders from connecting to this network.

Type the key, and then click Connect.

Network key: ••••••••

Confirm network key: ••••••••

[Connect]   [Cancel]

You're connected now — congratulations! You can confirm this by noting that the word Connected appears next to your network in the list of wireless networks or by hovering your mouse over the network icon in the system tray.

Configuring wireless, the longer way

Sometimes the network you're connecting to doesn't advertise its existence, even though it's still there. This is often the case at businesses, where at one point in time, hiding your wireless network was considered a security bonus.

Hiding your network doesn't solve any security problems; all it does is make it slightly harder to connect.

If you're playing around as you go, you might find a faster way of getting to certain menus than the way I'm showing you — which is great! I'm showing you the foolproof one.

Follow these steps to connect to a network when you know its configuration but don't see it in your list of available wireless networks:

1. **Right-click on the wireless adapter icon in your system tray and select View Available Wireless Networks.**

2. **Select Change Advanced Settings.**

   The Wireless Network Connection Properties dialog opens.

3. **Select the Wireless Networks tab shown in Figure 6-6.**

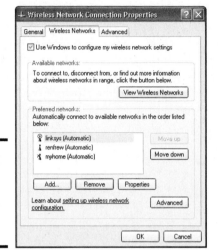

Figure 6-6:
The
Wireless
Network
Properties
window

This dialog is used to manage all the preferred networks.

4. **Create a new profile by clicking Add, which is found at the bottom of the window.**

The window shown in Figure 6-7 pops up has three tabs: Association, Authentication, and Connection. Most of the work is in the first tab; in fact, we're just going to glance at the last two.

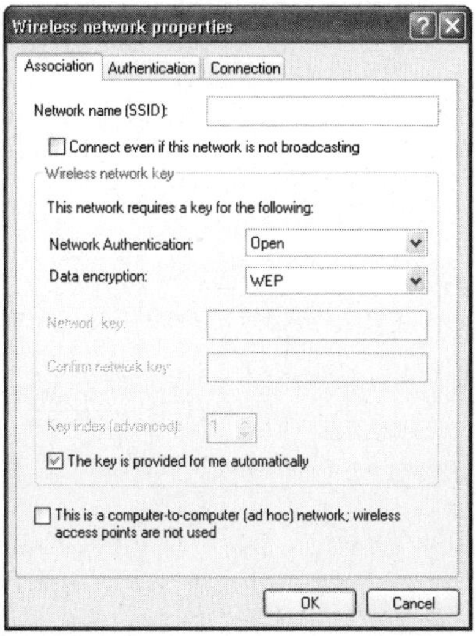

Figure 6-7:
The new
network's
properties
window.

5. **In the Association tab, type the SSID of the network you're trying to connect to, which is the same as the name of the network.**

   This value is case sensitive, so "myhome" is different than "MYHOME" and "MyHome."

6. **Make sure the Connect Even If This Network Is Not Broadcasting checkbox is selected.**

   This option is important for networks that are hidden. Checking this option tells Windows to actively look for the network rather than waiting to hear the network announce itself.

   The Wireless network key section is the trickiest part. If you set up your network following the instructions earlier on, you will be using WPA2-PSK authentication and AES data encryption. Make sure to choose WPA2-PSK and not WPA2! The PSK means Pre-Shared Key, which refers to the password you set up on your router. The non PSK version is used in enterprise networks where you are authenticating against a directory server.

7. **Type the network password in the section that asks for the network key. Confirm this value in the next line.**

   If you are unsure of this information, plug back into your router and make sure. It'll save a lot of frustration later.

8. **Make sure that the This Is a Computer-to-Computer Network checkbox is not selected.**

   Figure 6-8 shows a dialog that's been filled out. In the Authentication tab, everything should be grayed out if you are using WPA2-PSK or WPA-PSK.

Figure 6-8: A network that's been configured.

9. **In the Connection tab, make sure that the Connect When This Network Is In Range checkbox is selected.**

If you don't have a WPA2-PSK option, then your computer's software might be out of date. Upgrade Windows XP to at least Service Pack 2, which includes WPA2 support. Alternatively, search http://microsoft. com for KB893357, which is the patch that provides WPA2.

10. **Click the OK button to exit the configuration and then click OK again to exit the properties window.**

If you have configured the network correctly, and the network is within range, Windows connects.

Managing your preferred networks

A computer can only be connected to one wireless network at a time. Sometimes, you run into a situation where your computer can see two networks that it knows how to log into, and the computer must decide which network to log into. You control this decision by ordering your preferred networks. Windows chooses the network that's highest on the list.

If you ever connect to a default network like NETGEAR, D-link, or Linksys, make sure that you move it down to the bottom of your list of preferred networks. Your computer doesn't know the difference between the network you connected to at the coffee shop and your neighbor's insecure wireless network, because all it has to go on is the name. With the defaults at the bottom, you avoid the embarrassing situation where you connect to your neighbor's network when you should be connecting to your own.

Go back to the Wireless Network Connection Properties dialog by right-clicking on the wireless adapter in the system tray, selecting View Available Wireless Networks, and then Change Advanced Settings. Figure 6-6 shows this dialog. Look at the Preferred Networks section. You can select any network and move it up or down using the appropriate buttons on the right. If you want to view the connection's settings, highlight the name of the network and click on the Properties button.

You may adjust the priority of any network you have used, no matter if you configured it manually or let Windows set it up for you.

Using Wireless Utilities

The Windows Zero Configuration method isn't too difficult, but you need to do a lot of clicking to find what you want. Wireless support in Windows XP was almost an afterthought, so it's no surprise that there are some annoyances.

Modern network adapters come with a utility for managing the network connections which takes over from Windows Zero Configuration. You must choose to use one or the other — both cannot be active at once. The wireless utility from the manufacturer has its own configuration database, meaning that if you switch back to WZC at some point, you lose all your settings.

Still, I prefer to use the manufacturer's utility because it usually has a nicer interface and often provides more troubleshooting tools than does Windows.

If you are running an earlier version of Windows, such as Windows 2000 or Windows95, then you're pretty much stuck with using the manufacturer's utility.

Finding a network

Just like the WZC procedure, you connect to a network by picking it from the list of available networks.

I'm using a NETGEAR USB adapter and the associated utility called the NETGEAR Smart Wizard. If you're using a different adapter, your screens are going to be different. Most of the utilities are similar, so just click around until you find what I'm talking about.

To find a network, follow these steps:

1. **Open the utility by finding it from your Start menu, or by double-clicking the icon in the system tray.**

   I'm not talking about the Windows network adapter icon, but the new icon that was created when the software was installed.

2. **Select the Networks tab to see the list of available networks.**

   The NETGEAR utility is the only one I've used in which I had to click on a tab to get to the list of networks; all the other ones started off at that screen. The screen is shown in Figure 6-9.

   You get a list of all the available networks, along with an indication of what wireless standard is used, the security mode, and the strength as measured by a percentage. The column marked N indicates 802.11n capable networks.

3. **Double-click on your SSID (*linksys* in this case), which brings up the dialog box you see in Figure 6-10.**

   Wi-Fi Protected Set up (WPS) is a simplified method of connecting to wireless networks. Rather than typing in passwords and any other security settings, a different approach is used. A WPS capable router has a PIN number printed on it, a WPS button, or both. If you supply the PIN during the connection, then your computer can negotiate the shared secret directly with the router. Alternatively, you can press the WPS button on the router, which puts it in a mode ready to pair up with your computer.

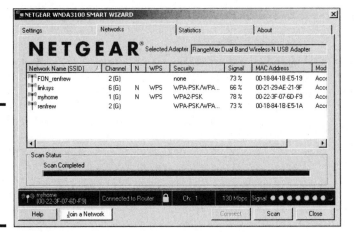

Figure 6-9: The list of available networks as seen by the Smart Wizard.

Book II
Chapter 6

Getting Your PC
On the Net

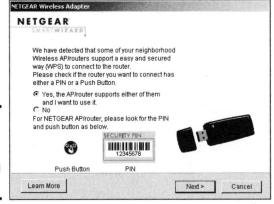

Figure 6-10: The Wi-Fi Protected Setup dialog box.

4. **Select Yes in response to the dialog box shown in Figure 6-11, which then prompts again to see if the router has a push button.**

5. **The router does indeed have a push button, so click Yes.**

   The next screen, shown in Figure 6-12, asks you to press that button.

Figure 6-11: Do you have a WPS button?

Figure 6-12: Press your WPS button!

6. **Press the WPS button on the router and then come back to the dialog box and click on the icon where indicated.**

   Your computer thinks for a moment and then connects you to the wireless network.

   The WPS method is very easy because you don't have to remember any settings. All you need to do is press a button or read a PIN off a sticker.

Configuring Vista

Microsoft's Vista operating system came several years after Windows XP, and Microsoft decided that they should build wireless support in from the ground up. As such, wireless configuration is much smoother in Vista than it is in XP.

Rather than choosing between using Windows for configuration or the manufacturer's utilities, Vista integrates the two. You are free to use either approach because the two integrate with each other. Because of this integration, Microsoft has changed the technology's name from Wireless Zero Configuration to Native Wi-Fi.

Listing available networks

Start off by displaying the list of available networks. To do so, follow these steps:

1. **Click Start and then click Connect To.**

You get a familiar-looking window showing the list of available networks, as shown in Figure 6-13.

Figure 6-13: Vista's list of wireless networks.

Just like the Windows XP version, you can see the name of the network, a signal strength, and a list of the security measures used on the network.

2. **Double-click on the network you want, and if it's a secure network, you'll be prompted for the password just as in Figure 6-14.**

Note that this time around, you only have to type in the password once. If you select the Display characters button, then everything you type will be echoed to the screen instead of just displaying stars.

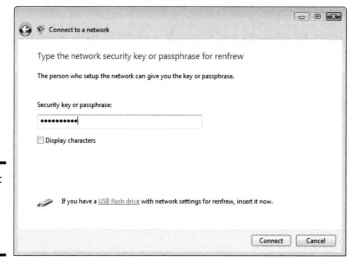

Figure 6-14:
Vista's
prompt for
a network
password

3. **Click OK to save the connection and have it start automatically.**

   Vista introduces more security features, one of which requires you to assign a context to a network connection. After you have connected to a network, you are prompted to assign a location, which you can see in Figure 6-15.

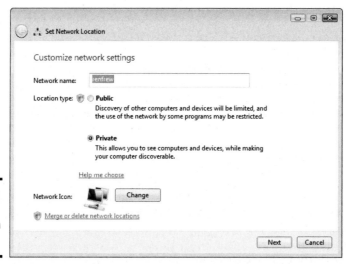

Figure 6-15:
Assign a
location to a
network.

You have three options:

- **Home**: You are using this on a private network, such as at home. Your computer can be discovered on the network, and firewall restrictions are somewhat relaxed.

- **Work**: You are using this connection at work, where your computer is managed by an IT department. This location is virtually identical to the Home location, except that the firewall is further tuned to allow management connections in.

- **Public location:** You are using your computer in an untrusted network that's outside your control. The computer will be hidden, and the firewall is very restrictive. The shields are up, and phasers are set to kill!

4. **Select the Home option.**

Confirming and changing settings

Figure 6-16 shows the Vista system tray. Look at the picture of the two computers with the globe. The icon indicates you are connected to a network (otherwise there would be a red X on top), and the globe indicates that you have a path to the Internet through this connection.

Figure 6-16:
The Vista
system tray.

Hovering over this icon gives even more details. From the box that appears, you can see that this computer is connected to the *renfrew* network and has access to both the local network and the Internet. The house to the left tells you that the security location is Home. Finally, the signal strength is four bars out of five, otherwise known as Very Good.

To the Control Panel!

Launch the Control Panel by choosing Start⇨Control Panel. Then choose Network and Internet⇨Network and Sharing Center. (If you haven't noticed by now, everything in Vista seems much cleaner than before, just harder to find!)

The Network and Sharing Center is shown in Figure 6-17. Along the top you can see the same information you learned from the icon in the system tray. The bottom half shows you all the security settings. In Figure 6-17, you can see that this machine is configured for very limited sharing. You may click on each row to change the setting.

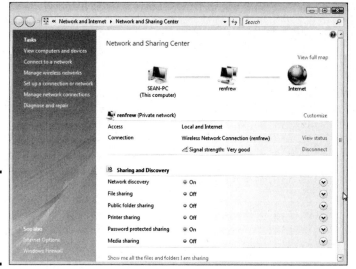

Figure 6-17:
The
Network
and Sharing
Center.

To the left are several tasks, the most important of which is the Manage Wireless Networks task. Clicking this takes you to a menu that does much the same as the Wireless Network Properties from Windows XP. Figure 6-18 shows this menu.

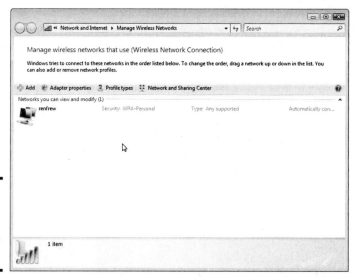

Figure 6-18:
Managing
Wireless
Networks in
Vista.

The Manage Wireless Networks menu shows a list of all the currently con-figured networks; in the example above, there is only one. If you need to reorder the networks, so that one is tried before another, then click and drag the network to the place in the list you want (Windows XP had Up and Down buttons to achieve the same thing). The Add button adds a network in much the same way that Windows XP does it.

But what's my address?

Our final stop in the Vista configuration is to find your network information, which is helpful to know if you ever call your service provider for help. From the Network Sharing Center, choose the Manage Network Connections option. Double-click the wireless adapter, and you see Figure 6-19.

Figure 6-19:
Viewing
the adapter
status.

This dialog box is almost exactly like the Windows XP counterpart. You can see that this adapter has access to the Internet through IPv4 but has limited IPv6 connectivity (this is nothing to worry about, as most of the Internet uses the IPv4 connections, and Vista's trying to get ahead of the curve by setting IP version 6),

Again, just like Windows XP, you can see the connection timer, speed, strength, and packet counters.

The Details button shows the exact IP addresses involved.

Pushing Boundaries

At some point, you're going to venture out of your house and connect to another network, such as one in a hotel, airport, coffee shop, or another building.

Your computer is perfectly capable of keeping track of multiple configurations, so connecting to a new network won't cause any problems when you return home.

Most public networks are wide open and have no security. They employ a *captive portal*, which lets you connect to the network but immediately redirects you to a login screen where you must log in, pay, or otherwise identify yourself before getting on the Internet. Remember that your wireless session is available for anyone else to capture, so be careful about typing in credit card numbers and passwords unless the Web site is protected with *Secure Sockets Layer* or *Transport Layer Security* (you see a lock in your browser window if this is the case, and the address bar might even change, depending on which browser you use). Book IV, Chapter 1 discusses browser security in more depth.

Also, pay attention to which network you are connecting to. If you are at a hotel, you may want to check with the front desk to find the SSID of the network you should connect to. There may be other open networks you can connect to, but you'd be using someone else's network, and you can't be sure what they're doing to your traffic.

Chapter 7: Setting Up Other Hardware

In This Chapter

✓ **Printing wirelessly**

✓ **Using wireless file storage**

✓ **Adding an access point**

*O*ne drawback of being wire-free is that carrying your printer everywhere you go is a little tricky! Rather than plugging into the printer every time you need to print, let's get your printer on the network, too! Many printers come with network adapters, so there's no reason you shouldn't be able to print from wherever you happen to be.

Having your computers on the same network also means they can share files. In this chapter, you discover a way to have a permanent file server on your network.

Finally, if your wireless network doesn't reach somewhere, I look at adding another access point to your network to expand that reach.

Printing Wirelessly

Several years ago, the traditional way to get a printer on the network was to shell out big bucks for a printer that supported it, or to buy an adapter that had a parallel cable on one end and a network cable on the other. These devices cost between $50 and $100. I'm not sure about prices in your area, but that's as much as an entry-level printer.

Over the past few years, printers have both dropped in price and become more feature rich. One of the features you can expect to see on some new printers is a wireless network card. This means that the printer can be placed anywhere there's a power outlet. The extra cost to get a model with the wireless card is minimal, and it's only going to get lower.

For example, the device I'm demonstrating here is a color inkjet printer that also copies, scans, and faxes. It's got an 802.11g wireless adapter that can be found online for $150.

Just like the network adapter you installed earlier, you'll need some drivers for your printer. This time, the drivers tell your computer how to communicate with the printer over the network and how to operate the extra features such as scanning and faxing.

As usual, if you've got a different printer than the one I'm using, your screens will be different. However, the steps are similar.

Before you get started, have a look at the documentation that comes with your printer. The printer I'm using comes with a note that says if you intend to use the printer on a network that you should ignore the quick start guide and refer to the network installation guide.

Plug your printer in and install the ink cartridges per the directions in the manual.

To set the wireless configuration on the printer, you first have to get it set up on the wired network. To do so, follow these steps:

1. **Plug the Ethernet cable that came with the printer into the back of the printer and the other end into your wireless router.**

Figure 7-1 shows the network port on the back of the printer.

Figure 7-1:
The wired
port on the
printer.

Your printer picks up its initial address from DHCP.

If your printer is nowhere near your router, bring your router to the printer rather than the other way around. The only thing you lose is Internet access, which isn't needed for the installation anyway.

2. **Put the CD that came with the printer into your CD drive, and you see the initial screen, shown in Figure 7-2.**

Figure 7-2: The initial printer installation screen.

3. **Click the Install button to begin the installation.**

After accepting the license and going through the introductory screens, you are prompted to indicate if this is a network installation or not.

You see a couple more screens of information, after which you are asked how you're connected to the printer (shown in Figure 7-3). Method one is the simplest, as you are already set up that way (despite the picture in Figure 7-4 showing the computer plugged into the network, it works just as well over wireless).

4. **Select Next and the software attempts to discover the printer.**

If your computer has the Windows firewall enabled, then a dialog box appears so that you can make a firewall exception. Figure 7-5 shows the dialog box, to which you should select Unblock.

5. **After a moment, your printer will be discovered, and you can continue clicking Next until you are asked how you want to print, as shown in Figure 7-6.**

Figure 7-3:
Is this a network installation?

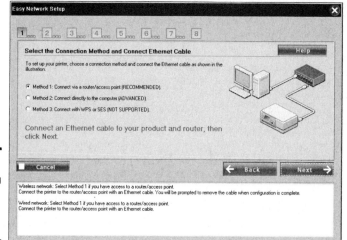

Figure 7-4:
How are you connected to the printer?

6. **Even though the printer is plugged in now, you eventually want to get it on the wireless network, so select Wireless.**

   The software will scan for available wireless networks and then present a list of SSIDs that you can connect to, which is shown in Figure 7-7. This is almost identical to how you chose which network to connect your computer to.

7. **Click on your network name to select it and then click the Next button.**

   If your network uses WEP, WPA, or WPA2, you must enter a password.

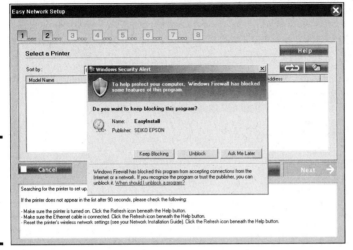

Figure 7-5:
Unblocking
the
application
from the
firewall.

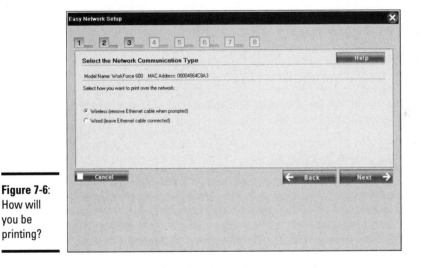

Figure 7-6:
How will
you be
printing?

8. **Type your password, confirm the settings, and then the printer will be configured by the software.**

9. **After the software has confirmed that the printer is configured, you can unplug the wired connection and print a test page when prompted.**

   Your default printer is set to the wireless printer.

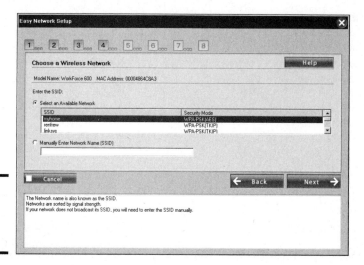

Figure 7-7:
The list of
wireless
networks

 If you noticed the WPS option during the setup, then good for you! For some reason, the current documentation specifically tells you not to use WPS, but after you've done the initial installation it works fine. This way would be handy, for instance, should you move the printer to a different network. From the control panel on the front of the printer, select Setup ⇨Network Settings⇨Wireless LAN setup. From there, you can change the network settings, including performing a WPS setup. You still need the driver on your computer to print, though.

Sharing Files Wirelessly

Sharing files between computers over a network, wired or wireless, is nothing new. However, you do find a few disadvantages:

✦ **The computer with the files on it has to be turned on.** The current trend is to save energy by turning off computers when they're not in use — which is good.

✦ **The computer with the files on it has to be connected to the network.** If the file you need is on a laptop that's not at home, you've got a problem.

✦ **It's more difficult and less secure to share files with the Internet.** If you want to grab some of your home files when you're at work, for example, the usual solution is to expose one of your home computers to the Internet.

Add to this that external USB storage is becoming larger and cheaper. For much less than $200, you can get a 1TB disk that can be used on any computer in your house, without having to take anything apart. Unfortunately, after you plug one of those bad boys into your laptop, you have no more mobility!

With the latest crop of home you simply plug the external hard drive into the router, configure file sharing, and presto! You have a permanent file server that you can store your stuff on. In Figure 7-8, I show a picture of the back of a Linksys WRT610N which has such a feature.

Figure 7-8:
A USB
port on a
router for
an external
storage
device.

A router draws far less power than a computer, is always available, and its position in the network is ideal for performance. The router is also able to share files to both the internal network and the Internet at large because it sits on both of those networks.

Setting up file storage

Start by plugging your USB storage device into the USB port on your router and then log in to your router's administrative interface. On the Linksys WRT610N you access the storage configuration from the Storage menu, which is shown in Figure 7-9.

The menu shows you details about the disk that's currently plugged in. Above, you can see I have a 2GB flash disk drive plugged in. This is a good sign because it means the router has recognized the drive. If you don't see any drives, double-check that the USB cable is plugged in all the way and that the hard drive has power.

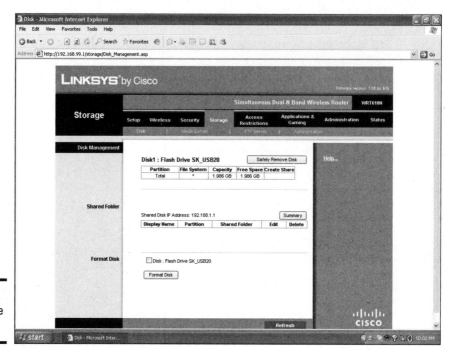

Figure 7-9:
The storage menu.

The disk details, shown in Figure 7-9 also include a column called Create Share. Depending on how your disk is set up, you may or may not see a button in that column that also says Create Share. If you do see the button, then you can skip the next section. If your view is like that shown in Figure 7-9, you need to format the disk.

Formatting the disk

Disks must be formatted and partitioned before they can be used. This process lays out certain structures on the disk that the computer uses to remember where files are placed and which parts of the disk are free.

You can format a disk many different ways; however, not all formats are supported by the router. It's easy to determine if you have to format your disk again — if you have the option to create a share, then you don't have to format the disk. Additionally, you can see some partitions listed in the top table.

Formatting a disk deletes everything on that disk. Gone! Kaput! Copy your stuff off the disk to another computer before you format; otherwise, it's gone!

Follow these steps to format a disk:

1. **After you back up your data, look down to the Format Disk section of the Web interface. Check the button next to the name of the disk and push the Format Disk button.**

You receive a warning indicating that everything on the disk will be deleted, as shown in Figure 7-10.

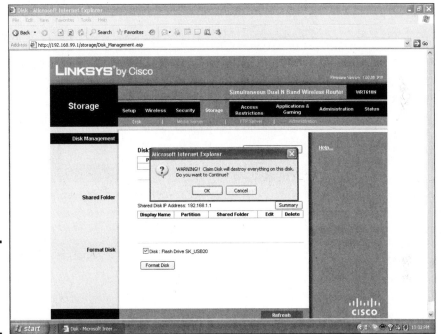

Figure 7-10:
A warning before formatting a disk.

2. **If you are sure you're ready to format the disk, click the OK button.**

After you've done that, you are asked to supply the name of a partition (see Figure 7-11).

A partition is a way to split out a disk into multiple logical disks. This formatting process assigns one partition to the disk, using all available space, so the name of the partition isn't that important.

3. **Type the name of a partition and click the Format button.**

You are asked again to confirm that you're okay with any data on the disk being wiped clean, after which the router can chug away while it formats the disk. This may take a few minutes, depending on the size of your disk.

After the formatting is complete, you are returned to the main storage menu (see Figure 7-12) showing the partition that was just created. Note that the Create Share button shows up along with the partition.

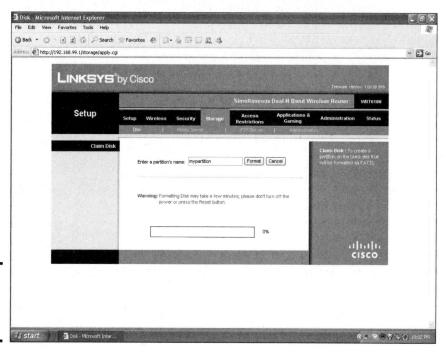

Figure 7-11: Supplying the name of a partition.

Figure 7-12 also shows that a shared folder called *public* has been created. Before you can use this share, though, you must take care of some of the default security settings.

Dealing with security

After you format the disk, the router creates a directory called public and shares it out with the name of Default. When you connect to a network share you must provide a username and password to connect with, which prevents the wrong people from getting at your data.

The router has created two users by default and given them access to the share. One user, *guest*, can only read the data, while the *admin* user can read and write. This is okay, but you want to set the passwords to something you know and control. To do so, follow these steps:

1. **Select the Administration submenu (the one to the right of FTP server, not the one to the left of Status) to see a list of the users and groups as shown in Figure 7-13.**

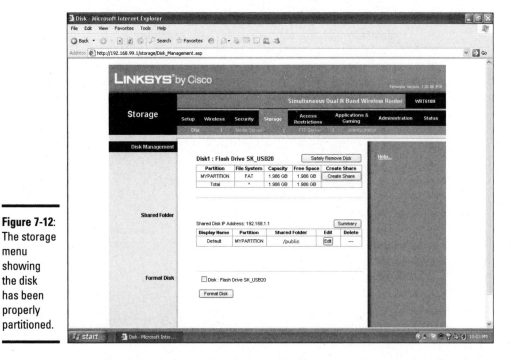

Figure 7-12:
The storage
menu
showing
the disk
has been
properly
partitioned.

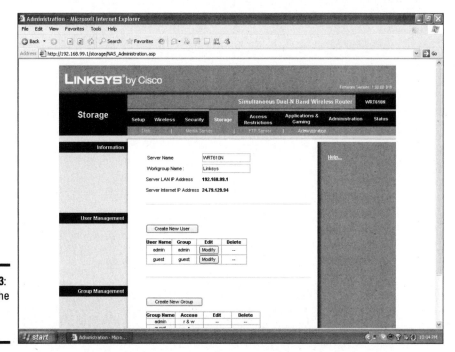

Figure 7-13:
Showing the
users and
groups.

2. Click on the Modify button next to the Admin user, and a new window, like the one in Figure 7-14, appears.

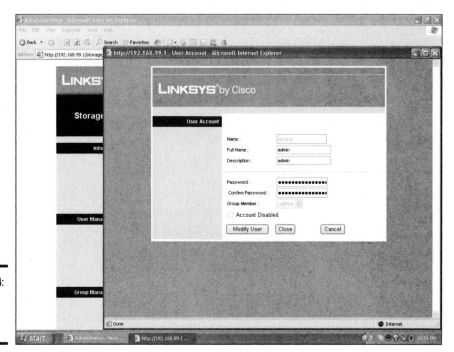

Figure 7-14: Modifying the admin user.

3. Type a new password in the Password field and then confirm it in the field below.

4. Finally, click Modify User to save the change. Repeat this process for the Guest user.

Connecting to the file share

While you're in the administration menu, make a note of the *Server LAN IP Address*. It's the address of the router, which will now be your file server address.

1. From the Start menu, select Run, then two backslashes followed by the IP address of the router. I've shown this in Figure 7-15 using the IP address of my router, which is 192.168.99.1.

2. After you click OK, you are asked to log in (see Figure 7-16).

3. Type the admin user and password where prompted and select OK (you can also select the Remember my password box if you don't want to have to log in all the time).

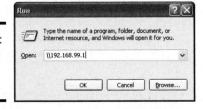

Figure 7-15:
Connecting
to the file
share.

Figure 7-16:
Logging in
to the file
share.

After you've logged in, you see a list of file shares available (see Figure 7-17). The Config file share contains a link to the administrative interface of the router; the Default file share is the one you set up earlier.

Figure 7-17:
The list of
file shares

With this all done, you have a centralized place to put your files that never goes away!

Make sure to back up your data, either by periodically burning files to DVD or making copies on other computers. Or, the other way around, this central file share makes a fine backup site for your local files, should something happen to your laptop.

Some of these devices have some features on top of the file sharing. For instance, the Linksys WRT610N can act as a media server which will be auto-detected by Windows Vista and some other universal plug and play capable software. Any media files on the shared hard drive will be instantly accessible to your audio software!

Adding an Access Point

Chapter 1 pointed out that wireless waves don't travel forever, especially if dense objects like walls are in the way. It's possible that you've got some wireless dead spots in your network, or even a whole area such as an outside workshop. Moving your router around might help things out, but at some point you need a second access point.

The general idea behind a second access point is that you plug it into your internal wired network and give it the same wireless settings as the router. If the radios are on two different channels, then your computer will pick which radio to associate with, based on signal strength. If you roam from one radio's space to the other, then your computer moves over to the other access point.

That's the theory, anyway. In practice, I've found that the built-in Windows wireless software doesn't do a great job here, and that you're better off using your manufacturer's software if you plan on roaming between wireless zones. The worst case is that you have to reconnect when you move from one zone to the other.

This is a very effective technique for expanding your network. Your only requirements are an access point and a cable to go from wherever the access point is back to your Internet router.

The trouble I've found with access points is that they're hard to find. I was at an office supply store doing some research, and I found a dozen varieties of wireless routers, but no access points.

Fear not! You'll soon learn how to turn a router into a simple access point. If you're upgrading your router anyway, you can keep your old router to provide lower-speed coverage to a different area of your place.

We're going to be turning off some features that make it easier to connect to your router, but nothing that's irreversible. If you're stuck, do a factory reset on the router and you'll be able to connect again. Usually this involves pushing the reset button while rebooting your router. When in doubt, check the product documentation.

Converting a router into an access point

A wireless router is really a regular wired router with a built-in access point. All you need to do is avoid using the router part, and you've got yourself an access point.

Wireless routers generally have one Ethernet port that goes to the Internet, and about four ports for connecting wired devices into your internal network. These four internal ports are bridged to the wireless side, meaning that they are on the same network.

With that in mind, if you connect the internal ports of two routers together you've got yourself two wireless networks that are connected. See what I mean in Figure 7-18. The goal here is to provide some extra coverage in the basement where the signal is low.

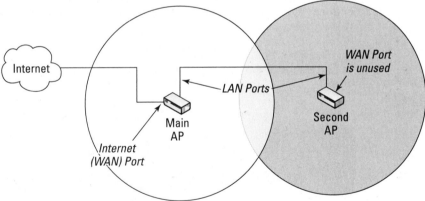

Figure 7-18:
Connecting
two routers.

As long as those two radios are on different channels, it doesn't matter which one you're connected to because you'll always be in the same network. A few things to keep in mind, though:

✦ Only one of the routers can be connected to the Internet. The other router's Internet port is not used.

✦ You need a special cable called a crossover cable to connect two routers together. It looks the same as a regular cable but one of the ends has some of the wires crossed.

✦ Only one DHCP server is needed for the whole network. If you had two DHCP servers going, there would be a lot of confusion. To make things simple, the DHCP server goes on the router that's connected to the Internet.

✦ The two routers must have different IP addresses. If they were the same, they'd fight, and your computer would not know how to get out to the Internet. Again, in the interests of simplicity, the router connected to the Internet will keep its address; the other router will pick a new one.

Despite having these four caveats, it's not too hard to do, especially if you do it in the right order.

To keep things straight, the router that connects to the Internet is called the Internet router. The new router is called the expansion router.

Reconfiguring the expansion router

The first order of business is to reconfigure the expansion router. The easiest way to do this is to plug your computer into the router on one of the Internal ports, with the Internet disconnected.

The router I'm using is an older Linksys device that I'm repurposing to expand my wireless footprint. As usual, it may look different than yours, but the concepts are still the same. To reconfigure the expansion router, follow these steps:

1. **Navigate to the Wireless menu and change the network name (SSID), so that it is the same as that on your Internet router.**

Remember that case matters! See Figure 7-19.

Figure 7-19: Reconfiguring the SSID on the expansion router.

2. **After you've set the SSID, move over to the Wireless Security menu and change the security mode and key to the same thing as what you're using on the Internet router, as shown in Figure 7-20.**

   Disable DHCP on the expansion router and change its address to something that doesn't conflict with the Internet router.

   On this access point, both tasks happen on the same screen. If your router has the features split, then make sure to change the address last! After you change the address, you won't be able to connect to the router until you hook it into the Internet router, at which point you'd have two DHCP servers, which wouldn't be great!

   Figure 7-21 shows the screen to disable DHCP and change the IP address.

3. **Change the Local DHCP Server setting to Disable.**

4. **Change the local IP address to something different than that of the Internet router.** My Internet router's address is 192.168.99.1, so I'm using 192.168.99.2 for the expansion router. Note that the first three numbers are the same, only the last one differs.

Book II
Chapter 7

Setting Up Other
Hardware

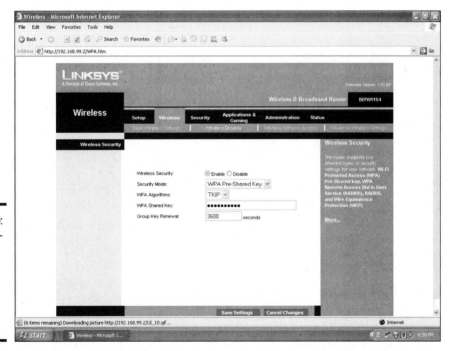

Figure 7-20: Reconfiguring the wireless security on the expansion router.

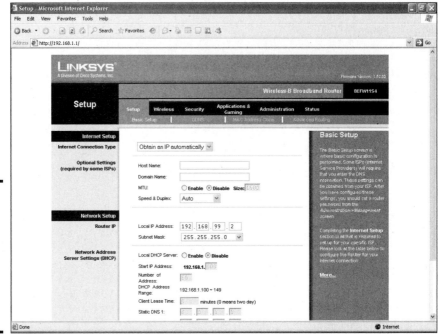

Figure 7-21: Disabling DHCP and changing the IP address on the expansion router.

You might also note that the Internet connection stays on Obtain an IP automatically. This setting doesn't really matter anymore because the expansion router won't be plugged into the Internet.

5. Click the Save button.

After you save the settings, you will lose connection to the router because it's using a new address. (This is expected, and it'll come back in the next step.)

You should already have a crossover cable run from your Internet router to the expansion router.

6. Plug this cable into an internal port on each router.

The port number doesn't matter, but it has to be the internal port. Don't use the Internet port on the expansion router!

You can now connect to either router using their address in your Web browser. You can access the Internet, and any other computer on your network, while associated to either of the access points. In fact, you shouldn't even know which network you're on!

Chapter 8: Troubleshooting Network Hardware

In This Chapter
- ✓ Isolating network problems
- ✓ Troubleshooting problems in order
- ✓ Upgrading drivers and firmware

Technology always works, right? I don't believe that either. Many pieces have to come together correctly to put a Web page on your computer and get your e-mail delivered so that it's a wonder that it works at all.

Sometimes parts break or just don't work the way you want them to. You've just built a wireless network; it's quite probable that something needs to be fixed.

In this chapter, we look at fixing your network problems, or at least getting far enough that you can point the finger at your service provider.

Before You Begin

Was your wireless network working, then you did something, and then it stopped working? Even if you did something, that shouldn't have made a difference. Maybe you installed some new software, changed a name, or were rearranging some cables.

If so, undo what you did. If it's not undoable (such as moving cables around), make sure everything was exactly the way it was before.

Most computer problems happen because something was changed. It's okay to change things, but when the change makes your computer break, backing out of the change is faster than fiddling around.

Coming Up with a Plan

Successful troubleshooting means following a plan. I'm not talking about a detailed written plan — most often a picture on a scrap of paper can suffice.

Generally, you start at one end of the network and work your way through to the other end until you've found the problem.

Defining the problem

Before you start anything, define your problem. Framing this definition in terms of what you are trying to do that's not working is important. Some good descriptions are

- ✦ I'm trying to browse to http://example.com, but my Web browser says "Host not found."
- ✦ I'm trying to get my e-mail, but Outlook tells me "Invalid password."
- ✦ I'm trying to get the sports scores, but my Web browser just returns a white screen.

Note that in all cases the problem description includes an error message, or at least a description of what you are seeing, along with a description of what you're trying to do. This information helps guide your troubleshooting and will be essential information if you have to call someone for support.

A few bad problem descriptions are

- ✦ The Internet is down.
- ✦ My e-mail is broken.
- ✦ My site doesn't work.

These phrases don't communicate anything to people trying to help, nor do they describe the problem.

If you have multiple computers in your house, then you should check to see if the problem exists on some of those. Doing this helps differentiate a computer problem from a network problem.

Drawing a picture

It may sound corny, but drawing a picture can help your troubleshooting considerably. A picture helps you understand how all the parts go together, which guides your problem solving.

You can see a sketch of my network in Figure 8-1:

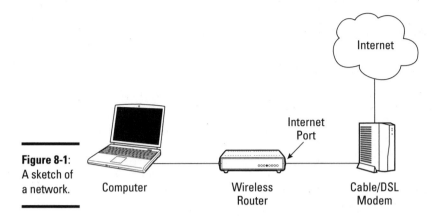

Figure 8-1:
A sketch of
a network.

See? It can be pretty simple. The computer connects over the wireless network to the router, which connects to the Internet, through the cloud known as the Internet to the Web site.

Is the error message trying to tell me something?

Now that the network layout is fresh in your mind, look at the error message that comes up when you try to perform your task. Is it pointing out something?

For example, if your e-mail client tells you that the username and password are wrong, you should jump straight to verifying those items. Sometimes, though, the error message doesn't make things any clearer for you, which means that you need to continue to troubleshoot.

Is the problem the same for all sites?

If your problem has to do with a Web site, then check another Web site to see if it has the same problem. Sites such as Google.com, yahoo.com, and ebay.com should generally be available, unless the problem is more local.

If you can get to other sites, then chances are your site is having problems, and you'll just have to wait it out. You could call a friend and ask if they're having the same problem, just to make sure.

If other sites seem to be down, too, then the problem is probably on your end, and it's time to fix it.

If Web sites work, but e-mail doesn't, then there's little point in following the guidelines in this chapter. You've shown that the Internet works and that it's a problem with your ISP. Skip straight to calling your ISP.

Looking at Your PC

Starting at the left of the network diagram, you want to make sure your computer's working correctly.

Before you start checking your PC's settings, can you log into the administrative interface of your router while connected to the wireless network? If so, your PC's probably okay, and you can skip to the next section. If not, it's time to troubleshoot the PC.

Repairing your network connection

In Windows XP, right-click on the network adapter icon in your system tray and select Repair. Your computer disables the network adapter and then brings it up.

In Vista, right-click on the network adapter icon in the system tray and select Diagnose and Repair.

Rebooting the computer

If resetting the network connection doesn't work, then reboot your computer. I know it's a pain, but this is Windows after all, and sometimes it needs the computer equivalent of a swift kick in the behind. Rebooting solves a lot of problems.

After a reboot, Windows gets a fresh chance to do things in its own order and from scratch, which is often enough to fix a problem with the computer.

Checking the wireless association

At this point, you've rebooted your computer so you know that it wasn't some sort of transient thing that most computers experience. Looking back at the network diagram, the problem must either be between you and your router, the router itself, or with the rest of the Internet.

If you can, try plugging your computer into the router using an Ethernet cable instead of using wireless. If things work with a wire, then the problem must be with the wireless connection. If not, you can troubleshoot the router.

Go back to your list of wireless networks (see Chapter 6) and make sure you're connected to the right one! If your computer loses connection to your original access point, it will try to find another one and associate with that, even if it doesn't belong to you or work properly. You might not even notice this happening at the time.

If you're not connected to the right wireless network, or you're not connected to any network, review Chapter 6 to configure your computer. Try it with both the built-in Windows configuration and your vendor's configuration tool.

Pay close attention to the signal strength as you configure your network. A low strength is a sign that you need to either move your router to a better spot or add a second access point for more coverage. Put your computer in the same room as the access point while configuring, just to make sure.

Incorrect passwords are often the culprit when dealing with association problems. Review the settings on the wireless router and make sure that they match those on the computer. If Wireless Protected Setup is available to you, then use that method.

If, after all that, you can't associate with your wireless network, skip ahead to the end of this chapter and upgrade your router firmware and your computer's drivers.

Verifying your IP settings

If you're able to associate with an access point and you are still having problems connecting to the Internet, then it's time to make sure you're getting a proper address.

In Windows XP, right-click on the adapter in the system tray and select Status. Then click on the Support tab and click Details.

In Vista, choose Start⇨Control Panel⇨Network and Sharing Center. Click on the Status link next to your wireless adapter and then click Details.

You are looking for the following information:

✦ IP address (or IPv4 address in Vista)

✦ DHCP Server

✦ Default gateway

✦ DNS Server

Checking the IP address

The IP address identifies your computer on the network. The IP address probably begins with 192.168, though it could also begin with 172 or 10. These are the reserved private network addresses and are used for people behind routers.

If your IP address begins with 169.254, then you aren't getting an address from your DHCP server. If a computer doesn't hear from a DHCP server, then it picks one of these addresses. This is okay if you have computers that want to talk to each other, but it will not work with your router.

Pay special attention if your computer roams between networks, such as home and work. Sometimes Windows doesn't pick up a new address when it changes networks, and it is vital to have a proper address. This is why the first step in troubleshooting is to initiate a repair operation on the adapter or reboot the computer.

DHCP and your gateway

Your DHCP server should be the address of your router. It should also be the same as your default gateway. If you don't have a DHCP server set, then your computer might be set with a static address. Generally, you want to pick up a dynamic address.

If you have an IP address beginning with 169.254, then it's possible that your router does not have the DHCP service turned on. If so, it's best to do a factory reset of your router and start from scratch.

If your DHCP server is different from your gateway, then you might have two DHCP servers running on your network. Recall from Chapter 7 that you only want one DHCP server, and it should be the device that also plugs in to the Internet (and should therefore be your default gateway).

You should also have a gateway set. The gateway is the device that your computer uses to send information to the Internet.

Changing to DHCP addressing

If you don't have a DHCP server set, then your computer is probably hard coded with an address (also called a *static address*). To work properly on your network, you want to use DHCP addressing.

If your computer was set up with a static address for a reason, such as to work with an office network, then you have to switch your settings every time you change networks. It would be worth your time to find out if you can use DHCP on the other network.

1. **In Windows XP, right-click on the adapter icon in your system tray and select Status.**

2. **From that dialog box, click the Properties button.**

   A dialog box like the one shown in Figure 8-2 appears.

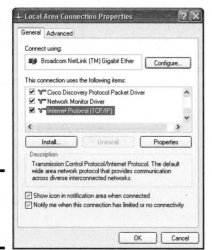

Figure 8-2:
Windows
XP adapter
properties.

3. **In the This Connection Uses the Following Items area, scroll down
until you see Internet Protocol (TCP/IP). Select that line and click the
Properties button.**

The dialog box in Figure 8-3 appears.

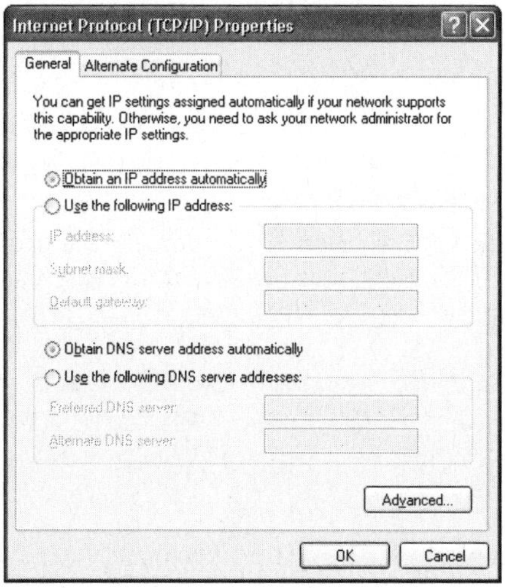

Figure 8-3:
Windows
XP TCP/IP
properties.

4. **The two radio buttons should be on Obtain an IP Address Automatically and Obtain DNS Server Automatically. If the buttons are on a different option, change them.**

5. **If you had to make changes, then continue clicking the OK button to get out of all the menus. You should be able to obtain an address now.**

Vista is slightly different.

1. **Go to Start⇨Control Panel⇨Network and Sharing Center.**

2. **From the Tasks menu, choose Manage Network Connections.**

3. **Select the adapter and choose Change settings of this connection.**

4. **Select Internet Protocol Version 4, as shown in Figure 8-4, and click the Properties button.**

   The dialog box shown in Figure 8-5 appears.

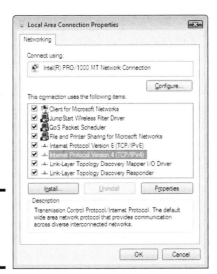

Figure 8-4: Vista adapter properties.

5. **Make sure that the automatic options are selected.**

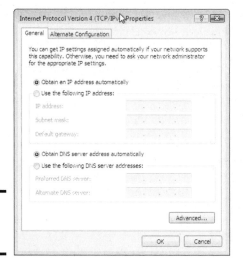

Figure 8-5:
Vista IPv4
properties.

Looking at Your Router

You should be able to connect over the wireless network to your router. If not, make sure of the following:

+ Do you have DHCP enabled on the router?

+ Is the computer able to associate with the wireless network?

+ Can you connect to the wireless router's Web interface using its address (such as 192.168.1.1) over the wireless network?

The "Looking at Your PC" section covers these three items in detail.

If you've got through the previous section and still can't connect to the router, then skip ahead to the end and look at updating drivers.

Look back at the network diagram. Because you can connect to the router, you know that your computer is all right and the wireless network works. So, the problem is either the router or the router's connection to the Internet.

Rebooting the router and ISP equipment

Reboots fix a lot of things, and your Internet connection is no exception. Pull the power from your cable or ADSL modem and your wireless router, count to five, and then plug them back in.

While you're at it, make sure that all the cables are plugged in properly. Ethernet cables have a tab on the connector that prevents the cable from falling out, so a gentle tug on the connector verifies that everything is locked in.

Also verify that the devices have power. All devices differ, but they all have some sort of light to indicate that they're on. If, after all this work, you realized that you forgot to plug something in, don't worry; it happens to the best of us!

Give things a few minutes to settle and check again.

Bypassing the router

By now, you've checked all the common problems with the router and you're getting close to the point where you're going to have to call someone for help.

Take your router out of the loop by plugging your computer directly into your Internet connection. For cable modems, this is fairly straightforward, but for ADSL connections you sometimes need some special software.

If you're able to connect to the Internet with your computer directly plugged in to your cable or ADSL modem, then your ISP is off the hook. The problem must be with your router. (I go over this in the next section.)

If you still can't browse the Web with your computer plugged in to the Internet connection, then your provider's probably at fault. You might want to skip down to the "Before Calling for Support" section.

If you've successfully connected to the Internet with the router before, and it just stopped working, then it's probably a problem with your provider. Make sure that you've rebooted everything, and then jump down to the "Before Calling for Support" section.

Setting the connection type

If you remember way back to when you set up the router, you were asked if your Internet Service Provider requires a username and password to log in. This information is required to authenticate to the provider and get your service. If this information is wrong, then you won't be able to log in.

Similarly, if the router is configured to log in, but your provider isn't expecting it, then you have problems.

First, check to see if you're getting an IP address from your provider. On the NETGEAR router, click on the Router Status link, which is in the Maintenance section and is shown in Figure 8-6.

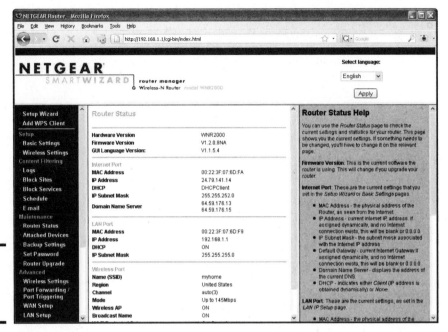

Figure 8-6:
The router
status
screen.

The section of the router status screen headed Internet Port contains the information pertaining to your Internet connection. You can see that an IP address of 24.79.141.14 has been assigned, and that DNS servers have also been given (it is all right that the IP address and the DNS servers look nothing like each other).

If you have an Internet address of 0.0.0.0, then it means that you're not connected to your provider, or your provider is having a problem.

In this event, check the cable between your router and the modem, and between the modem and the provider, to make sure they're attached and in the right port.

Go back to Chapter 3 and make sure your router is set up correctly. If everything seems fine on your end, see the next section to make sure the router's firmware is up to date, and then call your provider.

If at this point all indications are that things should be working but they aren't, you still can't pin the blame on your router or the service provider. In this case, it's best to work through your service provider first to verify that the Internet connection is working, and if that is successful, to call the support line for your router for further troubleshooting.

Upgrading Software

When software is written, the possibility of bugs being introduced exists. One of my favorite quotes about software development is, "If debugging is the process of removing bugs, then programming must be the process of putting them in."

Sometimes software is shipped with bugs (either knowingly or unknowingly), and sometimes changes to other software introduces new bugs.

Thankfully, most devices ship with the ability to upgrade software in the field. For routers, this means that you can upgrade the firmware that runs the hardware. For wireless adapters, this means that you can upgrade the drivers.

The downside is that you need to get on the Internet to get the latest updates. If you are upgrading to regain your Internet connection, then you have to use a working computer to get the appropriate software onto a USB pen drive or a CD-ROM.

To find the latest software upgrades, go to the home page of the device's manufacturer, and look for a link called either "Support" or "Drivers and Downloads." You'll need to know the model number of the device you have.

Upgrading router firmware

Your router is a special purpose computer and needs some special software to make it run, much like your computer needs an operating system like Windows to run. For routers, the manufacturer provides the operating system. The router comes with a version of the software, but periodically updates are released.

Updates are a good thing for you, the consumer. A few years back, when the wireless encryption standards were in a state of flux, manufacturers were able to release updates containing the latest standards. This way, customers could be using the latest security protocols without having to buy a new router. When the 802.11n standard makes it out of draft form, you should be able to download an updated version of your router code that will bring you into compliance.

The software that a router runs is called *firmware*, which is some geek's way of talking about something halfway between hardware and software.

Download the firmware from the vendor's support site and store it on your computer. If you got the file as a .zip file, then unpack it first.

Most manufacturers recommend doing upgrades while connected to a wired port rather than wireless. This is because if the connection is interrupted during the upgrade, the router will only have part of the new image, and it might not run correctly anymore. The technical term for this is called *bricking* your router, because a failed upgrade usually renders the device with the same functionality as a brick.

1. **Look for a menu item within the router's Web GUI that talks about upgrading.**

   Figure 8-7 shows the upgrade menu from the NETGEAR router.

2. **Click the Browse button to locate the image you downloaded and click OK.**

3. **Click the Upload button to send the software image to the router.**

   The next screen prompts you to confirm the version number on the router. In Figure 8-8, you can see that the current revision is 1.2.0.8, and I'm trying to upgrade it with the same version.

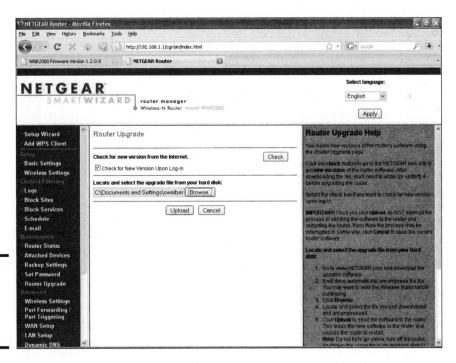

Figure 8-7: The NETGEAR router upgrade.

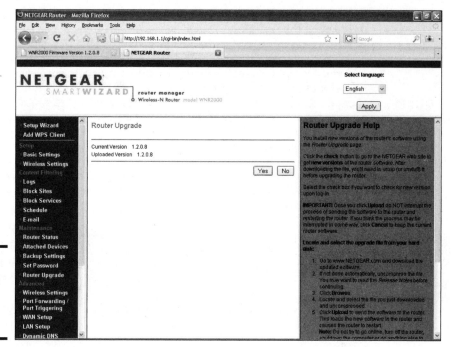

Figure 8-8:
Confirming
the
firmware
versions.

4. **Click Yes if you want to continue.**

   The router displays a progress bar and thinks for a while before reboot-ing and bringing you back to the main menu.

Don't touch your computer while this process is happening. Go grab a coffee or something. It'll finish on its own!

That was easy, wasn't it?

Upgrading your network drivers

The network drivers control how the physical adapter interfaces with the rest of the operating system. Changes to the operating system sometimes mean that you have to update your driver. Sometimes new wireless features are added to the adapter that allow you to be more compatible with other wireless networks.

While you're upgrading your drivers, you may as well upgrade the wireless utilities. In fact, doing both at once is usually easier than going the long way and upgrading your drivers.

Most manufacturers release a self-installing package that automatically updates your wireless drivers and the wireless utilities. It's remarkably simple to use.

For this example, I went to the Intel support site and searched for 3945ABG, which is the wireless card model I have. I know this because it's printed on the bottom of my computer. I was then asked to choose my operating system. Finally, I saw the screen shown in Figure 8-9.

The following options are available:

**Book II
Chapter 8**

Troubleshooting
Network Hardware

✦ The first option is to download only the wireless drivers. Doing this updates the adapter to the latest code, but it won't touch the management tools. The key words here are drivers-only.

✦ The second option is to download the drivers and management software. This includes both the wireless drivers and the connection utility. This option is the better choice in my humble opinion, even if you don't use the vendor's management utilities.

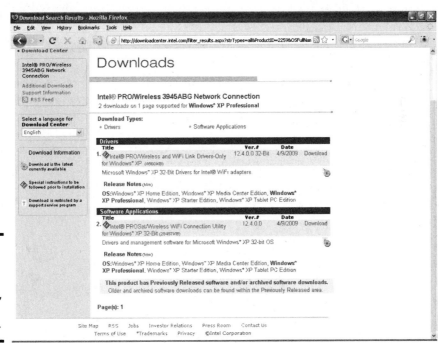

Figure 8-9:
Choosing
between
drivers only,
and drivers
and utilities.

Click the Download link, accept the agreement, and then save the file to a directory, such as your desktop. Run the program that you downloaded and follow the prompts. It's fairly uneventful.

Before Calling for Support

If you got this far, then you're calling either your ISP or your router manufacturer for support. That's all right, because that's what they're there for. You can do this before you call to make the process go quicker, though.

 Whatever you do, don't get mad at the person on the other end of the phone. Doing so just makes the repair take longer. Remember that he didn't cause the problem — they're trying to help you. Introduce yourself and greet them by name.

No matter who you're calling, make sure to have the following things handy:

✦ A concise description of the problem and what you think should be happening

✦ An estimate of when the problem started

✦ A list of what you've done so far

✦ A description of what your network looks like

If you are calling your service provider, make sure that you know the following:

✦ Your account number or billing address and what kind of service you have

✦ A description of which lights are on the modem and what color they are

✦ The last time you rebooted your computer and modem

If you are calling your router manufacturer, have the following handy:

✦ The model number of the router in question.

✦ A description of which lights are on and what color they are.

✦ A summary of what you've tried. Does the router work if you are wired in but not wireless?

The people on the phone will start by asking many of the same questions that have already been asked in this chapter. Just go with the flow — they're just trying to make sure the common problems have been covered.

Book III
Configuring Networks

The 5th Wave   By Rich Tennant

"You the guy having trouble staying connected to the network?"

Contents at a Glance

Chapter 1: Exploring Windows Networking

In This Chapter

✓ Windows XP makes wireless easy

✓ Plug and play . . . hopefully

✓ Choosing the kind of network you want

Microsoft introduced an easy wireless network setup and configuration with the release of Windows XP in 2001. Prior to that, installing any kind of network using Windows computers was often a hassle and usually unpredictable. Skip ahead to 2009, and subsequent editions of Windows (most notably Vista and the new Windows 7) have made things even easier! In many cases, it's as simple as turning on your computer or flipping a switch on your laptop.

If you have a typical setup, which includes a modern PC and networking equipment released in the past one or two years, creating a wireless network should be a snap. If all goes well, you can install a wireless network adapter in your PC, and you're almost ready to connect with your chosen wireless network. The best part is that once you set up your wireless network, it's completely low maintenance — don't expect to have to toy around with the settings very often. Now, cross your fingers (I'm watching, as is Microsoft) and venture into the relatively painless world of Windows XP and wireless networking.

Installing Is Child's (Plug and) Play

Most of the work of installing a wireless network is done by the computer as part of the operating system's plug and play feature. That means after plugging in your adapter, it should be installed automatically (or close to it). You may have to install a driver or supplemental piece of software to interact with the hardware, but it's a very easy procedure to perform.

With modern wireless technology, installing the necessary hardware into your computer is usually so-called plug and play. In other words, the process is supposed to be mostly automated: You plug in your network adapter (a card that transmits and receives signals over your wireless network), and the operating system is supposed to recognize, install, and configure it with minimal action on your part.

If you have newer hardware, this should be the case most of the time. If you're trying to use an older or obscure network adapter (stay away from the bargain bins!) or own a computer that you bought more than, say, eight or nine years ago, this might not be the case.

And remember that I'm talking about Windows XP Service Pack 2 or later here. If you're running an older operating system, all bets are off. My advice: Upgrade to Windows Vista before you pursue this course called wireless networking. If you're one of those home computer users that just isn't comfortable using Windows Vista for whatever reason, then you'll want to make sure you're using Windows XP Service Pack 2 at the very minimum or plan on upgrading to Windows 7 upon availability. In order to remain consistent with Microsoft's current offering at the time of publishing, I work with Windows Vista in any relevant procedures.

Just because Windows can configure your network adapter doesn't mean you want it to do so. You may find that the utility software that came with the adapter provides more features and better feedback about signal strength and other basics. For example, the Intel Pro Wireless Network Connection is a more than capable alternative to Windows' Network and Sharing Center.

In that case, let Windows' plug-and-play feature handle the installation, and you can look to the network equipment maker for the software to add any extra features that Windows doesn't add automatically. Just remember, if you decide to use a third-party application to manage your computer's wireless capabilities, it completely shuts Windows out of the picture until you decide to revert.

Working with the Network and Sharing Center

My Network Places is replaced in Windows Vista with the Network and Sharing Center, as shown in Figure 1-1.

The Network and Sharing Center is really a one-stop shop for all of your network needs; it truly is the hub of your broadband experience. When you first access the center, as discussed in the following sections, you will find out a lot about your network. For example, Windows draws a basic schema of your network connection that shows your computer, the name and type of network location, and finally to what you're connected (the Internet!).

Book III
Chapter 1

Exploring Windows
Networking

Figure 1-1:
The new
Network
and Sharing
Center.

From the main panel in the Network and Sharing Center, you can find out more information about your network, such as the name and access you have. While it's a more text-based version of the aforementioned schema, this section lets you rename your network. Remembering Mike's Network is easier than remembering Network 24, which is default Windows fashion. This section is also important because it indicates whether or not you actually have Internet access. When everything is running smoothly, it says Local and Internet. Should you see only Local only, you know you've got problems on your hands and you should consider rebooting either your computer or your wireless router.

The second section of the main pane concerns your file sharing options (Sharing and Discovery). By default, all available menus are collapsed but can be expanded to set your preferences. Each option is represented with a green light (on) or a gray radio button (off), indicating the status. The sharing options also extend to printers, media files, and public folder sharing. I recommend only enabling these options when you are working on a private network, such as at your home. If you are in a public place, you will really want to think twice about making key folders on your computer available to everyone within wireless range.

The left side of the Network and Sharing Center displays a series of tasks and related topics. With respect to wireless networking, these tasks allow you to either set up a new wireless network or connect to an existing, available wireless network within range of your computer.

What is a public folder?

If you grew up using Microsoft Windows as your primary (if not only) operating system over the years, you're undoubtedly familiar with the legendary Windows folders: My Documents, My Pictures, My Music, and so on.

Windows Vista offers a few new changes to that tried and true practice. First, you've likely noticed that Vista has dumped My. More importantly, Vista offers a second set of documents called Public folders. These folders, which include Public Desktop, Public Documents, Public Downloads, and so on, as shown in the figure, let you make specific files and folders available to others on your computer or your network. To use them, simply drag and drop the file or folder into the corresponding Public folder. These folders are accessible from Windows Explorer.

So, when do we actually get to meet the Network and Sharing Center? How about right now? The following sections provide several ways for you to access it in Windows Vista.

Accessing from the Windows taskbar

Here's how you access the Network and Sharing Center from the taskbar:

1. **Right-click the network icon (two screens joined with a planet Earth) in the right-side of the taskbar, as shown in Figure 1-2.**

The corresponding contextual menu appears.

2. **Click Network and Sharing Center.**

The Network and Sharing Center appears in a separate window.

Figure 1-2:
Accessing the Network and Sharing Center from the taskbar.

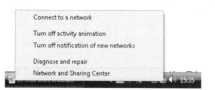

Connect to a network

Turn off activity animation
Turn off notification of new networks

Diagnose and repair
Network and Sharing Center

Accessing from the All Programs menu

Perhaps you are more old-school and like to use your keyboard to locate Windows features:

1. **Click the Start menu icon.**

The Start menu appears.

2. **Type Network in the Start search text box at the bottom of the menu.**

The entries are filtered to show only applications or elements displaying the word "network," as shown in Figure 1-3.

3. **Click Network and Sharing Center.**

The Network and Sharing Center appears in a separate window.

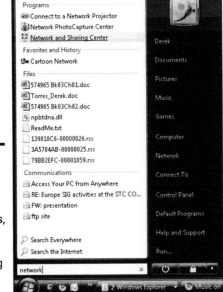

Figure 1-3: The returned list of applications, including Network and Sharing Center.

Mingling with Different Networks

You can create two kinds of networks with Windows:

✦ **Infrastructure:** Chances are you want to create an infrastructure network, which is the traditional network that uses a DSL or cable modem connecting to your computer directly or through a router.

✦ **Computer to computer:** You also see this called a peer-to-peer or an ad hoc network. It's a connection made directly between one computer and another.

As always, each has advantages and disadvantages.

Thinking about an Infrastructure Network

Most likely, when you think of a wireless network, you're thinking about an infrastructure network. Book II is essentially about creating an infrastructure network. I avoid repeating that information here.

However, anytime you communicate between a wireless access point (such as a wireless router) and a wireless network adapter, you're moving information over an infrastructure network. When you're on the road and using a coffee shop's wireless access, you're connecting to an infrastructure network. Your computer is connecting through a wireless access point, which in turn connects to the Internet.

In most cases, it just makes more sense at home to set up and run this kind of network instead of a computer-to-computer network.

Creating a Computer-to-Computer Network

A computer-to-computer network means exactly that: Your computer is wirelessly connecting directly to another computer. This is known as an ad hoc network. Both PCs need wireless adapters, of course. Windows XP also will need to be set up to handle a computer-to-computer network connection.

At one time, a computer-to-computer network may have been cheaper to create because you didn't need a router. Instead, one computer can connect to the Internet and the other PC can wirelessly share that connection. Declining hardware costs provide no reason to use a computer-to-computer network when what you really need is an infrastructure network, which requires a router and possibly other hardware.

You can use a computer-to-computer network in your home or on the road, but a wireless network usually has specific applications, including the following:

✦ On a business trip, you and a colleague can connect your laptops wirelessly, allowing you to share files without the use of a router or other wireless access point.

✦ Anytime you're mobile, the network moves with you because you don't have to lug routers or other hardware (aside from your laptop).

✦ Anywhere an infrastructure network's wireless access point is unreachable; a computer-to-computer network provides an Internet connection, provided one of the computers is connected to the Internet.

✦ If you don't want to rely on the hardware in an infrastructure network, a computer-to-computer network provides redundancy. If a router goes down on an infrastructure network, the whole network stops working.

With a computer-to-computer network, another computer can always share the load. (This assumes more than two computers are in the computer-to-computer network.)

Creating a network for work

Depending on your network configuration at work, it may be possible for you to connect to your servers or computer at the office from home or on the road. To do this, you must first connect to your office's network and then use the Remote Desktop Connection application, which allows you to connect directly to a specific machine or server.

Before trying to create a connection to your office's network, verify with your IT or helpdesk team that you are authorized to create such connection. You also want to make sure that you have the parameters and login settings necessary to log on successfully. Of course, for security reasons, be sure to log off from the network or your remote computer when you are done with your session.

To connect to a work network, you need to first connect to a Virtual Private Network (VPN), which lets you act as if you were plugged in at the office. This type of network is covered in Book V, Chapter 6.

After you are connected to your VPN, go to Start➪All Programs➪ Accessories➪Remote Desktop Connection. Once you add your credentials (available from your company's network administrator, if you don't already know these details), you can access your computer exactly as if you were at work.

Enabling Internet sharing

After you have a computer-to-computer network set up, you can configure one computer to share an Internet connection with the other computers. I don't recommend using this fast and dirty way to share broadband access unless you have no other choice. It's slow compared to using an infrastructure network with a router.

If you can, try to build an infrastructure network where a router does the work of divvying out IP addresses to each computer and, most importantly, hides the network behind a firewall.

This method is really a last-ditch effort when you need to share an Internet connection. With the advance of networking and wireless technologies in recent years, it's hard to believe that this option is still available!

Book III Chapter 1

Exploring Windows Networking

Chapter 2: Managing Available Networks

In This Chapter

✔ **Finding out about wireless networks**

✔ **Adding a preferred network**

✔ **Watching your network**

✔ **Setting some advanced preferences**

A good thing about wireless networks is that you don't have those pesky Ethernet cables to tie you up in knots. I can still remember back in the old days when I'd have those drab, gray cables running from room to room. I also remember constantly tripping over said cables; fortunately, those days are gone! That doesn't mean that wireless networks are always easy to set up and use. Hopefully, you've made it past the rough spots and are ready to actually transfer data around your home.

Maybe your wireless network is ready to send data between your living room and second-floor bathroom. If so, make sure your PC can see the router and any other access points. That's where Windows Vista's Connect to a network feature in the Network and Sharing Center, formerly known as Available Networks for Windows XP, enters the picture.

I also discuss some ways to monitor your network's signal strength and capacity. Other chapters discuss similar network troubleshooting and maintenance topics:

✦ Book II, Chapter 8 gives you some help troubleshooting network adapters.

✦ Book III, Chapter 5 discusses how you confirm your wireless network is working.

✦ Book IV, Chapter 3 gives you some tips for solving wireless networking problems.

Discovering What's Out There

Notice that the title doesn't say who is out there. After all, this chapter's about wireless networks, not dating. If you're still interested in finding what's out there, read on, because you're in the right place.

The Connect to a network feature lets you see what networks are available — for dial-up, VPN, and wireless. Available means that they're out there, probably close by. The list should include one or more of your own networks, if all goes well. If you don't see your networks, be concerned.

If you sort the list to only display available wireless connections, the list is displayed by signal strength, which is indicated by a series of bars (much like the ones used by mobile phones to display signal strength).Your network(s) should be at the top of this list; if it's not, it should be quite closer; otherwise, we should discuss where your wireless router is stored, not to mention where it is that you tend to do most of your work.

In some cases, you see neighbors' wireless networks. That doesn't mean that you can connect to those networks, though. (I tackle that issue in more detail, along with other security topics, in Book IV.)

You likely won't see wireless networks where the owners have intentionally made them invisible to public viewing. The geeks can still discover your network name, but it's one tool in your security toolbox. After I tell you about monkey wrenches and screwdrivers (I'm trying to milk this toolbox metaphor), I talk about how you can make your network mostly invisible in Book IV.

1. **Right-click the network icon in your Windows notification area.**

A menu appears.

2. **Select Connect to a network.**

You see something like Figure 2-1. The dialog box lists Available Networks. In this case, Dog is the network and Livebox-bbcc is the neighbor (possibly the one with the barking dog and who insists on partying every weekend).

Figure 2-1:
The Connect To a Network dialog box displays all available wireless networks, or rather all those in range of your computer.

3. **Click the name of the desired network and click Connect.**

If the selected network requires a network key, now's the time to type it in this screen of the dialog box, as shown in Figure 2-2.

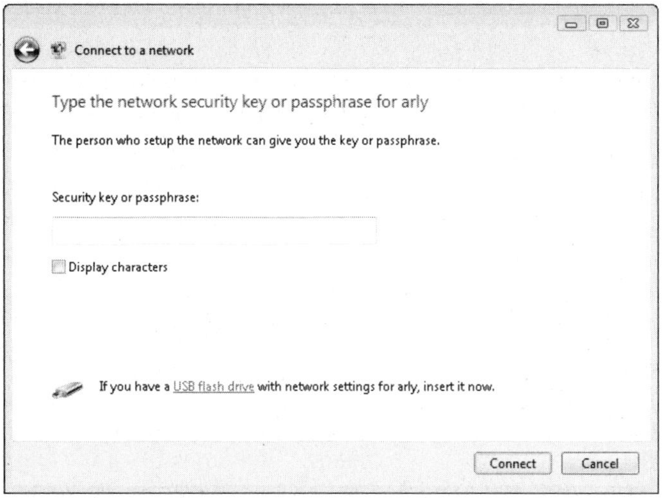

Figure 2-2:
You need
to know the
security
key for a
secured
network
before you
can use it.

Some networks require a network key, which is basically a password with so many unrelated letters and numbers that only a Jeopardy contestant can remember it. You can tell if the network requires a network key because it is labeled as a security-enabled network.

What if an available network requires a network key, but you don't have one? If you're sure it's your network or one you've been invited to use, you should ask its administrator for The Magic Key. Unfortunately, "abracadabra" doesn't work here.

4. **If a network doesn't require a network key (labeled as an Unsecured network), click the Connect Anyway link as shown in Figure 2-3.**

If you do use an unsecured network, be aware that your data may be visible to other parties. Though there is some security risk in using unsecured networks, you can take precautions (and others that Windows automatically takes for you in this case, which I will discuss later).

It's a scary option, I know, but select it for now. I tackle security issues in another chapter. That's it! You're done.

**Book III
Chapter 2**

Managing Available Networks

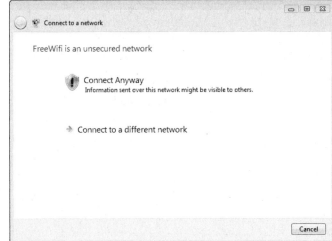

Figure 2-3:
If you are going to use an unsecured network as a wireless connection, Windows makes sure that you realize what you're getting yourself into.

You can do something that ensures almost always having a working Internet connection. In one word, it's called redundancy. Say a DSL line now comes into your house. Well, call up the cable company and order its cable modem service, too. Now use one connection for your wired network and the other connection for your wireless network. If one goes down, you can easily switch to the other Internet connection. Too bad you can't do that with electrical service!

What the heck is a, b, g, n?

When you went to your local electronics store to buy a laptop, or a wireless router/card, you likely noticed that 802.11 (followed by a/b/g/n) appeared on the box. These are wireless protocols that are used to designate a set of standard for wireless communications. For example, if you are using 802.11a (which is very unlikely these days), you know that your wireless connection is operating on a certain frequency and has a set data transfer rate.

There are currently four protocols used for wireless communications. The oldest are "a" and "b" — which are also the least powerful.

I'd say that "g" is the most commonly used protocol, but it will quickly be replaced by the "n" protocol, which has only been available for a relatively short amount of time. When you buy a wireless router, you must make sure that your laptop computer or wireless card is compatible with the router. If you buy an 802.11n wireless router, but only have a "g" compatible card, you won't be able to take advantage of the high performance of the "n" protocol.

To get a good idea of the difference between the various protocols, here are some facts and figures:

✔ (A) 802.11a

Frequency 5 GHz

Typical Data Rate 23 Mbit/s

Max Data rate 54 Mbit/s

Range 115 feet

✔ (B) 802.11b

Frequency 2.4 GHz

Typical Data Rate 4.5 Mbit/s

Max Data rate 11 Mbit/s

Range 115 feet

✔ (G) 802.11g

Frequency 2.4 GHz

Typical Data Rate 19 Mbit/s

Max Data rate 54 Mbit/s

Range 125 feet

✔ (N) 802.11n

Frequency 5 GHz and/or 2.4 GHz

Typical Data Rate 74 Mbit/s

Max Data rate 300 Mbit/s (2 streams)

Range 230 feet

Viewing Available Networks

If you followed the previous set of instructions, you've made it past the initial gatekeeper. You can view all available networks now. After following the steps in the preceding section, you find yourself in the Wireless Properties dialog box.

As I mention earlier, you may see your neighbors' wireless networks on the list. Ignore them, as it's the right thing to do. Hopefully, they'll do the same for you. Besides, you were wise enough to enable security on your wireless network, so there's no chance of them getting on, right?

If the stars are aligned, you see your wireless network along with other kinds of networks on the list, as shown in Figure 2-4. Again, in the example the network is dubbed Dog, which does not reflect on myself, my cat, or my network hardware.

You can refresh the list of available networks by clicking the — yes! — Refresh button, which is above the list of networks, to the right (across from the Show scroll-down list). If you're in a neighborhood with lots of wireless networks, you'll probably see this list constantly change as some networks go live and others shut down.

Book III
Chapter 2

Managing Available
Networks

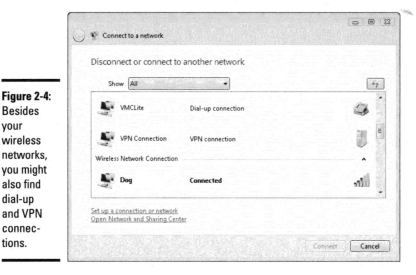

Figure 2-4:
Besides
your
wireless
networks,
you might
also find
dial-up
and VPN
connec-
tions.

You can configure an available network from the Manage Wireless Networks page, which is available from the Tasks list in the Network and Sharing Center. Configuration options include changing the network name (which is also called the SSID) and the wireless network key. Here's how you configure an available network:

1. **In the Network and Sharing Center, click Manage wireless networks under the Tasks list.**

2. **Click the name of the network you wish to configure.**

3. **Right-click and select Rename. (The network name becomes an enter-able text box, as shown in Figure 2-5.) Rename the network and click outside the box.**

A dialog box appears warning you of the consequences of such actions. Validate this dialog box. The network appears in the Manage Wireless Networks page with its new name.

4. **Right-click the name of the network and click Properties; click the Security tab.**

The following dialog box appears, as shown in Figure 2-6.

5. **You can make one or more changes to Association settings:**

- Toggle Network Authentication between Open and Shared.

- Change the Data Encryption setting to Disabled or WEP. If you select WEP, you can enter a network key and make other related changes. WEP is discussed in Book IV, Chapter 3, which covers the implemen-tation of wireless network security.

6. **Click OK.**

Whew! That's it for configuring available networks. Now, onward to preferred networks.

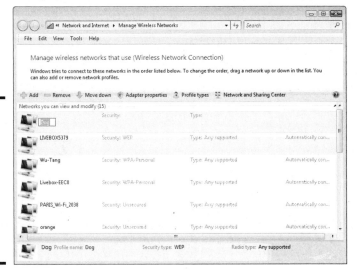

Figure 2-5:
You can rename your SSID, or wireless network, to make it more recognizable.

Figure 2-6:
The Properties dialog box lets you make some pretty important security decisions.

Managing Preferred Networks

You also can make an available network a preferred network. This gives some networks priority over other networks in case Windows has several from which to choose. It also lets you save custom configuration settings so you don't need to make them twice for the same network. When you find yourself in an area covered by a particular wireless network you used in the past, you'll be all set to connect.

In Windows XP, there was actually a dialog box called Preferred Networks. Now it's handled from the Manage Wireless Networks page. Here's what you can do from this page:

✦ Add a network

✦ Remove a network

✦ View a network's properties

✦ Reorder a preferred network's position

Each time you connect to an available network, the network is added to the list of preferred networks. But just because a network appears under Available Networks does not mean it's automatically added to the Preferred Networks list.

Connecting with your peers

Most wireless networks are called access point, or infrastructure, networks. That means your computer connects to the Internet through a wireless router or other access point. Chances are, this is how you'll set up your wireless network.

But there's another way (isn't there always?) you can create a wireless network by connecting two or more computers together. A computer-to-computer network lets you skip wireless network routers and other access points. Instead, PCs talk directly with one another, transmitting and receiving data through their network adapters.

A computer-to-computer network is also known as a peer-to-peer or ad hoc network.

One name wasn't enough, so the Lords of Geekdom bestowed it with three names.

The obvious advantage is cost: You don't pay for as much networking hardware. One computer usually serves as the gateway to your Internet connection, assuming some of the duties of a dedicated hardware router. Peer-to-peer networking also is handy for connecting a PC to a wireless print server, or networking two TiVo units.

If all you want is to wirelessly connect to PCs in your home, it may be the answer. I discuss the actual set up of these networks in Book III, Chapter 1.

Of course, the Add a network feature lets you do more than just add your own network. For example, let's say that you've been using a new wireless connection that is available to you, but your computer insists on always looking for, and connecting to, an older wireless connection. You can add this network while it's in range, and it adds it to the list of preferred wireless connections. From there, you can use the Move up and Move down buttons to rank its priority. You can also create an ad hoc connection (computer-to-computer) from the Add a network feature in this page.

Adding a preferred network

Follow these steps to add a preferred network:

1. **Click the Add button.**

   A Wireless Network Properties dialog box opens, as shown in Figure 2-7.

2. **Enter the network's name and other details.**

3. **Click OK.**

   You're done. That's all there is to adding a preferred network.

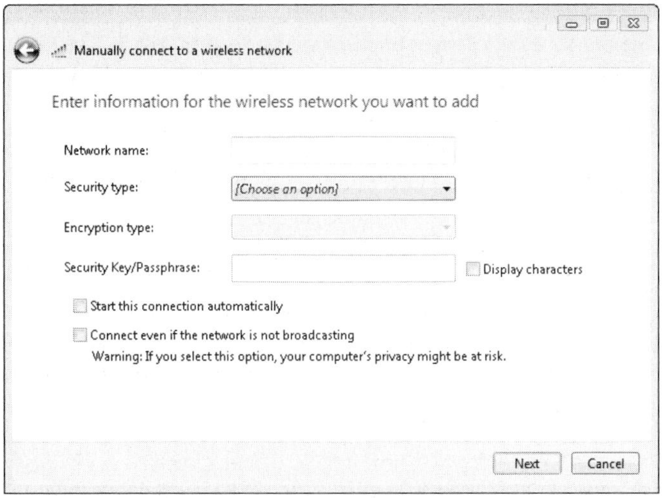

Figure 2-7: You can manually add your own preferred network from scratch.

Removing a preferred network

This is how you remove a preferred network:

1. **Select the network you want to remove.**

2. **Click the Remove button.**

Viewing a network's properties

You can view a preferred network's properties by following these steps:

1. **Select a preferred network.**

2. **Click Properties.**

   That now-familiar Wireless Network Properties dialog box appears. Make whatever changes, additions, or deletions you like to properties.

3. **Click OK to finish.**

Reordering preferred networks

Windows (XP, Vista, and 7) starts with the first network and moves down, so you'll want your most-used networks toward the top of the list. Here's how to move preferred networks on the list:

1. **Select a preferred network.**

2. **Click either Move Up or Move Down. You can also drag-and-drop a network from the list to its preferred location in Vista.**

   The preferred network is reordered in the Preferred Networks list.

3. **Repeat as many times as necessary to rearrange the order of preferred networks.**

Now you've reordered your life — or at least your list of preferred networks. It's a good start, though!

Viewing an Available Network's Signal Strength

You'll be happy to know there's a simple way to view the strength of your wireless network's signal. It doesn't provide a great deal of information, but it's enough to know whether you ought to, say, move your wireless router closer to your computers.

A good time to check your network's signal strength is when you first set it up and anytime you move your PCs or other network hardware. By moving components just a few feet from their original positions, you might find that the signal strength drops. In that case, you can scurry about, putting everything back in place.

Then, with thinking cap firmly applied, you can reconsider where you'll move your equipment.

There are other software and hardware tools for viewing your network's signal strength. I'll discuss them in a later chapter.

To view a simple but helpful visual graphic showing your network's signal strength, just follow these steps:

1. **Mouse-over the network icon in the Window notification area.**

   A pop-up menu appears.

2. **Look at your computer's connections; the strength is displayed next to your network's name.**

   A small bar graph provides a quick look at the strength of your wireless network's signal, as shown in Figure 2-8. If four or five bars are highlighted, you're enjoying strong, robust signal reception.

Figure 2-8: With four bars highlighted, this network is cranking.

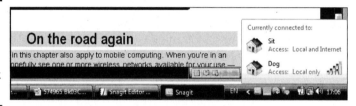

If three or fewer bars are highlighted, you have a pretty weak wireless connection. Read Book IV, Chapter 3, which helps you solve wireless network problems like this one.

On the road again

Many of the topics tackled in this chapter also apply to mobile computing. When you're in an airport, for example, you hopefully see one or more wireless networks available for your use — although some or all may require payment.

When you're in an airport or other public area (or even in one of your company's offices) where you expect to return on a future trip, you can add the network to the list of preferred networks. If you need to make any special configurations for accessing a particular network, you can save them for the next time you connect to the same network.

Monitoring signal strength becomes even more important on the road. Here are some examples:

- ✔ By moving just 50 feet to a new location, your airport connection may grow stronger.

- ✔ If you're in a strange office, you may not know that the steel walls are blocking a nearby network. By moving around and checking signal strength on your laptop, you find the best spot for (wireless) networking.

Chapter 3: Creating Bridges

In This Chapter

✔ **Bridging two or more networks**

✔ **Building the bridge with hardware**

✔ **Doing what you wish with a bridge**

*N*o, this isn't a chapter on civil engineering. And I'm not going to tell you how to build a bridge on the River Kwai, although I may in an upcoming sequel. (Naturally, I'll be playing William Holden's part after I shed a few pounds.) Instead, this chapter is about bridging two or more networks.

Huh? A bridge is software or hardware that connects two or more different networks together.

Huh is exactly what I said when I first learned about creating a bridge between, say, a wired Ethernet network and a wireless network. What is it? Why do I need it? Is the Big Bang overrated?

If all goes well, instead of "Huh?" your response by the end of this chapter will be "Duh!" These are times when I would want to bridge two or more networks:

✦ You're adding a wireless network and want it to piggyback on an existing wired Ethernet network. The wireless network has access to the same things — hardware and data — as the wired network does.

✦ You want to bridge two wired Ethernet networks. This occurs mostly in business environments, but it could occur in a home, too. The wired networks are physically separated and the most convenient way to connect them is by creating a bridge.

✦ You want to extend the range of a wireless network. By bridging two wireless access points, you can expand the signal range without laying any wires.

You can use a wireless access point as a bridge, if the access point's hardware is equipped to handle the task. Not all wireless access points can be used as a bridge; it must specifically say it can be used as one.

Bridging with Windows Vista

Windows Vista makes it easy to create a bridge between two or more networks connected to the same computer.

You need a network adapter, which serves as a communications point between your computer and the network, for each network you want to bridge. If you're bridging a wired network with a wireless network, your computer needs two adapter cards: one for the wired network and one for the wireless network.

Creating a bridge

Use the following steps to bridge two networks in Windows Vista:

1. **Click Start.**

The Start menu appears.

2. **Click Network and Sharing Center; click Manage network connections from the Tasks list.**

The Network Connections dialog box appears, as shown in Figure 3-1. Be sure not to click Network from the Start menu; it opens the Network page. (I know, it gets confusing!)

3. **Select the networks you want to bridge.**

The networks you select are highlighted. You can select multiple connections by holding down the Ctrl key as you click each network.

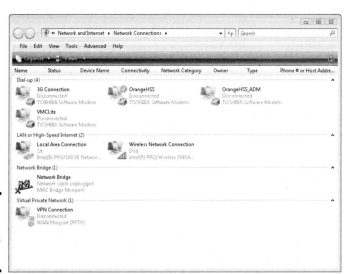

Figure 3-1:
Network
Connections
dialog box.

4. **Right-click one of the highlighted networks and select Bridge Connections, as shown in Figure 3-2.**

Figure 3-2:
Bridging the
networks
you
selected.

Windows Vista bridges the connections, as it indicates with the dialog box shown in Figure 3-3.

Figure 3-3:
Windows
bridging the
connec-
tions.

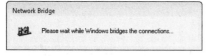

The network connections are bridged, as shown in Figure 3-4.

**Book III
Chapter 3**

Creating Bridges

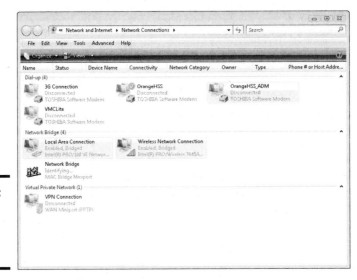

Figure 3-4:
These
bridges
aren't
burning.

Adding a network to a bridge

You can easily add a network to an existing network bridge. Just follow these
steps:

1. Click Start.

The Start menu appears.

**2. Click Network and Sharing Center; click Manage network connections
from the Tasks list.**

The Network Connections dialog box appears.

**3. Right-click the network you want to add to the bridge and select Add
to Bridge.**

Windows Vista adds the network to the bridge. The Status column in the
Network Connections column shows Bridged once the network has been
added to the bridge, and it also appears in the Network Bridge section of
the page.

Removing a network from a bridge

Maybe you've added a bridge by mistake, or maybe you're ready to burn a
bridge or two. Follow these steps to get rid of a network from a bridge:

1. Click Start.

The Start menu appears.

2. **Click Network and Sharing Center; click Manage network connections from the Tasks list.**

The Network Connections dialog box appears.

3. **Right-click the network you want to remove from the network and select Remove from Bridge, as shown in Figure 3-5.**

Windows Vista removes the network from the bridge.

Book III
Chapter 3

Creating Bridges

Figure 3-5:
Removing
a network
from a
bridge.

Deleting a bridge

If you need to delete a bridge, here are the steps for doing so:

1. **Click Start.**

The Start menu appears.

2. **Click Network and Sharing Center; click Manage network connections from the Tasks list.**

The Network Connections dialog box appears,

3. **Right-click the network bridge and select Delete, as shown in Figure 3-6.**

Windows Vista deletes the network bridge.

Figure 3-6:
Deleting
a network
bridge.

Chapter 4: Configuring Printers

In This Chapter

✔ **Sharing a printer on your network**

✔ **Adding a network printer**

✔ **Switching the default printer**

A wireless network is about more than just sharing Internet access and your multimedia files. You also can do things like share a printer among all the computers on your wireless network. I don't need to tell you how helpful that can be these days, especially when more and more households are using multiple computers.

In this chapter, I explain how to set up printer sharing across a network, as well as how to add a new printer and change the default printer.

Learning to Share

You can add and select printers that you will use over your wireless network. For instance, you might be sharing a laser printer on your network and want to add a color inkjet printer that's connected to another computer to your network. Here's how to share a local printer on your entire network:

1. **Click Start.**

The Start menu appears.

2. **Click Control Panel.**

The Control Panel appears.

3. **Click Printer in the Hardware and Sound section.**

4. **Do one of the following:**

- Right-click the printer you want to share and select Sharing.
- Click Change sharing options and confirm the operation.

5. **Select the Share This Printer button.**

6. **Type a name for the shared printer, in the text box as shown in Figure 4-1.**

Try to choose a name that's meaningful to you and to others who use the network. Printer is simple, but not very meaningful, especially if you have more than one printer on the network. Better examples include Upstairs Laser and Basement Color.

Figure 4-1:
A meaningful name is better than a short name.

There is no longer a character limitation when naming your shared printer; however, be mindful that there are some characters that cannot be used. For example, the uses of slashes or other special characters are not allowed. If you use an *illegal* character, don't worry about it, Windows shows you the error of your ways. It is then up to you to correct it. It's important to learn from one's mistakes.

7. **Click OK.**

An image of two people appears, which fortunately replaces the open-palm hand that appears superimposed on the printer's icon, as shown in Figure 4-2. (I think the shared icon looks like a guy in a rather boring family portrait, but that's me. I may die young from cynicism, but at least there won't be any nasty surprises ahead.)

You're all done here. Move along, move along.

Name	Documents	Status	Comments	Location	»

Brother MFC-685CW Printer
0
Ready

Brother PC-FAX v.2
0
Ready

Brother PC-FAX v.2 #2
0
Ready

Fax
0
Ready

Microsoft XPS Document
Writer
0

Adobe PDF
0
Ready

PaperPort Image Printer
0
Ready

SnagIt 9
0
Ready

Figure 4-2:
Share and
share alike:
The printer
is ready.

Feeling Selfish and Turning Off Sharing

Just as you giveth, you can taketh. It may occasionally be a good idea to turn off your printer sharing. For example, if you know that you're running a bit low on ink or paper (and hey, those cost a lot of money these days!), you may want to limit access to your printer. If you know that you're going to be tying up the printer for a few hours and can't bear the thought of anyone encroaching on your territory (or simply sliding in a quick print job), then you may want to pick up your marbles and go home, or simply un-share your printer.

If, after setting up printer sharing on your network, you decide that you no longer want to share the printer, you can easily switch it off. Just follow these steps:

1. **Click Start**.

The Start menu appears.

2. **Click Control Panel.**

The Control Panel appears.

3. **Click Printer in the Hardware and Sound section.**

4. **Do one of the following:**

- Right-click the printer you want to share and select Sharing.
- Click Change sharing options and confirm the operation.

**Book III
Chapter 4**

Configuring Printers

5. **Deselect the Share This Printer button.**

6. **Click OK.**

   The sharing symbol disappears from the printer's icon. That's it for switching off printer sharing. If you want to add a network printer, mosey on over to the next section, please.

Adding a Network Printer

Windows Vista usually installs printers for you automatically if you're connecting the printer directly to your PC; if you've been around computers since the Windows XP (or even Windows 95) days, then you likely know this. Of course, this might not be enough. There are other computers out there just waiting for you to print your prose. If you want to add the ability to use a printer that's connected to another computer on your network, rather than one connected directly to your computer, you need to follow these instructions for each printer you want to add.

Sharing must be enabled before you can add a network printer. You must enable sharing from the computer that connects to the printer you want to share.

To add a new network printer, follow these steps:

1. **Click Start.**

   The Start menu appears.

2. **Click Control Panel.**

   The Control Panel appears.

3. **Click Printer in the Hardware and Sound section.**

4. **Click Add a Printer from the menu just under the file menu.**

   The Add Printer wizard appears.

5. **Click Add a network, wireless or Bluetooth printer.**

   The list of available printers appears, as shown in Figure 4-3.

6. **Select a printer and go to Step 7; otherwise, if you cannot find the printer you want, click The Printer I Want Isn't Listed option and carry on.**

7. **Do one of the following:**

   • Select Browse for a Printer if you don't know the printer's name and network address.

• Use Select a shared printer by name, if you know the printer's name, and Add a printer using a TCP/IP address if you know the network address. Skip to Step 10.

The Browse for Printer dialog box appears.

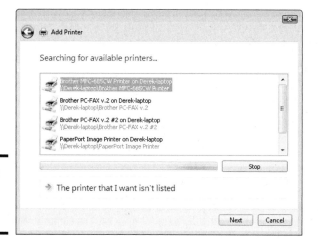

Figure 4-3: Selecting a network printer.

8. **Wait for the newly selected printer to go ahead and configure, and think of a new name for your printer.**

9. **Type the name in the dialog box shown in Figure 4-4 (or leave the default name, it's really up to you!) and then click Next.**

The congratulatory message appears, letting you know that your network printer is now installed.

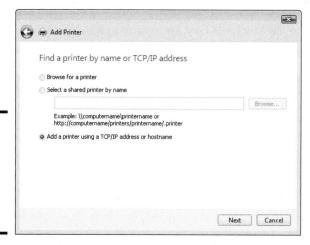

Figure 4-4: Finding the desired printer by TCP/IP address or hostname.

10. **Do one of the following:**

- Select Finish if you want to finish any remaining work with the wizard.

- Select Print a test page if you want to make sure your new printer really works!

You just added a network printer to your personal computing arsenal!

Changing the Default Printer

You can change the printer that Windows Vista uses as its default printer. The default printer is the one where your print jobs automatically go. Although you can always choose another printer on the network (if there is one), doing nothing means your default printer handles the job.

Usually, your default printer is your local printer (the one hooked up to your computer), but you can choose to make a network printer the default printer. Of course, you may want to look twice and make sure that you're online; otherwise it's likely that your network printers won't appear. Here's how you do it:

1. **Click Start.**

The Start menu appears.

2. **Click Control Panel.**

The Control Panel appears.

3. **Click Printer in the Hardware and Sound section.**

4. **Right-click the printer you want to have as your default printer.**

5. **Select Set as Default Printer.**

A white check mark on a green circle appears on the printer icon. It indicates that the printer is now the default printer, as shown in Figure 4-5. You're done.

Figure 4-5:
This
printer's
your default.

Chapter 5: Confirming Your Network Works

In This Chapter

✔ **Checking your signal strength**

✔ **Monitoring your network's activity**

✔ **Avoiding possible signal obstacles**

✔ **Handling interference**

"*E*ureka!" That's what you hope comes out of your mouth after setting up a wireless network. You may want to yell from the rooftops, or wherever you can find the tallest antennae that your new wireless network is running without any problems. Hold that thought: First check on your network's health. That includes viewing the signal strength as well as monitoring its activity (that is, the network traffic). After all, what's the point of having a wireless network if it is an underachiever?

Flexing Your Signal Strength

You'll be happy to know of a simple way to view the strength of your wireless network's signal. This method doesn't provide a great deal of information, but it's enough to know whether you ought to move your wireless router closer to your computers. Sometimes that's all you really need to know. Don't forget — a wireless connection is always weaker than a traditional, wired connection. In other words, you'll experience slower download speeds than a wired connection. That's why it's important to make sure your signal strength is as strong as possible, to guarantee the best possible results from your wireless network.

You should check your signal strength at two different times:

✦ When you first set up your network

✦ Anytime you move your PCs or other network hardware

Moving components just a few feet from their original positions may cause signal strength to drop. In that case you can scurry about, putting everything back in place. Then, with thinking cap firmly applied, you can reconsider where you'll move your equipment. You also have to take in to account the realities of where you installed your network; for example, the layout of your house if this is a home network. For example, I live in a building from the early 1800s; the walls are quite thick, so if I put my laptop on my desk, next to the wall, I don't get a very good signal. If I move my laptop just a few feet behind me, the signal jumps to full strength.

Windows Vista has several built-in tools for testing your network. I discuss these in Book IV, Chapter 3.

To view a simple but helpful visual, just follow these steps:

1. **Right-click the network icon in the Windows Vista notification area.**

   A pop-up menu appears.

2. **Identify the desired network.**

   Next to the network connection is a small bar graph that provides a quick look at the strength of your wireless network's signal, as shown in Figure 5-1. If four or five bars are highlighted, you're enjoying robust signal reception. This is much easier than in past versions of Windows, where you actually had a procedure to work your way through simply to see if you had a decent connection or not.

Figure 5-1:
With four bars highlighted, this network is cranking.

If only three or fewer bars are highlighted, you have a pretty weak wireless connection. You'll want to read Book IV, Chapter 3, which helps you solve wireless network problems like this one.

3. **When you're done viewing your signal strength, move your mouse away from the pop-up menu.**

You can also find out the strength of your network using a more procedure-intensive way. The Network and Sharing Center, shown in Figure 5-2, opens and tells the strength with text. Here's how that text breaks down compared to the bar graph:

✦ **Excellent:** Your network is just full of energy. This is equivalent to four or five bars.

✦ **Good:** Your network is doing a fine job. This is equivalent to three bars.

✦ **Fair:** Your network is doing an OK job, but it's not living up to its potential. This is equivalent to two bars.

✦ **Poor:** Your network is an underachiever. You may want to start shifting things, because you likely only have one bar.

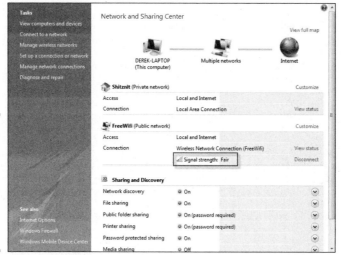

Figure 5-2:
The
Network
and Sharing
Center
also shows
signal
strength.

A more sophisticated way of measuring signal strength is discussed a little later in this chapter. Using a third-party software program, you can get a pretty accurate read on the strength of nearby Wi-Fi access points.

Monitoring Your Network

After you've decided which wireless networks you want to connect to, some Windows Vista tools can monitor those networks. One of these tools is in the same dialog box that shows your signal strength. Another is a real-time graphical network monitor that's part of Windows Task Manager. In the following sections you learn how to use these tools. Most people use these tools simply to establish that their network is up and running properly. For example, if your network seems a bit sluggish, these tools will show you whether or not data is getting in or out.

Viewing your network's activity

In the Wireless Network Connection Status dialog box, you can see how much data is moving in and out of a PC over your wireless network.

Here's how you view it:

1. **Confirm that your wireless network is enabled.**

   If it's not, enable it. If you're also running a wired network, disable it. If you're using a laptop computer, it may be as simple as flipping a switch.

2. **Right-click the network icon in Windows Vista notification area.**

   A pop-up menu appears.

3. **Select Network and Sharing Center.**

   The Network and Sharing Center appears.

4. **Click View status on the Connection row of your wireless connection.**

   Select the General tab if it's not already selected.

5. **The Wireless Connection Status window appears.**

   In the Activity area you can monitor bytes sent and received, as shown in Figure 5-3. If there's a number below Sent but a zero is beneath Received, your wireless network may not be working properly. If there are at least three-digit numbers under both Sent and Received, your network should work.

6. **Click Close.**

   That's it for one view of network activity!

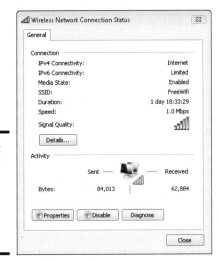

Figure 5-3:
A network showing signs of activity is a healthy network.

Viewing a real-time networking graph

To monitor your wireless network, just follow these steps:

1. Press Ctrl+Alt+Delete.

This is affectionately known by many as the Vulcan death grip. But in Windows Vista, instead of immediately rebooting your PC, it displays the Windows Task Manager dialog box. If that still freaks you out, you can always use Ctrl+Shift+Esc or right-click an open space on the Windows taskbar and go on to Step 2.

2. Select Task Manager.

You see several tabs at the top of the dialog box. By default, you are in the Applications tab.

3. Select the Networking tab.

A graph like that in Figure 5-4 shows your wireless network's activity in real time. In this example my wireless network is using about 1 percent of its capacity. The bandwidth I'm using appears consistent because I'm streaming music over the Internet.

Figure 5-4:
A graphics display shows your network's heartbeat, while a text area supplies other useful information.

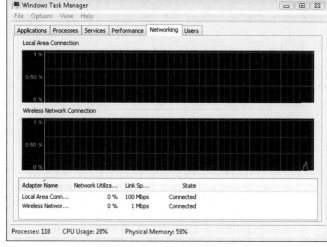

If you also have a wired Ethernet network active, you see two graphic windows. One window shows the wired network while the other window shows the wireless network.

The bottom window shows a bunch of information about your wireless network. For starters, you see the Adapter Name, Network Utilization, Link Speed, and several columns displaying your network's throughput (how much of the network's capacity is actually being used).

4. **When you're done viewing your wireless network's activity, close the Task Manager.**

That's it! See how easy it is to monitor your wireless network's activity?

Changing the networking information you see

When viewing the Networking screen in Windows Task Manager, you see some detailed text information below the glitzy graphical display. It's easy to change the columns displayed there:

1. **In the Windows Task Manager, choose View⇨Select Columns.**

The Select Networking Page Columns dialog box appears, as shown in Figure 5-5.

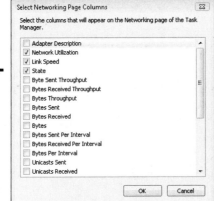

Figure 5-5: Choosing the information you'll see in the networking graph

2. **Select or deselect the boxes next to columns you want to display.**

The default selections are usually sufficient. However, you may want to see something specific, or your network administrator may ask you to add columns while diagnosing a problem with your network. For example, you might want to see the number of bytes that were sent or received in order to see exactly how much data has been flowing across your network.

3. **Click OK.**

Any column changes appear in the text area.

4. **If you added columns, you may need to resize the Windows Task Manager dialog box to see them. Point the mouse over the Task Manager's outline until you see a double-headed arrow and click and drag to resize.**

5. **Close the dialog box when you're done viewing the Networking screen.**

   You're done — and you're one step closer to becoming an experienced wireless network administrator.

Stumbling Upon NetStumbler

Although you can get a rough reading on your signal strength from Windows and monitor your network, another tool gives you a more detailed view: NetStumbler. It's free for home users (commercial and government users are encouraged to donate $50 per copy). This application is recommended for any users who are still working with Windows XP. At the time of printing, NetStumbler does not support Windows Vista, which makes support for Windows 7 even less likely.

Written by Marius Milner, NetStumbler runs under Windows and monitors the signal strength of nearby access points. You can select an access point and NetStumbler displays a real-time graph showing the strength.

You can use it on your desktop PC to see if it's close enough to the transmitter and if the signal is too noisy, which indicates interference or physical obstacles. Better yet, you can install the software on a laptop computer, moving around your house or business to measure signal strength in various places.

**Book III
Chapter 5**

**Confirming Your
Network Works**

Downloading and installing NetStumbler

To download the program, follow these steps:

1. **Go to www.netstumbler.com.**

   The NetStumbler Web page loads.

2. **Click Downloads (located on the left side of the main menu).**

   The Downloads page appears.

3. **Click NetStumbler and save the program to your desktop or to another location you can remember.**

4. **Double-click the downloaded NetStumbler setup program.**

   The Setup dialog box displays the license agreement, once Windows Vista knows that it's fine to install the program.

5. **After reading the agreement, click I Agree.**

   The Choose Components screen appears.

6. **Select the type of installation.**

   Complete is the default type.

7. **Click Next.**

   The Choose Install Location screen appears.

8. **If the installation directory is acceptable, click Install.**

   You can click Browse to choose another directory. The program installs when you click Install.

9. **When it says Installation Complete, click Close.**

Using other apps

Windows offers some solid, yet not stellar, networking monitoring tools, as we've seen in this chapter. Some other viable alternatives are available if you want to get a second opinion.

Be careful, not all third-party applications are decent quality simply because they're "not" Windows. Also, many are likely to either come at some cost and work only for a limited amount of time (either a full- or limited-access version). Be sure to check into such details before trying other applications.

For Windows Vista users, or any Windows 7 early adopters, you may want to try WirelessMon. This application, which is also available on a trial basis, works well under Windows Vista (even 64-bit). It is available at `www.passmark.com`.

The best advice I can give you is to perform a Web search for network monitoring applications and see what works best for you. Many applications offer the same or similar features for varying prices. In many cases, it's simply a question of personal preference.

Book IV
Security and Troubleshooting

The 5th Wave   By Rich Tennant

"We take network security here very seriously."

Contents at a Glance

Chapter 1: Looking at Internet Threats

The Internet is a great place; you can read about any subject you want to (and many you wish you'd never heard of). You can buy anything online and have it delivered to your door. You've got immediate access to your bank, credit cards, investments, and other financial information. Heck, you don't have to leave the house if you don't want to.

With all these new ways of doing business on the Internet come people trying to make a dishonest buck. On the Internet, some people are trying to part you from your hard-earned money without leaving their keyboard.

Not to scare you, but a whole lot of bad stuff is on the Internet. Fortunately, knowing about it goes a long way to avoiding it.

Finding Out about Bad Software

Software is the stuff you load on your computer to do work and have fun. Your word processor, Web browser, and spreadsheet are all software. Someone (or a group of people) sat down and wrote the software with the goal of trying to solve a problem you had in exchange for you buying the software.

What if those people didn't care about helping you, but thought they could write software that stole your online bank account number and password? Or what if they just thought it would be fun to delete all the files on your hard drive?

Software like this is called *malware,* which is short for malicious software. (Have you ever noticed how computer people like to make up words?) *Malware* is any software that intentionally does harm to a computer, without the computer owner's consent.

There are many different types of malware out there, and I cover these in the following sections.

Understanding viruses

In the physical world, someone gets sick, coughs on you, and the next thing you know, you're in bed for a couple of days. Computer viruses are much the same, just without the bonus of time off work.

When you happen to run a piece of infected software, the virus tries to replicate itself. Maybe it infects a few other programs on your system, maybe it hijacks your e-mail client and e-mails itself to 100 of your closest friends. Either way, the virus tries to make its way onto other machines.

Before the Internet, viruses traveled pretty slowly because you'd have to share the program over a floppy disk to move the virus around. With the advent of the Internet, viruses started incorporating network functionality.

Viruses aren't limited to programs, such as games and word processors. They can be hidden in e-mail attachments that look normal, or inside documents themselves. Newer viruses don't even need to be run; they spread by taking advantage of network services built into your machine.

One day in 1999 people started to get e-mails from friends containing a Microsoft Word document as an attachment. As soon as the document was opened, special code called a *macro* was run that made the user's e-mail software send the virus to the first 50 people in the user's address book.

This virus was very effective for several reasons:

+ The e-mail came from the victim, so people were inclined to trust it.
+ People weren't careful in what they opened because nothing like this had ever happened before.
+ It took very little effort on the user's behalf to propagate the virus because the macros were an integrated part of the word processor.

Viruses don't necessarily do damage by themselves; what matters is the payload. If the virus' objective in life is to replicate, it's merely annoying. If the payload deletes your computer's files on April Fool's Day, that would be bad.

Getting protection from viruses

Software called *anti-virus software* runs on your computer and is constantly on the lookout for virus activity. Most anti-virus (AV) software inspect all the files on your hard drive periodically and also give a quick scan to any programs you run, at the time that you run them.

I cover AV software later in this chapter. Not only do you need it, but you need to keep it up to date. AV software works by looking for *signatures*, or patterns, of viruses. To update your AV software means to get the latest set of signatures. Fortunately for you, any decent AV package will automate this.

The second way to keep virus-free is to keep on top of your operating system patches. In late 2008 and early 2009, a virus called Conficker was running around the Internet. Conficker spread by many different means, but one of the most effective was by exploiting a problem with Windows that had been patched several months prior. Because most people didn't install the latest operating system updates, they were vulnerable. We look at patching in the next chapter.

Finally, the first line of defense against virus infection is to use your head. If you receive a random e-mail with an attachment, don't open the attachment. Only get software from reputable sources, or friends. And use your anti-virus software to scan things after you download them.

Spyware and adware

Spyware and adware are two types of malware that hide in the background and try to make money for the creator. Spyware tracks the Web sites you go to and uses that data to make money. The author might be interested in the data themselves, or they might be able to sell the information to someone who is.

Adware is software that displays advertising inside it. This initially wasn't bad — some instant messaging services originally displayed small ads to keep their service running. As usual, though, people started writing code that would force itself upon the machine and change the ads that a user saw. For example, an ad for jewelry on a Web site might be replaced with an ad for something else, with the owner of the adware getting a cut if you buy anything.

This last scenario might seem like it's not a problem; but even so, adware takes up resources on your computer and makes it slower. Adware also cheats Internet businesses out of their money.

Other types of spyware, called *keyloggers*, take your keystrokes and send them to the creator. This includes anything you typed into your online banking site.

The lines between adware and spyware have blurred to the point where it's all generally called spyware now. Whatever it's called, you don't want it on your computer.

Most of the lesser forms of spyware come from toolbars that you randomly happen across on your Internet travels. Anything offering free smileys, "free screensavers, or something that enhances your Web browsing experience with a free deal finder toolbar probably contains some hidden nastiness. The program may work as advertised, but it will probably leave spyware that will be around long after you get bored with the software you downloaded.

These spyware packages are often distributed through a technology called ActiveX that is only supported by Microsoft Internet Explorer. There are few ActiveX components that are worth using, and a good part of the rest is spyware.

Spyware is often found in illegal downloads, especially software that purports to crack the copy protection on various legitimate pieces of software. Say what you will about the legal aspects of copyright protection, but the level of malware out there is atrocious.

Somewhat tied to the illegal downloads of software is downloads of illegal movies. The movies themselves don't contain anything bad because they're just data. However, trying to view the movie prompts you to download some software to properly decode it in the form of a piece of software called a *codec*. Guess what's in that software? Figure 1-1 shows a user being prompted to download a new codec in order to watch a copy of a new movie that was downloaded over the Internet.

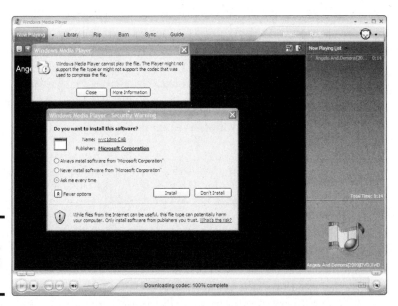

Figure 1-1:
A prompt to download a codec.

Does the codec contain malware? To find out, you should enter some of the details into your favorite search engine and see what other people have to say. Or, just stay away from media files like that.

Be selective about what you download and run. No matter what the ad says, you can't download a current version of Microsoft Office for only $4. Even if it does contain an illegal version of Office, it's bound to contain a bunch of nasty malware that you don't want.

Try to find an anti-virus package that includes anti-spyware functionality, too. This software tries to block the installation of the spyware and also prevents spyware from calling home to transmit the sensitive data that was stolen.

Don't download any extensions to Internet Explorer. In fact, don't run Internet Explorer at all. Firefox is a much faster browser and does not suffer from as many attacks as Internet Explorer. Whichever browser you choose, make sure you're up to date.

Be careful when installing software that has been suggested from a recent download. When you are prompted to download anything, take a moment to research what is being offered to make sure it's not malware.

Zombies and botnets

The final stop in our whirlwind tour of bad software brings us to zombies and botnets. In the movies, zombies are dead people that have been reanimated and spend their time looking for tasty human brains to eat. They're especially fond of groups of people who decided to split up so that they could find a way out of the abandoned building faster. I've never understood why people do that.

Anyway, a zombie computer is one that has been infected with some sort of malware that allows it to be controlled remotely. The infection is such that the owner of the computer doesn't know what's going on because the computer operates normally (but maybe slower).

Take a few thousand (or a few hundred thousand) of these zombified computers and you have yourself a *botnet*. The people who run these botnets make their zombie computers send e-mail spam, try to defraud advertisers, and even try to take down major Web sites. They may do this for their own uses or rent out their botnet to people who are in need of such services.

Needless to say, you don't want your computer to be a zombie! There's no upside, and you don't want to be giving out system resources for sending spam and taking down Web sites.

Zombie software gets on your computer the same way that other malware gets there, such as through strange e-mail attachments or in infected files taken from unscrupulous Web sites.

Avoiding Bad People

The last section talked about bad software. Bad people made that software, but there's another class of bad guys that are out to scam you directly.

Most of these schemes aren't new; they're just some old classics that have been adapted for the Internet. People have been writing bad checks for decades: the Internet just allows them to expand their reach.

Spam

If you've had an e-mail address for more than 10 minutes, then you've seen some spam. Spam is an *unsolicited commercial e-mail*, which is a fancy way of saying that someone you don't know sent you an e-mail trying to sell you something.

The nature of e-mail means that it costs about the same to send out a million e-mails as it does a handful. There are no stamps to buy, no envelopes to stuff, and no address labels to print. A single computer can generate thousands of spam e-mails per hour, and if you use the services of a botnet, you can blast out a few million e-mails in no time at all.

Spam is sometimes hard to differentiate from regular commercial e-mail. Sometimes you get added to a mailing list from a company that you dealt with, and you start getting a monthly newsletter. As inconvenient as it is, spam is a much bigger problem.

The idea behind spamming is that the spammer sends out an offer for a product. The types of products usually associated with spam are

+ Pharmaceuticals, especially male performance enhancing pills
+ Knockoff watches or clothing
+ Illegal software
+ Financial products such as loans
+ University degrees

All good stuff, right?

Spam is bad for several reasons, including

+ The sheer volume of spam makes your ISP do extra work to process the e-mail, and you do more work to find the e-mails you're really looking for. This makes e-mail less efficient as a communications medium.
+ The way that spammers send the e-mails out is often destructive to mail servers.

✦ The products being sold are usually a scam, illegal, or just plain low quality.

As tempting as it may be to be able to lose weight with only a small pill being sold at a ridiculously low rate, stay away.

Also be careful about how you give out your e-mail address. Posting to public forms sometimes exposes your address, which spammers harvest for their lists. Free Web-based e-mail providers are plentiful; it helps to have a separate account for posting to public forums.

Spam is often the vehicle for phishing attacks, which I look at next.

Phishing

Ever received an e-mail from your bank telling you that it was important that you go to their Web site and fill in some missing personal information? Ever received the same information from a different bank, one that you don't deal with?

These e-mails were probably part of a *phishing* scam. Phishing is a play on fishing, as in "fishing for suckers who will give me their bank information" (and another made up word!) With this personal information the bad guy can get into your bank account or can get credit cards in your name (also called *identity theft*).

Here's a step-by-step look at a scam:

1. Bad guy sets up a Web page that looks a lot like a particular bank's Web site, with a form asking for your credit card number, social security number, mother's maiden name, bank PIN, and anything else he can think of.

2. The bad guy sends out millions of e-mails that look official and that ask you to visit your bank's Web page using the link in the e-mail.

3. You just happen to use that bank, so you click on the link and fill in the form.

4. The bad guy cleans out your bank account from the safety of an Internet café in a foreign land.

That e-mail from the bank may look authentic, but here's what you might not know:

✦ Making an e-mail look like it came from whoever you want, including your bank, is easy.

✦ Making an e-mail look official and important is easy.

✦ Making the link shown on the screen take you to a different site is easy.

✦ Scammers can use many ways to trick people into thinking they're on their bank's Web site, when in fact they're on the bad guy's site.

Figure 1-2 is an e-mail that looks like it came from an auction site I use. It looks a lot like other e-mails that come from the site, but if you look where my mouse is hovering on the link, and the link that shows up in the status bar, they're different!

Figure 1-2:
An e-mail
from an
online
auction site.
Or is it?

What's happening here is that the phisher is trying to trick me into going to his site, where he'll try to get me to log in using my real username and password, at which point he can do bad stuff.

That hover trick is not always reliable, though. The only way to be certain is to copy and paste the URL that shows on the screen instead of clicking.

If you are presented with such an e-mail, it pays to view it with some skepticism. Keep the following in mind:

✦ Some sites that are especially prone to phishing attacks will include your username in the subject or e-mail to show you it's not a phishing scheme. If you don't see this, beware.

✦ Banks will not request personal information over an e-mail or on a random Internet page. When in doubt, call your bank and ask.

✦ Most Web sites that deal with sensitive information post a policy on their Web page describing whether or not they do send such e-mails out and what sort of protections they use.

When in doubt, pick up the phone or just delete the e-mail.

If you use the Firefox Web browser, or Internet Explorer version 7 or later, it adds some additional phishing protection. Clicking on the link in the previous figure brings you to Figure 1-3.

Figure 1-3: Trying to view a phishing site.

This screen is presented by your Web browser, and it indicates that the site in question is known to be a phishing site. It's not perfect, but it's an additional layer of protection.

Be very careful about what private information you give over the Internet, no matter what format. Scammers are getting cleverer. Identity theft is serious and can cause you a lot of trouble.

Rebills

The rebill, or the *negative option billing* scam, is usually legal but very shady.

The essence of the scam is that you sign up for a free trial of some product and only have to pay a couple of dollars shipping. What you missed in the reams of fine print is that after your trial expires, you'll be charged a hefty sum every month to continue on the program. It's usually a couple of months before you know and can get off the program.

This type of deal has been around for a while, especially for music clubs. The scammy version is different, though:

✦ The terms of the agreement are not made clear. You might have to go to another page or scroll down to see the catch.

Book IV
Chapter 1

Looking at Internet Threats

✦ Often the trial starts from the day you sign up, not from when you get the product. People find that their credit card has been billed for the first month before they've even received the trial item.

✦ The product itself is poor, either by not living up to the medical claims made or, in the case of make-money-fast type offers, is simply public domain information.

✦ The company's contact information is not made clear in case you want to complain or cancel your subscription.

✦ It takes several hours of dialing to get through to customer service to get off the product.

These types of scams are all over, from advertising on popular Web sites to spam. Often you see the product on a personal Web site from a person purporting to have used the product to lose weight or make thousands of dollars. This person probably doesn't exist; the seller has just made them up to try and get you to sign up for the trial.

Beware of anything offering a free trial that requires a shipping charge, and always check the fine print. Check your credit card balance online periodically (having a separate credit card for Internet purchases is also helpful), and call your credit card company at the first sign of abuse.

Another version of this involves your cell phone. You are given a free ring tone, or told that you need to provide your cell phone number to get the results of a test you just did. After you provide your cell phone number you are quietly signed up for a service on your cell phone that bills you every month.

You won the lottery!

Ever got an e-mail like one of the following?

✦ Congratulations! You won the Internet lottery!

✦ You have just inherited $1 million from a long-lost relative.

✦ I need you to help me get $5 million out of my country. You can have 40 percent for your efforts.

These are all scams.

The way these go is that you chat back and forth with the person, and at some point, they come up with a story for needing a few dollars, such as $50 to process some paperwork. If you pay that, more charges keep piling up for various things until you realize you've been had. This is called the *advance fee scam*. See Figure 1-4 for an example.

> **Dearest One** Spam | x
> 🖶 Print all ⚡ Turn off highlighting
>
> PHILIP POWELL to sea_marine   show details Apr 17 ↩ Reply | ▼
>
> Dearest One
>
> Please permit me to introduce my self you . am Mr Frank 22 year old . i need your urgent assistance in Dubai to save my inheritance fund 6.3m from United Nation (U N)diplomats .
>
> Before my late father died he arranged with U.N diplomat to ship a trunk box that contains 6.3m dollars under special arrangement nobody knows that the box contain money believe me .
>
> All i need from you is to help me to cliam the box from the diplomats here in Dubai and also to see everything clear with your eyes as you claimed the box
>
> Everything am telling you now is secret nobody knows that the box contains money i have the airwaybill issued to my late father by the UNITED NATION from my country .
>
> Please please, if you want to verify i can give you the full contact of the diplomat for you to reach them and verify if they have my late father's box to their custody . but you must not tell them that the box contains money inside for security reasons .
>
> Please help me out if the box claim and we have access to the money i will give you 20% while the balance 80% goes for investment I arraved here in Dubai for few days now .
>
> Please help me i pray before contacing you and i need good respond from you .
>
> I waity for your reply .
>
> Thanks

Figure 1-4:
The advance fee scam.

I really don't think that Mr. Frank has the $6.3 million dollars. Just ignore e-mails like this.

These types of scams have been around for years, but the Internet has made it easier for scammers to find their victims. At one point many of the scammers were based out of Nigeria, so you will find this called the *Nigerian scam* or the *419 scam* (419 is the section of the Nigerian criminal code dealing with such fraud). An Internet search for these terms uncovers a variety of different ruses used for the scam, along with some hilarious stories of people getting the scammers to do all sorts of silly things.

Looking at the amount of spam I get involving this scam, I can only assume that people are still falling for it. Indeed, I have seen a few stories in the news. One person was taken for $150,000, which gives you some idea of how bad it can get.

Check washing and the overpayment scam

Check washing is a process where a check that has been written on has the payee and amount removed (washed off), and a new value and payee put on. This was around before the Internet, but again, the Internet has made it easier to find victims.

Intercepting the check is surprisingly easy, so the scammers have a wide variety of potentially blank checks to choose from.

This scam generally works two ways. The first is that you are offered a job to process paperwork at home, which ends up being to cash some company checks. You send the money to your "employer," sometimes minus a small commission to you.

What has happened is that a legitimate check has been intercepted and washed, and your name has been put on it with a new dollar amount. You deposit the check, your bank advances you the funds, and then you send the money away. Usually you are told to use Western Union, which is an untraceable system.

Eventually the bank finds out when the check bounces and takes the money back from you. But you've already sent the money away!

The second way this happens is that you offer something for sale online, and someone buys it from you. When it comes time to pay they try to give you a check for more than the sale price with some excuse for why. You are asked to send the difference back to them.

Of course, the check bounces, and you're out whatever you sold and the cash.

To avoid this scam:

+ Beware of any deal where you get a check and have to send money back.

+ Never accept a check in response to an online dealing unless you know the person. Look into trusted systems, such as PayPal.

+ Never send any payment to someone you don't know by an untraceable method, such as Western Union.

+ Keep your checkbook safe and watch your bank account for the checks you issue. This will help prevent one of your checks from being used for the scam.

+ Remember that if it sounds too good to be true, it probably is.

Credit card stealing

Compared to all the other types of scams, this one is downright uninspiring:

1. You buy something online using your credit card.

2. The Web site you bought it from is hacked into and your credit card number is stolen.

3. Your credit card number is used to buy stuff, sticking you with the bill.

Fortunately, most countries have laws dealing with credit cards such that if you notice the fraudulent transaction before your bill is due, you can dispute the charge and not have to pay it when it's shown to be fraudulent. Still, it's an inconvenience to have this happen.

One sign to look for when paying over the Internet is that you are using a secure connection. A secure connection means that anyone watching your traffic will not be able to see the information inside because it is encrypted. Figure 1-5 shows an Internet Explorer window that is using a secure connection.

Figure 1-5:
A secure
connection.

In the address, note that the URL begins with https instead of http. This indicates the connection is encrypted. Also note the picture of the lock. This indicates that the site you are browsing is the same one that was certified to use the security. Some older Web browsers place the lock in the bottom status bar instead of in the URL.

The certificate itself is no protection against someone coming in after the fact and stealing the data. This is an unfortunate part of the Internet and security. The credit card companies are still rolling out their security standards across their merchants, which will enforce rules protecting your information.

It is a good idea to keep a credit card for use only on the Internet, and to keep the limit fairly low. This makes it easier to spot fraudulent transactions and limits your liability should problems arise.

It's Not All Doom and Gloom

This chapter has shined a spotlight on some of the darker parts of the Internet. I didn't lead off with it to scare you. In the next couple of chapters, I cover tools you can use to protect yourself.

Tools by themselves won't help you, though. You need to be smart before you open that attachment, or get your credit card out. The bad guys prey on greedy people. Don't be one of them.

You can find a lot of good stuff on the Internet, and the bad guys shouldn't keep you from it.

Chapter 2: Using A Safety Net

In This Chapter

✔ Understanding why your network should stay private

✔ Using your router's security features

✔ Protecting your wireless network

When networks were all wired, you'd know exactly who was on your network because they'd be connected by a cable to your switch. Unless someone snuck a 200 foot cable out your window, you could rest pretty soundly knowing that you and your family were the only users on the network.

With wireless, your neighbor's teenage son (never did trust the kid. . .) could be sneaking into your files, or that strange, white unmarked van across the street could be spying on you. Maybe I'm just getting paranoid. Or am I?

Knowing Your Network

If you want to defend your network, then you need to understand how it's put together. Each component has different properties and is defended differently. You can look at your network as if it were made up of two parts:

✦ The Internet connection

✦ All the stuff on the inside, like your computers

The next sections cover each of these in turn.

Protecting the Internet connection

What happens on your Internet connection is your responsibility. If someone on your network does something bad, willingly or unwillingly, then the Internet service provider has your name on their billing records and will talk to you first. If cops get involved, you get the first interview.

Problems are not unheard of. Consider the following scenarios:

✦ ISPs sometimes implement a cap on the amount of data that can be transferred on a given connection as part of the monthly rate, after which they charge a fee based on usage. Most people will never touch this cap, but if someone were to use your connection to download movies all month, you could blow past this limit without knowing.

✦ You've been following the advice in this book about keeping your computer safe, but the person borrowing your Internet connection hasn't. They get infected, their computer becomes a zombie, and the next thing you know you can't send e-mail because your provider has turned off your e-mail because of spam complaints.

✦ A scammer finds that they can use your Internet connection if they park their car across the street. They use it to commit fraud, and the police get involved. The ISP traces the messages back to your address.

Although the scenarios may seem far-fetched, they have happened.

I'm not saying you can't share your Internet connection with your neighbor, or that you should rigorously inspect everyone's computer that enters your door. You can still lock down your network and share the password so that just your neighbor gets on while keeping the bad guys out. If the neighbors aren't that computer savvy, maybe you could lend them this book (or better yet, get them their own copy!).

War driving

War driving is a play on a pre-Internet activity called War Dialing. In War Dialing, someone dials every phone number in a particular range of telephone numbers, looking for computers that answer instead of humans. This technique used to be very effective at finding unprotected computers because the systems administrators used to use dial-in modems as a way to remotely manage their systems and were often not very thorough in their security practices.

If you've ever seen the movie *War Games* you'll recognize this. If you haven't, you should look

it up. Despite being over 25 years old it's still a great flick!

War driving involves driving around a city with a computer and a wireless card, looking for open (or easily crackable) wireless networks. It's been refined to the point where you can tie in a GPS unit and end up with a map of all the networks, with the exploitable ones highlighted.

The bad guys will use war driving to find open access points they can use and abuse. Make sure you're not on their list!

Hackers versus crackers

Throughout this chapter and others, I might use the term hackers and crackers. You've probably heard the term hacker before and have heard it being used in the context of a bad guy trying to break into your computer.

The word hacker has a long and distinguished history, however. Hackers were the people that advanced computer science not by exploiting weaknesses and doing harm, but by using their intelligence to pull off feats of skill (called hacks). Hackers would build computers out of spare parts or come up with brilliant ways around limitations.

As other intelligent people used their skills for evil, the media applied the name of hacker to them. These are the bad guys: the people writing software to steal information, or coming up with ways to game systems to their advantage.

It's insulting to the hacker community to associate these bad people with them, so we use the term cracker, much as in a safe cracker.

In this book, I don't have the need to refer to people in the hacker sense, so I'll just use cracker, attacker, or, even better, bad guy.

There's a third class of people that I'll call researchers. These people try to find weaknesses in systems in the name of improving them. They're trying to break the security systems before the crackers do, so that the systems can be fixed. These guys are on your side.

Unfortunately, the public nature of research means that the crackers eventually learn about the problems and use them to their advantage.

The stuff on the inside

Your network may include your computers, video game consoles, and maybe a file sharing device or two. If someone can connect to your wireless network, then they can connect to your computers and file storage servers.

More sophisticated attackers can pretend to be your gateway and force all your Internet use through their computer using a process called *spoofing*. Anything you look at on your computer is passed through the attacker's computer. Even though your bank uses encryption when you view their Web page, you still have to be careful to make sure that the attacker isn't feeding you bad information.

WARNING!

Your computers have files on them that you'd probably rather keep private. You may not have anything to hide, but you still don't want to share all your files with people. Tax returns? Letters to the lawyer? If you wouldn't stick it to your front door, then it's worth spending some time to protect.

People from the Internet

So far I've been talking about people trying to get into your home network over the wireless connection. There are also people trying to get in from the Internet. Fortunately your firewall blocks any connections from the outside coming in, unless you deliberately turn that feature off. Don't do that!

Most of the attackers coming from the Internet are computer programs that are scanning your service provider's network, looking for vulnerable hosts. Your firewall protects you against these scans because it only allows connections that your computers make out to the Internet and not new connections from the Internet to the inside of your network.

All that said, if you run a program that's got a virus in it, all bets are off. We talk about getting anti-virus protection in the next chapter.

Choosing Wireless Security

Wireless networking, by nature, involves throwing your data over the airwaves and hoping only the recipient is the one listening. As more people used wireless, more important information was carried over the air. As more important information was sent, the incentive for people to try and listen to it increased. As people tried to listen, the engineers in charge of the wireless standards tried to keep up.

Here's a summary of the wireless security protocols available to you.

WEP

When 802.11 was introduced by the Institute of Electrical and Electronics Engineers (IEEE) in 1997, the standard called for vendors to optionally provide security through *Wired Equivalent Privacy* (WEP). WEP encrypted the data that was sent over the radio so that people listening in couldn't read it without the key.

WEP had some problems from the start. The key used to decrypt the data was static, meaning it never changed. To get on a WEP-protected network, everybody had to share the same key. As you can imagine, it became easy to figure out the key because it often got posted to the wall so people wouldn't forget it.

Secondly, the United States had some rather peculiar regulations at the time dealing with the export of encryption capable products to other countries. Back in 1997, encryption fell under the International Traffic in Arms Regulations (ITAR), which regulated the export of weapons out of the country. You couldn't export missiles, nuclear weapons, night vision goggles, and any encryption the government couldn't break.

As such, WEP went out the door with pretty weak encryption, even for 1997. But it was all we had. Some people used it, some people didn't.

Fast-forward a few years, and people are starting to look closely at the security of WEP. The U.S. government relaxed their position on encryption, and WEP was upgraded to something less embarrassing. However, some researchers found that by listening to enough traffic you could deduce the shared key. As people poked deeper into WEP, they found that even less traffic was needed, and you could even cause the access point to generate it if the clients weren't generating traffic. The time to crack a WEP key is now down to a minute, even with the stronger encryption in use.

Yes, you heard me right. Someone can listen to a WEP-protected network and have the key before you even notice they're there. With the right antenna, they could be farther away.

This isn't going to do. Something better is needed.

WPA

The IEEE started work on the 802.11i standard, which dealt with wireless security. As usual, trying to get a bunch of engineers to agree on something takes its time, so the Wi-Fi Alliance took some of the in-progress work from 802.11i and came up with the *Wi-Fi Protected Access* standard (WPA).

WPA solves the key problems that were the downfall of WPA with a protocol called the *Temporal Key Integrity Protocol* (TKIP). TKIP's job is to rotate keys constantly so that the problems WEP had won't happen again.

WPA had a major constraint in that it was intended to run on older access points by means of a firmware upgrade. This was because WEP was so broken that the industry wanted to protect access points in the field. Therefore WPA uses some of the same encryption techniques as WEP, just implemented in a better fashion.

WPA also introduced the concepts of a pre-shared key mode (PSK) and an enterprise mode. PSK mode requires a key that's known to all participants in the wireless network, just like WEP. Enterprise mode allows you to use your enterprise login credentials to log in to the wireless network, eliminating the need for a shared key.

Even though enterprise mode is better security, it requires servers and services that people at home just don't have. The acronyms and standard names required to implement this mode are astounding. So, you'll always want to use PSK mode if you're ever given the option.

WPA was a significant improvement upon WEP. Eventually, researchers found ways to mess with WPA networks. WPA is not as completely broken as WEP, but it is possible to inject packets into a WPA-protected network. With this ability, an attacker could still redirect the entire network's traffic through a computer of his choosing.

WPA2

Third time's the charm, right?

The IEEE finally finished 802.11i, and the Wi-Fi Alliance called it WPA2. The Alliance also made implementation of WPA2 a mandatory part of Wi-Fi compatibility testing. Without WPA2, vendors couldn't put the Wi-Fi logo on the box.

WPA2 got rid of TKIP and went with the *Advanced Encryption Standard*, which is the same that the U.S. government uses for protecting its secrets. The earlier WPA standard was also revised to allow AES to be used instead of TKIP.

To date, there are no direct attacks against WPA2. That hasn't stopped people from trying, though!

Even though the bad guys can't exploit weaknesses in WPA2, they can try to guess your password. So pick a good one!

Deciding what to choose

If you're setting up a wireless network, you want to be using WPA2. Most access points have a mode that allows both WPA2 and WPA to be used. If you have older clients that only support WPA, then this mode will work.

It's easy enough for me to say "use WPA2" when you're setting up your own network, but what about when you use other people's networks?

Hotel networks generally have no encryption or security at all. Anyone can connect, anyone can read the packets in the air, usually called *open mode* or an *open network*. Access to the network is usually protected by a *captive portal*, which intercepts you when you first start using the Internet, and only lets you through after you've registered.

Captive portals provide no protection for you; they're there only for the convenience (and usually, profit margin) of the hotel.

Connecting to these unprotected networks is okay as long as you've protected your computer (see Chapter 3) and realize that anything you send over the network is visible by anyone. Browsing the Web is fine. Logging into your secure bank account is secure as long as you validate the site's certificate like I showed in Chapter 1.

WEP should be considered in the same boat as an open network.

Exploring Network Security Features

As technology advances, the CPUs going into routers get faster and faster. The processing power required for the basic routing and firewalling is negligible, so there's ever increasing room left for more features.

You'd think that manufacturers would cut back and put the bare minimum CPU in, but the way the industry works is that older chips cost more to buy, so it ends up being cheaper to put more oomph inside the box.

Most manufacturers have several features in common, though some may implement them slightly differently. Some features are handy, some not so much, and some will completely expose your computer to Internet attackers. In the following sections, I identify when and where you'd want to use them.

Understanding the SSID and password

The network name (SSID), password, and security protocol (such as WPA2) are your first line of defense against attackers. You've seen earlier how WPA2 is currently the best protocol to use, and you probably gathered that the password is important.

The only known way to break into a WPA2 PSK (pre-shared key) network is to guess the password. The crackers know this and have come up with ways to guess passwords at incredible speeds.

The WPA/WPA2 key that encrypts all the data in the air is derived from both the password and the SSID. One of the optimizations the crackers use is to pre-compute these keys by using a list of popular SSIDs and popular passwords.

If you make sure that your SSID is unique, such as the name of your street, your pet's name, or something else unique, perhaps followed by a number, you'll be sure to stay off this list.

The most important thing to do is to choose a complex password. If you're using Wi-Fi protected setup (WPS), you don't even have to remember it!

Figure 2-1 shows where you configure the SSID, protocol, and password for the network. Here the SSID is "walberghome," the password is "W1r3l3ssB00k," and the network uses WPA2.

Search the Internet for "top 1000 ssids" and you should find, surprisingly enough, a list of 1000 of the most common SSIDs out there.

With a unique SSID and an unguessable password, the crackers will have to find another way in!

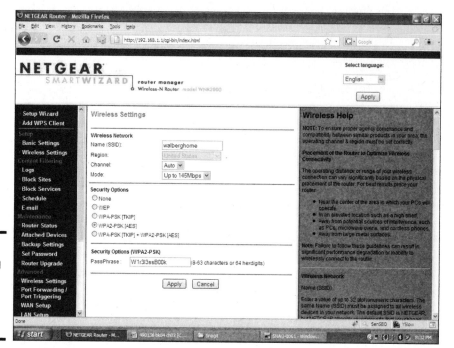

Figure 2-1:
Configuring
the SSID,
password,
and
protocol.

SSIDs and passwords are case sensitive. Use a lowercase SSID, and work in some uppercase letters and some numbers into your password.

Using advanced wireless settings

When wireless first came out and the low-strength version of WEP was all that was available, people came up with a few methods to increase the security of their network.

Security is always a tradeoff between protection and convenience. As you add more security measures, it becomes more complex to use whatever it is you're protecting.

And so, too, it is with wireless. Two ideas that people came up with were

✦ Hide the existence of the SSID

✦ Find the hardware addresses of the machines you want to connect and only let those in

With today's technology, both of these are poor protections against attack. Not only do they make your wireless network terribly inconvenient for you to use, but they don't improve your security.

On the surface, hiding your SSID makes some sense. Your wireless access point broadcasts its network name periodically so that your computer can know when it should connect. Turning off this feature means that someone driving by won't know the access point is there and won't try to break into it.

The problem with this is that it is still possible to deduce the presence of a wireless network because of the wireless traffic. After that, there are various ways to figure out the SSID.

The second idea involves making a list of the hardware addresses of the wireless cards and telling the router to only allow those addresses to use the network. Figure 2-2 shows the properties of a wireless card. The hardware address is the same as the physical address.

Figure 2-2: Showing the hardware address of a wireless NIC.

Not only is it a pain to administer, spoofing a MAC address is trivial. *Spoofing* in this example means that the attacker is using your MAC address instead of his; your access point is none the wiser.

Browse to Wireless Settings to see where these features are configured (See Figure 2-3). The Enable SSID Broadcast controls whether or not your SSID is broadcast. Click the Setup Access List button to set up the MAC addresses that can connect.

These features don't do much to protect your network but do cause serious usability concerns. At one point, using these features were requirements for companies transmitting credit card data over wireless networks, but the requirements were dropped in late 2008 because the tradeoff wasn't worth it. If even the credit card companies don't think it helps security, then it's not worth doing.

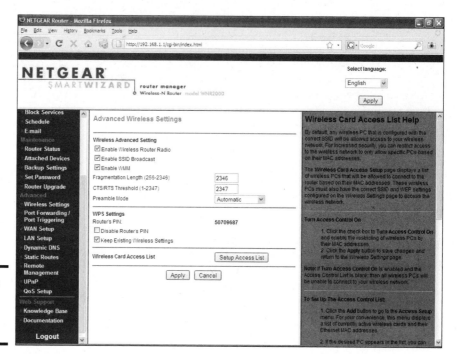

Figure 2-3:
Advanced
wireless
settings.

So why did I even bring it up? If you do some reading on the Internet, you may come across a page talking about it. I wanted to make sure you knew the reasoning and history behind the recommendation and the tradeoffs involved.

Allowing incoming connections

A firewall's job is to block bad packets and allow good packets. At the very simplest level your router's firewall does this by blocking any connections that were initiated by outside hosts and allows anything that was initiated from the inside. That's why you can request Web pages from your computer, but people can't open your file shares from the outside.

Most applications behave under these circumstances. Firewalls have been around for ages, even before the first home router. The nature of the Internet is also *client-server*, which means you (the client) request stuff from the server, and not the other way around.

That's not to say there aren't applications that break this mold. Peer-to-peer file sharing and online gaming are two notable examples. In these applications, the server sometimes has to push data to you, or you must accept a connection from another client to pull a piece of data. The firewall prevents this.

Port forwarding is a feature that lets you take certain inbound connections and forward them to a particular host on the inside of your network.

The firewall is preventing incoming connections for a good reason — they're usually insecure. When setting up port forwarding, be careful to only forward what you need.

To set up port forwarding, follow these steps:

1. **Determine the port to be forwarded, which should be provided by the application or its documentation.**

   Figure 2-4 shows a dialog from a file-sharing program, indicating that the incoming port is 59534.

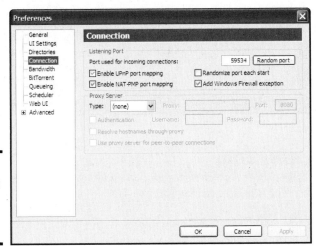

Figure 2-4: Determining the port to be forwarded.

Every application is different, and some (like the one above) choose random inbound ports. Just because the example above uses port 59534 doesn't mean that your application will.

2. **Navigate to the Port Forwarding menu in your wireless router's administrative interface, which is shown in Figure 2-5.**

3. **Ensure that Port Forwarding is selected. Check under Service Name to see if the name of the protocol is there.**

   (If it is, skip over the next section.)

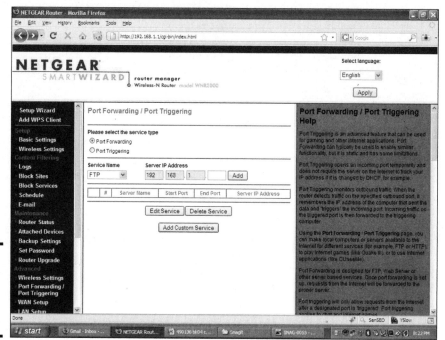

Figure 2-5:
The port
forwarding
configura-
tion screen.

Adding a custom service

The NETGEAR router comes with some predefined port forwarding protocols. If your protocol isn't on the list, you have to add it.

1. **Select the Add Custom Service button to get to the screen shown in Figure 2-6.**

2. **Fill in the details about the port to be forwarded.**

   The name of the service is what you want it to be. In this case, I used the name of the application.

   There is only one port to be forwarded, so I've put that in as both the starting and ending ports. Finally, the traffic is to be forwarded to 192.168.1.100, which is my laptop.

3. **Click Apply, and you are taken back to the port forwarding screen showing your new configuration (see Figure 2-7).**

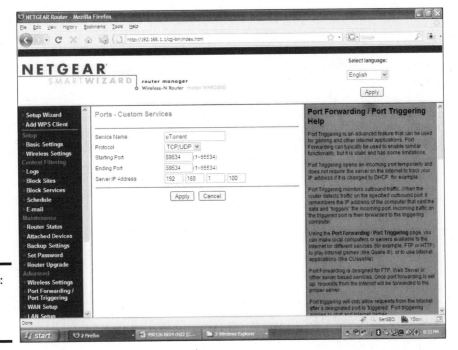

Figure 2-6:
Adding a
custom
service.

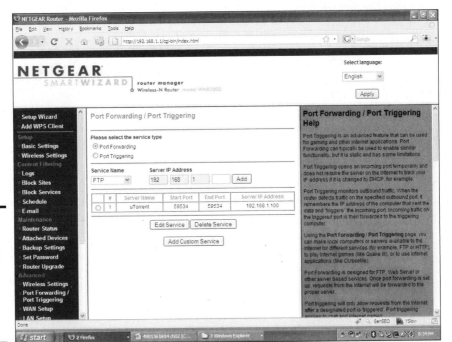

Figure 2-7:
The port
forwarding
screen
showing
the new
configura-
tion

Forwarding a known service

If the service is already known to the router, such as FTP, then you can select it from the main menu and enter the address of the server. Allowing incoming FTP traffic would be helpful if you wanted to set up a file server on the inside of your network.

Port triggering

The downside to port forwarding is that you have to know the address of the computer that wants to use the forwarding. This inconvenience is usually minor, but if it is a problem for you, then port triggering is an option.

Port triggering waits for an internal computer to make a predetermined type of connection to the outside. Upon seeing the connection, the router sets up a port forward to that computer.

The configuration of a port trigger is similar to that of a port forward, except that you must identify the outbound traffic, and you don't need to specify an internal host.

Usually a port forward will suffice, though, and if you need a port trigger, then your application's documentation will specify that.

DMZ server

In the security field, a demilitarized zone (DMZ) is a network that's in between the inside and the outside, and all traffic must pass through a firewall. Companies put servers that they want to be Internet accessible in there, such as Web and e-mail servers. The servers can't be trusted as much because they're exposed to the Internet, so the firewall also dictates how the server can talk back to the company's internal network.

The DMZ server on a home router is the catch-all host that all unknown traffic gets sent to. Think of it as a port forward of all the ports to one server. Good or bad, incoming traffic gets sent to the server you specify.

Browse to the WAN Setup screen shown in Figure 2-8 to set up a DMZ server. Select the check box and type the address of the server, and all the bad guys can talk to your internal device.

Avoid using this feature. That computer is going to get a lot of attacks. That same computer is also free to talk to any computer on your internal network, so if it gets compromised, you can expect more to follow.

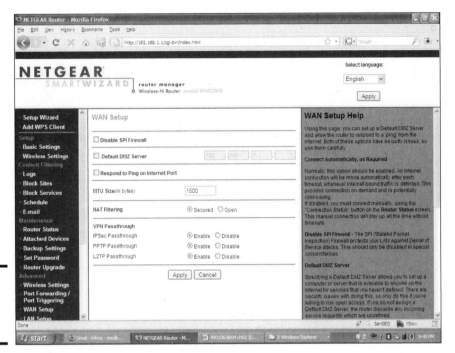

Figure 2-8:
The WAN
setup
screen.

VPN passthrough

Your employer might let you work at home using a virtual private network (VPN) tunnel. This gives your computer a secure tunnel over the Internet back in to your place of employment.

VPNs don't always play nicely with home routers. If you're having problems with your VPN, check to make sure that the VPN passthrough options are enabled (also shown in Figure 2-8).

Reviewing Internet policies

Your router is likely able to perform some more extensive filtering on what goes in and out, rather than just assuming everything that goes out is good. Some of this functionality is rather advanced and specialized, but some of it falls under the "why didn't they think of that before?" category.

One of the more handy features allows you to block Web sites based on key-words in the site's name, or in the page itself. If you've got kids around, this is especially helpful to make sure they don't wander into some of the seedier parts of the Internet.

**Book IV
Chapter 2**

Using a Safety Net

It is technically possible to block other applications, such as instant messaging, but chances are your router won't be able to do it. Chat programs are notorious for evading firewalls, even going so far as to masquerade themselves as Web traffic. For that matter it is possible to get around the Web filtering, so it should not be considered a substitute for proper supervision.

To block sites based on their content follow these steps:

1. **Navigate to the Block Sites menu, which is shown in Figure 2-9.**

2. **Enable blocking by selecting the Always option.**

3. **Enter your keywords one by one into the keyword box where indicated, pressing Add Keyword in between each one.**

   Figure 2-10 shows a screen where blocking has been enabled and netgear has been added. If the word netgear appears in either the URL bar or the page itself, the site will be blocked.

   Different routers are configured differently. For example, the Linksys routers maintain two separate block lists, one for the URL and one for keywords in the Web page.

   If you know the name of the site you want to block, you can enter it as a keyword. If you just want to block individual words, that's fine, too. You can do both at the same time.

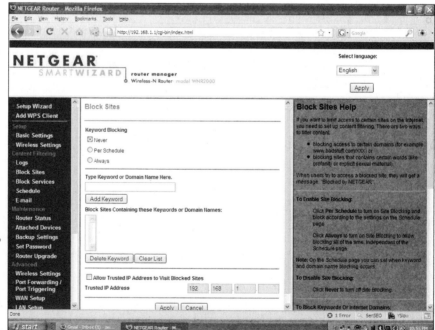

Figure 2-9:
The "block sites" configuration screen.

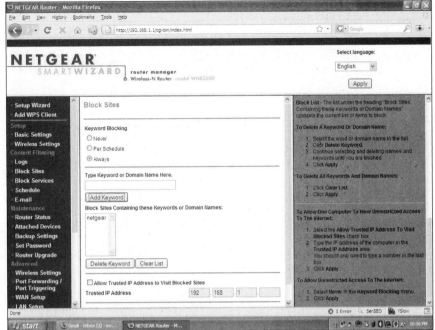

Figure 2-10:
Enabling site
blocking,
and adding
a keyword.

4. **When you're done with the list, click the Apply button at the bottom of the screen.**

   You can always come back and adjust the list.

If someone attempts to go to a blocked Web site they will see the message shown in Figure 2-11.

This message, in no uncertain terms, tells you the site has been blocked.

Some routers do not display a message. Instead, they reset the connection to the Web server, triggering an error in the Web browser. It's not as obvious to the user but still has the same effect.

Finally, if you would like to know what sites that people are going to, and if there were any blocks, click on the Logs menu (see Figure 2-12).

Here, you can see that someone tried to go to netgear.com but was blocked. The time of the infraction and the address of the computer are also logged.

Figure 2-11:
A site that
has been
blocked by
the firewall.

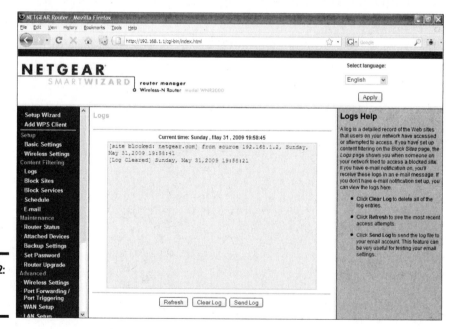

Figure 2-12:
Reviewing
the logs.

If you need more control

Blocking Web sites containing one of a handful of keywords is a pretty simple way of attacking the problem of keeping your kids from bad Web sites. If that's not good enough for you, then consider a subscription service that categorizes Web sites and lets you decide which categories are good and bad.

These services are used by either installing software on the computer that's to be filtered or by integrating with the router. Few routers support this integration, so go looking for a router that supports URL filtering with an external service if you want that option. Be forewarned, the router will probably cost a bit more than a router without the feature.

In addition to the cost of the router or software, you'll probably have to pay a regular subscription fee for use of the block list, which would include updates to the list.

Many business grade routers with integrated firewalls are starting to incorporate Web filtering, virus scanning, and more advanced (and automatic) firewalls. It's only a matter of time before this technology makes its way into home routers.

Whatever software or hardware you use, it's not a substitute for proper supervision. Putting the family computer in the living room, where everyone can see it, might be a cheaper and easier option.

Chapter 3: Protecting Your Computer

In This Chapter

🖙 **Keeping your computer up to date**

🖙 **Getting the right security software**

🖙 **Understanding browser security**

🖙 **Working with the User Account Control**

Security is a process, not a product. Even the best software out there won't protect you if you don't use it properly. Fortunately, there's a lot of good software built right into the operating system, and this chapter focuses on making it work for you.

Security is also a tradeoff between convenience and risk, so I look at a few places where you can choose to take a less aggressive security posture in return for less intrusion on your life. It's a fair trade — there are no wrong answers.

Throughout this chapter, I focus on the Windows Vista security tools. Other than a basic firewall, the older Windows XP has virtually nothing built in and therefore relies on third-party tools. Vista isn't perfect, but it's leaps and bounds ahead of XP.

Visiting the Windows Security Center

The Windows Security Center (WSC) was introduced to Windows XP in Service Pack 2, and was improved as it was carried forward into Vista. The job of the security center is to monitor the status of various security-related settings and to give you an easy-to-read view of your security posture.

The picture of the shield with the exclamation mark in Figure 3-1 is your first indication of a problem.

Figure 3-1:
The
Windows
Security
Center
alert in the
system tray
showing a
warning.

If your computer has a more serious security problem, you see a red X instead of a yellow shield, as shown in Figure 3-2.

Figure 3-2:
The
Windows
Security
Center alert
showing
a serious
problem.

The difference between warnings and serious problems in this case is subjective. Either case should prompt you to check and see what's going on, though.

Double-click on the Security Center alert icon to bring up the security center, which is shown in Figure 3-3.

The WSC is broken down into four separate areas:

✦ **Windows Firewall:** This area protects your computer against incoming and outgoing connections, which is an additional layer of defense if you've already got a hardware firewall.

✦ **Automatic updating:** This service automatically downloads and applies patches if you'd like, which ensures your computer is always up to date.

✦ **Malware protection:** This area shows the status of both anti-virus and anti-spyware software.

✦ **Other security settings:** This area is a grab bag of extra security features.

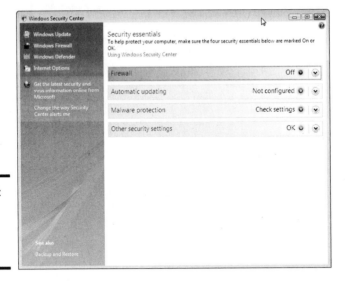

Figure 3-3:
The
Windows
Security
Center.

Each item in the Windows Security Center is shaded according to its status and also provides a line of text to further describe the status. Based on the dark shading, you can see that Figure 3-3 has a serious problem with the firewall because the firewall is turned off. The other elements seem to be healthy.

If you don't see an icon in your system tray, your computer probably meets all the requirements of the Windows Security Center. If you still want to check, go to the Control Panel and then click on the Check this computer's security status link.

Exploring the Windows firewall

The Windows firewall's job is to inspect the network packets that go in and out of your computer and to decide if they're allowed or not, based on the configured policy. The policy is changed over time based on feedback from the user. For example, using a new program might prompt you for permission to allow that particular program to make the network connections.

The firewall tracks down connections to the application. One application may be permitted to make a Web request, but another application might not. By doing so, you have an increased chance of spotting malware because you will be prompted when the application tries to make a request that is out of character.

Turning on the firewall

Turning on the firewall is a straightforward process.

1. **From the Control Panel, click the security icon to take you to the security menu within the control panel.**

   This is shown in Figure 3-4.

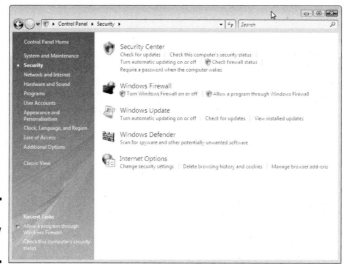

Figure 3-4:
The Security
menu.

2. **From the Security menu, select Turn Windows Firewall on or off to take you to the firewall settings menu shown in Figure 3-5.**

3. **From the Firewall Settings window, select the On (Recommended) option and click the OK button.**

   Your shields are now up!

Living with the Windows Firewall

If firewalls were foolproof, then you'd never have been given the option of turning it on — it would be just a part of Vista you never thought about.

Unfortunately, the firewall is not perfect, and it can't react to every situation. By default, the firewall blocks incoming connections. But what if you need a connection to come in?

When an application requests the ability to listen for incoming connections, and the policy would block that, you are given the opportunity to override the block through the dialog box shown in Figure 3-6.

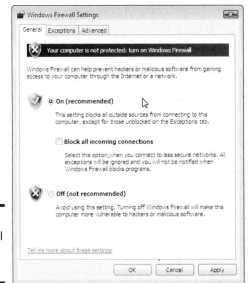

Figure 3-5:
The Firewall
Settings
window.

Figure 3-6:
Vista
prompts
to allow a
connection.

The dialog box shown in Figure 3-6 is light on details. You're being asked to decide whether or not an application should accept connections. If you allow it, the Windows firewall will allow incoming connections into this application.

To be clear, the application has requested the privilege of accepting connections. The first question you should ask is "Did I just launch that application?" If the query came while you were in the middle of browsing the Web, then you should be extra cautious. However, in this case, I ran the program. If you're not sure which program generated the alert, then check the dialog box because it's listed there.

After you determine that the alert was as a result of a program you chose to run, you should ask "Is this the type of program that accepts network connections?"

On the Internet, a client (your computer) connects to a server to get some information. The connection is always made from one side to the other, and having a connection come in to you if you're a client is rare.

Therefore, if you see an alert asking you if you'd like to accept connections, you should qualify the last question by asking yourself why someone would want to connect to me.

You want incoming connections on the following scenarios:

✦ When you're running some server software such as an FTP server.

✦ When you're running a peer-to-peer (P2P) file-sharing program that shares out parts of the file as you download the rest.

✦ When you're running some remote control software and want people to be able to control your computer.

It's also important to note that if you're behind a router, then people from the Internet can't make direct connections to you and wouldn't be able to connect to the application anyway. There are exceptions to this, such as if you've enabled port forwarding (see Book IV, Chapter 2).

If you want to allow the application to receive connections, then click Unblock. If not, click Keep Blocking.

Using automatic updates

Software isn't perfect. Actually, if you spent some time as a software developer, you'd be continually surprised when it works at all. A popular quote among developers is "If we built buildings the same way we built software, the first woodpecker that came along would destroy civilization."

Despite Microsoft's biggest efforts, bugs exist in Windows. Some of them are pretty tame such as "screen doesn't redraw properly." But some of them are pretty bad like one that surfaced in late 2008 that allowed anyone that could connect to your machine to take it over. Oops.

Patches are pieces of software that fix bugs. Think of using patches as patching up a hole in a wall, or in a bike tire. Microsoft releases these patches every month, and you can download them to make sure your computer's software is up to date.

The problem is that Microsoft software often has bugs and, therefore, it tends to release a lot of patches. Chances are you won't remember to download every single patch every month. Figuring out which patches are necessary is also a problem. So Microsoft introduced Windows Update some time ago, and more recently, made it install patches automatically, should you allow it.

In Figure 3-7, the line corresponding to automatic updates has been pulled down to show some more details.

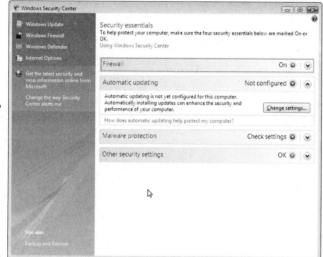

Figure 3-7:
The
Windows
Security
Center
showing the
automatic
updates
option

Click on the Change settings button to bring up the automatic updates configuration, which is shown in Figure 3-8.

From here, you have two options:

✦ **Install updates automatically:** In this mode, Windows checks for updates periodically and installs them.

✦ **Let me choose:** Gives you more flexibility on how you apply your updates.

If you choose the Let Me Choose option, the screen in Figure 3-9 appears. You can select one of the following options:

✦ **Install automatically:** This option is almost the same as the one in the previous menu. Updates are downloaded and installed without your intervention. The difference between this and the previous menu is that you get to choose the time the updates happen.

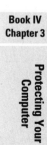

**Book IV
Chapter 3**

**Protecting Your
Computer**

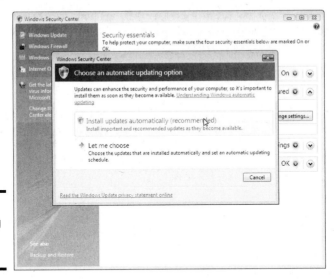

Figure 3-8:
Configuring
automatic
updates.

Figure 3-9:
Showing the
available
options for
Windows
Update.

✦ **Download updates but let me choose whether to install them:** If you're
not comfortable with updates happening without your knowledge,
choose this option. When new updates are released your computer
downloads them and then prompts you to download them.

✦ **Check for updates, but let me choose whether to download and install
them:** This option is similar to the last option, except that the updates

aren't downloaded automatically. I find this option to be troublesome because I like having the updates happen when I'm not using the computer.

✦ **Never check for updates:** If you want to do it by hand, choose this option.

I recommend setting your system up for automatic updates, so you won't miss an update.

Checking for updates manually

The automatic updates only download the patches that Microsoft deems critical. Every so often, check for updates manually; doing so lets you download all the optional updates.

Going through the process manually after you first install your computer is a good idea. Usually, you have some updates that require the presence of earlier updates, so even after going through the updates once, you may find that you're not fully patched. Only the manual process gives you the confidence that you're up to date. To do so, follow these steps:

1. **From the Control Panel, select Check for Updates from the Security menu.**

The screen shown in Figure 3-10 appears.

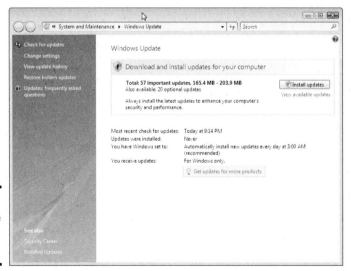

Figure 3-10: Showing the available updates.

Book IV
Chapter 3

Protecting Your Computer

In Figure 3-10, you can see that the system has 57 important updates to download. If you are curious about what they are, you can click the View available updates link.

This screen also lets you confirm your automatic update settings. Here you can see that the system is configured to update nightly at 3 a.m., and that it's never been updated.

2. Ignore the optional updates for now and click the Install Updates button to begin the update process.

Sometimes the updates come with a license that you must accept to use. In Figure 3-11, the license is for the Windows Malicious Software Removal Tool, which is the built in anti-spyware product. I look at this later, but for now, you have to accept the license terms and click Finish.

Figure 3-11: Accept the license terms.

3. Wait while your system downloads and installs updates.

The time it takes to do this depends on the speed of your computer and how many updates you have.

Your computer will be usable during the update process, but don't expect peak performance. There's a lot going on during the update process, and at times your computer might feel sluggish.

After the updates are installed, you get confirmation, as shown in Figure 3-12.

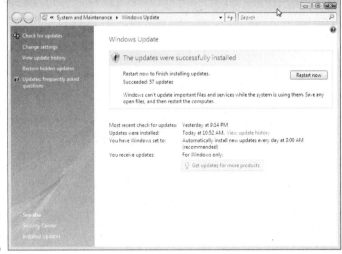

Figure 3-12:
A confirmation that the updates were successfully installed.

If you read the message on the screen, you can see that you're being prompted to reboot to finish the updates. You can do so now, or close the window to reboot later.

If you choose to reboot later, then you are periodically reminded to reboot by means of a dialog box that pops up from the system tray, shown in Figure 3-13.

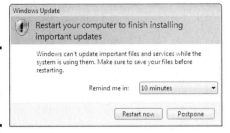

Figure 3-13:
Vista prompts you to reboot.

You can continue to postpone the reboot as long as you want.

When you finally reboot, the process takes longer than normal because updates are being processed.

Some updates depend on other updates already having been applied. The first time you apply updates you should go back and check to make sure all updates were applied correctly.

Book IV
Chapter 3

Protecting Your Computer

1. **After the reboot, go back to the updates window by going to the Control Panel and selecting Check for Updates from the Security menu.**

   Figure 3-14 shows that there is one important update and 20 optional updates.

2. **Click on View available updates to get details of these 21 updates.**

   Figure 3-15 shows the available updates. The important update is a security update, and most of the rest are regular system updates. If you are curious, you can enter the identification next to the update, such as KB931099, into the search engine at Microsoft.com to find out the details.

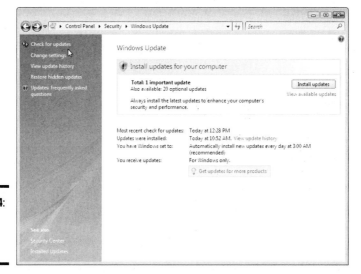

Figure 3-14: There are still more updates.

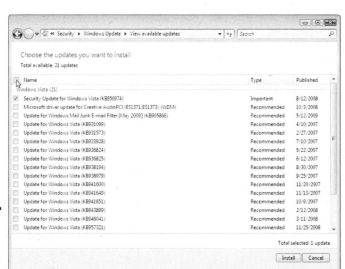

Figure 3-15: Viewing all the updates.

3. **Choose the updates you want to install by checking the box next to the name. If you want to select them all, you can check the button at the top of the dialog.**

4. **Finally, click on Install to begin the update process.**

   You might have to go through this a couple more times before you're all up to date. However, after you're done, you are told that there are no new updates available, as in Figure 3-16.

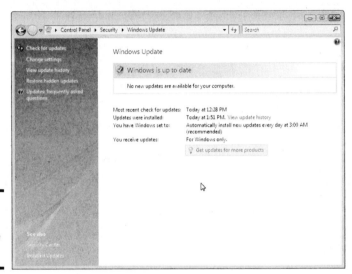

Figure 3-16:
No new updates are available.

After all of that, your automatic updates take care of you, and all you have to worry about is performing the odd reboot.

Protecting against malware

Microsoft Windows spawned an industry of malware authors eager to make a buck off of computer users. The malware authors were fairly successful, which itself was the drive behind the good guys to come out with anti-malware products.

Anti-virus products have been available long before the Internet was commonplace and have managed to keep pace with the virus authors. Anti-malware software has not been as successful as its anti-virus brethren. Finally, with the release of Windows Vista, Microsoft bundled its own anti-malware software with the operating system.

Microsoft calls this software Windows Defender. It is bundled with Vista and also downloadable from Microsoft.com for Windows XP and 2003.

Book IV
Chapter 3

Protecting Your Computer

Bundled security software

If you've bought a computer recently, especially from a retail outlet, you might find that it comes with anti-virus and anti-malware software. If so, great! But, please check carefully, because many of these are time-limited trials and will stop working after 30, 60, or 90 days.

If, after the trial, you're happy with the software, then by all means buy it. Windows Vista

was designed to work with third-party anti-virus and anti-malware products. Make sure that you understand what you're signing up for, such as recurring billing.

If you don't want to keep the software, make sure to uninstall it to avoid being nagged about buying it.

Sadly, Windows Defender doesn't do anything for viruses. You're on your own there, so I've got a free alternative for you later on in this chapter.

Looking at Windows Defender

1. **From the Control Panel choose Security and then click on Windows Defender to open Windows Defender, shown in Figure 3-17.**

   In the figure you can see that everything is just fine according to Defender.

2. **If you want to scan your computer right away, click the Scan button at the top. If anything pops up, you can deal with it right there.**

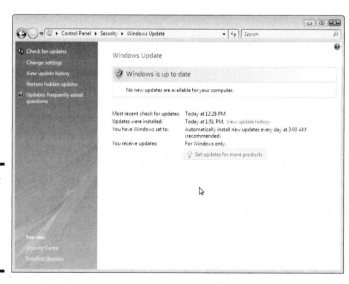

Figure 3-17: The Windows Defender main screen.

Other than that, Windows Defender doesn't provide a whole lot of options. It's nowhere near as interesting as anti-virus.

Installing anti-virus software

Many companies are selling anti-virus software. You can expect to pay around $30–$60 for the software, depending on the features, and to pay that every year for upgrades and updates to the virus signatures. Packages at the upper end (and higher) include more than just anti-virus and anti-spyware; they help you with spam, identity theft, and a whole host of other problems.

There is, however, a free anti-virus package out there. AVG is a company that produces anti-virus and anti-spyware software with various features. They offer their base package free for noncommercial use. If you don't already have anything else, I highly recommend AVG.

If you scroll to the bottom, you can see the download link, which is shown in Figure 3-18.

Upon clicking the download link, you are redirected to another site for the download. If you are using Internet Explorer, you might get the warning shown in Figure 3-19. If so, click on the warning bar and then click Download File.

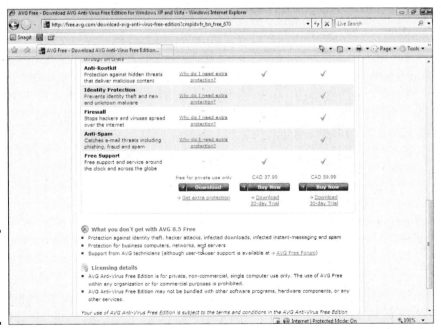

Figure 3-18: The download link at free. avg.com.

Warning or not, the next dialog box you get prompts you to save or run the file, as shown in Figure 3-20. Clicking Run is easy.

Figure 3-20:
The Run or
Save dialog
box.

Grab a coffee, because the download takes a couple of minutes. If you want to grab one for me, I take mine black, please, and thank you.

Configuring AVG

The installation program starts as soon as the download begins and you see Figure 3-21.

The next few screens prompt you to accept the license and remind you that you are using the free edition of the package. Click Next to advance screens until you come to Figure 3-22.

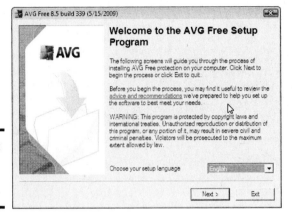

Figure 3-21:
Beginning
the AVG
installation.

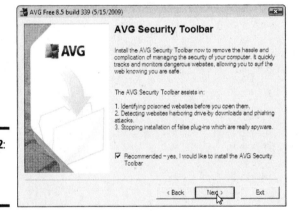

Figure 3-22:
Installing
the AVG
toolbar.

The AVG toolbar provides some enhancements to Internet Explorer that can help keep you safe, so it is worth installing the toolbar.

Be careful about which toolbars you install because you don't know if they contain malware. The AVG toolbar is a helpful toolbar and alerts you if you try to install a toolbar containing malware.

Continue following the prompts until the software reports that installation is complete.

Configuring the first run

After you install the AVG anti-virus software, you are prompted to configure it through the first run wizard. For the most part, you can accept all the defaults, though there are a couple of screens where you might choose to select an alternate option to the default.

**Book IV
Chapter 3**

Protecting Your
Computer

The first screen is shown in Figure 3-23. Click Next to continue.

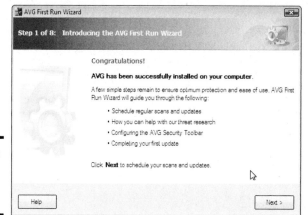

Figure 3-23:
Beginning
the first run
wizard.

The next screen is the most important, because it schedules the periodic update and daily scan (see Figure 3-24). One update a day should be enough.

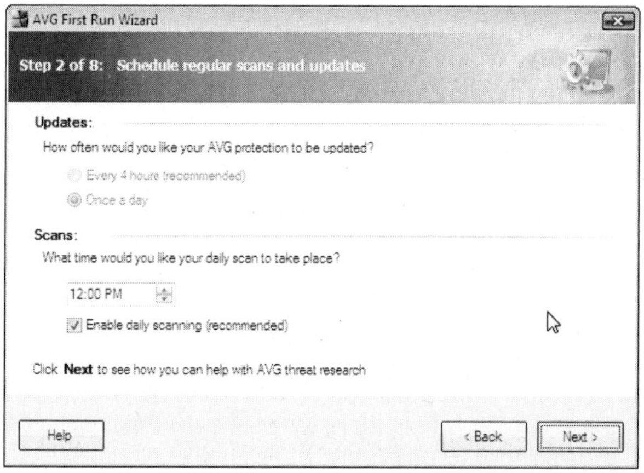

Figure 3-24:
Configuring
the time
and type
of scan.

Configure the scan for a time that works for you and make sure that the Enable scanning check box is selected. Your computer is slower than normal because of all the disk reads, so pick a time where you don't expect peak performance. Lunchtime works well for me.

Follow the instructions on the screens to complete the installation. You may or may not want to choose the following options:

✦ **Agree to provide information about detected threats to AVG:** This option is disabled by default, and you may want to consider enabling it. Turning on this option sends information about what the software finds back to AVG for product improvements and virus research. Any information that could identify you is stripped before it is sent.

✦ **Change my default search engine to Yahoo!:** If you installed the toolbar, this option changes your default search engine to Yahoo!. By default this is selected; if you prefer a different search engine, then deselect it.

You go through a few screens, the software updates itself with the latest virus definitions, and then you are protected.

Verifying that you're protected

You know you're protected from viruses two ways, as shown in Figure 3-25.

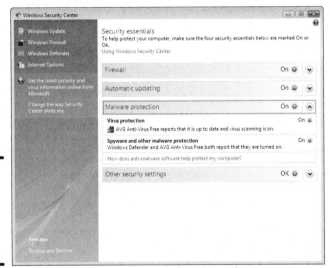

Figure 3-25: Verifying that the anti-virus software is working.

The first indication is that the Windows Security Center isn't complaining about the anti-virus (go to the Control Panel and then find Check this computer's security status, or see the earlier section called Visiting the Windows Security Center). In fact, if you look at the Malware protection section, you see the following:

✦ **Virus Protection**: AVG Antivirus Free reports that it is up to date and virus scanning is on.

✦ **Spyware and other malware protection**: Windows Defender and AVG Anti-Virus both report that they are turned on.

Finally, look in the system tray to see the new AVG icon (the four colored boxes).

You've got virus protection. You've got spyware protection. Let's move on.

Other security settings

By now you've set up some pretty good defenses. Your computer updates itself regularly. It has a firewall, and its anti-virus and anti-spyware sensors are busy looking for any signs of malware.

You could stop right here and be fairly worry free when browsing the Internet. But being safe on the Internet is much more than the software you run; it's also the decisions you make.

I'm pretty sure you're going to approach the Internet with a cautious eye and make good decisions, but even the best of us clicks the odd dialog box without reading it too closely. So, I'm going to show you a couple of safeguards that you can use to further protect yourself against the bad things out there.

Creating separate accounts for administrators and users

Windows Vista is a multiuser operating system. This means that the system recognizes that you are different from someone else based on a username that you provide. Vista recognizes you by your *account*, which has a name and a password.

Using separate accounts means that you can keep your files separate from other people that use your computer. Maybe you want to protect stuff from being deleted; maybe you want your nosey sister to stay out of your stuff. Either way, one user can't touch another user's stuff.

Accounts also have privilege levels — either a standard user or administrator — in Vista. The account you're using now is probably the one you created when you set up the system and is an administrator. In this section, you create a standard user account for day-to-day use which limits your exposure if something gets by your malware filters. Follow these steps:

1. **Go to Control Panel and select Add or Remove user accounts.**

   The list of user accounts appears, as shown in Figure 3-26.

   In the figure you see that there is a user called Sean, who is an administrator and has a password. You can also see a disabled guest account that you will not use.

2. **Select Create a new account to start creating the new account.**

   The form you see is shown in Figure 3-27.

Figure 3-26:
The initial
list of user
accounts.

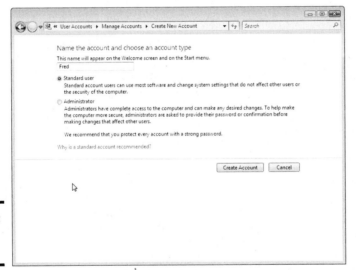

Figure 3-27:
Creating an
account.

The username I have selected is "Fred." Note that the account is to be
created as a standard user rather than an administrator (which is the
default).

3. **Click on the Create Account button to continue.**

You are taken back to the previous menu, and you can see the new user
(see Figure 3-28).

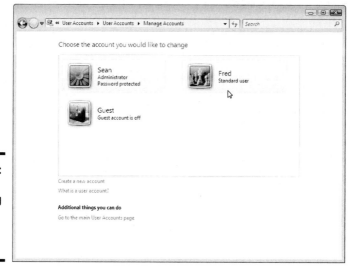

4. **Click on the new user's name and then click the Create Password button, shown in Figure 3-29.**

Figure 3-29:
Setting the
password
on the new
account.

5. **You must enter the password twice, and you can also give a password hint to be used if you forget the password.**

It is possible to reset passwords as an administrator, but heed the warning in Figure 3-28. If you end up using the encrypted file feature, you risk losing your files.

Logging in

The next time you start your computer (or if you select Logout from the Vista menu) you will see your new user available to use. Log in with that user and do your work as normal.

Should you need to assert your administrative might, you don't have to log out and back in again as your administrative user. Simply right-click on the icon you want to run, and select Run as administrator, just like in Figure 3-30.

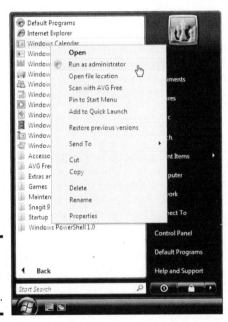

Figure 3-30:
The Run as administrator option.

After you release the mouse button, you are prompted to log in as your administrative user, as shown in Figure 3-30.

Simple, eh?

Running as a regular user makes sure that any software you run can't do too much damage. It's just a good thing to do.

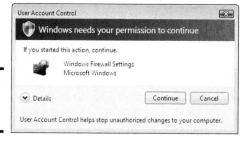

Figure 3-31:
Logging
in as the
adminis-
trator.

User Account Control

User Account Control (UAC) was introduced in Vista. Formerly, if you
were an administrator, you had rights to modify anything on the system. If
you weren't an administrator, you were constantly running into problems
because, well, you couldn't modify anything.

As a result, people just logged in as administrators because it was the path of
least resistance. UAC tries to solve this problem by withholding administrative
access from a user (even an administrator) until they approve the action.

You've probably noticed dialog boxes like the one in Figure 3-31.

Figure 3-32:
The UAC
dialog box.

If you see something like that, then you know you're being asked to do something at the administrative level. Programs that need administrative access
have a special shield icon next to them in the control panel.

Go ahead and click on Continue if you had run the program indicated. If it
pops up for no reason, or on a file you downloaded from the Internet, it's
time for caution! Fire up your anti-virus software and scan the file first.

Chapter 4: Troubleshooting Network Problems

In This Chapter

✔ **Verifying your settings**

✔ **Checking hardware**

✔ **Finding information about a Web site**

✔ **Exploring the command line**

*W*eb sites can be temperamental. Sometimes they work, sometimes they don't. I think it's related to how badly you need the information on the page, but the scientific community is still undecided on that one. Either way, we live in an imperfect world, and not everything works all the time.

In this chapter, I present a few ways to find out if Internet problems are your fault or that of the other end and provide some general guidance on how to proceed after that.

If a Web site isn't working for you, the most obvious thing to do is try a different one. If that one works, then maybe you should just try your first Web site later.

Confirming Your Network Settings

Before you go blaming the other guy, look at your network settings to make sure that you're actually connected to your network.

1. **From Vista's Control Panel, select the View Network Status and Tasks option.**

   This takes you to the Network and Sharing Center, shown in Figure 4-1. The Network and Sharing Center is the starting point for configuring various aspects of Vista's networking features.

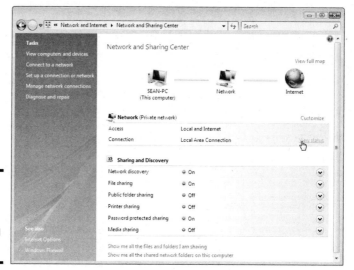

Figure 4-1:
The
Network
and Sharing
Center.

2. **From the Network and Sharing Center, select the View Status option on the right side of the window.**

You can view details about the Local Area Network, as shown in Figure 4-2.

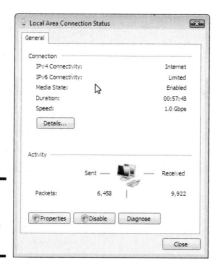

Figure 4-2:
Local Area
Connection
Status.

From this window, you can see that Windows Vista considers that you have Internet access to the IPv4 network.

IPv4? IPv6?

Computers and networks are constantly evolving. Network *protocols* are standardized ways of talking between computers. Standardized protocols let your mobile phone request a Web page from a supercomputer across the ocean — they're both speaking the same language.

When the Internet as we know it began, it ran a protocol called IP — the Internet Protocol — Version 4. Guess what version we're running 30 years later? That's right, Version 4.

IPv4 works great, but the problem is that it wasn't designed to be used as much. The addresses used in the protocol, which identify the sender and the recipient of the packet, are only 32 bits long, which roughly works out to be a number between 0 and 4 billion.

Therefore, you could have 4 billion hosts on the Internet. However, various rules governing how hosts get laid out and how stuff works together bring that number down significantly.

With something like 6 billion people in the world, cell phones, and multiple computers per house, a lot of pressure is placed on those 4 billion addresses. It's not possible to make the address field bigger, so something has to be done.

The smart people that keep the Internet going managed to tweak the way the protocol works to extend the life of the addresses. One of these ways is the use of private addresses like 192.168.1.1 that you see in your home network. Private addressing has done a remarkable job of extending the time before all the IPv4 addresses are depleted. The so-called "death of the IPv4 Internet" has been predicted for years, and somehow we always make it through another year.

In the early 1990s work was started on the next-generation IPv4, which was eventually called IPv6 (IPv5 is something completely different and isn't used). Windows Vista supports IPv6, but chances are your service provider doesn't, nor do most of the Web sites you want to go to. So for now, don't worry that your IPv6 network doesn't work.

Even though Vista thinks you have Internet access, you want to verify this yourself. Click that Details button at the bottom of the window to see the network details shown in Figure 4-3.

There are a few important numbers here:

✦ **IPv4 IP Address:** Your Internet address

✦ **IPv4 Default Gateway:** Where you send all your packets to in order to get onto the Internet

✦ **IPv4 DNS Server:** The machine that takes care of resolving names like http://www.dummies.com to the IP address of the machine

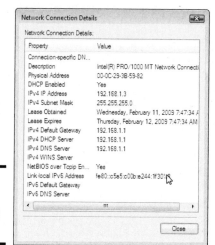

Figure 4-3:
Network
connection
details.

Your IP address probably starts with 192.168, but don't fret if it doesn't. However, if it begins with 169.254, then you've got a problem.

169.254.x.x is called the DHCP Autoconfigure Network. If a computer isn't given a proper address by the network, then it makes up an address in the 169.254 space. An address like this is a sure sign that your computer can't find its DHCP server.

If you're getting one of these addresses, then the problem is between you and your ISP. Begin by rebooting your wireless router and then your computer. If that doesn't solve the problem, refer back to Book II, Chapter 8 for instructions on how to troubleshoot your computer and wireless network.

Pinging Around

Underwater sonar relies on measuring sounds to determine where an object is and what it looks like. Active sonar generates sounds and measures the reflections that come back.

The Internet has its own version of a sonar ping called the ICMP Echo Request (ICMP being the Internet Control Message Protocol, which is like the traffic signals of the Internet). If you want to see if a host is alive, you send it an echo request. If it responds with an echo reply, then you know the host is there.

Of course, no one goes around saying "I'm going to send an ICMP Echo Request to that host and see if it comes back"; they say, "I'm going to ping that host." Unsurprisingly, the command to initiate these tests is called *ping*.

Your host generally responds to pings automatically unless this feature is disabled or blocked.

Be careful about relying on negative ping results. If a ping doesn't come back, then it's possible that the site is down or that the pings are being blocked somewhere. It's a fairly common (but not terribly effective) security policy to block ping requests going to servers.

Ping is a command line tool, which means it doesn't have a point-and-click interface. But don't worry, it's easy to use.

Getting to the command line

The first step is to open up a command prompt (sometimes called a shell, DOS prompt, or command line).

Choose Start➪All Programs➪Accessories➪Command Prompt.

You are rewarded with a black window, like the one you see in Figure 4-4.

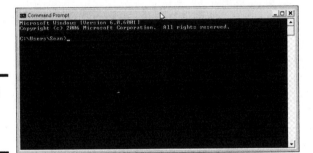

Figure 4-4:
The
command
prompt.

This window is the command prompt. Way back when, you used to interact with a computer by typing in commands rather than using a mouse. Things have changed since then, but Windows maintains a command line for the benefit of people managing the computer and troubleshooting.

Pinging your default gateway

The first order of business is to make sure that you can ping your gateway. You know the gateway's address from when you looked at the network connection details earlier.

Simply type **ping** followed by the IP address of the gateway, separating the two with a space. Then press enter. You should see something like Figure 4-5.

Figure 4-5:
A
successful
ping of the
gateway.

By default, the ping command tries four times and reports on the status of each one. In Figure 4-5, you can see that all four tries are reported as successful because the ping program indicated that the replies were received. The bytes and TTL (time to live) are uninteresting now, but the time field tells you how long each ping took from the time the request was issued to the time it was received. The first ping took 21 milliseconds, and the rest took 4 ms or less. It is normal that the first one takes longer.

If you lose some or all of the pings, you see a message like the one in Figure 4-6.

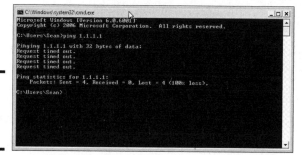

Figure 4-6:
An
unsuccess-
ful ping.

"Request timed out" means that no response came in the allotted time, which is usually 2 seconds. Most sites on the Internet are within 350 ms of you, so 2 seconds is almost like forever! Because you're pinging the gateway, you should expect less than 10 ms, except possibly for the first response.

If you receive a few replies and a few timeouts, that's usually a sign of packet loss. Losing a few packets here and there is normal, but again, if this is the gateway, then you might have interference and should go back to Book II, Chapter 8 for instructions on troubleshooting interference.

Pinging your Web site

Now that you've got this magical tool that can tell you whether or not a computer is alive, you can apply this to test if your Web site is there or not.

Ping only verifies that the computer is there; it doesn't check to see if the Web site works.

When pinging a Web site, ping only the name of the Web site. For example, with `www.dummies.com/some/page.html`, the name of the server is `www. dummies.com`. The http:// says that the address describes a Web page, and everything between that and the first slash (/) is the server name. The rest, including that first slash, is the path to the file. In this case, it's /some/page. html.

Behind the scenes, ping is going to translate `www.dummies.com` into an IP address. If it is unable to do so, then you will get the error message shown in Figure 4-7.

Figure 4-7: Ping is unable to resolve www. dummies. com.

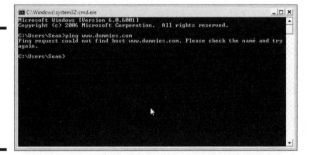

Both Figure 4-6 and Figure 4-7 show unsuccessful pings, but they were unsuccessful for two different reasons.

Although the pings that timed out knew the destination address, they just never came back. When ping couldn't find `www.dummies.com`, that meant that it had no idea who to send the pings to.

If you get the second error about the hostname, then it means you've either typed in the hostname wrong or you're having a problem with your DNS server.

DNS, the domain name system, resolves names like `http://www.dummies. com` to an IP address that your computer can communicate with. If that link isn't made, then you're not going to be able to reach the Web page.

Assuming that you can ping your gateway, you should reset your ADSL or cable modem and then your wireless router. Doing this resets the path between you and the name server.

If the name resolution is successful, you either get your replies back or you won't. If you get your replies back, then you know you can reach the other side. If not, it's possible that the site is blocking the pings, or they might really be down.

If you don't receive any replies to your ping, try a couple of other Web sites to see if the situation is more widespread.

Tracing the route

The Internet is made up of big, expensive computers called *routers*, and their sole purpose is to send your traffic to an adjacent router that's one step closer to your destination. Therefore, you're sending your data to your ISP's edge router, who will forward that inside their core, probably to another provider, and so forth, until it's time to send the response back the other way.

You can trace the path to your Web site to see how far along the path you get. Keep in mind that these traces are meant to be read by network engineers, but you can still get an idea if the problem is close to you or not.

Use the curiously named *tracert* command to trace the route. You must also specify the name or address of the site to trace.

Why not *traceroute*? If you were on pretty much any system other than Microsoft Windows, you would use *traceroute*. But way back in the old days, Windows only allowed file names to be eight characters long. That requirement has long been eliminated, but you still see a few commands with slimmed-down file names.

The first example is a site that successfully works. Figure 4-8 shows the path from my home to www.unpluggedandonline.com, a site by the author about consumer wireless.

The first hop is 192.168.1.1, which is the wireless router, and then to the wireless router's default gateway. Hops 3, 4, and 5 have names (on the right) ending in shawcable.net, which is my Internet service provider. The traffic is then handed off to ThePlanet, which is another service provider. The final hop, number 11, is the Web server itself.

The trace completed successfully, which means we know there is end-to-end connectivity. We could have just used *ping* to find the same information, but *tracert* gives the whole path. The numbers on the left give the cumulative latency (maximum, average, and minimum) up to and including the particular hop. Between hops 3 and 4, you can see latency takes a jump, presumably because it is a long haul link from my city to the coast.

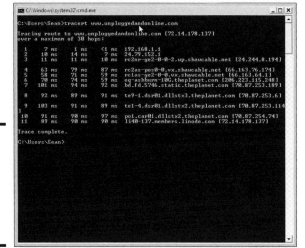

Figure 4-8:
Tracing
the route
to www.
unplugged
andonline.
com

Remember earlier that site that could not be pinged? Figure 4-9 shows a trace route to it.

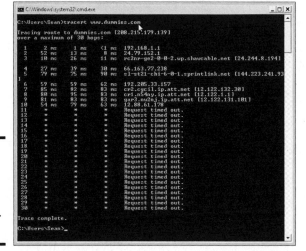

Figure 4-9:
Tracing
the route
to www.
dummies.
com

The trace starts the same and then diverges at hop 3. Hop 11 claims that the request timed out, which is the same response that *ping* gave. *Tracert* will look for up to 30 hops, so the rest of the path is more timeouts.

Even though the *tracert* failed, you can conclude that the packets are getting out of your Internet service provider and out onto the Internet. Any problems are likely going to be out of the control of your service provider.

The names on the right generally give some idea of where that hop is. For the path to www.unpluggedandonline.com, the path was probably going East to Asburn, Virginia, then to Dallas, Texas, where the server is located. www.dummies.com seems to be going Chicago to New York to New Jersey. It's entirely possible that you might see paths crisscrossing the country.

Figure 4-10 shows a trace to an address that dies right after hop 2. This is generally the point where all the subscribers are collected into the ISP core network, so for the trace to die here indicates your provider is stopping something.

In this case, it turns out the address being traced is unknown.

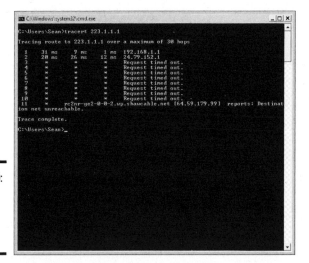

Figure 4-10: The traceroute dies very quickly.

The final pattern you see is called a *routing loop*. The trace bounces between the same few hops until the trace times out. This occurrence is rare; if you see it you should just wait for it to clear itself out.

Finding Out if Other People Are Having Problems

I've suggested earlier that one way to check if a Web site is really down is to ask someone else. If you can't get to it, and they can't get to it, chances are the problem lies closer to the Web site than it does for you (for this to work, the other person should really be in a different house).

That said, it's somewhat intrusive to keep on asking someone to check a Web site for you whenever you have a problem. That's why I really like `http://downforeveryoneorjustme.com`. This is a Web site where you can type in the name of another Web site, and it'll happily tell you if it can reach the site or not.

Figure 4-11 shows `http://downforeveryoneorjustme.com` loaded, with `www.dummies.com` typed into the input field.

Figure 4-11: http:// downfor everyoneor justme.com about to check a site.

Press the Enter key to check your Web site. Figure 4-12 shows that `www.dummies.com` was up when the Web site checked it, so the problem must be on my end.

However, if you check a site that is actually down, you get a different message shown in Figure 4-13.

When using this service, you can get reliable results without having to bother your friends!

Figure 4-12:
Dummies.
com is up.

Figure 4-13:
unplugged
andonline.
com is
down.

Getting Information About a Web Site

Have you ever wanted to contact the owner of a Web site, but couldn't find out whom to call or e-mail? Maybe you're trying to get more information about a product, or get in touch with the owner of a Web page. Sometimes it's hard to get someone on the phone.

I've got two ways for you to find a name.

Using a search engine

Search engines are huge farms of computers that comb the Web and keep track of what's out there. When you need to find something, the search engine looks in its index of Web pages and pulls out what you're looking for.

Most people go to a search engine and type in query phrases such as "real estate agent," which tells the search engine to find all the pages that are about real estate agents. Search engines also support some other ways of querying them that let you be more specific.

One of these ways is to use the *site* operator, which limits your search to a given Web site. You then look within the site for common strings like "contact us" or "e-mail."

Most search engines support the site operator, which is simply the word site, followed by a colon (:), then the name of the web site you're looking for. To look for the phrase "contact us" on the dummies.com Web site, you would search for site:dummies.com contact us, as shown in Figure 4-14.

Figure 4-14: A Web search for site: Dummies. com contact us.

Fortunately for me, the first result was the one I was looking for. Sometimes you have to try some of the other results or try a variant of "contact us," but if the page exists on the Web site, you'll find it.

This technique is also good for finding other information. If you were to search for "site:dummies.com wireless all in one," you would see all the results for this book on the Dummies.com Web site.

Checking the domain registration

If you were to get a domain name of your own (as opposed to using space on someone else's), then you'd have to register the name. The registration process requires that you give some contact information, which is stored in a public registry. People can query this registry, called the *Whois database,* in order to find out how to contact the owner of a domain.

Depending on the company that owns the domain, the name you get back might be a generic phone number or it might be the owner of the company. Most larger companies will register as a generic entity like "Name registrations," but the e-mail address and phone number will go to a real person. This prevents the company from having to update all their domains when people change jobs.

That's no problem, because half the battle is finding a living, breathing, human being to talk to. After you've got someone on the line, a few kind words should get you the person you're looking for.

Figure 4-15 shows the front page of http://dnstools.com, which is a site that automates the lookup of a domain's owner. Browse to the site and enter the name of the domain you want to search. You can see that I've already filled out "dummies.com" and have made sure that the *Whois (Domain Name)* check box is checked.

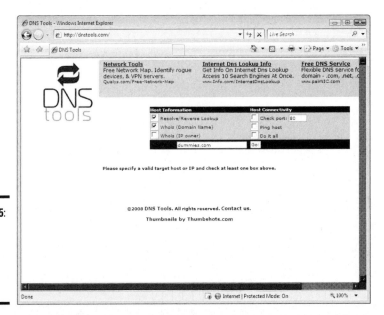

Figure 4-15: Searching for the owner of Dummies. com.

When you click the Go! button, you are given the registration information for the domain. You usually get several names back:

✦ **Technical contact:** This is the person you're supposed to call with technical problems about the name, so it usually leads to the company's IT department.

✦ **Billing contact:** This is usually the accounts payable team. "Billing" refers to who pays the bills for the cost of the domain registration and not about customer billing.

✦ **Administrative contact:** This is a generic business contact.

If you don't see all of these, don't fret. Sometimes, companies combine several of the roles into one contact record. Doing this makes it easier for you, as there are fewer people you have to try!

When contacting these people, explain how you found their name and what it is you're looking for. Chances are this person won't be the exact person you need, so try to get them to put you in touch with the person you do want to talk to.

Book V

On the Road Again — But Without Wires

It's an e-mail from my mother. She wants me to know how happy she is for us.

Contents at a Glance

Chapter 1: Putting a Network in Your Lap (top)

In This Chapter

✔ **Installing and using a wireless card**

✔ **Power backup on the road**

✔ **Printing while on the road**

✔ **Feeling at home**

*I*f you think of the network as only being something that you have in your home, you're missing an awful lot. Having the ability to connect your laptop PC to a network opens up whole new worlds for you. A networked laptop PC not only shares files on your home network, but connecting a networked laptop PC is also far easier while you're on the road. In this chapter, you read about a number of options that make your life on the road with a laptop a lot more convenient.

In many ways, a networked laptop PC is identical in operation to a networked desktop PC. Topics such as network security, user accounts, and basic network setup, covered earlier, also apply to a networked laptop PC. Therefore, this chapter concentrates on topics that are specific to your laptop PC and its use while you're away from home.

Discovering Your Options for Wire-Free Access

Connecting on the road is not necessarily the same thing as connecting at home. You have different options that might work better in some circumstances than in others. To some extent, the options that are best for you depend on a number of factors that you have to weigh carefully.

Before choosing your on-the-road connection options, you should ask yourself a number of questions:

✦ Do I need to be able to connect wherever I am?

✦ How important is my connection speed?

✦ Do I need real-time Internet access?

✦ What is my budget?

The following sections take a look at a number of options that are based on your answers to these questions.

Choosing the expensive option

Wireless data plans sure have come a long way over the years. With the arrival of 3G and 3G+ in the United States and in Europe, wireless broadband cards for PCs are all the rage. Most often this means setting up an account with a provider, such as AT&T Wireless, Sprint, or Verizon Wireless. With this type of service you can connect wherever there's network service — almost any urban/suburban area and even in rural areas. If you need to get broadband service from the top of a mountain in the heart of the Rockies, then perhaps you need to learn what vacation is all about.

Each network provider offers a similar plan, but you should definitely do your homework and make sure that you pick a provider that's right for you. You should research things like equipment compatibility with your machine, network coverage, and terms of the contract. As with most things in life, the devil is in the details.

What makes this type of connection more expensive than most other options is the service contract that you have to sign with the service provider. Not only do you get the oppressive service contract, but you might also be stuck with a rather high monthly rate and potentially limited service. For example, you may have download restrictions, in order to prevent network saturation, or your monthly fee may go up, depending on your bandwidth usage. Even though you might not think that you download a lot of data, if you enjoy streaming video or audio, then you likely use more than you think! Also, you're likely to spend a monthly fee compatible to the price of a mobile phone subscription. Therefore, if you don't end up using your wireless broadband card much one month, your price per megabyte becomes quite costly!

This option is good for road warriors, but it's really not a viable option for a full-time home solution. You'll want to enjoy the benefits of a traditional high-speed internet connection, which is still much, much faster than the speeds offered over wireless internet broadband.

Choosing somewhat limited option

If connection speed is the factor that's most important, you probably need to consider a solution that trades off long range to provide higher speed. In this case, a Wi-Fi connection is probably your best option.

Wi-Fi hotspots are pretty easy to find, especially in most large cities. Coffee shops, fast food restaurants, hotels, and even quick print shops offer access. In some cases this access is free, while in others you have to pay a small fee.

Many mobile phone providers also offer hotspot coverage on their network on a monthly or per-use basis. This option is good for those who travel occasionally or work at coffee houses.

If you have a home network, you probably already have all of the equipment you need to connect to a Wi-Fi hotspot. You know that this type of connection provides speed, but that the signal only travels a limited distance. You can't, for example, generally expect to connect several miles away from the hotspot.

Choosing the gimme-it-all option

Okay, I can hear you saying, "I want it all." In other words, you want to connect wherever you are and you want high speed, but you don't want to spend a lot of money.

I wish I could offer that option. What I can offer you is the good news that wireless is now a widely embraced technology in the United States, which means it's hard to go someplace and not have a wireless connection within earshot, or phone/computer shot.

Many of these services are free, but some still require some sort of payment. Most travel-oriented places, such as hotels, airports, and convention centers, offer free Wi-Fi connections to customers. Eventually, we should get to a point where free connection is always available, even if it isn't always the best option.

Getting Carded

Installing and using your wireless card is very similar to installing and using any other PC Card in your laptop. The process consists of three main steps, but the order of those steps depends on a number of factors. The steps (in no particular order) follow:

✦ Install the necessary driver software in your laptop PC.

✦ Insert the card into the slot on the side of your laptop.

✦ Configure your laptop for the selected service.

Reading the user manual that came with your wireless card is extremely important. That manual tells you the correct order for performing the installation steps, and the order is often dependent on the operating system version that's installed on your laptop. That is, you may have to install the software drivers first on some operating system versions, and you may have to insert the card first on others — and this is for the exact same wireless card!

No matter what type of wireless card you use, you can greatly extend the battery life in your laptop PC by either turning the card off or removing it when it is not in use.

Using a wireless data card

If you've ever bought a mobile phone, you're probably aware that each device that uses the network has to be activated before it can be used. Buying a wireless data card and installing it into your laptop is only the first part of the task.

Although different mobile carriers follow different procedures, generally once you sign up for service you have to provide the unit ID for your wireless card to the carrier, who activates the card. As is the case with cell phones, the activation is specific to a particular unit ID, and this means that if you replace the wireless card, you need to cancel the old activation and then activate the new wireless card.

Wireless data providers offer a broad range of service plans (just as they do for voice service). In general, though, you sign up for either a specific amount of monthly data transfer or a specific amount of connect time. Running over your allocation can become quite expensive, so it's important to not only sign up for the correct plan but also to monitor your usage to ensure that you don't run up huge overage charges. Of course, any provider worth its salt also offers unlimited plans at a robust price.

Depending on the network that you're connecting to, you'll likely find that the wireless cellular data card functions much like a dial-up modem, only without wires. That is, you'll use a small application (provided by your service provider) to connect to the cellular network as needed and then disconnect once you no longer need the connection. These days, most wireless data cards are USB, so plug-and-play technology means that you're up and running in no time.

Using a wireless network card

Using a wireless network card in your laptop is really the same thing as using your wireless home network on any of your PCs. The primary difference with a laptop PC is that it's portable, and this enables you to take your laptop places where you can connect to other networks besides your home network. In fact, this means that the whole world of Wi-Fi hotspots becomes available to your wireless networked laptop PC.

Before you buy a wireless network card for your laptop PC, remember that many laptops now come with a wireless network adapter built in. Also, Windows Vista has quite capable wireless networking features built in, so you probably don't need to rely on additional applications to help you locate

Wi-Fi hotspots. In fact, you're not likely to find many laptop PCs made within the past couple of years that don't already have a sufficient network card already built in. However, if you are using a laptop PC that is older, it is possible that it might not have an integrated network card, or even more likely, it might not be compatible with today's more advanced wireless protocols.

You may have read about wireless security in previous chapters. Wireless security when you're on the road with your laptop PC can be somewhat of a mixed bag: Some Wi-Fi hotspots are wide open, and others use the full range of available security features. In some cases you may be given a username and password that function for a limited period of time, or you may need to enter a security key to match that in use by the access point.

Even when you have all of the information that you need, making the connection can sometimes be a bit difficult — especially if you need to enter the WEP or WPA security keys, because the configuration methods for wireless network cards can be rather confusing. In the past, a third-party application may have proved helpful in managing your wireless networks on your laptop PC. However, Microsoft has gotten their act together, and Windows Vista offers a wonderful Manage Wireless Network window, as shown in Figure 1-1.

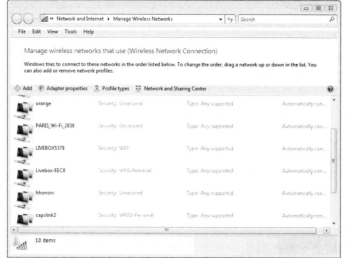

Figure 1-1:
The Manage Wireless Network window helps you keep track of all those hotspots.

Not only does it remember all those routers to which you've connected over time, but it remember vital connection information, such a security keys, and keeps a pecking order, so that you always connect to the right network and the right time.

Getting Out and About

Laptop PCs are made for travel, but that doesn't mean life on the road is always easy. After all, a lot can go wrong — especially if you're depending on your laptop to help you do business or even just keep you from becoming lost in some strange locale.

I won't bore you by repeating a bunch of pretty obvious information, such as how attractive laptop PCs are to thieves. Rather, look at some topics that can help you get more use from your laptop while you're on that road trip.

Finding Wi-Fi hotspots

Because this book's focus is on wireless topics, it makes sense to begin the discussion on traveling with a laptop PC with the subject of finding Wi-Fi hotspots. Quite simply, Wi-Fi hotspots are likely your primary means of connecting to the Internet and for sending and receiving e-mail.

A number of Web sites have lists of Wi-Fi hotspots. A quick Google search produces hundreds of hits. Some of these sites are better than others, but none of them are up-to-date enough to be your single source of information. Most of these sites depend on information supplied by volunteers, although some use lists of hotspot providers that are in some way affiliated with the site. Still, the lists do give you a starting point.

If you're going on a road trip you may want to print out a couple of hotspot lists for your destination before you set out. That way, you have some idea of where to begin looking for an Internet connection.

Once you're in the general area of a Wi-Fi hotspot, you have several choices for locating a usable signal:

✦ Break out your laptop PC and see if the built-in software can find the Wi-Fi signal and allow you to connect.

✦ Fire up your laptop and use a program or feature like Manage Wireless Network window (as mentioned earlier in this chapter) to locate any nearby Wi-Fi signals and then to make a connection to one of them.

✦ Visit a Web site, such as www.thegobutton.com, and download a Wi-Fi finder. This quickly finds any free hotspots for you to connect or shows you the strongest ones available.

Of these three options, they are all equally good. Again, it comes down to a question of personal preference. There are some users who prefer using the out-of-the-box solutions that Microsoft provides. Other users may feel more comfortable using a third-party application, such as the Go Button, as shown in Figure 1-2. At the end of the day, these options all provide the same services, even if they don't always follow the same path to get there.

Figure 1-2:
The Go Button quickly finds the availability and strength of Wi-Fi signals.

Power backup on the road

Although not strictly a wireless issue, keeping your laptop powered while you're on the road can be a challenge. Even the most power-stingy laptops don't last through a full day of constant use on battery power, and if you've opted for one of the more power-hungry units, you are lucky to get more than about two hours on a full charge.

When you're traveling, the weight of all of your equipment can become a real issue. It seems like the longer the trip, the heavier all of those separate little power adapters and cables seem. Sure, each one might weigh just a few ounces, but when you're dragging everything down a long airport concourse to the farthest gate, that can feel like pounds.

One way to cut down on your travel weight is to buy a single power supply that works with all of your portable devices and with the power outlets in your hotel, your rental car, or in an airplane. While it's true that the manufacturer of your laptop probably doesn't offer such a great power supply solution, some companies do. For example, iGo Mobility Electronics, Inc. (www.igo.com) has just such a product. You can see it in Figure 1-3.

If you're really going out to get away from it all (but can't quite give up on your laptop), you might want something like the Notebook Solar Laptop Computer Charger from Sierra Solar Systems (www.sierrasolar.com/manufacturers.php?manufacturer_id=144) shown in Figure 1-4. This handy unit can charge other devices like your cell phone when it isn't powering your laptop and does good things for the planet by using solar power, too.

You may find that the higher-capacity solar charger is a good investment because it charges your laptop's battery faster.

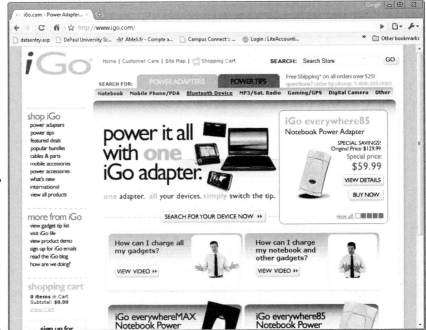

Figure 1-3:
The iGo
Web site
offers
power
solutions
that every
road warrior
needs.

Figure 1-4:
Power your
laptop from
the sun and
you never
worry about
finding an
outlet.

Printing while on the road

Some years ago when e-mail was first becoming popular, a number of pun-dits predicted that we were rapidly moving toward the "paperless office" of the future. It probably would have been a good idea to invest in the stocks of paper companies at that time, because it's pretty clear that we're a long way from eliminating paper.

When you're on the road, it can be difficult to find a convenient way to print those documents that simply can't wait until you get back home. Sometimes there simply is no choice — you have to get a printout.

Carrying your own printer

There are those who like to carry their own printer with them on the road. Personally, I think it's a great idea weighed down by reality. Even the most travel-compatible personal printers still require space in my travel bag.

If you do opt to bring along a printer, you shouldn't expect the sort of print speed or paper-handling capabilities in a portable printer that you take for granted with a desktop printer, but then I really don't want to try packing along my HP Color LaserJet on a trip, either.

The available models are always changing, but you can find a quick list of what's available on Amazon.com and by searching for "small travel print-ers." It's hard to stay one step ahead of technology, where new hardware is always becoming smaller, cheaper, and offering better performance.

For true road warriors, you are better served by using the print services that are available in your hotel.

Using a printing service

Another on-the-road printing option you may want to consider is a printing service such as PrintMe (`www.printme.com`). This service is available at some Wi-Fi hotspots, and it enables you to print to a printer at the hotspot without loading any printer drivers.

If a FedEx Kinko's print shop is nearby, you may find their printing service pretty handy, too. See `www.fedex.com/us/officeprint/main/index.html` for more information on getting signed up for this service.

Printing using a USB key

Any office you visit probably has a printer you could use if only you had a way to get your document to that printer. Few people are likely to want to open up their network so you can access it, but there's no reason you can't use a little innovative thinking to get around that problem.

One very simple solution is to use a USB memory key such as the SanDisk MiniCruzer (`www.sandisk.com`), shown in Figure 1-5, to transfer your document to a PC on the network and print it from that PC. You can even open the document directly from the USB memory key so that you aren't storing a copy of the document on the PC connected to the printer.

Figure 1-5:
A USB memory key makes it very easy to transfer data between different PCs.

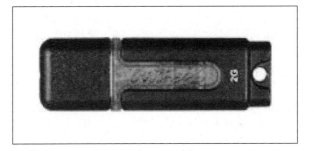

USB memory keys are extremely handy because they enable you to quickly exchange data between different PCs using a very tiny package that easily fits into your pocket. All modern PCs have USB ports, and the USB key simply appears as an additional disk drive. To a great extent. USB keys have replaced floppy disk drives, and they've become very popular because they hold so much more than a diskette and work with any PC.

Faxing: Your last resort

If you can't find any other way to print but absolutely must have a printout of an important document, the desperate have one last resort: sending a fax to a nearby fax machine. True, the quality of the printout probably won't win any awards, but when you're out of options, it pays to be resourceful.

To send a fax, you either need a modem in your laptop PC and access to a phone line or Internet access and an account with an Internet-based fax service, such as eFax (www.efax.com).

Lounging at Home

Thus far this chapter has primarily focused on the mobile uses for a networked laptop PC. However, no law says you can't have a little fun with your laptop when you're at home. Consider the following ways that having a wireless laptop PC might enhance your home life:

✦ On a nice, summer afternoon when you're stuck working on a report for that boss who always drops a bomb on you just before the weekend, why not take your laptop out to a shady spot in the backyard and work out there? You still can do your online research, thanks to your wireless Internet connection, and who knows — maybe the fresh air will inspire you.

✦ If you're having some friends over for a cookout on your deck, take your laptop and a set of speakers out, too. Then you can listen to an Internet radio station and never have to worry about changing CDs on your stereo system.

✦ It's amazing how much information is available on the Internet these days. If you need to recalibrate your underground sprinkler system, tune up your furnace, or track down the wiring harness layout in your car so that you can add a CD changer, the information is probably online somewhere. If you take your laptop to your job you can view the information onscreen as you work and have easy access in the event you need a bit more detail.

✦ When you're absolutely out of ideas of what to make for dinner, bring your laptop into the kitchen. With the multitude of cooking-related sites, you can quickly find a whole bunch of ideas for recipes using ingredients you have on hand.

Wireless laptop PCs are awfully handy, whether you're a road warrior or simply want a convenient PC that you can move anywhere in your home without a second thought.

Chapter 2: Connecting Wireless Devices to Networks

In This Chapter

✔ **Connecting a wireless device**

✔ **Configuring your network**

✔ **Using advanced configurations**

*I*t's hard to believe how widespread the use of wireless devices is these days. In fact, not so long ago (try as few as five years ago), you were pretty limited in options. At the time, your options were basically limited to a Pocket PC or Palm personal digital assistant (PDA). If you we're in luck, the device may have had Wireless access but likely few places to actually use it.

Fast-forward a few years to the present and, my, has the world changed! First, the former market leaders barely have a seat at the table anymore. Technology moved quickly and combined the best of both products to create a new series of smartphones. Of course, wireless devices aren't limited to souped-up mobile phones; Apple offers the iTouch, which is basically a smartphone without an actual phone. The current kings are Windows Mobile and Google's new Android operating systems.

Any device that is Internet-driven offers wireless capability. If it doesn't, it's not worth discussing. After all, even printers offer wireless capability these days! Wireless devices offer widespread Wi-Fi connectivity, so that you can connect to your network or a wireless hotspot while at home or on the road. These devices let you truly organize and manage your life, which may be a troubling sign for our future, if you think about it.

In this chapter I talk about connecting both a handheld computer and a functioning router to a wireless network. After you're on the network, you can do just about anything you can on your desktop computer:

✦ Check your e-mail.

✦ Surf the Internet (albeit on a much smaller screen).

✦ Access PC files located on your network. This includes documents, as well as video and music files.

You also can skip the cradle you normally use to synchronize information between your handheld computer and desktop computer. Instead, you can do it over your wireless network.

Want to check your mail but the ballgame is in the ninth inning? No problem, as now you can connect to your network and access your messages (and the scores of other games) while lying on your couch. It's a rough life, and I feel your pain.

Reaching Out to the Wireless World

Connecting your wireless device to a wireless network is very easy. In fact, the wireless connectivity aspect is so important to wireless devices that it's been that device makers minimize your role in connecting to a network. For more devices, connecting to the Internet isn't much different from how you do it with your personal computer.

Here's how you connect your wireless device to a network:

1. **Turn on wireless networking if it's not already enabled.**

   This step is different for each device. Some devices may require you to call up a connectivity-related settings page or perform some sort of key manipulation to turn on your wireless connection. For example, in Figure 2-1, an HTC mobile device simply offers a switch-type button. Alternatively, you can also use Start⇨Settings⇨Connections⇨Wi-Fi and select the check box to enable wireless connectivity.

2. **Select an available hotspot that is detected by your wireless device and validate it.**

3. **Select Internet Explorer or any other Web browser of your choice that is supported and available on your wireless device.**

4. **Browse to a Web page to confirm your wireless connection is working. That's all there is to it.**

When traveling, your mobile device can connect to a Wi-Fi network as easily as Windows Vista can since Windows Mobile and Vista share similar zero-configuration technology. This makes it simple for them to detect and connect to nearby Wi-Fi networks.

This saves you the hassle of configuring your device every time you're in range of a wireless network. Of course, as with Windows Vista, once you connect to a wireless network with your wireless device, most devices will remember the security key (WEP/WPA) so that you can quickly recall a frequently used network. If you connect to a new network, you'll still need to know the security key to connect the first time.

Figure 2-1:
The connec-
tivity option.

Using other devices

The first section of this chapter was designed for those of you using
Windows Mobile devices. However, accessing your network is just as easy,
or sometimes even easier, using other platforms.

For example, if you are using an iPhone, simply access the Settings button
on the touch screen and select Wi-Fi. From this page, you can opt whether
or not to turn it off. When Wi-Fi is enabled and connected to a network, the
standard Wi-Fi connection icon appears on the phone. What's particularly
cool about the iPhone is that it always tries to connect to the last connected
network. If it can't find it, it will go through its list of known networks until it
finds one that works. Otherwise, you can always select the desired network
and enter its password (if necessary).

If you're using Android, things can be even easier. If you use Android's Wi-Fi Toggle widget, it's as simple as clicking a button on the phone's toolbar. Otherwise, you have to go through the Settings menu, which is accessible from Home⇨Menu⇨Settings⇨Wireless controls. The Wireless controls page lets you turn on or off your wireless connection.

Manually configuring your network

You can manually configure the wireless network settings if you are using Windows Mobile, which is helpful if the automatic network connection feature is not working or you have some special situation. Here's how you access the configuration settings:

1. **Click the selectivity icon, shown in Figure 2-2, at the top of the screen.**

Figure 2-2:
The selectivity icon.

A connectivity window appears, as shown in Figure 2-3.

2. **Click Wi-Fi to bring up the wireless network settings.**

3. **Click Settings.**

   The Wi-Fi screen appears, as shown in Figure 2-4.

4. **Click the name of the wireless network to configure. Enter the network key.**

   The current strength of your connection is also indicated, as shown in Figure 2-5.

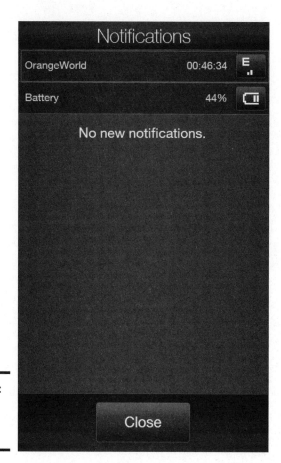

Figure 2-3:
The connectivity window.

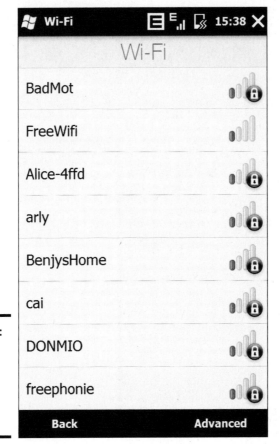

Figure 2-4:
The Wi-Fi screen displays the list of available networks.

You can click Wireless Networks to perform advanced configurations. However, these configurations should only be performed by advanced Windows Mobile and networking users. Most readers of this book will likely not need to use these configurations.

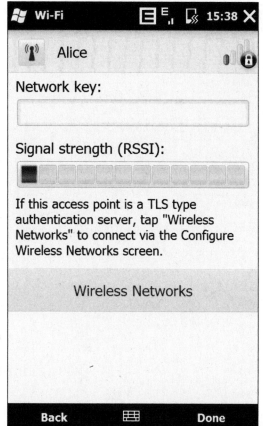

Figure 2-5:
The strength
of your
network
connection.

Using Advanced Configuration

If you want to manually add a new wireless network from a Windows Mobile device, you can do so by choosing from the list of wireless networks and selecting Advanced. If you can do this, you are either very patient, have nimble fingers, or surgeon-like accuracy with a stylus.

Go back to of the list of wireless networks, which is accessible from the Wi-Fi settings page. Click Advanced to open the Wireless LAN window, as shown in Figure 2-6.

Settings   🏁   H   H,   ☐⟲   15:40   OK

Wireless LAN

SSID: | BadMot
Change Network
Mode: | Infrastructure
BSSID: | 06-1D-6A-56-F4-66
Tx Rate: |
Rx Rate: |
Channel: | 6

Signal Quality:

| Main | Advanced | Power Mode | LEAP | Enroll |

Back   ☷

Figure 2-6:
The
Wireless
LAN screen.

Select LEAP from the tabs that appear across the bottom of the window,
as shown in Figure 2-7. The Wireless LAN window appears, as in Figure 2-8.
Then do the following:

Figure 2-7:
Let's add
our own
wireless
network
manually
in this next
procedure.

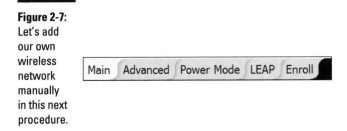

| Main | Advanced | Power Mode | LEAP | Enroll |

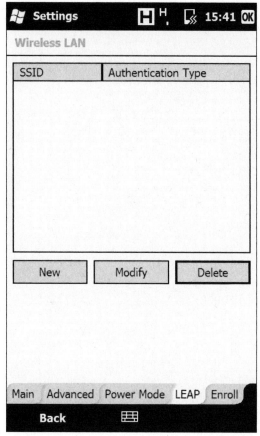

Figure 2-8:
The
Wireless
LAN
window is
your starting
point.

1. Click New.

The Wireless LAN Settings page appears with empty fields.

2. Add a SSID, domain, username, and password as shown in Figure 2-9.

3. Select whether or not the new wireless network should be open (no key) or require authentication.

If you want to encrypt (a good idea), select EAP.

4. Click OK.

If necessary, refer to your device's manual for troubleshooting tips or contact the manufacturer for help.

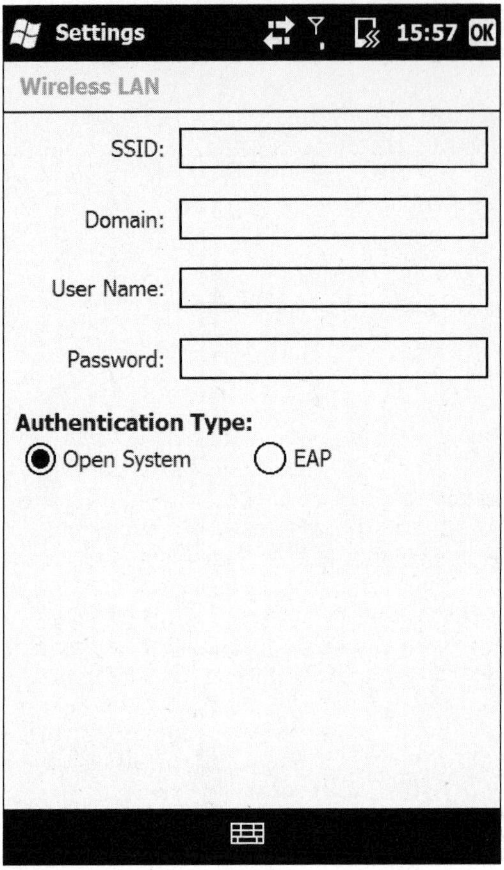

Settings	⇄ Y, ⊏⊱ 15:57 OK

Wireless LAN

SSID: [_____]

Domain: [_____]

User Name: [_____]

Password: [_____]

Authentication Type:

● Open System   ○ EAP

Figure 2-9:
Enter a
SSID and
username
at the very
least.

Chapter 3: Synchronizing Devices over a Network

In This Chapter

✔ **Synchronizing with Windows Mobile**

✔ **Synchronizing with other operating systems**

✔ **Using RSS feeds**

I'm assuming that you've successfully connected your wireless device to your wireless network and are ready for the next step: actually using that wireless link to move data across the network. If you're not there yet, check out Book V, Chapter 2, which provides the instructions for connecting.

In this chapter, I discuss synchronizing your wireless device with information on your desktop PC. Wireless synchronization has made some progress, but it has also taken a few steps back at the same time. While that may sound contradictory, it's very much true. For example, most systems (hello, Symbian and iPhone) don't have any wireless synchronization options available at the time of press. Windows Mobile, on the other hand, does offer a wireless synchronization, but not everyone can use it.

I also tell you how you can add content to your wireless device (such as news and articles) using RSS feeds and your RSS hub. You can update your wireless device using the RSS hub and take reading material when you travel.

Getting Windows Mobile to Coordinate

You can synchronize your wireless device using Windows Mobile with your computer in two ways. You can

✦ Connect the device to your computer using a USB cable.

✦ Connect wirelessly and update your device.

If you are running Windows Vista, you will use the Windows Mobile Device Center to synchronize your device with your computer. The version that shipped initially with Windows Visa has been updated, so be sure to update. It's important to make sure you have the most up to date version for compatibility with the most recent wireless devices, which is available at `www.microsoft.com/windowsmobile/en-us/help/synchronize/` `device-center-download.mspx`.

How often you synch really depends on how often you update your wireless device and computer. Personally, I tend to only sync data such as contacts and appointments, so I only need to sync when I update Outlook. However, I use my wireless or 3G+ connection to update other applications, such as RSS Hub, which I discuss later in this chapter.

Running with Windows Mobile Device Center

Windows Mobile Device Center is the new and improved version of ActiveSync, which went the way of the dodo bird when Windows Vista was released. It has a much more intuitive, graphic-friendly interface that is easy and comfortable to use. The first time you plug your wireless device to your computer running Windows Vista, it automatically opens the Mobile Device Center and configures your device with Windows.

If you still need to start the Windows Mobile Device Center, here's how to do it:

1. **Choose Start↷All Programs.**

2. **Select Windows Mobile Device Center.**

   The application opens and displays the name and a picture of your wireless device, if properly connected, as shown in Figure 3-1. If no device is connected, a generic image of a wireless device is displayed and says "not connected." Your wireless device is automatically synced.

3. **Select Mobile Device Settings.**

4. **Click Connection settings.**

   Make sure that Allow USB connections is selected. If you want to be able to sync wireless using Bluetooth, make sure that the Allow connections to one of the following option is selected with Bluetooth in the drop-down menu.

5. **Click OK.**

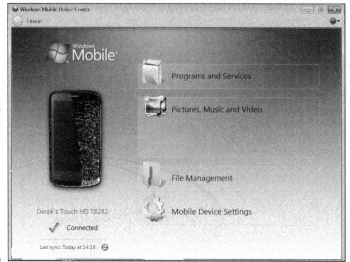

Figure 3-1:
Your
wireless
device
picked up
in Windows
Mobile
Device
Center.

6. **Click Mobile Device Settings.**
7. **Click Change content sync settings.**
8. **Select which content should be synced, as shown in Figure 3-2.**
9. **Click Save.**

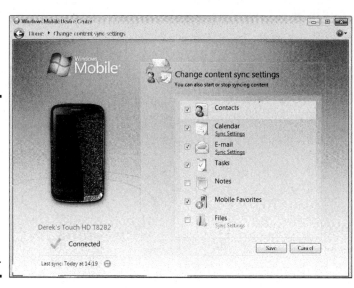

Figure 3-2:
The
Windows
Mobile
Device
Center lets
you pick
and choose
what you
want to
synchronize.

Running with ActiveSync

You can use Microsoft's ActiveSync software to wirelessly synchronize information between your wireless device and your desktop computer. Usually I don't discuss Windows XP in this book, but since there are enough users still working with this operating system, do keep in mind that you must install Microsoft ActiveSync before you can synchronize your wireless device with information on another computer on your network. You can download the latest version of ActiveSync from www.microsoft.com/windowsmobile/en-us/downloads/microsoft/activesync-download.mspx.

Before you can synchronize your wireless device, make sure the settings are correct on the ActiveSync software running on your desktop PC.

Now, let's synchronize:

1. **Click Start➪All Programs.**

2. **Click Microsoft ActiveSync.**

   The ActiveSync dialog box appears.

3. **Click File.**

4. **Click Mobile Device, if you have more than one device connected or registered with Active Sync.**

   Menu of available wireless devices appears.

5. **Select the wireless device that you want to synchronize, if necessary; otherwise your device appears as shown in Figure 3-3.**

   In this case, there is only one device, and it's called HTC87. (Sometimes even computer stuff is easy to follow.)

6. **Click File.**

7. **Click Connection Settings.**

   The Connection Settings dialog box appears.

8. **Confirm that this choice is selected: Allow Network (Ethernet) and Remote Access Service (RAS) Server Connection with This Desktop Computer.**

9. **Click OK.**

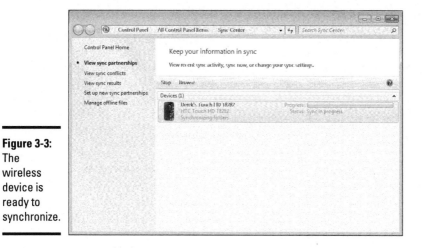

Figure 3-3:
The wireless device is ready to synchronize.

Syncing information for your wireless device

Here's how you initiate synchronization from your handheld computer from your wireless device. Be careful, though, this shows you how to initiate the synchronization from your wireless device and not your computer; it doesn't show how to do it on a wireless network. In other words, you need to have a USB connection to do this. Follow these steps:

1. **Choose Start⇨System.**

The System dialog box appears.

2. **Click ActiveSync.**

ActiveSync screen appears.

3. **Click Sync.**

Your wireless device shows Connecting and then Synchronizing, shown in Figure 3-4.

When it's done, the screen displays Not Connected. The ActiveSync software on both your PC and handheld show the last date and time they connected to each other. If the synchronization is not occurring, make sure you have a working wireless connection and that your Pocket PC is close enough to a wireless access point.

Figure 3-4:
Windows
Mobile
synchro-
nizing with
desktop PC.

Make sure Microsoft ActiveSync is also running on your desktop PC.

Syncing information wirelessly

You also can synchronize your wireless device by using Bluetooth wireless technology instead of a Wi-Fi connection. Bluetooth works over a much shorter range — about 30 feet — but can be an easier way to connect your handheld to your desktop PC at close distances. In addition, with the introduction of more and more Bluetooth-enabled cellular telephones, it's also a way to synchronize information between your laptop computer and your mobile phone.

Getting Other Platforms to Coordinate

This chapter demonstrates how you can synchronize your wireless device if you are using the Windows Mobile operating system, but it's worth remembering that all mobile device platforms offer this capability as well.

Each platform has its own proprietary software package that allows you to transfer data (e-mails, contacts, files, pictures) between your computer and the wireless device. In most cases, this is done using a USB connection. I recommend using the documentation provided for your wireless device that will certainly show you how to set up synchronization.

Generally speaking, your wireless device ships with a CD-ROM that allows you to install the necessary software on your computer. Once you connect your phone to the computer using USB, your computer automatically launches and recognizes the wireless device.

For example, if you are using a Nokia N95, a suite of applications is provided to let you synchronize your data quickly and easily, as shown in Figure 3-5. Not only do these proprietary applications provide you with synchronization tools, but also additional applications to help you handle other often-used features, such as for photos and music.

If you are using a Palm-based wireless device, such as the Treo, you can use Treo Desktop to synchronize your data, as shown in Figure 3-6. This device is a little more complicated, as it also requires you to have Palm desktop installed, along with a sync user. In other words, you need two separate applications to sync your device!

Figure 3-5:
Nokia also
allows
you to
synchronize
files, music,
and photos.

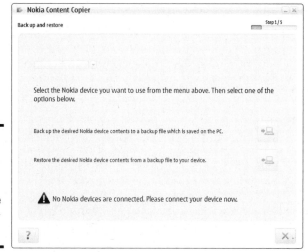

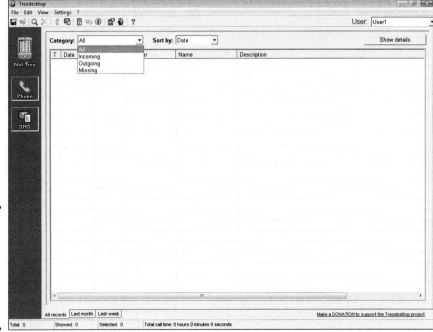

Figure 3-6:
For Treo, you need two applications to synchronize data.

If you want to synchronize your device wirelessly, you'll need to make sure that both your computer and the wireless device support Bluetooth technology.

Using RSS Feeds

When wireless devices first became the rage, there was a program called AvantGo that was extremely valuable to users. It allowed you to take reading material when you traveled, or to update the information from your device while you were on the road over a wireless connection and read a miniature version of the newspaper.

Of course, like all good ideas, it became copied and was soon made obsolete by its peers. This is the sad story of AvantGo, which was made redundant and eventually stopped publishing in June 2009. Though there are a number of imitators available to take AvantGo's place, the most useful application for obtaining information on the go is the RSS feed.

This publishing format is a widely used standard for publishing Web content – including blog posts, news articles, and multimedia – as an XML file or feed that can be read by a reader on your desktop computer or wireless device. Likewise, you can also "subscribe" to RSS feeds on Web sites that allow you to track its content easily from your e-mail client or an RSS reader.

Similar to AvantGo, an RSS reader (such as RSS hub) allows you to select content sources (for example, Yahoo and BBC News) called channels to which you can subscribe. Using your wireless network connection, you can update the channel's content, which is displayed as a list of entries, as shown in Figure 3-7.

By double-clicking the article header, you can obtain the first few lines of the article as shown in Figure 3-8, followed by a link, which can be clicked to display the rest of the article in your device's Web browser.

Figure 3-7: Each channel provides a list of its latest content in an easy-to-follow format.

Figure 3-8: An article header saves bandwidth by displaying just a bit of the article.

Using RSS Hub on a wireless device

A number of RSS readers are available for use with wireless devices. Most of them offer a similar group of features; the right one really depends on your personal preferences. I choose to use RSS Hub because it was included on my wireless device and satisfies my requirements for getting information quickly.

To use RSS Hub on Windows Mobile:

1. **Click Start⇨Web⇨RSS Hub.**

The program launches and displays All Categories.

2. **Click Refresh to update each channel in the list for the category.**

If you wish to organize your categories, click Menu⇨Categories⇨ Menu⇨New. You can also use this menu to rename an existing category by clicking it and selected Rename, or to delete it by clicking Delete.

3. **Using your preferred input method, enter a name for the category.**

4. **Click Done.**

   The new category appears in the list of categories.

5. **To change categories, return to the list of channels and click the desired channel.**

6. **Click Menu⇨Chanel⇨Change Category and select the desired category.**

7. **Click OK.**

   If you sort the list of channels using the drop-down menu, as shown in Figure 3-9, the new category appears.

8. **Select the desired category.**

   The channel now appears in a filtered list.

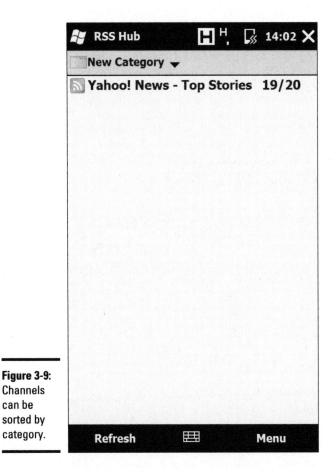

Figure 3-9:
Channels
can be
sorted by
category.

To add a new channel to RSS Hub:

1. **Choose Start⇨Web⇨RSS Hub.**

   The program launches and displays All Categories.

2. **Choose Menu⇨Channel⇨New.**

   The New Channel Wizard appears.

3. **Select how you wish to select your new channel.**

   If you do not know the Web address to the channel's RSS feed, you can either search for the channel or choose from a list of known channels. Click Next.

4. **Use the scroll bars to select the channel(s) to select, as shown in Figure 3-10.**

5. **Click Finish.**

   The newly selected channel(s) appear in the list of channels.

If you have an unlimited data plan and have the necessary battery life on your phone, you may want to set RSS Hub's options to auto-update feeds. This is of value if you find that you like to catch up on the news and read RSS feeds regularly. The advantage is that the information is always up to date (you can determine how often it is refreshed), but it can also be a disadvantage. First, if your data plan is not unlimited, you must watch that you do not download too often lest you go over your allotment for the month. Also, every time your mobile device performs a content refresh, it uses battery power. If you need to use your phone frequently during the day and don't have the ability to charge your device until the end of the day, this could waste valuable batter life.

To set auto-update settings, from RSS Hub, do the following:

1. **Choose Menu⇨Options.**

2. **From the Auto Update Mode drop-down, select the desired update cycle.**

3. **Using the next group of drop-down menus, select the frequency for the automatic update.**

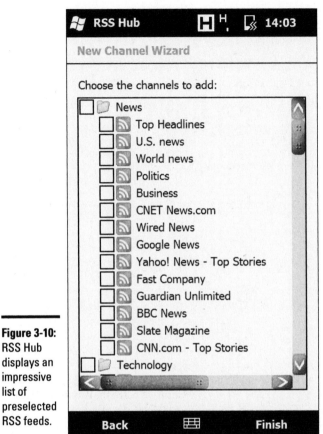

Figure 3-10:
RSS Hub
displays an
impressive
list of
preselected
RSS feeds.

4. **Click the Notify tab.**

5. **Select how, or if, you should be notified of new content.**

6. **Click OK.**

   This button is located at the upper-right side of your mobile device, as shown in Figure 3-11.

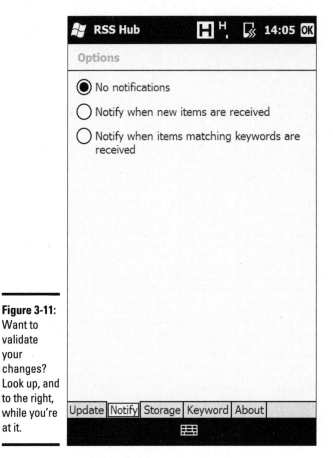

Figure 3-11:
Want to validate your changes? Look up, and to the right, while you're at it.

Hopefully, now you have a good idea on how to keep your wireless device up to speed — and in sync with your desktop computer. Having a wireless device that has information, such as e-mail addresses, that isn't available when you use your desktop can be pretty frustrating. Save yourself some time, tears, and gray hair by making sure the two have the same information.

Chapter 4: Picking a BlackBerry

In This Chapter

- ✔ Setting up the BlackBerry
- ✔ Grabbing your e-mail
- ✔ Using BlackBerry as a phone
- ✔ The future of BlackBerry

Technology can be quite an amazing thing, especially when you think about how far Internet and mobile technology have come in relatively so little time. Not so long ago, a little device that hooked on your belt and could make calls around the world, surf the Internet, and send e-mails seemed like something out of the year 3000.

One device, called the BlackBerry, helped realize that future. If you look back just a few short years, sure, it lacked many of the standard features that most people take for granted today, but it still was one of the first devices out there that truly helped you go mobile!

Of course, BlackBerry faces some stiff competition from other device manufacturers. This competition resulted in BlackBerry improving and updating their offering to be more in line with what mobile office users really need today, including wireless capabilities and touch screen technology.

Whether or not to make the move to BlackBerry really depends on you, your preferences, and how you actually plan on using your mobile device. For those who like the all-in-one nature of the device (e-mail. Internet, applications), but also prefer having a keyboard for typing, you may want to check out the BlackBerry Web site at www.blackberry.com and see what's cooking!

Avoiding a Raspberry

A BlackBerry is a suitable way to communicate for several reasons:

- ✦ It's wireless, so you can take it with you wherever you go.
- ✦ It's small and light, fitting in a holster you can wear on your belt.
- ✦ It gives you around-the-clock access to your e-mail.
- ✦ It provides 24-hour access to the Web.

✦ It works well with corporate e-mail systems, so workers can easily use their BlackBerrys to stay in touch.

✦ Newer models provide touch screen technology, which makes navigating your device even easier

Of course, these features were once hot selling points, but now they are so standard that I wouldn't even tout these features. As I said before, what really sets the BlackBerry apart from the rest — even after all these years — is its keyboard feature.

You can read more by visiting the BlackBerry Web site at `www.black berry.com`.

Which carriers offer the BlackBerry? Here's a short list, which doesn't include smaller telecommunications (or telecom, if you want to be sleek, too) providers:

✦ AT&T Wireless

✦ Cingular

✦ Nextel

✦ T-Mobile

✦ Verizon

When you subscribe to BlackBerry from one of these services, make sure you read the fine print carefully. Some providers may offer a voice and data plan that allows you unlimited Web and messaging access, as well as a certain number of minutes per month. Other plans may only offer data plans and charge you a higher-than-normal voice rate for calls made using your BlackBerry.

Picking a Model, Any Model

The decision about which BlackBerry model to use may be made for you if you have a particular cellular phone carrier in mind. Whichever model that carrier has is the one you will get. They may sell more than one model. (Models with built-in cell phones are similar to the PalmOne Treo 600, which is one of the mobile phones I discuss in Book VI, Chapter 1. They also are similar to the Sidekick II, which I write about later in this chapter.)

Ask yourself some of these questions when deciding which BlackBerry model to purchase:

✦ Is the newest technology important to me? Or do I just want functionality and can leave the stylish technology to the hipsters?

✦ Which models are available from my carrier of choice? If you like ABC Wireless, but they don't have the model you want, you may need to go with another carrier or settle with the BlackBerry model they provide.

✦ Do I want a color screen or is a monochrome screen okay? Remember that e-mail messages, for better or for worse, read the same either way.

✦ Do I want to have a touch screen to easily access my applications or can I live with the standard kind of screen?

Currently, Blackberry is definitely a competitor with other smartphone vendors; though it seems that they are more in catch-up mode than innovation. For example, the most recent model, Storm, doesn't offer Wi-Fi capabilities, something that is corrected in the upcoming Storm2 release. BlackBerry also released their first touch screen device a full 18 months after LG, then HTC.

The current series available is the 8900+ GPS Wi-Fi Series. This series includes the BlackBerry Bold (9000), BlackBerry Curve 8900, BlackBerry Tour (9630), and BlackBerry Storm (9500/9530).

What makes these models so popular is that they offer everything a professional or high-end phone should: decent graphics, high-speed Internet/wireless capabilities, e-mail (including push mail), and GPS capabilities.

Navigating a BlackBerry

BlackBerry owes much of its popularity to its ease of use. Other than the traditionally laid out keyboard — although much smaller, so get those thumbs in shape — the device has very few buttons. It has three non-keyboard buttons:

✦ **Phone button:** Push this button to go to the screen where you either can pick a phone number from your address book or enter a phone number from the keyboard.

✦ **Trackwheel:** You can whirl the wheel with your thumb and then press when you reach something you'd like to do, such as run an application.

✦ **Escape key:** Press this when you're in an application and want to return to the main menu. Think of it as the key that helps when you get lost: You can escape to safety.

Turning it on and off

Start where all things BlackBerry start: the on button. On some models, it's the silver button on the far-bottom right of the keyboard. On the Storm, it's the button on the side of the device. If you press and hold this button, the BlackBerry turns off. Push it again and the BlackBerry turns on.

Sending and receiving e-mail

Sending and receiving e-mail through the BlackBerry certainly is what has made the brand name synonymous with portable, mobile e-mail messaging.

You can receive e-mail through a BlackBerry three ways:

✦ Personal e-mail account access through the BlackBerry Web client. This is for e-mail addresses like my@emailaddress.com.

✦ Business/corporate e-mail access through the BlackBerry Enterprise Server, which lets workers grab their messages from Microsoft Exchange or IBM Lotus Domino.

✦ BlackBerry e-mail via an e-mail address that looks like mlelrick@black berry.net. You receive messages through BlackBerry Web client. These addresses are assigned to you by BlackBerry.

Reading e-mail messages

E-mail is the first application on the BlackBerry screen, so it's fast and easy to jump right in and check for messages. Just follow these steps:

1. **Making sure the e-mail icon is highlighted, click the trackwheel.**

The e-mail message screen appears, as shown in Figure 4-1.

Figure 4-1:
The e-mail
messages
screen.

2. **Double-click the trackwheel to open the message.**

3. **Click the Escape button when you want to return to the main menu.**

Otherwise, use the menu to perform another function on the e-mail message. That's it.

The first click of the trackwheel opens a menu that, in addition to opening a message, lets you do these things:

• File a message

• Mark a message as unopened

- Save a message
- Reply to a message
- Forward a message
- Delete a message

Composing a message

Now you know how to read your e-mail messages. How do you send one? Just follow these steps:

1. **Scroll to the Compose icon.**

2. **Click the icon using the trackwheel button.**

   A Compose Message screen appears. Click Use Once if the address you need is not listed.

3. **Select E-mail from the menu.**

   One Time E-mail screen appears.

4. **Type the e-mail address.**

   You can use the spacebar to insert the @ sign into the e-mail address. Clicking the spacebar a second time inserts a period into the address. This lets you enter an address quicker because you don't need to press any special keys to access the symbols and punctuation keys.

5. **Press the Return key.**

   The Subject line appears.

6. **Enter a subject.**

7. **Press the Enter key.**

   The cursor moves to the body of the e-mail.

8. **Enter your e-mail message, as shown in Figure 4-2.**

9. **Click the trackwheel.**

   The menu appears.

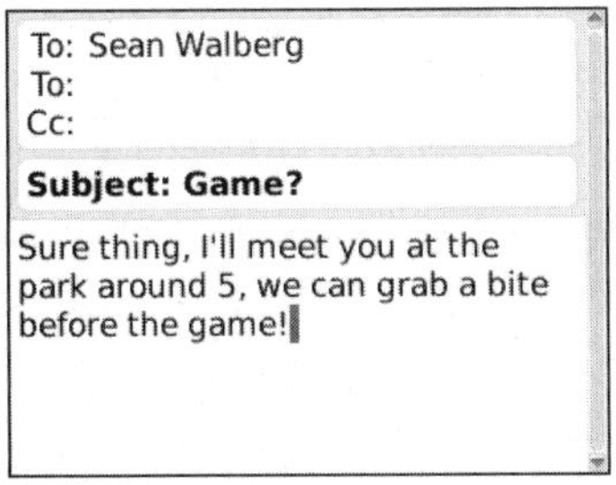

Figure 4-2:
Compose
an e-mail's
address,
subject, and
message.

To: Sean Walberg
To:
Cc:

Subject: Game?

Sure thing, I'll meet you at the park around 5, we can grab a bite before the game!

10. **Click Send.**

    That's how you send an e-mail message with your BlackBerry!

    You also can Save Draft or add addresses in the To, Cc, and Bcc fields. If you clicked Send, you are taken to the e-mail screen, which shows your outgoing and incoming messages.

Tables 4-1 and 4-2 provide shortcuts to help you navigate the BlackBerry landscape.

Table 4-1	General Shortcuts
Do This	*To Do This*
Press Alt while rolling the trackwheel	Scroll horizontally in any screen where you enter text
Press Alt while rolling the trackwheel	Scroll a screen at a time in the Messages, Address Book, Calendar, Tasks, and MemoPad screens
Type the first letter of an item in an option list or menu	Jump directly to the item option list or menu
Type the first letters of a name	Find a contact in the address book or To screens (or the initials separated by a space)
Press the Escape key	Exit any screen, menu, or dialog box

Table 4-2	Messages Shortcuts
Do This	*To Do This*
Press Alt + I	View all incoming messages
Press Alt + O	View all outgoing messages
Press T	Go to the top message in the Messages screen
Press B	To go to the bottom message in the Messages screen.
Press N	Go to next unread message in an open message.
Press C	Compose a new message and Saved Messages screens
Press S	Start a search for a message in the Messages and Saved Message screen
Press P	Learn the corresponding date in the Messages previous screen

Do This	*To Do This*
Press R	Reply to the sender with text
Press G	Return to the last cursor position (if you previously closed a message before you finished reading it)

Making a phone call

You can make a phone call from the BlackBerry a couple different ways. One way uses the dedicated phone call button on the top of the unit, while the other involves selecting the Phone icon on the device's Home screen.

To use the dedicated phone call button, follow these steps:

1. **Click the dedicated phone call button on the top of the BlackBerry.**

   The Phone screen appears.

2. **Select One Time Dial or begin entering the number.**

   The Enter Phone Number dialog box appears.

3. **Enter a phone number.**

4. **Select Call.**

   BlackBerry dials the number.

To place a phone call from the Home screen, follow these steps:

1. **Click the Phone icon.**

   The Phone screen appears.

2. **Select One Time Dial or begin entering the number.**

   The Enter Phone Number dialog box appears.

3. **Enter a phone number.**

4. **Select Call.**

   That phone on the other side should be ringing.

Clicking a telephone number in an e-mail, for example, makes the BlackBerry call that number automatically. In addition, if you click an e-mail address inside a message, the BlackBerry automatically composes a message with that address. It also works with Web addresses; clicking them fires up the browser.

Adding a person to Contacts

You can add someone to Contacts in two different ways: add a contact from scratch or add a contact from a message you received from that individual.

Follow these steps to add a contact from scratch:

1. **From the Home screen, click the Contacts icon.**

   The Find screen appears.

2. **Click the trackwheel to bring up the menu.**

3. **Click New Address.**

   The New Address screen appears.

4. **Enter information into the address book fields, which are shown in Figure 4-3.**

   Press Enter or use the trackwheel to move between fields.

5. **When you're done entering contact information, click the trackwheel to bring up the menu.**

6. **Click Save.**

   The contact information is added to your address book.

Figure 4-3: Enter information into Contacts.

Follow these steps to add a contact to the address book from an e-mail message:

1. **Open the e-mail message.**

2. **Click the trackwheel to view the menu.**

3. **Select Add to Contacts.**

   The New Address screen appears with the e-mail address filled in.

4. **Add any other contact information you'd like.**

5. **Click the trackwheel to bring up the menu.**

6. **Select Save; the contact information is saved in your Contacts.**

Security help

If you're strolling through Boston's Logan International Airport and you look a little shady to Massachusetts State Police officers, a BlackBerry may be unholstered long before a gun is drawn. The state police are using the devices to perform background checks on suspicious individuals. The BlackBerry connects to a database called LocatePlus, which contains information from various sources about more than 200 million U.S. residents. The database, based on the data, assigns a security rating to everyone. All of this information is available via the BlackBerry.

Browsing the Web

Using a BlackBerry to access the Internet used to be like using a spoon to dredge the ocean. Most Internet sites are not designed for viewing on such a small screen, although the BlackBerry is a way to read Web content in a pinch. Fortunately, the newer Blackberry models have improved browser rendering, and more and more Web sites are developing mobile versions of their Web sites to facilitate surfing on these small, handheld devices.

There are several ways to open a Web page. Here are the steps for entering a Web address in the BlackBerry and visiting that Web site:

1. **From the Home screen, click the Browser icon.**

The Browser Bookmarks screen appears.

2. **Click the trackwheel to view the menu.**

The menu appears.

3. **Click Go To, which brings up the Go To dialog box.**

4. **Enter the Web address.**

I already told you about the trick of pressing the Space key to insert a key. You also can press Shift + Space to insert a forward slash (/).

5. **Click OK.**

BlackBerry's browser loads and, hopefully, the Web site you requested appears.

Special versions of two popular Web sites are designed for small Web browsers l: www.google.com/wml and mobile.yahoo.com/home. I discuss many of these Web services and others in Book V, Chapter 2.

Chapter 5: Finding Wi-Fi Hotspots

In This Chapter

✔ Using Wi-Fi directories

✔ Dreaming about airports, hotels, and clouds

✔ Thinking about security

Your laptop and your smartphone are set up for wireless networking, and you're restless to connect to the Internet somewhere outside your home or office. You've heard about hotspots, which are places with public Internet access. How can you find them?

Luckily, you can turn to several places for this information before venturing from home. In this chapter I talk about Wi-Fi directories, as well as some public projects that are trying to make wireless access available to everyone. Of course, with the preponderance of hot spots these days, it's really easy just to turn on your wireless device and see what's available! From restaurants, to hotels, to bookstores, more and more businesses are offering some sort of Wi-Fi coverage — some free, some paid.

Getting Thee to a Directory

How do you find Wi-Fi heat in the spots you plan to travel? The quickest way is to do some homework before you leave, searching one of several large databases on the Internet for hotspots. Table 5-1 describes some of the largest online directories. WAP is a security protocol that scrambles your wireless communications to keep them from prying eyes.

Table 5-1	Online Wi-Fi Directories	
Site	*URL*	*Description*
JiWire	www.jiwire.com	This large online directory of world-wide hotspots lists more than 272,000 hotspots in 140 countries. You can search for a hot spot using several criteria. A search results page is shown in Figure 5-1. A group of mini directories separates free hotspots. Offline versions are available. You can download Windows, Macintosh, and Linux versions from www.jiwire.com/hotspot-locator-laptop.htm. A third version for Web-enabled mobile phones connects live with the JiWire directory.
Wi-FiHot SpotList.com	www.wi-fi hotspotlist.com	Calls itself the definitive list of hot-spots. Though some find it to be slow to return results, I've found it to be satisfactory.
The HotSpot Haven	www.hotspot haven.com	Counts 107,799 hotspots in its directory. The United States has the largest number of hotspots, but the European and Asian directories also return a decent number of hotspots.
Wi-Fi Marine	www.wifimarine.org	Do marinas float your boat? Then you might check out this site. It covers everything related to boaters and wireless Internet access.
Web In-Flight	www.webinflight.com	Has information about Wi-Fi service available on airlines.
NodeDB.com	www.nodedb.com	If you're heading overseas, NodeDB.com seems to be one of the largest directories that focuses on hotspots outside the United States.
WiFiMaps.com	www.wifimaps.com	This site was a little slow for me. But the site is a little different from the others in that it displays hotspots on interactive U.S. and world maps. You can search by station name, U.S. state, or by geographic region.

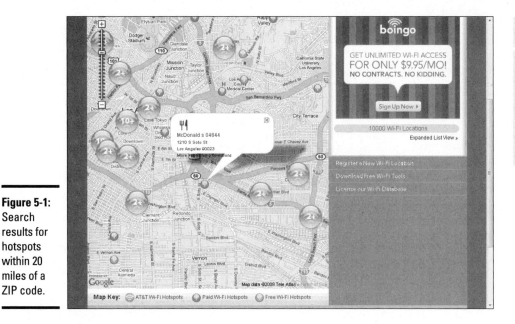

Figure 5-1:
Search
results for
hotspots
within 20
miles of a
ZIP code.

Paying for the Goods: Commercial Providers

I wish everything were free (except this book!), but sometimes you need to turn to commercial Wi-Fi providers when you travel. I present you with a list of the major ones:

✦ **T-Mobile at** www.t-mobile.com/hotspot/. The nation's largest public hotspot provider sells Wi-Fi access at 45,000 locations worldwide, including Starbucks, FedEx Kinko's copy centers, and Borders bookstores. It also provides service in some major airports, as well as the frequent-flyer club lounges for Delta Air Lines, American Airlines, and United Airlines. As I write this, T-Mobile has three different ways to pay for access:

• T-Mobile Unlimited national. The subscription includes unlimited minutes for $9.99 a month for qualifying T-Mobile voice customers.

• Unlimited national. The subscription includes unlimited minutes for $29.99 a month if paid a year in advance or $39.99 a month if paid month to month.

• DayPass. You can purchase this prepaid access for no minimum commitment. It costs $7.99 for 24 continuous hours.

• Pay as you go. It costs $6 per login for the first hour with a minimum user session of 60 minutes, with additional minutes costing 10 cents each.

✦ **Boingo Wireless at** www.boingo.com. This large provider of hotspots boasts more than 100,000 locations. Boingo charges $9.95 a month for unlimited connection time in North America. For world travelers, there are more sophisticated (read: expensive plans) that run $59.00 per month.

✦ **Wayport at** www.wayport.com. Wayport is now AT&T Wireless, which offers a national plan for $19.99 per month. Plans for Europe are also available to national customers.

Paying for the Goods: Making a Commitment

If you're a road warrior, as I have been over the years, it's likely that you're going to want something a little more reliable than rolling the dice on a free Internet connections or an underperforming, yet expensive, option. Up until a few short years ago, hotspots were our best option. Of course, the problem was that arranging your schedule to only be in places that offered a Brand X hotspot was hardly convenient or practical.

Entering the 21st century, wireless providers took a new approach and stopped advertising their hotspot access and replaced it with a full-blown wireless broadband service. Rather than depending on your wireless device, these subscriptions were solely for laptop or netbook users and depended on a USB-device that you would use — along with an application — to connect to your provider's broadband network over a GSM, 3G, or 4G network. The download speeds for these connections are more than adequate for most business travelers; however, it's important to note that performance is still not as fast as at home over your wireless connection. Currently, most providers in the United States provide connection speeds of up to 1.4MB/1.5MB.

Searching made easier

T-Mobile used to offer a helpful tool called Connection Manager, which helped you find a nearby hotspot. It was replaced by Web Connect, which doesn't appear to offer this feature — rather, it's a plug in and go feature — but you can still download Connection Manager online if you're really interested in using it; just don't expect any support from T-Mobile.

Boingo Wireless has similar software available for Windows computers and Pocket PCs. You can download it from www.boingo.com/download-boingo.php, though a mobile version is also available for download. It also helps you connect to Boingo's virtual private network (VPN) service, which means you make a secure connection to the company's network so that all of your Internet traffic is encrypted (read: jumbled and hence safer). It's a virtual loincloth for public hotspots.

A handy feature that both utilities share: They detect all nearby Wi-Fi signals, whether or not they're part of the companies' network. You can easily connect to any of these detected hotspots.

There are five major mobile broadband providers in the United States; you might recognize them because most of them also offer voice plans. They are

✦ **Verizon Wireless:** One of the major players on the mobile broadband scene, Verizon offers a variety of plans for mobile devices such as netbooks, laptops, and USB modems that range from a day pass ($15/session) to monthly plans ($39.95–$59.99) that offer 250MB and 5GB monthly allowances, respectively. Verizon also offers a variety of plans for other mobile devices, including handsets or smartphones (`www.verizonwireless.com/b2c/mobilebroadband/`).

✦ **AT&T:** A solid network with a good coverage page; AT&T offers a number of data plans for handheld wireless devices, such as smartphones and BlackBerry devices. There is also a single data plan for mobile laptop broadband. This package offers up to 5GB traffic per month for $60. (`www.wireless.att.com/cell-phone-service/cell-phone-plans/data-connect-plans.jsp`).

✦ **Sprint:** Another one of the major players; it is now teamed up with Nextel to offer pretty impressive coverage. Sprint offers a variety of plans for mobile devices, including its Sprint wireless broadband cards, which let you connect to Sprint's national wireless broadband network. The mobile broadband connections range from $59.99 to $69.99 (if you're a voice customer) (`http://nextelonline.nextel.com/NASApp/onlinestore/en/Action/DisplayPlans`).

✦ **T-Mobile:** T-Mobile offers a pretty reliable network that always seemed to be around when I needed it. They offer not just standard data plans for wireless devices, but also BlackBerry and SideKick (a T-Mobile original) wireless data plans. These plans range from $39.98 to $59.99 per month (`www.t-mobile.com/shop/plans/Cell-Phone-Plans.aspx?catgroup=Indvidual-cell-phone-plan&WT.mc_n=Individual_PlanFirstTile1&WT.mc_t=OnsiteAd`).

✦ **U.S. Cellular:** This is probably the least robust option available in terms of coverage, but it does offer some good plans for the budget conscious. Data plans (not all high speed) range from $9.95 (bare bones service) to $49.95 (`http://easyedge.uscc.com/easyedge/jsp/plans.jsp`).

Going Public

The beauty of Wi-Fi networking is its mobility. It gives you the freedom to wander far from home and still have a solid connection to the Internet. You can find Wi-Fi hotspots around the globe, with the United States, Europe, and Asia leading the way as they add thousands of new access points every year.

In airports

Second to your hotel room, where do you spend most of your time during a business trip? It's probably not in the meeting or at the conference. More likely, it's the airports you pass through, especially with the increased security that forces you to arrive earlier and stay longer. Of course, layovers add to the fray.

That's why it's a good idea to know, before you leave on your trip, which airports offer what Wi-Fi services. Some may offer free access, a combination of limited free access and commercial access, or commercial access only.

Generally speaking, paid wireless access will run you about $9.95 for 24 hours or $49.95 per month for unlimited service. If you're stuck in one of these airports for several hours, ten bucks may seem like a bargain as you pull out your laptop to check your e-mail.

Here's a list of major airports and some of the wireless Internet services they offer:

+ **Chicago O'Hare International.** Concourse and Boingo are the providers here, which cover terminals 1, 2, and 3. Unlike many other airports, these services don't come for free.

+ **Los Angeles International Airport.** Boingo Wireless rules the roost here and covers no less than seven terminals.

+ **Dallas-Ft. Worth International Airport.** Boingo and T-Mobile provide coverage in various areas throughout the airport, though Boingo is your cheaper option if you plan on surfing more than an hour.

+ **Atlanta Hartsfield International.** A-town offers one of the most extensive airport wireless lists, offering Boingo, Concourse, Sprint PCS, Access, Opti-fi, and T-Mobile. I forgot to mention that none of them are free.

+ **Denver International Airport.** Not surprisingly, Boingo is the mile-high Wi-Fi provider (are you sensing a trend?).

Obviously, any of these services can change in an Internet minute. However, these snapshots of Wi-Fi access available in the larger airports at least gives you an idea of what's out there. As with other hotspots, you can check availability on one of the hotspot directories listed in Table 5-1.

In hotels

Not so long ago, it was a pretty big deal when I found a hotel offering high-speed, wired Internet access. It beat a slow, dial-up connection, and I was able to work better in my hotel room.

Now it's almost expected, especially among mid- to high-end hotels, that you'll have wireless Internet access from your room and possibly the lobby, too. Note that wireless access outside the United States is generally not free and can cost upwards of $25 per day. For example, these large hotel chains offer some services (if you're in the U.S.):

✦ **Hyatt.** Most of the chain's more than 200 hotels have Wi-Fi access; currently there are 414 properties that offer wireless. The service is available in the lobby, other public areas, and some guest rooms. Hyatt charges a daily rate that varies by location.

✦ **Marriott.** More than 1,200 of Marriott's hotels have wireless Internet access. Hotels include Marriott Hotels & Resorts, Renaissance Hotels & Resorts, Courtyard, Residence Inn, TownePlace Suites, Fairfield Inn, and SpringHill Suites. Access is available in hotel lobbies, meeting rooms, and public spaces.

✦ **Hilton.** As one might expect, almost every Hilton property (including Hampton Inn and Hilton Garden Inn) offer wireless access. Generally speaking, the Hilton properties charge a daily fee for Internet access; however, its partners (notably the two mentioned here) offer complimentary wireless access.

✦ **Sheraton.** Owner Starwood Hotels & Resorts has Wi-Fi connectivity in more than 150 Sheraton, Westin, and W hotels in the United States. It also provides access to about 40 properties in 10 countries and regions across Asia Pacific.

✦ **Omni.** All U.S.-based Omni hotels offer high-speed wireless access. In some hotels, this is limited to certain rooms or public areas.

✦ **Best Western.** Yep, you read that right. Even the lower end of the hotel industry is embracing Wi-Fi. And how: Best Western plans to install wireless access in 2,300 properties throughout North America.

In the (city) clouds

A new movement is equipping many city centers with Wi-Fi access. The Wi-Fi service areas, called city clouds or hot zones, are a way for cities to differentiate themselves from other business and tourism centers. In many cases, the hot zones are dual use, with police and fire workers using it along with residents and visitors.

It is good PR: If you can check your e-mail on your Wi-Fi–enabled laptop or PDA while visiting a city's downtown, aren't you more likely to remember your visit and have good feelings about the hospitality? Covering several or more blocks beats isolated hotspots at coffee houses and other limited locations.

Hot cities and countries

Not surprisingly, the United States is the nation with the most hotspots. In fact, it has more hotspots than the next nine nations on the worldwide top ten list combined. The source of this list, JiWire (www.jiwire.com), counts over 273,000 hotspots worldwide.

- United States: 66,312
- China: 28,678
- United Kingdom: 27,458
- France: 25,573
- Russian Federation: 14,457
- Germany: 14,434
- South Korea: 12,813
- Japan: 11,607
- Sweden: 6,634
- Taiwan: 5,386

When it comes to U.S. cities with the most hotspots, New York City tops the list. Interestingly, half of these cities are in either California or Texas, as the map shows.

- New York City: 885
- San Francisco: 871
- Chicago: 788
- Seattle: 624
- Houston: 600
- Los Angeles: 499
- Atlanta: 451
- San Diego: 422
- San Antonio, TX: 416
- Austin, TX: 411

Here's a small selection of cities and states offering wireless access:

✦ **New York City.** In the Big Apple, thinking big is part of living. Officials are planning a Wi-Fi network for public safety employees. The price tag: a staggering $500 million to $1 billion. For the general public, you can find wireless access virtually anywhere just due to the sheer size of the city.

✦ **Washington, D.C.** You can get free Wi-Fi access from the front of the Supreme Court, the Library of Congress, and the Capitol visitors' site. The nonprofit group deploying the network has a hot zone stretch from Capitol Hill to the Washington Monument.

✦ **San Francisco.** The real San Francisco treat is the city's plan to install 360 solar-powered bus stops with Wi-Fi across the city over the next couple of years.

✦ **Seattle.** If you're sleepless in this city, sometime in the future you might be able to access what city officials hope will be border-to-border wireless Internet access. Of course, this city has what seems like a limitless number of coffee shops ready to provide you with Wi-Fi coverage in the meantime.

✦ **Spokane, Washington.** Its dual-use Wi-Fi network covers a 100-block area that is a mile long and a third of a mile wide.

✦ **Rio Rancho, New Mexico.** This is the first city to offer city-wide, free wireless access. It's also home to Intel's primary manufacturing center.

✦ **Austin, Texas.** A volunteer effort is under way here to keep Wi-Fi free.

✦ **St. Cloud, Florida.** The city is offering free Internet access, with its hot zone covering an area about 20 city blocks.

✦ **Paris.** For those of you traveling in Europe, there is an extensive public wireless access system in Paris. Many parks and other public spaces offer free wireless internet access. It's not uncommon to see people in parks with their laptops, working.

McWireless and others

What's left after the other locations? In many places, such as Seattle, Wi-Fi–equipped coffee shops are all the rage. (If you live in Seattle, check out the Caffeinated and Unstrung Web site at `www.seattle.wifimug.org`.) Wireless Internet access is also making inroads to fast-food restaurants and sports venues.

Retailers

Schlotzsky's Delis, Apple retail stores, Panera Bread, and Krystal Restaurants are among the national chains that have Wi-Fi in at least some of their locations. Not only can you buy goods and services from these places, you can go online:

✦ **Starbucks:** While this national coffee shop famously keeps its customers wired, it also offers Wi-Fi access. The company says that Wi-Fi users stay in its stores longer, with the average wireless session lasting about 45 minutes. Now it's safe to drink and (hard) drive.

✦ **McDonald's:** I'm not sure how many people take their laptops or PDAs to a McDonald's to get some work done, but 15,000 of the restaurants worldwide now offer wireless access. I'll have a salad, a large fry — and my e-mail, please.

✦ **FedEx Office:** It took T-Mobile six months to wire (unwire?) this copy center's 1,000 U.S. locations. They welcome your use of the stores as surrogate offices.

✦ **UPS Stores and Mailboxes Etc:** After starting with AT&T to offer high-speed access to customers, they were unceremoniously dropped, and I'm not quite sure what's on the menu anymore.

Stadiums and arenas

During baseball game broadcasts, I'm surprised how many people I see in the stands chatting on their cell phones. Maybe providing wireless Internet access is the next logical step? The San Francisco Giants is offering free Wi-Fi access to its baseball fans. Now you can attend a day game while checking your e-mail, making it appear you're working. You also can check on scores and stats — anything you can do at home is available. The Charlotte Bobcats basketball team offers a similar service. Other stadiums and arenas have toyed with the idea, too.

On the road

You can be between points A and B and still get online:

✦ **Airplanes:** German airline Lufthansa has on-board Wi-Fi access. With regards to the U.S. market, Delta and Virgin America are the most advanced so far. This service is provided by Gogo Inflight, which is available at `http://gogoinflight.com/`.

✦ **Truck stops:** Truck drivers need Wi-Fi access, too. There's family to e-mail and paperwork to file. Offering access differentiates one truck stop from the other, providing a competitive advantage.

✦ **Highway rest areas:** Texas, Iowa, and Maryland think they know how to encourage tired drivers to stop more often at highway rest stops: Offer them wireless Internet access from the comfort of their vehicles. It's especially a boon to truckers and RVers. With the security lines in airports being so long, the highways may become an important alternative to business travelers.

✦ **Campgrounds:** The state of Michigan installed Wi-Fi access in a state park campground. It plans to do this in other state parks, as well. I'm sure this is happening elsewhere, too. My idea of roughing it is watching TV on anything other than a big screen, so battling insects in a tent and foot fungus in the shower is not within my definition of reality. Yet I understand many folks like this return to precivilization days. Now they can swat the mosquitoes while surfing the Web. Progress!

Clenching Your Security Blanket

Most, if not all, of the public hotspots I discuss in this chapter provide unsecured wireless Internet access. That means you're out there naked, baby. The guy with the tall latte at the next table can easily access your laptop or PDA files if you're not careful. Use a firewall and buckle down your file access, as I discuss in Book IV, Chapter 1. If you're connecting to a corporate network, do so through a virtual private networking (VPN) connection, which I discuss in Book V, Chapter 6.

Don't send out personal information like credit card numbers unless you're connecting to a Web site that encrypts the data before sending it. You can tell if it's a secured site by the Web address, which usually begins with https, and a closed padlock icon appears in your browser.

T-Mobile, which operates hotspots in Starbucks locations, is very clear that you're on your own when it comes to security. "The T-Mobile HotSpot network is based on evolving wireless technology and is not inherently secure," it says in a security statement posted on Starbucks' Web site. "We therefore cannot guarantee the privacy of your data and communications while using the HotSpot service." The statement cautions that an unexplained loss or deterioration of your connection could mean that a nearby hacker has gained free access to the Internet using your HotSpot username and password. If you suspect that's the case, logging out knocks the freeloading hacker off the Internet. T-Mobile suggests you then call its customer service department.

While I cover many of these security issues elsewhere, they're worth mentioning here as you consider connecting to a public hotspot. There's no need to be paranoid (believe me, I know), but vigilance is diligence. T-Mobile makes these security recommendations:

✦ Don't leave your computer or device unattended. (Duh! The worst security is a stolen laptop.)

✦ Don't loan your computer or device to someone unfamiliar to you. (You might be a Dummy, but you're not an idiot.)

✦ Watch for over-the-shoulder viewing of your login, credit card number, or other personal information.

✦ Log out of Web sites by clicking Log Out instead of just closing your browser or typing in a new Internet address.

✦ Create passwords using a combination of letters and numbers, and they should be changed frequently. (This is always good advice.)

✦ Keep passwords and account numbers secure; don't store them on your computer or device or share them with anyone.

✦ Avoid using Web-based e-mail or instant messaging that uses clear, unencrypted text to send confidential information.

✦ Remove or disable your wireless card if you're working offline and you are not planning to connect to a hotspot.

Any way you sip it, it's worth letting this advice brew and considering it the next time you connect to the Internet through a public Wi-Fi hotspot.

Book V
Chapter 5

Finding Wi-Fi
Hotspots

Chapter 6: Setting Up a VPN Connection

In This Chapter

✔ **Creating a VPN connection**

✔ **Using VPN to connect to a far away computer**

✔ **Putting together an incoming VPN connection**

*W*ireless networking security is an evolving area. Though wireless networking has some built-in security features, you can't be as confident with it as you can with wired networking. What if you want to wirelessly move information from your PC to a computer located elsewhere? You're in an airport, using public Wi-Fi access, and you want to connect to an office computer — and don't want anyone to see the information you're sending. How can you pull this off? I'm glad you asked.

I show you how to create and use what's called a virtual private network (VPN) to move your data safely over a public network such as the Internet. When you create a VPN connection, you're creating a virtual tunnel. Everything moving through this tunnel is encrypted, or scrambled, so it's safe from prying eyes. Once the data reaches the computer on the other end, the information is decrypted so users can see what you sent.

Setting Up a VPN Connection

Follow along with these steps and you find it's pretty easy to set up a VPN connection (one of which is shown in Figure 6-1). If you have set up other network connections using Windows Vista's Network and Sharing Center, it is even easier for you.

Here's how you set up the VPN connection:

1. **Click the Start menu and select Control Panel.**

   The Control Panel opens.

2. **Click Network and Internet.**

   The Network and Internet dialog box appears.

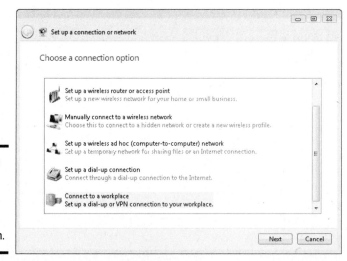

Welcome to SSL-VPN Service

Fortinet SSL VPN Client 1.0

Link Status	Bytes Sent	Bytes Received
Up	22700	187

Install Uninstall Connect Disconnect Refresh now

FortiClient SSL VPN connected to server

Tools

Test for Reachability(Ping)   Go
Telnet to Host   Go
Vnc to Host   Go
Rdp to Host   Go

Figure 6-1:
Data moving
through a
secure VPN
tunnel.

3. **Click Network and Sharing Center.**

   The Network and Sharing Center appears.

4. **Under Tasks, click Set up a connection or network and then Connect to a workplace.**

   Figure 6-2 shows this being done. The Network Connection dialog box appears. Despite the menu selection's name, the VPN connection can be made anywhere, not just to a company network.

5. **Select whether to create a new connection or use an existing connection, as shown in Figure 6-3.**

   This procedure creates a new connection.

Set up a connection or network

Choose a connection option

Set up a wireless router or access point
Set up a new wireless network for your home or small business.

Manually connect to a wireless network
Choose this to connect to a hidden network or create a new wireless profile.

Set up a wireless ad hoc (computer-to-computer) network
Set up a temporary network for sharing files or an Internet connection.

Set up a dial-up connection
Connect through a dial-up connection to the Internet.

Connect to a workplace
Set up a dial-up or VPN connection to your workplace.

Figure 6-2:
The first
step in
creating
a VPN
connection.

Next   Cancel

Figure 6-3:
Selecting
a VPN
connection.

6. **Click Next.**

   The Connection dialog box appears and lets you choose how to connect,
   either using your Internet connection or dial-up.

7. **Select your Internet connection, as shown in Figure 6-4.**

8. **Enter the domain name or IP address of the computer to which you
   are connecting, as shown in Figure 6-5.**

   You can get this information from your network administrator.

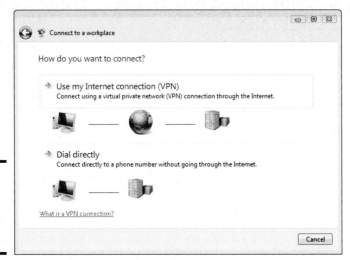

Figure 6-4:
Entering
a VPN
connection
name.

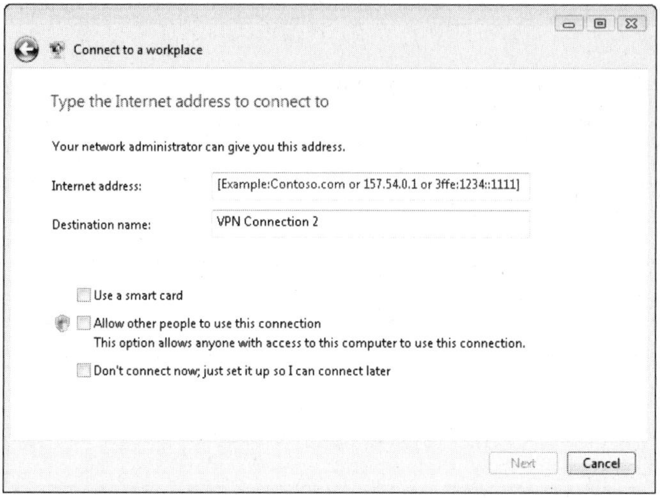

Figure 6-5:
Entering
a domain
name or IP
address.

9. **Click Next.**

You can enter the login name and password for the VPN connection.

10. **Click Create.**

Your new VPN connection appears in the Network Connections dialog box, as shown in Figure 6-6.

Figure 6-6:
You created
a VPN
connection.

Connecting to a Remote Computer Using VPN

If you've set up a VPN connection on your computer, you can connect to a remote computer that accepts incoming VPN connections. Ask your network administrator whether a remote computer accepts VPN connections. (In the next section I show you how to create an incoming connection for a Windows Vista machine.)

Here's how you connect to a remote computer using VPN:

1. **From the Network Connections dialog box, double-click the VPN connection.**

A connection dialog box appears.

2. **Enter the remote computer's username and password, as shown in Figure 6-7.**

You can get this information from your network administrator.

If you select Save This User Name and Password for the Following Users, everyone with access to your PC can connect to the remote computer. The username and password are saved on your computer, so users won't need to know that information to connect.

Figure 6-7:
Entering a
username
and
password.

3. **Click Connect.**

You see the Connecting dialog box shown in Figure 6-8.

If the connection is a success, your Virtual Private Network icon in the Network Connections dialog box says Connected.

Figure 6-8:
Connecting
with a
remote
computer.

You can disconnect a VPN connection by right-clicking the VPN connection icon and selecting Disconnect. You can use the icon to reconnect whenever you want by clicking it.

Creating an Incoming VPN Connection

Windows Vista lets you create an incoming connection so that other users — maybe even yourself while on the road — can connect to your computer using a VPN connection.

The Home edition of Windows Vista can only accept one incoming VPN connection at a time. The Professional version allows multiple incoming connections.

These steps create an incoming connection:

1. **In the Network Connections dialog box, click File⇨New Incoming Connection.**

The following dialog box appears, once you get past the User Account Control, as shown in Figure 6-9.

2. **Select the user(s) with an account on the machine and click Next.**

The network will accept incoming calls from these users. Once you click Next, the Allow connections to this computer dialog box appears.

3. **Select Through the Internet, as shown in Figure 6-10.**

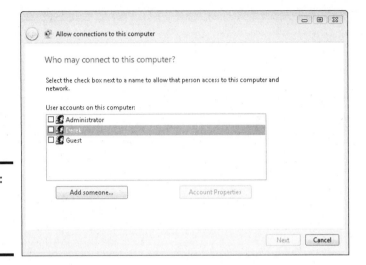

Figure 6-9:
Allow
incoming
connec-
tions.

Figure 6-10:
Internet or,
um, dial-up.
The choice
is yours.

4. **Click Next.**

   The Network selection dialog box appears. Leave everything selected, as shown in Figure 6-11.

5. **Click Next.**

   The Devices for Incoming Connections dialog box appears. You can ignore this dialog box.

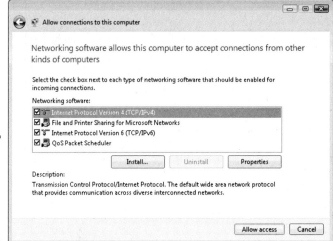

Figure 6-11:
Accepting
incoming
connections
using these
protocols.

6. **Click Allow Access.**

The procedure is completed, and your selected users can now access the network, as shown in Figure 6-12.

Your new incoming connection shows up in the Network Connections dialog box like you see in Figure 6-13. That's it: You just set up an incoming VPN connection.

Figure 6-12:
Be sure to
note this
information
down!

Figure 6-13:
Success!
The
incoming
connection
is shown.

Chapter 7: Taking Home with You

In This Chapter

✔ **Watching TV around the world**

✔ **Taking off with Slingbox**

✔ **Making the most of the experience**

1 know this sounds bad, but I love watching American television. Except for the abundance of commercials, it's like hunting through a junk shop. You've got loads of channels and only a handful of shows worth watching. One of the things I missed about home when I moved to Europe was all the shows that I would miss.

Thinking back a few years to my first stint living abroad in the late 1990s, technology was nowhere even remotely close to where it is today. Back in the day, phone calls back to America were outrageously priced, dial-up was the norm here, and streaming technology? Forget it.

Jumping ahead to 2009, times certainly have changed. For starters, my ISP has download speeds that I hadn't dreamt possible just a few short years ago. Thanks to VOIP technology, I am able to have a local number from the United States so family and friends can call me for the price of a local call. Finally, thanks to one great leap for mankind, I can watch my beloved sit-coms (and here's a special shout-out to DVR technology for surmounting the seven-hour time zone difference).

This chapter explores my latest toy, the Slingbox, from Sling Media, which allows me to watch television remotely with very little setup. Thanks to Slingbox, VOIP, and Web cams, I can feel like home even when I am thousands of miles away.

Watching TV around the World

The Slingbox, in my humble opinion, has to be one of the coolest, more practical gadgets for road warriors of the past 20 years. It's especially useful for those who travel out of the country frequently.

Once you take care of the hardest part (finding someone who will share their television with you), installation is easy, and you're on your way within minutes. Of course, there is some mild inconvenience for the host, as I discuss later in this chapter.

Using proprietary software, you can log on to your account, where you register your Slingbox, and then watch television live through your computer or wireless device. When you are connected to the Slingbox, you literally take over the television on the other end of the internet connection. This means that you control the sound, and more importantly, the channel!

The benefits are in spades, however, as you can enjoy the feeling of sitting on your favorite sofa back home watching your favorite shows. The only thing missing is a batch of mom's homemade chocolate chip cookies. There are no geographical limitations to using the Slingbox; you can live in the U.S., Germany, or Japan and log in to watch a Slingbox that is hosted in France, Brazil, or Canada. It's proven to be quite useful when out shopping with the kids; I can log on to the application on my smartphone and watch cartoons in the United States as we're shopping in Paris.

Taking Off with the Slingbox

There are a few items that you'll need to buy before you are up and running. Even though the installation process is pretty straightforward, you'll have to have some familiarity with wireless technology and a general level of patience for computers.

To get an idea of what you're going to need to get started, visit the Web site `www.slingmedia.com`. From a technical standpoint, you're going to want to make sure that you have a wireless network already configured in your home, or wherever you intend on installing the Slingbox itself. This means that the Slingbox is expecting to find a wireless router to which it can plug in.

After the network requirements are met, you can pick what kind of Slingbox you want to buy. The SOLO model allows you to broadcast your incoming satellite television transmission both over the local television and though authorized users over the Internet. The PRO-HD model lets you go one step farther — you can connect multiple devices, so that you can include DVRs, DVD players, satellite television, and so on in high-definition quality.

The Slingbox provides ample online documentation, but the following is a quick and dirty way to get started. Again, while it's not difficult to set up, it's like preparing a fancy recipe. The individual ingredients may be easy to prepare, but mixing them together at the right time may prove to be a more difficult maneuver to make. These instructions apply to the host — in other words, the person kind enough to share their television with you.

1. **Make sure that you have all the necessary equipment.**

   Locate the back of your satellite receiver, where input and output cables are plugged in.

2. **Plug the cables from the Slingbox to the back of your satellite receiver.**

   This allows the incoming satellite signal to be processed by the receiver (decoder) and then be sent as output to your Slingbox.

3. **Plug the Ethernet cable from the back of your Slingbox to an open port of your router.**

You may want to plug in the Slingbox to an electrical socket for good measure. Experience has taught me that a little bit of electricity also helps move things along. Once plugged in as described above, you should notice lights on in front of the Slingbox, which means that the Slingbox is receiving data and able to broadcast it.

If you have set up your home network in a way that your television/satellite television connection is not in the same room as your wireless router, do not fret. Slingmedia offers a dapper little device called a SlingLink that you can connect between your wireless router and your Slingbox to create a wireless connection between the devices when they are not in the same room.

Now that your host is ready to broadcast, it's now up to you to get things ready on your end. This is a simple process, but it does require a little bit of configuration on your end, so look sharp!

1. **Sign up for a free Sling account.**

   You can do this at `https://betasecure.sling.com/account/login`.

2. **Download the Slingbox software.**

   You can do this at `http://downloads.slingmedia.com/`. You'll want to first download SlingPlayer software for either Windows or Macintosh.

3. **Install the software.**

   This is a straightforward installation; double-click the installer that you downloaded in Step 2 and follow the instructions.

You're almost ready to go at this point! Click the icon that is installed on your desktop to launch the SlingPlayer software. The SlingPlayer appears as shown in Figure 7-1.

The first step is to click Log In, which is in the upper-right corner of the window. If you do not log on, you cannot configure the Slingbox now, nor will you be able to watch the SlingPlayer in the future. The Log In dialog box appears, as shown in Figure 7-2.

Figure 7-1:
The
SlingPlayer
interface.

Figure 7-2:
The
SlingPlayer
login
window.

Once you are logged on to your Sling account, you will need to configure the Slingbox. This is something that you will likely only need to do once (unless you have to reinstall the software one day), and it will require some help from your Slingbox host.

1. **Choose Connect⇨Slingbox Directory.**

2. **Click Add.**

The New Slingbox Entry Properties window appears, as shown in Figure 7-3.

Figure 7-3:
Add your
Slingbox
to your
account.

3. **In the Connection section, add the Slingbox ID.**

You guessed it; you need to get this number from the back of the Slingbox. Pick up the phone and call the person hosting your Slingbox for you, or go to the room with the Slingbox in it and jot that ridiculously long ID number down.

4. **You can add an administrator password if desired.**

This is helpful if you want to watch the Slingbox and boot someone else off who is already watching it.

5. **Click OK.**

The new Slingbox appears in the directory, as shown in Figure 7-4.

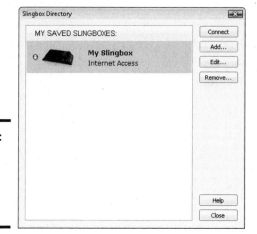

Figure 7-4:
The
Slingbox
directory
with new
addition.

The Setup Assistant is available to help you set up your Slingbox connection; this is notably where you'll confirm the satellite connection/input device connection and make sure it is properly configured, as shown in Figure 7-5.

Figure 7-5:
The Setup
Assistant
lets you
make sure
everything
is properly
set.

Once you are set, you can go back to the Connect menu and select the Connect to my Slingbox. Once it connects to the Slingbox next door or half-way around the world, it optimizes for the best possible.

Making the Most of the Experience

You're finally all set to watch your streaming television from anywhere around the world. What is strangest for me is watching shows in Europe and seeing the advertisements for stores or restaurants back home that do not exist here. More than once, I've said to myself, "grab your coat, kids, we're heading out! Wait a minute, doh!"

I should also point out that although the SlingPlayer software is free, you can purchase a version for mobile. If you have a wireless device that supports Internet access (a given, these days), you can buy a version of almost any mobile operating system, as well as iPhone. For more information on this version, check out www.slingmedia.com/go/spm.

As a frequent user of the mobile version, I still marvel at the fact that I can watch NBC from the comfort of the subway with amazing clarity. Given the advances in smartphone technology, I can watch on a rather generous-sized screen, without having to sacrifice sound quality.

The Slingbox itself can be somewhat pricey, admittedly. However, if you do enjoy watching television and are frequently on the road or not in the country, its money well spent.

To truly make the most of the experience, I recommend watching on a computer with a proper screen size. I also hooked up some high-end speakers to my laptop so that I could enjoy the full cinema-like sound of what I was watching.

Depending on your computer's capabilities, it's also possible to hook up your PC/netbook/laptop to your television and to watch the SlingPlayer through your own television instead of a small PC screen.

As technology teaches us, where there's a will, there's a way. With Slingbox, I now have yet another piece of home closer to me, which really does prove that the world is indeed getting smaller.

Book VI

Other Networking Technologies

The 5th Wave   By Rich Tennant

THE NEXT EVOLUTION IN PALM-TOP ORGANIZERS

The PatchPilot

Delivers a preset amount of data into your bloodstream which quickly rushes it to your brain and subconscious.

I have to go now. I suddenly got the feeling I'm supposed to be at a meeting in 10 minutes.

Contents at a Glance

Chapter 1: Choosing and Using Cordless Phones

*I*t's bad enough that buying a cellular phone and wireless networking equipment is so complicated. Now, with new options for cordless phones, even that once straightforward purchase is forcing you to reach for the aspirin. Consider me the aspirin — and you don't even have to call me in the morning. In this chapter I discuss the different kinds of cordless phones, the advantages of one over the other, and a technology term or two.

You have choices when it comes to buying a cell phone and choices when installing wireless networking. Now, consider your standard telephone: when you decide to cut its cord and go wireless, you also have choices. Thankfully, cordless phones aren't nearly as complex as smartphones or Wi-Fi networks, but there are different types of cordless phones that use various technologies.

Cutting the Cords

If you're over 35, you probably remember the days when one of the only telephones in the house was a corded model mounted on the wall, possibly with a rotary dial. The only way to increase your distance from the phone was to purchase a longer cord. Although it might be possible, wrestling with a 300-foot cord so you can chat as you move from the kitchen to the garden to the garage is a bit impractical.

Around 1990, when the FCC assigned bandwidth in the 900 MHz frequency range, cordless phones first became a real alternative to corded telephones. While there were cordless phones before that (usually with big, metal, telescoping antennae), the newer frequencies were a big jump in clarity and range from the old 43–49 MHz band.

As manufacturers began making digital models, cordless phones grew even more practical; they were more secure (allowing for less eavesdropping) than analog versions. Also, more channels are available for use by the cordless phone to communicate between the base station and handset. A wider range of channels means interference is more easily thwarted. The breakdown is as follows:

✦ 10 to 25 channels for inexpensive 900 MHz phones.

✦ 20 to 60 channels for most 900 MHz phones.

✦ 50 to 100 channels for high-end 900 MHz phones and for 2.4 and 5.8 GHz phones.

Table 1-1 breaks down the megahertz and gigahertz by range.

Table 1-1:	Cordless Phone Ranges
Frequency Band	*Range*
900 MHz	75 to 400 feet
900 MHz with DSS	200 to 1,500 feet
2.4 GHz with DSS	300 to 2,000 feet
5.8 GHz with DSS	300 to 2,000 feet

Analog phones

Analog cordless phones act like a plain, old AM/FM radio. They convert sounds waves into radio waves, transmitting them between the cordless phone and its base station. Anyone with a converter and a radio scanner can eavesdrop. (Selling police and fire radio scanners that pick up 900 MHz transmissions is illegal; 2.4 GHz and 5.8 GHz phones are out of range of most radio scanners.)

When you and an analog handset get too far from the base station, you hear static over the conversation until you can no longer communicate with the base station. These phones also are prone to static from interference. Figure 1-1 shows analog versus digital communications methods.

What is this DSS?

Many new cordless phones — and I recommend making sure this is true of the one you purchase next — use a technology called DSS, or digital spread spectrum. The digital part of DSS means your conversation is converted from analog sound waves to digital 1s and 0s. (You can buy a digital phone that does not use DSS, however.) The spread spectrum part is less clear, though it has something to do with the radio spectrum. This technical term is vague until you discover what it is, how it works, and why you want it.

First, why you want it: DSS-equipped phones are much more secure than analog and plain digital phones. In fact, it's nearly impossible to listen to a conversation taking place on a DSS phone because the listener only hears quick bursts of data that transmit very quickly across multiple frequencies. In other words, one data burst will be at frequency A, then next at B, and so on — and only the phone knows what frequency the next data burst will occur on. Everything happens so fast that it's impossible to follow conversations sent with DSS unless the eavesdropper has very expensive and sophisticated snooping equipment. You can feel pretty confident that the personal information you reveal during a telephone call (credit card numbers, social security numbers, and so on) on this phone is safe.

Second, phones using DSS suffer from less interference. Depending on different factors, they may also have a greater range than similar phones that don't use DSS technology. In addition to being more secure, DSS is a more efficient use of the radio spectrum.

A DSS phone may also be referred to by frequency hopping spread spectrum or FHSS.

**Book VI
Chapter 1**

Choosing and Using Cordless Phones

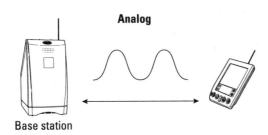

Analog

Base station

Figure 1-1:
Analog and digital phones work differently.

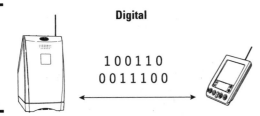

Digital

100110
0011100

Digital phones

Digital phones convert sound waves into digital signals, which consist of a lot of 1s and 0s. If you tune into a conversation transmitted digitally, you can't hear it without using equipment that converts the output into something humans can understand. When you go out of range with a digital phone, the conversation terminates suddenly with dead air. Digital phones offer no gray area between a good signal and a lousy signal. Their existence shows up on the time lines in Figure 1-2.

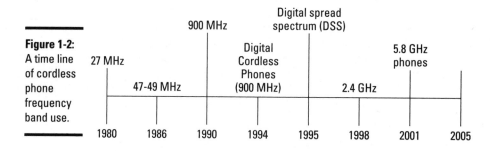

Figure 1-2: A time line of cordless phone frequency band use.

Some digital phones use something called digital spread spectrum (DSS). See the "What is this DSS?" sidebar in this chapter for further information. Not all digital phones have DSS, but all DSS phones are digital.

Choosing Your Frequency

Can you imagine if when purchasing a cell phone and a calling plan, you had to tell the company what technology you want to use? Of course, you have some choices when it comes to handsets and choosing a particular carrier for its network. You don't have to tell the cell phone provider at what frequency you want the phone to operate.

When you purchase a cell phone and calling plan, you make some technical decisions. These mainly concern the handset and its features, plus a carrier for the network. Cordless phone shoppers have their own set of technological decisions to make, above and beyond the features offered by the model.

When shopping for cordless phones, you choose the frequency and sometimes whether the radio signals are analog or digital. Shopping for the phones in a store does little to narrow your decision making, other than deciding on the look and feel of the phone. Table 1-2 can help you start your comparison shopping before you set foot in a store.

Table 1-2:	Pros and Cons of Cordless Frequency Bands	
Band	*Pros*	*Cons*
900 MHz	Cheap, won't interfere with Wi-Fi	Usually little or no security, limited range
2.4 GHz	Price is right, more secure than 900 MHz secure	Possible conflicts with Wi-Fi
5.8 GHz	Clear, likely more secure	More expensive

You have an array of choices when purchasing a cordless phone. The important option is the frequency band on which the phones operates. Cordless phones are available in 900 MHz, 2.4 GHz, and 5.8 GHz models. Generally, as the frequency goes higher, so does the maximum distance you can take the handset from the base station, and the clarity gets better. Watch out, however, for interference from other sources of radio waves, physical structures like walls, and the weather.

Here are what the three frequency bands offer.

900 MHz

You can buy one of these phones pretty cheaply, but many manufacturers are phasing them out, favoring instead the 2.4 GHz and 5.8 GHz models. If you're on a budget, you can buy one of these analog models for less than you paid for this book — but I wouldn't recommend it (the phone, not the book).

Why? The prices of 2.4 GHz phones are very reasonable and cover a larger area with less likelihood of interference. Also, higher frequency phones offer more conversation security: It's fairly simple to listen in to a 900 MHz analog signal with the right equipment.

2.4 GHz

Quality and price meet here. This is the sweet spot for cordless phones; most of them made today operate in this frequency range. They offer more clarity and range than you get with a 900 MHz phone.

Given the number of 2.4 GHz models, you can find them in a wide variety of configurations, choosing the features you want and not paying for ones you don't need. You can buy 2.4 GHz phones in analog and digital models. These phones are also available in multiple-handset models, which let you add more handsets as you need them. Some models let you have as many as eight — seemingly enough for every room of your house. While the additional phones need a nearby AC outlet, they don't each need a phone jack.

You can find 2.4GHz phones in a huge variety of configurations with any number of features. Some contain digital answering machines. Some allow you to add up to eight handsets to the same base. Extra handsets usually come with a charging dock for which you need an AC connection, but you only need a phone jack for the base station itself.

Unfortunately, phones that operate in the 2.4 GHz range can interfere with some Wi-Fi wireless networks (802.11b and 802.11g, but not 802.11a or 802.11n).

5.8 GHz

These phones have an exceptionally notable advantage over the other two kinds of phones: The 5.8 GHz band is less populated, but that's changing quickly. Along with an increase in clarity and distance, cordless phones using this frequency are the perfect fit for a home that has a Wi-Fi network and other interference on the 2.4 GHz band.

The 5.8 GHz phones tend to be feature-packed affairs that get expensive quickly, although with the frequency growing in popularity it's only a matter of time before cheaper 5.8 GHz phones emerge.

Featuring Cordless Phones

If the confusion over frequencies isn't bad enough, you have to decide between a myriad of features when shopping for a cordless phone. From caller ID displays to multiple-handset models, you have much to discover before plopping down your greenbacks.

You find some of the features on cordless phones:

✦ **Caller ID.** If you subscribe to caller ID service through your local phone company, this feature is a must. If the phone's not enabled for caller ID, subscribing doesn't make any difference. When you get an incoming call, the caller's phone number and possibly the name (if you pay for this service) appears on the handset's display.

✦ **Call waiting ID.** Call waiting ID is a cool feature. While you're on the phone with someone else, you can see who is trying to reach you by glancing at the display on your phone. If you want to take the new call, you flash over to the other line. When you're done, if the first caller is still waiting, you can flash back to him or her.

✦ **Digital answering machine**. I thought everyone who needs to record calls signed up for voicemail through their phone company. I guess not. Long gone are the days of cassette tapes; the answering machines built into these phones are digital, which have far less recording capacity. One benefit is that long-winded callers have fewer seconds to leave their messages, sparing you some rambling. Sometimes you can even set the length of messages your answering machine will take before cutting off the caller.

✦ **Multiple handsets**. You can do several things with these phones:

- Add up to eight handsets (depending on the model) for use throughout your home.

- Answer a call using any one of the phones.

- Transfer a call to and from a handset.

- Page a handset, making the setup similar to an intercom system.

- Plug each handset's cradle into a power outlet; they don't require separate phone jacks.

✦ **Two-line phones.** These models can handle multiple phone lines. If you have a second line in your home, consider this feature. My household uses a two-line phone — one for business and faxing and the other for personal calls.

✦ **Speakerphone.** This feature is always handy, especially when stuck on hold with a credit card company or other sadistic entity. You can push the appropriate button and leave the handset in its cradle, using the speakerphone located in the base station. Better still are handsets with speakerphone built-in; you can carry them around and have speakerphone conversations while you do other stuff.

Book VI
Chapter 1

Choosing and Using
Cordless Phones

Avoiding Interference

As I mentioned earlier, if you have a Wi-Fi network in your house, I don't recommend the purchase of a 2.4 GHz cordless phone. If your household is constantly using a baby monitor, that could be a problem, too. Even microwave ovens, which operate on the same frequency, can create problems. Never situate the base of your phone near a microwave, because if somebody decides to heat up last night's dinner while you're on the phone, you'll experience loud and annoying interference.

If your analog phone has interference, you hear it as static and hisses. A digital phone will probably fade in and out or have a shorter range, or even cough up sounds like buzzing or beeping (but not technically static).

The best way to eliminate or reduce these kinds of interference problems is to move the phone's base station around the house, seeing if a different location makes any difference. If you already have a Wi-Fi network and purchased a 2.4 GHz phone without reading my wise admonitions beforehand, you still have hope. Just turn off the network when you're using the phone and vice versa (as annoying as that can be). However, you may find the two coexist peacefully.

Chapter 2: Picking Peripherals

You may be focusing on Wi-Fi and Bluetooth networks and forgetting some of the more "peripheral" uses of wireless technology. In this chapter, namely, I'm literally referring to peripherals — for your computers.

A peripheral is really anything that's not an internal, integral part of your desktop or laptop computer. Examples include keyboards, mice, trackballs, external hard drives, speakers, and game controllers. (It also includes printers, but they're covered in Book III, Chapter 4.) While these all once were tethered to your PC via wires, more and more of them are sold in cordless versions. In this chapter I highlight a few of the cordless peripherals you can buy.

Unplugging Your Desktop

Logitech, one of the largest manufacturers of cordless mice and keyboards, has shipped literally tens of millions of cordless peripherals worldwide, including keyboards, mice, and trackballs.

You may see peripherals called cordless or wireless. I guess I like wireless because this book isn't called Cordless All-in-One Desk Reference For Dummies. It's a good thing, too, as I picture a cordless phone disguised as a Dummies book. I'd love the look — I'll gladly take a black-and-yellow phone any day — but holding a book to my head for an hour could be tiring.

Of course, some cordless peripherals still come with cords. The base stations usually plug into a USB port (found on the back or front of your computer) on your computer and then sit somewhere on your desk — but probably out of the way and out of sight. Others simply require USB dongles to communicate with your computer — no wires at all.

Seems logical

Logitech introduced the first radio-frequency (RF) cordless mouse in 1991 and the first cordless keyboard-and-mouse combination in 1998. Logitech cites a study showing that eight out of ten U.S. consumers know about cordless peripherals.

It's a sizeable market, with Logitech estimating that retail sales of cordless mice and keyboards total $230 million a year. That's a growth rate of nearly 50 percent. It seems I'm not the only one cutting the cords and opting for a wireless desk.

One of the annoying things about corded, or wired, peripherals is when you attempt to move a mouse but the cord is hung up on something else on your desk. As you pull the mouse toward you to move the cursor down, the mouse stops, the cursor stops, but your eyes (and sometimes your hand) keep going. This little disruption can totally throw off your suspension of disbelief if it happens when you're in the middle of a game.

Switch to a cordless mouse, and you'll never experience that particular problem again. Of course, cordless mice have their own issues, but I'll get to them a bit later.

Using a Cordless Mouse

Microsoft and Logitech are two of the largest makers of cordless mice. Various other companies manufacture similar cordless peripherals, including game controllers, which are described later in this chapter.

Microsoft mouse

Microsoft has a massive line of cordless mice, including things like the Wireless Laser Mouse 7000, the Wireless Laser Mouse 8000, and the SideWinder X8 gaming mouse. It also has cordless notebook mice, which are more compact versions of standard mice, such as the Arc Mouse and the Mobile Memory Mouse 8000. Many of these operate in the 2.4 GHz range and allow for up to 30 feet of wireless range.

Bluetooth peripherals work similarly to the cordless mice and keyboards I mention in this chapter A Bluetooth base station can simultaneously interact with several devices, including appropriately equipped cell phones and handheld computers. I discuss mice and keyboards that use Bluetooth wireless technology in Book VI, Chapter 5.

SideWinder X8 Mouse

A dedicated gaming mouse, the SideWinder X8 Mouse is equipped with a 2.4GHz connection, a tilt scroll wheel, 12 buttons (7 of which are programmable), and something called Play and Charge. That's a charging cable that allows you to continue playing even if the built-in battery dies during a gaming session.

The grooviest thing about this mouse is that the thumb buttons, traditionally placed horizontally along the left side of the mouse, are, in this mouse's case, vertically placed for easier access. With programmable mice, gamers can program stuff they'd normally have to do with the keyboard to mouse buttons. This includes in-game actions like jumping, changing movement speeds (walk/run), ducking, and so on.

Wireless Laser Mouse 8000

This killer mouse goes beyond optical tracking. Like most high-end, modern mice, it doesn't use a ball or a visible LED for movement; it uses a laser. This makes for much more precise tracking over just about any kind of surface you can imagine. The Wireless Laser Mouse 8000 also includes 2.5 GHz Bluetooth technology, a rechargeable battery, and more.

Logitech mouse

Logitech also has a wide range of wireless mice. You can order them online at www.logitech.com.

This itty-bitty, portable mouse is the exact mouse I use with my notebook computer. It's small, yet features big technology. It's a laser mouse, it comes with a USB receiver the size of a nickel (literally), it's oddly palm-friendly for its size, and it runs on two AAA batteries.

I just leave the little receiver plugged into my notebook's USB port all the time. When the computer goes to sleep, I just wiggle the mouse and it wakes right up. The mouse has two main buttons, two buttons nestled to the left of the standard left mouse button, and a scroll wheel with tilt sensors. (See Figure 2-1.)

It really has just about everything a full-sized mouse might feature, but it's pocket-sized and easy to bring around the house, or even anywhere to which I may travel, and to use with my Wi-Fi enabled notebook for computing all over the place.

**Book VI
Chapter 2**

Picking Peripherals

Figure 2-1:
The
Logitech
VX Nano
Cordless
Laser
Mouse

Trackballs

I'm no expert, but I'd say trackballs are a niche market. If you haven't seen one, it's basically a mouse with the ball on the top rather than the bottom. The unit stays in place as you move the ball (and hence, the onscreen pointer) with your fingers.

Trackballs are good for precision work (graphical work) and certain games. However, if you don't know if you need one, you probably don't. Logitech has two wireless trackballs. One is the Cordless TrackMan Optical and the other is the Cordless TrackMan Wheel. The TrackMan Optical is the fancier of the two and costs about $10 on the street. The TrackMan Wheel has a street price of about $50. Both models have lots of buttons. The TrackMan Wheel has its ball on the left side instead of on top. You use your thumb to operate the ball, rather than your fingers.

Finding the Home Row: Keyboards

You also can find keyboards that are wireless. Want to know more? Read on!

Microsoft wireless keyboards

Microsoft sells wireless keyboards and mice as a set. It offers about a dozen sets, some of which are Bluetooth enabled. The sets have different features, depending on the price tags. They range all over the place, from basic sets to elite sets.

Some of the keyboard sets come in ergonomic models, which I can't stand. If you don't know what ergonomic means, you probably have seen one of the keyboards, anyway: The keys are split into two groups, positioned at angles that more closely mimic the normal angles of your wrists. They cut down on injuries to your wrist but also typing precision. Bury me with my Logitech Wave keyboard (below).

Logitech wireless keyboards

Logitech also has a range of cordless keyboards and keyboard/mouse sets. The standout is called the Cordless Desktop Wave (See Figure 2-2). The Wave keyboard comes in a corded version; the Wave desktop has the same keyboard in a cordless form and a mouse to go with it. I prefer a different mouse, so I use the Wave keyboard without the mouse that came with it. Call me a rebel.

**Book VI
Chapter 2**

Picking Peripherals

Figure 2-2:
Cutting the cord with Logitech's Cordless Desktop Wave keyboard (it looks beat up, but it's actually well loved)

Book VII

Wireless Home Technology

The 5th Wave   By Rich Tennant

"Good news! I found a place where the router works with the PC upstairs and the one in the basement."

Contents at a Glance

Chapter 1: Entertaining Yourself Wirelessly

In This Chapter:

- ✔ Starting out with digital music
- ✔ Deciding between wireless and wired
- ✔ Finding out about digital media adapter basics
- ✔ Using other gadgets

Your network is set up and ready to go. You're surfing the net wirelessly from your laptop. Maybe you've got music streaming from your desktop PC to your laptop.

One problem: the home theater is in your family room. You have content on your PC that you'd love to see on the big screen TV, but getting said content from one to the other seems like a major chore.

The real chore is not streaming the video or music to your home theater. Once you have your network set up to talk to your entertainment system, streaming is easy. What's hard, then?: asking the right questions.

In the next few chapters, I take a look at specific devices and show you how to set them up and connect to your wireless network. Think of these as examples; you may choose different gear, but the principles of installation and setup are the same.

In this chapter, I cover some basic knowledge, so you can understand exactly what I'm trying to do.

Entertaining the Wireless Way

The goal for a wireless entertainment experience falls somewhere between listening to audio on your $20 computer speakers and having a full-featured home media PC running a special version of Windows XP connected to your entertainment system. With the former, you get poor sound but few setup hassles. With the latter, you must invest much more money — at least around $1,000 — to get a computer that directly feeds music, photos, and videos into your home entertainment center. (In fact, the home media PC becomes part of your home entertainment center.)

Instead, you want to take the content that already lives on your PC and deliver it to that home entertainment center. Most of the products I discuss are a compromise between those two extremes. You get the advantages of a dedicated device that does a few things very well with minimal hassle and that costs less than a full-fledged Media Center PC. Figure 1-1 shows a typical media player configuration on a wireless network.

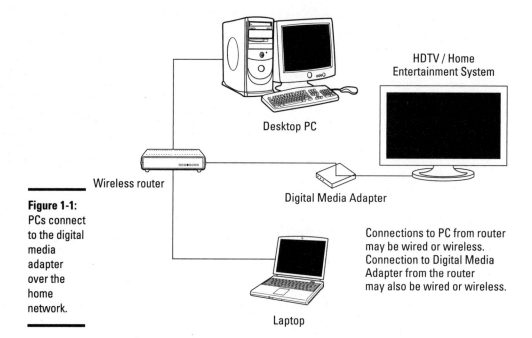

HDTV / Home
Entertainment System

Desktop PC

Wireless router

Digital Media Adapter

Connections to PC from router may be wired or wireless. Connection to Digital Media Adapter from the router may also be wired or wireless.

Laptop

Figure 1-1:
PCs connect to the digital media adapter over the home network.

Starting out with digital music

You choose your media adapter based on the type of content you want to play. If most of your music is bought or ripped from CDs using iTunes, you want a player capable of playing back music encoded with Apple's AAC format. If your music is in Windows Media Audio (WMA) format, make sure that your player can handle WMA playback.

A word on formats

CDs are easy: There's really only one type of audio CD, known as Red Book Audio CD, which is the actual color of the cover defining the CD audio standard. You buy a CD, and you can pretty much pop it into any CD player and feel confident that it will play.

The world of digital music is less well defined. When you rip a CD onto your computer, it may be stored an one of a number of different competing formats. Apple's iTunes, for example, uses AAC (Advanced Audio Coding) as its normal format. Windows Media Player and Microsoft's Zune software encode music in WMA (Windows Media Audio).

The reason for competing formats is so that the companies can protect the music from unauthorized copying — this is also called DRM (digital rights management).

The closest thing to a universal standard for compressed music files is MP3. MP3 is MPEG-1 Audio Layer 3 and was developed by the Moving Pictures Expert Group, a standards organization that has developed a number of audio and video standards over the years.

So if you want to buy hardware to play back the music you've stored on your PC, you'll need to understand what format is being used.

Note that all digital media players understand MP3, which is perhaps the most common format for storing digital music.

There are wrinkles and variations to even the most common formats. For example, WMA can rip music from CDs *losslessly*. Apple's iTunes also has a lossless ripping format available. Most music compression schemes throw away some data — usually not data that affects the actual sound. However, audio purists prefer formats that keep *all* the data. These lossless formats include Apple Lossless, WMA Pro Lossless, and FLAC (free lossless audio codec). Even players capable of playing WMA sometimes can't play back music files encoded in WMA Lossless format, so be aware of your digital music players' limitations.

Another potential sore spot is *digital rights management*, or DRM. DRM is a way of preventing unauthorized copies of digital content. Until recently, all music bought from the iTunes store was protected with a DRM scheme called FairPlay. Most digital media players that can play back AAC-encoded music can't play back music protected with FairPlay DRM.

Hardware support for playlists

In addition to the music itself, everyone makes playlists. You might be hosting a party and want to have a long playlist of catchy songs to set the mood. You might be working and want a background music playlist. There are three common playlist formats: M3U, PLS, and WPL. If you do make extensive use of playlists, you'll want your DMA to handle the format you use.

The good news is that Apple now offers most of the music you can buy from the iTunes store in unprotected AAC. Microsoft is a little behind the curve but is starting to add unprotected music. Note that Amazon.com's MP3 download service sells all its songs in MP3 format with no DRM added.

Every picture tells a story

You know that big box of photos you have somewhere that you plan to organize any day now? Well, that day has arrived. Now that you can view your photos on your TV screen, why not take the time to scan in your photos so they're available for use by these gizmos?

Both Windows and Mac have some fine software packages that help you organize your photos. You can scan them on a scanner, make some changes (like eliminating that dreadful red eye that happens when you use a flash), and organize them.

Adobe Photoshop Album (www.adobe.com; about $50) and Google's free Picasa (www.picasa.com) software are both excellent photo management applications. Your printer may have shipped with one as well. The popular formats for photos include the following:

✦ **JPEG:** JPEG is the most common compressed format for digital pictures and was developed by the Joint Photographic Experts Group. High levels of compression can reduce picture quality.

✦ **TIFF:** TIFF (Tagged Image File Format) is a picture format originally developed for scanners. TIFF supports file compression, but not at the cost of image quality.

✦ **BMP:** BMP stands for "bitmap" and was a picture standard developed for Microsoft Windows.

✦ **PNG:** PNG, or Portable Network Graphics, uses lossless compression to make picture files smaller but maintains a high level of image quality. It's not commonly used in cameras but is used often in Web design.

✦ **RAW:** This is the pure, unaltered digital sample recorded by the camera during exposure. Every camera company uses a different raw format. RAW format is used mostly in digital SLRs.

The good news is that most digital media adapters capable of showing pictures handle most of the common picture formats. The confusion and variations in standards that prevail in the digital music world aren't quite as common in the arena of digital photos.

Hollywood on a hard drive

Video and wireless networking are not quite like water and oil, but they're close. If you're going to move around video files on a wireless network, bandwidth on the wireless network becomes important. If you have enough bandwidth, your video playback is smooth and uninterrupted. If you don't, the video will become jerky, frames will be dropped, and the whole experience will be terrible.

Early wireless routers and access points supported a standard called 802.11b, which maxes out at 11 megabits per second (mbps). At first blush, 11 mbps sounds good enough, but it really isn't. The best DVD quality video pushes a maximum of over 9 mbps, and high-definition video can exceed 20 mbps.

When 802.11b was released, another standard known as 802.11a also became available. Although 802.11a supported bandwidth up to 54 mbps, it wasn't common in home networking products, since it was mainly targeted for corporate use.

Since 802.11b, two newer wireless networking (Wi-Fi) standards have emerged suitable for home wireless networks: 802.11g and 802.11n. 802.11g boosts bandwidth up to 54 mbps (double that for some products), while 802.11n supports throughput as high as 600 mbps, although most current products max out at around 256 mbps.

Book II, Chapter 2 talks about 802.11 options in depth.

The throughput differences between the technologies (b, g, and n) are striking, and you'll definitely see an improvement with 802.11g networking equipment, and even more with 802.11n. If you're streaming video in real time you almost certainly need 802.11g equipment or better.

What kind of video can you watch on media players? Just about anything your media player can read. You may want to watch some home movies you've converted into digital format, for instance. A number of online movie rental and streaming services now exist, including services from Amazon, Hulu, iTunes, Xbox 360, and Netflix.

More video services are sure to follow, especially given Hollywood's concern about content transferring illegally over peer-to-peer networks. As Apple's iTunes music store has shown, people will pay for content. They're willing to go the legal route as long as the options are there.

Book VII Chapter 1

Entertaining Yourself Wirelessly

Some of the more popular video formats include the following:

+ **MPEG (MPEG-1, MPEG-2):** Commonly used in Web video, DVDs, and other common commercial applications.

+ **MPEG4:** AVCHD high-definition standard, plus portable media players, including the iPod and Sony PSP.

+ **WMV (Windows Media Video):** Used by Microsoft's Windows Media Player.

+ **ASF (Advanced Systems Format):** Another Microsoft standard for digital containers for streaming video.

+ **AVI:** Audio/video interleave is an earlier format for Windows video file.

+ **Xvid / DiVX:** These are based on MPEG-4, but with proprietary extensions. They support high levels of compression with good quality.

There are more wireless media players that play only music than that play both music and video. That's partly because manufacturers — at least until recently with the growing popularity of 802.11g — probably felt they couldn't meet the expectations of non-geeky consumers. After all, video takes substantial bandwidth, which wired Ethernet and, in most cases, 802.11g can deliver.

Ultimately, though, keep it simple. It may sound really cool to first rip a DVD onto your PC's hard drive and then stream that movie wirelessly to your home entertainment system. In practice, it's far easier to just pop the DVD into your home theater system's DVD player — and you have all those nifty extras, which is often the real reason to own the disc.

What's important is to create an environment that works seamlessly and without a lot of unnecessary tweaking. If you have video content that is only available by streaming, by all means, go for it. But if you have to turn on your PC every time you simply want to watch a movie, there may be easier solutions.

Chapter 2: Streaming Digital Music in Your Home

In This Chapter

✔ Serving up your digital music

✔ Sharing over your network

✔ Exploring digital music hardware options

Wouldn't it be great to walk from your kitchen to your bedroom, then down to your family room, and be hearing music throughout your house? What if you could be listening to Miles Davis in your home office while your daughter listens to her favorite music in her bedroom? You can have all of this, using your wireless network, your PC, and networked digital music players.

This chapter explores the ins and outs of listening to music stored on your PC, anywhere in your home. You've invested your time and money to buy and download music from iTunes, Microsoft's Zune service, Rhapsody, or other music services. Or maybe you've spent all that time ripping your massive CD collection onto your PC. Sure, you can listen to it in your portable music player, but why not listen to it on your home theater system, too?

Serving Up Your Digital Music

You've been busy ripping your entire CD collection using your favorite music player software. You've also bought digital music, perhaps from a variety of sources. That iPod or Zune player is an inseparable companion. But you can't help thinking that something is missing, as you pop one of your music CDs into your CD player in your home entertainment system.

Stop right there. Why are you still using CDs to play music on your large format audio speakers? You can have your entire digitally ripped music collection, with your customized playlists, playing on those superb-sounding home theater speakers that grace your living room. Banish your CD player forever, and replace it with a modern digital music player.

Dealing with DRM

One of the problems with iTunes and other paid music services was the issue of content protection, known as DRM (digital rights management.) A song bought from the iTunes store was almost always protected with Apple's own DRM scheme, known as FairPlay. Although you could play that music on Apple players — iPods and iPhones — you couldn't play protected music on networked devices.

Note that both WMA and AAC can have DRM assigned to specific music files. Networked digital music players usually cannot play DRMed content, so I suggest either paying a little extra money to buy DRM-free music, ripping your music from CD or burning an audio CD, then re-ripping that CD into a DRM-free format.

Recently, though, Apple has removed content protection from most iTunes music. There's still a lot of music out there on players that still have FairPlay DRM, however, so unless all those users re-buy their music, FairPlay will be with us for some time.

The choice of the best digital music player depends on what digital format you've been using for your music, which I discussed in Chapter 1 of this minibook. The other piece of the puzzle is how music is delivered from your PC (or another source, such as network attached storage) to your home entertainment system. That also depends on the digital music format you use and what software.

Using music software

More people use iTunes than any other digital music application. It's available on both Macintosh- and Windows-based PCs. iTunes is tightly linked to the iTunes Store, where content can be purchased for instant download. But you can also use iTunes to rip your CD collection.

iTunes uses two different formats, depending on how you rip the music from your CD. One is known as Advanced Audio Coding (AAC), the other is Apple Lossless. Apple Lossless offers better sound quality, because its compression doesn't throw away data. AAC, like MP3, discards what it thinks is redundant data. Usually, the result can sound pretty good, but I'd suggest using the highest possible bit rate for the best results.

Microsoft's Windows Media Player and the Zune player both use Windows Media Audio (WMA) audio format. Windows Media also offers a lossless compression option for the best possible sound quality.

One other option for lossless compression is known as FLAC (free lossless audio codec). FLAC is, as the acronym hints, free. It's widely supported by many digital media players, but you need either a plug-in for Windows Media Player or some standalone application to rip your collection into FLAC format.

You can use a number of ways to get your music from your PC to your home entertainment center; all do require additional hardware. I look at two examples of how you can do this: Logitech's Squeezebox and the Sonos Music System.

The Logitech Squeezebox

The original Squeezebox was developed by a company called Slim Devices prior to being acquired by peripheral manufacturer Logitech. The philosophy behind the Squeezebox was to make it simple to play your digital music anywhere in the house and to make the options flexible.

Currently, a number of Squeezebox products exist: Squeezebox Classic, Squeezebox Duet, Squeezebox Touch, Squeezebox Radio, the Squeezebox Boom, and the Squeezebox Transporter. In this section, I cover how to set up the Squeezebox Duet, a compact, two-piece unit with a remote control that behaves much like a portable digital music player, shown in Figures 2-1 and 2-2.

The Duet's receiver fits easily into small spaces and connects up to either an A/V receiver or to powered speakers. In our hookup, the Squeezebox duet is connected to an A/V receiver equipped with a pair of stereo speakers.

Figure 2-1:
The Squeezebox Duet consist of the receiver box and a remote with iPod-like controls and a small LCD screen.

The Squeezebox can be connected via Wi-Fi but also has a built-in wired Ethernet connection. Audio output is either through a pair of analog stereo RCA connectors (for powered speakers) or your choice of digital coax or digital optical cables (for connecting to an A/V receiver).

That's the Squeezebox Duet hardware. I show you how to use the hardware shortly. But first, you have to set up the software that enables music play-back on the Squeezebox, which is called *SqueezeCenter*. (You may see references online to *Slimserver*, which is the old name for SqueezeCenter.)

Setting up SqueezeCenter

You can install SqueezeCenter from the CD that ships with the Squeezebox or download the latest version from the Logitech Web site (`www.logitech.com`).

The installer is a standard Windows installer, so after launching the installation, just click next and pick the default locations. At the end of the installation process, SqueezeCenter will launch. SqueezeCenter is actually a Web-based application, so don't be surprised if your favorite Web browser fires up at this point.

Now you have to make a decision: Where is your music?

Most people have their digital music stored in whatever default location used by their digital music software. For iTunes running in Windows Vista, that's usually Users⇨<your user name>⇨Music⇨iTunes⇨iTunes Music. For Zune, it's Users⇨<your user name>⇨Music⇨Zune.

Alternatively, you may choose to have your music live on a home server or network-attached storage device (NAS.) That's my choice for storing music. It's convenient, safer than my desktop PC, since the NAS unit offers redundant storage, and accessible even when my PC is turned off. However, SqueezeCenter does require your PC to be running.

To use a network storage location, you first need to set up your network location as if it were a hard drive on your local PC; this is known as *mapping a network drive.* Simply open up your network location as you usually do, then right-click on the network folder and choose Map Network Drive, as shown in Figure 2-3.

Windows Vista calls user directories simply "music" or documents. Windows XP called its user folder "My Documents" or "My Music." Windows 7 returns to this naming convention. So the iTunes music folder above would be Users⇨<your user name>⇨My Music⇨iTunes⇨iTunes Music.

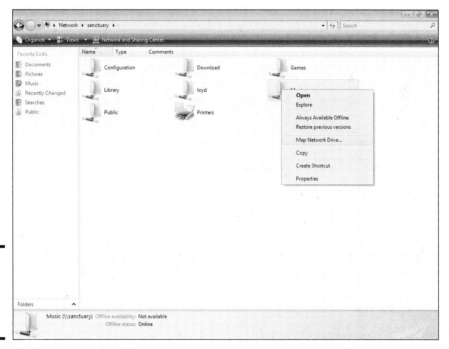

Figure 2-3:
Mapping a network drive to a drive letter

For the purpose here, I assigned drive letter G: to the music folder on the network. Any drive letter will do.

Now that a drive letter is assigned, let's set up SqueezeCenter. If the application hasn't already launched, go ahead and run it from the icon on your desktop or the start menu. I'm skip the Internet access bits for the time being and get to what that means in Book VII, Chapter 4. Right now, you just want to play the music you've stored on our local system or home network.

1. **Because my own music is ripped in Windows Media Lossless format, I click the first check box. If you're an iTunes user, click the second box, which allows SqueezeCenter to use iTunes. (See Figure 2-4.)**

2. **The next two steps look identical: Choose a folder for your music location and then repeat the step for your playlist location.**

   In most cases, your music and playlists are in the same root folder. If you've stored your playlists in a different location than your music, you need to specify this in the second window, Local Playlist Folder shown in Figure 2-5.

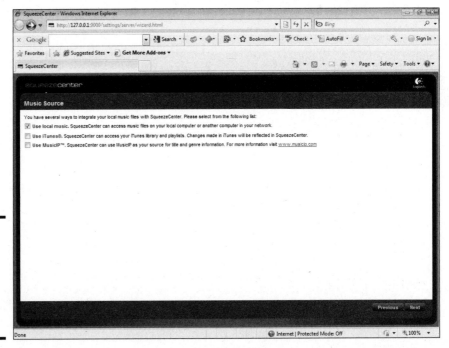

Figure 2-4:
Squeeze-
Center
setup:
choosing
your media
type

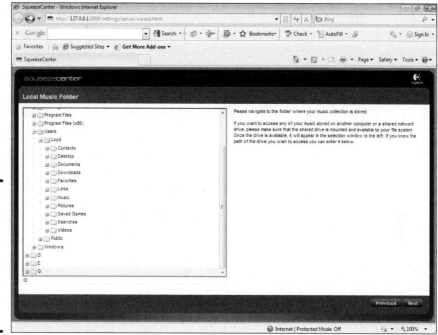

Figure 2-5:
Squeeze-
Center
setup:
choosing
your music
and playlist
folder
location.

When you click next after choosing your music folder, the screen will look the same, but the screen title changes to Choose Playlist Folder.

3. **Now you can just click through.**

SqueezeCenter scans your music folders, which can take a few minutes or over an hour, depending on how much music you have. Eventually, you'll see the main SqueezeCenter screen populated with album art (if you click on "Albums"). (See Figure 2-6.)

SqueezeCenter for network storage

Customized versions of the SqueezeCenter exist for non-Windows PCs and other digital appliances. For example, a version exists for NETGEAR's ReadyNAS line of network-attached storage devices, which have a version of SqueezeCenter running directly on the ReadyNAS hardware. If you have such a supported device, then your Squeezebox can play music directly from the NAS device, and you don't need to have your PC running. Check the Logitech support site for more information. Note that the number of devices supported is limited, so if you like this idea, make sure the NAS box you're considering supports SqueezeCenter.

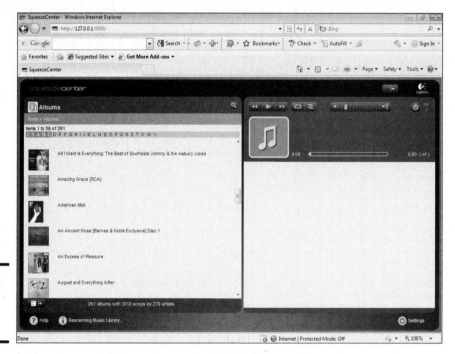

Figure 2-6:
Squeeze-
Center
running

Setting up your Squeezebox Duet

Connecting up the Squeezebox hardware is simple:

Attach the analog stereo RCA cable or the correct digital cable to the input
on the powered speaker or receiver. For example, on my system, I have the
Squeezebox connected via a copper RCA digital coax cable to an input on my
Onkyo A/V receiver — one that's set up normally for a CD player.

If you've just unpacked the Squeezebox Duet, plug in the charging stand and
charge the remote control for a few hours. The unit ships with two small
power bricks — one for the remote charging cradle and the other for the
Duet receiver. While the receiver needs to be near your home audio system,
the charging stand for the cradle can be located anywhere in your home.

While the physical connections are easy, connecting to your wireless network is a little more work. The Duet Remote has a small color LCD display
and controls that allow you to navigate through the setup process. Stepping
through the setup is pretty straightforward, but you have to know three
things to connect the Squeezebox:

✦ **Your SSID.** The SSID is the name that your router assigns to the wireless network. It may be something as simple as your router's model name (such as D-Link DGL-4500) or some name you entered when you first set up the router.

✦ **Your security code.** If you're using WEB or WPA security, to prevent outside intruders from gaining access to your router, you'll need to enter the WEP or WPA key.

✦ **The system name or IP address of the system that's hosting the SqueezeCenter software.** Note that the Squeezebox remote will try to find this, but you may need to manually enter it.

All this assumes your router is set up to automatically assign IP addresses to new devices on the network — most routers do.

After your Squeezebox is connected to the network, you can use the scroll wheel and buttons to easily navigate to albums, artists, or playlists and begin listening to your digital music collection on your home audio system. Now you can enjoy your audio collection using the full range of your best speakers.

Using the Sonos Music System

The Squeezebox is a cool standalone digital music player, but what if you want to have your digital music play back in multiple locations throughout your home? One solution is the Sonos Music System (`www.sonos.com`.)

The Sonos Music System can be wired or wireless but works very well in a wireless environment. Each Sonos unit can find other Sonos devices on the network, creating what's known as a *mesh network*. If you have a large house that may have spotty Wi-Fi coverage, each Sonos box can relay the signal to the next one, filling in those Wi-Fi holes in your network coverage.

Why would you want a Sonos system? Simple: It's easy to control multiple ZonePlayers using a single remote control. You can have different ZonePlayers play different songs or playlists in different rooms. If you like, you can add additional remotes, so your spouse can have his or her own. But one remote can control multiple players, wirelessly (see Figure 2-7). And the remote is not an IR remote, but uses a radio signal, so you don't need line of sight.

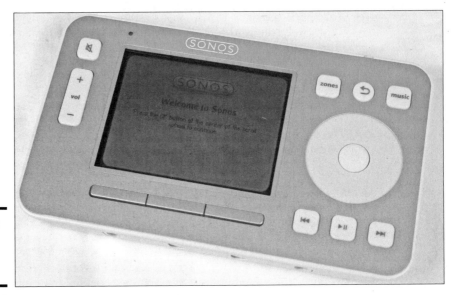

Figure 2-7:
The Sonos
remote
control.

The basic Sonos bundle consists of a ZonePlayer 120, a ZonePlayer 90 (Figure 2-8), and a controller. The ZP120 actually has a built-in digital amplifier, so you can connect them to bookshelf speakers anywhere in the house. The ZP90 is designed to connect to either powered speakers or a home audio system with an A/V receiver.

Figure 2-8:
The Sonos
ZP90 does
require
either
amplified
speakers or
connection
to an A/V
system.

Setting up a Sonos system is even simpler than setting up a Squeezebox. First, plug in the remote control cradle into wall power and charge the control unit. While that's charging, set up the ZonePlayers. In my house, I used a pair of ZP90s attached to two different rooms. One was attached to my home theater system, with a large A/V receiver and a 7.1 surround sound system. The other was attached to a smaller powered receiver that only had stereo speakers.

In both cases, the ZP90s were connected to the receivers via digital audio connections.

Once the remote is charged and the ZonePlayers connected, you pop the Sonos installation CD into your PC and run the setup application. Follow the prompts — they're very simple.

During setup, the Sonos software will locate all the ZonePlayers and config-ure them. You may need to verify a player's existence by walking up to it and pressing a button on the front during setup. (See Figure 2-9.)

As with SqueezeCenter, you need to tell the Sonos software the location of all your digital music files, which can be on the local PC or on a network storage device.

**Book VII
Chapter 2**

**Streaming Digital
Music in Your Home**

Figure 2-9: The Sonos software interface. You can set up playlists and manage music on your PC.

Unlike the SqueezeCenter, the Sonos natively recognizes file systems on network-attached storage devices. So if your music is on an NAS device, you don't need to have your PC running.

Sonos now offers an iPhone/iPod Touch application to control ZonePlayers, so you don't even need to use the bulkier Sonos control unit, though the Sonos remote is a little easier to use than the iPhone app.

At first, spending $999 or more on a Sonos bundle seems pricey. After you get whole-house audio running, controlled by a single remote control, you'll wonder why it costs so little.

A Word on Audio Quality

The era of digital music began when most people connected to the Internet via 56kb per second (or slower) modems. At that time, a 40GB hard drive was considered huge. So it was natural that the first digital music formats available on the Internet were highly compressed files.

When iTunes first started, the only format supported by the iTunes store was 128kbps AAC audio. On some music, you could actually hear artifacts in the music created when the compression software threw away what it thought was empty data.

Now, you have high-speed broadband connections and hard drives as large as 2TB. There's no need to squeeze your music so hard that it loses real data.

Today, several formats exist that compress audio *losslessly*. This means that any data that represents actual music is retained. However, music compressed with WMA Pro Lossless, Apple Lossless, or FLAC (free lossless audio codec) are considerably larger than the highly compressed music you buy from the iTunes or Zune stores.

If you like the idea of lossless compression, you can set iTunes, Windows Media Player, or the Zune Player to compress in the company's respective lossless format. One source for buying digital music is losslessly encoded, MusicGiants (www.musicgiants.com). The library at MusicGiants isn't as large as the iTunes or Zune stores, however.

After broadband becomes ubiquitous, maybe losslessly compressed options will become part of the mainstream stores as well. Your ears will thank you.

Chapter 3: Networking Your Television: From PC to HDTV

In This Chapter

✔ Understanding PC video formats

✔ Maximizing your viewing experience

✔ Digital Media Adapters: Getting video from the PC to your HDTV

✔ Game consoles for watching PC video

Streaming video over wireless networks is much more challenging than audio. Even full CD audio only pushes 176KB (that's kilobytes) per second — hardly enough to challenge even an old 802.11b network in home environments. Newer 802.11g or 802.11b networks can handle multiple users and multiple CD-quality audio streams.

Video is another beast entirely. DVD-quality video, which is already compressed with the lossy MPEG-2 codec, can consume as much as 9.8MB, or over 1.2MB. If you're thinking about streaming high-definition video, you're looking at bit rates that can approach 20 Mbps. Some pristine, well-mastered Blu-ray discs approach 40 Mbps.

Then there's the issue of quality of service. Quality of service, or QoS, is a nebulous term that tries to capture the idea that your video should look good. If you've ever watched a video streamed from the Internet, and noticed lots of interruptions or breakups in the picture, that's poor quality of service. All the bandwidth in the world isn't useful if your video stream keeps getting interrupted. Modern wireless routers and streaming applications are built to try to maintain a high level of QoS.

In this chapter, I show you how to maximize your viewing enjoyment while streaming video captured on your PC to your living room over your network. You find out about video formats, how to enhance your PC to maximize throughput, and examine a couple of sample scenarios using existing hardware.

Understanding PC Video Formats

As with audio, video is captured and stored on your PC in multiple different formats. My goal is not to exhaustively cover all possible formats, but to explain the basic concepts in the context of getting that video from your PC to your home entertainment center.

In the old, pre-digital TV days, television was broadcast in purely analog formats. If you wanted to record and store an analog TV signal on your PC, it needed to be digitized. A number of different encoding methods emerged to convert the analog TV signal to digital format.

The key commonality is that all of these formats used some form of compression — usually lossy compression, which meant some of the data was actually discarded. Techniques such as MPEG-1, MPEG-2, WMV, and H.264 can predict what the pixel will look like five frames after the current one is displayed, so don't try to save the pixels in the four intervening frames.

What this actually means is that lossy compression can help reduce the bandwidth needed to stream video. Unfortunately, HDTV streams are *already* heavily compressed. A typical over-the-air high-definition broadcast can hit 20 Mbps. A cable or satellite HD stream ranges from 5 to 13 Mbps.

Windows Media Center in Windows Vista and Windows 7 can capture high-definition broadcasts using PC capable tuners. If you want to capture digital cable TV shows, you need a tuner capable of ClearQAM capture. Those shows need to be unencrypted.

There are PC models built with Windows Vista that can use CableCard to capture premium shows which are encrypted by the cable TV provider. But you have to buy those PCs as a unit — you can't add CableCard support to an existing PC.

Of course, you won't want to simply watch TV shows streamed from your PC. While the PC can work perfectly well as a DVR (digital video recorder), it's more interesting to use the PC to store and show videos you, your family, and friends have shot using digital and high-definition camcorders.

However you get the video into your PC, the tricky part is streaming it from your PC to your family room.

Using a PC to Maximize Your Viewing Experience

Before diving into how to display the video streamed from the PC to the home entertainment system, I need to talk about the PC that will be delivering the video.

People often just take whatever PC is handy — the home office PC, their laptop — and try to stream video to the TV from a general purpose PC. The result is often choppy video with strange compression artifacts. Now, you don't need a dedicated video server. Your home office PC might be good enough, but you'll need to tweak it a bit for best delivery of video content.

Here's a brief rundown on common digital video formats:

✦ **MPEG (including MPEG-1, MPEG-2, and MPEG-4):** Developed by the Motion Pictures Expert Group, the various MPEG formats are perhaps the most common encoding scheme. DVDs use MPEG-2; some Blu-ray discs are encoded in MPEG-4. Satellite and cable TV often deliver their video in MPEG-4 format.

✦ **WMV (Windows Media Video):** Microsoft's proprietary video compression format.

✦ **H.264:** This is a variant of MPEG-4, used in some Blu-ray movies and online video.

✦ **AVCHD:** This format is common to high-definition camcorders and is actually one form of H.264/MPEG-4.

✦ **DiVX:** This compression format is most commonly used on the Web, so if you download videos from the Web to your PC, they may be DiVX encoded.

✦ **Flash and Silverlight:** These are almost exclusively used for streaming video over the Web, and it's unlikely you'll be doing much downloading of Flash or Silverlight video. Flash is a proprietary video format owned by Adobe, while Silverlight is a Microsoft product.

✦ **AVI, QuickTime, and Transport Streams:** These are container formats — that is, they are wrappers around a compressed video stream (like MPEG, WMV, or DiVX). If you've ever wondered why your system can play some AVI files but not others, it's probably because the codec (*compressor-decompressor*) needed to decode a particular format isn't on your system.

To properly decompress and view a video file, you'll need the right codec software. As noted above, just because you can play a container format like QuickTime doesn't mean that you have the correct codec. Modern operating systems, like Windows 7, have become much smarter about codec support, so it's worth running Windows 7 if only to avoid having to hunt and download the right codec to playback your video.

CPUs versus GPUs

You may have heard that graphics processors — the chip that powers the graphics card in your system — are capable of handling those processor intensive transcoding chores. That's true, to an extent. A high-end graphics processor, such as an AMD Radeon 4890 or Nvidia 260 GTX Core 216, is actually a lot faster at most video transcoding than even fast quad-core CPU. However, only a few applications support the use of video cards for transcoding on the fly, and none of them are streaming applications — yet. But it's worth keeping an eye on this rapidly developing area.

Now that you have some understanding of video formats, you need to know what your eventual target device will be. For example, if you know that you're using a Windows Media Center extender, you know it will support Windows Media Video, MPEG-1, MPEG-2, and possibly MPEG-4. It may not directly support AVCHD, which is the format that high-definition camcorders use. For our purposes, this is really all you need to know about compression schemes.

If you are sure all formats you use are directly supported by the digital media adapter, then the PC just becomes responsible for streaming the data. That's a fairly straightforward process, and optimizing for sending out one or two video streams is fairly simple — I'll get to the specific shortly.

On the other hand, if your target device doesn't support the format directly, you'll need software on the PC that will *transcode* the format on the PC to one that the display device will understand, then stream it to the device. What's more, the transcoding will typically happen in real time.

It works like this. As you request a video from your PC, the PC knows that it needs to transcode the file to a format the display hardware understands. The transcoding is performed on the fly and then streamed to the TV. Some software needs to do this every time the video is streamed. Other software will cache the transcoded files, so the next time you want to watch, it becomes an exercise in simply streaming the file.

All this sounds complicated, but the right combination of hardware, once properly set up, just works. All the transcoding, streaming, and other background tasks occur silently, without fuss, when you press the Select button on your remote control to play the video.

Maximizing streaming performance

You want the video stream to flow without interruptions. Ensuring your PC can send the video stream consistently, and without hiccups, is fairly straightforward. Here's what you need to do:

✦ **Set up a regular schedule to defragment the hard drive.** As video is recorded to the system's hard drive, then deleted, then re-recorded, parts of newly recorded videos can be spread out over large areas of the drive. This can result in poor streaming performance and choppy playback.

✦ **Use a big hard drive.** If you're capturing high-definition video streams, the bigger the hard drive, the better. Part of the problem is that a drive that's almost full (or more than three-quarters full) tends to fragment more easily.

✦ **Minimize background services.** This is particularly true if you have an older or lower performing processor. For example, a typical desktop PC really doesn't need to run SmartCard services, telephony services, remote desktop services, Tablet Input Services, and others. Shutting those down will save memory and CPU cycles.

Maximizing transcoding performance

If your needs require the system to transcode a file into a different format before streaming, then you'll need a beefy CPU and lots of memory. If you can swing a midrange quad-core processor or a high-end dual-core CPU, and 4GB of RAM, you'll be in good shape.

This is particularly true if you plan on transcoding and streaming high-definition formats. For that, you'll definitely want a quad-core CPU, with at least 4GB of RAM, running a 64-bit operating system.

Why a 64-bit OS? The streaming and transcoding apps, like those that ship with products like the Sage TV HD Media Extender, aren't really 64-bit apps yet. But a 64-bit operating system (such as Windows 7 Home Premium 64-bit) actually gives a little more memory to 32-bit applications. And it won't be long before media applications move to 64-bit.

Of course, you'll also want to apply the tips and tricks I mentioned earlier for purely streaming applications as well.

Now that you've taken a look at video formats and system tuning, let's look at three examples of hardware and software combinations for watching PC video on your HDTV.

Media Center Extenders

I'm using the term *media center extenders* generically, not just the Microsoft Windows Media Center variety. I show you two scenarios. One is based on a Windows Media Center Extender by D-Link. The other is the Sage HD Media

Extender. Then I'll look at the issue of using a game console to stream video from the PC to the HDTV. Figure 3-1 shows some example hardware.

Sage TV HD Media Extender

Sage TV has made something of a reputation for being an alternative to Microsoft's Windows Media Center. On the one hand, the user interface tends to be just a little less polished than Windows Media Center. On the other hand, it's more powerful and flexible, allowing for heavy customization and offering very granular settings.

While you can use the Sage TV software on our PC, our focus here is using it in conjunction with Sage TV HD Media Extender. Setup is somewhat convoluted. First, you need to install two pieces of software on the PC that serves up the content: Sage TV and Sage TV Placeshifter. Installed along with Sage TV is the Sage TV server. The server is somewhat inflexible in that all content must reside on the PC where Sage TV is running. So you can't use network-attached storage to store your video content.

What Sage TV offers is control over a vast array of features. The setup menu is one of the most complete I've ever seen (see Figure 3-2).

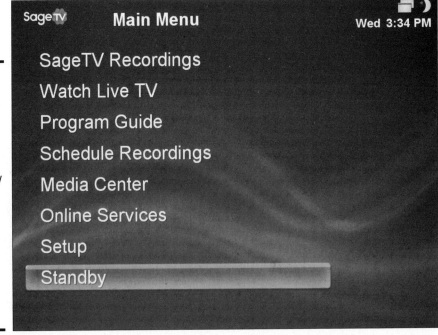

Figure 3-1: Streaming video hardware: from top to bottom, the Xbox 360, the Sage TV HD Media Extender, and the D-Link HSM-750 Windows Media Center Extender.

SageTV   **Main Menu**   Wed 3:34 PM

SageTV Recordings

Watch Live TV

Program Guide

Schedule Recordings

Media Center

Online Services

Setup

Standby

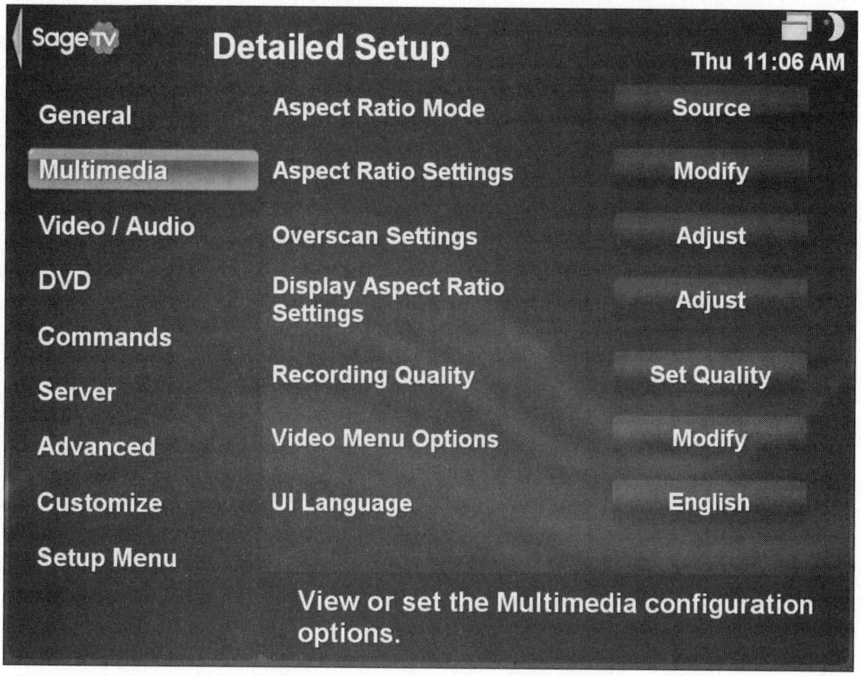

Figure 3-2:
Sage TV's
setup menu
offers a
wealth of
detailed
settings.

Each submenu within Sage TV breaks options down into very granular detail. You can adjust overscan settings (useful if the PC is attached directly to a TV), pick the DVD rendering method, and more (see Figure 3-3).

The real problem is trying to figure out which settings are actually important. It's best to leave things at their default settings when you first start, then adjust settings as needed. For the most part, though, you can leave the PC software at their defaults and make changes in the Sage TV HD Media Center setup screen.

Many of these settings exist because of the differences in PC hardware. The Sage TV HD Media Extender itself also has a rich set of options you can change, though it's somewhat simpler since the hardware is a known quantity. The menus themselves, however, look and operate in a similar way, but you'll use the remote control to configure settings, rather than a mouse and keyboard.

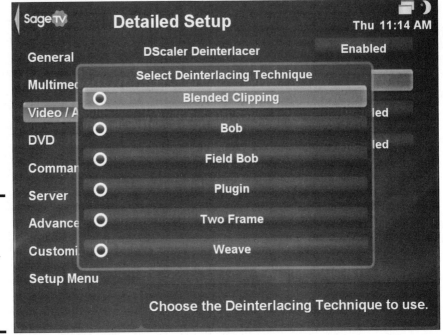

Figure 3-3:
Digging
deep with
Sage TV —
setting up
deinter-
lacing
settings.

Installing the hardware itself is simple. You can use the included analog cables, but it's much better to attach the device to your system using an HDMI cable. An HDMI cable doesn't ship with the unit, so you'll need to obtain one separately.

Getting the unit running with the Sage TV software is an exercise in running back and forth between the computer and the location where the HD Media Center is installed. You need to enter a code in the Media Center Extender that's supplied by the Sage TV software, and that particular HD Media Center extender is locked to that specific PC.

After recording shows off the air, the Sage TV server software streams the media to the HD Media Extender. Note that the software doesn't transcode formats, so if you have a video or audio format that's not recognized by the HD Media Extender, the video won't play back.

Once the device is set up, using the extender is pretty straightforward. You use the remote to navigate the onscreen menus, playing back recorded content, as you would any digital video recorder.

D-Link Wireless N HD Media Center Extender

Most flavors of Windows Vista and Windows 7 used by consumers have built-in support for Microsoft Windows Media Center. Table 3-1 sorts out the different Windows versions.

Table 3-1:	Windows Versions with Media Center	
Windows XP	*Windows Vista*	*Windows 7*
Windows Media Center Edition	Home Premium	Home Premium
Windows Media Center 2005	Ultimate	Professional
		Ultimate

Windows Media Center Extenders are pretty much what they sound like — you're essentially running Windows Media Center remotely, on dedicated hardware.

The D-Link Wireless N HD Media Center, also known as the D-Link HSM-750, is one such gadget. It attaches to your HDTV or A/V receiver via either HDMI or analog video. Curiously, if you use HDMI for video, you still need to attach a digital audio cable (either optical or coax) to your TV or receiver for audio; the HSM-750 uses HDMI for video only.

When you plug in the HSM-750 to a power outlet and turn it on, a Windows Media Center–equipped PC will automatically discover the device through Windows Universal plug-and-play capability, if the device is plugged into a wired network. If you're planning on using the wireless option, you need to first configure the HSM-750 to connect to your wireless network, entering the SSID and security information (WEP or WPA key). After that's done, the Windows system can discover the Media Center extender. (See Figure 3-4.)

Follow these steps to finish the process:

1. **Click on the bubble to open a dialog box.**

If you simply want to use the default settings, just click on the button labeled Allow, shown in Figure 3-5.

2. **The next step is to connect the Windows Center software with the Windows Media Center extender.**

When you first start up the extender, one of the setup screens should walk you through this. If not, scroll through the user interface with the remote and select setup, then select the Windows Media Center icon and press the OK button. You are eventually presented with an eight-digit key, which you'll write down and enter on the PC. (See Figure 3-6.)

3. **After entering the eight-digit key, you can click Next several times to accept the defaults, shown in Figure 3-7.**

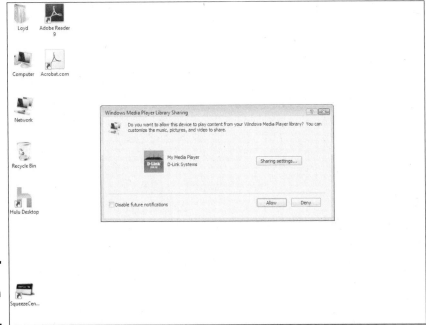

Figure 3-5:
Just click on
Allow.

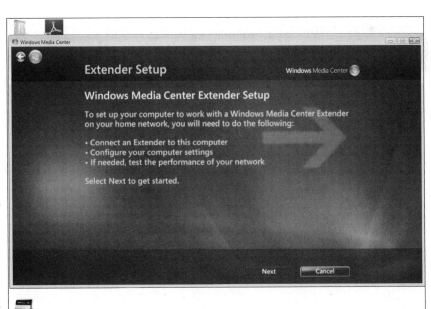

Figure 3-6:
Just click
next to
start the
process of
connecting
the extender
to the PC.

Figure 3-7:
Enter the
eight-digit
key supplied
by the
Windows
Media
Center
extender.

4. **You also want to configure additional options on the extender, including aspect ratio (usually 16:9 for an HDTV).**

    Once connected, the HSM-750 behaves much like a Windows Media Center PC. The user interface behaves much the same. However, the HSM-750 may not support all the file and compression formats that the PC might support. For example, Microsoft's own Windows Media Lossless compression codec for audio isn't supported.

    The HSM-750 can also act as a more general digital media adapter. If you're an iTunes user, you can navigate (outside of the Windows Media Center interface) to any PC running iTunes. You'll have to enable sharing in iTunes, but then you can play your ripped or non-DRM music. Network-attached storage with built-in iTunes or plug-and-play capability are also visible to the Media Center extender.

    Finally, the HSM-750 connects to a number of different online streaming services, such as Youtube, so you can watch content directly streamed from the Internet, no PC needed.

Game Consoles as Digital Media Adapters

Game consoles can be used as general purpose digital media extenders. I'm not going to walk through the setup process for these consoles, but I will discuss each of the major consoles that support Media Center capabilities briefly.

Original Xbox

In its out-of-the-box form, Microsoft's first Xbox lacked any Media Center capability. However, since the system was essentially a cut-down PC, enterprising programmers developed XMBC (originally the Xbox Media Center). XBMC is an open source project that's free.

The XBMC team strongly suggests that the Xbox have a *mod chip* installed. This is an aftermarket chip that's installed in the Xbox to bypass some of the DRM and other restrictions imposed by Microsoft. Installing a mod chip voids the warranty, but since most Xboxes are out of warranty by now, that's not a big deal. You also can't call Microsoft for help.

Also, XBMC doesn't support high-definition playback unless the Xbox has been modified to upgrade the CPU.

For more on XBMC, check out http://xbmc.org.

Xbox 360

The Xbox 360 can connect as a Media Center extender in several ways. A Windows-based PC running Windows Media Connect (available with Windows Media Player 11 or later) can connect to an Xbox 360. Navigation is a little cumbersome, but it all works fairly well.

If the PC is a Windows Media Center capable PC, the Xbox 360 can also act as a Windows Media Center extender, similar to the D-Link HSM-750. Configuring the Xbox 360 Windows Media Extender is like any WMC extender hardware — generate an eight-digit code, enter it on the PC, and you're off and running.

You can extend the capabilities of Windows Media Center 11 by adding an application called TVersity (www.tversity.com) on your PC. TVersity will even transcode formats that the Xbox 360 doesn't natively understand into supported formats before streaming.

All in all, the Xbox 360 is a versatile media center extender, whose capabilities can be enhanced by third-party software.

Sony PlayStation 3

The PlayStation 3 is a DLNA (Digital Living Network Alliance) capable device. DLNA builds on the Universal plug-and-play standard to allow easy communication between disparate devices and PCs with media stored on them.

The PS3 is a capable media center extender, but lacks some of the tighter integration available with the Xbox 360. But if you have DLNA compliant media server software on the PC, or DLNA-enhanced network-attached storage, it's easy to navigate and playback media. As of Windows 7, Windows Media Connect is DLNA compliant, so you don't need third-party software if you're playing back supported formats.

Chapter 4: Listening to Music and Audio from the Web

In This Chapter

✔ Finding good entertainment on the Web

✔ Watching on your PC

The world of audio and video is changing. In the past 30 years, we saw the shift from broadcast TV to cable and satellite sources. Now, we're starting to see the shift to Internet-based channels for TV and music. It's even possible to forego paid services and get all your entertainment from the Web.

Alas, it's not easy. There are a huge variety of sources, from user-created content like YouTube to repackaging of commercial TV and movies on Hulu. Help is at hand, however, with software that can help you sort through the choices and stream the content you want to watch directly to your TV from the PC.

In addition, companies that make Blu-ray players and HDTVs are now building the capability into their sets to directly access some of the content streamed from the Internet.

The biggest problem is the walls that content providers put up. Want to watch NASCAR? You need to go to www.ESPN.com. Trying to find your favorite movies? Hulu is one place — but not all movies are on Hulu.

In this chapter, I show you how to find that content plus explore some sources for music and video. Then I take a look at the hardware you might need to get that Internet content from your PC to the TV. Finally, we'll take a look at some software packages that make life a little easier in getting your favorite audio or video to your home entertainment center.

Finding Content

The show you want to watch is almost certainly somewhere out there on the Internet. We're not talking about illegal downloads. Instead, there's a wealth of video and music legally available for your entertainment pleasure.

The problem is finding all that content. Sure, you can search on Google or Bing to find a particular show, but doing so is a tedious process.

This issue of locating your favorite shows exists because the content providers seriously guard their intellectual property. So they put up walls that make it difficult to get to what you want to watch from a single source.

Progress is slowly being made to aggregate all the balkanized world of copyrighted video, movies, and music. Some of these solutions require a particular piece of hardware, while others are software based. Finding the best solution for your viewing and listening pleasure is still something of a compromise, but instead of dozens of Web sites, all you need is a PC and the right hardware attached to your home theater system.

In the next section, I begin with solutions that exist on the PC for watching movies, TV, and listening to music available on the Web. Then I show you how you can get that from the PC to the living room.

Watching on Your PC

You've almost certainly watched hilarious or moving user-created videos on YouTube. If you want to watch commercially produced shows, however, you need to look elsewhere.

Two providers of streaming content that also rent or sell hard goods, such as DVDs, are Netflix (www.netflix.com) and Amazon (www.amazon.com). I take a closer look at the Netflix streaming service shortly.

Recently, Hulu, shown in Figure 4-1, has become increasingly popular. Hulu. com is a Web site that aggregates vast amounts of video — movies, TV shows, trailers, short subjects — into one easy-to-navigate site. Like broadcast television, Hulu pays for the shows by requiring you to watch advertisements. The good news is that Hulu ads are generally shorter and less intrusive than broadcast TV ads.

If you are a serious sports fan, or perhaps love watching NASCAR, the individual Web sites for the different leagues will often stream video. For example, if you want to subscribe to an entire season of baseball, you can head over to the Major League Baseball site, www.MLB.com. The sports sites, such as MLB.com, do a great job of integrating stats, video, and interactive features.

Figure 4-1:
Hulu lets
you watch
a variety of
movies and
TV shows
free, but
with short
ad breaks.

Sitting in front of your PC isn't the ultimate goal, however. You want to get that great streaming content onto your TV. There are ways of getting substantial amounts of entertainment to your living room with the right hardware — hardware that's easier to set up and use than a PC.

We're going to assume that you've got an HDTV and possibly an audio-video receiver and a surround sound speaker setup. It all looks and sounds great when watching broadcast shows or DVDs. I explain how to go further by streaming video in the next sections.

Using Xbox 360 for media

I touch on using the Xbox 360 as a Windows Media Center Extender (WMCE) in Chapter 3 of this minibook.

But the Xbox 360 offers additional streaming and downloadable video services. These include a variety of TV shows, music videos, independent videos, and movies. Some are somewhat obscure, some popular. Curiously lacking is sports content, which seems heavily weighted toward combat sports.

While some of the content is free, most of it is paid through Microsoft Points, Microsoft's attempt to manage pricing. If you can get the same content in different parts of the world, the point cost is the same — but the amount of money each point costs in real terms may differ. In the U.S. currently, 80 points is equivalent to one dollar.

Movies range in point costs from 200 points for older, obscure movies in standard definition to 480 points for newly released Hollywood movies. However, movies are rented — which means the movie is watchable for any number of viewings in the first 24 hours and expires after 14 days.

TV shows are another matter. Prices are widely divergent, ranging from free to a staggering 4400 points for the UFC Live show, one of a number of fighting shows on the 360. Unlike movies, TV shows don't expire, so you can keep them on the Xbox 360 hard drive as long as you want — as long as you have drive space available.

The issue of drive space is a crucial one. The original Xbox 360 Pro had a 20GB hard drive, barely large enough to hold a handful of high-definition TV shows. Watching a series — and keeping them on the system — was problematic. However, with TV shows, you can re-download a show to the same Xbox 360 if you've paid for it. The maximum amount of storage available is 120GB for the Xbox 360 Elite — better, but in the era of terabyte hard drives, hardly substantial.

Also available on the Xbox 360 is the Netflix Watch Instantly streaming service. You do have to have a Netflix subscription, and that subscription has to be a minimum $8.99 one, which leaves out those with a basic, two-disc per month plan.

You also need to set up the Watch Instantly queue on your PC using a Web browser. Although you can edit top lists in the Xbox 360 directly, it's a bit clumsy, so using the PC Web browser is still easier.

Standalone devices exist that can accept streaming media from the PC. These include Windows Media Center Extenders, such as D-Link's DSM-750, which supports 802.11n wireless connectivity. These devices generally layer some capability in addition to supporting WMC streaming from a PC. For example, the previously mentioned DSM-750 (Book VII Chapter 3) directly supports YouTube videos, provided your home has a broadband connection to the Internet.

Another interesting device is the SageTV HD Media Extender (www.sagetv.com). The SageTV HD Media Extender is a combination of the SageTV software running on the PC and the Media Extender hardware, which streams video captured by SageTV's software.

If all you want is Netflix Watch Instantly on your HDTV, Roku (`www.roku labs.com`) offers a $99 box that supports Netflix Watch Instantly plus Amazon's own Amazon Video on Demand service.

DLNA hardware

DLNA is an acronym for Digital Living Network Alliance. DLNA is both an organization of technology companies and a standard developed by that organization for sharing media between the PC, HDTV, music players, cameras, and other consumer electronic devices.

Hundreds of DLNA-certified devices, including a number of network-ready HDTV units, are available. DLNA is a pretty basic standard and has suffered from implementation differences between hardware manufacturers. In addition, even though the PC was a key component of the DLNA standard, no Microsoft Media Player or (see Figure 4-2) Windows Media Center supported the standard.

Figure 4-2: Windows Media Player 12 now supports DLNA 1.5 devices as part of its standard sharing protocol.

Having DLNA-compliant hardware means removing any intermediary devices. Although having a Windows Media Center Extender or game console has its own benefits, soon you'll be able to attach your HDTV, Blu-ray disc player, or set-top box to your network and stream content directly to your home entertainment system.

Some newer devices even have built-in services. For example, some LG HDTVs and Blu-ray players have the Netflix Watch Instantly service available on the unit.

Watching Internet TV in Your Living Room: PlayOn

Let's say you've got a Windows Media Center Extender (WMCE) or an Xbox 360 attached to your HDTV. Anything you can get on Windows Media Center on the PC is available in your console or WMCE device, right?

Not quite. As it turns out, services like Hulu and Netflix don't stream from Windows Media Center to an extender or console. However, software exists which takes those video streams, transcodes their formats into a format that your device can understand, and pipes it directly to your networked home theater.

The software is called PlayOn and is available from MediaMall Technologies (www.themediamall.com). PlayOn is a PnP (universal plug-and-play) media server that runs on the PC.

PlayOn supports a variety of streaming Internet services, including Hulu, YouTube, CBS, ESPN, CNN, and Netflix Watch Instantly. Setting up PlayOn is simple. You download the software from PlayOn's Web site and install it on your PC. (See Figure 4-3) Some services, such as Hulu, require login names and passwords, and you can enter these into the PlayOn configuration control panel. Others, like the CBS network, just stream directly from a virtual folder on the PC.

Figure 4-3:
PlayOn
Setup.
There are
relatively
few settings
you need to
worry about;
the defaults
work well
in almost all
cases.

PlayOn has two issues that keep it from being more widely used: minimum PC requirements and limited hardware playback support.

PlayOn converts video formats on the fly as they stream from the source on the Web, to a format that the playback device can understand, a process known as *transcoding*. What this means is that you need a pretty beefy system. PlayOn recommends a dual-core CPU with 2GB of RAM at a minimum for standard definition transcoding. High-definition transcoding requires a high-performance dual-core or quad-core CPU.

PlayOn support for playback devices is limited. Currently, PlayOn officially supports the following hardware for playback:

✦ DirecTV HR21-100 HD DVR and HR20 receiver

✦ D-Link DSM-510, DSM-520, and DSM-750 media extenders

✦ Pioneer Elite Pro-1140 HDTV

+ Popcom Hour A-100

+ SageTV HD Theater

+ VuNow VNHD100HD Hi-Def POD, VN100SD Std-Def POD

+ XBMC (Xbox Media Center)

+ Xbox 360

+ PlayStation 3

Other devices are unofficially supported, and you can find discussions about additional devices in the PlayOn forums.

PlayOn costs about $40, although they occasionally offer half-price specials on the MediaMall Web site. It's really an elegant solution, slowly garnering wider support on a variety of networked playback devices due to its PnP and DLNA support.

Radio Internet: Web Radio in the Living Room

A wealth of radio-style programming exists on the Internet. These range from traditional radio stations simulcasting over the Web, to podcasts, to a range of other audio services, like the music recommendation service Last.fm.

In Chapter 2, we talked about devices like the Logitech Squeezebox and the Sonos Music Player. If you have one of these products, or something similar, you should be comfortable streaming music from your PC. What about all that Internet radio?

Now, take a look at the Squeezebox Duet as an example of something that can also act as an Internet radio player. First, you need to create an account on Logitech's SqueezeNetwork (www.squeezenetwork.com).

After your account is created, you set it up in SqueezeCenter on your PC. Follow these steps:

1. **Click on the Settings button on the lower right of the SqueezeCenter main window, shown in Figure 4-4; then click the SqueezeCenter tab.**

2. **Enter your SqueezeNetwork login information and click Apply and then Close. (See Figure 4-5.)**

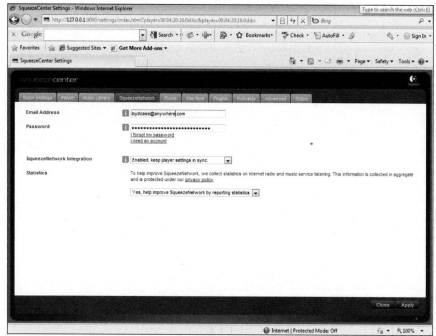

Figure 4-4:
The
Squeeze-
Network
login screen

3. **Now that your account information is entered, you can select SqueezeNetwork as one of the music sources.**

   You can do this in the SqueezeCenter browser or directly in the Squeezebox Duet.

   Other devices, such as those from Sonos or Roku, also allow access to Internet radio in your living room or family room.

   Internet radio and video have come a long way since the days of choppy, highly compressed content. Now you have access to a vast array of content, from traditional media sources to edgy, new media producers working out of their homes and garages. Grab that remote, plop yourself down, and take it all in.

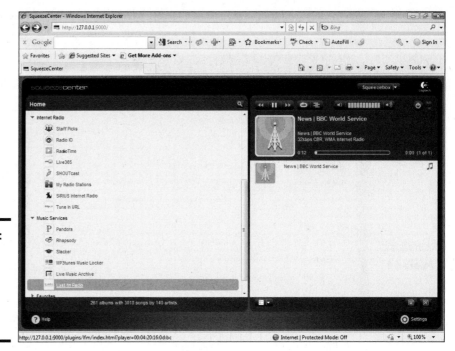

Figure 4-5:
Internet
Radio
playback
from
Squeeze-
Network.

Chapter 5: Exploring Digital TV and Satellite Radio

In This Chapter

✔ Understanding digital TV

✔ Deciphering HDTV terms and jargon

✔ Listening to satellite radio

*O*n June 12, 2009, a remarkable thing happened in the United States: All analog television signals vanished. The digital television revolution, which began years before, has reached its climax. The federally mandated switch to digital television ended the more than half-century reign of analog TV. Not only were the old, bulky CRT TVs a thing of the past, but the very way TV signals were transmitted and processed inside the TV had changed.

A similar revolution was also occurring in radio. Over-the-air digital radio lagged behind satellite radio services such as Sirius XM, but both satellite radio and the emerging over-the-air HD radio bring radio firmly into the 21st century. I'll look at the various options for digital television and radio, so you can understand the choices and better enjoy the wealth of digital content available from a wide variety of providers.

Making HDTV Choices

Purchasing a television used to be so simple. All you needed to know was what size you wanted. All analog TVs were built pretty much the same.

Then home theater became popular, and TVs became more complicated — but only a little. The TVs were still pretty much the same, although some big screen TVs used three small CRTs (cathode ray tubes) to project the image onto a screen, rather than one large CRT as the main screen. More choices of connections also became available. In addition to the little, yellow plug — composite video — you also had S-Video and component video. Many users simply connected their antenna or cable box directly to the antenna input on the TV.

Then HDTV arrived, and the complexity of choices exploded by an order of magnitude. Several different display technologies arrived on the scene, the number of ways to connect to those displays exploded, and confusion reigned. On top of that, different methods of delivery have competed for viewers' attention, including cable, over-the-air, and satellite television.

The latest wrinkles include direct streaming of video over the Internet, and Blu-ray, the replacement for the highly popular DVD disc format.

Part of the mix also includes multichannel audio — 5.1 or 7.1 surround sound — once the purview of movie theaters. Now that you can buy TVs as big as 65 or more inches (diagonally measured), adding surround sound brings the theater into your family room.

The key thing to remember is that if you don't have a TV with an over-the-air tuner, whether it's built into the TV itself, an external DTV converter box, or part of a cable or satellite digital tuner, then you cannot receive over-the-air (OTA) DTV and high-definition broadcasts. Whatever else you buy, don't forget this simple rule.

Understanding All Those Terms

The list of features that are printed on the side of an HDTV box seems to consist of a mind-numbing array of acronyms, numbers, and indecipherable terms. Surprisingly, you can ignore a lot of those features if all you want is a straightforward high-definition television. Many of the terms you see have more to do with issues like image quality or overall visual fidelity, rather than the basic stuff you need. In the following sections, I cover the basic terminology.

Display technology

When HDTV first became popular, flat panel TVs — plasma and LCD TVs — were very expensive. So rear projection was popular for a time. A rear projection system consists of a big screen inside a large box that's mostly air. Inside the box is a small projector that projects the image through a series of lenses and prisms onto the large screen.

Rear projection HDTV

Because you need all that volume, rear projection TVs are bulky, even though the technology used in the projectors is small. There were two main types of rear projection TVs that were popular: DLP (Digital Light Processing), a technology developed by Texas Instruments, and LCoS (liquid crystal on silicon). In actual practice the differences are minor, but LCoS TVs are pretty much extinct. DLP still exists, but mostly in very large screen HDTVs.

Rear projection TV is still a great bargain if you want a really big screen. You can typically buy a 65-inch or larger DLP RPTV for less than $2,000. Some other features, such as 3D movies (those movies that require you to use the special glasses) may serve to keep DLP alive for a time.

But the real action these days are flat panel TVs. Two different types of flat panel technologies coexist today: LCD and plasma. Plasma HDTVs have tiny cells, each of which behaves almost like a tiny CRT. LCD TVs are much like the flat panel screens used on personal computers, but much larger.

Flat panel TVs: Plasma versus LCD

Until recently, the differences in image quality between plasma and LCDs were substantial. LCD TVs were great in bright rooms but not so good for light-controlled environments — particularly a darkened room where you might be watching a high-definition movie with lots of low-light content. Plasmas were also much better for high-motion content, like sports.

Advances in LCD technologies have narrowed the gap considerably, though some differences still exist. Higher refresh rate — the speed at which frames are displayed on the screen — and new backlighting technologies, like LED backlighting, have made LCD TVs much more attractive. Today, the real difference is size: If you want something 50 inches and larger, plasmas are a better buy. On the other hand, 55-inch and smaller LCDs can be found at reasonable prices.

At that crossover size — 50 to 55 inches — the choice becomes a matter of taste. Better quality LCD TVs cost nearly as much as (sometimes more than) a good plasma.

One issue that dogged plasma TVs for years was the problem of *burn in*. If you left the TV on for a long time — say, on ESPN — that little ESPN "bug" at the lower right of the screen would eventually become a permanent ghost image that overlaid everything else. That problem no longer exists. Similarly, plasma TVs had a reputation of consuming more energy than LCD TVs, something that's a concern with green-aware consumers. But big LCD TVs use nearly as much juice as newer plasmas.

Both LCD TVs and plasma panels had issues with the overall life span, but today's models typically have life spans in excess of 50,000 hours to half-bright. That means a good eight years or more. The technology is evolving so rapidly, that you'll likely get a new TV before you notice any issues with fading images on plasma TVs.

Book VII Chapter 5

Exploring Digital TV and Satellite Radio

Ultimately, which technology you want is really a matter of preference and budget. The best advice is to take the time to view lots of content on the TVs you're considering before buying.

Resolution

Display resolution as it applies to HDTV is simply a measure of the number of pixels on the screen and is typically shown as (number of horizontal pixels) x (number of vertical pixels). For example, many large-screen LCDs are 1920 x 1080.

Early HDTVs shipped in a variety of resolutions, including oddball pixel formats such as 1366 x 768, 1440 x 900, and even 1024 x 1024 (using nonsquare pixels.) A number of digital TVs also supported something called EDTV (extended-definition TV), which was 720 x 480 pixels, but progressively scanned (see below). Thankfully, this silly bit of confusion has all but disappeared.

Today, it's much simpler: You typically have 1920 x 1080 and 1280 x 720. These are often shortened to 1080p and 720p.

That *p* stands for *progressive,* as in progressive scanning. Progressive scanning simply means that the display is generated by displaying the entire image at once. This differs from interlaced scanning, which displays alternate images that are actually one-half the frame height. You'll see references to 1080i, in which two images of 1920 x 540 are rapidly displayed in succession; each interlaced frame actually comprises one complete image frame.

This idea of interlaced versus progressive scanning is actually a holdover from the old days of CRT displays, when an electron beam painted the image on the screen by rapidly scanning the beam over the inside of the screen. Modern digital TVs can now just display the entire image at once.

Interlacing works because the two half-frames are thrown up on the screen so fast, your eye is fooled into seeing it as a single frame. This idea of progressive versus interlaced is important because broadcasters transmit HDTV images in either 720p or 1080i; there are no HDTV broadcasts in the U.S. that are 1080p.

Why, then, do you see so many larger displays that describe themselves as 1080p? That's because circuitry built into the TV itself combines the two interlaced half-frames into a single image *before* they're displayed; this is known as *deinterlacing.* While home theater enthusiasts often argue about how well different HDTVs deinterlace signals, most current generation TVs do it well enough that the majority of viewers don't notice problems.

The new Blu-ray high-definition disc standard, on the other hand, does support 1080p, so Blu-ray content can take advantage of the full resolution of a 1080p display.

The bottom line: if you're getting a larger HDTV — above 32 inches — it's a good idea to opt for 1080p display.

Understanding standard definition

Standard definition TV is simply TV as it was shot and produced before the HDTV era. All your old favorites were shot in standard definition. SDTV, as it's sometimes called, had very low resolution — 480i — and was designed to be displayed on old CRT televisions with electron beams that scanned across the interior of the tube.

This very low resolution relative to true HDTV is challenging for HDTVs to display well, but a good quality HDTV can at least show a presentable SDTV signal. Similarly, DVDs were also 480i, but the production quality of DVDs is typically much higher, so the problems aren't as glaring when watching DVD movies.

Understanding aspect ratio

While the issue of available resolution of HDTVs has simplified a bit, understanding aspect ratios is still a confusing topic. Aspect ratio is simply the horizontal resolution divided by the vertical resolution, and is typically displayed as (some number):(some number).

For example, 1920 x 1080, which is the maximum HDTV resolution, is 1.78:1 (sometimes also referred to as 16:9); 1280 x 720 is also 1.78:1. This ratio of 1.78:1 is actually built into the industry standard for HDTV.

So if all available HDTVs are 1.78:1, what's the big deal?

There are two sources of confusion: movies and standard definition TV.

Movies are shot in a variety of aspect ratios. In fact, there are too many to really discuss here; if you're interested in the topic of movie aspect ratios, a good source is the Widescreen.org aspect ratio page: www.widescreen.org/aspect_ratios.shtml.

Standard definition TV was modeled on the original Academy movie aspect ratio, or 4:3. You'll also see 4:3 reduced to 1.33:1 — either format is correct and means the same thing. Worse, standard definition TV is effectively 480i, or 640 x 480 interlaced. So not only is the aspect ratio different, the effective resolution is much less. As Figure 5-1 shows, if the SDTV image is displayed on an 1920 x 1080 display, this is what you see.

Figure 5-1:
An SDTV image displayed on an HDTV would look very small.

You really want to avoid this, and most HDTVs will allow you to stretch the image but maintain the correct aspect ratio, as in Figure 5-2.

You'll still see black or gray bars on either side.

Many HDTVs try to intelligently scale the 4:3 image to fit the *entire* screen, but this can result in a distorted image. Many viewers don't seem to actually care, preferring not to fiddle with the HDTV settings. It's entirely personal preference, though image quality purists may cringe at this.

Figure 5-2:
SDTV image scaled up to a larger image.

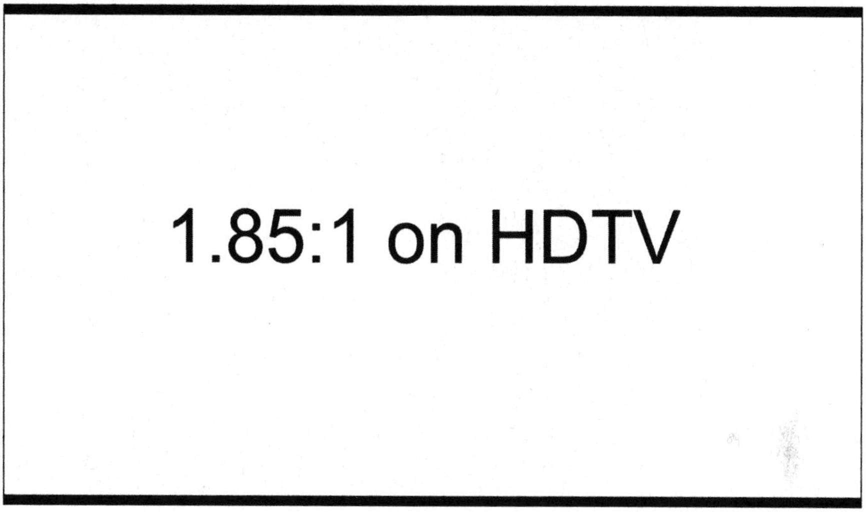

Figure 5-3:
A 1.85:1 movie will show small black or gray bars at the top and bottom.

1.85:1 on HDTV

Wide-screen movies will show letterboxing at the top and bottom, rather than the left and right sides. Just briefly, this is what you'd see with the two most common wide-screen movie aspect ratios, 1.85: 1 and 2.35:1, shown in Figures 5-3 and 5-4.

Again, most current HDTVs try to scale the image to use the entire screen, with some distortion. Again, whether you do that or not entirely depends on how you value image quality.

Figure 5-4:
A 2.35:1 movie will show larger black or gray bars at the top and bottom.

2.35:1 on HDTV

**Book VII
Chapter 5**

**Exploring Digital TV
and Satellite Radio**

That's resolution, interlacing, and aspect ratios in a nutshell. There are many more considerations when buying an HDTV. Mostly, though, take along some content (DVDs or Blu-ray movies) with you when buying an HDTV or at least insist on watching some content that you tend to view often. Then choose the TV based on what *you* see on the screen.

Shopping for an HDTV

Now that you have an understanding of several key technical terms, let's go shopping!

Consider the following items when shopping for an HDTV:

✦ **Budget:** How much money are you willing to spend? Your budget determines what feature set you can afford and also affects the ultimate screen size of the HDTV you purchase.

✦ **Physical size:** Have a huge living room and a small budget? Maybe a large format, DLP rear projection TV would work. On the other hand, if you have tight space constraints, perhaps because you have a particular piece of furniture that will house the HDTV, then that will dictate the maximum size of the unit.

✦ **Content Source:** What's the source of the HD content? If you want to use an over-the-air antenna exclusively, you'll need an HDTV with a built-in tuner or you'll have to make sure that an external tuner is part of the package. If you plan on watching exclusively through cable, then you may not need a built-in tuner.

✦ **Connections:** Finally, if all you want to connect is a cable or satellite box, you may not need many inputs. Similarly, if you're connecting multiple devices through an A/V receiver, one input on the HDTV will suffice. But if you want to have many devices connected directly to the HDTV, then you want to have multiple inputs — as many as you have devices to connect.

Prices of HDTVs have dropped considerably in the past several years, and it's not uncommon to find a 50-inch LCD for around $1,000 and a 50-inch plasma at nearly the same price — and those are the prices for 1080p. Above about 55 inches, prices increase much more rapidly, due to manufacturing constraints. Again, determine your budget and space constraints before going shopping.

A word about HDMI

I'm assuming your entire setup is fairly current. Whether your cable company is supplying you with a cable box or you're using a home theater A/V receiver, the best way to connect your HDTV today is HDMI (high-definition multimedia interface). HDMI carries both audio and video signals, so you only need one cable connecting a single source to the HDTV. It's far more convenient than component video cables with separate digital audio cables, for example. Plus, HDMI can carry all the newer high-definition audio standards, such as Dolby TrueHD and DTS-HD Master Audio.

As I noted earlier, make sure to watch some content on the HDTVs you're seriously considering buying. Even good quality HDTVs may handle color, brightness, and contrast a little differently, so personal preference often has a strong impact on what you buy. Note also that most HDTVs in showrooms typically have their controls set to be very bright, with very saturated colors, so that the images "pop" on the showroom floor.

One final word about buying: you should also make sure to buy your HDTV from a store with a solid return and exchange policy, in case the unit you buy simply won't work in your viewing environment.

Understanding Content Sources

Assuming you actually want to use your HDTV to view shows, you need a content source. The three primary sources of HDTV programming are over-the-air (OTA), cable TV, and satellite TV. A fourth source, streaming video from the Internet, is in its infancy but is rapidly becoming a popular alternative. Take a look at the options in the following sections.

Receiving TV over the air

Getting your programming over the air, using an antenna, has one key benefit: it's free. Depending on your location, you may have access to few or many channels of digital programming. Large urban areas can have access to 30 or more digital TV channels.

HDTV versus HDTV ready

Until recently, you could buy an HDTV without a built-in, over-the-air tuner. These were really just large monitors, not true TVs, and were often labeled "HDTV ready." You had to add your own content source. Most HDTVs today ship with an included OTA tuner, but you may still stumble across the occasional model that lacks a tuner. Be aware of what you're buying, since you need some source of HDTV content if you want to actually watch anything on your shiny new display.

All you need for OTA reception is a tuner and an antenna. Typically, you can buy a good antenna from the same source where you bought your HDTV. Note that some antennas are directional, while others can gather signals in all directions (omnidirectional.) Make sure to consult your dealer for the type of antenna best for your local area.

A good source of information on antennas and ways to help maximize your HDTV over the air reception is antennaweb.org, a Web site cosponsored by the Consumer Electronics Association (CEA) and the National Association of Broadcasters (NAB).

If you're lucky, you may only need an indoor antenna. Could the days of the rabbit ears be returning?

Even if you have cable or satellite TV, you may still want to have OTA reception. The reason is that over-the-air broadcasts actually offer better image quality, since satellite and cable providers often use heavy compression on their HD signals, reducing image quality. So if you have a choice of receiving a particular show through an OTA source, for from cable/satellite, get it from the local broadcast.

You also need an over-the-air tuner. OTA tuners are built into most modern HDTVs, but they're also often included in satellite or cable TV set-top boxes.

There is one difference between getting digital TV over the air and the old analog broadcasts. With DTV, you either get a picture or you don't. There's no fuzzy image because of poor reception. Poor reception means no picture at all, with DTV.

Premium services: Satellite and cable

Satellite and cable TV providers are pay services, usually requiring a monthly subscription fee. If you want to add HDTV and premium channels (such as HBO or Showtime), you may need to pay additional monthly fees. The advantage of premium services is the lack of commercial interruption.

Note that cable and satellite often offer similar mixes of HDTV programming, though there is some exclusive content on the different providers.

Receiving HDTV via satellite TV

Both local and cable channels broadcasting in HDTV are available from two satellite TV service providers, DirectTV and Dish Network. For an additional fee, you subscribe to local stations, receiving them via your satellite provider rather than over the air. However, the satellite set-top boxes also include OTA tuners, so you can hook up an antenna to them to get OTA HDTV from a single source.

Along with cable TV providers, satellite TV services are offering a package of HDTV content that goes beyond these local stations. They include new channels, such as ESPN HD, Discovery HD, HDnet (movies), HBO HD, and Showtime HD.

You usually need to purchase or rent a new set-top box that receives HDTV content. This investment is on top of the one you make for the high-definition TV. One popular option is the DVR (digital video recorder), which enables you to time-shift your viewing. A DVR contains a large capacity hard drive that stores shows for later viewing, much like people did in the analog era with VCRs.

Receiving HDTV over cable TV

Receiving HDTV programming over cable TV is similar to getting it from a satellite TV provider. In some cases, you could have trouble receiving all of the local HDTV channels directly on cable, if the local cable provider hasn't signed contracts with local TV stations to offer local content. However, you can still get those local channels through an OTA tuner.

As with satellite TV, local cable providers often offer DVR capability if you want to record shows for later viewing. A few cable companies are experimenting with virtual DVRs. A virtual DVR doesn't actually store the show in a local set-to box, but flags it back at the cable provider's server farm for later viewing.

**Book VII
Chapter 5**

Exploring Digital TV
and Satellite Radio

To CableCard or not?

A new standard for connecting HDTVs to cable TV, known as CableCard, emerged several years back, but it wasn't widely adopted. CableCard theoretically allowed TV producers to embed a digital cable tuner in the HDTV itself that was independent of the cable provider. Once the TV was installed, you would call your local cable provider who would supply you with the proper CableCard for your area. The problem was that the first CableCard standard was one way, which meant that interactive services like video on demand still required a telephone connection. CableCard 2.0 attempts to address this key issue, but future adoption remains in doubt. For the moment, the better option is to buy an HDTV without a built-in digital cable tuner and go with the set-top box supplied by the local cable provider. If you want to use TiVO HD, though, you'll need to get two CableCards from your local provider, one for each of the cable tuners built into a TiVO high-definition DVR.

Some HDTV TV sets offer CableCard slots. With one of these cards, you can bypass the set-top box and plug the coaxial cable into your TV. You insert a card into a CableCard slot, which carries information about the services you are allowed to view, as well as any limitations on the programming you can record.

TV over the Internet

A generation of new streaming video services, some free, some fee based, is emerging. Free services like Hulu (www.hulu.com) are gaining in popularity. Like broadcast television, the Hulu service uses commercials to pay for the programming, though the commercial interruptions are typically briefer than broadcast television.

Companies such as Amazon and Netflix also offer streaming services. Amazon's streaming service is pay-per-view. Netflix, on the other hand, offers their Netflix Watch Instantly service free to any current Netflix subscriber who has more than the most basic subscription.

Image quality ranges from poor, if you have a slow, unreliable Internet connection, to high definition, if you have a high-speed broadband connection. However, not all shows or movies are available from any single service.

Getting streaming Internet services to your TV is something of a challenge. You can use your Wi-Fi network to deliver content streamed to your PC to the TV. Some services, like Netflix's Watch Instantly service, are available in a standalone set-top box which connects directly to your TV, or on the Xbox 360 game console.

The Xbox 360 itself offers downloadable TV shows and movies for a fee. Similarly, Apple TV uses Apple's own iTunes service to deliver video and music to your HDTV from the Apple TV box itself.

Emerging classes of HDTV and accessory products now have some of these services built into the unit itself. For example, some HDTV and Blu-ray players have Ethernet connections and can connect directly to the Internet, offering services like Watch Instantly directly on your TV — no PC needed.

Heavenly Radio

The era of driving in your car and listening to crackling and hissing radio stations interfering with each other is almost gone. The new era of digital radio, whether from satellite services like Sirius XM or the emerging generation of HD radio stations, will forever change the way we listen to radio.

Satellite radio

If you're looking for all the possible radio programming you could ever want, you need look no farther than Sirius XM, which provides satellite radio service nationwide. Most newer cars and many aftermarket automobile radio receivers offer Sirius XM. Of course, you do have to pay a monthly subscription fee of $12.95 per month. The service does offer a lifetime membership for around $500, but you can only switch receivers three times during that "lifetime."

HD radio

Digital radio is quietly, but rapidly, supplanting traditional AM/FM radio. It's quiet, because digital radio coexists alongside AM/FM, but you do need new hardware to receive the HD radio signals. Many newer cars and home audio receivers now have HD radio tuners built in. The audio quality of HD radio is substantially better than typical AM/FM radio and nearly as good as satellite radio.

Chapter 6: Exploring the Kindle

*I*magine being able to carry dozens of books around with you, without the weight and bulk of actual books. Now imagine you can buy those books anywhere, anytime, and have them delivered nearly instantaneously, whatever your location.

That's the promise of Amazon's Kindle. I get into more detail about what an eBook is, but for the moment, think of it as a thin, portable device for storing and reading anything that can be converted into electronic text. The Kindle revolutionized eBooks by adding the capability to buy books and have them automatically transferred wirelessly to the Kindle.

I explain how eBooks work in this chapter.

Understanding eBooks

When people first look at eBook readers and compare their prices to other devices, like Netbooks (small, Internet-connected laptops), the initial reaction is negative. After all, the second-generation Kindle 2 costs $299, the same price as many Netbooks. If you want the larger-screen Kindle DX, that costs a hefty $489.

Electronic book readers are built around a technology known as e-paper, or electronic ink. These are unlike the LCD displays in laptops in several ways:

✦ The image requires no refresh, which means the text or image is constant (no flickering). That makes it easier on the eyes and uses much less power than LCD displays.

✦ The surface of e-paper is reflective, rather than requiring a backlight (as a standard LCD) or emitting its own light (as with OLEDs).

✦ Current e-paper implementations are monochrome or shades of gray only, though color versions are working in research laboratories.

The extraordinarily low power draw, coupled with the reduced eyestrain relative to LCD displays, makes eBook readers compelling for actually reading. I've read very long books on the Kindle for hours at a time, with almost none of the eye fatigue associated with extended computer use.

A variety of eBook readers exist, from companies like Sony, iRex, Samsung, and others. Amazon launched the original Kindle in 2007. The Kindle offered a 6-inch screen and four shades of gray. The Kindle's key innovation was its built-in Whispernet capability, which uses Verizon's CDMA cell network to wirelessly transmit books bought on the Amazon.com store to the Kindle.

The Kindle was followed up with the notably thinner and slightly lighter Kindle 2. The Kindle 2 offers longer battery life, 16 shades of gray, and faster page turning. Like the original Kindle, it has a small keyboard and a 6-inch screen. The Kindle 2 also has built-in text-to-speech capability and an audio output jack, which can be used for headphones or speakers. So you can enjoy having books read to you, even if you're in the dark, or want to listen while driving.

Amazon also offers the Kindle DX, a larger, heavier version with a 9.4-inch display. Almost twice as heavy, at 18.9 ounces, and more expensive than the Kindle 2, the DX is targeted at students and others requiring more robust graphics support and native support for PDF files (the Kindle and Kindle 2 do not natively support PDF).

The Kindles uses a proprietary file format which includes DRM (digital rights management) capability to protect authors from having their works illegally distributed. The format is actually based on the open Mobipocket standard. The Kindle readers can also natively read Mobipocket formatted files. Many free eBooks are available as Mobipocket files.

Now that we understand a bit more about the various Kindles, keep reading to find out how to use them.

Reading on the Kindle 2

The Kindle 2 (Figure 6-1) is a compact device weighing just a shade over 10 ounces. The 6-inch screen seems small at first, but it's easy to read, and page turning is fairly quick.

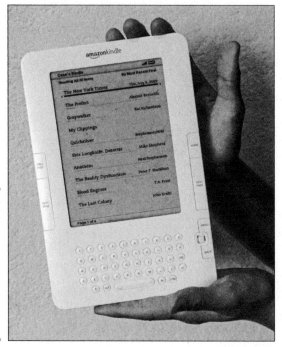

Figure 6-1:
The Amazon Kindle 2 delivers books bought from the Amazon. com site wirelessly.

The power switch on the Kindle 2 has two purposes. If you quickly flick it, the Kindle 2 is put into a very low power sleep mode. The sleep mode still uses a little power, but the Kindle 2 can still remain in suspended animation for weeks without a recharge — provided you've also disabled Whispernet.

If you leave Whispernet on while the Kindle 2 is in sleep mode, Kindle books you buy from www.Amazon.com will still download automatically, but battery life will be reduced.

If you move the power switch, but hold it for several seconds, the device completely powers down. If you do this while the system is powered off, it powers up.

You buy Kindle books from Amazon's Web site. That's the only place to buy currently published work in Kindle format. However, other sources of free — as in zero cost — books are available in Kindle or other recognized formats. See "Reading free eBooks" later in the chapter.

The Kindle home page simply consists of a list of books, with the most recently read books at the top, as in Figure 6-2. One of the best features of a Kindle book is the automatic bookmarking. Whenever you exit a book, the reader will remember the last page read. When you return to that book, you can take up reading where you left off.

Navigating the book list is simple. A little nub in the lower right, between the MENU and BACK buttons, behaves like a tiny four-way joystick. You can navigate down the book list by moving the nub toward the bottom of the Kindle. Moving it right opens a book; moving it left asks you if you want to delete a book. You can also open the book by pressing the nub into the Kindle, like you would a mouse button. If you do delete a book, you can always re-download eBooks you own from Amazon at no charge.

If you have multiple pages of listings — something that's easy to do if you buy more than a few books — the Next Page button will take you to the next part of the book list. The Prev Page button takes you back.

Case's Kindle	
Showing All 30 Items	By Most Recent First
Greywalker	Kat Richardson
My Clippings	
The New York Times	Thu, Aug 6, 2009
The Prefect	Alastair Reynolds
Quicksilver	Stephenson,Neal
Kris Longknife: Deserter	Mike Shepherd
Anathem	Neal Stephenson
The Reality Dysfunction: ...	Peter F. Hamilton
Blood Engines	T.A. Pratt
The Last Colony	John Scalzi
Page 1 of 4	

Figure 6-2:
The Kindle book list.

The Menu button has two functions. When you're in the book list, you can search the Kindle, shop for books (shown in Figure 6-3), change settings, and peruse the Experimental section, which includes a crude Web browser, an MP3 player, and the text-to-speech function.

When you're reading a book, the menu shows alternative navigation possibilities, including creating custom bookmarks, looking at the table of contents, or even adding annotations to what you're reading. Each note is marked in the book with a footnote-like number. One very useful feature in the in-book menu is the ability to change the text size, making it easier to read in dimmer light or if your eyesight isn't as good as it used to be. See Figure 6-4.

You can also use the joystick nub to move a cursor through the text. Pausing over a word causes a brief definition of the nearest word at the bottom of the Kindle page. Pressing the return key takes you to the Kindle's built-in dictionary, if you want a more detailed definition.

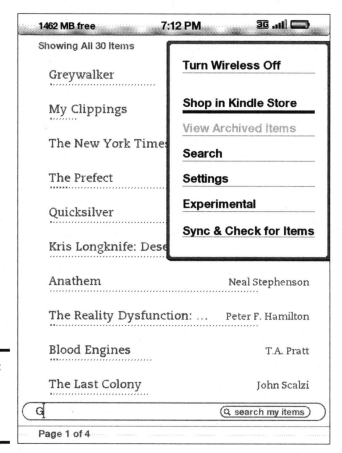

Figure 6-3: The Kindle menu on the main screen.

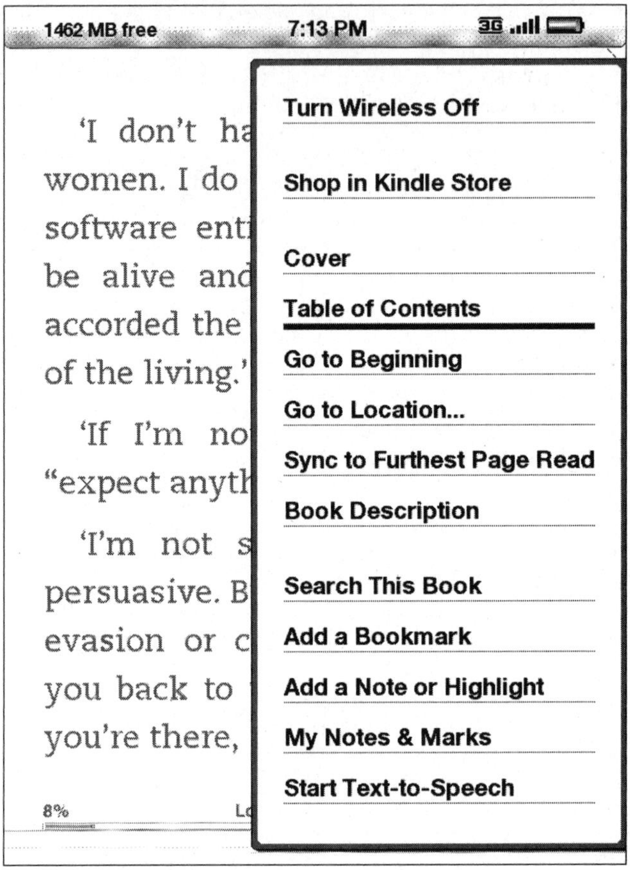

1462 MB free	7:13 PM	3G .ıll ▭

'I don't ha

women. I do

software ent

be alive and

accorded the

of the living.'

'If I'm no

"expect anyth

'I'm not s

persuasive. B

evasion or c

you back to

you're there,

8%

Turn Wireless Off

Shop in Kindle Store

Cover

Table of Contents

Go to Beginning

Go to Location...

Sync to Furthest Page Read

Book Description

Search This Book

Add a Bookmark

Add a Note or Highlight

My Notes & Marks

Start Text-to-Speech

Figure 6-4:
The Kindle menu when reading a book.

Every time you read a book, that book's title pops up to the top of the book list.

That's pretty much it. The Kindle 2 is an extremely simple device to use — another advantage of using a dedicated eBook reader rather than a small laptop.

Reading Blogs, Newspapers, and Magazines

In addition to books, other content is available for the Kindle 2, as shown in Figure 6-5. These include popular newspapers such as *The New York Times*, *Washington Post*, *Chicago Tribune*, *Le Monde* (if you can read French), and many more. You pay a monthly subscription fee, which varies, depending on the publication. Color pictures are rendered in 16 shades of gray, so those don't look as good. But a newspaper supports most of the book-reading features, making reading easy and convenient.

Subscriptions to popular blogs, like boingboing.net, Slashdot, Gizmodo, and tons of other blogs, are also available. Unlike reading them for free on the Internet, you do pay a subscription fee, but it's typically only $1.99 for the more popular blogs and less for others.

If blogs and newspapers are available, what about magazines? In fact, a wide array of magazines are available. Text-heavy magazines, like those specializing in fiction, work best, while art heavy magazines are probably best avoided unless you have a Kindle DX.

Figure 6-5:
The New York Times on the Kindle 2.

Reading eBooks for Free!

So you have your Kindle 2. If you're like most first-time users, the ability to have hundreds of books in your backpack, purse, or messenger bag probably went to your head. You bought a bunch of books you're meaning to read.

Then your credit card bill arrives. Ouch.

Luckily, you don't need to spend hundreds of dollars on Kindle books. A vast array of books are available for free in either the Kindle's own format or the Mobipocket format, which the Kindle can natively display.

Amazon itself has a large number of free Kindle books. Most are in the public domain. For example, you can download most of William Shakespeare's plays for free (though only one at a time — the collected works cost a little money). Similarly, other classic authors, ranging from Charles Dickens to Alexander Dumas to Jules Verne, are downloadable for no charge.

Another source of free books in Kindle format is manybooks.net (`www.manybooks.net.`) There are many more sources, too numerous to mention, but you can find a unified list of free eBook sources for the Kindle at ireader-review.com (`http://ireaderreview.com/2008/01/19/free-books-for-the-amazon-kindle/`).

Amazon also has a large assortment of titles that are not quite-free. Numerous classic titles from the golden age of science fiction (1930–1960) are available for 99 cents, for example.

So you don't need to bankrupt yourself in order to completely fill up your Kindle with more interesting books than you'll be able to read in a lifetime.

Converting PDF Files for the Kindle

If that's not enough, there are even more books available in Adobe Acrobat PDF format. Although the Kindle DX natively reads PDF format, the original Kindle and Kindle 2 do not. So how can you gain access to the staggering number of PDF books (and other PDF documents) for the Kindle?

Two utilities exist to convert PDF files. One is Mobipocket Creator, which can be downloaded for free personal use from the Mobipocket Web site (`www.mobipocket.com`). Mobipocket Creator doesn't actually convert to Kindle's .AZW format but converts to the open Mobipocket format, which the Kindle can read. Mobipocket is extremely flexible, allowing for substantial tweaking of the final output, but it is also a bit difficult to use because of all the options that must be manually set.

Another free tool is Stanza (`www.lexcycle.com/`). Stanza runs on the Mac, Windows PCs, and the iPhone. It's also a tool for reading and downloading eBooks. Converting files is very simple, but the formatting is sometimes odd.

With either Stanza or Creator, you need to connect your Kindle 2 to your PC or Mac. If it's a Creator Mobipocket file, you copy it manually to the Kindle 2 document folder. With Stanza, you export it to the correct folder.

By far the simplest way to convert PDF files to Kindle format is to use Amazon's own "experimental" service. When you buy a Kindle 2, you register an e-mail address: yourname@kindle.com. You don't have to worry about any settings, and the formatting usually looks correct.

If you take the PDF file (it must be a PDF file free of DRM protection) and e-mail it to yourname@kindle.com, you'll get back a file in Kindle format, delivered to your Kindle through Whispernet. Amazon charges 10 cents for each conversion.

If you're converting numerous, small files, 10 cents can add up pretty quickly. If you're willing to connect your Kindle to your PC and manually download the file, you can use the Amazon service for free by e-mailing the PDF to yourname@free.kindle.com. Amazon e-mails the converted file back to your Amazon contact e-mail (the one you use for your Amazon.com account). You'll have to manually download the file to your Kindle 2.

In the end, the Kindle line of eBook readers represents a new way of reading, coupling the benefits of a large, online book retailer with an eBook reader. That makes the process of buying and reading books substantially easier than previous readers. Much of that ease of use is due to the Kindle's built-in wireless service. So, what are you waiting for?

**Book VII
Chapter 6**

Exploring the Kindle

Book VIII
The Global Positioning System

The 5th Wave   By Rich Tennant

...WHILE ADJUSTING HIS DASHBOARD GPS...

©RICHTENNANT

Hey - look out!
Ahhhhhhhhh!

Contents at a Glance

Chapter 1: Getting Uncle Sam to Ante Up

In This Chapter

✓ Getting a handle on your position

✓ Knowing your options

✓ Making a connection with your PC

*E*very once in a while, the U.S. federal government gives its citizens — and sometimes the entire world — a gift. When the government financed, launched, and began running the Global Positioning System (GPS), it did just that: gifted us.

GPS is a system for finding your place anywhere in the world. As long as you have a fairly clear view of the sky, where the two dozen (or so) satellites orbit the Earth, you have a pretty good chance of getting a GPS reading and finding your way to where you want to go.

Its uses are almost limitless:

✦ Navigate the roads, letting more advanced GPS receivers lead you along street by street. Some models even speak the directions so you can keep your eyes on the road and not on the receiver's display. You also know which direction you're traveling in and how fast you're driving.

✦ Find a remote fishing hole — and then find your way back to your car. You can even keep your favorite hot fishing spot a secret because with GPS you've no need to leave any sort of marker that might tip off other anglers.

✦ Hike in the woods without getting lost. Or at least if you do get lost, your GPS receiver helps you get un-lost. It's the modern version of Hansel and Gretel, but the bread crumbs in this case are virtual, displayed on your GPS receiver as waypoints.

✦ Find a lost child who is wearing a GPS receiver on his or her wrist.

✦ Run or jog and collect precise information about your workout.

✦ Make an emergency call with your new GPS-equipped cell phone and help the 911 dispatcher locate you even if you aren't sure of your precise location.

Knowing Where You Are

Where are you? I know you're there because you're reading this book. You have to be somewhere to do that. But where are you really? In precise terms.

I can tell you where I am in precise terms:

N 42.96506 W 085.92599 Elevation: 744 feet above sea level

That's with an accuracy of about 30 feet. Just enough to throw off a stalker or an angry editor. (I'm just kidding about the stalker part.) In the next chapter, I explain how to understand that reading, but for now I just want you to see how accurate GPS can be.

How'd I get this reading? By using a very inexpensive GPS receiver called the Garmin eTrex. It was a $79 Christmas gift. It doesn't talk to me and doesn't display any maps other than a very rudimentary one, but it's enough to get a basic reading from the GPS system. Figure 1-1 shows the eTrex. You can find out more about Garmin GPS receivers at www.garmin.com.

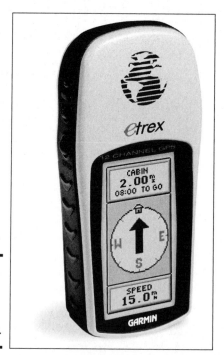

Figure 1-1: Garmin's eTrex GPS receiver is inexpensive.

Many other GPS receiver models do show quite detailed maps. For example, Sony (www.sony.com) sells a broad range of GPS receivers The Sony GPS receivers and mapping programs not only tell you where you are, but they can tell you the best route from where you are to where you want to go. Figure 1-2 shows the Sony NV-U44 GPS receiver that not only shows your current position but can also keep a log of where you've been for later playback. Furthermore, it can hold a bunch of photographs on an SD card and use its screen to show off your family memories.

Figure 1-2: The Sony NV-U44, well-worn and loved.

Achieving Missile Precision — Almost

Book VIII Chapter 1

Getting Uncle Sam to Ante Up

Do you have a chimney somewhere in the world at which you'd like the U.S. military to fire a long-distance missile? Using GPS, they can do it. Assuming all goes well, the missile will find the chimney, make a downward turn, and take a ride straight down. GPS is relatively new, although Santa Claus has been using a similar technique for years.

How the military uses GPS

How do you think the U.S. military makes those precision strikes during confrontations? Soldiers take a GPS reading of the target, transmit it to artillery and air forces, and get the heck out of the way. The GPS coordinates and very expensive ammunition do the rest — at least they do if no one in the area is using one of the GPS jammers available from Russia.

Being selective

On May 1, 2000, President Bill Clinton signed an order turning off the Selective Availability feature of the GPS system. Selective Availability was designed to degrade the GPS signal that was received by nonmilitary users so that the location information provided by civilian GPS units would be less precise than that of military GPS receivers. The U.S. military still has the ability to use a similar Selective Deniability feature in war zones or when there is a global terror alert, but this feature is targeted at specific areas rather than affecting all civilian users worldwide. See the article on GPS at wordiQ.com (`www.wordiq.com/definition/Global_Positioning_System`) for more information on GPS precision.

The military has an advantage over civilian GPS users: It uses some additional information to gain even more precision in GPS readings. The information is encrypted so that civilians — read: enemies — can't get the same precision. The U.S. military uses GPS in its missiles, its tanks, and other ground and air resources, and probably in ways that if I knew about they'd have to kill me.

Civilians can find their way, too

The precision the U.S. military achieves when using GPS for its guidance systems isn't quite as precise when a civilian uses the service. It's close enough for finding a fishing hole or navigating your way out of the woods, though.

The difference is so small, at least from a civilian perspective, that if I gave you the GPS coordinates for my front door, you might wind up at my back door — just enough precision to foil enemies without harming hapless hikers lost in the woods.

Actually, even civilian GPS receivers can have extremely precise measurements using a system known as Wide-Area Augmentation System (WAAS). This system relies upon ground-based transmitters whose position is very precisely known. These transmitters broadcast a signal that is matched with the satellite-transmitted GPS signal so that the normal positioning errors are reduced to such an insignificant degree that a WAAS-enabled system can be used to land an airplane in zero-visibility conditions. The WAAS system currently is only available in North America, but WAAS-enabled GPS receivers provide normal GPS accuracy even when they're used in areas where WAAS isn't available.

Most GPS receivers enable you to monitor the current signal to determine how accurately your position is being reported. Typically this information is reported using the following values:

✦ **PDOP (Position Dilution Of Precision):** A number representing the relationship between the error in user position and the error in satellite position using three coordinates. Smaller values are better.

✦ **HDOP (Horizontal Dilution of Precision):** A number similar to PDOP, but relating only to your horizontal position.

✦ **EHPE (Expected Horizontal Position Error):** The error in horizontal position, which you can assume under current conditions. For example, Figure 1-3 shows that the GPS receiver is probably accurate to within about 27 feet when I captured the image.

Figure 1-3: The GPS receiver has my position located within about 27 feet of my actual location.

Sat	El	Az	SNR	Stat	3D
8	63	326	39	NET-	
31	9	188	28	NET-	
29	7	320	27	-ET-	
0	0	0	0	----	
0	0	0	0	----	
27	71	32	32	NET-	
13	40	155	29	NET-	
19	37	69	28	NET-	
28	43	237	30	NET-	
10	22	290	27	NET-	
3	15	42	0	----	
124	0	0	0	----	

PDOP:	HDOP:	EHPE:
N/A	1.0	27.1 ft

Street Atlas USA · 12:40

Data GPS Tools

Using GPS

What can you do with GPS and its receiver? As the list at the beginning of this chapter shows, the number of ways to take advantage of this free service are numerous. Here I go into detail on a few of the more popular uses.

Taking a hike

A GPS receiver is a must-have accessory for the outdoor types among you. It helps get you to where you want to go like a map cannot and prevents panic when all of those trees start looking alike.

Still, as my Garmin manual cautions, it's important to carry an old-fashioned compass and map with you whenever you hike in new territory. If your batteries die or the trees prevent you from getting a good lock on the satellite signals, your GPS receiver isn't much help. Also, if you're trekking into some back country or there's a possibility that the weather might turn sour, be sure to tell someone where you're planning on going so they know where to start looking for you if you don't return when you told them you'd be back.

If I was an outdoors person, and I'm not (although I do go outside to get the daily mail), I would buy one of the fancy, new two-way radios that combine a communications transceiver with a GPS receiver. I discuss these in Book VI, Chapter 3, which is about Family Radio Service and other two-way radios.

On the road again

I have a horrible time getting to new destinations. Actually, I have a horrid time finding places I've already visited, too. I don't know how many times I've driven to some strange city and found myself in the less glamorous parts of town rather than where I should be, safely in my friend's driveway.

GPS to the rescue!

Instead of relying on memory and getting all of those numbered highways mixed up in my head, I can rely on a GPS receiver to provide turn-by-turn directions. I tell the receiver where I'm going — it knows where I am, of course — and it tracks my direction and speed and lets me know when it's time to make a turn onto another highway or road.

If you're hungry on the way, some advanced models can tell you where the nearest restaurant is located. The DeLorme Street Atlas programs include information on literally thousands of points of interest including restaurants, gas stations, parks, campgrounds, and so on to make your trip far more enjoyable.

On a bike ride

It might not seem obvious at first, but a portable GPS receiver (or a PDA with a GPS accessory receiver) can be a wonderful addition for your bicycle. This is especially true if you set off on a road trip, but even mountain bikers can appreciate the way that a GPS receiver helps them find the trail in rugged back country.

If you do decide to bring along your GPS receiver on your bike, keep in mind that a bike presents something of a challenge to fragile electronic gear. Your local bike shop can probably supply a strong handlebar mount for the GPS receiver, but you may also want to shop carefully for a GPS receiver that's rated for rugged use.

It's a bird, no, it really is a plane

Private pilots travel in a world where the ordinary landmarks simply look a whole lot different than they do from ground level. It's awfully hard to read road signs from several thousand feet in the air, so getting a little extra help in determining exact position is really important to a pilot.

GPS technology has become a very important tool for pilots over the past several years. Products like Anywhere Map from Control Vision (www.controlvision.com) have simply revolutionized the general aviation world because they've made it possible for virtually every flyer to realize the benefits of GPS mapping at a fraction of what it would have cost even a few years ago.

Just for fun

In the next chapter I talk about two other fun uses of GPS: finding goodies in a hobby called geocaching and finding your ancestors and their haunts in genealogy. I just mention them here briefly so you can decide whether you want to read more details in the next chapter.

Geocaching

By using your wits and a cheap GPS receiver, you can participate in something called geocaching. It's really a high-tech treasure hunt. The treasure, or cache, is usually inexpensive items, but the fun is in the chase. With coordinates in hand, you can drive to nearby locations, finding your way to the cache with GPS receiver in one hand and perhaps a can of bug spray in the other.

Genealogy

The use of GPS technology is just starting to catch on in the hobby of genealogy, which is the search for your family roots. With a GPS receiver, you can make the drive to old family homesteads easier and even find relatives' graves. Instead of requiring other researchers to retrace your steps on their own, you can provide precise GPS coordinates to make their hunt for family information and physical remnants easier.

Exploring Your Options

A wide variety of GPS receivers are available in all kinds of styles and with different levels of features. What you buy mostly depends on what its main use is, because a hiker's GPS receiver must be much smaller than one meant to rest on your vehicle dashboard.

**Book VIII
Chapter 1**

Choosing a portable unit

When choosing a portable unit, these are some of your choices:

Getting Uncle Sam
to Ante Up

✦ Magellan at www.magellangps.com/en/

✦ Garmin at www.garmin.com

✦ Cobra at www.cobra.com

Each of these manufacturers offers an assortment of models aimed at different types of users. You probably want to look at several different GPS receivers before choosing because the extra features that are included in the slightly more expensive models can greatly improve the convenience of using a portable unit.

If you intend to use your portable GPS receiver with your laptop PC, be sure to buy a unit that includes the necessary cables or adapters. These are typically not included with the least expensive models.

Driving around with a vehicle GPS unit

In the car, you have lots of options for using GPS, but don't pay it so much attention that it turns you into a reckless, dangerous, inattentive driver:

✦ You can buy a new car that has a fancy built-in navigation system. This is by far the most expensive option, of course, but it's the only one that's guaranteed to impress the neighbors (or make your boss start wondering if you're being paid too much). Built-in navigation systems often have a hidden cost your dealer may "forget" to mention, though. In most cases you need to buy expensive map add-ons if you want maps for the entire country.

✦ If you like the idea of a built-in GPS navigation system but aren't in the market for a new car, the manufacturers of portable GPS receivers offer aftermarket units that can be added to your existing car. While these might not have quite the panache of a factory-installed GPS navigation system, they're a lot more affordable, and you can move them to a new vehicle in the future.

✦ You can also use a Bluetooth or another GPS receiver with a laptop PC and carry it along in your car. This option is far less expensive than the other two vehicle options I mentioned, and it has one feature that trumps both of them in a big way — the laptop PC's screen is far bigger than that on any built-in vehicle GPS system. In addition, GPS mapping software for your laptop is far less expensive to update, so it's far easier on your wallet when you want to know about the newer roads.

✦ If you want the small size of a portable GPS receiver but you also want most of the advanced mapping options available with laptop PC GPS mapping software, you might want to consider pairing up a GPS receiver with a PDA. I talk about using a GPS receiver with a PDAPDA shortly, but this is an excellent choice in many cases.

No matter what type of GPS navigation system you use in a vehicle, it can be very dangerous to you and everyone else on the road if you don't take the time to get to know the unit before you begin driving. In fact, unless the GPS navigation system uses voice prompts to tell you when and where to turn, it's far safer to have a passenger handle the navigation duties than to try to watch the screen while you're driving.

Merging your laptop with GPS

I've already mentioned how you can use your laptop PC for navigation in your vehicle. This is a very popular option among RV owners because they usually have plenty of room for the laptop and at least one passenger who can handle the navigation while driving. In addition, GPS mapping software for laptops generally includes the locations of RV parks so you may not need a big, printed RV park directory.

Another way to use GPS with your laptop is to combine your search for Wi-Fi hotspots, which I discuss in another chapter, with GPS. Using your laptop, you can drive around, essentially mapping hotspot locations. To aid in this quest, you may want to download a trial version of WiNc from Cirond (www.cirond.com/winc.html). This extremely handy program quickly identifies all Wi-Fi connections within an area and helps you determine if you can connect to them. Cirond even offers a PDA version called pocketWiNc, shown in Figure 1-4.

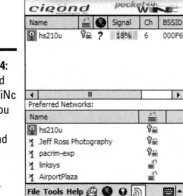

Figure 1-4: WiNc and pocketWiNc enable you to easily locate and connect to Wi-Fi hotspots.

Using GPS with a PDA

I've mentioned several times that a PDA and a GPS receiver make an excellent pairing. With the two, you have most of the size advantages of stand-alone portable GPS receivers and a whole raft of capabilities that you won't find in most portable GPS units. (You may want to pick up a copy of iPAQ For Dummies or PDA For Dummies — both written by Brian Underdahl and published by Wiley Publishing — to read more about what you can do with a PDA.)

Because different PDA models offer different expansion options, you'll find several types of GPS receivers that work with various PDAs. I recommend checking out the products that are available from the following:

+ **DeLorme** at www.delorme.com
+ **Sony** at www.sony.com
+ **Teletype** at www.teletype.com
+ **PocketMapStore** at www.pocketmapstore.com
+ **ALK Technologies** at www.alk.com

In each case you should specify the type of PDA you own so you can get the proper GPS receiver.

GPS maps can eat up a lot of memory on a PDA. If you don't already have a PDA, try to get one with built-in Bluetooth, so you can use the expansion slot for a memory card to hold your maps.

Using a GPS-enabled cell phone or smartphone

Nextel has a service called TeleNav that provides audible driving directions, automatic notification when you've gone off course, and locations of nearby businesses like gas stations and restaurants. You can read more at www. nextel.com/about/enterprise/wbs/gps/navigate.shtml. Other carriers have similar services. Visit your carrier's Web site or call to see if they sell any GPS-enabled phones.

One very popular phone with a GPS integrated is, of course, the Apple iPhone. In fact, my doctor often brags to me while I'm lying on his table that he and his daughter went hiking in some backwater area of the United Kingdom, and when they got lost, she whipped out her iPhone and led them home. My doctor is an interesting fellow.

Saying Goodbye to AAA

Even though GPS devices rule so thoroughly, I recommend you don't take AAA or any other paper map out of the loop just yet, especially when you're using a GPS unit in the car. There's still the chance the map data you upload is not up to date, that your batteries will go dead, or that you'll have some other technical problem. Having a map gets you to the Grand Canyon long after your GPS receiver stops working. If you're hiking, a compass and a map are essential, even if you have the best GPS receiver available. In that case, your life is possibly at stake, and you don't want to rely on an electronic gizmo to get you out of the woods and back home.

GPS mapping programs for laptop PCs generally offer the option to print out both ordinary maps and those that show your selected route. These printed copies can serve as an excellent backup for your GPS unit and save you a trip to the auto club office.

Making a Connection with Your PC

There are quite a few reasons why I think you'll find that having a connection between your GPS receiver and your PC awfully handy. Examine a few of them.

Upgrading software and maps

As I mentioned in the previous section, once you move beyond the most basic portable GPS receivers, you quickly get into units that display maps rather than simply numbers to indicate your position. You may have noticed, however, that maps have a certain amount of obsolescence built in. For some reason people want to build new roads, change the course of old ones, or even just rename existing roads. That's one reason many GPS receivers offer the option to connect to your PC — so you can update the maps in the GPS receiver.

Downloading your life's movements

Virtually all GPS units can store some record of where they've been. By downloading this tracking information to your PC, you can map out the route you took in getting somewhere. Here are some possible uses for this type of information:

✦ Imagine how useful it would be to be able to print out maps of the trail to some hidden but beautiful picnic spot so that you could share those maps with your friends.

✦ If you have a consulting business where you must visit your client's locations, you could use your GPS track to justify the travel expenses you bill to the customers or that you claim on your tax returns.

✦ Because the GPS track also includes information about the speed of travel, you might try to beat an unwarranted speeding ticket by convincing a judge that the GPS track is an accurate representation of how you were driving. I don't think I'd bet on that working, but you're welcome to try. (Just don't blame me if the judge throws the book at you — remember, I'm not offering anything resembling legal advice here.)

✦ You could put your GPS receiver in your car before you let your teenager drive to the library and remind him or her that the unit tracks both speed and location. Who knows? It might just make your kid drive a bit more carefully.

**Book VIII
Chapter 1**

Getting Uncle Sam to Ante Up

Using your GPS with your laptop

Don't you just love it when you can get the best of both worlds out of a product? Well, when it comes to GPS, it's entirely possible for you to do so. There's no reason why you can't buy a small, portable GPS receiver that's perfect for taking on hikes and then connect that same GPS receiver to your laptop PC to use with the far more comprehensive PC-based GPS mapping software for trip navigation in your vehicle.

Sure, you probably have to buy a portable GPS receiver that's slightly above the bottom of the line, but virtually any of the portable units that include a PC connection cable as standard equipment can likely do the job. (You can check the PC-based GPS mapping software manufacturer's Web site to verify if a particular portable GPS unit is considered compatible.)

GPS receivers work the best in vehicles when the receiver has a clear view of the sky. The optimal location in most cars is at the front of the dashboard as close to the windshield as possible. A small piece of rubberized drawer liner (like you find in the housewares section at your local store) goes a long way toward preventing the GPS receiver from sliding around as you drive.

Chapter 2: Finding Your Way in the World

In This Chapter

✔ **Taking a quick mapping course**

✔ **Coordinating your coordinates**

✔ **Deciphering a GPS display**

✔ **Understanding waypoints**

In the preceding chapter, I give you an overview of the global positioning system (GPS). Hopefully, that chapter gives you a good understanding of what GPS is, how you can use it, and how to pick a GPS receiver. It also shows you a number of different options to fit different circumstances so you also realize that GPS isn't something just for a few dedicated hobbyists.

Now I'm going to take you to the next step, which is understanding how to read a GPS display. Most importantly, I give you a quick lesson in longitude, latitude, and related mapping terms so you know what your GPS receiver is telling you. You probably learned most of this in school, but if you're like me, you slept through most of it.

Still, while this information is interesting, it's more important to understand your GPS receiver so you can figure out how to get found when you've become lost. After all, it's unlikely a latitude and longitude reading will help much when you're lost in the middle of, say, the Adirondack National Park without any idea of how you got to wherever it is you are.

Giving Some Latitude to Your Longitude

Maybe you remember latitude and longitude from geography class, maybe you don't. It's an international way to indicate your location in the world. I don't think in international terms too much, though, so let's take a few minutes to review what latitude and longitude mean.

Figure 2-1 shows a world map divided by latitude and longitude lines. If you know the latitude and longitude values of any location on the planet, you can use those values to find that location on the map.

A GPS receiver does its magic by listening to signals from the GPS satellites and then tells you where you stand, also in the geographic sense, by determining your precise latitude and longitude. In fact, that's how a GPS receiver is able to display your location on a map. It simply takes your latitude and longitude numbers and figures out where that position is on the map.

 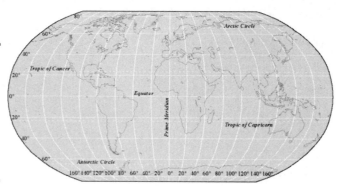

Figure 2-1:
Latitude and longitude lines help you find your location on Earth.

A Quick Course on Mapping

This isn't a book on mapping or geography or even GPS, so this is a very short introduction to the three things you should know about: latitude, longitude, and elevation. Even so, this basic information should enable you to begin using your GPS receiver for simple navigation. It also helps you remember a few easily confusing facts.

A bit of simple geometry

Okay, you knew this was coming, didn't you? Yes, it's necessary to have just a brief review of geometry to make certain that we're all speaking the same language:

✦ When you divide a circle into degrees, there are 360 degrees in a complete circle.

✦ Both latitude and longitude are measured in degrees, which is often shown using the ° symbol.

✦ For the purposes of navigation, the Earth is considered to be essentially round. Flat Earth societies don't have a leg to stand on.

✦ Because latitude and longitude both indicate a position on a round planet, the total number of degrees around the Earth in either latitude or longitude is 360 (even though, as you discover shortly, the values are expressed a bit differently, they do add up to 360).

✦ Fractions of degrees are measured in minutes, with 60 minutes in 1 degree. The symbol for minutes is '. Don't get geometrical minutes mixed up with temporal minutes.

✦ Likewise, fractions of minutes are measured in seconds, with 60 seconds in a minute. The symbol for seconds is ". That's to further confuse people who use the clock on their GPS devices.

✦ Sometimes, though, fractions of degrees are expressed using decimal values rather than minutes and seconds. The results are the same, but just a bit of math is involved in converting between the two. For example, 39 degrees and 30 minutes could also be shown as 39.5 degrees (because 30 minutes is one-half of a degree). It could also be shown as 39° 30'.

That wasn't too bad, was it? Now that you've got the simple geometry out of the way, see how it applies to latitude and longitude.

Latitude

The lines of latitude run east and west around the globe. The equator is basically a line of latitude. Latitude is shown as degrees north in the Northern Hemisphere and as degrees south in the Southern Hemisphere. Starting at the equator, which is zero, when you go north, the north latitude rises to 90 degrees when you reach the North Pole. When you go south of the equator, the south latitude reaches 90 degrees when you hit the South Pole.

So, for example, Reno, Nevada, is located at approximately 39 degrees and 30 minutes north latitude, while Los Angeles, California, is at about 34 degrees north latitude. From these two values you can tell that Reno is farther north than Los Angeles — and that's without looking at a map.

Longitude

The imaginary lines of longitude run north and south. The zero-degrees longitude line runs through Greenwich, England, which is called the prime meridian. If you went west of the prime meridian and a friend went east, you'd eventually meet up at the International Date Line. You would go 180 degrees in both directions. (Remember how I told you the numbers would add up to 360?)

In the Eastern Hemisphere, the longitude is given as degrees east. In the Western Hemisphere, longitude is given as degrees west. You may also see west longitude expressed as a negative value. That is, W119° is the same as –119°.

Going back to the earlier example, you find that Reno is at about W119° 50' while Los Angeles is approximately W118° 15'. Hey, wait a minute! That puts Reno west of Los Angeles, doesn't it? Well, yes it does, and that's exactly why understanding a little bit of geometry is so important. (Go ahead, look on a map and you see that Reno actually is farther west than Los Angeles — you can win a bar bet with this one.)

434 Coordinating Your Coordinates

Elevation

Elevation is basically the distance you're standing above the level of the world's oceans, called sea level. If you're on a high mountain, you're obviously at an elevation much higher than sea level.

When using a GPS, you must receive signals from a fourth satellite to measure your elevation. You only need three visible satellites if all you need is your two-dimensional position in the world. GPS receivers typically display 2D to indicate a two-dimensional fix and 3D to indicate a three-dimensional fix. A fix is simply the navigational term for knowing your precise location.

Coordinating Your Coordinates

Latitude lines are always parallel to the equator and to each other. Longitude lines, however, are not really parallel to each other because they meet at the north and south poles.

One important result regarding the difference between latitude and longitude lines is that a one-degree change of latitude is always equal to the same distance (ignoring elevation differences, of course), but a one-degree change of longitude varies. Look at how this can be:

✦ Going directly north or south changes your latitude but not your longitude. One degree of latitude change equals just about 70 miles. You could figure out the circumference of the Earth and divide that by 360 to verify this, but your number comes pretty close if you do.

✦ Going one degree east or west at the equator changes your longitude but not your latitude. Again, if you're at the equator, one degree of longitude change is also about 70 miles (because the Earth is round, so the circumference around the equator is virtually the same as it is on one of the longitude lines).

✦ Now, to blow your mind. Imagine that you are standing exactly at the north pole. Take one step south (that's any direction from where you are). That places you about 3 feet away from the north pole. If you stay the same distance out and walk all the way around the pole, you'll go about 20 feet. *But that 20 feet brought you all the way around the world so you traveled through 360 degrees of longitude!* A little math tells you that one degree of longitude change here is a bit less than an inch. How can this be? Well, the latitude lines are parallel (running east and west, remember), so the circles going entirely around the world are much shorter than they are at the equator. Because the longitude lines all meet at the poles, each of them is exactly the same length.

It's easy to see how this could be confusing, so aren't you glad that your GPS receiver does all of the math for you? And aren't you glad that I went to the north pole to do the measurements so you wouldn't have to?

Explaining How GPS Works

I'm not an engineer or anything close, but I think I can describe in simple terms how the GPS system works. It's not like it's — well, actually, in this case it really is — rocket science, but the general idea is fairly easy to understand.

Imagine for a moment that you have found three posts pounded into the ground in a triangular pattern somewhere in your yard. One day you're down at the library, and you come across some historical records that mention that the town recluse used to live on your property and that before he died he told someone that he had buried some treasure exactly 100 feet from the posts. Can you figure out where to dig without ruining all of the land-scaping you've so carefully added to your yard?

Actually, that's a pretty simple problem because there's only one solution. If you tie a 100-foot string to each post and then see where the three ends meet, you've found the spot because there is no other place that's exactly 100 feet from all of the posts (as shown in Figure 2-2).

The GPS system works something like those three strings. Of course, it uses satellites instead of posts, but using several satellites, it can determine where you are, as you see in Figure 2-3. The rocket scientists figured out how to calculate the precise position of each GPS satellite, all of which are in geo-synchronous orbit, at each point in time, and they know that radio signals travel at the speed of light, so throw in a little fancy math, and bingo!

Now, it takes not three, but four GPS satellites to fix your location. That's because you need one more measurement than the number of dimensions to rule out multiple positions in the remaining dimension. Get it?

In the example of using three strings to find the buried treasure in your yard, you assumed that where the three strings touched the ground was where the treasure was buried. If you held onto those three strings and raised them up above the ground, you would find that they would still meet, even if you held them above your head. The same thing happens with the GPS satellite signals, but once you add a fourth signal there's only one point that can be your location.

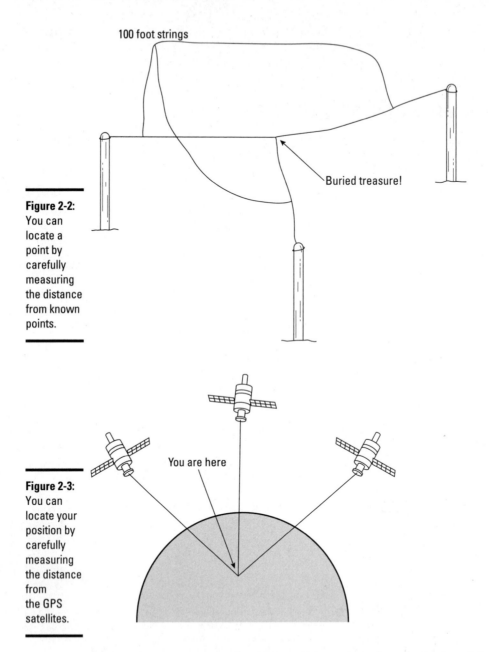

100 foot strings

Buried treasure!

Figure 2-2:
You can
locate a
point by
carefully
measuring
the distance
from known
points.

You are here

Figure 2-3:
You can
locate your
position by
carefully
measuring
the distance
from
the GPS
satellites.

Figure 2-4 shows an example of how a GPS receiver shows a display of the satellites that are being tracked. In this case the display symbols indicate that four satellites are being used for navigation, and the 3D indicator near the upper right of the display tells you that the unit has a 3D fix. GPS receivers often have more satellites in view than are being used for navigation simply because the data from some of the satellites might not be coming through reliably enough for navigation purposes.

Figure 2-4: The GPS receiver is tracking seven GPS satellites and using four of them for navigation.

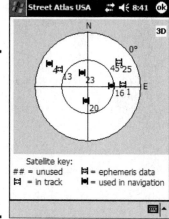

Reading a GPS Display

I own a Sony NV-U44 GPS device, but these examples are from my old Garmin eTrex GPS receiver. Like most modern GPS receivers, you can choose how to display your coordinates. That is, you can choose degrees, minutes, and seconds or you can opt for degrees and decimal fractions.

For example, my location in a digital format, according to the display on my GPS receiver, is this:

N 42.96506 W 085.92599

Using the degrees, minutes, and seconds display, the following represents the same location:

42° 57' 54.4" N 85° 55' 33.6" W

That means I'm in the Northern and Western hemispheres. To be exact, I'm in this location:

42 degrees, 57 minutes, and 54.4 seconds north of the equator

85 degrees, 55 minutes, and 33.6 seconds west of the prime meridian

That puts me in West Michigan. If you look at the digital equivalent of my location you can see how the 42 degrees, 57 minutes, and 54.4 seconds were simply converted to 42.96506:

N 42.96506 W 085.92599

The same was done with the second half of the coordinates. It's 57 minutes of one way and 0.96 of the other. In other words, they're the same coordinates, just expressed differently.

That's important to know because you may see coordinates expressed one way, but your GPS receiver may be set to display them another way. Usually, you can make a quick conversion to the coordinates of your choice by going into your receiver's setup menu and selecting Units or something similar.

Figure 2-5 shows how a GPS receiver display might look using the degrees and decimal degrees option, and Figure 2-6 shows the display when the degrees, minutes, and seconds option is selected. Note that these two readings do not show precisely the same location.

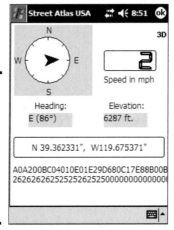

Figure 2-5: The GPS receiver is displaying coordinates using degrees and decimal degrees.

Due to rounding errors, you may not get precisely the same values when you try to convert between the two types of display. It's always best to pick one method and stick with it to avoid these types of errors.

Figure 2-7 shows one very good reason why you may prefer to use a GPS receiver that displays your position on a map rather than using latitude and longitude coordinates. I don't know about you, but it's a lot easier for me to determine my location by looking at the map display than by reading the coordinate display.

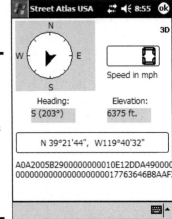

Figure 2-6: The GPS receiver is displaying coordinates using degrees, minutes, and seconds.

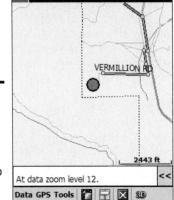

Figure 2-7: The GPS receiver is my current location using a map display.

Finding Your Waypoints

Waypoints are the essence of basic GPS navigation. At the simplest level waypoints are just the various points along the route between where you are and where you want to go. Even if you've never used a GPS receiver before, you've certainly used waypoints — you probably just didn't use that name for them.

Understanding how waypoints work

To understand how waypoints work, consider the following set of directions:

1. Take Highway 395 south to the junction of Highway 341.

2. Turn left on Highway 341.

3. Turn left at the intersection with Cartwright Road.

Those directions seem clear enough, don't they? Well, waypoints work pretty much the same way except that waypoints are often indicated using geographical coordinates in place of the names or numbers of roads or other physical objects. In fact, that same set of directions could be expressed using two waypoints (because the directions tell you to turn in two places) as in the following:

1. Go to N39° 24' 10.1", W119° 44' 46".

2. Go to N39° 21' 59.1", W119° 39' 59".

3. Turn left.

Although it's true that both sets of directions get you to the same place, the directions that use waypoints offer one distinct advantage over the directions that use highway names and numbers. Can you spot the important difference? The first set of directions is pretty useless without additional information — such as an assumed starting point. The sets of directions using waypoints need no other details because anyone with a GPS receiver can follow them, no matter where the trip began.

Even though this example only uses two waypoints, that doesn't mean that you necessarily want to set off on a cross-country hike directly between the two waypoints. You might find a number of obstacles in your path that prevent that sort of straight-line approach. If you use a GPS receiver that displays maps, you might want to choose the option to create a route that uses roads rather than to create a direct route. (The method for choosing this varies according to the type of GPS receiver you use.) But even if you choose the direct route option, your GPS receiver shows you the distance and direction to your next waypoint, just as you see in Figure 2-8. This means that if you have to navigate around a steep hill, a lake, or even a large building, your GPS receiver shows you how to reach the waypoint.

Creating waypoints

You can create your own waypoints a number of ways. The precise methods depend on your particular GPS receiver, of course, but generally you'll probably find that you have at least some of these options available:

✦ Enter waypoints manually by entering latitude and longitude coordinates before you set out with your GPS receiver. This method requires that you know the coordinates, of course, but it allows you to set very accurate waypoints.

✦ The manual process may also be as simple as clicking points on an on-screen map. This generally won't be quite as accurate as entering specific latitude and longitude values, but it's far more convenient.

✦ Most GPS receivers allow you to manually set waypoints at your current location. This method is very handy if you're out for a walk in a strange city and want to be sure that you can find the way back to your starting point.

✦ Many GPS receivers offer an automatic tracking option. Typically, this option creates waypoints at specific time intervals so you can later play back a record of your travels. If you use this option it's a good idea to learn how to set the recording interval. That way, you can set a value appropriate to your mode of travel — shorter intervals for vehicular travel and longer intervals when you're on foot.

Portable GPS receivers typically have a limited amount of available memory. If you set the recording interval too short you can lose your earlier recorded waypoints when the memory becomes full. As you can imagine, this could make it difficult for you to backtrack in unfamiliar terrain.

The popularity of GPS receivers has generated a whole new hobby — exchanging lists of useful and interesting waypoints. Web sites such as GPS Waypoint Registry (www.waypoint.org) are dedicated to collecting and sharing lists of these waypoints.

This chapter has helped you understand a bit more about how to use your GPS receiver. Although there wasn't room for an entire course on the finer points of GPS usage, I'm sure that you're far more comfortable about how you can use your GPS receiver to get from where you are to where you want to be.

**Book VIII
Chapter 2**

**Finding Your Way
in the World**

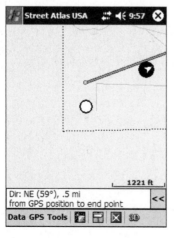

Figure 2-8:
The next waypoint is a half-mile to the northeast from my current position.

Chapter 3: Exploring with the Rest of GPS

In This Chapter

✔ **Exploring geocaching**

✔ **Using GPS to find cemeteries**

✔ **Finding your ancestors' homesteads**

A popular hobby called geocaching uses your GPS receiver to track down plots of small prizes hidden around the globe. GPS stands for Global Positioning System, and it can be used for more than simply finding your way out of the forest.

The second use is a more practical one. You can use GPS coordinates in genealogy research, both for finding cemeteries (and even specific gravestones) and your ancestors' old homesteads, schools, churches, and other sites.

Seeking and Hiding with Geocaching

GPS is not only about using the technological equivalent of bread crumbs to find your way out of the forest. It also helps provide the basic navigational tools for geocaching, helping you pinpoint within feet the location of hidden caches that others have left for you to find.

When you've mastered the seeking, you may want to try the hiding part. You can create your own caches, maybe right in your backyard, that others can seek. There are even groups and Web sites dedicated to this hobby. Here are some popular geocaching Web sites:

✦ www.geocaching.com

✦ www.navicache.com

✦ www.terracaching.com

✦ www.earthcache.com

Check these out, lurk in their communities, and see which one is most exciting for you.

Playing it safe while playing

Having fun shouldn't lead to forgetting about good old common sense. Consider these things before heading off:

✔ Travel in pairs.

✔ Let someone know where you're going if you go out to look or hide a cache.

✔ Carry ID, water, and a flashlight if you're hiking.

✔ Make sure you get permissions to hide a cache on property if it's not yours.

✔ Make sure you know what the park rules are for hiding things.

✔ Follow your instincts, and don't do something if your gut is saying not to.

Nabbing the cache

Given the choice, you probably would rather nab cash. But geocaching leads to its own treasures, many of them you keep while others you take to the next cache location and exchange for something else. You can do this on and on, traveling across the United States and other countries (but mind the oceans, lest you find yourself with some wet cache).

For those who love technology, the outdoors, and a good quest, it's a perfect hobby. It's a little like a modern-day version of scouting, where you might have earned an orienteering badge for your skills with a map and compass. Now you're using your map, compass, and GPS navigational skills. You can do it with friends and family; you breathe the clean air of mostly remote areas and improve your navigational skills for the day you might need them. (On the other hand, staying inside is safer and dryer. But I'm assuming you like the outdoors.)

In most instances the hidden caches are tucked away in a hidden location in a public place. Don't expect to be digging for buried treasure in someone's yard — if you do, you're probably looking in the wrong place, and you're likely to get arrested, to boot.

You don't need an expensive GPS receiver for geocaching. An inexpensive model that's $75 or even less is enough to get you going. Later, if you want a better GPS receiver that allows you to carry pictures and music and stuff, you always can spend a little more money ($150 to $200) for an advanced model. See Book VIII, Chapter 1, for more information about your options in buying a GPS receiver.

TIP

You can find nearby caches by searching on the one of the Web sites listed above. At most such sites, you can search by ZIP code, state, country, and other variables. Once you find a cache you want to find, www.geocaching.com, for example, has some suggestions for hunting it down:

✦ Research the cache location. Buy a topographical map for remote cache locations. Use services like Google Maps (maps.google.com) or MapQuest (www.mapquest.com) to get driving directions for more easily accessible ones. Google Maps even has street level views of many locations, so you can familiarize yourself with the terrain in advance.

✦ If you're familiar with the area, navigate there using mostly the readings from your GPS unit. The site www.geocaching.com doesn't recommend this for first-time hunters. However, you may need to use a combination of all three strategies to find a cache. Bringing along a compass is a good idea, too.

✦ Drive as close to the cache location as you can. When you get within 300 feet, check your GPS receiver's margin of error. It could be between 25 and 200 feet. The smaller the error, the more you can rely on your receiver's reading. For the last 30 feet or so, circle the area to find the cache. For higher error rates, the circle is larger.

✦ When you find the cache, at least write your name in the enclosed log book. If you want to take an item from the cache and replace it with another, that's great, too. This is all done under the honor system, of course. You're not supposed to find the cache, take all the loot, and run off for an early retirement.

✦ **When you leave your car, mark a waypoint on your GPS receiver.** This way, you can find your way back to the car. Otherwise, you may need to wait for the next person who finds the cache, so they can lead you back to civilization. (For more information on waypoints, see Book VIII, Chapter 2.)

Hiding the bounty

Once you have mastered the art and science of geocaching, you may want to try your hand at hiding your very own cache.

As for goodies, you can put just about anything in your cache. Yes, even cash — which would make you a very popular person indeed on the geocaching circuit! Many caches contain inexpensive toys, CDs, and any other knickknacks you can imagine and that fit into the container used in the cache. Some people even include one-time-use cameras, asking all the finders to take a photo of themselves (and, of course, then leave the camera for the cacher).

The site www.geocaching.com makes these recommendations for hiding your own cache:

✦ **Research the location.** Look for someplace that may require some hiking, rather than an easy-to-find place close to well-traveled areas where someone may discover the cache accidentally.

✦ **Prepare your cache.** Your best bet is a waterproof container. You can place the actual items inside sealable plastic bags like those you use for sandwiches. Include a log book (small spiral notebook) and pen or pencil so seekers can record their find. Consider including a goodie that finders can take with them, and asking them to leave something behind, via a note in the cache container.

✦ **Hide the goods.** This is where you use your GPS receiver. Get the cache's coordinates by taking a waypoint reading. For better accuracy, you should average the waypoints. If you're using a low-end GPS model, this may require taking a waypoint up to ten times — you take a waypoint and then walk away, returning to do another one — and then finding the average waypoint measurement. This average is what you write on your container and in the log book, keeping a copy for the next cache you find.

✦ **Leave a note**. Figure 3-1 shoes a typical geocache note.

✦ **Report the cache.** This involves filling out an online form on www.geocaching.com or another site. Information includes cache type, size, coordinates (of course!), overall difficulty and terrain ratings, a description, and optionally, hints.

Letterboxing: Geocaching sans batteries

What do you get if you take geocaching and substitute the GPS receiver with a compass? Letterboxing, a low-tech version of geocaching. And in this case, letterboxing has nothing to do with black bars on your TV set.

Instead of taking a trinket and leaving one, as you do in geocaching, letterboxing involves leaving your mark at every treasure location by stamping a log book with your own customized rubber stamp. You use another rubber stamp, stored in the cache box, to stamp your own book, like a passport.

If you wake up one Saturday morning and find your GPS receiver's batteries are dead, a similar hobby awaits you. That is, if you're handy with a compass.

You can read more about letterboxing at www.letterboxing.org.

GEOCACHE SITE - PLEASE READ

Congratulations, you've found it! Intentionally or not!

What is this hidden container sitting here for? What the heck is this thing doing here with all these things in it?

It is part of a worldwide game dedicated to GPS (Global Positioning System) users, called Geocaching. The game basically involves a GPS user hiding "treasure" (this container and its contents), and publishing the exact coordinates so other GPS users can come on a "treasure hunt" to find it. The only rules are: if you take something from the cache, you must leave something for the cache, and you must write about your visit in the logbook. Hopefully, the person that hid this container found a good spot that is not easily found by uninterested parties. Sometimes, a good spot turns out to be a bad spot, though.

IF YOU FOUND THIS CONTAINER BY ACCIDENT:

Great! You are welcome to join us! We ask only that you:

- Please do not move or vandalize the container. The real treasure is just finding the container and sharing your thoughts with everyone else who finds it.
- If you wish, go ahead and take something. But please also leave something of your own for others to find, and write it in the logbook.
- If possible, let us know that you found it, by visiting the web site listed below.

Geocaching is open to everyone with a GPS and a sense of adventure. There are similar sites all over the world. The organization has its home on the Internet. Visit our website if you want to learn more, or have any comments:

http://www.geocaching.com

If this container needs to be removed for any reason, please let us know. We apologize, and will be happy to move it.

Figure 3-1:
A copy of
a letter you
can leave in
your cache
box.

Finding Your Ancestors

GPS receivers can help you find your way, plot your course, and always let you know where you stand in the world. One thing it can't do is help you find your soul. Believe me, if it could, I'd be in better shape.

Enough about lost souls. I have something pretty close to a soul, and that's discovering my past by tracking down where my ancestors have tread. Even if you know where deceased relatives lived, it's often difficult to find their old homesteads.

A very grave matter

Speaking of souls, you can use your GPS receiver to find burial sites. Some kind people have already logged the latitudinal and longitudinal positions of some cemeteries and share them with others on a Web site called The U.S. GeoGen Project (www.geogen.org).

In many cases, it's an even more difficult task to find old cemeteries, some of which aren't as preened and tended to as those where our closest relatives rest. They may be in heavily wooded areas. Or, worst of all, vandals or developers may have tipped over or removed headstones so that you're not even sure that what you're visiting is a cemetery. If you have a map that lists the cemetery, have jotted down its longitude and latitude coordinates, and are heading there with a GPS receiver, you have a much better chance of actually finding it, like the person shown in Figure 3-2.

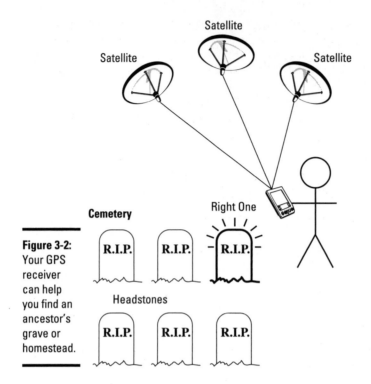

Figure 3-2:
Your GPS
receiver
can help
you find an
ancestor's
grave or
homestead.

The original author of the first edition of this book enlisted his adventure-some mother in a quest for a great-grandfather's grave. They knew the cemetery, but not the location of the gravestone.

The author had the cemetery's name, so I bet you're thinking the rest was easy. Far from it. It was a large cemetery. There were thousands of gravestones, many of them flat against the ground so you could see them only after walking up to each and every one. And just finding the cemetery wasn't easy.

Now imagine you have the GPS coordinates for the cemetery and that, maybe from another genealogist's efforts, you even have the latitude and longitude of the actual grave. Now that's something! Imagine the time you'd save. Even with GPS readings that have a margin of error of 20 feet or so, you have narrowed down the search considerably.

This isn't a book on genealogy, and I'm assuming you can figure out how to narrow down your search of cemeteries where your ancestors may be buried. GPS technology isn't going to help you find these sites unless you know they are places to look for family headstones.

Once you have a good idea of which cemeteries are good bets, either because they are close to where ancestors lived or are located on the family land, you can use maps and other tools to find the coordinates. From there, it's a matter of using your GPS navigational skills to reach each one and check them out.

In addition to the U.S. GeoGen Project's Web site mentioned earlier, a good place to look for coordinates of cemeteries is the Geographic Names Information System (GNIS). The GNIS contains information about nearly 2 million U.S. physical and cultural geographic features. Many of these include associated latitudinal and longitudinal coordinates to enter into your GPS receiver to help you find them.

Here's how you do a quick search of the GNIS:

1. **Point your browser at http://geonames.usgs.gov/.**

   The GNIS home page appears.

2. **On the top, click Search Domestic Names (if you are looking for U.S. landmarks).**

   A query form appears.

3. **You can search many different ways. To search for a specific cemetery, as shown in Figure 3-3, do the following:**

   1. Type in the name of the cemetery.

   2. To narrow it down a bit, type in the county name and choose the proper state.

   3. Select Cemetery under Feature Type.

   4. Click Send Query.

   The site can sometimes take a painfully long time to search, but eventually it displays a list of search results, as shown in Figure 3-4.

Where is (old) home sweet home?

As I do a bit of genealogical research to find the source of my genes, I sometimes come across confusing maps showing where this or that ancestor made his home. I can't go to the grocery store without getting lost, so you can imagine my confusion when reading these homestead maps, let alone actually traveling to an old homestead.

Wouldn't it be easier if I knew the longitude and latitude of places I want to visit and then use my GPS receiver to find them? Why, yes, it would be easier.

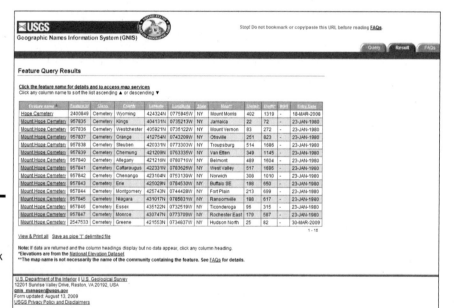

Figure 3-3: Searching for a particular cemetery

Figure 3-4: A list of cemeteries in New York State with the name Mount Hope.

Just like finding cemeteries with Uncle Sam's (celestial) help, you can use GPS coordinates to help locate where your relatives migrated within the United States. Why not just use a map? Like I said, I get lost on the way to the bathroom, so simply finding a location on a map, perhaps in another state, and driving there is not a reasonable expectation.

Instead, you can use the GPS navigation skills you discovered in the preceding chapter to travel to locations you want to visit as part of your genealogy research. Remember, these towns may be so small that they are difficult enough to find on a map. By using your GPS receiver, especially one designed for automobile use, you can find those homesteads quicker by following the coordinates.

Don't forget to write down and make available the locations' coordinates to genealogists, homesteads, farms, county courthouses, and local libraries.

Glossary

802.11 series: Wireless standards that include 802.11a, 802.11b, 802.11g, 802.11n, and other current and future related standards. Generally, 802.11g and 802.11n are used for Wi-Fi hotpots.

802.11a: The first 802.11 standard in the 5 GHz range, which offers 54 Mbit/sec.

802.11b: The original 11Mbit/sec wireless standard in the 2.4 GHz spectrum.

802.11g: An improvement on 802.11b that gives 54 Mbit/sec.

802.11i: A standard that dictates how wireless security is to be handled. This is currently implemented in WPA2.

802.11n: The latest wireless standard that, as of this book's publishing, is still a draft standard. When the standard is complete, you might need a firmware upgrade to your router to comply.

802.1x: An authentication scheme for Wi-Fi. Mostly used in corporate environments.

access point: A wireless device that serves as a communications hub for Wi-Fi clients.

ad hoc mode: A mode in Wi-Fi networking where one computer connects directly to another computer, bypassing a central access point.

adware: Software that interferes with Internet advertising, or that which inserts extra advertising into your Web browser.

analog: Something that relies on wave forms that can take on many values, such as human speech or radio waves.

antenna: A metal rod or wire used to transmit and receive radio signals. All wireless technologies use some kind of antenna, even if it's so small you cannot see it.

band: A group of frequencies.

BlackBerry: A handheld device made by Research in Motion (RIM) that lets you access your e-mail and browse the Web anywhere there is wireless coverage.

Bluetooth: A wireless technology operating in the frequency range of Wi-Fi communications, but has a much shorter range. Mostly used as a substitute for cables on the desktop (keyboards, mice) and in cell phone applications (wireless link between a headset and phone).

botnet: A collection of computers infected with malware that forces the computer to do work on behalf of the botnet owner. This work might be attacking a Web site or sending out e-mail spam.

bridge: Lets you connect two or more networks together. For your purposes, it usually means connecting a wireless network to a wired network.

cable modem: A device that connects between your cable TV company's Internet connection and your network or computer. It enables you to send and receive information over the Internet using a coaxial cable that runs into your home.

cellular phone: A mobile telephone that uses a network of short-range transmitters to communicate with the landline phone system.

coaxial cable: Cable used for cable TV and some other applications.

cordless phone: A wireless phone usually used inside the home or yard that operates over one of three frequency bands: 900 MHz, 2.4 GHz, or 5.8 GHz.

cracker: Someone who hacks into a network with malicious intent.

DHCP: The dynamic host configuration protocol provides a way to automatically allocate IP addresses to computers on a network.

digital: A signal, composed of 1s and 0s, used to transmit information.

Digital Media Adapter: A device that plays back audio or video files streamed over a network that have been encoded in some digital format.

DLNA: Short for Digital Living Network Alliance, an industry consortium. DLNA defines protocols for consumer electronics devices to connect to PCs and each other.

Domain Name Service (DNS): A global system of computes and a protocol that lets you convert names like www.dummies.com to an IP address.

driver: Software that allows hardware to communicate with your computer's operating system. Each piece of hardware, such as a network adapter, has its own driver. The manufacturer usually provides the driver.

DRM (Digital Rights Mangement): Methods to protect digital media from unauthorized copying.

DSL: A digital subscriber line which allows you to receive the Internet over the same wires as your telephone service. This is one way to get broadband Internet access.

DSL modem: A device that connects between your telephone company's DSL connection and your network or computer. It enables you to send and receive information over the Internet using a telephone line that runs into your home.

eBook: Also, eBook Reader. eBook readers are hardware consisting of an electronic paper display suitable for reading documents.

encryption: Scrambling information as a way to secure it.

ePaper: ePaper is a display technology that's reflective, rather than generating its own light. These displays do not require that the display be refreshed, so they use very little power.

Ethernet: A protocol that describes how most computers can talk to each other, either over wired or wireless medium.

ExpressCard: The next generation of PC cards for laptops. ExpressCards are around the same size as a PC Card but have a different pinout.

firewall: Software that inspects incoming and outgoing traffic, and allows or blocks it, depending on your security policy.

firmware: A small software program inside hardware, such as routers, that controls the hardware.

Fiber optics: long glass fibers that carry network signals in the form of light instead of electricity. Fiber optics have much greater range than copper wire.

GHz: Gigahertz. A wave with a frequency of 1 GHz oscillates 1 billion times per second.

global positioning system: Worldwide network of satellites operated by U.S. Defense Department that enables civilian and military users to pinpoint their location on Earth.

GPS: *See* global positioning system.

hacker: Originally referred to a person who was able to perform great technical feats. In recent times, it has become synonymous with "cracker." *See* cracker.

HDTV: High-definition TV.

hotspot: A wireless access point that's found in a public place such as a library or coffee shop.

hub: A hardware device used to connect two or more network devices.

IEEE: The standards body responsible for Ethernet and most wireless protocols. Pronounce this as "eye triple e."

infrastructure mode: A mode in Wi-Fi networking where computers connect through one or more access points. This is the most popular way of creating a wireless network.

instant messaging: IM. A technology that allows for real-time, two-way text communications between two or more individuals. Yahoo!, MSN, and AOL operate the largest IM networks.

interference: Electrical noise or conflicting radio signals that cause a deterioration in the radio signal in Wi-Fi and other wireless communications.

Internet service provider (ISP): A company that sells you access to the Internet. This is usually a cable or telephone company.

IP address: A number in the format *xxx.xxx.xxx.xxx* that designates a host address on the Internet. Each domain name, such as `www.google.com`, has one or more associated IP addresses.

KB: Kilobytes.

Kb: Kilobits.

kHz: Kilohertz. A wave with a frequency of 1 kHz oscillates 1,000 times per second.

Kindle: Amazon's eBook reader, which is tied closely to Amazon's book-shopping service. Two current versions are available, the Kindle 2 and Kindle DX, with different-sized screens.

LAN: Local access network. A network found inside a home or a single building.

malware: Malicious software that tries to do something bad to your computer, such as steal information or delete files.

MAC address: Media Access Control. A wireless hardware device's unique number that identifies it on a network.

MB: Megabytes.

Mb: Megabits.

Mbps: Megabits per second.

mini-PCI adapter: A wireless network adapter that can be installed in newer laptops that include a mini-PCI slot, freeing the laptop's PC card slot for other uses.

multimedia: One of many forms of media. Can include photos, video, and music.

network: A way to connect two or more computers.

network adapter card: A wireless device that allows a laptop, desktop, or handheld computer to connect to a Wi-Fi network. Also called a network interface card (NIC), a network adapter card transmits and receives data over the network.

network-attached storage (NAS): A NAS drive is a standalone device to store data and programs, which are accessible over a network.

network interface card: NIC. *See* network adapter card.

number portability: The ability to keep your current cell or landline phone number when you either switch carriers or move to a new residence.

OTA: Also, over-the-air. Receiving digital TV signals from local broadcast stations via an antenna.

PC Card: An adapter inserted into a laptop slot to allow the computer to receive and transmit Wi-Fi radio signals.

PCI adapter: An adapter card inserted inside a desktop computer to allow the computer to receive and transmit Wi-Fi radio signals.

PDA: Personal digital assistant.

peer-to-peer mode: *See* ad hoc mode.

peripheral: A device that connects to a computer.

phishing: A technique where someone sends you an e-mail pretending to be from your bank or other service. When you follow the instructions in the e-mail, you are giving your personal information to the bad guy, not the bank.

ping: A method of sending a packet to a computer to see if it's accessible.

Pre-Shared Key (PSK): An authentication method for wireless networks that relies on the computer and the access point having a secret that they both know.

QoS: Quality of Service. This refers to technology that can prioritize streaming media packets, so the audio or video stream is delivered without dropped video frames or lost audio.

range extender: A piece of wireless gear that acts as a repeater for wireless signals so that you can be farther from the access point.

RF: Radio frequency. Electromagnetic waves that operate on frequencies from about 3 kHz to 300 GHz. Every wireless device uses a frequency.

router: A device that sits between your Internet service provider and your network, routing Internet traffic to its proper destination.

satellite radio: Paid services that stream large numbers of radio channels from orbiting satellites to satellite-capable receivers. The service most common in the United States is Sirius XM Radio.

Service Set Identifier: An identifier that a Wi-Fi network uses to identify itself.

SmartWatch: A wristwatch produced by one of several manufacturers that can receive news and information using a wireless network. Created by Microsoft.

SMS: Short message service. A text service offered on phones using the GSM digital cellular telephone system. The messages are limited to 160 alphanumeric characters.

spyware: Software that captures information such as your keystrokes and Web browsing habits and sends them to someone else.

SSID: *See* Service Set Identifier.

streaming: The process of sending multimedia information between two or more computers.

TCP/IP: Transmission Control Protocol/Internet protocol. A suite of protocols for sending information over the Internet and local networks. Because everyone on the Internet speaks TCP/IP, your computer can talk to any other computer that allows it.

universal serial bus: USB. A standard for sending and receiving data between a computer and a peripheral device, such as a wireless access card. USB 1.1 moves data at up to 12 Mbps, while the newer version (2.0) can handle up to 480 Mbps.

USB: *See* universal serial bus.

virtual private network: A technology that permits secure communications between two points. A VPN tunnels through the public Internet, sending and receiving encrypted information.

virus: A piece of malware that replicates itself to spread, and usually attaches itself to another piece of software.

VPN: *See* virtual private network.

WAN: Wide-area network. In the larger sense, this refers to a network that connects different cities. Most routers label the port that connects to the Internet as the WAN.

WEP: *See* wired equivalent privacy.

WPA: *See* Wi-Fi protected access.

Wi-Fi: Wireless fidelity. Wi-Fi permits communications over the 2.4 and 5.0 GHz bands within a radius of up to 300 feet. Wi-Fi is used to create wireless networks and hotspots, allowing anyone with the proper wireless equipment to connect.

Wi-Fi protected access: WPA. A transition mechanism to fix problems in the WEP protocol until the full 802.11i specification could be implemented.

Wi-Fi protected access version 2: WPA2. The current generation of wireless privacy extensions, based on the IEEE 802.11i standards. WPA2 fixes problems with WPA and WEP that would let crackers get into your network.

Wi-Fi Protected Setup (WPS): A mechanism to automatically configure a wireless device to a supported access point.

wired equivalent privacy: WEP. The first encryption standard, vulnerable to hackers, for securing Wi-Fi networks. WPA2 is now supported by all manufacturers, so WEP should not be used anymore.

Windows Vista: Microsoft's latest operating system, which provides many built-in wireless networking functions.

wireless: Communications that use radio waves rather than wires.

zombie: A computer that has been infected with malware that causes that computer to operate as part of a botnet.

Index

Numerics

Notes

Notes